Keith's Radio Station

"Hendricks and Mims are to be congratulated for a superb update to Keith's long-successful text. *Keith's Radio Station* has been given a fresh makeover, written in a student friendly and engaging manner with every chapter updated to reflect the latest trends and issues in radio."

– Michael Brown, Professor, University of Wyoming, USA

"In the current era, when we're bombarded by new media inventions, it's easy to forget that nothing replaces the ubiquity and potency of audio—whether it's distributed as traditional radio or via other platforms. Those who seek a thorough understanding of radio's borderless power and how to master it need to read the this-just-in (as we say on the radio) edition of *Keith's Radio Station*."

– Peter Laufer, James Wallace Chair in Journalism, University of Oregon, USA

"Hendricks and Mims took the pre-eminent book for future industry professionals and made it even more relevant for today's students. As their updates attest, the future of sponsored audio content (i.e., radio) has never looked brighter or been more deserving of study and practice."

– Dr. Joseph Blaney, Associate Dean, College of Arts and Sciences, Illinois State University, USA

"This edition is valuable to students given the authors' efforts to take a serious look at radio's future, mixing in essays from industry leaders, an examination of various listening devices, and a companion website that makes for significant collaboration between faculty and students."

– Joe Misiewicz, President/CEO, Indiana Broadcasters Association, USA

Keith's Radio Station

Broadcast, Internet, and Satellite

Ninth edition

John Allen Hendricks
Bruce Mims

Focal Press
Taylor & Francis Group
NEW YORK AND LONDON

First published 1986 by Focal Press

This edition published 2015
by Focal Press
70 Blanchard Road, Suite 402, Burlington, MA 01803

and by Focal Press
2 Park Square, Milton Park, Abingdon, Oxon OX14 4RN

Focal Press is an imprint of the Taylor & Francis Group, an informa business

Library of Congress Cataloging in Publication Data
Hendricks, John Allen.
Keith's radio station: broadcast, internet, and satellite/
John Allen Hendricks, Bruce Mims.—Ninth edition.
pages cm
1. Radio stations. 2. Radio broadcasting.
I. Mims, Bruce. II. Keith, Michael C., 1945– Radio station.
III. Title.
HE8698.K45 2014
384.54′53—dc23 2014002609

ISBN: 978-0-240-82116-0 (pbk)
ISBN: 978-0-240-82462-8 (ebk)

Typeset in Giovanni and Franklin Gothic
By Florence Production Ltd, Stoodleigh, Devon, UK

Printed in Canada

Contents

Foreword

You're reading the most acclaimed and widely used guide into the world of audio communications, broadcast, satellite, the Internet, and mobile. *Keith's Radio Station* is a lucid, accurate, up-to-the minute survey examining all aspects of today's expanding world of radio and audio communications. Experienced broadcasters and teachers John Allen Hendricks and Bruce Mims collaborated with pioneering author Michael C. Keith to update and revise this ninth edition. Thanks to their combined expertise and connections, you'll enjoy a rich narration of radio's past and present, highlighted with insights from dozens of industry leaders.

Keith's Radio Station is no ordinary text; this expansive collaboration might inspire your own future in communications!

From the vacuum tube to the transformative leap into the digital integrated circuit, technology evolved and then revolutionized radio, literally spawning new competitors. That pace of change is accelerating. Audio distribution systems not envisioned a few decades ago—satellite and Internet radio, MP3 players, customized "stations," and radio apps—abound. Yet surprisingly, 92% of Americans still listen to AM and FM radio every week.

Although technological developments have transformed the industry, its success is largely a human story. Technology can enhance the experience, it can distribute the audio, it can "create" in some ways, but it requires people to truly communicate. Ask yourself, what did you hear on the "radio" (or Pandora, TuneIn, iHeartRadio, SiriusXM, etc.) today? Maybe you heard a personality, a news reporter from inside a wartorn nation, or a conversation about sustainable foods. You listened to people-created content.

Yet technology presents tantalizing opportunities—now and for the future. "Big data" has unlocked detailed information about current and potential consumers, unleashing a future of highly customized content. Technology also facilitates real-time interactivity to capture unique and spirited user-created content, enhancing involvement and engendering loyalty.

So it's this combination of technology and "content" that subconsciously helps you decide what to listen to, for how long, and when to switch. Technology builds the restaurant; the chef's creations tempt the customers.

Yet many in radio today are flummoxed. Intimidated by technology, some find it difficult to morph from the old "broadcast" model to new configurations, from past success into the unknown. Terrestrial broadcasters are scrambling to make their stations more interactive, capitalize on social media, and adapt to mobile. Most cling to terminology like "listeners" and "audience estimates" when they should be empowering their "brands" and recruiting more "fans" across multiple platforms. Others, rather than investing, are cutting costs to protect existing margins.

As you read this book, think about how *you* might solve these problems. The industry today needs fresh thinking people who can integrate new technology with an understanding of the consumer and the power of radio.

When compared to periods of innovation in other industries, radio's current tension should not be surprising. Kodak, for 100 years the world's dominant camera and film manufacturer, failed to adapt to a digital future that it actually saw coming! BlackBerry, once ubiquitous, took its focus off innovation. Instructively, photography and handheld devices have never been more popular. But others seized the lead.

Every generation creates, embraces, and then becomes ensnared by the technology of the day. Importantly, many have also forgotten that throughout the history of radio and media, superior content—engaging, relevant, and compelling—invariably prevails, generates followers, and makes money.

From Socrates to Lincoln, we've learned the immense power of communicating thoughts and ideas. But it was radio, the most breathtakingly advanced technology of the day, which enabled these ideas to travel worldwide instantaneously. During World War II, FDR's "Fireside Chats," together with Winston Churchill's speeches that "mobilized the English language and brought it into battle," stirred their nations to action and changed the course of history by harnessing the power, immediacy, and intimacy of radio. In 2012, after Hurricane Sandy slammed into 15 states leaving millions without power for days, draining phone batteries and destroying Internet connections, only radio remained to serve as the singular lifeline to those reeling from the devastation.

The power of radio is waiting to be used. Technology will continue to enlarge the distribution systems and enhance the listening devices we use, but the human mind and soul will always be drawn to exceptional creativity, imagination, and spontaneity. As *Keith's Radio Station* guides you into the world of radio and audio communications, introducing you to its array of parts and players, imagine yourself in this world. Opportunity awaits your preparation.

Jay Williams, Jr. was VP/GM of WVBF (FM) Boston before co-owning and managing a New England radio group for 20 years. He also co-founded DMR/Interactive and is now president of Broadcasting Unlimited, radio/audio content consultants. Jay serves as a trustee at Wabash College (Indiana) where, as a student, he helped launch the college station, WNDY (FM).

About the Authors

John Allen Hendricks (PhD, University of Southern Mississippi) has nearly 20 years of experience as an electronic media educator. He currently serves as chair of the Department of Mass Communication and holds the rank of professor at Stephen F. Austin State University in Nacogdoches, Texas.

Dr. Hendricks is the author/editor of eight books including: *The Palgrave Handbook of Global Radio* (Palgrave, 2012); *The Twenty-First-Century Media Industry: Economic and Managerial Implications in the Age of New Media* (Lexington, 2010); *Social Media: Usage and Impact* (Lexington, 2012), and *Social Media and Strategic Communications* (Palgrave, 2012). One of his books received the 2011 National Communication Association's Applied Research Division's *Distinguished Scholarly Book Award*.

He is an active member of the Broadcast Education Association (BEA) and served as BEA vice-president for Academic Relations for 2014–2015 and Secretary/Treasurer from 2013–2014. From 2009–2013, he was on the BEA board of directors representing District 5 which included Arkansas, Kansas, Missouri, Oklahoma, and Texas. He is past chair, vice-chair, and secretary of the BEA Radio and Audio Media (RAM) Division. Also, he is a past president of the Oklahoma Broadcast Education Association (OBEA).

Dr. Hendricks has experience in both commercial and noncommercial radio. From 1997 to 2009, he was responsible for the oversight of programming, budgeting, and personnel at a noncommercial, university-owned radio station.

Bruce Mims (PhD, University of Southern Mississippi) began his career as an electronic media educator in 1977. He currently holds the rank of professor at Southeast Missouri State University in Cape Girardeau, Missouri.

Dr. Mims has authored articles published in the *Journal of Radio Studies, Journalism and Mass Communication Educator*, and *Journal of Media Education*. He was a contributor to the Michael C. Keith-authored book *Tuning In: Radio in Society Since 1945*. In addition, Dr. Mims also has published in professional trade magazines, including essays that have appeared in *Billboard, Broadcast Management/Engineering,* and *Radio World.*

He is an active member of the Broadcast Education Association (BEA) and recently served as chairperson of its Management, Marketing and Programming Interest Division. He is a past president of the National Broadcasting Society-Alpha Epsilon Rho and is a charter member and past president of the Missouri Broadcast Educators Association (MBEA).

Dr. Mims began his commercial radio broadcasting career in 1971 and transitioned to public radio broadcasting seven years later. Since 1989 he has served as faculty advisor to the student radio station licensed to Southeast Missouri State University.

Preface

A Note from Michael C. Keith

When I proposed *The Radio Station* to Focal Press three decades ago, I hoped it would find an appreciative audience. To my delight it far exceeded my expectations. Just a year after its publication, it had become the most widely adopted text on its subject in the country. How did this happen? As a new college teacher—following a dozen years as a radio broadcaster—it struck me that no existing text on the medium accurately or sufficiently conveyed the true nature of the industry. The most widely used book on the subject at the time seemed grossly out of step with the realities of the radio profession. Furthermore, the text failed to include the insights and perspectives of broadcasters or portray the unique *visual* nature of the audio medium—yes, radio *is* a visual medium. These were two components that I felt were absolutely necessary in an instructional volume focused on the operations of a modern radio station.

Focal had recently entered the broadcast publications arena in the US, so needless to say it was more than thrilled with the new text's performance. It is hard for me to believe it is now in its fourth decade of existence. That it has flourished for so long—both nationally and internationally—is attributable to a number of factors, not the least of which are the invaluable contributions of those in both the industry and academia. The input of students and the dedication of Focal Press editors played a central role in the tome's success and longevity as well.

This legacy text now turns a significant corner in its heralded life with a slightly revamped title (how flattered can an author be to see his name in the marquee of a work he originated?) and an extensively updated and refashioned interior courtesy of its new coauthors. In 2011 Focal Press conducted an extensive search for qualified individuals to assume authorship of the next edition of the volume.

I had produced eight editions over three decades and felt it was time to hand it over to someone else. Quite frankly, I no longer felt up to the task, nor did I feel fully informed of the digital influences that had dramatically transformed the medium.

To be sure it was not an easy decision to turn my "baby" over to others. The next caretakers had to possess a myriad of knowledge, skill, and vision to take on the formidable responsibility. Moreover, the individuals had to have a finite grasp of the volume's essence—what made it so important and irreplaceable to thousands of users worldwide. To my great satisfaction, my good colleagues John Allen Hendricks and Bruce Mims were chosen to reinvigorate the text for the next generation of users, and they have done an extraordinary job their first time out. Based on what they have accomplished in this new incarnation of this landmark publication, I am convinced they will maintain its long tradition of excellence.

Michael C. Keith
Boston, Massachusetts

Acknowledgments

The first edition of this book was published in 1986 and as the radio industry evolved, so did this book. Michael C. Keith was the creator and primary author of the first edition as well as the seven subsequent editions. He was assisted by broadcaster Joseph M. Krause on the first two editions. The ninth edition of the book has two new authors who are most appreciative to Michael for entrusting us with his legacy textbook on the radio industry. Moreover, the ninth edition has a revised title to reflect and honor the seminal contribution to radio study that Michael has made over the course of his academic career.

Although changes are abundant in this new edition, the mission of this book has not changed since 1986; it remains the result of an effort to provide the student of radio with the most complete account of the medium possible, from the insider's view. It is presented from the perspective of the radio professional, drawing on the insights and observations of those who make their daily living by working in the industry. It has been that formula that has made this book so successful for nearly three decades. Accordingly, we choose to stay with that strategy.

Like Michael C. Keith, we have sought to create a practical, timely, illustrative, and accessible book on radio station operations; to do so, hundreds of radio professionals have contributed to this effort to disseminate factual and relevant information about the medium in a way that captures its reality and evolution. These professionals represent the top echelons of network and corporate radio, as well as the rural daytime-only outlets spread across the country. Because the strategy of the book is to draw upon the experience of countless broadcast and allied professionals, our debt of gratitude to them is significant.

Therefore, we wish to express sincere appreciation to the many individuals and organizations that assisted in so many important ways. Foremost among them are Jay Williams, Jr. and Ed Shane, who freely and frequently shared with us their counsel, assistance, and expertise. It also goes without saying that the help of the following individuals was invaluable: John Alfonso, Phil Barry, Gary Begin, Frank Bell, Gary Berkowitz, Chuck Bethea, Mike Bloxham, Ted Bolton, Brian Buckley, Alan Burns, Ian Burns, George Capalbo, Drew Carey, Brad Carson, Gregg Cassidy, Kevin Cassidy, Lynn Christian, Kaitlin Ciphery, Greg Clancy, Dawn Cohen, Ed Cohen, Randal Crow, Andrew Curran, John David, Glenn Davies, Tim Davis, Joel Denver, Mike Dougherty, Rick Ducey, Robert Dunlop, Bruce

DuMont, Tripp Eldridge, Doug Erickson, Erica Farber, Jim Farley, Doug Ferber, Norm Feuer, Paul Fiddick, Donald Fishman, Ty Ford, Ann M. Fotiades, Mark Fratrik, Ken Frommert, Radhika Gajjala, Kevin Geary, John Gehron, Valerie Geller, Josie Geuer, Natalie Gheit, Thomas Gibson, Carolyn Gilbert, Andrea Gils, Paul Goldstein, Matt Grasso, Kelli Grisez, Ralph Guild, Jeff Haley, Donna Halper, Stephen Hartzell, Mike Henry, Juan Carlos Hidalgo, Derrick Hinds, David Holland, Jason Insalaco, Fred Jacobs, Mike Janssen, Leah Kamon, Paul Kamp, Mark Kassof, Larry Keene, Dick Kent, Kimberly Kissel, Valerie Komor, Wolf Korgyn, Kent Koselke, Weezie Kramer, Michael A. Krasner, Erwin Krasnow, Warren Kurtzman, Megan Lazovick, Stephanie Wai Lee, Lori Lewis, Guy Low, Leah Luddine, Andy Ludlum, Luke Lukefahr, Jeff Magram, Robin Martin, Chea McGee, John McGrath, Paul McLane, James McMahen, Mike McVay, Christine Merritt, Larry Miller, Ken Mills, Thomas Mocarsky, Allen Myers, Dave Neugesser, Vicki Nichols, Clark Novak, Criss Onan, Dick Oppenheimer, Otabek, Lorna Ozmon, Ben Palmer, Simon Peacock, Wayne Pecena, Henry Peirse, Michael Pelaia, Tom Pierson, Darryl Pomicter, Laura Jane Prendergast, Ward Quaal, Robert Quicke, Joel Raab, Dick Rakovan, Mark Ramsey, David Reese, Skip Reynolds, B. Eric Rhoads, Nicole Ribaudo, Alice M. Rios, Jim Robertson (for his vast Rolodex), Ron Rodrigues, Sophie Rompré, Luke Russert, Tim Scheld, Rebecca Schnall, Dave Scott, Tom Severino, Michael Shane, Larry Shannon, Glenda Shrader Bos, Bill Siemering, Evelina Simanonyte, Jeff Smulyan, Mark St. John, Emily Stephens, Chris Sterling, Peter Stewart, Robert J. Struble, Marlin Taylor, Tom Taylor, Jay Tyler, Martin Vacher, Dave Van Dyke, Chris Vane, Rob Vining, Karen Volkman, Girish Warrier, Ned Waugaman, Mike Whalen, Thomas White, Audra Wiant, Stephen Winzenburg, Richard Withers, Jack Zibluk, et al.—the list is endless.

Countless companies and organizations contributed to the body of this work. They include: a2x, ABC Radio Networks, Ad Council, Air America, Alan Burns & Associates, *All Access*, Apple Corporation, Arbitron Ratings Company, Arrakis Systems, Associated Press, Auditronics Inc., Backbone Networks Corp., The Benchmark Company, Berkowitz Broadcast Consultants, BIA/Kelsey, BMI, Bolton Research, Bonneville Broadcasting, Borrell Associates, Inc., Boston Acoustics, BPME, Broadcast Company of the Americas Radio San Diego, Broadcast Electronics, Broadcast Programming, *Broadcasting and Cable*, Broadcasting Unlimited, Burkhart Douglas and Associates, C-SPAN Radio, CBS, CFM, CIPB, Clear Channel Communications, Clear Channel Sucks.com, Coleman Insights Media Research, Communication Graphics, Comrex, CRN, Crown Broadcast IREC, Cumulus, David Sarnoff Library, Deer River Group, Denon, Direct Marketing Research, Donna Halper and Associates, Edison Media Research, Electro-Voice, Emmis, Enco, Entercom Communications Corp., Erickson Media Consultants, ESPN Radio, the FCC, *FMQB*, FMR Associates, Focusrite, Geller Media International, Global Radio News, Goldwave Inc., Greater Media, GRN-live, Halper and Associates, Harker Research, HD Radio, Hear2.0, Herald Media Inc., Holland Cooke Media, Hooks Unlimited, iBiquity Digital, IGM Inc., iHeartRadio, Infinity Broadcasting, *Inside Radio*, Interep Radio Store, International Demographics, iTunes, Jacobs Media, Jefferson Pilot Data Systems, Jelli, Joel Raab Country Radio and Media Consulting, Jones Radio News, Katz

Media Group, KD Kanopy, Kelton Agency, KHWL, KIRO, KISS-FM, KKWE, Library of American Broadcasting, Lund Consultants, *The Mancow Show*, Mark Kassof & Co., Marketron Inc., McVay New Media, Mediabase, Media Behavior Institute, Mercury Research, Metro Traffic Network, MF Digital, Ken Mills Agency, MMR, Moose Lake Products Company, Museum of Broadcast Communications, National Association of Broadcasters, Nautel, NBCU, NextMedia, NPR, NuVooDoo Media, Omnirax Furniture Co., Orban, Oxysys, Pandora Radio, Paragon Media Strategies, Pew Internet & American Life Project Surveys, Premiere Radio Networks, Prophet Systems, Public Radio International, QuickHitz, Quik-Stats, Radeo, Radio Advertising Bureau, *Radio and Internet Newsletter*, *Radio Business Report*, Radio Computer Systems, *Radio Daily News*, *Radio Ink*, Radiolandia, *Radio & Records*, Radio SAWA, *Radio World*, RCA, *RTDNA*, Satellite Music Network, SCS Unlimited, Shane Media, Spotify, 360 Systems, SiriusXM Radio, Skyline Satellite Services, Society of Broadcast Engineers, Sound Exchange, Spanish Radio Group, Jim Steele, Annette Steiner, Strategic Radio Solutions, Sun Broadcast Group, Superaudio, Sysndication.net, *Talkers Magazine*, Talk Radio Network, Tapscan, The Telos Alliance, Tieline, TM Studios, *Tom Taylor Now*, WBTZ-FM, Westinghouse Broadcasting, WestwoodOne, Wheatstone, WIZN, WOR-AM, WTOP-FM, Xaxis, and Zapoleon Media Strategies.

We made every effort possible to locate industry professionals who contributed to earlier editions of this book and request updated information and, in almost every chapter, you will notice that their essays are new and analyze the radio industry from a fresh perspective. We sincerely express appreciation to all who assisted us in this process.

This book's manuscript was blind, peer reviewed. After the review process, we learned the identity of our reviewer. Accordingly, appreciation is extended to Michael Laponis, professor of communications at the University of La Verne and general manager/adviser of LeoFM Radio. His thoughtful and knowledgeable comments throughout the review process made this book more robust and accurate.

We especially wish to thank our editor at Focal Press, Kathryn Morrissey, who spent an enormous amount of time fielding phone calls, promptly answering emails, and helping with formatting issues when our computers simply would not cooperate with us. She provided helpful guidance throughout the entire process and possesses a keen editor's eye. We were most fortunate to work with Katy.

We wish to express appreciation to Denise Power, Production Editor at Taylor & Francis in the United Kingdom, for her diligence and guidance with our manuscript as it made its way through the production department. She is responsible for the book's wonderful new interior design.

Lastly, and perhaps most importantly, we wish to acknowledge and express appreciation to our families for being patient and understanding as we worked long hours on weekends and nights at our computers. We thank them for their continued love and support.

John Allen Hendricks, Nacogdoches, Texas
Bruce Mims, Cape Girardeau, Missouri

What's New to this Edition of *Keith's Radio Station*

Keith's Radio Station, successor to the well-respected eighth edition of *The Radio Station*, extends its examination of information, issues, and trends pertaining to the contemporary broadcast, satellite, and Internet radio environment. The entire text has been updated and refreshed with new facts, observations, and insider essays. Most noticeable to the new edition are the color figures and photos appearing throughout the book, which provide enhanced examples and demonstrations for the reader. Some additional highlights:

Chapter 1—Internet radio, online music services, and satellite radio are discussed more extensively in terms of their prospects for competing with the terrestrial radio market. New essay contributions from Eric Rhoads and Paul Goldstein provide readers with interesting viewpoints of how the radio industry is evolving in an era of rapidly changing technology. Dr. Rob Quicke's essay discusses the objective of College Radio Day and Glenda Shrader Bos discusses the impact of mobile listening on radio in her essay.

Chapter 2—Technological advances have forced station management to continually adjust and evolve to remain financially competitive. The updates to the chapter includes examining strategies being implemented and challenges being faced by radio station managers as a result of the Internet and social media technologies. All essays have been updated by industry professionals and a new essay has been added to the chapter by radio leader Erica Farber, president and CEO of the Radio Advertising Bureau. There are updated figures and images throughout the chapter.

Chapter 3—Updates about existing and evolving formats in FM, AM, and HD Radio are presented. New and revised commentaries from respected American essayists Lorna Ozmon, Frank Bell, Fred Jacobs, Mike Janssen, and Ed Shane and from British journalist Peter Stewart address trends and practices in commercial and non-commercial radio at home and abroad. Sections on satellite and Internet programming have been updated and expanded. Station website content and broadcaster uses of social media, podcasts and blogs also are examined in this context.

Chapter 4—A fresh examination of the importance of generating advertising revenue is presented with a focus on new media technologies increasingly competing for a percentage of the ad dollar. New essay contributions by key industry sales executives such as Dr. Rick Ducey, BIA/Kelsey's managing director; David Gleason, a radio programming consultant and former executive vice-president of Univision Radio; Wolf Korgyn, general manager of KHWL-FM; Jason Insalaco, a media lawyer and talent manager representing personalities from morning show radio, talk radio, and public broadcasting; and Weezie Kramer, responsible for operations in ten Entercom markets, refresh this chapter. There are updated figures and images throughout the chapter.

Chapter 5—The examination of the role of radio news is significantly expanded. Prominent industry leaders share with readers their expertise of radio news, including New York's WCBS-AM director of news and programming, Tim Scheld; co-anchor of KRLD-AM Morning News in Dallas, Alice Rios; and Jim Farley, vice-president of news and programming at WTOP-FM in Washington, D.C.,. Andy Ludlum, director of news programming at KNX 1070 Newsradio and KFWB News Talk 980 in Los Angeles, CA, provides an insightful essay on what makes a successful news station and Jay Williams, Jr., president of Broadcasting Unlimited, Inc., provides a fascinating essay on the *Boston Herald* and its venture into the radio business. There are updated figures and images throughout the chapter.

Chapter 6—New information about listener patterns that have emerged from data collected by and retrieved from Nielsen Audio's (formerly Arbitron) electronic audience-measurement device, the Portable People Meter, is presented. Essayists Dr. Ed Cohen of Nielsen Audio and Mike Henry of Paragon Media Strategies examine industry changes that are rewriting the rules of radio research and pose the challenges that professionals confront in measuring online and mobile listening. Industry veterans Warren Kurtzman and Ted Bolton present essays about the role research plays in understanding the dynamics of the contemporary radio environment.

Chapter 7—The updated content in this chapter examines the many ways in which radio stations promote themselves using both traditional and new media technologies such as social media and smartphones. Radio station website usage for promotional purposes is also expanded with a new essay by Glenn Halbrooks on how a station can build a website that gets results. Lori Lewis, director of digital and social strategies at Jacobs Media, provides an essay on how stations can effectively use social media to promote themselves. Ed Shane, CEO of Houston-based Shane Media, provides a new essay on enhancing the image of both the radio station and the client. Importantly, there is also a new section titled "Promotions in the Digital Era." There are updated figures and images throughout the chapter.

Chapter 8—The content is considerably expanded giving full recognition to the importance of an efficient and technologically advanced traffic and billing department. The twenty-first-century traffic director's role and responsibilities are updated with an examination of the availability and importance of sophisticated traffic and billing software. The important contributions of Dave Scott, a leading radio industry developer of traffic and billing software, are explored. Also, Larry Keene, founder of the Traffic Directors Guild of America, provides an essay that clearly enunciates the importance of the traffic department. There are updated figures and images throughout the chapter.

Chapter 9—An emphasis on Internet Protocol (IP) audio technology anchors a significantly revised discussion about today's studio environment. The role that networked audio plays in distributing content within and among studios and station clusters is examined within the context of the audio console and the growing number of peripheral devices that connect to it. Discussions about the contributions that studio furniture, telephone equipment and remote pick-up units (RPUs) make in ensuring station success are presented for the first time.

Chapter 10—Surrounding a centerpiece examination of digital transmission technologies are revised passages about FCC regulations and licensee-compliance requirements. Special emphasis is directed to an examination of the future of the station-engineering career, and the important role the Society of Broadcast Engineers (SBE) performs in recruiting and educating next-generation technologists.

Chapter 11—Some of the industry's leading station consultants share their expertise about managing programming and operations in an increasingly competitive, interconnected, mobile listening environment. Also discussed are emerging syndicated programming services, including an essay penned by founder Mike Dougherty about Jelli—an approach to music programming fueled by social-media interaction.

CHAPTER 1

State of the Fifth Estate

IN THE AIR—EVERYWHERE

The competitive landscape of AM and FM radio broadcasting has changed dramatically in the last few years. Satellite and Web radio, along with mobile multimedia devices (smartphones, tablets, and portable media players), have transformed the listening environment and the listening experience. Yet, well into the second decade of this new millennium, broadcast radio—the original portable electronic medium—continues to exhibit a dominant presence in the face of these newer, competitive audio technologies. Seismic shifts in radio's management and operational structure, a result of the elimination of long-standing ownership caps, fostered sea change in ownership consolidation and led to the operational clustering of thousands of stations. Jay Williams, Jr., president of Broadcasting Unlimited, states: "Buoyed by deregulation, consolidation and Wall Street money, then buffeted by increased competition and new technology, terrestrial radio executives are bracing for a challenging future by exploring programming and format options, more sophisticated advertiser relationships, and new digital distribution platforms to more robustly compete and grow."

Radio listenership remains resilient and robust across all delivery platforms. While overall listening to AM and FM stations declined 15% in the period between 1990 and 2008 the number of listeners began to rebound in 2012. Arbitron, the radio audience measurement company, reported that the upward trend continued in 2013, when AM and FM stations attracted an estimated 243 million listeners, with the greatest gains occurring in the teen-listener demographic. Arbitron's data are referred to frequently throughout this edition of the book. In September 2013, Arbitron was purchased by Nielsen and was rebranded "Nielsen Audio." Despite new ownership and a new name, this edition of the book will continue to refer to the entity as "Arbitron."

Younger listeners who gravitated toward alternative listening opportunities also helped propel satellite and Internet audio providers to new heights. Online music provider Pandora reported that its share of radio listenership measured

Monday, September 30, 2013

» **ALERT: Arbitron becomes Nielsen Audio as deal closes.**

Nielsen today closed on its $1.26 billion deal to buy Arbitron. Arbitron is being rebranded Nielsen Audio, and it will become part of Nielsen's U.S. Watch business segment that also includes the TV ratings business. "This is a great day for Nielsen and a natural step in our evolution," Nielsen CEO David Calhoun says.

FIGURE 1.1
Arbitron was purchased by Nielsen and rebranded as Nielsen Audio. Courtesy of AllAccess.com.

slightly more than 8% of all radio listeners in the U.S. in October 2013, an increase of approximately two share points over the previous 18-month period. Pandora continues to deflect criticism that its minimal reliance upon local content precludes the service from achieving "radio station" status. Apple announced its iTunes Radio service already had streamed to 11 million unique listeners within weeks of its September 2013 launch; its most-listened to song during this period was "Hold On, We're Going Home" by Drake. Satellite broadcaster Sirius/XM shook away investor fears in 2013, reporting larger-than-anticipated increases in subscribership and revenues. Riding on the success of an auto sales revival, the combined satcasters reached out to 25 million subscribers with more than 140 channels of mostly commercial-free programming. Radio—whether it be of the terrestrial, satellite, online, or mobile variety—continues to be one of the most pervasive media on earth, even more so than the Internet, which is virtually non-existent in many parts of the world, especially in Third World countries.

It is a position the radio industry vigorously and aggressively promotes. The National Association of Broadcasters (NAB) is its trade organization, and it lobbies government from its Washington, D.C., headquarters. President Gordon Smith, speaking to attendees at the group's 2012 national convention, noted "more than 241 million people listen to free radio every week." Speaking at the same event, FCC chairman Julius Genachowski affirmed radio's resilience in the new-media environment, observing that "even with the many new digital sources of audio, radio ad revenue is up 9% since 2009." Smith also affirmed radio's role in helping listeners discover new music, saying, "Even in an era of Pandora and Spotify, local radio is by far the number one source for new music.

FIGURE 1.2
University students communicate using hand signals while preparing for a broadcast.
Courtesy Studio École de France and the Telos Alliance.

And this is just using our existing business model. Radio has new opportunities including on mobile phones." Results of a 2013 study conducted by Edison Research and Arbitron reinforce the NAB president's claim: more adults overall consider AM/FM radio to be their number one source for learning about new music (AM/FM, however, is second to YouTube for listeners in the 12–24 age demographic).

There is no patch of land, no piece of ocean surface untouched by the electromagnetic signals beamed from the more than 40,000 radio stations worldwide. The United Nations Educational, Scientific and Cultural Organization (UNESCO), sponsor of World Radio Day, recognizes on its website the pervasive nature of radio, observing:

> Radio is the mass media reaching the widest audience in the world. It is also recognized as a powerful communication tool and a low cost medium. Radio is specifically suited to reach remote communities and vulnerable people: the illiterate, the disabled, women, youth and the poor, while offering a platform to intervene in the public debate, irrespective of people's educational level. Furthermore, radio has a strong and specific role in emergency communication and disaster relief.

Today more than 15,000 stations in this country, including more than 10,800 commercial AM and FM outlets, reach 99% of all households. Less than 1% of households have fewer than five receivers (most have at least eight). Over the previous decade the total number of commercial FM stations increased 5% while the number of commercial AM stations declined 1%. There are nearly a billion working radios in the United States.

Modern radio's unique personal approach resulted in a shift of the audience's application of the medium: radio went from family or group entertainer before 1950 to individual companion after the debut of the video medium. Although television usurped radio's position as the number one home entertainment source more than five decades ago, radio's total reach handily exceeds that of the video display. More people rely on radio for its multifaceted offerings than on any other medium—print or electronic, although the Internet is quickly gaining ground. Practically every automobile (96%) has a radio. "There are twice as many car radios in use (approximately 140 million) as the total circulation (50 million) of all daily newspapers, and four of five adults are reached by radio each week," contends Kenneth Costa, former vice-president of marketing for the Radio Advertising Bureau (RAB).

Arbitron noted in the 2012 edition of its annual "Radio's All Dimensional Audience Research" (RADAR) national listening report a reversal of declining audience sizes, indicating that the radio audience of listeners aged 12 and above grew by 590,000 persons in the previous year. Among the significant statistics to emerge from the findings is the news that, for the first time in several years, the size of the teenage audience increased to a cumulative 22.8 million weekly listeners. Similar improvement was achieved with young adult listeners although listening by older adults declined.

More than six in ten listeners aged 18 and over tune in to radio in their cars on a typical weekday; during the typical week eight out of ten adults are reached by car radio.

FIGURE 1.3
Weekly radio listening by Americans approaches near-universality. Courtesy Arbitron/Edison Research Infinite Dial 2013. ©2013 Arbitron, Inc.

According to Arbitron's *Radio Today* report, the medium "reaches more than 93% of the U.S. 12+ population each week, with an ever-increasing amount of listening taking place away from home." Radio has always been the most portable mass medium and it continues to be a vibrant mobile listener companion. Nighttime radio listening by adults, an activity that has lingered in the shadow of television viewing for more than half a century, also exhibited growth, according to Arbitron. As the new millennium proceeded, this computed to well over 230 million Americans, although some recent audience studies have suggested that listening figures for radio, in particular time spent listening (TSL), are on a noteworthy decline due to new competing audio media. A RADAR report also found that working women account for nearly 60% of radio listening by females, a statistic that reflects the times.

Meanwhile, radio continued to be tremendously popular among African Americans and Hispanics, where the medium's weekly reach is about 95% of that population. Radio's vibrancy in attracting the attention of minorities is reflected by the increase from 2011 to 2012 of more than 2.5 million listeners 12 and older.

The number of radio receivers in use in America has risen by more than 50% since 1970, when 325 million sets provided listeners with a wide range of audio services. In recent years, technological innovations in receiver design alone have contributed to the ever-increasing popularity of the medium. According to *The New York Times*, Americans bought nearly 60 million radios annually in the last years of the 1990s, but that trend slowed in the new century, due to mobile music services. Radio's ability to move with its audience has never been greater. Out-of-home listeners account for more than 60% of the average audience Monday through Friday. In addition, the RAB concluded that seven out of ten computer purchasers and wine and beer drinkers tune into the medium daily.

Radio appeals to everyone and is available to all. Its mobility and variety of offerings have made it the most popular medium in history and, while this popularity has been on the wane in recent years, it continues to be high. To most adults, radio is as much a part of their day as morning coffee and the ride to work. It is a companion that keeps us informed about world and local events; gives us sports scores; provides us with the latest weather and school closings and a host of other information, not to mention our favorite music; and asks for nothing in return. A Katz Radio Group study concluded "only radio adapts to the lifestyle of its audience." The report dispelled the belief that radio listening drops during the summer, as does TV viewing, proving that radio is indeed a friend for all seasons.

It is difficult to imagine a world without such an accommodating and amusing cohort, one that not only has enriched our lives by providing us with a nonstop source of entertainment, but has also kept us abreast of happenings during times of national and global crisis. To most Americans, radio continues to be an integral part of daily life.

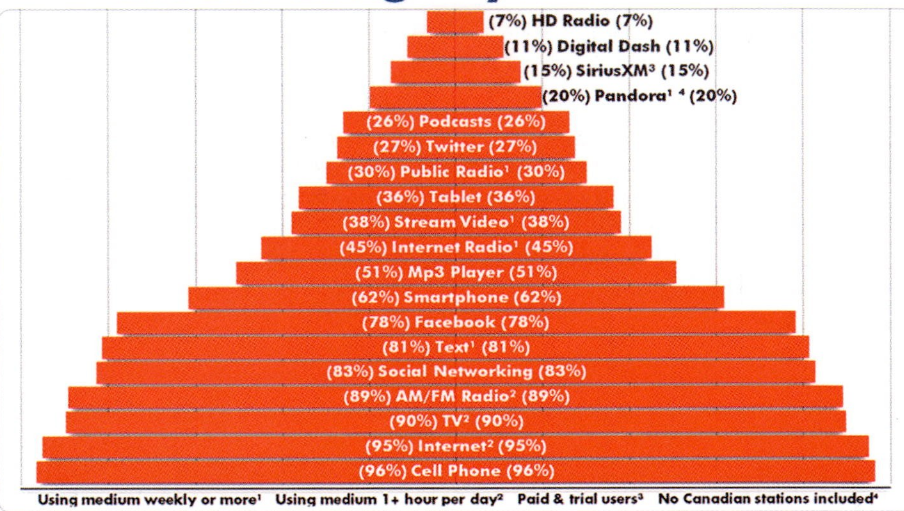

FIGURE 1.4
AM-FM radio listening remains an important media activity, according to this 2013 study: 264 stations across the U.S and Canada; 12 formats; 78,111 radio listener responses; four generations. Survey dates: January–February, 2013. All responses were collected online and solicited via email or social media channels. Courtesy Jacobs Media. ©2013. Used by permission.

WHAT DO YOU BELIEVE?

Eric Rhoads

FIGURE 1.5
Eric Rhoads.

You and I are living in perhaps the fastest-changing times in history. While much of the "old media" business still exists, the new world of media is vastly more powerful and more influential—and it's moving so fast that even the experts cannot track the rate of change.

From the perspective of my friends in Silicon Valley, you and I are employed in dinosaur media. They respect what we have done, and they want to steal our audiences and advertisers for their online audio services, but they think we're being silly when we cling to our transmitters. After all, the concept of "broadcasting" one signal to many radios is so very 1920s. They believe our model is broken, and it's just a matter of time before we lose our audiences and our advertisers—to them. What do you believe?

Is Radio Immune to the Changes?

Many broadcasters I speak with think the radio industry is immune to the sea change that has been seen in other industries. They feel that, because it hasn't happened yet, audience loyalty has saved our industry from its digital downfall.

But maybe we've just been lucky. Many buy the argument that radio has weathered the storms of other past attacks—8-tracks, cassettes, CDs, cell phones—so it will weather any new attacks, too.

The newspapers believed they were safe, too. And although they pretended to embrace digital and were among the first to launch websites, the mistake they made was trying to create a "hybrid media." They should have fearlessly cannibalized the print papers and developed the next big thing so they could control it. *Newspapers* should have put newspapers out of business, rather than allowing others to launch competing services and take their businesses away.

When you live with one foot in the old world and one in the new, the tendency is to approach every decision based on the way things have always been done. For far too long, newspapers refused to allow their news to hit their websites until after it had been in print. Is radio acting the same way?

Are You Willing to Cannibalize?

What you believe matters now more than ever, and radio's success as an industry will rely on our willingness to cannibalize ourselves. You can try to maintain the status quo, or assume that your station website is your digital insurance policy, but the real danger for all of us is ignoring facts and trends. Are you writing off Pandora, saying it won't last? Or are you looking to invent something better—not a copy, but something consumers will embrace even more?

Though I think aggregation services like TuneIn and iHeartRadio are important and believe every radio station needs to be a part of one of these services, we also need to follow other listening trends. Although an aggregated player allows the listener to pick from a variety of station types, that's still repurposing a broad product in a narrow, personalized digital world. The only reason we have broad formats is because there is a limit on the number of signals we can have in a market. Radio needs to be reinvented for the personalized experience of a digital environment.

Can You Say Audio?

My passion for radio began as a kid who was fascinated by stations with entertaining personalities and my favorite music. To me, radio is audio entertainment, and whether it comes from a car radio, a home radio, a tablet, a mobile device, or a transmitter is irrelevant. If you're clinging to your transmitter or have an idea that you don't want to stream to out-of-market consumers, you're missing a lot of opportunity.

Are You Admitting the Game Has Changed?

I continually hear complaints about change, about how big radio companies are cutting out local personalities and changing the way they do business. Although it's sad to see so many displaced radio soldiers, the reality is that this environment, this economy, and improving technology will increase this trend. Those who are caught in the crossfire need to realize the game has changed, certain positions will never return, and you'll have to keep reinventing yourself in order to stay employable. You don't want to be an out-of-work telegraph operator in a smartphone world.

The Past Will Return . . . Sure

I'm a nostalgic guy, and I love to think about the days when radio personality was at its peak and we had 15-share radio stations. They were fun times. I appreciate them, but I don't pine for their return, because there is no force in this industry big enough to make that happen. Big companies are not finally going to come to their senses and add back what they've cut out over the last ten years.

It's Time to Become Relevant Again

Every industry is facing tremendous change. Every industry is seeking efficient ways to survive through technology—and that results in jobs lost. Those of us in radio who have seen jobs eliminated, and those who have lost jobs, should not just try to shift to another station, we should realize that change will follow us all of our careers, and the only way to remain relevant and employable is to stay ahead of change.

So What Do You Believe?

Although I embrace change personally, I also find myself fighting it daily. It's human nature, and overcoming it requires a personal plan to embrace and make change for change's sake. We cannot wait for our companies to implement change. We cannot follow everyone else. We as professionals need to step up and force ourselves to reinvent, time and again. The way you reinvent yourself today may become irrelevant in another year. As Bob Pittman said, "Change is in our DNA." It should be in your DNA, and you need to force it to occur in your career.

Are You a Follower or a Leader?

I always used to think radio people were trendsetters, and some still are, but it seems that many today are no longer leading the pack. The same people who put radical FMs on the air, spat in the face of traditional AM programming, and changed the world are now the people protecting their turf rather than inventing the next radical change. Even though it's frightening, history tells us that someone else will reinvent us if we don't do it ourselves. It's happening all around us. You can't prevent it, but you can embrace it.

Radio—audio entertainment—will change, and if we don't each individually embrace and seek change, we will never catch up. We'll be remembered like the newspaper industry: changed, but by someone else.

Eric Rhoads is a career entrepreneur with 30 years of launching companies and media brands, creating start-ups and building businesses including more than 40 years' experience and leadership in the radio broadcasting field, 25 years in the publishing business, and 15 years in the art industry. Rhoads serves as chairman of the board of Streamline Publishing, Inc., which he founded in 1985. He also serves or has served as a consultant and advisor to companies in media, technology, digital media, and art. He has been recognized by the Broadcasters Foundation and was inducted as a "Broadcast Pioneer," one of the industry's highest honors.

Radio Reaches All Ages

Weekly Cume Rating
Listeners 12+ (Mon-Sun 6AM-Mid)

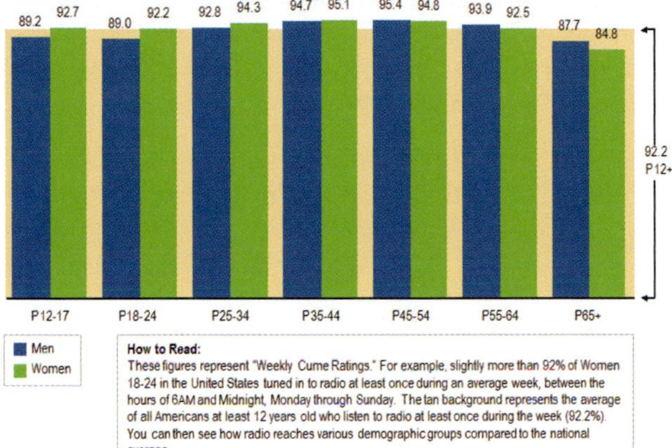

How to Read:
These figures represent "Weekly Cume Ratings." For example, slightly more than 92% of Women 18-24 in the United States tuned in to radio at least once during an average week, between the hours of 6AM and Midnight, Monday through Sunday. The tan background represents the average of all Americans at least 12 years old who listen to radio at least once during the week (92.2%). You can then see how radio reaches various demographic groups compared to the national average.

continued ▶

RADAR 115, December 2012; Radio Usage; Mon-Sun 6AM-Midnight

FIGURE 1.6
Courtesy Arbitron. Source "Radio Today 2013: How America Listens to Radio." © 2013 Arbitron, Inc. All Rights Reserved.

Hour-by-Hour Listening

Hour-by-Hour Listening, AQH Rating
Listeners 12+
Percent of Persons Using Radio
Mon-Fri, Sat-Sun, Total Day (5AM-5AM)

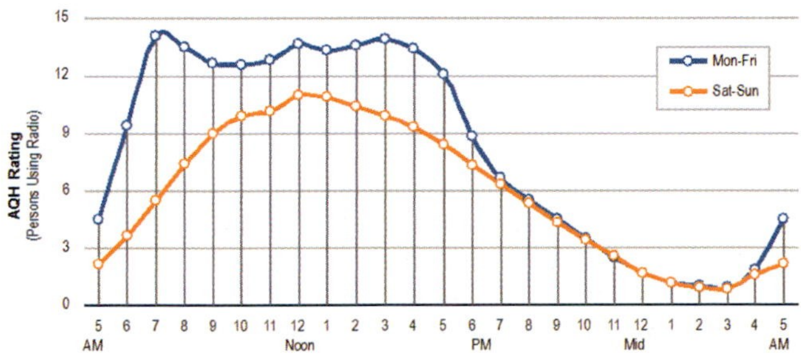

Source: TAPSCAN™ Web National Regional Database, Spring 2012

FIGURE 1.7
Courtesy Arbitron. Source "Radio Today 2013: How America Listens to Radio." © 2013 Arbitron, Inc. All Rights Reserved.

NON-COMMERCIAL/PUBLIC RADIO

More than 1,500 stations operate without direct advertiser support. Non-commercial stations, as they are called, date back to the medium's heyday and were primarily run by colleges and universities. The first "non-coms" broadcast on the AM band but moved to the FM side in 1938. After World War II, the FCC reconstituted the FM band and reserved the first 20 channels (88–92 MHz) for non-commercial facilities. Initially, this gave rise to low-power (10-watt) stations known as Class Ds. The lower cost of such operations was a prime motivator for schools that wanted to become involved with broadcasting.

In 1967, the Corporation for Public Broadcasting (CPB) was established as the result of the Public Broadcasting Act. Within three years National Public Radio (NPR) was formed. Today, more than 900 stations use the syndication services of NPR, which provides programming. In 2010, it adopted a new name, shortening "National Public Radio" to just "NPR." Many NPR affiliates are licensed to colleges and universities, and a substantial number are owned by non-profit organizations. To balance its budget, in 2013, NPR offered buyouts to 10% of its employees.

ABOUT

PRI Public Radio International℠

Public Radio International (PRI) is the source of more public radio programming than any other distributor in the United States. Founded in 1983 as American Public Radio, PRI is steadily moving forward with its second decade goal to "provide expanded global perspectives on world news, current events, and culture to public radio audiences."

In addition to acquiring finished programming from station-based and independent producers around the globe, PRI actively shapes and develops new programs and program formats. PRI also seeks to expand the reach, impact, and relevancy of public radio for audiences who have not traditionally been public radio listeners.

The network emphasizes programming in three general areas:

- News and information
- Classical music
- Comedy/Variety and contemporary music

PRI also distributes an average of four special programs per month.

Keep us in mind and on file. We look forward to talking with YOU.

PRI Public Radio International℠

Public Radio International
100 North Sixth Street, Suite 900A
Minneapolis, Minnesota 55403
Telephone: 612.338.5000
Facsimile: 612.330.9222

This recycled paper is made from 50% waste paper and contains 10% postconsumer waste.

FIGURE 1.8
A Public Radio International promotional piece. Courtesy PRI.

Member stations are the primary source of funding for NPR, contributing 60% of its operating budget. Affiliates in turn are supported by listeners, community businesses, and grants from the CPB. Program underwriting (the equivalent of sponsorships) is a primary way that public stations meet their operating budgets. These on-air announcements run approximately 15 seconds and include sponsor name and information but no direct selling or hype. They are purchased by sponsors in much the same way that spots are sold on commercial stations—from a rate card based on ratings. (Public radio station websites usually provide more detail on this subject.)

The CPB claims that 22.2 million listeners tune into public radio stations on a weekly basis. NPR claims that more than 13 million Americans tune into their member stations. Their literature states that "NPR's news and performance programming attracts an audience distinguished by its level of education, professionalism, and community involvement." (Programs such as *All Things Considered* and

Morning Edition have become the industry's premier news and information features, achieving both popular and critical acclaim.) Public radio consultant Ken Mills declares:

> The growth of public radio news listening is one of the biggest success stories in terrestrial radio of the past two decades. Since the early 1990s, listening to NPR News stations has more than doubled. As of 2005, more than 26 million listeners hear NPR News each week. NPR News stations are often among the most-listened-to stations in most markets. The growing demand for public radio news has created an opportunity for public radio consultants such as myself. News/talk programming and documentaries—the types of programming I specialize in—will likely continue to be in demand.

Research shows that NPR listeners are consumers of information from many sources and are more likely than average Americans to buy books. They are motivated citizens involved in public activities, such as voting and fundraising. They address public meetings, write letters to editors, and lead business and civic groups.

Public Radio International (formerly American Public Radio) debuted in 1983 and operated much like NPR. It provided listeners with additional non-commercial options, airing popular programs such as Garrison Keillor's *A Prairie Home Companion* and many others.

ON PUBLIC RADIO

William Siemering

Although the distance between commercial and public radio has narrowed in recent years, they remain notably different. As the largest single source of income for public radio stations is listener contributions, the programming is listener-driven and the program directors read the Arbitron ratings just as their commercial colleagues do. However, their programming must be significantly different in content and quality from commercial programs to elicit freewill contributions. (In many European countries, public service broadcasting is supported by a tax on receivers, not voluntary contributions.) Commercial stations, although often involved in community service, have one goal: make a profit. Public stations have a mission to serve unmet cultural, information, and community needs.

FIGURE 1.9
William Siemering.

The most listened-to programs on public radio are news and information programs: *Morning Edition*, *All Things Considered*, and *Fresh Air*. These are characterized by both the thoroughness of their coverage and the breadth of subjects. They regard news of the arts/popular culture to be as important to understanding the world as news of politicians.

No commercial network comes close to replicating these programs. Local stations frequently sponsor town meetings on important public affairs issues or sponsor concerts in the community to strengthen their local links. Local stations may broadcast jazz, Triple A (Adult Alternative Album), bluegrass, acoustic, classical music, or an array of talk programs. Some stations are directed to specific audiences such as Hispanic or Indian.

Public radio listeners tend to be educated and to include decision-makers and influentials in their communities, so their influence is great. Eight out of ten newspaper editors rely on it as an important source of information, as do network television producers and anchors. *Publishers Weekly* said public radio is the single most important medium for the book business.

In addition to support from listeners, public radio also receives corporate and business underwriting, and grants from foundations and the CPB, which was created in 1967 to distribute federal funds and protect stations against political pressure on programming. Managing a public radio station is, therefore, more complex because its funding is so diverse. At the same time it must protect the independence of the programming from the influence of the funders.

Recently, some politicians have questioned continued federal funding for public broadcasting, and various alternative systems of this support are being explored.

William "Bill" Siemering was the first Director of Programming of National Public Radio where he developed the long-running and well-known radio program, All Things Considered. He currently serves as president of Developing Radio Partners, an organization dedicated to supporting independent radio stations in young democracies through professional development in journalism, programming, station management, and finance.

Non-commercial stations can be divided into at least three categories: public, college (non-commercial educational), and community. A fourth category, non-commercial religious stations, has emerged during the past couple of decades and continues to grow in the 2010s.

Many public radio stations, especially those affiliated with NPR, choose to air classical music around the clock; others opt to set aside only a portion of their broadcast day for classical programming. According to the pre-eminent association of college broadcasters, the Intercollegiate Broadcasting System (IBS), more than 800 schools and colleges hold non-commercial licenses. The majority of these stations operate at lower power, some with as little as 10 watts. Since the late 1970s, a large percentage of college stations have upgraded from Class D and now radiate signals with powers of hundreds of watts or more. Most college stations serve as training grounds for future broadcasters while providing alternative programming for their listeners.

Community non-coms are usually licensed to civic groups, foundations, school boards, and religious associations. Although the majority of these stations broadcast at low power, they manage to satisfy the programming desires of thousands of listeners.

THE STORY OF COLLEGE RADIO DAY . . .

Dr. Rob Quicke

In December, 2010, I watched a movie called *The Social Network* about the story of Facebook. I was tremendously inspired and wondered whether there was a singular idea that could unite and excite the college radio community in the same way that Facebook initially united the college community. The next day I woke up with the idea of College Radio Day (CRD). The idea seemed so obvious that I searched online to see if there was precedent for a day of national unity for college radio, and I could not find any previous attempts to do so.

FIGURE 1.10
Dr. Rob Quicke.

The idea percolated throughout the first half of 2011 and in May 2011 I launched a website (collegeradioday.com) and put the call out for college stations in America to join together for the event. The biggest fear was that no one would participate.

I knew we had my college station, WPSC at William Paterson University (where I am GM and associate professor), and my friend Peter Kreten, GM of WXAV at Saint Xavier University in Chicago, was the only other station who had pledged to participate from day one. When I sent that first email out to as many college radio stations as possible I could only hope that we could persuade 50 of them to join the event. What happened in the next four months is that 365 stations in America, Canada, and Jamaica signed up for the October 11 event! Quickly I formed a CRD "Cabinet" with students and faculty advisors from across America as leaders helping guide, advise, and promote the event. We used free social media tools to recruit and spread the word about the event. We had no budget, save for the money that I had personally invested to get the website off the ground.

FIGURE 1.11
World College Radio Day 2013: More than 700 stations in 43 countries. Courtesy Dr. Rob Quicke.

Our mission is simple: the aim of College Radio Day is to harness the combined listenership of hundreds of thousands of college radio listeners throughout the world and to celebrate the important contributions of college radio by uniting for this one day. We encourage people who would not normally listen to college radio to do so on this day.

Around the summer of 2011, I had been reading *The Long Tail* by Chris

Anderson and was intrigued by the idea that if many fragmented organizations and people come together to unite in a common cause, collectively they can generate significant interest and have a larger impact because of their union. I experienced this theory work first-hand when I came to work and found voicemails requesting interviews from *The New York Times*, *The Washington Post*, *USA Today*, *Los Angeles Times*, and more, all wanting to know more about College Radio Day. This was during a difficult economic time when some college radio stations had been shut down and sold off by their owners. I believe that College Radio Day was an event that coincided with the need for college radio to make a collective statement that it was still around and was going to survive the turmoil of that time. With CRD we challenged the media narrative that suggested college radio was perhaps doomed. Not so!

College Radio Day was originally conceived as, and continues to be, a genuine celebration of college radio. Another surprise was how quickly the event caught on internationally. For some countries college radio is a relatively recent development—and in Europe and South America student radio stations are flourishing!

For the second CRD in 2012 we had 585 stations in 28 countries join us, all speaking in different languages but essentially all making the same point: that college radio is one of the last remaining bastions of creative radio programming, free from the constrictions of having to be commercially viable, and a place where those involved in its programming believe passionately in its mission. College radio is still an important training ground for future professional broadcasters. I love how participating stations are free to celebrate CRD by broadcasting whatever they want during the day, really unleashing their inventiveness.

College radio is the only free live medium brave enough to play unsigned, local, and independent artists on a regular basis. Indeed, many famous and successful bands today owe their initial break to being played on college radio. Put simply, college radio is an important part of the media landscape because of its unique and fearless programming.

The potential for our reach is enormous. I will never forget spending the morning with Coldplay and their lead singer Chris Martin who launched CRD 2012 by recording an interview and special message of support for college radio. With more than 700 stations in 43 countries, we are a growing, grassroots non-profit organization that has a voice that cannot be ignored! For college radio, the future is very bright indeed.

Dr. Rob Quicke is founder of College Radio Day and is also a tenured associate professor of communication at William Paterson University where he also serves as general manager of WPSC 88.7 FM in Wayne, New Jersey. In 2013, Rob won the "Outstanding Service Award" from the Intercollegiate Broadcasting System (IBS) for his dedication to academic broadcasting.

In some instances, non-coms pose a ratings threat to commercial stations. However, this threat is usually in the area of classical music and news programming. Consequently, commercial and non-commercial radio stations manage a fairly peaceful and congenial coexistence. (See "Suggested Further Reading" at the end of this chapter for additional information on non-commercial radio.)

RADIO STATION FORMATS

The list below includes all of the radio formats measured in Arbitron listening surveys.

FORMATS

80s Hits	New AC (NAC)/Smooth Jazz
Active Rock	New Country
Adult Contemporary (AC)	News/Talk/Information
Adult Hits	Nostalgia
Adult Standards/MOR	Oldies
Album Adult Alternative (AAA)	Other
Album Oriented Rock (AOR)	Pop Contemporary Hit Radio
All News	Religious
All Sports	Rhythmic AC
Alternative	Rhythmic Contemporary Hit Radio
Blues	Rhythmic Oldies
Children's Radio	Smooth AC
Christian AC	Soft AC
Classical	Southern Gospel
Classic Country	Spanish Adult Hits
Classic Hits	Spanish Contemporary
Classic Rock	Spanish Contemporary Christian
Comedy	Spanish Hot AC
Contemporary Christian	Spanish News/Talk
Contemporary Inspirational	Spanish Oldies
Country	Spanish Religious
Easy Listening	Spanish Sports
Educational	Spanish Tropical
Family Hits	Spanish Variety
Gospel	Talk/Personality
Hot AC	Tejano
Jazz	Urban AC
Latino Urban	Urban Contemporary
Mainstream Rock	Urban Oldies
Mexican Regional	Variety
Modern AC	World Ethnic

FIGURE 1.12
Format descriptors currently recognized by Arbitron. ©2013 Arbitron, Inc.

PROLIFERATION AND FRAG-OUT

Specialization—*narrowcasting* or *nichecasting* as it came to be called—salvaged the medium in the early 1950s. Before that time, radio bore little resemblance to its sound during the age of television. It was the video medium that copied radio's approach to programming during its golden age. "Sightradio," as television was sometimes ironically called, drew from the older electronic medium its programming schematic and left radio hovering on the edge of the abyss. Gradually, radio station managers realized they could not combat the dire effects of television by programming in a like manner. To survive they had to change. To attract listeners they had to offer a different type of service. The majority of stations went to spinning records and presenting short newscasts. Sports and weather forecasts became an industry staple.

Initially, most outlets aired broad-appeal music. Specialized forms, such as jazz, rhythm and blues, and country, were left off most playlists, except in certain regions of the country. Eventually, these all-things-to-all-people stations were challenged by what is considered to be the first popular attempt at format specialization. As legend now has it, radio programmer Todd Storz and his assistant Bill Steward of KOWH-AM in Omaha, Nebraska, decided to limit their station's playlist to only those records that currently enjoyed high sales. The idea for the scheme struck them at a local tavern as they observed people spending money to play mostly the same few songs on the jukebox. Their programming concept became known as "Top 40." Within months of executing their new format, KOWH topped the ratings. Word of their success spread, inspiring other stations around the nation to take the pop-record approach. They too found success.

By the early 1960s other formats had evolved, including Beautiful Music, which was introduced over San Francisco station KABL, and All-News, which first aired over XETRA located in Tijuana, Mexico. Both formats were the progeny of Gordon McLendon and were successfully copied across the country.

The diversity of musical styles that evolved in the mid-1960s, with the help of such disparate performers as the Beatles and Glen Campbell, gave rise to myriad format variations. Although some stations focused on 1950s rock 'n' roll ("blasts from the past" and "oldies but goodies"), others stuck to current hits, and still others chose to play more obscure rock album cuts. The 1960s saw the advent of the radio formats of soft rock and acid and psychedelic hard rock. Meanwhile, country, whose popularity had been confined mostly to areas of the South and Midwest, experienced a sudden growth in its acceptance through the crossover appeal of artists such as John Hartford, Bobbie Gentry, Bobby Goldsboro, Johnny Cash, and, in particular, Glen Campbell, whose sophisticated country-flavor songs topped both the Top 40 and country charts.

As types of music continued to become more diffused in the 1970s, a host of new formats came into use. The listening audience became more and more fragmented. *Frag-out*, a term coined by radio consultant Kent Burkhart, posed an ever-increasing challenge to program directors (PDs) whose job it was to attract a large enough piece of the radio audience to keep their stations profitable.

The late 1970s and early 1980s saw the rise and decline of the disco format, which eventually evolved into urban contemporary, and a wave of interest in synthesizer-based electropop. Formats such as soft rock faded from the scene only to be replaced by a narrower form of Top 40 called "contemporary hit." New formats continue to surface with almost predictable regularity. Among the more recent to appear (and, in some instances, disappear) are Adult Standards, New AC/Smooth Jazz, Eclectic-Oriented Rock, All-Weather, Churban, All-Motivation, and All-Business.

Although specialization saved the industry from an untimely end half a century ago, the proliferation in the number of radio stations (which have more than quadrupled since 1950) competing for the same audience has brought about the age of hyperspecialization. Today, there are more than 100 format variations in the radio marketplace, compared to a handful when radio stations first acknowledged the necessity of programming to a preselected segment of the audience as the only means to remain in business. Also, programming options offered via smartphone apps (iHeartRadio and radio.com) and satellite (SiriusXM) provide even more options for listeners (for a more detailed discussion on radio formats, see Chapter 3).

PROFITS IN THE AIR

Although radio has been unable to regain the share of the national advertising dollar it attracted before the arrival of television, it does earn far more today than it did during its so-called heyday. About 7% of all money spent on advertising goes to radio. This computes to billions of dollars.

Despite the enormous gains since WEAF introduced the concept of broadcast advertising, radio cannot be regarded as a get-rich-quick scheme. Many stations walk a thin line between profit and loss. Although some major market radio stations demand and receive more than $1,000 for a one-minute commercial, an equal number sell time for the proverbial "dollar a holler."

Although the medium's earnings have maintained a progressive growth pattern, radio has also experienced periods of recession. These financial slumps or dry periods have almost all occurred since 1950. Initially, television's effect on radio's revenues was devastating. The medium began to recoup its losses when it shifted its reliance from the networks and national advertisers to local businesses. Today, 70% of radio's revenues come from local spot sales as compared to half that figure in 1948.

By targeting specific audience demographics, the industry remained solvent. In the 1980s, a typical radio station earned $50,000 annually in profits. As the medium regained its footing after the staggering blow administered to it by television, it experienced both peaks and valleys financially. In 1961, for example, the FCC reported that more radio stations recorded losses than in any previous period because it began keeping records of such things. Two years later, however, the industry happily recorded its greatest profits ever. In 1963, the medium's revenues exceeded $636 million. In the next few years earnings would be up 60%, surpassing the $1.5 billion mark, and would leap another 150% between 1970 and 1980. FM profits have tripled since 1970 and have significantly contributed to the overall industry figures.

The AM daytimer segment of the industry has found it the most difficult to stay in the black. The FCC requires these radio stations to commence operating no earlier than local sunrise and to cease broadcasting around the time of local sunset so as not to interfere with other AM stations. Of the approximately 2,000 daytimers in operation, nearly a third reported losses at one time or another in the 1980s.

Concerning the challenges of programming an AM daytimer, station manager Dan Collier observes:

> You don't have the money for staff. You don't have the budget for talented people. You don't have the resources for new equipment or to even maintain the equipment you have, which is typically in disrepair. These stations are a very tough sell to advertisers, so they lapse into decline and many eventually go silent. It doesn't have to be that way, but good management of this type of station is almost as scarce as advertising dollars.

The unique problem facing daytime-only broadcasters has been further aggravated by FM's dramatic surge in popularity. The nature of their license gives daytimers subordinate status to fulltime AM operations, which have found competing no easy trick, especially in the light of FM's success. Because of the lowly status of the daytimer in a marketplace that has become increasingly thick with rivals, it is extremely difficult for these stations to prosper, although some do very well. Many daytimers have opted for specialized forms of programming to attract advertisers. For example, religious and ethnic formats have proven successful.

Over the years, the FCC has considered a number of proposals to enhance the status of AM stations. One such proposal suggested that the interference problem could be reduced if certain stations shifted frequencies to the extended portion (1605–1705 kHz) of the AM band. FCC Docket 87–267, issued in the latter part of 1991, cited the preceding as a primary step in improving the AM situation. It inspired many skeptics who regarded it as nothing more than a bandage. Other elements of the plan included tax incentives for AM broadcasters who pull the plug on their ailing operations and multiple AM station ownership in the same market.

As a consequence of the formidable obstacles facing the AM daytime operation, many have been put up for sale, and asking prices have been alarmingly low. However,. many fulltime metro-market AMs have sold for multimillions, for the simple reason that they continue to appear in the top of their respective ratings surveys. Meanwhile, the price for FM stations has skyrocketed since

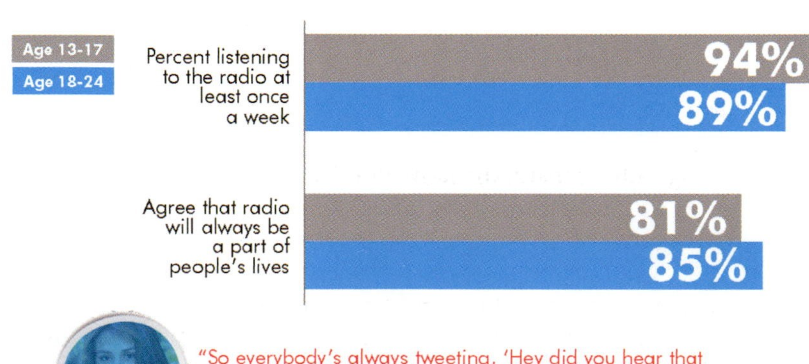
YOUNG PEOPLE ARE LISTENING TO RADIO A LOT AND SEE RADIO AS INTEGRAL TO THEIR LIVES
Young consumers listen as much as the rest of us, and majority expect it to always be part of their lives.
Age 13-17
Age 18-24
Percent listening to the radio at least once a week
94%
89%
Agree that radio will always be a part of people's lives
81%
85%
"So everybody's always tweeting, 'Hey did you hear that new song on Z100?' And they want to go look and see so they can tweet about it, too – and look cool."

clearchannel
iHeart RADIO

FIGURE 1.13
Data appearing in the 2013 iHeartRadio/Clear Channel study *The State of Listening Today* suggest connections between radio and young listeners remain strong. ©2013 Clear Channel.

1970. To illustrate FM radio stations increasing value as a business venture, in May 2012, Boston's WFNX-FM was sold to Clear Channel Communications for an estimated $14.5 million in cash.

In general, individual station profits have not kept pace with industry-wide profits due to the rapid growth in the number of outlets over the past two decades. To say the least, competition is keen and in many markets downright fierce. It is common for 30 or more radio stations to vie for the same advertising dollars in large cities, and the introduction of other media in recent years, such as cable, satellite, radio aggregators, and Internet-Only (IO) radio, intensifies the skirmish over sponsors.

ECONOMIC TURBULENCE

Like all businesses, the radio industry experiences times of economic uncertainty. The end of the twentieth century and the early part of the twenty-first century were tough financial times for the industry. Following the general financial euphoria and binge-buying of the 1980s, the early 1990s experienced a considerable economic downturn, which had a jarring impact on the radio industry. Had the medium become a "top-down" industry, to use the vernacular of the day?

Many people consider 1991 to have been one of the worst years ever for radio. "As a result of the proliferation of stations, the excessively high prices paid for them during the deregulatory buying and selling binge of the late 1980s, and the recession, more than half of the stations in the country ran in the red," observed Rick Sklar of Sklar Communications.

Producer Ty Ford agreed with Sklar, adding:

> The price fallout of the late 1980s and early 1990s was due in great part to the collapse of the property-value spiral that was started by deregulation and the negative effect that investors had on the broadcasting business. This resulted in depressed or reduced salaries and an inability to make equipment updates due to the need to pay off highly leveraged station loans.

According to leading radio consultant Kent Burkhart:

> The recession in the first third of the 1990s crippled financing of radio properties. The banks were under highly leveraged transaction (HLT) rules regarding radio loans; thus the value of stations dropped by one-third to one-half. The recession created advertising havoc too. Instead of five-deep buys, we were looking for one- through three-deep. Emotional sales pitches were rejected. Stations streamlined costs due to the economic slump. Airshifts were expanded and promotion budgets slashed. The top 10 to 15 markets did reasonably well in the revenue column, but

> those markets outside of the top majors went searching for new ad dollars, which were difficult to find.

The total value of radio station sales declined 65% in a six-month period between 1990 and 1991, and radio revenues dropped 4% during the same period, according to statistics in *Broadcasting* magazine (September 9, 1991). All of this took place during a time when operating expenses rose. These were troubling figures when compared to the salad days of 1988 when $5.8 billion was paid for 955 radio stations.

Cash flow problems were the order of the day, and this resulted, as Ty Ford pointed out, in significant budgetary cuts. This was made very evident by a report in the December 1991 issue of *Broadcast Engineering* magazine that stated, "All radio budgets show a decrease." The survey showed that budgets for equipment purchases were being delayed and that "planned spending for most areas is somewhat below last year's."

To counter the sharp reversal of fortunes, many broadcasters formed local marketing (also called *management*) agreements (LMAs), whereby one radio station leases time and/or facilities from another area station. The buzzword in the early 1990s became LMAs.

LMAs allowed radio stations to enter into economically advantageous, joint operating ventures, stated the editors of *Radio World*. They believed that LMAs should remain the province of the local marketplace and not be regulated by the federal government. The publication asserted that LMAs provide broadcasters a means of functioning during tough economic times and in a ferociously competitive marketplace.

Those who opposed LMAs feared that diversity would be lost as stations combined resources (signals, staffs, and facilities). A few years later, the relaxation of the duopoly rules would raise similar concerns. Proponents argued that this was highly improbable given the vast number of frequencies that light up the dial. In other words, there is safety in numbers, and the public will continue to be served. However, radio station general manager Pat McNally presciently observed, "In the long run LMAs and consolidation may cause a loss of available jobs in our business and help to continue the erosion of creative salesmanship and conceptual selling. Radio station sales staffs will become like small rep firms."

In the 1990s, radio programming software developer Dave Scott observed that LMAs had inspired some interesting arrangements.

> Some of the novel partnerships include a suburban station north of Atlanta that bought a suburban station south of Atlanta and created one studio to feed them both. A similar situation occurred in San Francisco/San Jose, and I believe they're on the same frequency (or maybe a notch apart). Around Los Angeles, someone got two or three stations on the same frequency. Necessity is the mother of invention, they say.

Although many industry people were guardedly hopeful about the future of radio, many saw change as inevitable. "Major adjustments are being made as the consequence of the recent mini-crash. In the future, we will depend on fewer non-revenue producers at stations. We'll see less people per facility. The belt will be tightened for good," notes Bill Campbell, former vice president and general manager of WSNE-FM in Providence, Rhode Island.

Rick Sklar accurately predicted that satellite-supplied stations would have a role in this. "To save money and stay in business, large numbers of stations are going satellite and others are turning to suppliers of 24-hour formats for their programming because of the economic environment." (See Chapter 11 for more on syndicated programming.)

Fred Jacobs, president of Jacobs Media, assessed the state of the Fifth Estate:

> In the first third of the 1990s, everything seemed to be converging, and radio's future was up in the air. Many operators were in debt and were feeling the pressures of a long economic recession. Similarly, the FCC was not providing regulatory focus. There was no consensus about the legality of LMAs, multiple station ownership in the same market, and so on. Format fragmentation had made for a more competitive environment in most cities, including medium markets. The available revenue pie was now being split among more players. Like cable television, radio has become very niche-oriented.

Then came the financial crash of 2008. The dramatic downturn in the economy impacted radio station values and brought a decline in advertisers, who were adjusting their budgets in light of the recession. Among the casualties was the Tribune Company whose COO at the time, Randy Michaels, had observed, "We aren't quite on the ropes yet. We're restructuring our debt, so we'll be around for a while yet." In the end, observes Entercom's Operations Manager, Dave Neugesser:

> While the economy may be wreaking havoc, just as important are the new audio platforms that have grown over the past five years. Radio has the unfortunate and unfair image of being viewed as old media. There are newer, shinier objects that have become even sexier than radio, so the tide has turned away from the medium on multiple fronts. Hard work and ingenuity are key to its future success and survival.

Overall Radio Revenue Inched Upward in 2012

In Millions of Dollars	Dollars Spent	Percentage Change	Percentage of Total Radio Revenue
Spot	$14,205	1%	86%
Digital	$767	8%	5%
Off-Air	$1,510	1%	9%
Total	$16.482	1%	100%

FIGURE 1.14
Profits for radio appear to be on the rise for digital audio. Courtesy of the Pew Research Center.

Media Post, citing a BIA/Kelsey radio report, predicts "total over-the-air revenues will reach $15.2 billion in 2013, $15.8 billion in 2014, $16.3 billion in 2015, and $17 billion in 2016," which, if accurate, indicates a relatively stable forecast and perhaps is an indication of a more robust stream of revenue for the radio industry.

CONSOLIDATIONS, DOWNSIZINGS, AND CLUSTERS

As the medium entered the mid-1990s, it was doing more than just fine. The headlines in the industry trade publications revealed exactly how well the medium had recovered: "Radio Draws Advertisers as Economy Strengthens" (*Broadcasting,* May 1994), "Recovery" (*Radio Ink,* December 1993), "Radio Revenues Hit One Billion in May" (*Radio World,* August 1994), "National Spot Revenue up 38%" (*Broadcasting,* May 1995).

The primary cause of this dramatic upsurge was the relaxation of FCC rules, foremost among them station ownership caps and duopoly. With the advent of the Telecommunications Act of 1996, individual companies could own several stations in the same market (up to eight in large markets and no limits on national totals—at this writing, radio station ownership limits were being reviewed by the FCC), and this spurred active trading and mergers of broadcast properties. The idea was to reduce competition and thus overheads. The consolidation and downsizing prompted by LMAs would pick up steam with the elimination of the duopoly rule, which prevented dual station ownership in the same market. Greater Media's David Pearlman says, "The Telecommunications Act of 1996 is the biggest piece of legislation in radio history. It has changed everything."

Observes Lynn Christian, "Consolidation—market by market—is the word best describing what was happening in commercial radio in the 1990s. The legal authority to own and operate several radio stations in almost every market has rapidly changed radio's landscape. Radio station operators have become more like local cable operators, offering a variety of formats on the FM and AM dials."

One alarming effect of consolidation and subsequent downsizing for aspiring broadcasters is the reduction of available jobs. "Individual station staffs get small as companies grow in station holdings. A direct result of consolidation and the increase in ownership limits is fewer jobs, more generalization, and less specialization. Multitaskers will be valuable. Group presidents will be taking jobs as station managers, especially in clusters or multiple station operations," observes Ed Shane, president of Shane Media.

Another concern inspired by consolidation is the potential loss of programming diversity. Christian adds, "While cost savings and profits are central to the concept behind downsizing and multiple ownership, the creative forces in radio are taking a hit. In point of fact, in the past few years no exciting new programming ideas have been developed."

On this topic, Jay Williams, Jr., observes:

> Many argue that consolidation is bad, charging that radio programming has become less innovative and diverse, that local radio news is in decline, and the lack of competition within each local market has driven up rates for advertisers. Others counter that radio "research" combined with the demand for higher ratings had already eliminated programming innovation. Proponents for consolidation point to the stations previously competing in the same format head-to-head that are now co-owned allowing one of the stations to carve out a new format. They suggest that television and 24-hour cable news competition, plus the rising costs of radio news programming, had already precipitated the decline of radio news well before consolidation, and that new technologies, such as the continuous news updates on the Internet, have only accelerated the pace. And they point to the increasing variety of other media and promotional options open to advertisers as the reasons that radio rates will always remain competitive. It might be better if consolidation were viewed as being neither good nor bad but as a reaction to the changing realities of business.

Williams gives a brief overview of a major West Coast cluster inspired by the consolidation approach:

> Clear Channel's greater San Diego cluster consists of 13 stations. They also oversee two additional suburban stations in Temecula, California about 50 miles away. The Temecula stations simulcast two of the San Diego stations but add local content. The two suburban stations have a local sales manager and local sales staff. In addition to the stations, they also operate Clear Channel Traffic (similar to, but competitors of, Shadow and Metro traffic) and the Padres sports network as separate business entities out of this facility.

Despite the many concerns, business improved after the mid-1990s. The dollar volume of station transactions (number of stations changing hands) approved by the FCC soared. At the beginning of the new millennium, the radio business was robust, to say the least. Annual revenues were heading toward the $20 billion mark. A handful of radio corporations, many owning hundreds of stations, recorded yearly earnings in the billion-dollar range. However, by 2006, due to a variety of factors—namely increased competition—*Radio Business Report* and other industry publications were charting the downward trajectory of the medium's annual revenues. And, as already indicated, the 2008 recession hit and created economic hardships for the industry.

Meanwhile, the large radio station holdings groups began downsizing the number of properties they owned. In fact, many mega radio groups (Clear Channel is one example) returned to private ownership, forsaking Wall Street.

The trend in what is called "deconsolidation" was well underway as this edition was being prepared.

BUYING AND SELLING

Today, brokerage firms handle the sale of many radio stations. "It's difficult to overlook the importance of Wall Street and the financial community in the future of radio," notes Ed Shane. Bill Campbell, co-owner of Blue River Communications, says the future is now.

> Wall Street is where much of the buying and selling of radio outlets occurs nowadays. Things have changed to where stations are sold through lawyers and brokerage houses more than they are from broadcaster to broadcaster. Those are pretty much bygone days, and that is kind of sad. It became the "three-piece-suiters" game in the 1990s. There is little direct negotiating, no bargaining between owners over a drink at the corner pub. Stations are commodities to be bought and sold by people who sometimes have little appreciation or understanding of what radio is really all about. Of course, the economic inertia of the first part of this decade inspired more direct negotiations (strategic alliances) between owners, and I think that is good. I'm also detecting a move to drive the MBAs out of our business. Broadcasters who gain general experience beyond just management are the future.

For their services, brokers receive an average commission of 7–8% on sales, and in some cases they earn additional incentives based on the size of the transaction. In recent years, brokers have been very successful in negotiating large profits for their clients.

Brokerage firms promote the sale of stations through ads in industry trade magazines, direct mailings, and appearances at broadcast conferences. Interested buyers are provided with all the pertinent data concerning a station's geographical location, physical holdings, operating parameters, programming, and income history, as well as economic, competitive, and demographic information about the area within reach of the station's signal.

Another recent approach to the buying and selling of radio properties is the auction method, although this means of selling a station is perceived by some as a kind of last-resort effort at getting rid of profitless stations, most of which are AM. Owing to the upsurge in radio's fortunes, this approach has declined.

The average price for FM stations is higher than it is for AM. In the early 1990s the average price for an FM station exceeded several million, and in the 2010s was in the tens, if not hundreds, of millions. Meanwhile, at this writing, many AM outlets sell in the hundreds of thousands. In 2012, radio stations sold for as much as $50 million for five FM stations in large media markets owned by CBS Radio and as little as $100,000 for KWRD-AM in Henderson, Texas. Many

AM broadcasters look for fulltime status, improved reception, and stereo to increase the value of their properties in the coming years, although the stereo conversion of the band is hardly seen as the panacea it once was. In 2000, Clear Channel paid $24 billion for AMFM's group of radio stations.

Despite the bullishness of the station acquisition market, Robin Martin, retired CEO of the Deer River Group, expressed concerns about the tactics used by station owners to keep property values high.

> The radio industry is too defensive and is not pursuing innovative strategies for creating new streams of revenue. How the industry in general is responding to more competition and new technologies does not inform the average owner (not a major group owner) about how to succeed in this changing environment on a local level. Each market, each owner, and each station will have unique sets of circumstances that would define the optimal strategies for that situation. As I visit different markets and talk with station owners and managers, I find that there are creative plans for success of many different types in markets of all size and characteristics. Forget what the overall industry pundits and reports say. Study the specific target market to understand how to develop the strategies that will begin or continue to generate advertiser loyalty and the willingness to commit with more advertising and promotion money on the station. Radio generates enough revenues in most markets to give individual owners opportunities to make good returns on their investments. Regardless of the dire news on the national level, there are successes to be earned in many markets. The difficult truth is that, with some exceptions for turnarounds, gone are the days of easy double-digit increases in sales from traditional ad revenues. Cost control and the generation of creative concepts to increase advertiser stickiness and new types of revenues are necessary ingredients for financial stability, growth, and enhanced station values.

THE HD RADIO™ REVOLUTION

A predecessor to HD Radio was AM stereo. In its hope to help AM radio out of its doldrums, in the early 1980s the FCC authorized stereocasting on the senior band. However, the commission failed to declare a technical standard, leaving that task to the marketplace. This resulted in a very sluggish conversion to the two-channel system, and by the 1990s only a few hundred AM outlets offered stereo broadcasting. Those that did were typically the more prosperous metro market stations that ultimately featured talk and information formats.

Eventually, the FCC declared Motorola the industry standard-bearer, but by the mid-1990s the hope that stereo would provide a cure for AM's deepening malaise had dimmed considerably. By this time, many AM outlets, which may have benefited by having a stereo signal, were in a weaker financial state and unable to convert or were less than enthusiastic about any potential payback.

Many were just holding on in the hope that the impending conversion of radio to digital would help level the playing field for AM. In the 2000s, the C-QUAM (Compatible—Quadrature Amplitude Modulation) system grew in popularity and allowed for HD radio to broadcast AM stereo signals.

DAB, or HD Radio, makes analog AM and FM outmoded systems. With the great popularity of home and portable digital music equipment (CD, MP3s, iPods), broadcasters are compelled to convert their signals to remain competitive. Thus, DAB, known more popularly as HD Radio, a registered trademark of its developer, iBiquity Digital Corporation, looms large in the future of radio. The days of analog signal propagation are numbered. (For an explanation of both digital and analog transmission characteristics, see Chapters 9 and 10.)

In the mid-1980s, compact disc players were introduced to the consumer market. Today, CD players no longer rank as the top consumer item for home music reproduction, because they have all but been replaced by iPods and smartphones equipped to play MP3 files and other formats of compressed-audio files. Turntables, which were believed to have long gone by the board, have regained popularity with next-gen audiophiles, although few working tables are found in today's control rooms. The analog tape cassette market is consigned largely to the history books. Digital is here to stay, at least until something better comes along.

At first broadcasters viewed DAB as a threat. The National Association of Broadcasters (NAB) looked at the new sound technology as an adversary. In an interview in the July 23, 1990, issue of *RadioWeek*, John Abel, NAB's executive vice-president of operations, stated, "DAB is a threat and anyone who plans to stay in business for a while needs to pay careful attention."

As time went on, DAB was regarded as a *fait accompli*, something that was simply going to happen. Soon broadcasters assumed a more proactive posture regarding the technology, and then the concern shifted to where to put the new medium and how to protect existing broadcast operations.

Early on, NAB proposed locating DAB in the L-band portion of the electromagnetic spectrum. It also argued for in-band placement. Eventually the FCC saw fit to recommend that DAB be allocated room in the S-band, and it took its proposal to the World Administrative Radio Conference (WARC) held in Spain in February 1992. This spectrum designation spurred in-band terrestrial development. In-band, on-channel (IBOC) digital signaling, developed by iBiquity's Glynn Walden, permits broadcasters to remain on their existing frequencies. AM and FM station operators embraced the plan out of concern that satellite DAB signal transmission represented a significant threat to the local nature of U.S. broadcasting. On the other hand, many countries are fully supportive of a satellite DAB system because they do not have the number of stations the United States possesses and thus lack the coverage and financial investment.

FIGURE 1.15
Station frequencies appear on the lower portion of this HD Radio display. © 2013 iBiquity Digital Corporation; reproduced with permission from iBiquity.

Of course, digitized terrestrial radio (called HD Radio™) renders existing analog receivers obsolete. This is cause for some anxiety among broadcasters who wonder whether the buying public will convert. However, considerable confidence exists since consumers' appetite for new and improved sound shows no sign of abating.

Several manufacturers offer HD receivers at prices that are affordable and competitive and a number of car manufacturers provide HD Radio in their latest models. Digital converters are also available at a modest price. At the 2012 NAB conference, it was reported that there are more than seven million HD Radios in the market owned by listeners. More impressively, it was reported that an HD Radio-equipped car sells every 15 seconds. The HD Radio market is clearly growing and appears to have a strong future. The RAB reported that more than 2,100 radio stations were broadcasting in HD in 2012.

Considered another plus of digital radio is its capacity to do other things. For example, iBiquity has developed a technology that allows those stations broadcasting digitally to transmit data to portable digital services, including smartphones. This is attractive to the station operator's bottom line. The ability to multicast (provide side-channel transmissions) is yet another major plus for HD Radio. Known as HD2, it allows the medium to deliver additional program channels to the listening audience.

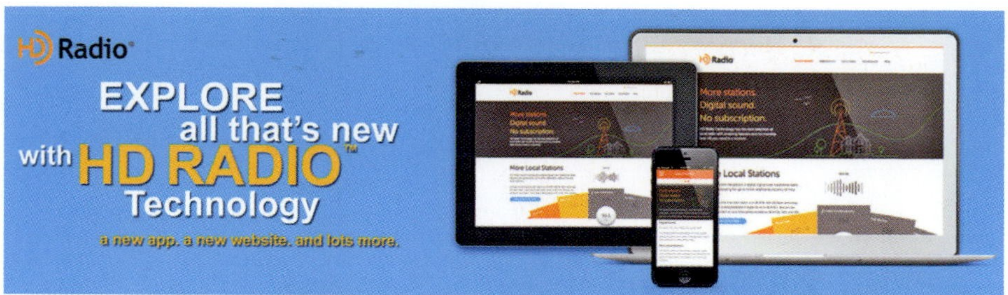

FIGURE 1.16
HD Radio uses all forms of social media technologies such as smartphone apps and Web pages to reach listeners© 2013 iBiquity Digital Corporation; reproduced with permission from iBiquity and Courtesy of *Inside Radio.*

America is a nation of audiophiles, demanding high-quality sound. Analog broadcasting cannot compete with the interference-free reception and greater frequency dynamics of digital signals. Digital signaling heralds a new age in radio broadcasting. Jeff Tellis, former president of the IBS, explains why. "The reason for the great interest in digital broadcasting is its considerable number of advantages." Among them are:

- Significantly improved coverage using significantly less power.
- Dramatic improvement in the quality of the signal; compare CD to vinyl.
- More precise coverage control using multiple transmitters similar to cellular phone technology.
- No adjacent-channel reception problems.
- On-channel booster capabilities eliminating the need to use separate frequencies to extend the same signal.
- Easy transmission of auxiliary services, including format information, traffic, weather, text, and selective messaging services.
- Sharing of transmitting facilities—common transmitter and antenna.

Telecommunications professor Ernest Hakanen expands on the cost advantages of digital broadcasting.

> DAB also promises to be economically efficient. Since there is no interstation interference between digital signals and because of the appeal of the spectrum efficiency provided by the interleaved environment, all of the channel operators in an area could utilize the same transmitter. The transmission facilities could be operated by a consortium for the construction, operation, and maintenance of the common transmission plant. Antenna height for DAB systems is also lower than current FM standards. Electrical power conservation and savings are a huge advantage of DAB.

FIGURE 1.17
AM & FM radio: A pervasive mobile-listening presence. Courtesy Arbitron/Edison Research Infinite Dial 2013. ©2013 Arbitron, Inc.

The digital quality combined with mobility is sure to help AM and FM radio to remain a popular medium.

Picking up on Hakanen's point about consolidating broadcast operations, Lynn Christian says, "The consortium (radio station malls or clusters) approach to maintaining and operating a station is commonplace because of economic reasons, and HD Radio is very conducive to a collaborative relationship among broadcasters."

Prior to the World Administrative Radio Conference (WARC) meeting in 1992, NAB's DAB Task Force proposed a set of standards to ensure that the technology would operate effectively. The specifications included:

- CD-quality sound.
- Enhanced coverage area.
- Accommodation of existing AM and FM frequencies.
- Immunity to multipath interference.
- Immunity to stoplight fades.
- No interference to existing AM and FM broadcasters.
- DAB system interference immunity.
- Minimization of transmission costs.

- Receiver complexity.
- Additional data capacity.
- Reception area threshold.

After nearly a century of analog signal transmission, radio is now in the digital domain, which will keep it relevant to the demands of a technologically sophisticated listening marketplace as it embarks on its next 100 years. Hundreds of radio stations across the country became early adopters and began offering digital signals. Additionally, the majority of them are also providing expanded listening options with HD2 service. At several industry gatherings in the first half of the 2000s, former NAB president Eddie Fritts presciently proclaimed HD Radio as the wave of the medium's future, saying "Transitioning to digital will give radio even better opportunities to serve [its] listeners." More than 2,000 stations offer HD and approximately half of them have taken the additional step into the world of multicast audio, bringing to listeners what the NAB says are "new and innovative formats" that give listeners "exactly what they want: more choices." The products of almost 50 consumer electronics and automotive manufacturers have aligned with iBiquity to produce HD-capable products. As one might expect, HD Radio listener habits mirror that of the traditional AM-FM audience, with the highest percentage of listenership concentrated in the on-the-go category. iBiquity predicted that one in every five new automobiles shipped to dealers in 2012—almost two million units—would be equipped with HD Radio receivers.

Today, not all industry observers see HD/HD2 as the solution to the drop in music radio listening. Mark Ramsey of Mercury Media Research observes, "Will digital help reverse radio's declining audience? Absolutely not." Dave Neugesser counters, "It's not something that's going to happen overnight. HD2 gives radio an infinite dial with incalculable choices, but it won't impact the market as fast as some would like. Before this happens, it has to be standard equipment in new cars, and people have to buy HD radios. It's a steep hill, but it can be surmounted."

Clearly, HD Radio has yet to achieve widespread acceptance. Despite the technological advancement it represents, the trade press has observed that the public simply is not clamoring for a radio service that provides increased fidelity and wider dynamic range, particularly when a purchase is required in order to achieve the improvement. One telling statistic about the progress of HD Radio adoption is reported by the Pew Research Center in its 2013 annual report on the state of the news media. For the first time since HD radios became available for purchase in 2004, the number of radio stations in 2012 that ceased broadcasting in HD exceeded the number of stations that had adopted the technology. Approximately 2,050 stations were broadcasting in HD Radio at the end of 2012, representing a loss of approximately 50 stations over the prior year.

Certain industry watchdogs attribute the slow diffusion of HD Radio to the government's decision regarding whether to require broadcasters to abandon analog transmission and replace it with digital signaling. Twice in the history of television broadcasting the FCC has taken action to stimulate the adoption and spread of emerging technologies. The first of these occurred following the passage of the 1961 federal All-Channel Receiver Act. To stimulate the growth of television in the ultra-high frequency (UHF) band, Congress empowered the FCC to require television receiver manufacturers to include UHF tuners in all sets manufactured in 1964 and thereafter. Decades later, the FCC required TV broadcasters in 2009 to turn off their analog broadcast and operate solely with digital (DTV) transmitters. Interestingly, neither Congress nor the FCC has imposed mandates on radio broadcasters to abandon terrestrial analog AM and FM transmissions. As the FCC observed in 2002, "broadcasters may begin interim IBOC operations on a voluntary basis, deferring costs as they deem appropriate . . . it is important to recognize that the endorsement of the hybrid IBOC transmission systems does not compel any broadcaster to make the investments necessary to initiate digital transmissions." More recently, proponents who support decommissioning the analog standard-band service in a process they term "AM sunset" have revived the debate. Vigorous discussion about establishing a cessation date for AM analog swirled around the 2013 convention of the NAB.

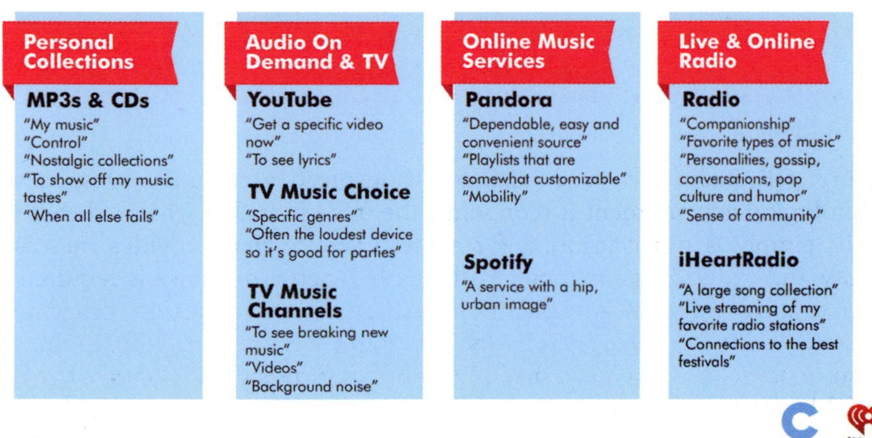

LISTENERS OPTIMIZE THEIR EXPERIENCES BY ENGAGING MULTIPLE PLATFORMS
Consumers are increasingly expanding their sources of audio content, and associate specific benefits with each.
Personal Collections
MP3s & CDs
"My music"
"Control"
"Nostalgic collections"
"To show off my music tastes"
"When all else fails"
Audio On Demand & TV
YouTube
"Get a specific video now"
"To see lyrics"
TV Music Choice
"Specific genres"
"Often the loudest device so it's good for parties"
TV Music Channels
"To see breaking new music"
"Videos"
"Background noise"
Online Music Services
Pandora
"Dependable, easy and convenient source"
"Playlists that are somewhat customizable"
"Mobility"
Spotify
"A service with a hip, urban image"
Live & Online Radio
Radio
"Companionship"
"Favorite types of music"
"Personalities, gossip, conversations, pop culture and humor"
"Sense of community"
iHeartRadio
"A large song collection"
"Live streaming of my favorite radio stations"
"Connections to the best festivals"
clearchannel
iHeart RADIO

FIGURE 1.18
Courtesy of Clear Channel.

SATELLITE RADIO

Radio broadcasters retain a wary eye on the ever-evolving digital audio services being made available by satellite. It is the threat of increased competition that inspires concern for the new and evolving audio options. Although broadcasters have long employed satellite programming and network services to enhance their over-the-air terrestrial signals, the idea of a direct-to-consumer alternative has not been greeted with enthusiasm, especially since these non-terrestrial signals are available in digital sound, something broadcasters are just beginning to offer. For several years, the FCC debated the question of satellite radio. In the waning years of the 1990s, the feds gave licenses to companies, such as CD Radio and XM Satellite Radio, to launch their services. Meanwhile, the NAB vociferously argued against its introduction into the local marketplace. Despite all the brouhaha, XM Satellite launched its service in September 2001 and a year later claimed nearly a quarter of a million subscribers. Less than a year after XM Satellite rolled out its audio service, Sirius Satellite Radio debuted. It quickly became clear to terrestrial broadcasters that there was a new kid in town, one who would further accelerate the splintering of the radio listening audience. In 2008, again against the protestations of the NAB, both satellite radio services merged, with Mel Karmazin at the helm of the renamed SiriusXM.

Over-the-air broadcasters contend that their local orientation betters the services of the satellite audio companies, which are nationally based programmers. Former Infinity Broadcasting senior vice president, David Pearlman, says, "Broadcast radio is locally rooted and the satellite companies can't fulfill that need at the present time. This will be its saving grace and aid in its ability to withstand this frontal attack. With its selling of local news, traffic, weather, events, personalities, and services, the product differentiation will work in the industry's favor."

Satellite radio is fee driven and offers a wide array of program options featuring an array of famous personalities that includes Oprah Winfrey, Bob Dylan, Martha Stewart, and the service's most-listened to talent, Howard Stern. In all, satellite radio provides some 200 channels to subscribers. Initially, subscribers were charged a monthly cost of $12.95 for the coast-to-coast signals (continuously in receiver range) and had to invest money for receiver equipment. Astutely, SiriusXM signed contracts with car manufacturers to install their digital receivers, predicting the acquisition of an impressive segment of the drivetime listening audience in the not-too-distant future. The *Los Angeles Times* reported that SiriusXM posted a $427 million profit in 2011, up tenfold from 2010. In 2012, SiriusXM boasted 23 million customers who pay from $8 to $18 monthly to gain access to 140 radio channels. Subscriptions to satellite radio continue to grow.

In the mid-2000s, many longtime broadcast radio listeners were making the switch to satellite for reasons similar to those articulated by media scholar and author Christopher Sterling:

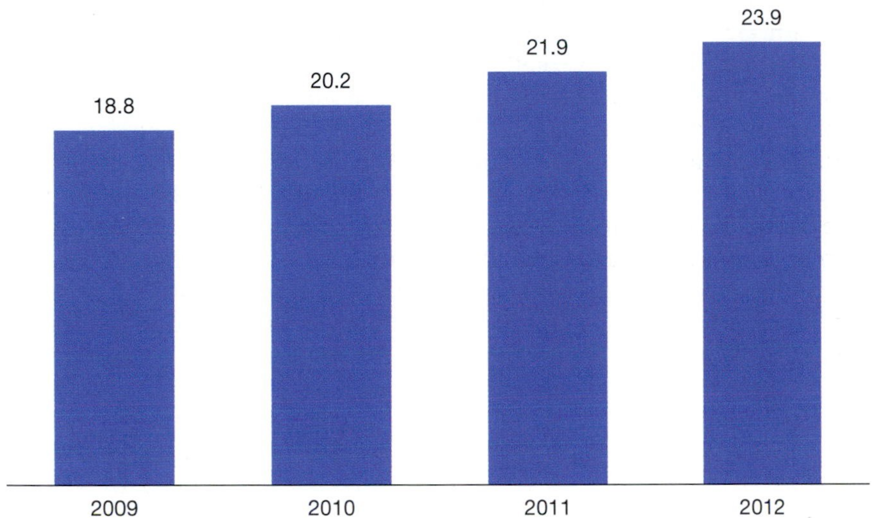

FIGURE 1.19
Subscriptions to SiriusXM continue to grow annually. Courtesy of the Pew Research Center.

> Like many older Americans, I used to listen to radio, especially in the car . . . but in the past year here in Washington, the medium has left me in the lurch. I used to listen to three stations (usually one at a time), but all have dumped friendly formats to slave after programming already available on other outlets in this market. The main public radio station dropped a decades-long classical music and talk format to rely totally on the latter—including British talk shows that keep giving me numbers I can call in London (I note with an "I told you so" feeling that their audiences and donations are down as a result). The remaining commercial classical music station got caught in a shift of Clear Channel station frequencies and now uses a fringe transmitter that can't put a decent signal into downtown. And most recently, the oldies station that had played music from the 60s and 70s "moved ahead" and now focuses on the late 70s and the 80s. Why do programmers presume nobody of 55 matters? Thank heaven for satellite radio where genuine choice thrives. I almost never turn on a radio anymore.

Former XM programming chief Lee Abrams discounted the potential impact on his medium of terrestrial HD Radio. "I'm pretty sure these guys will screw up HD. They'll add a blues channel but it'll play 200 blues songs and be run by guys who don't know much about the blues beyond Stevie Ray Vaughan." And about the potential of increased local programming on broadcast radio stations influencing the fate of his medium, Abrams said, "I doubt local radio will ever get back to the so-called 'community.' In fact, they're going the other way by cutting costs and taking on more remote voice track and syndicated programming."

To compound the competition for the listening audience, cable companies provide in-home music services for most of their subscribers. For example, Comcast cable users receive more than 45 channels of music and Suddenlink cable users receive nearly 50 channels of music that are often quite niche specific. These commercial-free channels of diverse non-stop music, replete with on-screen information about what is being played, are very attractive to subscribers and frequently result in the loss of yet another portion of traditional radio's listening audience. Despite competition from niche music programming choices such as cable radio stations, traditional terrestrial radio, and other multimedia audio choices, satcasters are in a strong position to do very well in the future.

INTERNET RADIO AND ONLINE MUSIC SERVICES

Although traditional radio still garners a larger share of the listeners than its online counterparts, many listeners now indeed access their favorite radio station via their computer, smartphone, iPod, or iPad. Despite the costly copyright royalty fees imposed on Internet stations streaming music, there are plenty of options for listeners such as online music service providers Pandora, iTunes, Spotify, and iHeartRadio.

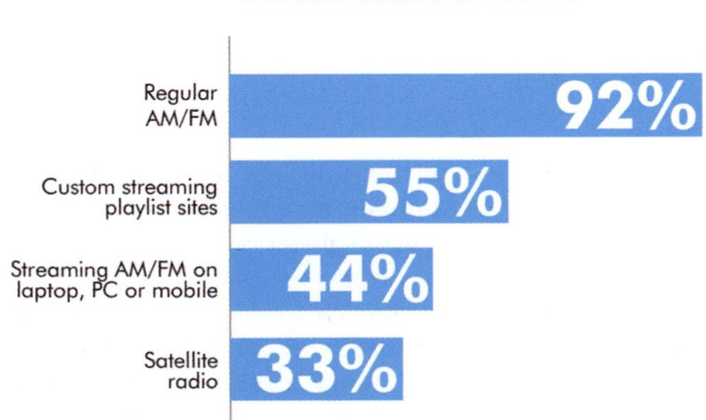

FIGURE 1.20
Courtesy of Clear Channel.

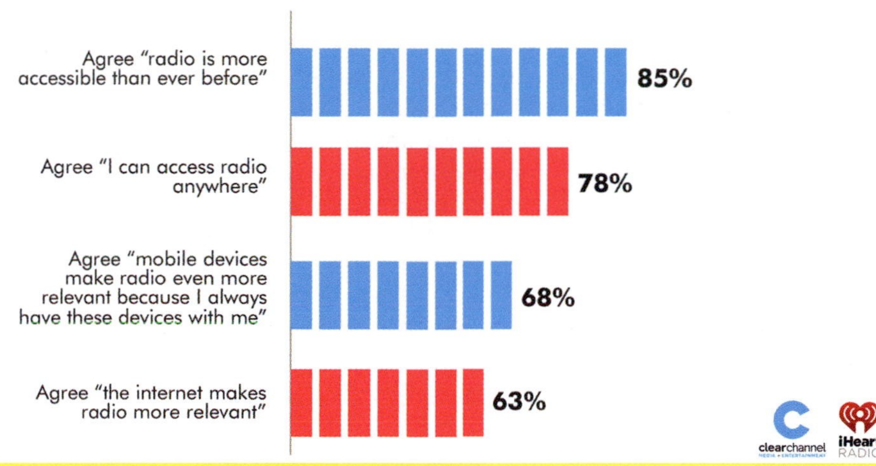
DIGITAL EXPANDS RADIO'S ACCESSIBILITY AND RELEVANCY
Access to radio via multiple platforms is enhancing its currency with listeners.
Agree "radio is more accessible than ever before"
85%
Agree "I can access radio anywhere"
78%
Agree "mobile devices make radio even more relevant because I always have these devices with me"
68%
Agree "the internet makes radio more relevant"
63%
clearchannel
iHeart RADIO

FIGURE 1.21
Courtesy of Clear Channel.

Pandora generates revenue from its music streaming. In 2013, *Advertising Age* reported that Pandora expected 80 percent of its revenue to be from advertising. "The internet-radio pioneer and its brethren hope they can divert a swath of local-radio ad dollars their way. But for that to happen, they have to get bigger in local markets and offer mobile ads tailored to local audiences. Kinda like radio," says *Advertising Age*. Thus, that's exactly what online audio services are doing: they are devising strategies to compete for local advertising dollars. If the strategy of going after local radio advertising dollars is successful, it could mean serious competition to the traditional radio industry. *Advertising Age* reports that the U.S. AM and FM advertising market is $15 billion with 75% of that devoted to local advertising. Moreover, Internet radio is experiencing growth in listenership.

Pandora reports more than 72 million monthly listeners while iTunes Radio is available on more than 200 million iPhones, iPods, and iPads. Unlike traditional radio, Pandora "combines users' registration data—age, gender, and ZIP code—with time, day and device as well as its so-called Music Genome Project," according to *Advertising Age*. The Genome Project's data are very attractive to advertisers to strategically target messages and therefore make ad dollars more effective. To further illustrate the potential Internet radio possesses, a 2013 *eMarketer* study estimated there were more than 145 million digital listeners, or nearly half of the entire nation's population.

FIGURE 1.22
Courtesy of the Pew Research Center.

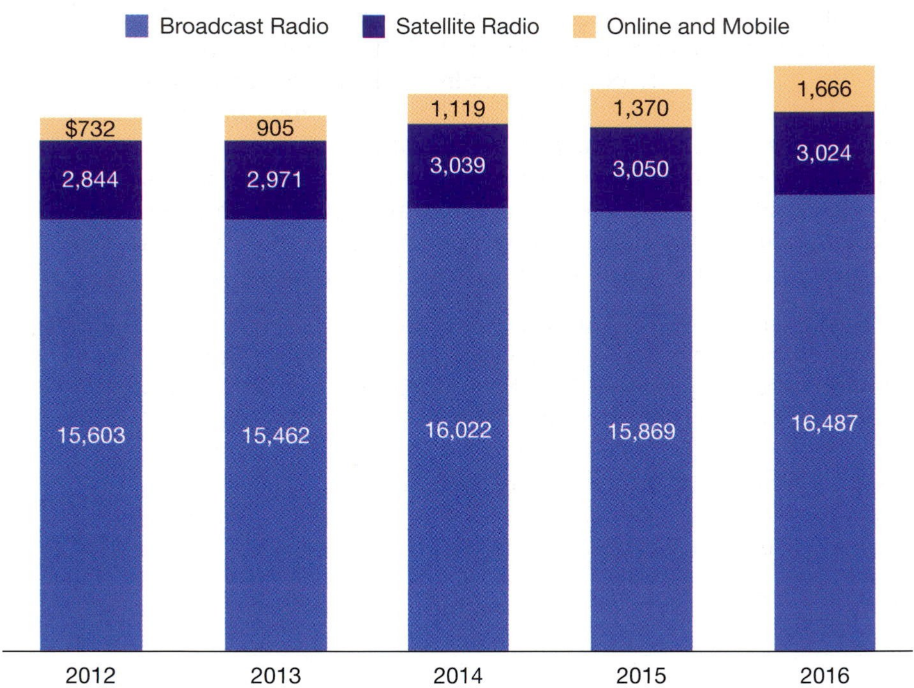

Recognizing Internet radio's ability to generate healthy advertising revenue, CBS Radio launched its Audio Ad Center in 2013, a digital platform designed for advertisers to purchase online audio advertising on CBS's 125 radio station audio streams. *Inside Radio* describes the Audio Ad Center as enabling "small businesses to buy and build audio ads for online and mobile radio listeners to run at specific times on specific station streams with frequency set by the client."

Traditional radio recognizes Internet radio's potential and has made efforts to have a presence where the listeners are migrating. For example, Clear Channel introduced iHeartRadio in 2008 and has more than 30 million registered listeners to its online stations. iHeartRadio offers its listeners more than 800 radio stations from which to choose. Streaming music online has caused some distress for the industry due to music royalty fees. In 2012, *The New York Times* reported that satellite and cable radio stations pay 8% of their revenue to royalty rates while online radio stations like Pandora pay a fraction of a cent every time a song is played, thus reducing how much music is played, considering that Pandora paid nearly 55% of its revenue that year. Indeed, Internet radio is now big business. To illustrate just how big, in 2012, *The New York Times* reported that more than $1 billion had been collected and paid to artists and record labels.

In spite of the formidable royalty issue confronting webcasters, the RAB determined that more than 6,000 stations were streaming their content as of 2012 to listeners. Meanwhile, Measure-Cast reported that Internet radio listening was continuing to grow a year later, so the practice was far from moribund. In 2012, the RAB reported that the U.S. Internet, or online, radio audience is reaching a staggering 103 million listeners each month. One year later, SoundExchange, the organization that collects and distributes royalties for streamed audio to recording artists and record labels, reported making the highest quarterly payment in its history. Payments distributed during the second quarter of 2013 totaled $149 million, half again as much as it paid the previous year.

Indeed, today stations continue to view the Internet as a viable supplement to their on-air signals, especially for promotion and audience research purposes. Interactive radio is a growing reality, as is the opportunity for everyone with the right computer and software to be a broadcaster or cybercaster. With an Internet encoder, the home user can transmit to an international audience. This prospect prompts a collective sigh from station managers, who are losing track of the new forms of competition.

Notes longtime broadcaster Lynn Christian:

> The major concern regarding the future of radio is centered on new competition from satellite, cable, and online sources. Those companies that are planning to partner with these new media choices, and develop data services, will undoubtedly be the big winners in the twenty-first century. Broadcast radio, as I have known it during the past 50 years, will not be the same in the next few years. But what American business is the same now? These are revolutionary times in radio and in the world.

Jason Insalaco observes:

> Radio executives programming in the rapidly changing media landscape must embrace the technological revolution that is upon them. Cell phones, the Internet, MP3 players, the iPod, and videogames are vying for the audience's attention. Programmers must heed these encroachments on terrestrial radio or else accept extinction. Rather than fear the new and evolving audio media, traditional radio needs to embrace it for its own benefit. Radio websites are great places for listeners to find out about the station's personalities, music, contests, and

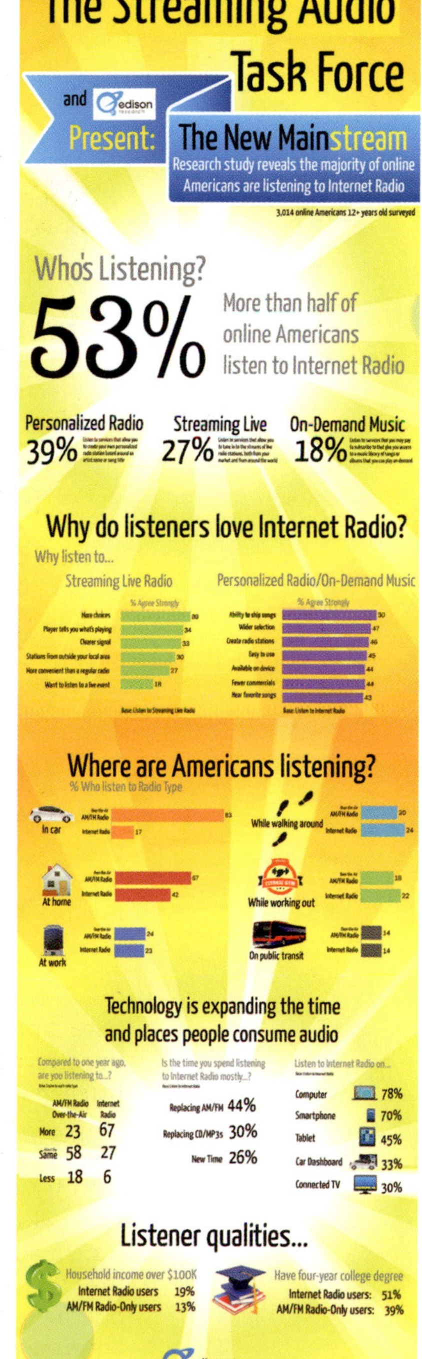

FIGURE 1.23
Courtesy of Edison Research.

> events. Websites are cyber-extensions of the over-the-air station brand. Station websites also enhance audience interactivity and constitute another revenue source for a station.

In 2013, the biggest challenge confronting Internet presence continues to be fees charged to provide music. States Paul Kamp of Backbone Networks, an Internet radio service provider:

> The performance royalty rate is probably the largest obstacle. Currently, in the U.S., there are a number of different rates and laws that apply to internet performance royalty rates. This includes the Small Webcasters Settlement that requires stations of a certain size to pay a percentage of their revenue. There is also the commercial Copyright Review Board (CRB) rate that requires internet radio stations to track performances of a particular piece. This rate escalates through [2015] when it is up for renewal again. The reason this is a big challenge for internet radio is that the rate is higher than for other broadcast media, like terrestrial and satellite broadcasts. If the rate was equal across all broadcast media we suspect there would be a rush to internet broadcasting because of the more precise listener statistics that can be generated and the opportunity to more precisely advertise to a particular target. The royalty rate discussion masks a broader issue that needs to be confronted. The strength of the internet is that it is worldwide. As such, an internet broadcaster would have to pay music composition performance royalties to all of the professional performing rights organizations where a connection terminates (the country from where the listener connects).

Cognizant of the many obstacles and challenges that exist in the age of the Internet, most radio broadcasters forecast a long-term relationship between the two media—one that will benefit both. As radio heads warp speed into this "future world," it is obvious that aspiring broadcasters will have to know their way around a computer, because the audio studio will exist both in the ether and in cyberspace, especially when considering the amount of revenue being generated from online radio stations. A BIA/Kelsey study indicated that online radio advertising revenues had reached nearly $500 million in 2012. Further, BIA/Kelsey predicted that by 2017 the online radio revenue would reach more than $800 million. "As the digital marketplace continues to rise in all sectors of advertising, radio is improving its listener engagement online and benefitting from the value of its web and mobile assets," said Mark Fratrik, vice-president and chief economist at BIA/Kelsey, in a press release. "Overall, the industry is still recognized as an important part of the media mix as it continues to meander around, rising slightly with the rate of inflation but not keeping up with the economy."

For those interested in this aspect of the medium, the *Radio and Internet Newsletter* (RAIN) provides a daily update on the key issues involving radio and the

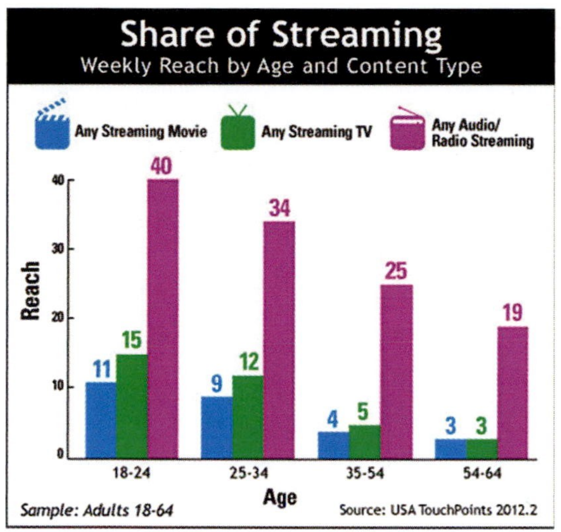

FIGURE 1.24
A comparison of audio vs. video streaming across four key demographics. Courtesy Media Behavior Institute. ©2013. Used by permission.

Internet. In fact, RAIN interviewed Larry Rosen, president of Edison Research, about the study Edison Research conducted, titled "The New MainStream," about online radio listening. Regarding the study, Rosen noted:

> The overwhelming point is this technology has brought audio to new places, new locations, and new times in people's lives that they weren't previously filling in with audio. This is the golden age of audio. If all audio were counted, people would see that never before—probably even going back to the twenties and thirties when radio had no competition—there is more audio listening going on today than ever before.

SEISMIC SHIFTS REMAKE THE RADIO INDUSTRY

Paul Goldstein

There is a tectonic shift undermining the very foundation of broadcast radio. Multiple metrics make it clear that serious threats imposed on the FM/AM platform by new online competitors are escalating exponentially.

For more than 25 years I've helped build audiences for some of the radio industry's most successful brands. But today, as online competitors like Pandora, iTunes Radio, and Spotify add fuel to their astonishing rise, it's questionable whether the strategies broadcasters have chosen can foster healthy growth. Furthermore, it's obvious that radical change to audio media is already underway.

FIGURE 1.25
Paul Goldstein.

As change happens all around them, radio broadcasters tout the health of their business and how the competitive threat of Internet rivals is overstated. I understand the need to present their case to advertisers. But their sales narrative, an echo chamber of their own making, cements complacency and fosters lack of innovation.

A new Edison research study warns that among the six most common places where listeners consume audio media, broadcast radio dominates in just two of them (in car, at home); is tied with Internet radio for two (at work, on public transportation); and is defeated by Internet radio in two (while working out, while walking around). Another red flag in the study for broadcasters is that 50% of at-work listeners who listen to Internet-radio-only stations/services (that is, stations/services that don't broadcast on FM/AM) have replaced their FM/AM listening time with Internet-radio-only stations/services.

Broadcasters can't afford to repeat mistakes made by companies like Microsoft that dismiss competitors and lack cultures of innovation. In 2007 Microsoft CEO Steve Ballmer said, "There's no chance that the iPhone is going to get any significant market share. No chance." With the absence of content innovation, the audience and revenue drain forced upon FM/AM stations by formidable competitors will only deepen.

In Google's "news" search section, query the phrase "content is king." From Forbes to CNBC, you'll see a wealth of articles reaffirming that notion, which is of vital importance to executives leading both the Internet and broadcast radio industries. In the words of Steve Jobs, "That's what makes great products. It's not process—it's content."

Behemoths like Apple, Google, Microsoft, and Amazon have joined the audio media ranks of Pandora, Spotify, Rhapsody, Rdio, Slacker, Stitcher, Songza, Beats Music, and others, heating up an epic battle for the hearts and minds of America's radio listeners. Who will win, and why?

In a memo to the staff of *The Washington Post*, the paper's new owner, Amazon.com titan Jeff Bezos wrote, "The Internet is transforming almost every element of the news business . . . There is no map, and charting a path ahead will not be easy. We will need to invent, which means we will need to experiment." Experimentation is the ethos of Silicon Valley yet the antithesis of broadcast radio.

Powered by hundreds of millions of dollars in investments, the venture capitalist and blue-chip-backed online entities storming broadcast radio's bastions are being embraced by a massive, rapidly growing audience. With few exceptions, an honest assessment can only conclude that the radio industry's response is lackluster, at best.

According to eMarketer, the combined monthly online radio audience is 147 million listeners at present; by 2017 that number is expected to rise to at least 179 million. This will enable audio media start-ups to gobble up even larger pieces of the advertising pie.

Hopefully, broadcasters recognize that their most significant innovation of the past decade, HD radio, reaches about just 3% of the U.S. radio audience because they didn't invest in content that's important to listeners.

With the FM/AM distribution platform diminished by audio media on the Internet, the companies that will create real value are those developing bold, original content. Great is no longer good enough; top performance requires content that's amazing. The lack of celebrated original content at broadcast radio, especially the scarcity of their original online content, stunts growth.

When HBO launched, it was all about non-original movies. Today, HBO is a highly profitable juggernaut whose groundbreaking success is based on its acclaimed original content, loved and paid for by tens of millions. Additionally, Discovery Communications CEO David Zaslav notes, "We're spending more money on content and a lot less money on everything else"—a strategy that doubled its stock price in two years.

As radio's venture capital-funded competitors digest the countless millions of FM/AM listeners they've consumed so far, if they follow the HBO/Discovery model before broadcast stations do, they'll have beaten them at what should be their own game. Audio media companies, broadcast or Internet, will gain a strong competitive advantage when they create original content so irresistible that in comparison listeners perceive competitors as disposable. It's especially urgent that broadcasters create dazzling content exclusive to the online platform; otherwise, they'll be fishing where there are fewer and fewer fish.

In her blog, Internet radio expert Jennifer Lane wrote about Apple's response to the success of the Pandora app on iTunes. iTunes music sales declined, so with the writing obvious on the wall, Apple wasted no time developing plans to get into the streaming game and invested substantially in yet another formidable competitor to broadcast radio, iTunes Radio. Apple was willing to cannibalize iTunes music sales by investing in iTunes Radio. Are broadcasters willing to invest in breakthrough content in order to secure their future online?

With the release of iOS7, Apple's brand-new operating system, more than 500 million iPhone, iPad, iPod Touch, Apple TV, Mac, and PC users now have iTunes Radio in their pockets, on their desks, in their cars, and in their homes. To fight off Apple's stampede into streaming, Pandora lifted its 40-hour listening cap.

The U.S. census confirms broadcast radio listening is declining, compounded by broadcasters' unremarkable influence in the online streaming space. According to Triton Digital, at any given moment among online listeners (M/F, 6:00 am–8:00 pm), Pandora has more than twice the audience of all of the radio stations owned by Clear Channel, CBS, Cumulus, Entercom, and the next seven broadcasting companies combined. Factor in tens of millions listening to iTunes radio, Google Play, Spotify, XBox Music, Rhapsody, and other audio start-ups (not measured by Triton)—not to mention SiriusXM and the explosive growth of streaming on smartphones—and it's clear that broadcast radio's monopoly has ended.

As the velocity of change accelerates, broadcasters need the equivalent of the Manhattan Project for content—particularly original online content. And among the increasingly crowded personalized radio/on-demand music services, companies that couple their appealing personalized/on-demand attributes with extraordinary original content will break out from the pack just as HBO and Discovery did.

The companies that best execute a strategy to build out-of-this-world, original content are the ones that will become the kings of audio media. The shakeout is well underway.

Award-winning audience development executive **Paul Goldstein** has directed programming and developed original content propelling local and network radio properties to market-leading ratings at Sony/Warner Networks in New York, KTWV/The Wave in Los Angeles, WNUA in Chicago, KKSF in San Francisco, and KOAI in Dallas, among others. His company, PG Audience Development, creates breakthrough, original content for new media companies, celebrities, brands, and radio groups: TheContentIsKing.com.

MOBILE MUSIC SERVICES

The biggest competitive challenge to radio today is posed by a range of interactive devices (smartphones, cell phones, tablets, and laptops) with downloading capabilities for song files and podcasts as well as the related but non-interactive devices such as iPods and other MP3 audio playback devices. As the Wi-Fi and WiMAX universe extends and expands, observers anticipate the competition will only increase. Online radio reached a tipping point in 2013. According to Triton Digital's *Online Audio Top 20 Ranker*, the amount of online audio content consumed on mobile devices exceeded 50% for the first time. Pandora, a perennial leader, topped Triton's list; Clear Channel's iHeartRadio, a newly revamped Slacker, and, to a lesser extent, Cumulus Streaming Network and CBS Radio, round out the list of the five most popular online services. Listener statistics for Apple's iTunes Radio, which launched as this edition went to press, were unavailable.

Recognizing the juggernaut of cell phone and smartphone devices used daily by millions of consumers, there have been legislative attempts to mandate an FM tuner be placed in every new mobile phone. This attempt to be a part of additional audio media platforms has been embraced by the radio industry. In June 2012, radio industry officials testified before the U.S. Congress subcommittee on Communication and Technology that having FM tuners in mobile devices is a "public safety" issue and would bring the United States in alignment with Europe and Asia. Greg Sandoval, a reporter for *CNET.com*, asserts that opponents to the FM tuner mandate "argue this is a cheap attempt by radio to piggyback on cell phones and avoid becoming more irrelevant in the digital age."

In 2013, Emmis chairman/CEO Jeff Smulyan announced that the company had partnered with Sprint to install an FM-enabled wireless device called NextRadio. This new application on Sprint phones will permit users to listen to radio stations on their smartphones. *AllAccess.com* reports, "The announcement by Sprint also marks the official launch of NEXTRADIO, the smartphone app that delivers a highly interactive artist and ad experience to FM-enabled smartphones." The software will allow stations to upload branding images, call letters, slogans, and other items that will promote the station.

Also, attempting to capitalize on the ever-expanding Internet music services, Cumulus Media Inc. announced, in 2013, a partnership with Rdio, a music subscription service with a website as well as mobile apps for all major smartphones and mobile devices. A press release from Cumulus explains the partnership:

> Today, people consume audio in many ways with local radio accounting for about two-thirds of all audio consumption. Other forms of audio include: Local Radio Streaming (station sites and apps, iHeart), On Demand (iTunes, Rdio, Spotify), Custom Playlists (Pandora, Rdio), National Radio Channels (Sirius and coming to Rdio). Our strategy of owning premium

> and exclusive content that we distribute across broadcast and digital platforms is designed to enable us to be relevant across the entire audio ecosystem.

Further, Cumulus states, "As the consumer's options and behavior continue to evolve, it's imperative that we be in a position to serve our listeners a premium quality audio experience wherever, whenever, and however they want it."

The Internet radio stations are also appealing to a younger demographic. During the last quarter of 2012, the NPD Group found that 24% of U.S. consumers aged 13 to 35 listened to music on traditional AM and FM radio stations while 23% of those surveyed used Internet radio stations as their primary means of listening to music. Satellite radio garnered only 5% of the listeners. The same study found that 39% of those surveyed preferred Pandora, 11% preferred iHeartRadio, while 9% preferred Spotify. In a February 2013 study, the NPD Group found that 56% of smartphone owners used the devices to listen to music while 65% of those surveyed used apps on their smartphones to listen to music rather than their own music collections. The study also found that vehicles are where most of the smartphone listening occurs among 13- to 35-year-olds.

Further, not only recognizing the growth but also the potential to generate revenue, the union that represents actors, announcers, broadcasters, journalists, dancers, deejays, news writers, news editors, program hosts, puppeteers, recording artists, singers, stunt performers, voiceover artists, and other media professionals began negotiating on its members' behalf a new pay structure for work done that is streamed online. The Screen Actors Guild and the American Federation of Television and Radio Artists (SAG-AFTRA), began the dialogue with broadcasters in 2013. No agreements were reached as of the publishing date of this book.

Michael A. Krasness, head of Oxysys, a mobile music networking service, expands on the virtues of his enterprise:

> For the listener, traditional music radio—both over-the-air and Internet delivery—is about listening to tracks the user already knows, plus music discovery by the radio station's playlist, driven by an ad-based revenue model. Mobile music services add to that by allowing interactive user selection of music, active participation in the music discovery process, and social networking. Similar ad-based revenue models may be augmented by e-commerce through integration of a store. Traditional radio certainly provides complementary services for our users. As a feature for our users, Oxy phling! includes simple, integrated access to a number of Internet radio stations. For the radio station, they now have access to our community of mobile users.

Spotify®

FIGURE 1.26
Courtesy Spotify.

Online Car Listening through Cellphones Is on the Rise
Percentage of Cellphone Owners Who Have Ever Listened to Online Radio in a Car by Listening to the Stream from a Cellphone Connected to a Car Stereo

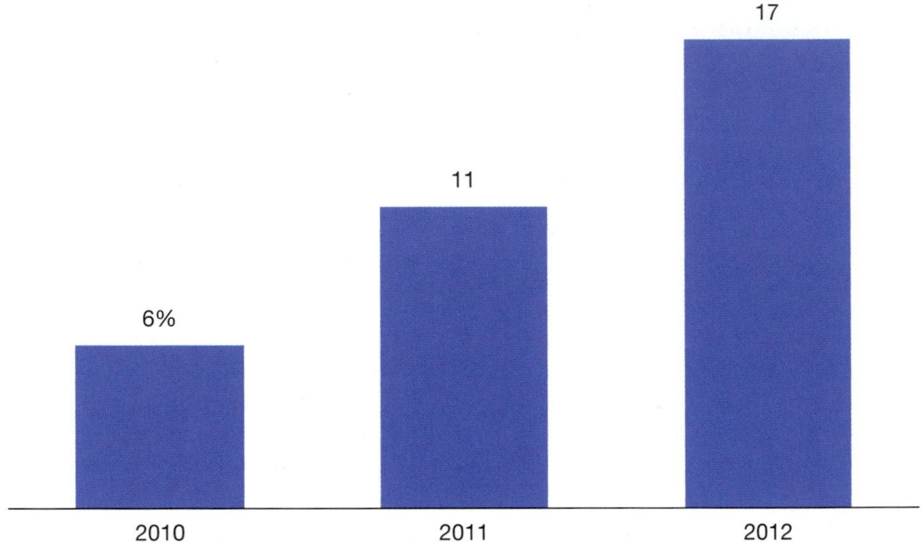

FIGURE 1.27
Listening to Internet radio stations in cars is growing in popularity. Courtesy of the Pew Research Center.

With Pandora, iHeartRadio and other mobile audio services likely venturing into non-music areas, such as talk and sports, the competitive threat to broadcast and satellite radio looms larger than ever. Mark Ramsey says, "We are fast-entering a time when 'radio' will become a feature of other things rather than simply a destination unto itself, as it has been up until now."

THE IMPACT OF MOBILE LISTENING ON RADIO

Glenda Shrader Bos

The growing use of smartphones like the iPhone will have a profound impact on radio use. Cell phones with radio apps mean that one day nearly everyone will have a radio with them at all times. Theoretically, this should increase radio consumption, but research suggests that the increased accessibility of radio may not have the positive impact that one might expect.

FIGURE 1.28
Glenda Shrader Bos.

Today's smartphone is used for so many tasks that a consumer might turn to listening only during rare times when the phone isn't used for some other task with a higher priority.

An analysis of Internet radio listening patterns over the current period of rapid smartphone growth gives us a glimpse of the potential impact of this phenomenon. The research shows a strong correlation between growth of mobile phone listening and a dramatic decline in listening spans. In 2010 when most Internet radio listening was done on a desktop computer, Pandora's average time spent listening was nearly one hour. By 2012, more than 70% of Pandora's listening was done on a mobile device, and average time spent listening had plunged to 46 minutes.

Broadcast groups have seen a similar decline in listening spans as more listening is done on smartphones. Broadcast radio groups have seen combined listening spans decline from 35 hours in 2010 to only 16 hours in 2012.

Radio advertising rates are determined by the average size of a radio station's audience, traditionally measured as the number of people listening during a quarter-hour (a metric that dates back to the days when radio shows were 15 minutes long). The longer a person listens to a station, the greater the number of quarter-hours of listening. This is why radio stations make an effort to create programming that encourages longer listening spans.

The growing use of smartphones combined with multitasking is fragmenting listening into smaller and smaller periods of time, which then depresses ratings, and therefore how much a radio station can charge for a commercial. Lower rates lead to lower income for a station. As a result, programming budgets are reduced. This could ultimately lead to lower quality programming.

This is the irony of mobile Internet radio listening. Radio apps on mobile devices are leading to greater radio accessibility. However, listening spans are lower on mobile devices, virtually canceling out the advantages of greater accessibility. This means that the impact of mobile listening may ultimately be negative for the radio industry.

The only solution is to push radio up the priority ladder for the mobile user, so that radio can successfully compete for a user's attention with emails, social media, and the like. The only way that will happen is if radio is able to create more compelling programming. This may become the single greatest challenge for radio in the coming years.

Glenda Shrader Bos is managing partner and co-owner of Harker Research, a firm that specializes in media research with companies such as CBS, Fox News, ESPN, and ABC. She joined the company in 1991 and has more than 20 years of research experience. Harker Research has grown from a three-person team to a full-service company that specializes in Internet, radio, television and cross-platform media research.

LPFM (LOW-POWER FM)

A microradio movement surfaced in the 1990s and raised the ire of both broadcast regulators and the industry. The debate positioned the NAB against what it labeled radio "pirates." After lengthy reflection, FCC chairman William Kennard proposed rule-making designed to legitimize these unauthorized, tiny-wattage outlets. The argument used to justify support of LPFMs cited the erosion of programming diversity in commercial radio as the consequence of widespread consolidation and mergers. According to Kennard this new species of broadcaster would give voice to those alienated or disenfranchised by mainstream corporate radio. The FCC's proposal sought to create two types of new licenses on the FM band. Power would span 10 (LP10) to 100 (LP100) watts with service areas restricted to three to nine miles. Among many stipulations, the FCC requires that LPFM licensees be non-profit organizations. This rule helped placate commercial broadcasters' concerns that the new category of stations would represent yet another competitive threat. The LPFM rules further require that this "sub" or "secondary" category of radio stations not interfere with the signals of regular full power outlets. As the FCC states, "LPFM stations are not protected from interference that may be received from other classes of FM station."

Perhaps the greatest threat to the existence of microstations is the looming conversion of regular radio outlets to IBOC digital. This will all but squeeze out any chance for the continued survival of the community-centric medium. Meanwhile, many proponents of LPFM have been alarmed by the micromedium's takeover by conservative religious broadcasters, which have been scooping up as many non-commercial frequencies (both primary and secondary) and translators as possible to spread their gospel.

Former executive director of now defunct Allston-Brighton Free Radio, Stephen Provizer, gives this view of the threatened medium:

> As an open platform for all voices, we had two goals: to disseminate programming that would otherwise be unavailable and to empower our participants which, to the greatest extent possible, encompassed the entire community. The first goal becomes increasingly important as the range of consumer choice becomes narrower due to ongoing corporatization and an obsession with demography-driven advertising. The second goal, participation, is driven by our belief that direct participation is the key to empowerment. If an individual in our media-drenched culture is going to be able to exercise critical judgment toward mainstream media, he or she must have the process demystified and clarified. Perhaps if media literacy education was more available in lower school this would not be necessary, but such is not now and has never been the case.

FIGURE 1.29
A new kind of radio via the Internet. Courtesy of Pandora.

RADIO AND GOVERNMENT REGULATIONS

Almost from the start it was recognized that radio could be a unique instrument for the public good. This point was never made more apparent than in 1912, when, according to legend (which was recently challenged by scholars who contend that others were involved), a young wireless operator named David Sarnoff picked up the distress signal from the sinking *Titanic* and relayed the message to ships in the vicinity, which then came to the rescue of those still alive. The survivors were the beneficiaries of the first attempt at regulating the new medium. The Wireless Ship Act of 1910 required that ships carrying 50 or more passengers have wireless equipment on board. The effective use of the medium from an experimental station in New York City's Wanamaker Building helped save 700 lives.

Radio's first practical application was as a means of communicating from ship to ship and from ship to shore. During the first decade of the twentieth century, Marconi's wireless invention was seen primarily as a way of linking the ships at sea with the rest of the world. Until that time, when ships left port they were beyond any conventional mode of communications. The wireless was a boon to the maritime services, including the Navy, which equipped each of its warships with the new device.

Coming on the heels of the *Titanic* disaster, the Radio Act of 1912 sought to expand the general control of radio on the domestic level. The secretary of commerce and labor was appointed to head the implementation and monitoring of the new legislation. The primary function of the act was to license wireless stations and operators. The new regulations empowered the Department of Commerce and Labor to impose fines and revoke the licenses of those who operated outside the parameters set down by the communications law.

Growth of radio on the national level was curtailed by World War I, when the government saw fit to take over the medium for military purposes. However, as the war raged on, the same young wireless operator, David Sarnoff, who supposedly had been instrumental in saving the lives of passengers on the ill-fated *Titanic*, was hard at work on a scheme to drastically modify the scope of the medium, thus converting it from an experimental and maritime communications apparatus to an appliance designed for use by the general public. Less than five years after the war's end, receivers were being bought by the millions, and radio as we know it today was born.

As explained earlier, the lack of regulations dealing with interference nearly resulted in the premature end of radio. By 1926 hundreds of stations clogged the airways, bringing pandemonium to the dial. The Radio Act of 1912 simply did not anticipate radio's new application. It was the Radio Act of 1927 that first approached radio as a mass medium. The Federal Regulatory Commission's five commissioners quickly implemented a series of actions that restored the fledgling medium's health.

The Communications Act of 1934 charged a seven-member commission with the responsibility of ensuring the efficient use of the airways, which the government views as a limited resource that belongs to the public and is leased to broadcasters. Over the years the FCC has concentrated its efforts on maximizing the usefulness of radio for the public's benefit. Consequently, broadcasters have been required to devote a portion of their airtime to programs that address important community and national issues. In addition, broadcasters have had to promise to serve as a constant and reliable source of information, while retaining certain limits on the amount of commercial material scheduled.

The FCC has steadfastly sought to keep the medium free of political bias and special-interest groups. In 1949, the commission implemented regulations making it necessary for stations that present a viewpoint to provide an equal amount of airtime to contrasting or opposing viewpoints. The Fairness Doctrine obliged broadcasters "to afford reasonable opportunity for the discussion of conflicting views of public importance." Later, it also stipulated that stations notify persons when attacks were made on them over the air.

Although broadcasters generally acknowledge the unique nature of their business, many have felt that the government's involvement has exceeded reasonable limits in a society based on a free-enterprise system. Because it is their money, time, and energy they are investing, broadcasters feel they should be afforded greater opportunity to determine their own programming. More recent justifications used by the radio industry include the fact that there is a proliferation of online and digital media choices for consumers. These additional choices for consumers, based upon traditional broadcasters' rationalization, means there is less need for the government to provide oversight to ensure the public interests and needs must be met solely via AM and FM signals. Thus, they allow the marketplace to dictate how the industry evolves.

In the late 1970s, a strong movement headed by Congressman Lionel Van Deerlin sought to reduce the FCC's role in broadcasting, to allow the marketplace to dictate how the industry conducted itself. Van Deerlin actually proposed that the Broadcast Branch of the commission be abolished and a new organization with much less authority be created. His bill was defeated, but out of his and others' efforts came a new attitude concerning the government's hold on the electronic media. President Reagan's anti-bureaucracy, free-enterprise philosophy gave impetus to the deregulation move already under way when he assumed office. The FCC, headed by chairman Mark Fowler, expanded on the deregulation proposal that had been initiated by his predecessor, Charles Ferris. The deregulation decision eliminated the requirement that radio stations devote a portion of their airtime (8% for AM and 6% for FM) to non-entertainment programming of a public affairs nature. In addition, stations no longer had to undergo the lengthy process of ascertaining community needs as a condition of license renewal, and guidelines pertaining to the amount of time devoted to commercial announcements were eliminated. The rule requiring stations to maintain detailed program logs was also abolished. A simplified postcard license renewal form was adopted, and license terms were extended from three to seven years. On August 4, 1987, the FCC voted to eliminate the 38-year-old Fairness Doctrine, declaring it unconstitutional and no longer applicable to broadcasters. A month before, President Reagan had vetoed legislation that would have made the policy law.

The extensive updating of FCC rules and policy was based on the belief that the marketplace should serve as the primary regulator. Opponents of the reform feared that with their newfound freedom, radio stations would quickly turn their backs on community concerns and concentrate their full efforts on fattening their pocketbooks.

Those who support the position that broadcasters should first serve the needs of society are concerned that deregulation (unregulation) has further reduced the medium's "good citizen" role. "Radio, especially the commercial sector, has long since fallen down on its 'interest, convenience, and necessity' obligation born of the Radio Act of 1927. While a small segment of the industry does exert an effort to address the considerable problems facing society today, the overwhelming majority continue to be fixated on the financial bottom line. There needs to be more of a balance," observes Robert Hilliard, former FCC chief of public and educational broadcasting. Proponents of deregulation applauded the FCC's actions, contending that the listening audience would indeed play a vital role in determining the programming of radio stations, because the medium has to meet the needs of the public to prosper.

Although the government continues to closely scrutinize the actions of the radio industry to ensure that it operates in an efficient and effective manner, it is no longer perceived as the fearsome, omnipresent Big Brother it once was. Today, broadcasters more fully enjoy the fruits of a laissez-faire system of economy, although they are not immune to commission actions.

In the spring of 1996, the Telecommunications Bill (later to become a Telecommunications Act) became a reality, and ownership caps were all but eliminated. The Act opened the floodgates for those radio groups wanting to vastly expand their portfolios. For example, by 2002, Clear Channel Radio had acquired nearly 1,400 stations. Consequently, by the mid-2000s, localism had taken a substantial hit, as many of the major radio groups had replaced the indigenous broadcasts of their stations with voice-tracking and "out-of-town" programming.

In terms of what interests the FCC most regarding station acquisition, radio group CEO Robin Martin offers the following view:

> [T]he Commission has relaxed the bureaucratic requirements for approval of the transfer of licenses to new owners. Most of the questions on the forms can be answered by checking boxes. However, simple as this process might seem, the check marks a new owner places in the boxes represent legal certifications by the proposed licensee and should not be

> taken lightly. The FCC has great interest in a certain few areas that qualify as threshold questions of eligibility to be a license holder. The percentage of foreign ownership is but one example. If the answers to these questions do not comply with FCC rules and regulations, the transfer will not be approved. However, all the non-threshold questions, while not necessarily individually disqualifying, may in the aggregate lead the FCC staff to inquire further about the response to clarify the details or to understand if the application is fatally defective or can be corrected or amended with supplemental information. The most important issue for the FCC is honesty. If an applicant answers a question dishonestly, the Commission will take swift action against the applicant should it discover falsehoods. The consequences of not being truthful with the Commission are more dire than if the answer was truthful and required more explanation or even a waiver of the rules. It's therefore important to understand the meaning or implications of the questions to avoid unwittingly answering incorrectly. Attorneys need to be consulted before applications are submitted.

Prominent broadcast attorney Erwin Krasnow provides the following summary regarding the downsizing trend by the FCC of regulating radio broadcasters.

> The world of FCC regulation has changed dramatically. No more ascertainment. No more Fairness Doctrine (William Paley once quipped that the Fairness Doctrine was like the Holy Roman Empire, which was neither Holy, Roman, nor an Empire). No regulation of call signs or submission of Annual Financial Reports. Virtually all applications and forms are now filed electronically, many without the assistance of a communication lawyer. Rather than terms of three years, licenses are now renewed for eight years (that's a long time; a common law marriage results after only seven years).

Krasnow waxes poetically about the situation in "Deregulation: A Lawyer's Lament":

> Martin, Tate, and McDowell are proceeding with deregulation en masse,
> But nobody's thought of the lawyers who subsist on the present morass.
> When Arcane comparative hearings
> Have been paying the partnership's bills
> It will not be an easy conversion to torts and divorces and wills.
> Plain language rules will be all that are left
> No "wherefores" and "hereins" and such
> Treasured old forms will be thrown on the fire
> And for lunch we'll be forced to go Dutch.
> So pity your struggling lawyer
> Who has served at your side for so long
> And write to your Congressman promptly to tell him that "deregulation" is wrong.

JOBS AND EQUALITY IN RADIO

Today, the radio industry continues to employ tens of thousands, but with all the downsizing and consolidation and the increase in new and competitive audio media, this figure has eroded and likely will continue to do so in the coming years. In 2013, the U.S. Department of Labor reported that the radio announcing industry was a source of nearly 62,000 jobs. The labor department predicted a 7% employment growth in the industry from 2010 to 2020. Former WBZ/WODS general manager Ted Jordan says, "Consolidation is causing a lack of a career path because so many middle and upper management positions have been eliminated." Jim Robertson, vice-president of Dix Communication, concurs and adds, "Consolidation has affected employment for on air positions and promotion jobs due to staffing cutbacks. However, if graduates are willing to hit the streets selling, things are better." Since 1972, 75,000 individuals have found full-time employment in radio. Today, opportunities for women and minorities are greater than ever. Until fairly recently, radio has been a male-dominated profession (and in some respects it still is). In 1975, men in the industry outnumbered women by nearly four to one. But that has changed; now women are being hired more than ever before, and not just for office positions. Women have made significant inroads into programming, sales, and management positions, and there is no reason to think that this trend will not continue. Ed Shane says, "Females have made exceptional inroads, especially in sales, but less so in station management."

Results of a recent study conducted by the industry trade organization Mentoring and Inspiring Women in Radio (MIW) affirm Shane's observation, yet also point toward an increasingly brighter future for females. Approximately one in every six station general managers (GMs), for example, is female—a statistic that has been trending upward for seven consecutive years. On the revenue-generating side of the business, where women have made great strides, one third of radio's general sales managers (GSMs) are female. Less optimistic are the study's data pertaining to women and the programming function. In the press release that accompanied the release of the findings, MIW observed, "The greatest challenge for women in radio management continues to be as programmers: women still only program 11.1% of all stations, which compares to 10.7% six years ago. In the top 100 markets, women are not doing much better, programming just 9.6% of all stations." It will take a while, however, before an appropriate proportion of women and minorities are working in the medium. The FCC's insistence on equal opportunity employment within the broadcast industry makes prospects good for all who are interested in broadcasting careers.

A common misconception is that a radio station consists primarily of deejays with few other job options available. Wrong! Nothing could be farther from the truth. Granted, deejays comprise an important part of a station's staff, but many other employees are necessary to keep the station on the air.

An average-size station in a medium market used to employ between 18 and 26 people, but today due to consolidation, a fraction of that number may be used where several stations form a cluster or radio mall, and on-air personnel may comprise most of that figure. Stations are usually broken down into three major areas: sales, programming, and engineering. Each area, in particular the first two, requires a variety of people for positions that demand a wide range of skills. Subsequent chapters in this book will bear this out.

Proper training and education are necessary to secure a job at most stations, although many will train people to fill the less-demanding positions. Hundreds of schools and colleges offer courses in radio broadcasting, and most award certificates or degrees. As in most other fields today, the more credentials a job candidate possesses, the better he or she looks to a prospective employer.

Perhaps no other profession weighs practical, hands-on experience as heavily as radio does. This is especially true in the on-air area. On the programming side, it is the individual's sound that wins the job, not the degree. However,

How FCC Rules Are Made

I. Initiation of Action

Suggestions for changes to the FCC Rules and Regulations can come from sources outside of the Commission either by formal petition, legislation, court decision or informal suggestion. In addition, a Bureau/Office within the FCC can initiate a Rulemaking proceeding on its own.

II. Bureau/Office Evaluation

When a petition for Rulemaking is received, it is sent to the appropriate Bureau(s)/Office(s) for evaluation. If a Bureau/Office decides a particular petition is meritorious, it can request that the Dockets department assign a Rulemaking number to the petition.

A similar request is made when a Bureau/ Office decides to initiate a Rulemaking procedure on its own. A weekly notice is issued listing all accepted petitions for Rulemaking. The public has 30 days to submit comments. The Bureau/Office then has the option of generating an agenda item requesting one of four actions by the Commision. If a Notice of Inquiry (NOI) or Notice of Proposed Rulemaking (NPRM) is issued, a docket is instituted and a docket number is assigned.

III. Possible Commission Actions

Major changes to the Rules are presented to the public as either an NOI or NPRM. The Commission will issue an NOI when it is simply asking for information on a broad subject or trying to generate ideas on a given topic. An NPRM is issued when there is a specific change to the Rules being proposed.

If an NOI is issued, it must be followed by either an NPRM or a Memorandum Opinion and Order (MO&O) concluding the inquiry.

IV. Comments and Replies Evaluated

When an NOI or NPRM has been issued, the public is given the opportunity to comment initially, and then respond to the comments that are made. When the Commission does not receive sufficient comments to make a decision, a further NOI or NPRM may be issued.

It may be determined that an oral argument before the Commission is needed to provide an opportunity for the public to testify before the Commission, as well as for the Bureau(s)/ Office(s) to present diverse opinions concerning the proposed Rule change.

V. Report and Order Issued

A Report and Order is issued by the Commission stating the new or amended Rule, or stating that the Rules will not be changed. The proceeding may be terminated in whole or in part.

The Commission may issue additional Report and Orders in the docket.

VI. Reconsideration Given

Petitions for reconsideration may be filed by the public within 30 days. They are reviewed by the appropriate Bureau(s)/Office(s) and/or by the Commission.

VII. Modification Possible

As a result of its review of a petition for reconsideration, the Commission may issue an MO&O modifying its initial decision or denying the petition for reconsideration.

Provided by FCC

FIGURE 1.30
Courtesy *Radio World.*

it is the formal training and education that usually contribute most directly to the quality of the sound that the program director is looking for when hiring. In reality, only a small percentage of radio announcers have college degrees (the number is growing), but statistics have shown that those who do stand a better chance of moving into managerial positions.

Many station managers look for college-educated candidates, particularly for the areas of news and sales. Before 1965, the percentage of radio personnel with college training was relatively low. But the figure increased as more and more colleges added broadcasting curricula. Thousands of communications degrees are conferred annually, thus providing the radio industry with a pool of highly educated job candidates. Today, college training is a plus (if not a necessity) when searching for employment in radio. The job application or resume that lists practical experience in addition to formal training is most appealing. The majority of colleges with radio curricula have stations. These small (low-power) outlets provide the aspiring broadcaster with a golden opportunity to gain some much needed on-air experience. Some of the nation's foremost broadcasters began their careers at college radio stations. Many of these same schools have internship programs that provide the student with the chance to get important on-the-job training at professional stations. Again, experience is the key, and it rates highly with the prospective employer. Small commercial stations often are willing to hire broadcast students to fill part-time and vacation slots. This constitutes professional experience and is an invaluable addition to the resume.

Entry-level positions in radio seldom pay well. In fact, many small-market stations pay near minimum wage. However, the experience gained at these small-budget operations more than makes up for the small salaries. The U.S. Department of Labor reported that the 2013 median salary of radio announcers was $27,010 or $12.99 per hour. The first year or two in radio constitutes the dues-paying period, a time in which a person learns the ropes. The small radio station provides inexperienced people with the chance to become involved in all facets of the business. Rarely does a new employee perform only one function. For example, a person hired as a deejay will often prepare and deliver newscasts, produce play-by-play sports coverage, write and produce commercials, and may even sell airtime.

To succeed in a business as unique as radio, a person must possess many qualities, not the least of which are determination, skill, and the ability to accept and benefit from constructive criticism. A career in radio is like no other, and the rewards, both personal and financial, can be exceptional. "It's a great business," says Lynn Christian, former senior vice-president of the Radio Advertising Bureau. "No two days are alike. I recommend it over other career opportunities."

CHAPTER HIGHLIGHTS

1. With nearly 15,000 radio stations in the United States, radio is the most available source of entertainment, companionship, and information.
2. The Corporation for Public Broadcasting was established in 1967. Three years later, National Public Radio began providing funding and programming to member stations. More than 800 schools and colleges hold non-commercial radio licenses. In 2010, the network's name officially became "NPR."
3. Narrowcasting is specialized programming. Frag-out refers to the fragmentation of audience because of numerous formats.
4. Highly leveraged transactions (HLTs) created economic problems for many stations. Local marketing agreements (LMAs) allowed broadcasters to form contracts with one another for mutually beneficial purposes.
5. Consolidation, downsizing, and mergers have been prompted by the FCC's relaxation of the duopoly and ownership rules.
6. Local spot sales account for 70% of radio's revenues.
7. Brokerage firms handle the sale of most radio stations. Brokers receive a commission of between 7% and 8% on sales.
8. HD Radio™ is supplementing the conventional analog system of signal transmission and reception.
9. Satellite radio services are providing listeners with options besides traditional terrestrial signal reception.
10. Radio webstreams, once beset by copyright issues, have become a central part of station operations; station websites promote programming and permit listener interaction. Websites also provide secondary revenue opportunities.
11. Mobile music services spawned by the Internet, Wi-Fi, and smartphones draw listeners away from traditional radio, although it is anticipated that broadcast and satellite radio will become an integral part of these audio sources. Online music services such as Pandora, iHeartRadio, Rdio, and Spotify are competing with traditional broadcasters for not only listeners but also for advertising revenue. Apps for smartphones, iPads, iPods, etc., are expanding the consumer's choice of music stations as well as offering an even more convenient way to listen to music.
12. Micro- or low-power FM stations constitute a new category of noncommercial radio outlets, but the conversion to IBOC digital by regular broadcast outlets and the takeover by religious broadcasters may mean the end to the community (neighborhood)-oriented medium.
13. In 1949, the FCC formulated the Fairness Doctrine, which obligated broadcasters to present opposing points of view. In 1987 the FCC declared the doctrine unconstitutional and eliminated it.
14. The Republicans wrote a new Telecommunications Bill designed to lift significant sanctions from broadcasters. The Telecommunications Act of 1996 all but eliminated radio station ownership ceilings, resulting in the reduction in the level of local programming. It was signed into law by President Bill Clinton, a Democrat.

15. The radio industry employs fewer people today due to consolidations and the subsequent downsizings. Women and minorities have made significant gains in recent years. A combination of practical experience and formal training remains the best preparation for a career in broadcasting.

16. Industry observers frequently cite the need for radio stations to become more proactive in developing innovative content as a means for sustaining relevancy in the competitive audio environment.

SUGGESTED FURTHER READING

Aitkin, H.G.J., *Syntony and Spark*, John Wiley and Sons, New York, 1976.

American Women in Radio and Television, *Making Waves: The 50 Greatest Women in Radio and Television*, Andrews McMeel Publishing, Chicago, IL, 2001.

Archer, G.L., *History of Radio to 1926*, Arno Press, New York, 1971.

Aronoff, C.E. (ed.), *Business and the Media*, Goodyear Publishing Company, Santa Monica, CA, 1979.

Baker, W.J., *A History of the Marconi Company*, St. Martin's Press, New York, 1971.

Balk, A., *The Rise of Radio, from Marconi to the Golden Age*, McFarland, Jefferson, NC, 2005.

Barlow, W., *Voice Over: The Making of Black Radio*, Temple University Press, Philadelphia, PA, 1999.

Barnouw, E., *A Tower of Babel: A History of Broadcasting in the United States to 1933*, vol. 1, Oxford University Press, New York, 1966.

Barnouw, E., *The Golden Web: A History of Broadcasting in the United States 1933 to 1953*, vol. 2, Oxford University Press, New York, 1968.

Barnouw, E., *The Image Empire: A History of Broadcasting in the United States from 1953*, vol. 3, Oxford University Press, New York, 1970.

Barnouw, E., *The Sponsor: Notes on a Modern Potentate*, Oxford University Press, New York, 1978.

Barnouw, E., *Media Marathon: A Twentieth-Century Memoir*, Duke University Press, Durham, NC, 1996.

Bergreen, L., *Look Now, Pay Later: The Rise of Network Broadcasting*, Doubleday, Garden City, NY, 1980.

Bianchi, W., *Schools of the Air*, McFarland, Jefferson, NC, 2008.

Bittner, J.R., *Broadcasting and Telecommunications*, 2nd edition, Prentice Hall, Englewood Cliffs, NJ, 1985.

Bittner, J.R., *Professional Broadcasting: A Brief Introduction*, Prentice Hall, Englewood Cliffs, NJ, 1981.

Blake, R.H. and Haroldsen, E.O., *A Taxonomy of Concepts in Communications*, Hastings House, New York, 1975.

Brant, B.G., *College Radio Handbook*, Tab Books, Blue Ridge Summit, PA, 1981.

Brown, R.J., *Manipulating the Ether: The Power of Broadcast Radio in Thirties America*, McFarland Publishing, Jefferson, NC, 1998.

Browne, B., and Coddington (consultants), *Radio Today—and Tomorrow*, National Association of Broadcasters, Washington, D.C., 1982.

Buono, T.J. and Leibowitz, M.L., *Radio Acquisition Handbook*, Broadcasting and the Law, Miami, FL, 1988.

Campbell, R., *The Golden Years of Broadcasting*, Charles Scribner's Sons, New York, 1976.

Cantril, H., *The Invasion from Mars*, Harper & Row, New York, 1966.

Carpenter, S., *40 Watts from Nowhere: A Journey in Pirate Radio*, Scribner, New York, 2004.

Chapple, S. and Garofalo, R., *Rock 'n' Roll Is Here to Pay*, Nelson-Hall, Chicago, IL, 1977.

Coe, L., *Wireless Radio: A History*, McFarland Publishing, Jefferson, NC, 2006.

Cox Looks at FM Radio, Cox Broadcasting Corporation, Atlanta, GA, 1976.

Craig, D.B., *Fireside Politics: Radio and Political Culture in the United States, 1920–1940*, Johns Hopkins University Press, Baltimore, MD, 2000.

Delong, T.A., *The Mighty Music Box*, Amber Crest Books, Los Angeles, CA, 1980.

Ditingo, V.M., *The Remaking of Radio*, Focal Press, Boston, MA, 1995.

Douglas, S.J., *Inventing American Broadcasting, 1899–1922*, Johns Hopkins University Press, Baltimore, MD, 1987.

Douglas, S.J., *Listening In*, Times Books, New York, 1999.

Dreher, C., *Sarnoff: An American Success*, Quadrangle, New York, 1977.

Dunning, J., *Tune in Yesterday*, Prentice Hall, Englewood Cliffs, NJ, 1976.

Edmonds, I.G., *Broadcasting for Beginners*, Holt, Rinehart, and Winston, New York, 1980.

Erickson, D., *Armstrong's Fight for FM Broadcasting*, University of Alabama, Birmingham, AL, 1974.

Eskanazi, G., *I Hid It Under the Pillow: Growing Up with Radio*, University of Missouri Press, Columbia, MO, 2005.

Fang, I.E., *Those Radio Commentators*, Iowa State University Press, Ames, IA, 1977.

Fisher, M., *Something in the Air: Radio, Rock, and the Revolution That Shaped a Generation*, Random House, New York, 2007.

Fones-Wolf, E., *Waves of Opposition*, University of Illinois Press, Champaign-Urbana, IL, 2006.

Fornatale, P. and Mills, J.E., *Radio in the Television Age*, Overlook Press, New York, 1980.

Foster, E.S., *Understanding Broadcasting*, Addison-Wesley, Reading, MA, 1978.

Fowler, G. and Crawford, B., *Border Radio*, University of Texas Press, Austin, TX, 2002.

Geller, V., *The Powerful Radio Workbook*, M Street Corporation, Washington, D.C., 2000.

Geller, V., *Beyond Powerful Radio: A Communicator's Guide to the Internet Age—News, Talk, Information & Personality for Broadcasting, Podcasting, Internet, Radio*, Focal Press, Burlington, MA, 2010.

Grant, A.E. and Meadows, J.H. (eds), *Communication Technology Update and Fundamentals*, Waltham, MA, 2012.

Hall, C. and Hall, B., *This Business of Radio Programming*, Hastings House, New York, 1978.

Halper, D., *Invisible Stars*, M.E. Sharpe, Armonk, NY, 2001.

Hasling, J., *Fundamentals of Radio Broadcasting*, McGraw-Hill, New York, 1980.

Hendricks, J.A. (ed.), *The Palgrave Handbook of Global Radio*, Palgrave Macmillan, Houndmills, UK, 2012.

Hilliard, R.L. (ed.), *Radio Broadcasting: An Introduction to the Sound Medium*, 3rd edition, Longman, New York, 1985.

Hilliard, R.L., *The Federal Communications Commission: A Primer*, Focal Press, Boston, MA, 1991.

Hilliard, R.L. and Keith, M.C., *Global Broadcasting Systems*, Focal Press, Boston, MA, 1996.

Hilliard, R.L. and Keith, M.C., *Waves of Rancor: Tuning the Radical Right*, Focal Press, Boston, MA, 1999.

Hilliard, R.L. and Keith, M.C., *Dirty Discourse: Sex and Indecency in Broadcasting*, Blackwell Publishing, Boston, MA, 2006.

Hilliard, R.L. and Keith, M.C., *The Broadcast Century: A Biography of American Broadcasting*, 5th edition, Focal Press, Boston, MA, 2010.

Hilmes, M., *Radio Voices: American Broadcasting, 1922–1952*, University of Minnesota Press, Minneapolis, MN, 1997.

Horten, G., *Radio Goes to War*, University of California Press, Berkeley, CA, 2002.

Hunn, P., *Starting and Operating Your Own FM Radio Station*, Tab Books, Blue Ridge Summit, PA, 1988.

Inglis, A.F., *Behind the Tube*, Focal Press, Boston, MA, 1990.

Keirstead, P.O. and Keirstead, S.K., *The World of Telecommunication*, Focal Press, Stoneham, MA, 1990.

Keith, M.C., *Signals in the Air: Native Broadcasting in America*, Praeger Publishing, Westport, CT, 1995.

Keith, M.C., *Voices in the Purple Haze: Underground Radio and the Sixties*, Praeger Publishing, Westport, CT, 1997.

Keith, M.C., *Talking Radio: An Oral History of Radio in the Television Age*, M.E. Sharpe, Armonk, NY, 2000.

Keith, M.C., *Sounds in the Dark: All Night Radio in American Life*, Iowa State University Press, Ames, IA, 2001.

Keith, M.C. (ed.), *Radio Cultures: The Sound Medium in American Life*, Peter Lang, New York, 2008.

Ladd, J., *Radio Waves*, St. Martin's Press, New York, 1991.

Lazarsfled, P.F. and Kendall, P.L., *Radio Listening in America*, Prentice Hall, Englewood Cliffs, NJ, 1948.

Leinwall, S., *From Spark to Satellite*, Charles Scribner's Sons, New York, 1979.

Lenthall, B., *Radio America*, University of Chicago Press, Chicago, IL, 2007.

Levinson, R., *Stay Tuned*, St. Martin's Press, New York, 1982.

Lewis, P. (ed.), *Radio Drama*, Longman, New York, 1981.

Lewis, T., *Empire of the Air: The Men Who Made Radio*, HarperCollins, New York, 1991.

Lichty, L.W. and Topping, M.C., *American Broadcasting: A Source Book on the History of Radio and Television*, Hastings House, New York, 1976.

Looker, T., *The Sound and the Story*, Houghton Mifflin, Boston, MA, 1995.

Loviglio, J., *Radio's Intimate Public*, University of Minnesota, Minneapolis, MN, 2005.

MacDonald, J.F., *Don't Touch That Dial: Radio Programming in American Life, 1920–1960*, Nelson Hall, Chicago, IL, 1979.

Matelski, M., *Vatican Radio*, Praeger Publishing, Westport, CT, 1995.

McCauley, M., *NPR: The Trials and Triumphs of National Public Radio*, Columbia University Press, New York, 2005.

McGregor, M.A., Driscoll, P.D. and McDowell, W.S., *Head's Broadcasting in America: A Survey of Electronic Media*, 10th edition, Pearson, New York, 2009.

McLuhan, M., *Understanding Media: The Extensions of Man*, McGraw-Hill, New York, 1964.

Mitchell, J.W., *Listener Supported: The Culture and History of Public Radio*, Praeger Publishers, Westport, CT, 2005.

Morrow, B., *Cousin Brucie*, Morrow, New York, 1987.

NAB, *Radio Station Salaries*, National Association of Broadcasters, Washington, D.C., 2004.

Nachman, G., *Raised on Radio*, University of California Press, Berkeley, CA, 2000.

Naughton, J., *A Brief History of the Future: From Radio Days to Internet Years in a Lifetime*, Overlook Press, Woodstock, NY, 2000.

O'Donnell, L.B., et al., *Radio Station Operations: Management and Employee Perspectives*, Wadsworth Publishing, Belmont, CA, 1989.

Orlik, P.B., *Electronic Media Criticism*, Focal Press, Boston, MA, 1994.

Paley, W.S., *As It Happened: A Memoir*, Doubleday, Garden City, NY, 1979.

Pease, E.C. and Dennis, E.E., *Radio: The Forgotten Medium*, Transaction Press, New Brunswick, NJ, 1995.

Phillips, L.A., *Public Radio: Behind the Voices*, CDS Books, New York, 2006.

Pierce, J.R., *Signals*, W. H. Freeman, San Francisco, CA, 1981.

Podber, J., *The Electronic Front Porch*, Mercer University Press, Macon, GA, 2007.

Pusateri, C.J., *Enterprise in Radio*, University Press of America, Washington, D.C., 1980.

Radio Facts, Radio Advertising Bureau, New York, 1988.

Ramsey, M., *Making Waves: Radio on the Verge*, iUniverse, 2008.

Rhoads, B.E., *Blast from the Past*, Streamline Press, West Palm Beach, FL, 1996.

Richter, W.A., *Radio: A Complete Guide to the Industry*, Peter Lang, New York, 2006.

Routt, Ed., *The Business of Radio Broadcasting*, Tab Books, Blue Ridge Summit, PA, 1972.

Rudell, A., *Hello, Everybody! The Dawn of American Radio*, Harcourt, New York, 2008.

Sarnoff, D., *The World of Television*, Wisdom, Agoura Hills, CA, 1958.

Schiffer, M.B., *The Portable Radio in American Life*, University of Arizona Press, Tucson, AZ, 1991.

Seidle, R.J., *Air Time*, Holbrook Press, Boston, MA, 1977.

Settle, I., *A Pictorial History of Radio*, Grosset and Dunlap, New York, 1967.

Shapiro, M.E., *Radio Network Prime Time Programming, 1927–1967*, McFarland, Jefferson, NC, 2002.

Siegel, S. and Siegel, D.S., *A Resource Guide to the Golden Age of Radio*, Book Hunter Press, Yorktown Heights, NY, 2006.

Sipemann, C.A., *Radio's Second Chance*, Little, Brown, Boston, MA, 1946.

Sklar, R., *Rocking America: How the All-Hit Radio Stations Took Over*, St. Martin's Press, New York, 1984.

Smith, F.L., *Perspectives on Radio and Television: An Introduction to Broadcasting in the United States*, Harper & Row, New York, 1979.

Soley, L., *Free Radio*, Westview Press, Denver, CO, 1999.

Sterling, C.H. (ed.), *Encyclopedia of Radio*, Fitzroy Dearborn, New York, 2003.

Sterling, C.H. and Keith, M.C., *Sounds of Change: FM Broadcasting in America*, University of North Carolina Press, Chapel Hill, NC, 2007.

Utterback, A.S., *Broadcasters Survival Guide*, Bonus Books, San Francisco, CA, 1997.

Vowell, S., *Radio On: A Listener's Diary*, St. Martin's Press, New York, 1997.

Wertheim, A.F., *Radio Comedy*, Oxford University Press, New York, 1979.

Whetmore, E.J., *The Magic Medium: An Introduction to Radio in America*, Wadsworth Publishing, Belmont, CA, 1981.

Whetmore, E.J., *MediaAmerica*, 4th edition, Wadsworth Publishing, Belmont, CA, 1989.

Winn, J.E. and Brinson, S.L. (eds), *Transmitting the Past: Historical and Cultural Perspectives on Broadcasting*, University of Alabama Press, Tuscaloosa, AL, 2005.

Woolley, L., *The Last Great Days of Radio*, Republic of Texas Press, Dallas, TX, 1995.

Yoder, A., *Pirate Radio Stations*, McGraw-Hill, New York, 2001.

CHAPTER 2

Station Management

NATURE OF THE BUSINESS

Continuous technological advancements have forced radio station management to adjust and evolve to ensure that radio stations remain financially competitive. In most media markets, especially in larger ones, managers have gone from managing a single or combo station to overseeing the operations of a half dozen or more, often clustered in the same building. Additionally, the station manager must now compete with new audio media that didn't exist at the start of this century yet quickly developed as a result of digital technology and the Internet. Were these challenges not enough, compounding the manager's task is a host of other external factors including the turbulent and anemic economy and constant changes in the regulatory landscape.

As has always been the case, the medium's unique character requires the manager to deal with a broad mix of people, from on-air personalities to accountants and from sales personnel to technicians. Few other businesses can claim such an amalgam of employees. Even the station manager of the smallest outlet with as few as four or five employees must lead and mentor individuals with very diverse backgrounds and goals. For example, a small Maine radio group or cluster may employ three or four full-time air people, who most likely were recruited from other areas of the country. Those deejays will gain valuable experience as they begin their broadcasting careers, but some will have plans to move on to larger markets. As a result, the station will probably be looking for replacements for these individuals within a few months.

Frequent turnover of on-air personnel at small stations is a fact of life. As a consequence, members of the air staff often are regarded as transients or passers-through by not only the community but also the other members of the station's staff. Less likely to come and go are a station's managerial and technical staff. Usually they are not looking toward the bright lights of the larger markets that provide larger salaries, since the town in which the station is located is often home to them. A small station's sales department may experience some turnover but usually not to the extent that the programming department does. Also, salespeople are likely to have been recruited from the local community, whereas air personalities more typically come from outside the community.

Running a small market station or group presents unique challenges (and it should be noted that half of the nation's radio outlets are located in communities with fewer than 25,000 residents). Stations in larger markets, however, are typically faced with more robust competition and jobs are kept or lost based upon ratings. In contrast to the small Maine radio group, where the closest competitors are 50 miles away, an outlet located in a metropolitan area may share the airwaves with 30 or more other stations. Competition in the larger markets is intense, and radio stations in large metro areas usually succeed or fail based on their showing in the latest listener surveys. The metro market station manager must pay close attention to competition, while striving to maintain the best on-air product possible to retain a competitive edge and prosper.

Meanwhile, the government's perception of the radio station's responsibility to its consumers, or listeners in the communities in which they are licensed to serve, also sets it apart from many other businesses. Since its inception, terrestrial radio has been Washington, D.C.'s business. Station managers, unlike the heads of most other enterprises, have had to conform to the dictates and whims of a federal agency specifically conceived for the purpose of overseeing their activities. Failing to satisfy the expectations of the Federal Communications Commission (FCC) can result in penalties that range from large fines to the loss of an operating license; as a result, radio station managers have been obliged to stay abreast of a fairly prodigious volume of rules and regulations that is constantly changing.

The 1980s and 1990s deregulation, actions designed to unburden the broadcaster of what had been regarded by many as unreasonable government intervention, have made the life of the station manager somewhat less complicated. Nevertheless, the government continues to play an important role in American radio, and managers who value their license wisely invest time and effort in fulfilling federal mandates and regulatory requirements. After all, a radio station without a frequency is just a building with a lot of expensive equipment.

The listener's perception of the radio business, even in today's technological era when almost every community with a small business district has a radio station, is often unrealistic. Film and television's portrayal of the radio station as a hotbed of quirky characters and bizarre antics has helped foster a misconception. This is not to suggest that radio stations are the most conventional places to work, however. Because it is the station's function to provide entertainment to its listeners, it must employ creative people, and where these people congregate, whether in a small town or a large city, the atmosphere is certain to be charged. "The volatility of the air staff's emotions and the oscillating nature of radio itself actually distinguishes our business from others," observes Kentucky station manager J.G. Salter.

Faced with an audience whose needs and tastes are fickle, today's radio station has become adept at shifting gears as conditions warrant. What is currently popular in music, fashion, and leisure-time activities will be nudged aside tomorrow by something new. This, says radio show coach Randy Lane, of the Randy Lane Company, forces radio stations to stay one step ahead of all trends and fads. "Being on the leading edge of American culture makes it necessary to undergo more changes and updates than is usually the case in other businesses. Not adjusting to what is currently in vogue can put a station at a distinct disadvantage. You have to stay in touch with what is happening in your own community as well as the trends and cultural movements occurring in other parts of the country." The complex internal and external factors that derive from the unusual nature of the radio business make managing today's station a formidable challenge. Perhaps no other business demands as much from its managers. Conversely, few other businesses provide an individual with as much to be excited about. It takes a creative person to run a radio station.

THE MANAGER'S CHALLENGE

Valerie Geller

In these uncertain economic times managing and motivating people can be challenging. It is easier to run *any* business when there is money around, when cutting costs and tightening belts is not the order of the day. All successful businesses must invest in product, and in broadcasting that product is personalities and content. But while the "fat" years may be in the past, radio still continues to thrive. And these are exciting times for the medium.

FIGURE 2.1
Valerie Geller. Courtesy of Valerie Geller.

Managing is a talent in its own right. It takes talent to lead, and it takes talent to find good people. If you find you enjoy leading and are excited by other people's good work, as much as from your own work, you may be a good candidate for management. There are many jobs in radio. Some people are naturally better "actors" than "directors." Those people should probably *not* be in management. But if you enjoy motivating others and running a team then management is something you should consider. The keys to managing staff include honesty, enthusiasm, creativity, and empathy.

Valerie Geller is president of Geller Media International, a broadcast consulting firm working with news, talk, information, and personality programming for radio and television throughout the world. Geller coaches talent, leads "Creating Powerful Communicators" workshops and seminars, and has helped more than 500 stations in 33 countries develop and grow their audiences by training communicators to work more effectively. She is a much-in-demand conference and keynote speaker and seminar leader and is the author of four books about broadcasting. Her latest, *Beyond Powerful Radio—A Communicator's Guide to the Internet Age*, is available from Focal Press.

THE MANAGER AS CHIEF COLLABORATOR

There are many schools of thought concerning the approach to managing a radio station. For example, there are the standard X (authoritarian), Y (collaborative), and Z (hybrid or chief-collaborator) models or theories of management (which admittedly oversimplify the subject but give the neophyte a basic working model). The first theory embraces the idea that the general manager is the captain of the vessel, the primary authority, with solemn, if not absolute, control of the decision-making process. The second theory casts the manager in the role of collaborator or senior advisor. The third theory forms a hybrid of the preceding two; the manager is both a coach and a team player, or the chief collaborator. Of the three models, broadcast managers tend to favor the third approach.

Lynn Christian, of L.A. Christian & Associates and former general manager of several major market radio stations, preferred working for a manager who used the hybrid model rather than the purely authoritarian model.

> Before I entered upper management, I found that I performed best when my boss sought my opinion and delegated responsibility to me. I believe in department head meetings and the full disclosure of projects within the top organization of the station. If you give someone the title, you should be prepared to give that person some authority, too. I respect the integrity of my people, and if I lose it, I replace them quickly. In other words, "You respect me, and I'll respect you," is the way I have always managed.

Randy Bongarten, of Bonten Media Group and former network chief, concurs with Christian and adds, "Management styles have to be adaptive to individual situations so as to provide what is needed at the time. In general, the collaborator or team leader approach gets the job done. Of course, I don't think there is any one school of management that is right 100% of the time."

Jim Arcara, former radio network head, also is an advocate of the hybrid management style. "It's a reflection of what is more natural to me as well as my company. Employees are capable of making key decisions, and they should be given the opportunity to do so. An effective manager also delegates responsibility."

General manager Pat McNally finds the collaborative approach suitable to his goals and temperament. "My management style is more collaborative. I believe in hiring qualified professional people, defining what I expect, and allowing them to do their job with input, support, and constructive criticism from me. My door is always open for suggestions, and I am a good listener. I consider this business something special, and I expect an extra special effort."

This also holds true for general manager Steven Woodbury. "I hire the best people as department heads and then work collaboratively with these experts. Department heads are encouraged to run their areas as if they had major ownership in the company. That instills a sense of team spirit too. Their energy level and decision-making efforts reflect this."

The manager/collaborator approach is one that allows radio to function at its full potential. "Since practically every job in the radio station is designed to support and enhance the air product, establishing a connectedness among what is usually a small band of employees tends to yield the best results," contends station manager Jane Duncklee. "I strongly believe that employees must feel that they are a valid part of what is happening and that their input has a direct bearing on those decisions which affect them and the operation as a whole. I try to hire the best people possible and then let them do their jobs with a minimum of interference and a maximum of support."

Marlin R. Taylor, founder of Bonneville Broadcasting System and former manager of several major-market radio outlets, including WRFM, New York, and WBCN, Boston, and most recently Sirius/XM enLighten's program director, believes that the manager using the collaborative system of management gets the most out of employees.

> When a staff member feels that his or her efforts and contributions make a difference and are appreciated, that person will remain motivated. This kind of employee works harder and delivers more. Most people, if they enjoy the job they have and like the organization they work for, are desirous of improving their level of performance and contributing to the health and well-being of the station. I really think that many station managers should devote even more time and energy to people development.

Station general manager and owner of Great Plains Media, Inc., Paul Aaron believes that managers must first assert their authority; that is, make it clear to all that they are in charge, before the transition to collaborator can take place.

> It's a sort of process of evolution. Actually, when you come right down to it, any effective management approach includes a bit of both the authoritarian and collaborative concepts. The situation at the station will have a direct impact on the management style I personally deem most appropriate. As the saying goes, "different situations call for different measures." When assuming the reins at a new station, sometimes it is necessary to take a more dictatorial approach until the organization is where you feel it should be. Often a lot of cleanup and adjustments are necessary before there can be a greater degree of equanimity. Ultimately, however, there should be equanimity.

Surveys have shown that most broadcast executives view the chief collaborator or hybrid management approach as compatible with their needs. "It has pretty much become the standard *modus operandi* in this industry. A radio manager must direct as well as invite input. To me it makes sense, in a business in which people are the product, to create an atmosphere that encourages self-expression, as well as personal and professional growth. After all, we are in the communications business. Everyone's voice should at least be heard," contends Lynn Christian.

WHAT MAKES A MANAGER?

As in all professions, the trajectory to the top is seldom a short and easy one. It may take many years to get there, and dues must be paid along the way. To begin, without a genuine affection for the business, knowledge, and a strong desire to succeed, it is very unlikely that the position can ever be attained. Furthermore, without the proper training and experience, the top job will remain elusive. So then what goes into becoming a radio station manager? According to Jim Robertson, vice-president and general manager of Dix Communications, the main personal and professional qualities a station manager should possess are honesty and integrity. As Robertson says:

> Everything else is moot without that to start. You must be willing to lead by example. Be a part of the process, not just an overseer. We are not a huge operation, which allows me to be much more a participant. As the size of the staff and the number of stations gets larger, the challenge of participation grows, and that brings us right back to honesty and integrity. These are core ingredients. Add to these the importance of leading a balanced life. One that allows you to share time with family, engage in leisure activities, participate in community, and so on. It is very important that a manager knows how to balance and prioritize these things.

Entercom's Dave Neugesser observes, "A station manager has to have a complete understanding of the three legs that support the body of radio—the listener, the client, and the station. While much of what we do in programming supports the station and listener, radio is a business and the client is just as crucial. A manager must have a clear vision, tight focus, and solid strategy to succeed. He or she must have a great team to be a great leader."

Longtime broadcast executive John Gehron shares his perspective on what makes for a successful manager. "He or she must understand what channels the audience is using and then match content to fit the channel. Deciding how to allocate resources among the many distribution sources is of utmost importance. At the same time the manager must not pull too many resources from the primary channel and diminish its popularity."

Emmis Communications chief, Jeff Smulyan, says the current times require special skills.

> A radio manager must be flexible. The media world is changing daily. Providing leadership that understands a rapidly changing world is the most important attribute. None of us understands how technology will change the industry. We have to provide content that can be deployed in several

different ways. Content that creates a unique listening experience and provides adequate results for advertisers. Being able to adjust to the shifting market scene is crucial for any manager.

First and foremost, a prospective manager needs a good foundation, and formal education plays a strong role in this background. Hundreds of institutions of higher learning across the country offer programs in broadcast operations. The college degree has achieved great importance in radio over the past decade or two and, as in most other industries today, it has become a standard credential for those vying for management positions. Anyone entering broadcasting with aspirations to operate a radio station should acquire as much formal training as possible. Station managers with Master's degrees are not uncommon. However, a Bachelor's degree in communications gives the prospective station manager a good foundation from which to launch a career.

In a business that stresses the value of practical experience, seldom, if ever, does an individual land a management job directly out of college. In fact, most station managers have been in the business at least 15 years. "Once you get the theory nailed down you have to apply it. Experience is the best teacher. I've spent 30 years working in a variety of areas in the medium. In radio, in particular, hands-on experience is what matters," says former station manager Richard Bremkamp, Jr.

To radio station manager Roger Ingram, experience is what most readily opens the door to management. "While a degree is kind of like a union card in this day and age, a good track record is what wins the management job. You really must possess both."

Jane Duncklee began her ascent to station management by logging commercials for airplay and eventually moved into other areas. "For the past 17 years I have been employed by Champion Broadcasting Systems. During that time I have worked in every department of the radio station, from traffic—where I started—to sales, programming, engineering, and finally management on both the local and corporate levels."

Since the ownership-consolidation era of the 1990s, most radio station managers are recruited from the sales area rather than programming. Because the general manager's foremost objective is to generate a profit, often from multiple operations, station owners usually feel more confident hiring someone with a solid sales or business background. Consequently, three out of four radio managers have made their living at some point selling airtime. It is a widely held belief that sales experience best prepares an individual for the realities encountered in the manager's position. "I spent more than a decade and a half in media sales before becoming a station manager. In fact, my experience on the radio level was exclusively confined to sales and then for only eight months. After that I moved into station management. Most of my radio-related sales experience took place on the national level with station rep companies," recalls Norm Feuer a vice-president for Broadcast Company of Americas in San Diego.

GENERAL SALES MANAGER

by miweco » Tue Sep 24, 2013 1:09 pm

Midwest Communications has an immediate opening for a General Sales Manager.

This position requires a proven track record and a track record for continuous growth. We are looking for an individual with prior management and sales experience with the ability to lead people. We need someone who can recruit and train the very best people and who can listen, coach, and provide feedback to motivate our talented, growing sales staff. We need someone who is an IDEA GENERATOR who will provide our Marketing Consultants with a multitude of revenue creating ideas. We need a coach who is ready to hit the streets with our team members and coach in the field. We need a coach who likes to make money and have FUN doing it...we work hard and we play hard.

We offer training, competitive salary and bonus structure, a full benefits package and unlimited opportunity for the right candidate. If you're ready to begin your future TODAY please send your resume, via email, to Mike.Klein@mwcradio.com...Or fax to General Sales Manager Opening/ Midwest Communications, Inc. C/O Michael Klein (517) 699-1880 or mail to Michael Klein C/O Midwest Communications 2495 North Cedar Street Holt, Michigan 48842.

Midwest Communications, Inc. is an equal opportunity employer

FIGURE 2.2
General sales manager job ad for Midwest Communications. A background in sales is a desired qualification in radio management. Courtesy of AllAccess.com.

Station manager Carl Evans holds that a sales background is especially useful, if not necessary, to general managers. "I spent a dozen years as a station account executive, and prior to entering radio I represented various product lines to retailers. The key to financial success in radio exists in an understanding of retailing."

It is not uncommon for station managers to have backgrounds out of radio, but almost invariably their experience comes out of the areas of sales, marketing, and finance. Broadcaster Paul Aaron, who worked as a fundraiser for the United Way of America before entering radio, contends that many managers come from other fields where they have served in positions related to sales, if not in sales itself. "Of those managers who have worked in fields other than radio, most have come to radio via the business sector. There are not many former biologists or glass blowers serving as station managers," says Aaron.

Although statistics show that the station salesperson has the best chance of being promoted to the station's head position (more general managers have held the sales manager's position than any other), a relatively small percentage of radio's managers come from the programming ranks. "I'm more the exception than the rule. I have spent my entire career in the programming side, first as a deejay at stations in Phoenix, Denver, and Pittsburgh, and then as program director for outlets in Kansas City and Chicago. I'll have to admit, however, that while it certainly is not impossible to become a GM [general manager] by approaching it from the programming side, resistance exists," admits station manager Randy Lane.

Many in the industry consider the programmer's role to be more an artistic function than one requiring a high degree of business savvy. However accurate or inaccurate this assessment is, the result is that fewer managers are hired with

Operations Manager - Missoula Cluster - Townsquare Media

by **scottrichman9** » Tue Sep 24, 2013 7:48 am

Townsquare Media of Missoula Montana has an opening for Operations Manager for our cluster of 6 radio stations here in Western Montana.

This position will report directly to the General Manager and Regional Operations Manager at the studios at 3250 S. Reserve Street, Missoula, Montana.

This job is much more than picking the hits. The successful candidate will be a great leader, a talent coach, and a highly organized strategist. You'll need exceptional teamwork skills to produce results with experienced talent, programmers, sales and digital teams. You'll need a sense for marketing and socialization, the ability to focus under fast-paced pressure, and the capacity for managing multiple tasks at once. Great communication skills, attention to detail, and a sense of humor are all a must. Strong working knowledge of music scheduling systems, digital audio systems and online media platforms are required. Duties will include: the day-to-day operations of the 6 station cluster (KBAZ, KYSS, KENR, KGVO, KLYQ, KMPT) managing the on-air staff and Promotions Department, scheduling personnel, work directly with the Digital Managing Editor, scheduling music for one or more stations (Country/Top 40), on air shift (on KYSS - Country).

Experience needed... minimum 5 years programming (preferably Country, Top 40), Music Scheduling, create and produce programming and promotional proposals, able to multi-task and communicate with all departments.

FIGURE 2.3
Operations manager job ad for a cluster of stations owned by Townsquare Media. Multiple skill sets are needed when managing a cluster of stations. Courtesy of AllAccess.com.

backgrounds exclusively confined to programming duties. Programmers have reason to be encouraged, however, since a trend in favor of hiring program directors (PDs) has surfaced in recent years, and predictions suggest that it will continue as new audio competition and added distribution channels for radio have put "product development" on par with sales and financial management.

Creative people may have an opportunity in radio as never before, especially if they are also able to grasp the essentials of the "other side" of the business: sales, marketing, personnel and financial management. The reason, says Broadcasting Unlimited's Jay Williams, is that "good program managers often have great vision, can determine a solid course for the station's programming, imaging and promotion, and can get people to follow their lead. More importantly, it's the program directors who are on the cutting edge of understanding and utilizing social media, building listener interactivity, harnessing the power of listener-generated content, and adding distribution channels. And that's the future."

In reality, the most attractive candidate for a station management position is the one whose experience has involved both programming and sales responsibilities. No general manager can fully function without an understanding and appreciation of what goes into preparing and presenting the air product, nor can he or she hope for success without a keen sense of business and finance.

Today's highly competitive and complex radio market requires that the person aspiring to management have both formal training—preferably a college degree in broadcasting—and experience in all aspects of radio station operations, in particular sales and programming. Ultimately, the effort and energy an individual invests will bear directly on the dividends he or she earns, and there is not a single successful station manager who has not put in 15-hour days or longer. The station manager is expected to know more and do more than anyone else, and rightfully so, since he or she is the person who stands to gain the most.

CBS Radio group president Dan Mason relates the qualities he sees in the most successful station managers: "A keen sense of what is 'good business,' humility to take the blame in bad times and to give staff credit in good times, fairness and passion for all, responsiveness to situations (not reactionary), passion for the industry, recognition and knowledge of staff (know by first names), and ability to keep personal problems out of the station."

THE MANAGER'S DUTIES AND RESPONSIBILITIES

A primary objective of the station manager is to operate in a manner that generates the most profit, while maintaining a positive and productive attitude among station employees. This is more of a challenge than it may seem, claims radio broadcaster Cliff Shank. "In order to meet the responsibility that you are faced with daily, you really have to be an expert in so many areas: sales, marketing, finance, legal matters, technical, governmental, and programming. It helps if you're an expert in human nature, too." Jane Duncklee puts it this way: "Managing a radio station requires that you divide yourself equally into at least a dozen parts and be a 100% whole in each situation." The Telecommunications Act of 1996 created an environment of consolidation where managers began providing oversight of many radio stations. Consultant Ed Shane observes: "The duties for station managers have changed radically. For example, at one time the manager of what became the Clear Channel cluster at Baton Rouge, had responsibility for several AM and FM stations in other parts of Louisiana and Texas. Talk about dividing yourself."

In today's consolidated environment, this is more common than not, says Jay Williams, "Mike Glickenhaus, a Clear Channel vice-president and market manager, originally oversaw nine FM stations in the San Diego cluster."

Station owner Bill Campbell says the theme that runs throughout the classic Tom Peters book, *In Search of Excellence*, is one that is relevant to the station manager's task today. "The idea in Peters's book is that you must make the customer happy, get your people involved, and get rid of departmental waste and unnecessary expenditures. A station should be a lean and healthy organism."

Station managers themselves generally must answer to a higher authority. The majority of radio stations, roughly 85%, are owned by companies and corporations that both hire the manager and help establish financial goals or projections for the station. It is the station manager's job to see that corporate expectations are met and, ideally, exceeded. Managers who fail to operate a facility in a way that satisfies the corporate hierarchy may soon find themselves looking for another job.

Fewer than 15% of the nation's stations are owned by individuals or partnerships. At these radio outlets, the manager still must meet the expectations of the station owner(s). In some cases, the manager may be given more latitude or responsibility in determining the station's fate, whereas in others, the owner may play a more direct role in the operation of the station.

A basic function of the manager's position is to formulate station policy and see that it is implemented. To ensure against confusion, misunderstanding, and possible unfair labor practices that typically impede operations, employees often receive a station policy manual. This manual states the station's positions on a host of issues, such as hiring, termination, salaries, raises, promotions, sick leave, vacation, benefits, and so forth. As standard practice, a station may require that each new employee read and become familiar with the contents of the policy manual before actually starting work. Job descriptions, as well as organization flowcharts, are commonly outlined to make it abundantly clear to staff members who is responsible for what. A well-conceived policy book may contain a statement of the station's programming philosophy with an explanation of the format it employs. The more comprehensive a policy book, the less likely there will be confusion and disruption.

Hiring and retaining good people are other key managerial functions. "You have some pretty delicate egos to cope with in this business. Radio attracts some very bright and highly talented people, sometimes with erratic temperaments. Keeping harmony and keeping people are among the foremost challenges facing a station manager," claims Norm Feuer.

Steve Woodbury agrees with Feuer, adding, "You have to hire the right people and motivate them properly, and that's a challenge. You have to be capable of inspiring people. Actually, if you are unable to motivate your people, the station will fail to reach its potential. Hire the best people you can and nurture them."

Cluster market manager Mike Glickenhaus says:

> You make sure you have a lot of great people. You need more key people who you can give lots of responsibility to because you don't have time to micromanage them. It's important to hire the right people and then clearly lay out the vision, goals, and many of the steps that will be necessary and agree on them. You need people who understand what it takes, what they have to do, and have the direction to get there. Then as manager you have to decide what (projects or problems) you're going to apply your time to.

NAB's executive vice-president for radio, John David, adds:

> There is no longer just one key to running successful radio stations. My advice would be to find as many creative people who have a real connection to the people in the audience. Hire them, treat them with respect, listen to their input, and pay them. Managers can hire people all day that agree with them. Hire people who have different ideas but are smart enough to carry out the plan with enthusiasm once the direction is determined. That goes for all departments of the team, including management. With this formula, you won't be constantly looking for people.

As mentioned earlier, managers of small-market radio stations are confronted with a unique set of problems when it comes to hiring and holding onto qualified people, especially on-air personnel. "In our case, finding and keeping a professional-sounding staff with our somewhat limited budget is an ongoing problem. This is true at most small market stations," observes station manager J.G. Salter.

The rural or small-market station is where the majority of newcomers gain their experience. Because salaries are low and the fledgling air person's ambitions are usually high, the rate of turnover is significant. Managers of small outlets spend a great deal of time training people. "It is a fact of the business that radio people, particularly deejays, usually learn their trade at the 'out-of-the-way,' low-power outlet. To be a manager at a small station, you have to be a teacher, too. But it can be very rewarding despite the obvious problem of having to rehire to fill positions so often. We deal with many beginners. I find

	Clear Channel	Cumulus Media Hldgs	Townsquare Media LLC	CBS Radio	Entercom	Salem Comm Corp	Saga Comm Inc	Cox Media Group	Univision
2012	841	507	242	126	113	98	91	82	69
2011	839	549	197	130	113	95	91	82	69
2010	845	305	175	131	112	93	91	84	70
2009	847	306	0	130	112	94	91	85	72
2008	851	308	0	134	112	94	91	85	69
2007	851	306	0	140	115	97	91	79	74
2006	1135	306	0	140	120	98	89	79	74
2005	1184	299	0	179	103	106	87	78	0
2004	1192	305	0	181	103	103	86	78	0

FIGURE 2.4
Change in Stations Owned by the Top Companies: 2004–2012. Courtesy of BIA/Kelsey.

it exciting and gratifying, and no small challenge, to train newcomers in the various aspects of radio broadcasting," says Salter.

Randy Lane also enjoys the instructor's role but notes that the high turnover rate affects product continuity.

> With air people coming and going all the time, it can give the listening public the impression of instability. The last thing a station wants to do is sound schizophrenic. Establishing an image of dependability is crucial to any radio station. Changing air people every other month doesn't help. As a station manager, it is up to you to do the best you can with the resources at hand. In general, I think small market managers do an incredible job with what they have to work with.

Managers of small-market stations must wrestle with the problems stemming from diminutive budgets and high employee turnover, whereas those at large stations must grapple with the difficulties inherent in managing larger budgets, bigger staffs, and facing stiffer competition. "It's all relative, really. While the small town station gives the manager turnover headaches, the major market manager usually is caught up in the ratings battle, which consumes vast amounts of time and energy. Of course, even larger stations are not immune to turnover," observes KGLD's Bremkamp.

It is up to the manager to control the station's finances. Knowledge of bookkeeping and accounting procedures is necessary. "You handle the station's purse-strings. An understanding of budgeting is an absolute must. Station economics is the responsibility of the GM. The idea is to control income and expenses in a way that yields a sufficient profit," says Roger Ingram.

The manager allocates and approves spending in each department (in cluster operations this also means for each station). Heads of departments must work within the budgets they have helped establish. Budgets generally cover the expenses involved in the operation of a particular area within the station for a specified period, such as a six- or 12-month period. No manager wants to spend more than what is absolutely required. A solid familiarity with what is involved in running the various departments within a station prevents waste and overspending. "A manager has to know what is going on in programming,

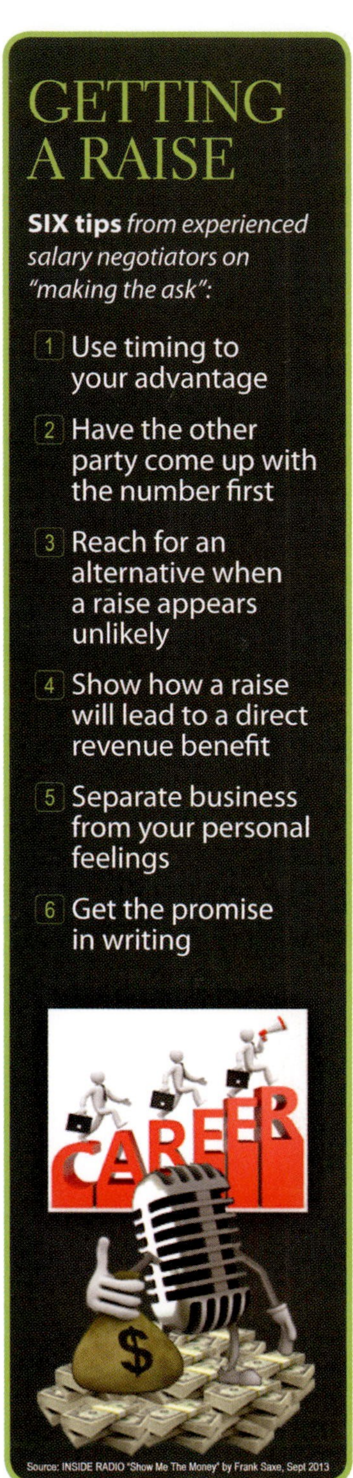

engineering, sales, actually every little corner of the station, in order to run a tight ship and make the most revenue possible. Of course, you should never cut corners simply for the sake of cutting corners. An operation must spend in order to make. You have to have effective cost control in all departments. That doesn't mean damaging the product through undernourishment either," says Evans.
David Saperstein, president of Metro Networks, observes that, "In the early days, radio was a mom-and-pop type of business. With the huge dollars in radio today, one mistake could cost a station hundreds of thousands or even millions of dollars in revenue."

GETTING A RAISE
SIX tips from experienced salary negotiators on "making the ask":
1 Use timing to your advantage
2 Have the other party come up with the number first
3 Reach for an alternative when a raise appears unlikely
4 Show how a raise will lead to a direct revenue benefit
5 Separate business from your personal feelings
6 Get the promise in writing
CAREER
$
Source: INSIDE RADIO "Show Me The Money" by Frank Saxe, Sept 2013

To ensure that the product the station offers is the best it can be, the station manager must keep in close touch with every department. Since the station's sound is what wins listeners, the manager must work closely with the program director and engineer. Both significantly contribute to the quality of the air product. The program director is responsible for what goes on the air, and the engineer is responsible for the way it sounds.

Meanwhile, selling the station to advertisers is vital. This falls within the province of the sales department. Traditionally, the general manager works more closely with the station's sales manager than with anyone else. In fact, in smaller stations, the general manager often is the sales manager.

An excellent air product attracts listeners, and listeners attract sponsors. It is as basic as that. "The formula works when all departments in a station work in unison and up to their potential," contends Marlin R. Taylor. "In radio our product is twofold—the programming we send over our frequency and the listening audience we deliver to advertisers. A station's success is linked to customer/listener satisfaction, just like a retail store's. If you don't have what the consumer desires, or the quality doesn't meet his standards, he'll go elsewhere and generally won't return."

In a quickly changing, dynamic industry like radio, where both cultural and technological innovations have an impact on the way a station operates, the manager must stay abreast of future trends. New technologies employed by stations compound the manager's task. For example, determining how best to employ a station's website and social media technologies such as Twitter and Facebook is ultimately the decision of the station manager. In terms of other new technologies, such as Facebook and Twitter, HD and its side-channels feature also known as multicasting, former radio manager Jim

FIGURE 2.5
Managers are responsible for the station's financial health including negotiating salaries with the station's staff. Courtesy of Inside Radio.

Robertson says that effective strategies for the implementation of such things are a part of what is expected of station managers. "You have to know what is going to enhance your product in the face of mounting competition. We are very excited about offering new opportunities for listening with our HD channels, and as manager you have to stay abreast of things all the time." As of March 2012, iBiquity Digital Corporation reported there were 2,144 radio stations broadcasting in HD. This technology approved by the FCC is designed to provide listeners with additional programming content such as real-time traffic or

FIGURE 2.6
Courtesy of AllAccess.com, Inside Radio, Radio Ink, and Radio and Television Business Report.

weather. But, it is the manager's responsibility to determine how to best leverage this technology to both the station's advantage and the listener's advantage.

Financial projections for future needs must be based on data that include the financial implications of prospective and predicted events. An effective manager anticipates change and develops appropriate plans to deal with it. Industry trade journals (*Broadcasting and Cable, Radio Ink, Radio and Television Business Report,* and a host of Internet newsletters such as *Radio and Internet Newsletter, All Access,* and *Inside Radio*) and conferences conducted by organizations such as the NAB and the Radio Advertising Bureau (RAB) help keep the station manager informed of what tomorrow may bring.

Regarding industry trade journals, Ed Shane observes, "Too many of the remaining trade publications are 'good news' journals, concentrating only on the most positive spin as opposed to providing balance or insight. It's as if they print news releases without vetting them."

Station consultants and "rep companies," which sell local station airtime to national advertising agencies, also support the manager in his or her efforts to keep on top of things. "A station manager must utilize all that is available to stay in touch with what's out there. Foresight is an essential ingredient for any radio manager. Hindsight is not enough in an industry that operates with one foot in the future," says Lynn Christian, who summarizes the duties and responsibilities of a station manager: "To me the challenges of running today's radio station include building and maintaining audience ratings, attracting and keeping outstanding employees, increasing gross revenues annually, and creating a positive community image for the station, not necessarily in that order." Richard Bremkamp is more laconic. "It boils down to one sentence: Protect the license and turn a profit."

THE QUALITIES THAT MAKE A STATION MANAGER

Norman Feuer

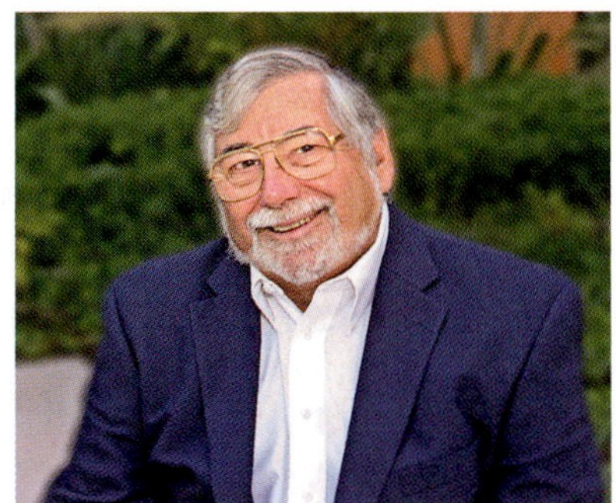

FIGURE 2.7
Norman Feuer. Courtesy of Norman Feuer.

1. **Smart/intelligent.** This is something that I cannot teach or help someone with; they are either smart or they are not.
2. **Organized.** A GM or GSM (general sales manager) has a lot on his or her plate, especially with the limited time available to accomplish what has to be done. An unorganized person will waste that time.
3. **Good communicator.** As a group head, I also have a lot on my plate. I must rely on my managers to communicate with

me quickly and efficiently. If they can do that, I have the comfort of knowing that they are able to communicate effectively with their staff on the station's missions and goals to be accomplished.

4. **Strategic thinker.** In today's world there's no such thing as a quick fix. Therefore, I need to have someone who can think through the long-term effects of each major decision that he or she makes.
5. **Motivated.** In my opinion, you cannot motivate people; they are either self-motivated or they are not. All I can do is set a work environment that motivates them to do their best.
6. **Business-like.** I need people who understand that this is a business, not a hobby, and that every decision that they make has a return on investment and will lead to a successful business conclusion.
7. **Leader.** I want a person who is a winner, for whom people want to work, with the ability to read personnel, hire the best people, and be able to maximize the potential of all his or her people.
8. **Good track record.** Although it is nice to be able to find someone who has a winning track record on all or most of his or her previous assignments, we also understand that no one is born a GM or GSM. Therefore, it is not always a criterion.
9. **High energy level.** I've always felt that you can determine a successful person by watching the way he or she walks down the hallway. I believe a person with a high energy level tends to get his or her people to move at a higher level also.
10. **Honest and with integrity.** It is absolutely critical that you trust your manager, and trust that he or she won't try to make excuses and place blame on other people. This is a very hard ingredient to determine up front and may have to be acquired eventually.

Norman Feuer is vice-president and market manager of Broadcast Company of Americas in San Diego that owns the cluster that features XPRS, XPRS-A, and XEPE-A. Feuer has had a 50-plus year career that includes executive leadership posts at Viacom, Noble Broadcast Group, Triathlon Broadcasting, Clear Channel, and Morris Communications.

MANAGING THE CLUSTER

A significant number of the nation's radio stations exist in cluster configurations that are several stations owned by the same company and are grouped together in one location. This has resulted in the downsizing of station staffs and the ultimate enhancement of the bottom line for the corporations licensed to operate these outlets. With clustering, some individuals often work for multiple stations. Thus, if there are four stations in a cluster, rather than having four separate staffs for each station, one set of staff members will do jobs at all four stations. This business model created a sweeping reorganization of the broadcast radio landscape. The longtime model of a single station run by a single manager is being eclipsed in major and medium markets by the post-Telecommunications Act of 1996 "cluster" paradigm in which a single market manager oversees the

FIGURE 2.8
CBS owns radio stations in media markets around the nation. When a company owns several stations in a market, this is called a radio cluster. In this example, CBS owns six radio stations in Dallas, Texas. Courtesy of CBS.

operation of many stations—in some cases up to eight. This creates a whole new set of challenges for radio managers. Perhaps the biggest challenge for the person responsible for the stations in a cluster is providing the appropriate amount of focus on each.

The late Tom Severino, Emmis Indianapolis Radio market manager, observed:

> While managing a single station or even two, you have more time to get involved with more detail in each department. When you manage a cluster of four or more, you have to stay focused on the biggest issues that move you toward goals. The right people have always been your most important asset, and that is even more critical in cluster management. You have to make sure you have the absolute right person in the right position

FIGURE 2.9
BCA Radio is a cluster in San Diego, California. Courtesy of Broadcast Company of the Americas.

HUMAN RESOURCES

Dick Oppenheimer

The management of station personnel is one of the manager's greatest challenges. The following is prominent Texas-based radio executive **Dick Oppenheimer**'s perspective on the subject:

FIGURE 2.10
Dick Oppenheimer.

One of the oldest sayings I can remember is that the more things change, the more they stay the same. Perhaps, but that adage certainly does not apply to the radio industry any longer.

Before there were LMAs, duopolies, and super-duopolies, you were the manager of one or, at most, two radio stations. Now the norm is to manage at least six in your market. This is an industry where the inventory is time and the commodity is people. In fact, radio is a business totally driven by people.

The typical radio station had perhaps 15 employees and although you had middle managers you were truly "hands-on." The manager was more than just the boss, he was priest, rabbi, psychologist, big brother, confidant, and so on. Today, with upward of 100 employees, you can no longer be "hands-on." You are now a corporate figurehead. You are responsible to and for your corporation for the day-to-day operations of your slew of radio stations.

Today's radio station is far different from the one of ten or 20 years ago. Now there's a host of considerations you as manager must keep a watchful eye on, including sexual harassment, job discrimination, hostile work environment, disabilities acts, and race, religion, and gender issues. That's just for starters.

The first thing a manager must do is learn all the rules and laws concerning areas that impact human resources. You shouldn't attempt this yourself. Hire and retain an attorney who specializes in labor law. Have the attorney write an employee manual and establish the policies that are necessary for you to be a competent personnel manager. Once you have done this, have an initial meeting with your management staff and your attorney to convey the information necessary to assist your people in their management of other people.

Next have your employees acknowledge receipt of the manual, and each and every quarter have reviews with your management staff regarding the various policies outlined in the manual as a means of detecting and assessing any potential problems.

Document everything. *Remember, if it is not in writing, it did not occur.* When an employee comes to you with a complaint, have someone else present to verify the discussion and its content. Keep in mind that in a courtroom, you are the defendant. All the employee has to say is that it happened. The burden of proof is yours.

Of course, one of the best ways to prevent problems is through proper hiring. It has been my experience that, often, the employee who files charges against you is a marginal or questionable employee, that is to say, an employee who should not have been hired in the first place. Unfortunately, it is not until a suit has been filed that you learn about an employee's history of filing complaints. However, there are times when a complaint is legitimate. Real problems can and do exist. You have to be mindful of this.

Handling people is one of the significant challenges of any manager. It is also one of the most rewarding.

Dick Oppenheimer was inducted into the Texas Radio Hall of Fame in 2012 and named the "2009 Pioneer of the Year" by the Texas Association of Broadcasters (TAB). He has had a long running career in the radio industry including managing Houston's KYOK-AM; starting Capitol Cities Broadcasting with radio stations in Austin, Baton Rouge, Little Rock, Mobile and Beaumont. Capitol Cities Broadcasting was sold for one of the highest prices ever paid for a group of its size. After selling Capitol Cities Broadcasting, he started Signature Broadcasting with numerous radio station holdings. He served on the TAB Board of Directors from 1981–87 and for eight years on the NAB Board of Directors. He also spent ten years (1996 to 2006) as an adjunct professor at the University of Texas, College of Communications, where he was voted by the students as the #1 professor in the college. He returned to the radio business in 2008 with the acquisition of two stations in the Austin market; which he sold in 2013 and retired "for real". (Bio information courtesy of Texas Association of Broadcasters).

because you have to rely on leadership at all levels more in a cluster situation. To manage this effectively everyone in the organization must know what the goals are, how they contribute to those goals, how we are doing in reaching those goals. Everyone needs to be familiar with the values of the company as well.

Dix Communications vice-president Jim Robertson shares many of Severino's views regarding the management of a station cluster.

The on-going balancing act of time and resources is by far top of the list from my perspective. I am fortunate to have two stations (93.7K Country/WOGK) and our three station classic rock simulcast (WNDD/WNDT/WNDN) that are capable of being number one in all of the key demographics. Each station rightfully demands and deserves equal attention. Admittedly, each station at times feels like the other is favored. I think that is good in a competitive environment. Good communication is essential in a cluster operation, especially at the department-head level. It allows each station's program director to understand why things are happening across the hall at the other station. A cluster has to function organically.

Severino offers a list of the pros and cons of the station cluster concept:

- **Pros:** As a manager, you can use each entity to cross promote each other (events, programming specials, news, formats, etc.; you can spread expenses); you can cross-utilize personnel; you can expand what is offered to advertisers; you can utilize each station's audience delivery and events to best serve the customer; you can combine resources to get better pricing from vendors (promotional items, outside marketing); and you can reduce expenses on support staff (business office, sales, and so forth).

- **Cons:** As a manager, you cannot get involved in the day-to-day detail of each entity; you cannot devote full focus on a single station; you cannot engage in long-term strategic thinking of each station enterprise.

THE MANAGER AND THE PROFIT MOTIVE

Earlier we discussed the unique nature of the radio industry and the particular challenges station managers face as a consequence. Radio, indeed, is a form of show business, and both words of the term are particularly applicable since the medium is at once stage and store. Radio provides entertainment (and information) to the public and, in turn, sells access to the audience it attracts to advertisers.

The general manager or market manager is answerable to many: the station's owners and corporate heads, listeners, and sponsors. However, to keep his or her own job, the manager must first please the owner or corporate manager. More often than not, that person's first concern is profit. As in any business, the more money the manager generates, the happier the owner. In May 2013, Emmis's Compensation Committee restructured the way in which the company's executives and managers were paid. In a filing with Security and Exchange Commission (SEC), Emmis proposes, "The Committee will award a quarterly bonus to each participant based upon the extent to which the quarterly performance goal was achieved, with no quarterly bonus to be paid under the plan if less than 95% of the quarterly performance goal was achieved. The quarterly bonus, if any, will be up to 20% of the participant's annual target bonus amount." In sum, in some situations, when managers accomplish goals they are financially rewarded, when the goals are not accomplished they see no financial rewards. Emmis owns radio stations in New York, Los Angeles, Austin, St. Louis, Indianapolis, and Terre Haute.

FIGURE 2.11
Strategic Radio Solutions works with managers to help develop winning programming and marketing strategies for radio stations based on listeners perceptions, tastes, and media behavior. Courtesy of Strategic Radio Solutions.

Profit is especially important with clustered stations due to their potential to generate vast sums of revenue and build equity quickly. To illustrate the importance of managers to build good teams to produce profits, *Inside Radio* reported, in 2013, that Sinclair Broadcast Group offered $373.3 million to purchase Fisher Communications. Fisher Communications' assets included three radio stations in the Seattle area along with other mass media businesses. The radio industry is big business and effective managerial oversight is imperative because so much money is at stake.

Ed Shane, a radio industry consultant and former manager, observes:

> The new radio paradigm is "manager as financial expert." Pressure from corporate ownership to feed stock prices has changed the way managers think about their stations. Budgets, once an annual affair, are reevaluated quarterly and even monthly. Managers now must be prepared at a moment's notice to cancel planned advertising expenditures or to move the expenditures into another quarter if the local cluster (or the company's region) is not making budgets. "Budgets" does not mean breaking even. It means achieving the percentage increase over the previous year's cash flow. Margins of 45–50% are not uncommon.

Critics have chided the medium for what they argue is an obsessive preoccupation with making money, which has resulted in a serious shortage of high-quality, innovative programming. They lament too much sameness. Meanwhile, station managers often are content to air material that draws the kind of audience that advertisers want to reach.

Marlin Taylor observes that too many managers overemphasize profit at the expense of the operation. "Not nearly enough of the radio operators in this country are truly committed to running the best possible stations they can, either because that might cost them more money or they simply don't understand or care what it means to be the best. In my opinion, probably no more than 20% of the nation's stations are striving to become the IBM of radio, that is, striving for true excellence. Many simply are being milked for what the owners and managers can take out of them."

Other detractors don't decry the "profit motive" for the problems of "sameness" as much as they do "consolidation," the result of the 1996 Telecommunications Act that allowed larger companies to buy up many smaller, individually owned and programmed radio stations in every market. Many independent stations, even in larger markets, did not have the resources to compete against group operators, and these were often the stations that provided the most eclectic programming. Conversely, group operators themselves are being challenged by other cluster operators in addition to a growing number of alternative audio sources that are taking a share of mind and dollars. Radio in its different forms is expanding, and that increases competition and puts pressure on profits.

The pursuit of profits forces the station manager to employ the programming format that will yield the best payday. In several markets certain formats, such as classical and jazz, which tend to attract small audiences, have been dropped in favor of those that draw greater numbers such as country. In some instances, the actions of stations have caused outcries by unhappy and disenfranchised listeners who feel that their programming needs are being disregarded. Several disgruntled listener groups have gone to court in an attempt to force stations to reinstate abandoned formats. Since the government currently avoids involvement in programming decisions, leaving it up to stations to do as they see fit, little has come of their protests. However, sometimes station managers listen to the public outcry, such as in the 2005 case of WHFS in Washington, D.C. Thousands of listeners signed petitions when WHFS went off the air prompting management to reverse its decision.

The dilemma facing today's radio station manager stems from the complexity of having to please numerous factions while earning enough money to justify his or her continued existence at the station. Marlin Taylor has suggested that stations reinvest more of their profits as a method of upgrading the overall quality of the medium.

> Overcutting can have deleterious effects. A station can be too lean, even anemic. In other words, you have to put something in to get something out. Too much draining leaves the operation arid and subject to criticism by the listening public. It behooves the station manager to keep this thought in mind and, if necessary, impress it upon ownership. The really successful operations know full well that money has to be spent to nurture and develop the kind of product that delivers both impressive financial returns and listener praise.

Although it is the manager who must deal with bottom-line expectations, it is also the manager who is expected to maintain product integrity. The effective manager takes pride in the unique role radio plays in society and does not hand it over to advertisers, notes station manager Bremkamp. "You have to keep close tabs on your sales department. They are out to sell the station, sometimes one way or the other. Overly zealous salespeople can, on occasion, become insensitive to the station's format in their quest for ad dollars. Violating the format is like mixing fuel oil with water. You may fill your tank for less money, but you're not likely to get very far. The onus is placed on the manager to protect the integrity of the product while making a dollar. Actually, doing the former usually takes care of the latter."

Conscientious station managers are aware of the obligations confronting them and are sensitive to the criticism that crass commercialism can produce a desert or "wasteland" of bland and uninspired programming. They are also aware that, while gaps and voids may exist in radio programming and that certain segments of the population may not be getting exactly what they want, it is up to them to produce enough income to pay the bills and meet the ownership's expectations.

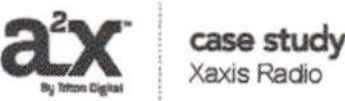

case study
Xaxis Radio

Digital Audio Drives Lift and Engagement for Product Launch

The Triton Digital® audio ad exchange, a2x™, is the industry's first exchange offering audience targeting for radio streams and pureplay audio. To deliver the most personal, targeted ads, a2x integrates consumer data from partner eXelate which provides data and insight on online purchase intent, household demographics and behavioral propensities.

Xaxis, a WPP agency, partnered with Triton Digital to create Xaxis Radio, enabling advertisers to incorporate online and mobile radio buys within their overall digital media campaigns. Triton's a2x technology provides Xaxis clients with access to the global inventory of over 44 million monthly unique listeners.

Objective
A top Financial Services Advertiser was looking to raise general awareness for a new Consumer Credit Card launch as well as drive deeper engagement beyond the landing page. This provided an ideal opportunity to activate the new channel, Xaxis Radio.

Target
Owners of competitive credit cards and new card prospects.

Execution
Baseline Media

- 2 Awareness Ad Networks
- 2 Premium Homepage Takeovers

Xaxis Brand Suite

- Xaxis Premium
- Xaxis Radio

Results
Users who were exposed to Xaxis Radio, interacted with the Advertiser's site at a significantly higher rate. Xaxis Radio users navigated to the Advertiser's site due to strong ad recall and quality targeting.

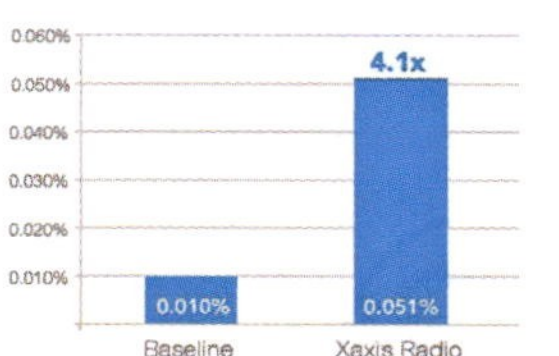

↑ 4.1x lift

Conclusion
Digital Radio has proven to be a legitimate addition to an awareness media plan and positively contributed to generating both awareness and engagement.

www.audioadexchange.com | a2x@tritondigital.com
UNITED STATES | CANADA | EUROPE | LATIN AMERICA | ASIA | MIDDLE EAST
A2X and TRITON DIGITAL are trademarks of Ando Media, LLC © 2013 Ando Media, LLC

FIGURE 2.12
The a2x software system is used by managers to increase profits. A top financial services advertiser saw a 4.1x lift in engagement and brand awareness by running highly targeted online audio ads on Xaxis Radio, powered by Triton Digital's programmatic audio ad exchange, a2x. Courtesy of Xaxis and a2x.

WHAT MAKES A SUCCESSFUL RADIO MANAGER?

Paul Fiddick

There are, in my experience, four indicators that correlate to high performance in radio managers.

In no particular order, one of these is a bias for action, what some industrial psychologists describe as task orientation. Entrepreneurism is closely related to this, as is the quality of decisiveness. The radio manager must be innately tuned to the necessity of taking the initiative if opportunities are to be exploited or—at a minimum—order is to be maintained.

Permit me one quick anecdote. On my first day in my first corporate-level job, the president of the company gave me this one piece of (unsolicited) advice: "Never be afraid to make a decision for fear of making a mistake. In worst case, you're wrong and you make another decision to fix things. But that's still better than being passive and letting the 'game play you.'"

FIGURE 2.13
Paul Fiddick. Courtesy of Paul Fiddick.

A second factor is intelligence. There is no substitute for being intellectually smart. A radio station manager is called upon to know many things about many subjects, and be many things to many people. This requires an agile mind. Generally speaking, smart people are better able to recognize and adapt to these demands.

Third, the increased complexity of and rate of change in the business climate—and our own reduced staffing and resources—require a manager to be more holistic than ever before. In other words, s/he needs to be fluent not just in all the disciplines (programming, marketing, sales, technology) inherent to radio, but knowledgeable about the larger business environment, as well. The successful manager is a lifelong learner—well-read and well-rounded.

That said, I've come to believe that our industry overvalues radio-specific product knowledge, the arcana that are unique to our business. Collectively, we have made many regrettable hiring mistakes because we were impressed by someone who speaks our tribal language, but otherwise lacked the necessary skills for the job.

The last quality is hardest to describe. I say it this way: successful managers take things personally. This may seem counterintuitive. Shouldn't managers retain a kind of cool objectivity towards their work?

What I've found is that the job is too demanding for that kind of detachment—at least at the highest levels. To overcome the frustrations that arise from so many aspects of your performance being outside of one's direct control, the successful manager is often a driven personality. I do not believe it coincidental that success and obsessiveness frequently go hand in hand!

Paul Fiddick has served as chief executive of four national media companies and also as a Senate-confirmed official in the U.S. government. Throughout his career, he has negotiated the acquisition (and occasional divestiture) of scores of businesses, and built every business he managed to record levels of profitability. Paul Fiddick is currently director and the immediate past president of Emmis International, a multinational broadcasting company. During his tenure, he expanded the company's footprint into three new countries and increased its operating income exponentially. Previously, he served as assistant secretary of the U.S. Department of Agriculture, and during the Clinton–Bush interregnum, as acting agriculture secretary. Pending his confirmation to government service, Paul Fiddick was executive vice-chairman and acting president of RadioWave.com, an affiliate of Motorola. He was also a co-founder of Heritage Media Corporation and president of its radio division from 1986 through its sale to News Corporation in 1998. He was recruited to Heritage from Multimedia Broadcasting, where he was president of the radio division from 1982. Paul Fiddick has served on many boards in both the commercial and not-for-profit sectors, and has taught at university level. He is an honors graduate of the University of Missouri School of Journalism.

THE MANAGER AND THE COMMUNITY

In the early 1980s, the FCC reduced the extent to which radio stations must become involved in community affairs. This deregulation process continued into the 1990s with the creation of the sweeping Telecommunications Act of 1996. Ascertainment procedures requiring that stations determine and address community issues have all but been eliminated. If a station chooses to do so, it may play musical hits 24 hours a day and virtually divorce itself from the concerns of the community. However, a station that opts to function independently of the community to which it is licensed may find itself on the outside looking in. Radio is, at its core, a local medium that relies on local audience ratings, so ignoring the needs of the public is seldom a good idea. This is especially true of small-market stations, which, for practical business reasons, have traditionally cultivated a strong connection with the community. Therefore, most stations do make an attempt to ascertain community issues and do so on a quarterly basis, maintaining the results of these surveys (often a list of the top ten issues confronting the community of license) in their Public Inspection File to attest to their good citizenship and to confirm that they are serving the public interests of the communities they are licensed to serve. This looks particularly positive at license renewal time.

A station manager is aware that it is important to the welfare of his or her organization to behave as a good citizen and neighbor. Although the sheer number of stations in vast metropolitan areas makes it less crucial that a station exhibit civic-mindedness, the small-market radio outlet often finds that the level of business it generates is relative to its community involvement. Therefore, maintaining a relationship with the town leaders, civic groups, and religious leaders, among others, enhances a station's visibility and status and ultimately affects business. No small-market station can hope to operate autonomously and attract the majority of local advertisers. Stations that remain aloof in the community in which they broadcast seldom realize their full revenue potential.

One of the nation's foremost figures in broadcast management, the late Ward Quaal, president of the Ward L. Quaal Company, observed:

> A manager must not only be tied, or perhaps I should say "married" to a station, but he or she must have total involvement in the community. This is very meaningful, whether the market is Cheyenne, Cincinnati, or Chicago. The community participation builds the proper image for the station and the manager and concurrently aids, dramatically, business development and produces lasting sales strength.

Cognizant of the importance of fostering an image of goodwill and civic-mindedness, the station manager seeks to become a member in good standing in the community. Radio managers often actively participate in groups or associations, such as the local Chamber of Commerce, Jaycees, Kiwanis, Rotary Club, Optimists, and others, and encourage members of their staff to become similarly involved. The station also strives to heighten its status in the community by devoting airtime to issues and events of local importance and by making its microphones available to citizens for discussions of matters pertinent to the area. In so doing, the station becomes regarded as an integral part of the community, and its value grows proportionately.

Surveys have shown that more than one-third of the managers of small-market radio stations are native to the area their signal serves. This gives them a vested interest in the quality of life in their community and motivates them to use the power of their medium to further improve living conditions.

Medium- and large-market station managers realize, as well, the benefits derived from participating in community activities. "If you don't localize and take part in the affairs of the city or town from which you draw your income, you're operating at a disadvantage. You have to tune in your audience if you expect them to do likewise," says Bremkamp.

FCC judge moves to pull radio licenses

By Chris McConnell

An FCC administrative law judge has decided to revoke the license

FIGURE 2.14
Job one: "Protect the license." Courtesy of *Broadcasting and Cable*.

The manager has to work to bring the station and the community together. Neglecting this responsibility lessens the station's chance for prosperity, or even survival. Station consolidation has influenced localism across the country, but most managers continue to recognize that community involvement is a key to their success.

THE MANAGER AND THE GOVERNMENT

Earlier in this chapter, station manager Richard Bremkamp cited protecting the license as one of the primary functions of the general manager. By "protecting" the license he meant conforming to the rules and regulations established by the Federal Communications Commission (FCC) for the operation of broadcast facilities. Since failure to fulfill the obligations of a license may result in punitive actions such as reprimands, fines, and even the revocation of the privilege to broadcast, managers have to be aware of the laws affecting station operations and see to it that they are observed by all concerned.

The FCC lists its fines in *47 CFR 1.80* and here are some examples of the base forfeiture amounts that can be decreased and/or increased at the commission's discretion per incident:

- Construction or operation without authorization: $10,000.
- Broadcasting telephone conversations without authorization: $4,000.

- Unauthorized substantial transfer of control: $8,000.
- Violation of transmitter control and metering requirements: $3,000.
- Violation of broadcast hoax rule: $7,000.
- Failure to permit FCC inspections: $7,000.
- Failure to respond to FCC communications: $4,000.
- Exceeding power limits: $4,000.
- EAS equipment broken or not installed: $8,000.
- Broadcasting indecent/obscene material: $7,000.
- Violation of EEO or political broadcast rules: $9,000.
- Violation of main studio rule: $7,000.
- Public file violations: $10,000.
- Failure to provide station ID: $1,000.
- Sponsor ID or lottery violations: $4,000.

Other examples of FCC fines were included in a 2013 newsletter from lawyer David Oxenford, of Washington, D.C. titled *The Cost of Little Things: FCC Fines for Regulatory Noncompliance*, it listed the following punitive amounts for rules violations:

- Quarterly issues programs lists: $9,000–10,000.
- Tower fencing: $4,000.
- Equal employment opportunity issues: $20,000.

In 2009, Clear Channel Communication's morning radio show *Bubba the Love Sponge* was levied the largest ever fine of $715,000 for sexually explicit content that aired during the morning hours of 6:30–9:00 am on radio stations in Florida. CBS News reported: "One segment featured the cartoon characters Alvin the chipmunk, George Jetson and Scooby-Doo discussing sexual activities."

The manager delegates responsibilities to department heads who are directly involved in the areas affected by the commission's regulations. For example, the program director will attend to the legal station identification (call letters and city of license), station logs, program content, and a myriad of other concerns of interest to the government. Meanwhile, the chief engineer is responsible for meeting technical standards, and the sales manager is held accountable for the observance of certain business and financial practices. Other members of the station also are assigned various responsibilities applicable to the license. Of course, in the end, it is the manager who must guarantee that the station's license to broadcast is, indeed, protected.

All rules and regulations pertaining to radio broadcast operations are contained in Title 47, Part 73, of the *Code of Federal Regulations* (CFR). The station manager keeps the annual update of this publication accessible to all employees involved

Payment Type Codes and Payment Amounts For FY 2012 Radio Station Regulatory Fees						
Population Served	AM Class A	AM Class B	AM Class C	AM Class D	FM Classes A, B1 & C3	FM Classes B, C, C0, C1 & C2
<=25,000	1217 $725	1223 $600	1229 $550	1235 $625	1241 $700	1247 $875
25,001 - 75,000	1218 $1,475	1224 $1,225	1230 $850	1236 $950	1242 $1,425	1248 $1,550
75,001 - 150,000	1219 $2,200	1225 $1,525	1231 $1,125	1237 $1,600	1243 $1,950	1249 $2,875
150,001 - 500,000	1220 $3,300	1226 $2,600	1232 $1,675	1238 $1,900	1244 $3,025	1250 $3,750
500,001 - 1,200,000	1221 $4,775	1227 $3,975	1233 $2,800	1239 $3,175	1245 $4,800	1251 $5,525
1,200,001 - 3,000,000	1222 $7,350	1228 $6,100	1234 $4,200	1240 $5,075	1246 $7,800	1252 $8,850
>3,000,000	1279 $8,825	1280 $7,325	1281 $5,325	1282 $6,350	1283 $9,950	1284 $11,500

FIGURE 2.15
FCC's AM/FM regulatory fees document. Note that the larger a licensee's market, the higher the fee. Retrieved from www.fcc.gov.

in maintaining the license. A copy of the CFR may be obtained through the Superintendent of Documents, Government Printing Office, Washington, D.C. 20402, for a modest fee or can be accessed for free from the FCC website at http://transition.fcc.gov/mb/audio/bickel/amfmrule.html. Specific inquiries concerning the publication can be addressed to the Director, Office of the Federal Register, National Archives and Records Service, General Services Administration, Washington, D.C. 20408.

To reiterate, although the station manager shares the duties involved in complying with the FCC's regulations with other staff members, he or she holds primary responsibility for keeping the station in compliance with FCC regulations and on the air.

Many of the rules and regulations pertaining to the daily operation of a radio station have been revised or rescinded. Since the CFR is published annually, certain parts may become obsolete during that period. Martha L. Girard, director of the office of the *Federal Register*, suggests that the *Federal Register*, from which the CFR derives its information, be consulted monthly. Subscriptions to the *Federal Register* are available; the publication also may be available at the local library.

Because the FCC may, without warning at any time during normal business hours, inspect a radio station to see that it is in accordance with the rules and regulations, a manager must make certain that everything is always in order. An FCC inspection checklist is contained in the CFR, and industry organizations, such as the NAB, provide member stations with similar checklists. Occasionally, managers run mock inspections in preparation for the real thing. Some stations are proactive when it comes to FCC matters and participate in the Alternate Broadcast Inspection Program (ABIP). The ABIP is a collaboration between the FCC and state broadcast associations in which the station goes through a mock inspection modeled after the one conducted by FCC field inspectors. If deficiencies are found, the station has a specific timeframe to correct the problems. Upon correction, or if no deficiencies are found, the station is issued a Certificate of Compliance and the station is exempt from random FCC inspections for three years. Essentially, the ABIP acts as an insurance policy for the station to protect itself from possible FCC compliance deficiencies. A state of preparedness prevents embarrassment and problems.

Christine H. Merritt, president of the Ohio Association of Broadcasters, explains how the ABIP works:

> The Alternative Broadcast Inspection Program (ABIP), established in cooperation with the Federal Communications Commission (FCC), helps radio and television stations ensure compliance with FCC regulations. Typically offered through state broadcasters' associations, the program provides stations with an inspection based upon the FCC Broadcast Station Self-Inspection Checklist. Inspections are conducted by a technical inspector approved by the FCC to conduct ABIP inspections. Stations certified to be in compliance with the FCC's technical rules are exempt from routine inspections by the FCC Field Office for three years.

THE MANAGER AND UNIONS

The unions most active in radio are the Screen Actors Guild-American Federation of Television and Radio Artists (SAG-AFTRA), the National Association of Broadcast Employees and Technicians-Communications Workers of America (NABET-CWA), and the International Brotherhood of Electrical Workers (IBEW). Major-market radio stations are the ones most likely to be unionized. The overwhelming majority of American stations are non-union and, in fact, union membership has declined in recent years.

Dissatisfaction with wages and benefits, coupled with a desire for greater security, are often motivators that prompt station employees to vote for a union. Managers seldom encourage the presence of a union since many believe that unions impede and constrict their ability to control the destiny of their operations. However, a small percentage of managers believe that the existence of a union may actually stabilize the working environment and reduce personnel turnover.

It is the function of the union to act as a bargaining agent working in good faith with station employees and management to upgrade and improve working conditions. Union efforts usually focus on salary, sick leave, vacation, promotion, hiring, termination, working hours, and retirement benefits. In 2013, SAG-AFTRA negotiated a deal on behalf of its members that was expected to generate $238 million in new salary increases for radio voiceover talent, health benefits, and retirement pensions.

A unionized station appoints or elects a shop steward who works as a liaison between the union, which represents the employees, and the station's management. Employees may lodge complaints or grievances with the shop steward, who will then review the union's contract with the station and proceed accordingly. Station managers are obliged to work within the agreement that they, along with the union, helped formulate.

As stated, unions are a fact of life in many major markets. They are far less prevalent elsewhere, although unions do exist in some medium and even small markets. Most small operations would find it impractical, if not untenable, to function under a union contract. Union demands and work rules would quite likely cripple most marginal or small-profit operations.

Managers who extend employees every possible courtesy and operate in a fair and reasonable manner are rarely affected by unions, whose prime objective is to protect and ensure the rights of station workers.

THE MANAGER AND INDUSTRY ASSOCIATIONS

Every year, the National Association of Broadcasters (NAB) and a variety of specialized and regional organizations conduct conferences and seminars intended to generate industry awareness and unity. At these gatherings, held at various locations throughout the country, radio managers and station personnel exchange ideas and share experiences, which they bring back to their stations.

The largest broadcast industry trade organization is the NAB, which was originally conceived out of a need to improve operating conditions in the 1920s. Initially only a lobbying organization, the NAB has maintained that focus while expanding considerably in scope. The primary objective of the organization is to support and promote the stability and development of the industry.

In the mid-1990s, however, the National Radio Broadcasters' Association, which merged with the NAB in the 1980s, threatened to break from the organization for its alleged overemphasis on non-radio matters.

FIGURE 2.16
NAB's Gordon Smith heads the nation's foremost commercial broadcasters' association.

Thousands of radio stations also are members of the Radio Advertising Bureau (RAB), which was founded in 1951, a time when radio's fate was in serious jeopardy owing to the rise in television's popularity. "The RAB is designed to serve as the sales and marketing arm of America's commercial radio industry. Members include radio stations, broadcast groups, networks, station representatives, and associated industry organizations in every market in all 50 states," explains Kenneth J. Costa, former RAB vice-president for marketing and the author of *History of the RAB*. In 2013, Erica Farber, former publisher and CEO of *Radio and Records*, was appointed president and CEO of the RAB.

FARBER'S RULES

Erica Farber

FIGURE 2.17
Erica Farber. Courtesy of Erica Farber.

1. The best person *does* get the job. *Be the best person!*
2. Do your homework. Learn about the company and make sure you like it and you fit in.
3. There are good bosses and bad bosses—look for best practices.
4. Do not complain. Ask for constructive feedback.
5. Offices have all kinds, from troublemakers to backstabbers.
6. SHOW UP! Be consistent! Be on time!
7. Have a sense of humor.
8. Treat people the way you want to be treated.
9. Ask for what you want, but remember: It requires you to *know* what you want.
10. Men and women are different: women re-visit decisions; men decide and move on.
11. Work hard—you are a role model.
12. Don't pretend—not knowing is *not* a weakness.
13. Make mistakes—decisions and growth depend on them.
14. Friends vs. co-workers: Socialize with friends; work toward respect with co-workers.
15. Balance sheets are the lifeblood of business. Learn to read profit and loss statements. Learn to understand budgets.
16. Continue to learn.
17. Have a plan. Set goals and update them. Careers need planning; jobs don't.
18. Learn the difference between public and private: information shared online never goes away.
19. Learn good phone etiquette. Phones are phones—leave messages. Check your own phone regularly.

20. Develop outside interests. You need to maintain YOU. Put things into your life to be whole.
21. TRUST and be trustworthy.
22. Get involved. Make a difference. Expose your life to others.
23. Learn to handle stress: it will always be in your life.
24. Be true to yourself.
25. Never compromise your belief system.

Compiled and edited by Dr. William Dorman, Millersville University

Dozens of other broadcast trade organizations focus their attention on specific areas within the radio station, and regional and local broadcast organizations are numerous. The following list is a partial rundown of national organizations that support the efforts of radio broadcasters.

- National Association of Broadcasters, 1771 N Street, N.W., Washington, D.C. 20036
- Radio Advertising Bureau, 125 West 55th Street, 5th Fl., New York, NY 10019
- National Association of Farm Broadcasters, 1100 Platte Falls Rd., PO Box 500, Platte City, MO 64079
- American Women in Radio and Television, 8405 Greensboro Drive, Suite 800, McLean, VA 22102
- Broadcast Education Association, 1771 N Street, N.W., Washington, D.C. 20036
- Broadcast Pioneers, 320 W. 57th Street, New York, NY 10019
- Clear Channel Broadcasting Service, 1776 K Street, N.W., Washington, D.C. 20006
- Library of American Broadcasting, PO Box 2749, Alexandria, VA 22301
- Native American Public Telecommunications, Box 83111, Lincoln, NE 68501
- National Association of Black Owned Broadcasters, 1201 Connecticut Avenue, N.W., Suite 200, Washington, D.C. 20036
- National Religious Broadcasters, 9510 Technology Drive, Manassas, VA 20110
- Radio Network Association, 1700 Broadway, 3rd Floor, New York, NY 10019
- Radio Television Digital News Association, The National Press Building, 529 14th Street, NW, Suite 425, Washington, D.C. 20045
- Society of Broadcast Engineers, 9102 North Meridian Street, Suite 150, Indianapolis, IN 46260.

NAB membership dues are based on a voluntary declaration of a station's annual gross revenues. The RAB and others take a similar approach. Some organizations require individual membership fees, which often are absorbed by the radio station as well.

CHAPTER HIGHLIGHTS

1. Radio managers constantly face challenges due to new audio competition and station consolidation. In addition, radio's unique character requires that station managers deal with a wide variety of talents and personalities.
2. The authoritarian (X) approach to management implies that the general manager makes all of the policy decisions. The collaborative (Y) approach allows the general manager to involve other station staff in the formation of policy. The hybrid or chief-collaborator (Z) approach combines elements of both the authoritarian and collaborative management models. The chief-collaborator management approach is most prevalent in radio today.
3. To attain management status, an individual needs both a formal education and practical experience in many areas of station operation—especially sales.
4. Key managerial functions include operating in a manner that produces the greatest profit, meeting corporate expectations, formulating station policy and seeing to its implementation, hiring and retaining good people, inspiring staff to do their best, training new employees, maintaining communication with all departments to ensure an excellent air product, and keeping an eye toward the future, especially in terms of how new technological applications—such as websites and HD—can enhance profitability.
5. Station clustering and consolidation have changed the personnel landscape at stations as radio groups often concentrate the operation of several stations in one central location. Some of the positions in a station cluster include a market manager, director of sales, general sales manager, director of operations, and controller.
6. In non-cluster station environments, the operations manager is second only to the general manager at those outlets that have established this position. This individual supervises administrative staff, helps develop and implement station policy, handles departmental budgeting, functions as regulatory watchdog, and works as liaison with the community.
7. Managers hire individuals who possess a formal education, strong professional experience, ambition, a positive attitude, reliability, humility, honesty, self-respect, patience, enthusiasm, discipline, creativity, logic, and compassion.
8. Says consultant Ed Shane, "The new radio paradigm is 'manager as financial expert.'"
9. Radio provides entertainment to the public and, in turn, sells the audience it attracts to advertisers. It is the station manager who must ensure a profit, but he or she must also maintain product integrity.
10. To foster a positive community image, the station manager becomes actively involved in the community and devotes airtime to community concerns—even though the FCC has reduced a station's obligation to do so via ascertainment.

11. Although the station manager delegates responsibility for compliance with FCC regulations to appropriate department heads, the manager is ultimately responsible for protecting the license. Title 47, Part 73, of the *Code of Federal Regulations* contains the rules pertaining to radio broadcast operations. Updates of regulations are listed monthly in the *Federal Register*. It can also be found online at the FCC's website at http://transition.fcc.gov/mb/audio/bickel/amfmrule.html.
12. The Screen Actors Guild-American Federation of Television and Radio Artists (SAG-AFTRA), the National Association of Broadcast Employees and Technicians-Communications Workers of America (NABET-CWA), and the International Brotherhood of Electrical Workers (IBEW) are the unions most active in radio.
13. The National Association of Broadcasters (NAB) and the Radio Advertising Bureau (RAB) are among the largest radio trade industry organizations.
14. A person must be a U.S. citizen to hold a broadcast license. The FCC investigates all would-be station owners. To put a new station on the air, a construction permit (CP) application must be submitted to the FCC.
15. Call letters and frequencies are assigned by the FCC.

SUGGESTED FURTHER READING

Agor, W.H., *Intuitive Management*, Prentice Hall, Englewood Cliffs, NJ, 1984.

Albarran, A., *Management of Electronic Media*, 5th edition, Wadsworth, Los Angeles, CA, 2013.

Appleby, R.C., *The Essential Guide to Management*, Prentice Hall, Englewood Cliffs, NJ, 1981.

Aronoff, C.E. (ed.), *Business and the Media*, Goodyear Publishing Company, Santa Monica, CA, 1979.

Boyatzis, R.E., *The Competent Manager*, John Wiley and Sons, New York, 1983.

Brown, A., *Supermanaging*, McGraw-Hill, New York, 1984.

Coleman, H.W., *Case Studies in Broadcast Management*, Hastings House, New York, 1978.

Cottrell, D., *Monday Morning Leadership*, Cornerstone Leadership, New York, 2002.

Creech, K.C., *Electronic Media Law and Regulation*, 5th edition, Focal Press, Boston, MA, 2007.

Czech-Beckerman, E.S., *Managing Electronic Media*, Focal Press, Boston, MA, 1991.

Elimore, R.T., *Broadcasting Law and Regulation*, Tab Books, Blue Ridge Summit, PA, 1982.

Goodworth, C.T., *How to Be a Super-Effective Manager: A Guide to People Management*, Business Books, London, 1984.

Kahn, F.J. (ed.), *Documents of American Broadcasting*, 4th edition, Prentice Hall, Englewood Cliffs, NJ, 1984.

Kobert, N., *The Aggressive Management Style*, Prentice Hall, Englewood Cliffs, NJ, 1981.

Krasnow, E.G. and Werner, E.T., *Radio Deals: A Step by Step Guide*, RBR Publications, Springfield, VA, 2002.

Lacy, S., et al., *Media Management: A Casebook Approach*, Lawrence Erlbaum Associates, Hillsdale, NJ, 1993.

McCluskey, J., *Successful Broadcast Station Management and Ownership*, Pearson Custom Publishing, Boston, MA, 1999.

McCormack, M.H., *What They Don't Teach You at Harvard Business School*, Bantam, New York, 1984.

Miner, J.B., *The Management Process: Theory, Research, and Practice*, Macmillan, New York, 1978.

Mogel, L., *The Business of Broadcasting*, Billboard Books, LA, 2004.

National Association of Broadcasters, *Political Broadcast Catechism*, 16th edition, NAB, Washington, D.C., 2007.

Pember, D.R., *Mass Media in America*, 6th edition, Macmillan, New York, 1991.

Pringle, P.K., Starr, M.F. and McCavitt, W.E., *Electronic Media Management*, 5th edition, Focal Press, Boston, MA, 2005.

Quaal, W.L. and Brown, J.A., *Broadcast Management*, 2nd edition, Hastings House, New York, 1976.

Rhoads, B.E., et al. (eds), *Management and Sales Management*, Streamline Press, West Palm Beach, FL, 1995.

Routt, E., *The Business of Radio Broadcasting*, Tab Books, Blue Ridge Summit, PA, 1972.

Schneider, C., *Starting Your Career in Broadcasting*, Allworth Press, New York, 2007.

Schwartz, T., *Media, the Second God*, Praeger, New York, 1984.

Shane, E., *Cutting Through: Strategies and Tactics for Radio*, Shane Media, Houston, TX, 1990.

Shane, E., *Selling Electronic Media*, Focal Press, Boston, MA, 1999.

Townsend, R., *Further up the Organization*, Alfred A. Knopf, New York, 1984.

Wicks, J.L., et al., *Media Management: A Casebook Approach*, LEA, Mahwah, NJ, 2003.

CHAPTER 3
Programming

PROGRAM FORMATS

"The devil is in the details," wrote famed French author Gustave Flaubert, and for our purposes in this chapter, we could say that the devil is in the *programming*. Indeed, designing a radio station's sound continues to be a bedeviling task, even as large radio companies cluster their outlets in the age of station ownership consolidation. More than 15,000 AM and FM stations compete for audience attention today and additional broadcasters continue to enter the fray. Other media have proliferated as well, resulting in a further distraction and dilution of radio's customary audience. The government's *laissez-faire*, "let the marketplace dictate" philosophy, concerning commercial radio programming, gives the station great freedom in deciding the nature of its air product, but determining what to offer the listener, who is often presented with dozens of audio alternatives, involves intricate planning. In the end, proffers Merlin Media LLC CEO Randy Michaels, "Programming is the key. Yes, I can hear my favorite songs on an iPod, but 'sometimes you like to drive, sometimes you like to ride.' A good programmer can create an experience that 'shuffle' cannot. The iPod won't bring play by play sports, breaking news, or introduce me to something new. It won't put events in context."

The bottom line, of course, is to air the type of format that will attract a sizable enough piece of the audience demographic to satisfy the advertiser. Once a station decides on the format it will program, then it must know how to effectively execute it. Ultimately, says Emmis programmer Jimmy Steal about the nature of music-based formats,

> Great programming remains a constant regardless of amount/source of competition and the type of ratings methodology. The core of successful programming has always been unique content, passionate/knowledgeable/distinctive/engaging personalities, a consistent source of new music (format-applicable, of course), and an overall presentation that eschews a sense of fun, a sense of energy, a sense of drama (positive drama—maybe suspense is a better word here), and an

> overall friend to, or oasis from, the daily challenges in the lives of our listening constituencies.

That said, programming in today's daunting marketplace is no easy task, observes consultant Ed Shane:

> The staff reductions in post-consolidation radio cause national chains to fill the time with something—often syndication or repurposed content from another market. Ryan Seacrest is a perfect example. Seacrest does his morning show at KIIS-FM (KISS) in Los Angeles, then portions of the program are edited and repackaged for other stations, mostly in the Clear Channel family (CC owns KIIS), although the show is available to stations owned by companies other than Clear Channel. That reduces local radio to "repeater," not machine originator.

Shane's oft-observed sentiment regarding the lack of localism underscores the fact that the distinction between AM and FM (terrestrial) broadcasting and its satellite and online counterparts is progressively blurring. A series of annual studies conducted by Edison Research and Arbitron focusing on radio's "Infinite Dial" attest to the melding of traditional radio with new forms of audio media. AM and FM stations, the most recent study says, remain in the best position of all forms of audio media to connect with listeners in local communities. Pandora, the much-talked-about online radio service, fares well with mobile listeners but, despite the inroads it has made in selling advertising in individual markets, still fails to achieve local granularity in terms of information and entertainment—the content that attracts an audience. If "location, location, and location" are the three keys to selling real estate then "local, local, and local" emerge as the guiding principles for creating compelling radio programming.

Brief descriptions of some of the most frequently employed formats in radio today follow. There are, however, more than 60 formats recognized by the audience research firm Arbitron (known today as Nielsen Audio; refer to details of this change in Chapter 1) and listed on its website. The reader should keep in mind that formats morph and evolve as new trends in lifestyle and culture emerge. Changes in audience measurement methodologies also can influence programming decisions. *Inside Radio*, an industry newsletter, reported in 2013 that format changes in markets measured by Arbitron's Portable People Meter (PPM) system are on the rise. Chapter 6 details PPM history and explains how Arbitron is transitioning from a diary-based, listener-recall method to an electronic, listener-exposure system for data gathering. Radio formats are anything but static, and the impetus for change is driven by various and largely economic factors.

Adult Contemporary

In terms of the number of listeners, Adult Contemporary (AC; also referred to as The Mix, Hot AC, Triple A, Urban AC, Soft AC, Spectrum AC, and Lite AC) continues its four-decade popularity trend. The AC format and its variants, according to Arbitron, was heard in 2010 by more than 76 million Americans on almost 850 stations, making it radio's most-listened to format. A notable characteristic of the format is its widespread appeal to women. AC, according to Arbitron, attracts radio's most evenly distributed audience of listeners aged 12 to 64. This format is ethnically diverse, and while its concentration is females aged 45 to 54, recent data suggest that AC popularity is improving with teens and young adults. Almost one-third of listeners are college educated. Says consultant Ed Shane, "Because the AC target audience is so diverse, the format has been most prone to fragmentation and competition."

Because AC is very strong among the broader 25–49 age group it is particularly appealing to advertisers due to this demographic group's significant disposable income. Also, some advertisers spend money on AC stations simply because they like the format themselves. In sum, the AC format is one of the most effective in attracting female listeners.

AC outlets emphasize current and not-so-current (all the way back to the 1970s at some AC stations) pop standards, sans raucous, or harsh beats—in other

FIGURE 3.1
Courtesy of Arbitron.

National Radio Format Shares and Station Counts

Fall 2012

Format	12+ Share	Total Stations	Primary			HD Radio					Streaming				
			FM	AM	Total	HF	HA	F2	F3	F4	IF	IA	G2	G3	G4
Country + New Country	14.2	2893	1426	301	1727	144	0	37	3	1	854	113	12	2	0
News/Talk/Info + Talk/Personality	11.4	3984	616	1337	1953	240	97	111	64	6	515	867	78	47	6
Pop Contemporary Hit Radio	8.2	1012	462	3	465	116	0	33	3	1	375	2	15	2	0
Adult Contemporary + Soft AC	8.1	1390	685	107	792	108	0	16	2	0	420	44	7	1	0
Classic Hits	5.2	883	422	88	510	51	2	17	1	0	250	45	6	1	0
Classic Rock	5.2	944	490	14	504	76	0	39	1	0	308	4	12	0	0
Hot Adult Contemporary	4.7	810	447	9	456	71	0	7	0	0	274	1	1	0	0
Urban Adult Contemporary	4.1	336	130	33	163	43	2	9	1	0	99	15	4	0	0
Rhythmic CHR	3.4	370	145	0	145	48	0	35	0	0	124	0	18	0	0
All Sports	3.1	1274	133	556	689	29	40	36	27	3	98	321	18	12	1
Urban Contemporary	3.0	274	121	16	137	28	0	13	0	0	80	9	7	0	0
Contemporary Christian	2.9	1691	871	32	903	18	0	27	8	0	690	16	23	6	0
Mexican Regional	2.9	550	204	132	336	24	2	7	0	0	121	55	5	0	0
Adult Hits + '80s Hits	2.2	395	180	15	195	34	1	22	4	0	124	4	9	2	0
Active Rock	2.1	356	164	2	166	32	0	20	0	0	129	2	7	0	0
AOR+Mainstream Rock	2.0	336	170	2	172	25	0	13	2	0	119	2	2	1	0
Alternative	1.9	614	266	6	272	33	1	55	10	0	199	6	30	8	0
Oldies	1.8	831	252	286	538	11	3	32	4	0	109	116	16	2	0
Spanish Cont. + Spanish Hot AC	1.5	224	75	35	110	20	2	10	3	0	52	21	3	3	0
All News	1.4	93	13	24	37	6	7	2	5	0	12	20	1	3	0
Classical	1.4	823	254	4	258	131	0	101	9	0	225	3	88	8	0
Religious	1.3	1739	828	384	1212	8	14	8	3	1	298	188	5	2	0
Album Adult Alternative	1.1	508	179	4	183	44	0	55	15	0	156	3	40	12	0
Variety	1.0	1579	746	105	851	111	4	23	12	0	502	54	18	4	0
Classic Country	0.9	472	106	201	307	6	2	25	2	0	44	77	8	1	0
Spanish Adult Hits	0.8	104	35	9	44	14	2	5	0	0	30	6	3	0	0
Gospel	0.7	454	80	219	299	3	7	10	0	0	32	96	7	0	0
Contemporary Inspirational	0.6	224	111	18	129	8	2	5	2	1	65	7	4	1	0
Adult Standards/MOR	0.5	289	36	172	208	0	6	4	1	0	13	55	2	0	0

Legend

FM	FM Station
AM	AM Station
HF	Digital (HD Radio) FM Station
HA	Digital (HD Radio) AM Station
F2	HD Radio Multicast Station
F3	HD Radio Multicast Station
F4	HD Radio Multicast Station
IF	Internet Stream of FM station
IA	Internet Stream of AM station
G2	Internet Stream of HD Radio Multicast F2
G3	Internet Stream of HD Radio Multicast F3
G4	Internet Stream of HD Radio Multicast F4

Source: Arbitron Radio Station Information Database, June 2012. These station counts include rated, unrated, commercial, and noncommercial stations. The AM & FM columns only include FCC-licensed stations and do not include translators.

words, no hard rock. Some AC stations could be described as soft rockers. However, the majority mix in enough ballads and easy listening sounds to justify their title. The main thrust of this format's programming is the music. Programming consultant Alan Burns specializes in the study of the relationship between females and radio. One of the more telling pieces of information to appear in his annual study "Here She Comes—Insights Into Women, Radio, and New Media," underscores the importance of music to adult females. Data from the 2012 study reveal that, for two of every three listeners surveyed, music is the primary reason for tuning in. Despite the popularity and perceived importance of the morning show to a station's success, only one in four listeners cite it as the principal reason for listening, according to Burns' study. More music is aired by deemphasizing chatter. Music is commonly presented in uninterrupted sweeps or blocks, perhaps 10–12 minutes in duration, followed by a brief recap of artists and song titles. High-profile morning talent or teams became popular at AC stations in the 1980s and remain so today. Commercials generally are clustered at predetermined times, and midday and evening deejay talk often is limited to brief informational announcements. News and sports are secondary to the music. In recent years, ACs have spawned a host of format permutations, such as Adult Hits and Adult Standards, as well as the iPod wannabe formats, known as Jack and Mike, which typically distinguish themselves from their AC counterparts by featuring a broader playlist, sometimes venturing as far back as the 1960s for music selections. In the late 2000s, according to Arbitron, the AC subgenre showing the most growth was Urban AC.

Adult Hits

Programmers in the new millennium seized the opportunity to meld aspects of traditional classic hits, pop and alternative radio, widening the depth of the playlist in creating what is popularly known as the Adult Hits format. An esoteric format derivative, known variously as "Jack," "Bob," "Dave," and by other names, predominantly of the male gender, is one of the more successful programming approaches to emerge. "Jack" and its masculine siblings represent attempts at humanizing a radio station, imbuing it with personality in efforts to evoke listener affinity. Influenced by the iPod experience, with its ability to shuffle the playback of users' massive song collections in creating a randomized playback sequence, "Jack," "Bob," and "Dave" programmers thumbed their noses at radio's tightly controlled playlist approach. By tapping into the mindset of listeners who had grown tiresome of the predictability and repetition of the music presentation, "Jack" outlets have proven to be particularly successful in attracting the attention of males and females aged 35 to 44. A commonly heard positioning catchphrase, expressed in slightly different versions by stations in their on-air imaging (i.e., the airing of creative audio elements that establish and promote station personality) alludes to this approach. Buffalo's 92.9 "Jack FM," Sacramento's 93.7 "Jack fm" and 101.1 "Jack FM" in Peoria, among many, proclaim that music variety is achieved by "Playing what we want." In Nashville,

96.3 "Jack fm" asserts, "We play what we want." Despite variations in the phrasing, the approach remains the same.

FIGURE 3.2
In the mid-2000s, radio conceived a format emulating iPod diversity. Courtesy of Jack FM 105.9.

Contemporary Hit Radio

Once known as Top 40, Contemporary Hit Radio (CHR) stations play only those records that currently are the fastest selling. CHR's narrow playlists are designed to draw teens and young adults. The heart of this format's demographic is 12–18-year-olds, although in the mid-1980s it enjoyed a broadening of its core audience. Like AC, it too has experienced fluctuations in popularity. The decade of the 1990s was particularly harsh for CHR. In the *Journal of Radio Studies* (1995–1996), Ed Shane observed that the format "was a statistical loser in the 1990s. What futurist Alvin Toffler called 'the demassification of media' affected CHR the most. There were too many types of music to play. No one radio station could create a format with elements as diverse as rapper Ice T, rockers like Nirvana, country artists like George Strait and Randy Travis, or jazz musicians like Kenny G or David Benoit. Each of those performers fits someone's definition of 'contemporary hit radio.' CHR lost its focus." The outcome? A number of stations abandoned the format. At one point only a couple of hundred CHR stations remained. Veteran broadcaster Rick Alexander of Main Line Broadcasting recalls a scarcity of programmable songs from that decade (a situation which seems to have improved). As Alexander put it, "the lack of playable 90s gold" created "a musical 'Swiss cheese' hole between the staunchly popular 80s and 00s." Alexander speculates the problem might have been attributable to "bad music" or "bad programming." While the former is a highly subjective judgment, the latter, he says, can be quantified: "We're in a business that has, for much of the time, relied more on the artistic side and minimized the science part. However, in order to be a mass appeal medium, we need to objectively be able to quantify the appeal of our product. So maybe what was missing in the 90s wasn't hit music but a way to measure it." The 1990s was a particularly troublesome decade in this regard: the sale of tangible music products (45-rpm records, cassette and CD singles) had faded into memory and downloadable digital song files had yet to materialize. Sadly, he muses, "We entered a period of relying solely on our gut and believing our own trade press." In 2010–2012, the format enjoyed resurgence in popularity with the expansion of Arbitron's Portable People Meter (PPM) measurement. Shane added, "Young audiences are prone to enjoy the pop music of CHR and to feel comfortable with the technology of the People Meter. Since younger consumers often listen in groups, listening is more likely to be detected by PPM, which favors the CHR format."

Consultant Jeff Pollack believed that CHR had lost ground because it was not in tune with what he called the "streets," and he predicted that the format would embrace a more dance-rap sound as well as develop more appreciation for alternative rock hits. The format is characterized by its swift and often unrelenting pace. Silence, known as "dead air," is the enemy. The idea is to keep the sound hot and tight to keep the kids from station hopping, which is no small task since many markets have at least two hit-oriented stations.

In a *Radio Ink* interview, programmer Bill Richards predicted that the high-intensity jock approach would give way to a more laid-back, natural sound. "The days of the 'move over and let the big dog eat' sweepers (positioning statements) are over. Top 40 will look for more jocks who sound like real people and shy away from the hyped deejay approach." CHR deejays have undergone several shifts in status since the inception of the chart music format in the 1950s. Initially, pop deejay personalities played an integral role in the air sound. However, in the mid-1960s, the format underwent a major change when deejay presence was significantly reduced. Programming innovator Bill Drake decided that the Top 40 sound needed to be refurbished and tightened. Thus, deejay talk and even the number of commercials scheduled each hour were cut back to improve the flow of the music sequence. Despite criticism that the new sound was too mechanical, Drake's technique succeeded at strengthening the format's hold on the listening audience.

In the mid- and late 1970s, the deejay's role on hit stations began to regain its former prominence, but in the 1980s, the format underwent a further renovation (initiated by legendary consultant Mike Joseph) that resulted in a narrowing of its playlist and a decrease in deejay presence. Super or Hot Hit stations, synonymous terms for the format, were among the most popular in the country and could be found either near or at the top of the rating charts in their markets.

At the moment, at least, CHR has a bit less of a frenetic quality to it and perhaps a more mature sound. Undergoing an image adjustment, the format is keying in on improving overall flow while pulling back on jumping aboard the fad bandwagon. The continued preening of the playlist will keep the format viable, say the experts. Reinforcing the mature-sound observation and bolstering the format's popularity is its return to offering what analyst Sean Ross terms "adult-friendly" music. In the Top-40 1960s and 1970s many stations enlarged listenership by connecting not only to a primary audience of teens but a secondary audience of parents who tuned in out of curiosity over their children's musical tastes and of adults who used radio as a means of reclaiming and preserving the feelings of their youth.

News is of secondary importance on CHR stations. In fact, many program directors (PDs) consider news programming to be a tune-out factor. "Kids don't like news," they claim. However, despite deregulation, which has freed stations of non-entertainment program requirements, most retain at least a modicum of news out of a sense of obligation. CHR stations are very promotion-minded and contest-oriented.

CHR stations in recent years have experienced multiyear growth patterns in ratings and share-of-audience. As of this writing more than 1,200 stations

MIX 105.1 FM
Picking You Up And Making You Feel Good

PROGRAMMING PROFILES
Tuning around the Orlando Radio Dial

AM	540	580	740	990	1030	1140	1270	1440	1600
	WQTM	WDBO	WWNZ	WHOO	WONQ	WRMQ	WRLZ	WPRD	WOKB

FM	92.3	93.1	94.5	95.3	96.5	97.5	98.1	98.9	100.3	101.1	101.9	103.1	104.1	105.1	105.9	106.7	107.7
	WWKA	WKRO	WCFB	WTLN	WHTQ	WPCV	WGNE	WMMO	WSHE	WJRR	WJHM	WLOQ	WTKS	WOMX	WOCL	WXXL	WMG F

JAMMIN OLDIES
WOCL

OLDIES
WSHE

ROCK
WJRR

ADULT STANDARD
WHOO

COUNTRY
WWKA
WPCV
WGNE

NEWS/TALK
WWNZ
WTKS
WDBO

CHR
WXXL

ADULT CONTEMPORARY
WOMX

URBAN
WJHM
WCFB

JAZZ
WLOQ

SPANISH
WONQ
WRMQ
WRLZ
WOKB
WPRD

CHURBAN
WTLN

SPORTS
WQTM

CLASSIC ROCK
WHTQ

SOFT ROCK
WMMO

LITE ROCK
WMGF

ALTERNATIVE
WKRO

am·fm

FIGURE 3.3
Market format breakdown. Courtesy of Mix 105.1.

(nearly all FM) call themselves CHR. Many of these stations prefer to be called Pop CHR; approximately one-third embrace the Rhythmic CHR format descriptor (Churban fell out of favor in the late 1990s; it was an approach that combined CHR and Urban hits).

Country

Since the 1970s, the Country format has been adopted by more stations than any other. Although seldom a leader in the ratings race until recent years, its appeal is exceptionally broad. An indication of country music's rising popularity is the fact that there are over ten times as many full-time Country stations today than there were 25 years ago. The station count now totals approximately 2,000 Country, New Country and Classic Country AM and FM broadcasters. This format is far more prevalent in the South and Midwest, and it is not uncommon for stations in certain markets to enjoy double-digit ratings successes. Although most medium and large markets in the North have Country stations, Country in the top five major markets appears among the lists of the top ten-rated stations in just two cities, Chicago and Dallas/Ft. Worth. Due to the diversity of approaches within the format—for example, classic, Cajun, bluegrass, traditional, and so on—the Country format attracts a broad age group, appealing to young as well as older adults. Listening percentages peak with persons between 45 and 54 and the demographic skews slightly (52 to 48%) to females.

Two related and encouraging trends for proponents of the format involve younger listeners. Country's derivative "New Country" offspring format continues to pull in strong ratings numbers, helping to propel the genre to the second-highest rated format nationally for teens. No doubt in response to immensely popular younger artists such as Taylor Swift and The Band Perry, stations are capitalizing on the promotional opportunity, staging what former Country Radio Broadcasters president Paul Allen termed "'high school spirit'-type contests to target the next generation of listeners."

Country radio has always been particularly popular among blue-collar workers. According to the Country Music Association and the Organization of Country Radio Broadcasters, the Country music format is drawing a more upscale audience today than it did in the past. Arbitron estimates than one in every six listeners is university educated. As many FM as AM stations are programming the Country sound in the 2010s, which was not the case just a few years before. Until the 1980s, Country was predominantly an AM offering. Depending on the approach they employ, Country outlets may emphasize or deemphasize air personalities, include news and public affairs features, or confine their programming almost exclusively to music.

Some programming experts point to the mid-1990s as the greatest period for the Country format, but its long-term history reflects periods of growth and retrenchment dating to the 1950s. Arbitron's "Radio Today 2011" report labels Country "America's most popular radio format" that is "far away no. 1 with more than double the ratings of no. 2 News/Talk and more than triple that of its nearest music competitor."

Soft Adult/Easy Listening/Smooth Jazz

The Beautiful Music station of the 1960s and 1970s became the Easy Listening or Soft Adult station of the 2000s. Playlists in this format have been carefully updated in an attempt to attract a somewhat younger audience. The term "Beautiful Music" was exchanged for "Easy Listening" in an effort to dispel the geriatric image the former term seemed to convey. Easy Listening is the ultimate "wall-to-wall" music format. Talk of any type is kept minimal, although many stations in this format concentrate on news and information during morning drivetime.

Instrumentals and soft vocals of established songs are a mainstay at Soft Adult/ Easy Listening stations, which also share a penchant for lush orchestrations featuring plenty of strings. These stations boast a devoted audience.

Efforts to draw younger listeners into the Easy Listening fold have been moderately successful, but most of the format's primary adherents are over 50 years old. Music syndicators provide prepackaged (canned) programming to approximately half of the nation's Easy Listening/Soft Adult stations. Easy Listening lost some ground in the 1990s and 2000s to AC and other adult-appeal formats such as Album Adult Alternative and New Age, which some

Country + New Country

Index of AQH Listening by Daypart

100 = Persons 12+, Mon-Sun, 6AM-Mid

Mon-Fri 6AM-10AM	Mon-Fri 10AM-3PM	Mon-Fri 3PM-7PM	Mon-Fri 7PM-Mid	Sat-Sun 6AM-Mid
132	143	125	41	80

Country + New Country appears to be a strong at-work format; it indexed highest in middays, 43% above its average. Its index grew slightly during evenings and weekends.

Share of Listening by Location

AQH Persons 12+, Mon-Sun, 6AM-Mid

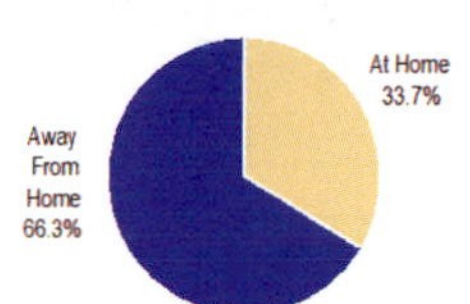

Two-thirds of consumer listening to Country + New Country took place away from home. That proportion has remained virtually unchanged for the past several years.

Audience Share by State

Persons 12+, Mon-Sun, 6AM-Mid, AQH Share

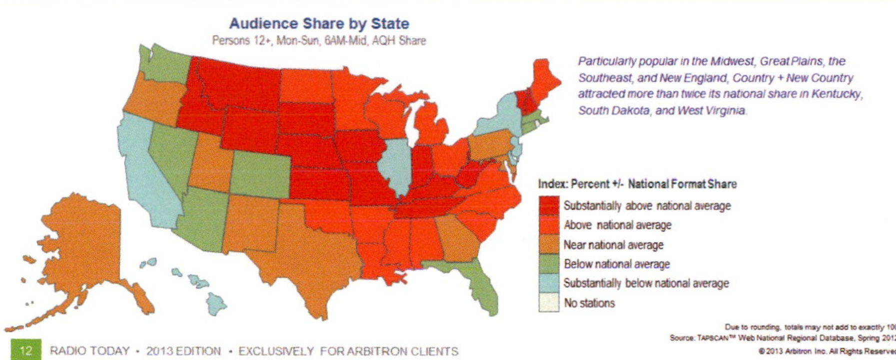

Particularly popular in the Midwest, Great Plains, the Southeast, and New England, Country + New Country attracted more than twice its national share in Kentucky, South Dakota, and West Virginia.

Index: Percent +/- National Format Share

- Substantially above national average
- Above national average
- Near national average
- Below national average
- Substantially below national average
- No stations

Due to rounding, totals may not add to exactly 100.
Source: TAPSCAN™ Web National Regional Database, Spring 2012

12 RADIO TODAY • 2013 EDITION • EXCLUSIVELY FOR ARBITRON CLIENTS

News/Talk/Information + Talk/Personality

Index of AQH Listening by Daypart

100 = Persons 12+, Mon-Sun, 6AM-Mid

Mon-Fri 6AM-10AM	Mon-Fri 10AM-3PM	Mon-Fri 3PM-7PM	Mon-Fri 7PM-Mid	Sat-Sun 6AM-Mid
158	153	123	41	59

News/Talk/Information + Talk/Personality indexed the highest in mornings as consumers awakened to the events of the day, 58% above its average. Its morning index was a close third of all 22 formats in this report.

Share of Listening by Location

AQH Persons 12+, Mon-Sun, 6AM-Mid

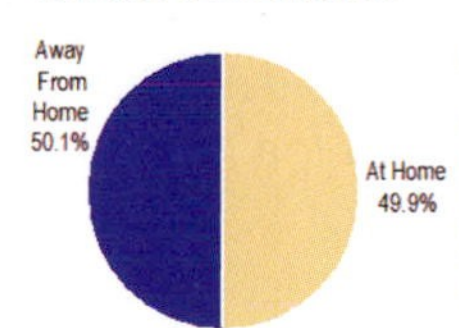

News/Talk/Information + Talk/Personality ranked No. 2 by a solid margin in its high proportion of at-home listening. It is consistently the only format with a nearly even split between at-home and away-from-home tune-in.

Audience Share by State

Persons 12+, Mon-Sun, 6AM-Mid, AQH Share

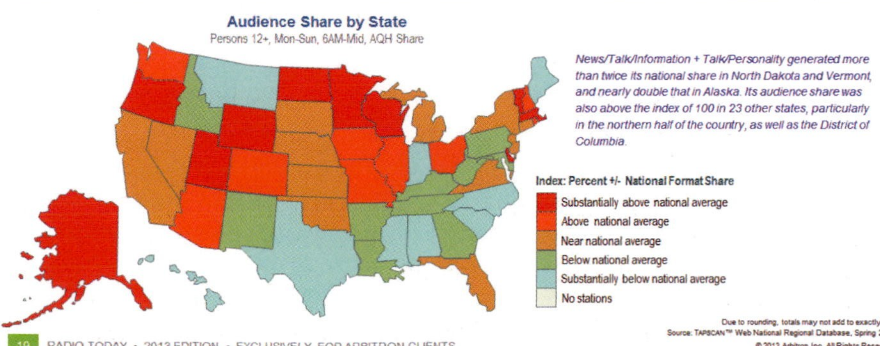

News/Talk/Information + Talk/Personality generated more than twice its national share in North Dakota and Vermont, and nearly double that in Alaska. Its audience share was also above the index of 100 in 23 other states, particularly in the northern half of the country, as well as the District of Columbia.

Index: Percent +/- National Format Share

- Substantially above national average
- Above national average
- Near national average
- Below national average
- Substantially below national average
- No stations

Due to rounding, totals may not add to exactly 100.
Source: TAPSCAN™ Web National Regional Database, Spring 2012

19 RADIO TODAY • 2013 EDITION • EXCLUSIVELY FOR ARBITRON CLIENTS

FIGURE 3.4A&B
Two top formats.
Courtesy of Arbitron.

media critics describe as "Easy Listening for Yuppies." Smooth Jazz fused the sounds of jazz, pop, rock, and other music genres in a low-key presentation featuring minimal announcer presence and interruption. Following a decade of popularity, the format waned in the mid-2000s. One reason for its decline, it appears, was that its core audience purchased few artist CDs. Devoted listeners, it appears, are satisfied instead by whatever selections their stations offer and aren't especially interested in product ownership.

Soft Adult, Lite and Easy, Smooth Jazz, Adult Standards, and Urban AC have become replacement nomenclatures for Easy Listening, which, like its predecessor, Beautiful Music, also began to assume a geriatric connotation.

Classic, Active, Modern, and Alternative Rock

The birth of the Album Oriented Rock (AOR) format in the late 1960s (also called Underground and Progressive) was the result of a basic disdain for the highly formulaic Top 40 sound that prevailed at the time. In the summer of 1966, WOR-FM, New York, introduced progressive radio, the forerunner of AOR. As an alternative to the super-hyped, ultra-commercial sound of the hit song station, WOR-FM programmed an unorthodox combination of non-chart rock, blues, folk, and jazz. In the 1970s, the format concentrated its attention almost exclusively on album rock, while becoming less freeform and more formulaic and systematic in its programming approach.

Today, AOR often is simply called Rock, or more specifically Modern Rock or Classic Rock, and although it continues to do well in garnering the 18–34-year-old male, this format has always done poorly in winning female listeners, especially when it emphasizes a heavy or hard rock playlist. This has proven to be a sore spot with certain advertisers. In the 1980s, the format lost its prominence owing, in part, to the meteoric rebirth of hit radio. However, as the decade came to an end, AOR had regained a chunk of its numbers, and in the 1990s, it renamed itself Modern Rock. Active Rock stations now adhere more faithfully to the AOR approach; as analyst Sean Ross noted, the two formats progressed lockstep in the 2000s until Modern Rock diverged and proponents advocated its distinction from the Alt Rock enthusiasts.

Generally, Rock stations broadcast their music in sweeps or at least segue two or three songs. A large airplay library is typical, in which 300–700 cuts may be active. Depending on the outlet, the deejay may or may not have "personality" status. In fact, the more-music/less-talk approach particularly common at Easy Listening stations is emulated by many album rockers. Consequently, news plays a very minor part in the station's programming efforts. Active Rock stations are very lifestyle-oriented and invest great time and energy developing promotions relevant to the interests and attitudes of their listeners. The Alternative Rock format tries for distinctiveness. That is to say, it attempts to provide a choice that is in contrast to the other Rock radio approaches. Creating this alternative sound is a challenge, says Stephanie Hindley, PD of Buzz 99.9: "The Alternative format is a great challenge for programmers. Think of the music you liked and the things you did when you were 18. Now think of the music you liked (or will like) and the things you did (or will do) at age 34. Despite the vast differences in taste in the 18–34 demographic, we need to play music that will appeal to as many people as possible within this diverse group." In comparison with other Rock variants, Alternative listeners typically are better-educated (two out of three have attended a university or have earned a degree). Additionally, the format attracts the highest percentage of Hispanic and black listeners within the "Rock" family of formats. As Hindley explains, "It's a constant balancing act. We have to play a lot of new music without sounding too unfamiliar. We have to be cool and hip without sounding exclusive. We have to be edgy without being offensive. Be smart without sounding condescending. Young and upbeat without sounding immature. As long as those balances are maintained on a daily basis, we will continue to have success in this format."

News/Talk/Information

There are News, News/Talk, News Sports, and Personality Talk formats, and each is distinct and unique unto itself. News stations differ from the others in that they devote their entire air schedule to the presentation of news and news-related stories and features. Chicago-based Radio Hall of Fame credits member Gordon McLendon, who achieved distinction for his innovative approach to formatic radio, with the introduction of the All-News format on the Windy City's WNUS. Because of the enormous expense involved in presenting a purely News format, requiring three to four times the staff and budget of most music operations, the format has been confined to larger markets able to support the endeavor.

The News/Talk format is a hybrid. It combines extensive news coverage with blocks of programming devoted to the airing of two-way telephone conversations. These stations commonly "daypart" or segmentalize their programming by presenting lengthened newscasts during morning and afternoon drive time hours and conversation in the midday and evening periods. The News/Talk combo was conceived by KGO in San Francisco in the 1960s and has gradually gained in popularity so that it now leads both the strictly News and the Talk formats. Talk radio began at KABC-AM, Los Angeles, in 1960. However, talk shows were familiar to listeners in the 1950s, since a number of adult music stations devoted a few hours during evenings or overnight to call-in programs. The motivation behind most early Talk programming stemmed from a desire to strengthen weak time slots while satisfying public affairs programming requirements. Like its non-music siblings, Talk became a viable format in the 1960s and does well today, although it too has suffered due to greater competition. In contrast to All-News, which attracts a slightly younger and more upscale audience, a marked characteristic of All-Talk formerly was its large following among blue-collar workers and retirees. This stereotype, however, no longer predominates. The format's core base of listeners has become better-educated; today, three of every four listeners is university educated. In markets measured by Arbitron's Portable People Meter (PPM) News/Talk is the leading format. News and/or Talk formats historically populated the AM band, where they proliferated in the wake of music-intensive format migration to FM. In recent years the number of non-music formats has significantly increased on FM, and this trend is predicted to continue as music listeners rely more and more on other audio sources.

Thanks in part to the fragmentation of the "News" and "Talk" franchises, the number of outlets has grown consistently for three decades. In the late 1990s, over 1,000 stations offered the information and/or news format. This was up nearly 300% since the late 1980s. In 2011, Arbitron estimated that almost 1,800 stations specialized in the talk format. More than 100 stations alone concentrated on sports exclusively, and dozens of others were beginning to splinter and compartmentalize into news/info niches, such as auto, health, computer, food, business, tourism, and entertainment.

National talk networks and syndicated talk shows, mostly of a conservative nature, continued to draw huge audiences in the new millennium, as more and more Baby Boomers became engaged in the political and social dialogues of the day. Despite the fact that a liberal talk radio network (Air America) debuted in the 2000s, the service faltered; its reception was anything but stellar. Right-wing hosts (Rush Limbaugh being the king among them) continued to rule the genre.

An indication that the information format is achieving equality in the balance of conservative and liberal viewpoints in the new-media environment emerged during the 2012 presidential election campaign. During that campaign one report about a study of listener patterns concluded that users streamed content labeled "liberal" almost two-to-one over "conservative" programming.

All-Sports

The trend in the last few years in the proliferation of the All-Sports format has boosted the popularity of non-music radio and significantly contributed to the dominance of "chatter" radio in the ratings. Propelling the trend are the new entrants into sports radio networking, including the 2013 launches of "major-league" broadcasters CBS Sports Network and NBC Sports Radio. ESPN, the dominant brand in sports media content, distributes programming to more than 700 stations, including more than 350 full-time affiliates. Fox Sports Radio and Yahoo!/Gow (formerly Sporting News Radio) also make the starter's list, ensuring the second decade of the 2000s is the format's most competitive. If AM radio is able to claim a younger demographic at all, it is because men 18–29 are big fans of sports radio. Overall listenership is well-distributed across all male demographics, helping the format to become one of radio's top ten in ratings in 2010 for males aged 25 and older. Male listeners outnumber females six to one and they tend to be more affluent and better educated than radio audiences in general. Meanwhile, All-Sports has begun to migrate to FM in significant numbers.

Consultant Ed Shane makes this observation regarding the success of the format. "The element of 'guy talk' is an important factor and one of the central ingredients that gives this format its special appeal. For our client stations, I define sports radio as 'beer, babes, and ball,' and not always in that order."

FM Talk

Although it's not recognized within the industry as a format descriptor *per se*, the approach adopted by FM stations to the presentation of information differs significantly enough from AM News/Talk to warrant its own discussion. The growing presence of FM talk is perhaps the most unique manifestation in non-music radio. This approach reflects industry awareness of the Gen Y and Gen Z audience, persons who likely came of age as radio listeners after music formats had migrated from the AM band to FM. The exchange of music for talk on FM dispels the long-held belief that the high-fidelity requirements for music reproduction necessitated its placement on FM, relegating talk programming to AM radio with its low-fidelity performance capabilities. Talent consultant Jason Insalaco gives his perspective on the rise of the *discourse* format on what has always been the dial for music:

> While traditional AM talk has been profiled in recent years for its explosion onto the radio landscape, FM talk radio has become a popular format for an audience previously ignored by talk programmers. FM talk's primary audience is 25–44 years old. This demographic likely did not grow up listening to AM talk radio. In fact, the FM talk audience has very likely tuned to AM very little during its lifetime. FM talk does not program itself like a traditional full-service AM talk outlet. There is not the emphasis on news and traffic, which is a staple of the AM talkers.

FM talk is inherently personality-driven by both nationally syndicated talkers such as Glenn Beck, Stephanie Miller, Michael Smerconish, and by a host of local talents. News and political discussion find their way into FM talk but the main focus is on entertainment and lifestyle. Insalaco adds:

> FM talk programs itself more like an FM music station than an AM talk station. It features shorter segments covering a variety of issues in contrast to the one-hour AM talk sweep. Issues discussed typically come from sources like *Rolling Stone* and *People* magazine and the local sports and entertainment sections of the newspaper. Topics are not necessarily caller intensive as with most AM talkers. Listener participation is a part of FM talk radio; however, there is not the typical topic-monologue-caller participation cycle of AM talkers. Moreover, the "bumper music" played to intro segments of FM talk comes from the latest alternative and rock artists found on the competing music stations. This gives the station a

youthful sound and grabs the potential talk listener who is scanning the dial. FM talk's competition comes from Alternative/Modern Rock/AOR and Classic Rock stations. The future of FM talk looks bright. Expect the format to become more widespread in the coming years.

Clearly, the number of FM talk outlets in major markets is on the increase. While ratings for stations in the top ten markets typically amount to about half of those earned by heritage AM talkers, FM talkers continue to trend upward and attract saleable and typically younger listeners.

Classic/Oldies/Nostalgia

While these formats are not identical, they derive the music they play from years gone by. Although the Nostalgia station, sometimes referred to as Big Band, constructs its playlist around tunes popular as far back as the 1940s and 1950s, the Oldies outlet focuses its attention on the pop tunes of the late 1950s and 1960s. A typical Oldies quarter-hour might consist of songs by Elvis Presley, the Everly Brothers, the Beatles, Brian Hyland, Three Dog Night, and the Ronettes. In contrast, a Nostalgia quarter-hour might consist of tunes from the pre-rock era performed by artists like Frankie Laine, Les Baxter, the Mills Brothers, Tommy Dorsey, and popular ballad singers of the past few decades.

"Music of Your Life" (MOYL) a vocal-intensive, 24-hour nostalgia presentation created in the 1970s by pop-music composer and performer Al Ham, continues to be heard nationwide on a network of approximately 50 stations, freshening its playlist to include softer pop hits of the 1960s and 1970s. Nostalgia is a highly syndicated format, and most stations go to MOYL or other out-of-house sources for programming material. Because much of the music predates stereo recording techniques, AM outlets are most apt to carry the Nostalgia sound. Music is invariably presented in sweeps, and, for the most part, deejays maintain a low profile. Similar to Easy Listening, Nostalgia pushes its music to the forefront and keeps other program elements at an unobtrusive distance. In the 1980s, Easy Listening/Beautiful Music stations lost some listeners to this format, which claimed a viable share of the radio audience.

The Oldies format was first introduced in the 1960s by programmers Bill Drake and Chuck Blore. Although Nostalgia's audience tends to be over the age of 50, the audience for Oldies skews somewhat younger. One-third of Oldies listeners grew up in the turbulent, rebellious 1960s and, unsurprisingly, the music of this decade constitutes the core of the song library. Unlike Nostalgia, most Oldies outlets originate their own programming, and very few are fully automated. In contrast with its vintage music cousin, the Oldies format allows greater deejay presence. At many Oldies stations, air personalities play a key role. Music is rarely broadcast in sweeps, and commercials, rather than being clustered, are inserted in a random fashion between songs.

Consultant Kent Burkhart noted that in the early 1990s, "Oldies stations are scoring very big in a nice broad demographic. These stations are doing quite well today, and this should hold for a while." That said, in 2012 Arbitron reported that the Oldies format continued its downward slide in audience share. In the 2000s the number of Oldies-formatted stations declined from more than 700 to approximately 570 as of this writing. Meanwhile, a more dance/contemporary approach that embraced the disco sound of the 1970s and 1980s, called "Jammin' Oldies," has attracted additional listeners.

The format descriptor "Oldies," according to Arbitron, is slowly being abandoned in favor of the label "Classic Hits." More pop than rock oriented, this 1960s-to-1980s-centric format has exhibited constant ratings growth in the 2000s on more than 500 outlets. Classic Hits stations are favored almost equally by male and female listeners, and particularly those aged 45 to 64. Classic Rock emphasizes the music of the iconic rock artists and attracts a predominantly (70%) male audience. By concentrating on tunes essentially featured by former AOR stations over the past three decades, the harder-edged Classic Rock format contrasts with the Classic Hits formula, which fills the gap between Oldies and CHR outlets with playlists that draw from 1970s, 1980s, and 1990s Top 40 charts.

Urban Contemporary

Considered the "melting pot" format, Urban Contemporary (UC) attracts large numbers of black listeners. Hispanic listeners, who constitute the largest minority in the nation, and Caucasians are also in the mix; together they account for one in five audience members. As the term suggests, stations employing this format usually are located in metropolitan areas with large, heterogeneous populations. Interestingly, however, the format currently exhibits higher-than-national average audience shares across the Deep South states, which include several urban markets, but only one of which (Atlanta) is considered to be "major market." A descendant of the heritage Black program format, UC was born in the early 1980s, the offspring of the short-lived Disco format, which burst onto the scene in 1978. At its inception, the disco craze brought new listeners to the Black stations, which shortly saw their fortunes change when All-Disco stations began to surface. Many Black outlets witnessed an exodus of their younger listeners to the Disco stations. This prompted a number of Black stations to abandon their more traditional playlists, which consisted of rhythm and blues, gospel, and soul tunes, for exclusively disco music. When disco perished in the early 1980s, the UC format emerged. Today, Progressive Black stations, such as WBLS-FM, New York, combine dance music with soulful rock and contemporary jazz, and many have transcended the color barrier by including certain white artists on their playlists. In fact, many Black stations employ white air personnel in efforts to broaden their demographic base.

What characterizes UC the most is its upbeat, danceable sound and deejays that are hip, friendly, and energetic. Although UC outlets stress danceable tunes, their playlists generally are anything but narrow. However, a particular sound may be given preference over another, depending on the demographic composition of the population in the area that the station serves. For example, UC outlets may play greater amounts of music with a Latin or rhythm and blues flavor, whereas others may air larger proportions of light jazz, reggae, new rock, or hip hop. Some AM stations around the country have adopted the UC format; however, it is more likely to be found on the FM side, where it has taken numerous stations to the forefront of their market's ratings.

The UC influence on the formats of traditional Black stations is evidenced by the swell in popularity of the Urban Adult Contemporary (Urban AC) and in the age alignment of audiences for the two formats. Urban AC listeners are predominantly middle-aged (35–54) African Americans who tend to stay tuned to stations for longer periods than do similarly aged listeners to other formats. UC has had an impact on Urban AC stations, which have experienced erosion in their youth numbers. More than a third of listeners to the nation's 270 UC stations are aged 23 and younger and a substantial amount of listening occurs in the after-school hours. Many UC stations have countered by broadening their playlists to include artists who are not traditionally programmed. Because of their high-intensity, fast-paced sound, UC outlets can give a Top 40 impression, but in contrast, they commonly segue songs or present music in sweeps and give airplay to lengthy cuts, sometimes six to eight minutes long. Although Top 40 or CHR stations seldom program cuts lasting more than four minutes, UC outlets find long cuts or remixes compatible with their programming approach. Remember, UCs are very dance oriented. Newscasts play a minor role in this format, which caters to a target audience aged 18–34. Contests and promotions are important program elements.

As noted earlier, several CHR stations adopted urban artists to offer the short-lived hybrid Churban or Rhythm Hits sound. Likewise, many Urban outlets have drawn from the more mainstream CHR playlist in an attempt to expand their listener base. Meanwhile, the old-line, heritage R&B and gospel stations still exist and can be found mostly on AM stations in the South.

Classical

Although there are fewer than two dozen full-time commercial Classical radio stations in the country, no other format can claim a more loyal following. Despite small numbers and soft ratings, most Classical stations do manage to generate a modest to good income. Over the years, profits have remained relatively minute in comparison to other formats. However, member stations of the Concert Music Broadcasters Association reported ad revenue increases of up to 40% in the 1980s and 1990s with continued growth, albeit modest, in the 2000s. Owing to its upscale audience, blue-chip accounts find the format an effective buy. This is first and foremost an FM format, and it has broadcast over the megahertz band for almost as long as it has existed.

In many markets, commercial Classical stations have been affected by public radio outlets programming classical music. Since commercial Classical stations must break to air the sponsor messages that keep them operating, they must

THE AMERICAN SOCIETY OF COMPOSERS, AUTHORS AND PUBLISHERS

ASCAP is

- a **performing-rights organization** whose function is to protect the **rights** of our members by licensing and collecting royalties for the public performance of their copyrighted musical works.
- the only U.S. society **created and controlled** by songwriters and publishers.
- the only U.S. society that gives writers and publishers **a voice**. ASCAP conducts open membership meetings, issues financial reports to its members, has writer and publisher member advisory committees.
- the only U.S. society that gives writers and publishers **a vote**. ASCAP is governed by an experienced Board of Directors composed of knowledgeable songwriters, composers and music publishers, each of whom is elected by the membership.
- the **largest** performing-rights society in the world in terms of **license-fee collections** and writer and publisher **performance-royalty payments**. 1995 income: more than $435 million.
- the **largest** performing-rights society in the world in terms of **constituency**. ASCAP has more than **75,000** U.S. writer and publisher members. Additionally, it represents more than **200,000** foreign-society writers and publishers.
- the industry **leader** since 1914 in negotiating license fees with the users of music.
- one of the most effective protectors of the rights of creators and music publishers. ASCAP **lobbies** in Congress and **litigates** in the courts, if necessary, on behalf of its constituents.
- the only society where writers and publishers sign **identical contracts**, with **the right to resign** every year of the contract.
- the only U.S. society with specific written rules covering **all types of performances on all types of media**, with all royalties distributed solely on that basis.
- the only U.S. society where payment **changes have to be approved** by the Board of Directors, the Department of Justice and in some cases by a U.S. Federal Court after an open court hearing. No changes are made without notice to the membership, and rates are not subject to arbitrary change at any time, as they are at other performing-rights organizations.
- the only U.S. society where your **royalties are determined objectively** over their entire copyright life and not by discretionary voluntary payments, short-term special deals or management discretion.

FIGURE 3.5
Radio stations pay an annual fee to music licensing services such as ASCAP, BMI and SESAC.

adjust their playlists accordingly. This may mean shorter cuts of music during particular dayparts—in other words, less music. The non-commercial Classical outlet is relatively free of such constraints and thus benefits as a result. A case in point is WCRB-FM in Boston, the city's only full-time Classical station. Although it was attracting most of the area's Classical listeners throughout the afternoon and evening hours, it lost many patrons to public radio WGBH's classical segments with fewer programming interruptions. In 2010 WGBH purchased WCRB-FM, relegating its classical music programming to the former commercially operated station and repositioning its programming approach to news and information.

Classical stations target the 25–49-year-old, higher income, college-educated listener. News is typically presented at 60–90-minute intervals and generally runs from five to ten minutes. The format is characterized by a conservative, straightforward air sound. Sensationalism and hype are avoided, and on-air contests and promotions are as rare as announcer chatter.

Religious/Christian

Live broadcasts of religious programs began while the medium was still in its experimental stage. In 1919, the U.S. Army Signal Corps aired a service from a chapel in Washington, D.C. Not long after that, KFSG in Los Angeles and WMBI in Chicago began to devote themselves to religious programming. Soon dozens of other radio outlets were broadcasting the message of God.

Religious broadcasters typically follow one of two programming approaches. One includes music as part of its presentation, and the other does not. Contemporary Christian-formatted stations feature music containing a Christian or life-affirming perspective. Almost 800 stations located in all U. S. regions attract listeners of all ages. The typical listener is almost twice as likely to be female than male and of above-average education. A notable presence to emerge in recent years is K-Love, the Contemporary Christian music service that operates a nationwide network of 400-plus FM full-power and translator stations. Operated by the California-based non-profit organization the Educational Media Foundation, K-Love offers a music-focused presentation with minimal interruption. Broadcast educator Janet McMullen finds that programming Contemporary Christian is a challenge for a number of reasons. "With the broad scope of denominations possessing varying beliefs, it is sometimes very hard to keep the listening public happy. It is a very fine line to walk. You have to be careful not to offend or alienate listeners, even in our format. This requires careful and thoughtful programming." Faith-affirming Gospel stations feature music that has its origins in the black church; Southern Gospel-formatted stations are mainstays of the South and Midwest; their music appeals to Caucasian listeners. Gospel programming can be heard on 500 stations, mostly on AM. In all instances, music-intensive stations include the scheduling of blocks of religious features and programs. Non-music Religious outlets concentrate on inspirational features and complementary talk and informational shows.

Religious broadcasters claim that their spiritual messages reach nearly half of the nation's radio audience, and the American Research Corporation in Irvine, California, contends that more than 25% of those tuned to Religious stations attend church more frequently. Two-thirds of the country's Religious radio stations broadcast over AM frequencies.

Hispanic

Hispanic or Spanish-language stations constitute another large ethnic format, reaching 95% of Hispanic listeners weekly. KCOR-AM, San Antonio, became the first All-Spanish station in 1947, just a matter of months after WDIA-AM

Leading Radio Formats Ranked by Demographic

AQH Share by Demographic
Mon-Sun, 6AM-Mid, AQH Persons 12+, Spring 2012

Persons 12-17		Persons 18-24		Persons 25-34	
Pop CHR	24.3%	Country + New Country	16.8%	Country + New Country	14.3%
Country + New Country	13.0%	Pop CHR	16.2%	Pop CHR	12.1%
Rhythmic CHR	9.2%	Rhythmic CHR	8.6%	Adult Contemporary + Soft AC	6.5%
Hot AC	7.3%	Urban Contemporary	6.6%	Rhythmic CHR	5.9%
Urban Contemporary	6.0%	Adult Contemporary + Soft AC	6.1%	Hot AC	5.6%
Adult Contemporary + Soft AC	5.5%	Hot AC	6.0%	News/Talk/Information + T/P	5.1%
Contemporary Christian	4.5%	Classic Rock	4.7%	Mexican Regional	4.9%
Classic Rock	3.1%	Active Rock	3.8%	Urban Contemporary	4.9%
Urban AC	3.1%	Alternative	3.4%	Classic Rock	4.6%
Mexican Regional	2.8%	Mexican Regional	3.4%	Alternative	3.8%
News/Talk/Information + T/P	2.7%	Classic Hits	3.2%	Active Rock	3.7%
Classic Hits	2.4%	Urban AC	3.1%	All Sports	3.6%
Active Rock	2.0%	Contemporary Christian	2.6%	Contemporary Christian	3.3%
Alternative	2.0%	News/Talk/Information + T/P	2.6%	Urban AC	3.2%
Spanish Contemp. + Span. HAC	1.7%	AOR + Mainstream Rock	2.4%	Classic Hits	3.1%
Adult Hits + '80s Hits	1.4%	Adult Hits + '80s Hits	1.8%	AOR + Mainstream Rock	2.7%
AOR + Mainstream Rock	1.4%	Spanish Contemp. + Span. HAC	1.7%	Spanish Contemp. + Span. HAC	2.4%
All Sports	1.1%	All Sports	1.5%	Adult Hits + '80s Hits	2.3%
Religious	1.0%	Oldies	0.9%	Album Adult Alternative	1.0%
Album Adult Alternative	0.7%	Album Adult Alternative	0.8%	Oldies	0.8%
Oldies	0.6%	All News	0.4%	Religious	0.6%
All News	0.5%	Religious	0.4%	All News	0.5%

continued ▶

Note: Top 16 formats listed
Source: TAPSCAN™ Web National Regional Database, Spring 2012

Leading Radio Formats Ranked by Demographic

AQH Share by Demographic
Mon-Sun, 6AM-Mid, AQH Persons 12+, Spring 2012

Persons 35-44		Persons 45-54		Persons 55-64		Persons 65+	
Country + New Country	12.6%	Country + New Country	13.7%	News/Talk/Information + T/P	17.1%	News/Talk/Information + T/P	26.4%
Pop CHR	9.5%	News/Talk/Information + T/P	10.9%	Country + New Country	14.1%	Country + New Country	15.4%
Adult Contemporary + Soft AC	8.2%	Adult Contemporary + Soft AC	9.1%	Adult Contemporary + Soft AC	9.8%	Adult Contemporary + Soft AC	8.5%
News/Talk/Information + T/P	7.7%	Classic Rock	8.3%	Classic Hits	8.2%	Classic Hits	5.1%
Hot AC	6.4%	Classic Hits	7.3%	Classic Rock	5.5%	Urban AC	3.3%
Classic Rock	5.7%	Pop CHR	5.2%	Urban AC	5.0%	Oldies	3.0%
Mexican Regional	4.4%	Urban AC	5.1%	All Sports	3.6%	All News	3.0%
Urban AC	4.4%	Hot AC	4.7%	Oldies	3.4%	All Sports	2.9%
Classic Hits	4.1%	All Sports	3.5%	Hot AC	3.1%	Religious	2.6%
All Sports	3.9%	Contemporary Christian	3.2%	Pop CHR	2.7%	Classic Rock	1.5%
Contemporary Christian	3.6%	Adult Hits + '80s Hits	2.8%	Contemporary Christian	2.5%	Hot AC	1.5%
Rhythmic CHR	3.3%	AOR + Mainstream Rock	2.5%	All News	2.0%	Contemporary Christian	1.3%
Urban Contemporary	3.2%	Mexican Regional	2.2%	Adult Hits + '80s Hits	1.9%	Pop CHR	1.3%
Adult Hits + '80s Hits	3.0%	Urban Contemporary	2.0%	Religious	1.7%	Mexican Regional	1.2%
Active Rock	2.9%	Oldies	1.9%	Mexican Regional	1.6%	Adult Hits + '80s Hits	1.0%
AOR + Mainstream Rock	2.7%	Active Rock	1.8%	Album Adult Alternative	1.5%	Spanish Contemp. + Span. HAC	0.9%
Alternative	2.5%	Rhythmic CHR	1.7%	AOR + Mainstream Rock	1.4%	Urban Contemporary	0.6%
Spanish Contemp. + Span. HAC	2.1%	Album Adult Alternative	1.6%	Urban Contemporary	1.1%	Album Adult Alternative	0.5%
Album Adult Alternative	1.1%	All News	1.4%	Spanish Contemp. + Span. HAC	1.0%	Rhythmic CHR	0.5%
All News	0.9%	Alternative	1.4%	Rhythmic CHR	0.8%	AOR + Mainstream Rock	0.4%
Oldies	0.9%	Spanish Contemp. + Span. HAC	1.3%	Active Rock	0.6%	Alternative	0.3%
Religious	0.9%	Religious	1.2%	Alternative	0.6%	Active Rock	0.2%

Note: Top 16 formats listed
Source: TAPSCAN™ Web National Regional Database, Spring 2012

FIGURE 3.6A&B
Radio format popularity according to demographic characteristics. Courtesy of Arbitron.

AM/FM Radio Is the Top Source to Learn About New Music
45% of Americans say it's important to learn about new music and nearly
8 out of 10 choose radio
to stay up to date with new music.
That's significantly more than YouTube, music television channels, Facebook, Pandora®, iTunes®, and satellite radio.
ARBITRON

FIGURE 3.7
Radio continues to be a "go-to" location for new music discovery. Courtesy of Arbitron.

in Memphis put the Black format on the air. Cities with large Latin populations are able to support the format, and in some metropolitan areas with vast numbers of Spanish-speaking residents—such as New York, Los Angeles, and Miami—several radio outlets are devoted exclusively to Hispanic programming. As Arbitron reported in 2008: "As their population continued to surge in the United States, Hispanics increased the percentage of their representation in 15 of the 20 non-Spanish-language formats in our report, averaging 1.1% more in audience composition than in spring 2006. The only formats where Hispanics made up a smaller proportion of a format's listenership were UC, Oldies, Alternative and Active Rock."

Programming approaches within the format are not unlike those prevalent at Anglo stations. That is to say, Spanish-language radio stations also modify their sound to draw a specific demographic. For example, many offer contemporary music for younger listeners and more traditional music for older listeners. Talk-Intensive formats parallel those popular with English-language stations and the approaches are similarly segregated by Arbitron. Thus, advertisers are able to differentiate and effectively target listeners who prefer Spanish News/Talk from other Spanish-language formats including Sports, Religious, and Variety.

Ed Shane concurs with the viewpoint that Hispanic radio is diverse and vibrant.

> An impressive multiplicity of programming styles and approaches are found in this format. Here in Houston, for example, we have two brands of Tejano, one of Exitos (hits), a lot of Ranchera, and a couple of Talk stations. In the Rio Grande Valley of Texas, there's a lush, instrumental-and-vocal "Easy Listening" station in Spanish. The LA dial is full of Hispanic nuance. Miami, likewise, and it has a totally different slant.

To find evidence of this diversity, Shane says, one need look no further than Houston and Miami. While Tropical is a dominant Hispanic format in Miami, it is absent from the roster of formats found in Houston, a market where Spanish Classic Hits prevails.

Spanish media experts predicted that there would be a significant increase in the number of Hispanic stations through the 2000s, and they were right. Much of this growth occurred on the AM band but later spread rapidly on FM. Leading the station count is the Mexican Regional format, found on 300 stations and heard by an estimated one in five Hispanic listeners.

Ethnic

Hundreds of other radio stations countrywide apportion a significant piece of their air schedules (more than 20 hours weekly), if not all, to foreign-language programs in Portuguese, German, Polish, Greek, Japanese, and so on.

Around 30 stations broadcast exclusively to American Indians and Eskimos and are licensed to Native Americans. Today, these stations are being fed programming from the American Indian Radio on Satellite (AIROS) service, which subsequently rebranded as the AIROS Native Radio Network, and other indigenous media groups predict dozens more Indian-operated stations to be broadcasting by the end of the next decade. Meanwhile, the number of stations broadcasting to Asians and other nationalities is rising.

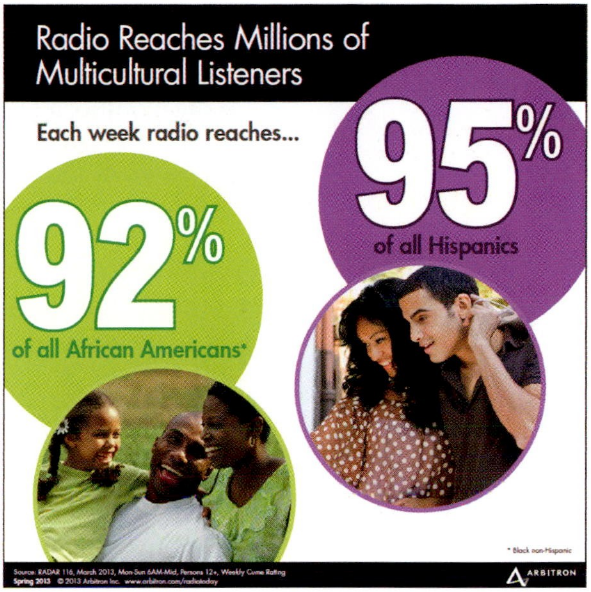

Radio Reaches Millions of Multicultural Listeners

Each week radio reaches...

95% of all Hispanics

92% of all African Americans*

* Black non-Hispanic

ARBITRON

FIGURE 3.8
Radio is a prominent information and entertainment source for multicultural audiences. Courtesy of Arbitron.

Full Service

The Full Service (FS) format (also called Variety, General Appeal, Diversified, etc.) attempts to provide its mostly middle-aged listeners a mix of all programming genres—news, sports, and information features blended with a selection of adult-oriented pop-music standards. This something-for-everyone approach straddled the "middle of the road" musically and subsequently became known as MOR. This format has attempted to strengthen its public service aspect through increased information programming. It is really one-stop shopping for listeners who would like a little bit of everything. Today, this type of station exists mostly in small markets where stations attempt to be good-citizen radio for everyone. It has been called the *bridge* format because of its "all things to all people" programming approach. The format has lost much of its large-market appeal and effectiveness due to the diversification and rise

FIGURE 3.9
A striking visual identity for Niijii Radio. Courtesy of KKWE.

in popularity of specialized formats. According to radio program specialist Dick Ellis, FS now has a predominantly over-40 age demographic, several years older than just a decade ago. In some major markets, the format continues to do well in the ratings mainly because of strong on-air personalities. But this is not the format that it once was. Since its inception in the 1950s, up through the 1970s, stations working the MOR sound often dominated their markets. Yet the Soft Rock and Oldies formats in the 1970s, the updating of Easy Listening (Smooth Jazz), and particularly the ascendancy of AC and Talk formats have resulted in severe erosion of Full Service, MOR and variety stations. According to Arbitron, stations with these formats collectively account for less than 2% of radio listening nationwide.

FS is the home of the on-air personality. Perhaps no other format gives its air personnel as much latitude and freedom. This is not to suggest that FS announcers may do as they please. They, like any other announcer, must abide by format and programming policy, but FS personalities often serve as the cornerstone of their station's air product. Some of the best-known deejays in the country have come from the FS (MOR) milieu. It would then follow that the music is rarely, if ever, presented in sweeps or even segued. Deejay patter occurs between each cut of music, and announcements are inserted in the same way. News and sports play another vital function at these stations. During drive periods, FS often presents lengthened blocks of news, replete with frequent traffic reports, weather updates, and the latest sports information. Many FS outlets are affiliated with professional and collegiate athletic teams. With few exceptions, FS is an AM format. Although it has endured ratings slippage in recent years, it will likely continue to bridge whatever gaps may exist in a highly specialized radio marketplace.

Niche and HD^2 Formats

When it comes to format prognostication, the term *unpredictable* takes on a whole new meaning. Indeed, there will be a rash of successful niche formats in the coming years, due to the ever-increasing fragmentation of the radio audience, but exactly what they will be is anyone's guess. A common thread that weaves throughout the industry is the almost surety that format experimentation is more active on the AM, satellite and HD bands and less so on FM.

A few years back, no one thought that All-Children's Radio (Radio Disney, whose affiliates mostly are on AM, and the "Kids Place Live" channel on SiriusXM) would draw an economically attractive segment of the listening public, but today it is one of the more successful format niches. New niche or splinter formats emerge frequently—Bluegrass, Christian Talk and K-Mozart Classical are good examples—in an industry always on the lookout for the next best thing and competing with a myriad of other listening options. Another interesting development involved the adoption of a successful Internet-only station format by the HD3 channel of Washington, D.C. FM, WTOP. The station's website describes variety-rich "The Gamut" as "a cross-section of all styles of music, made for lovers of music. Sample artists include Scissor Sisters, Doris Day, Mumford and Sons, Devo, Elvis Presley, Boney M, Johnny Cash, as well as Washington, D.C. area artists. Current music and its influences all the way back to pre-WWII are represented, selected and arranged to appeal to multiple generations of music lovers." In an MP3 and smartphone world, staying fresh and current gives radio an edge—one that is more and more necessary as the audio landscape changes.

In terms of future format innovations, the rollout of HD2 and HD3 side-channels (see the discussion of HD Radio™ in Chapter 10) has contributed somewhat to the development of new niche formats. Whether formats such as Japanese Pop or the Mormon Channel could become successful as primary-channel services is debatable, but as of this writing they had found a home on HD2 side channels. Experts remain divided in their opinions about the role HD Radio plays in enlarging format diversity. Says Lynn Christian, "Unique programming ideas or concepts best suited to an audio presentation with great potential in all-size markets, while utilizing the new HD/HD2/HD3 channels, have the greatest potential." However, some programmers, such as WIZN/WBTZ's Matt Grasso, don't expect much to change in the foreseeable future.

> I don't think the formats will change much. I think the change will be within each format. Stations will focus on being more local. It's our biggest strength against satellite. We're here. Let's entrench ourselves into the community and become an important and integral part of their lives. The only format I can see changing is the so-called "Jack" format. This knee-jerky response to iPods doesn't seem to fit the American culture. We want specific things, not a little bit of everything. We're picky, selfish, brand loyal people. Have buffets taken over the Italian, Indian, French, Chinese, and Thai restaurants? Of course not! Jack is the radio buffet—stale, lukewarm, and boring.

At best, the preceding is an incomplete list of myriad radio formats that serve the listening public. The program formats mentioned constitute the

FIGURE 3.10
Stations bring artists to the studio for live sessions. Courtesy of KEXP-FM.

majority of the basic format categories prevalent today. Tomorrow? Who knows? Radio is hardly a static industry, but one subject to the whims of popular taste. When something new captures the imagination of the American public, radio responds, and often a new format is conceived.

Public Radio

Like college stations, most Public radio outlets program in a block fashion. That is to say, few employ a primary (single) format, but instead offer a mix of program ingredients, such as news and information and entertainment features. National Public Radio (referenced nowadays as "NPR" during the network's on-air identifications), American Public Media and Public Radio International, along with state Public radio systems, provide a myriad of features for the hundreds of Public radio facilities around the country. Topping the list of prominent music genres are classical and jazz. Public radio news broadcasts, among them NPR's *Morning Edition, All Things Considered,* and PRI's *The Takeaway,* lead all radio in audience popularity for information focused on national and world events. The popularity of NPR and its programming is showing evidence of a shift in the way that listeners access the network's content. During the period from 2011 to 2012, NPR's average weekly cumulative broadcast audience was estimated at 26 million, a dip of 800,000 listeners from the year before. However, the network experienced growth in the number of monthly podcast downloads and in the number of its mobile app uses.

ON PUBLIC RADIO

Mike Janssen

FIGURE 3.11
Mike Janssen.

In the previous edition of this book, I wrote that public radio stations and networks in the U.S. were struggling to adapt to a media landscape rattled by the ascent of digital media. Today, it's a different story. Many stakeholders in public radio have realized the urgency of shifting gears to a multimedia approach, going beyond radio to serve their audiences. Public radio shows such as NPR's *Radiolab* and Chicago Public Media's *This American Life* regularly rank among the top podcasts on Apple's iTunes Store, and NPR has earned widespread recognition for its extensive website, in particular a companion music site that regularly features up-and-coming artists in many genres. In part to reflect this expanding digital presence, the network declared in 2010 that "NPR" no longer stands for "National Public Radio"—its name is now officially just its initials, the "radio" dropped from it.

These innovations stem from the realization that today's media consumers are getting news from a growing array of platforms and devices. Radio remains a popular medium on its own, but consumption on digital platforms continues to grow, particularly on portable devices such as smartphones and tablets. The emergence of a new platform demands that station and network leaders once again consider how to allocate resources to best take advantage of the opportunities presented. Managers often speak of the importance of being agile, innovative, and flexible as the system strives to remain relevant. Some stations paired with public television stations have responded by consolidating their newsrooms among all media, assigning their producers and reporters to create content for radio, TV, and online all at once. KPBS, a joint licensee in San Diego, was a trailblazer in this trend of "convergence." It has had such success that it now offers "boot camps" to other stations that seek to follow its example.

What kinds of programming are filling up all of these new platforms and broadcast schedules? NPR news programming has continued to expand its reach and popularity, while news stations that can afford the expense are developing their own midday news and talk shows to complement and extend the news offerings from NPR and its competitors, Public Radio International and American Public Media. In attempts to appeal to younger listeners and ethnically diverse audiences and keep pace with the growing diversity of the American public, stations and networks have also launched shows that aim for a fresher sound or take advantage of social and mobile media.

Public radio's traditional music formats of classical and jazz persist on many stations, while Adult Album Alternative (also known as Triple A) music has become a staple as well. But classical has lost ground on a number of stations as they have acquired or started to produce more news and talk programming. Regardless of format, for listeners seeking thoughtful, in-depth news and musical genres that get little airplay elsewhere, the lower end of the dial remains a go-to spot on FM radio and is likely to remain so for years to come.

Mike Janssen reports on trends and happenings in public media for Current.org, the website devoted to public media coverage. He describes himself as an educator, agitator and programmer in community media and is a member of the Washington, D.C. band The Boundary Stones.

THE PROGRAMMER

PDs are radiophiles. They live the medium. Most admit to having been smitten by radio at an early age. "It's something that is in your blood and grows to consuming proportions," admits programmer Peter Falconi. Longtime PD Brian Mitchell recalls an interest in the medium as a small child and for good reason. "I was born into a broadcasting family. My father is a station owner and builder. During my childhood, radio was the primary topic at the dinner table. It fed the flame that I believe was already ignited anyway. Radio fascinated me from the start." Entercom program manager (PM) Brad Carson confesses to this ulterior motive: "I was always glued to (hometown station)WSMI (Litchfield, Illinois) to find out on 'snow days' if my school was cancelled or not. (I always rooted for cancellations.)" As a teen Carson prepped for his first real job by producing "a series of 'fake' radio shows on a cassette player mixing music, announcing, and incorporating various entertaining 'impressions' of my high school teachers." What was the response? "My friends seemed to think they were hilarious," he says, "so I continued." The customary route to the programmer's job involves deejaying and participation in other on-air-related areas, such as copywriting, production, music, and news. It would be difficult to state exactly how long it takes to become a PD. For Dick Kent, former vice-president for programming at Nashville's WLAC AM-FM, the door to becoming a PD opened after achieving ratings success in three markets as a morning drivetime air personality. Success largely depends on the individual and where he or she happens to be. In some instances, newcomers have gone into programming within their first year in the business. When this happens, it is most likely to occur in a small market where turnover may be high. On the other hand, it is far more common to spend years working toward this goal, even in the best of situations. "Although my father owned the station, I spent a long time in a series of jobs before my appointment to programmer. Along the way, I worked as station janitor, and then got into announcing, production, and eventually programming," recounts Mitchell.

One of the nation's foremost air personalities and hall of famer was the late Dick Fatherly. *Billboard* magazine described him as a "longtime legend" who spent years as a deejay before making the transition. "In the 25 years that I've been in this business, I have worked as a jock, newsman, production director, and even sales rep. Eventually I ended up in program management. During my career I have worked at WABC, WICC, WFUN, WHB, to mention a few. Plenty of experience, you might say," Fatherly commented. Experience contributes most toward the making of the station's programmer. However, individuals entering the field with hopes of becoming a PD do well to acquire as much formal training as possible. The programmer's job has become an increasingly demanding one as a result of expanding competition. "A good knowledge of research methodology, analysis, and application is crucial. Programming is both an art and a science today," observes general manager Jim Murphy. Programmer Andy Bloom concurs with Murphy, adding, "A would-be PD needs to school him- or herself in marketing research particularly. Little is done anymore that is not based on careful analysis."

Radio Ink publisher B. Eric Rhoads echoes this stance:

> The role has changed. The PD used to be a glorified music director with some background in talent development. Today the PD must be a marketing expert. Radio marketing has become very complex, what with telemarketing, database marketing, direct mail, interactive communication, and so forth. Radio is changing, and the PD must adapt. No longer will records and deejays make the big difference. Stations are at parity in music, so better ways must be found to set stations apart.

Says Ed Shane, "The ultimate analogy for the PD is 'brand manager,' overseeing not only the product, but also the image and perception of the product. Since programmers now must work hand-in-hand with sellers to maximize station revenues, there's a new awareness of the marketing dimension." Rhoads, in his industry newsmagazine, *Radio Ink*, reported that Saga Communications, which corporately operates 90 AM and FM stations, would adopt the "brand manager" title, applying it to personnel formerly known as "program directors." The charge to the brand manager: take ownership of all delivery platforms, extend your oversight of content beyond the air signal by proactively managing your online presence as well as your social media activities.

The concept of "brand management," when applied to a day in the life of programmer Brad Carson's world, means multiple responsibilities.

> Right now I create the fun for our Classic Hits "brand" and two sports "brands." An average day might include scheduling music, writing, creating marketing plans/promotions with clients and creative partners, producing a sports show, deejaying, talent coaching, and answering emails from listeners. But obviously there's some inside "tricks of the trade" that we use to create the secret sauce just like every brand.

Cognizant of this change, schools with programs in radio broadcasting emphasize courses in audience and marketing research, as well as other programming-related areas. An important fact for the aspiring PD to keep in mind is that more persons entering broadcasting today have college backgrounds than ever before. Even though a college degree is not necessarily a prerequisite for the position of PD, it is clearly regarded as an asset by upper management. "It used to be that a college degree didn't mean so much. A PD came up through the ranks of programming, proved his ability, and was hired. Not that

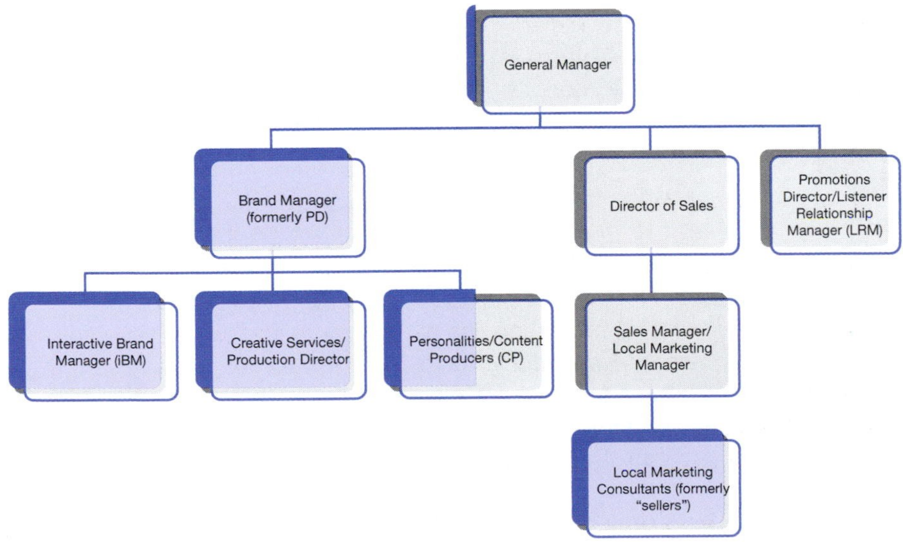

FIGURE 3.12
In this management-organization arrangement, the PD becomes the station's brand manager. Courtesy of McVay New Media.

that doesn't still happen. It does. But more and more the new PD has a degree or, at the very least, several years of college," contends Joe Cortese, syndicated air personality. "I majored in communication arts at a junior college and then transferred to a four-year school. There are many colleges offering communications courses here in the Boston area, so I'll probably take some more as a way of further preparing for the day when I'll be programming or managing a station. That's what I eventually want to do," says Cortese, adding that experience in the trenches is also vital to success.

His point is well taken. Work experience does head the list on which a station manager bases his or her selection for PD. Meanwhile, college training, at the very least, has become a criterion to the extent that if an applicant does not have any, the prospective employer takes notice.

Beyond formal training and experience, Chuck Ducoty, major-market station manager, says a PD must possess certain innate qualities. "Common sense and a good sense of humor are necessary attributes and are in rather short supply, I think." According to Dick Fatherly, the attributes of sensitivity, patience, compassion, and drive belong on the short list.

FIGURE 3.13
Program directors' cubicles inside the programming bullpen at SiriusXM offices in Washington, D.C. Courtesy SiriusXM and Marlin Taylor.

THE PD'S DUTIES AND RESPONSIBILITIES

Where to begin this discussion poses a problem because the PD's responsibilities and duties are so numerous and wide-ranging. Second in responsibility to the general manager (in station clusters, the individual station programmer reports to the director of operations, who oversees all programming for the various stations), the PD is the person responsible for everything that goes over the air. This involves working with the station manager or director of operations in establishing programming and format policy and overseeing their effective execution. In addition, he or she hires and supervises on-air music and production personnel, plans various schedules, handles the programming budget, develops promotions (in conjunction with the promotion or marketing director, if there is such a person in this role), monitors the station and its competition, assesses research, and may even pull a daily air-shift. The PD also is accountable for the presentation of news, public affairs, and sports features, although a news director often is appointed to help oversee these areas.

The PD alone does not determine a station's format. This is an upper management decision. The PD may be involved in the selection process, but, more often than not, the format has been chosen before the programmer has been hired. For example, the ownership and management of WYYY has decided on the basis of declining revenues that the station must switch from MOR to CHR to attract a more marketable demographic. After an in-depth examination of its own market, research on the effectiveness of CHR nationally, and advice from a program consultant and national advertising rep company, the format change is deemed appropriate. Reluctantly, the station manager concludes that he must bring in a CHR specialist, which means that he must terminate the services of his present programmer, whose experience is limited to MOR. The station manager advertises the position availability in various industry trade publications and their websites, interviews several candidates, and hires the person he feels will take the station to the top of the ratings. When the new PD arrives, he or she is charged with the task of preparing the new format for its debut. Among other things, this may involve hiring new air talent, acquiring a new music library or the updating of the existing one, preparing promos and purchasing jingles, developing external promotions and working in league with the sales, traffic, and engineering departments for maximum results.

On these points, Corinne Baldasano, senior vice-president of programming and marketing for *Take On The Day, LLC*, observes:

> First of all, of course, you must be sure that the station you are programming fills a market void, i.e., that there is an opportunity for you to succeed in your geographic area with the format you are programming. For example, a young adult alternative Rock station may not have much chance for success in an area that is mostly populated by retirees. Once you have determined that the format fills an audience need, you need to focus on building your station. The basic ingredients are making sure your

music mix is correct (if you are programming a music station) and that you've hired the on-air talent that conveys the attitude and image of the station you wish to build. At this stage, it is far more important to focus inward than outward. Many stations have failed because they've paid more attention to the competition's product than they have their own.

Once the format is implemented, the PD must work at refining and maintaining the sound. After a short time, the programmer may feel compelled to modify air schedules either by shifting deejays around or by replacing those who do not enhance the format. Metro Networks founder David Saperstein says, "You've got to continually fine-tune the station's sound. You must remove any and all negatives, like excessive talk, annoying commercials, technical weaknesses, and so forth. The most critical rule of thumb is that stations should always concentrate on bringing listeners to the station, keeping them tuned in, and providing the right balance of music, personalities, talk, information, and commercials so listeners do not have any reason to tune elsewhere." Adds WLAC/Nashville's Dick Kent, "A primary duty of the program director is the creation of the constant and consistently dynamic feeling of an on-air sound, with a seamless flow of the combined elements, all designed to attract a vibrant responsive target audience." The program director has the responsibility "to communicate these goals understandably to those persons responsible for the flawless execution of this seamless flow, whether it is in the production room, or maybe in the promotions department . . . or helping develop talent availability for the sales and promotion department's needs for personality appearances at station image/revenue-enhancing remotes." The challenge to becoming a successful PD, Kent believes, ultimately resides in shaping and conveying the programming philosophy to "everyone who is responsible for the station's sound" in order to preserve the "dynamic feeling."

The PD prepares weekend and holiday schedules as well and this generally requires the hiring of part-time announcers. A station may employ as few as one or two part-timers or fill-in people or as many as eight to ten. This largely depends on whether deejays are on a five- or six-day schedule. At most stations, air personnel are hired to work a six-day week. The objective of scheduling is not merely to fill slots but to maintain the continuity and consistency of sound. A PD prefers to tamper with shifts as little as possible and fervently hopes that he has filled weekend slots with individuals who are reliable. "The importance of dependable, trustworthy air people cannot be overemphasized. It's great to have talented deejays, but if they don't show up when they are supposed to because of one reason or another, they don't do you a lot of good. You need people who are cooperative. I have no patience with individuals who try to deceive me or fail to live up to their responsibilities," says Brian Mitchell. A station that is constantly introducing new air personnel has a difficult time establishing listener habit. The PD knows that to succeed he or she must present a stable and dependable sound, and this is a significant programming challenge.

Nowadays, the sometimes controversial practice of voice-tracking assists the PD in maintaining a consistent 24/7 on-air sound. Programmer Brad Carson defends the technology. "Talent-sharing from station to station," he says, "using voice-tracking and other methods (networks, for example) has helped many stations, regardless of market size or format, put the best voices and talent in radio markets across America." Detractors of voice-tracking criticize the practice, claiming that owners' primary objective in eliminating local talent is the reduction of expenses. Carson, however, believes that this viewpoint can be inconsistent with a PD's objectives. "While many have demonized voice-trackings and network radio because of cost reduction (which is not always the case when using these tools) radio groups want to put the very best content on the air. Content is still king. High quality content and entertaining content are always the goal."

Marlin R. Taylor, founder of Bonneville Broadcasting System and veteran major-market station programmer and manager, underscores the need for station personnel to support their non-local air talent:

> In most cases, if a station is to truly stay connected to the listener, "local" is an element that must be factored in. If you're talking about a voice-tracker from outside the market, he/she needs to be provided with information that enables the person to include content relevant to the local community. If it's a network music show, there should be timely local information included in the local breaks beyond just commercial spots. Otherwise, a properly run station that utilizes either of these extensively on weekends and even overnight hours needs to have someone available to communicate information should an emergency or other major newsworthy event occur in the community or region that the listener should be aware of.

Production schedules also are prepared by the programmer. Deejays are usually tapped for production duties before or after their airshifts. For example, the morning person who is on the air 6:00–10:00 am may be assigned production and copy chores from 10:00 am until noon. Meanwhile, the midday deejay who is on the air from 10:00 am until 3:00 pm is given production assignments for 3:00–5:00 pm, and so on. Large radio stations frequently employ a full-time production person. If so, this individual handles all production responsibilities and is supervised by the PD.

A PD traditionally handles the department's budget, which generally constitutes 30–40% of the station's operating budget. Working with the station manager, the PD ascertains the financial needs of the programming area. The size and scope of the budget vary from station to station. Most programming budgets include funds for the acquisition of program materials, such as subscription music services, network and syndicated program features, and contest paraphernalia. A separate promotional budget usually exists and this too may be managed by the PD. The programmer's budgetary responsibilities range from monumental at some outlets to minuscule at others. Personnel salaries and even equipment purchases may fall within the province of the program department's budget. Brian Mitchell believes that "an understanding of the total financial structure of the company or corporation and how programming fits into the scheme of things is a real asset to a programmer."

Devising station promotions and contests also places demands on the PD's time. While large stations often can afford to appoint a promotion director, the same cannot necessarily be said of situations in the smaller markets. In instances where fulltime promotions directors are employed, the PD and promotion director work together in the planning, development, and execution of the promotional campaign. The PD, however, retains final veto power should he or she feel that the promotion or contest fails to complement the station's format. When the PD alone handles promotions and contests, he or she may involve other members of the programming or sales department in brainstorming sessions designed to come up with original and interesting concepts. The programmer is aware that the right promotion or contest can have a major impact on ratings. Thus, he or she is constantly on the lookout for an appropriate vehicle. In the quest to find the promotion that will launch the station on the path to a larger audience, the PD may seek assistance from one of dozens of companies that offer promotional services.

The PD's major objective is to program for results. If the station's programming fails to attract a sufficient following, the ratings will reflect that unhappy fact. All medium and larger markets are surveyed by ratings companies, primarily Arbitron. Very few small rural markets, with perhaps one or two stations, are surveyed. If a small-market station is poorly programmed, the results will be apparent in the negative reactions of the local retailers. Simply put, the station will not be bought by enough advertisers to make the operation a profitable venture. In the bigger markets, where several stations compete for advertising dollars, the ratings are used to determine which is the most effective or cost-efficient station to buy. PDs constantly monitor the competition by analyzing the ratings and by listening. A radio station's programming is often constructed in reaction to a direct competitor's. For example, similarly formatted stations in the same market often counterprogram newscasts by airing them at different times to grab up their competitor's tune-outs. However, rather than contrast with each other, pop stations tend to reflect one another. This, in fact, has been the basis of arguments by critics who object to the so-called mirroring effect. What happens is easily understood. If a station does well by presenting a particular format, other stations are going to exploit the sound in the hopes of doing well also. WYYY promotes commercial-free sweeps of music and captures big ratings, and soon its competitor programs likewise. "Program directors use what has proven to be effective. It is more a matter of survival than anything. I think most of us try to be original to the degree that we can be, but there is very little new under the sun. Programming moves cyclically. Today we're all doing this. Tomorrow we'll all be doing that. The medium reacts to trends or fads. It's the nature of the beast," notes programmer Mitchell.

Keeping in step with, or rather one step ahead of, the competition requires that the PD knows what is happening around him or her at all times.

Jingles are an imaging element used as a means of establishing a station's position among listeners. Greg Clancy, GM and vice-president, creative, at TM Studios in Dallas, recounts the history of jingle pioneer and programming icon Gordon McLendon in the late 1950s: "Gordon pioneered the Top 40 format on the Mighty 7–90, KLIF in Dallas. He thought if people heard the station name put to a melody, they would have more top-of-mind recall of the station name. This was important when listeners filled out ratings sheets. It turns out Gordon was correct in his assumptions, and a cottage industry was born." Decades later, "jingling" continues to be a viable approach for creating and building station identity and position with audiences. "Jingles are heard on all formats," Clancy notes, and says "the music styles vary greatly. For example, we might use orchestral music for a news imaging package and use a full synthetic composition with effects for a CHR station. We use different vocal configurations for different formats as well."

Probably 60% of the nation's PDs pull an airshift (go on the air themselves) on either a fulltime or part-time basis. A difference of opinion exists among programmers concerning their on-air participation. Many feel that being on the air gives them a true sense of the station's sound, which aids them in their programming efforts. As PM Brad Carson sees it, being an on-air personality enables him to stay on top of a station's performance. "How could it not?" he questions. "Your colleagues you work closely with respect you more. Being 'hands on' helps with understanding. You know what is going on. I think there are obvious benefits." Others contend that the three or four hours that they spend on the air take them away from important programming duties. Major-market PDs are less likely to be heard on the air than their peers in smaller markets because of additional duties created by the size and status of the station. Meanwhile, small- and medium-market stations often expect their PDs to be seasoned air personalities capable of filling a key shift. "It has been my experience when applying for programming jobs that managers are looking for PDs with excellent announcing skills. It is pretty rare to find a small-market PD who does not have a daily airshift. It comes with the territory," says consultant and voiceover talent Gary Begin.

Whether or not PDs are involved in actual airshifts, almost all participate in the production of commercials, public service announcements (PSAs), and promos. In lieu of an airshift, a PD may spend several hours each day in the station's production facilities. The programmer may, in fact, serve as the primary copywriter and spot producer. This is especially true at non-major-market outlets that do not employ a full-time production person.

The PD must possess an imposing list of skills to perform effectively the countless tasks confronting him or her daily. There is no one person, other than the general manager, whose responsibilities outweigh the programmer's. The PD

MULTITASKING PROGRAM DIRECTORS AND THEIR NEED FOR AIR-PERSONALITY COACHES

Lorna Ozmon

When large groups of radio stations began being bought up by a handful of big companies the role of the program director in America began to change dramatically. Add to that the economic recession beginning in 2008 and the multi-tasking program director became the state of the industry. In today's radio environment it is not uncommon for a program director to be responsible for the day-to-day operations of two or more radio stations and pull an air shift as well, making complete attention to every programming detail an almost physical impossibility. Today most program director's days are filled with obligatory meetings having little or nothing to do with the actual programming of the station and dealing with whatever problems and issues arise at any given moment.

FIGURE 3.14
Lorna Ozmon.

One of the most disturbing results of this seismic shift in the roles of radio program directors is a lack of time to be proactive as it relates to coaching and developing their air personalities. A radio station's air personalities can be its most unique and valuable asset. But, because they are so time-challenged, program directors today tend to devote the little time they might find to spend with their air personalities on performance correction and no time on coaching and performance development.

It is for this reason now more than ever before that radio stations are employing an outside radio air-personality coach. An air-personality coach provides radio stations with a service that the program director once performed but no longer can. An outside air-personality or morning show coach has the time to dedicate hours or, as in my case, even days to just one morning show or other radio project. No program director today has even a spare hour much less a spare day to listen to, analyze and prepare a thorough air-personality coaching plan to execute with the air talent in this day and age.

Beyond the issue of time, great air-personality coaches also bring a unique set of specific performance skills to a radio station. These skills include improvisational technique, comedy and creative thinking training, episodic radio content execution tactics, how to build a successful ensemble cast, and character and role development. Most of today's program directors have little or no experience in any of these creative disciplines so the air-personality coach also provides them with a brand new set of skills which increase their value to their radio stations and in the industry in general.

Lorna Ozmon is president of Ozmon Media, Inc., a radio air-personality and morning show development company founded in 1990. She is one of America's leading radio air-personality development specialists working in every format in both commercial and public radio. She holds a BA in theater arts with an emphasis on theatrical direction and was a major market radio air personality, program director and general manager before establishing Ozmon Media, Inc. Her client list include stations owned by Alpha Broadcasting, CBS, Clear Channel, Cox Broadcasting, Emmis, Entercom, Lincoln Financial and NPR.

can make or break the radio station. Summing things up, chief programmer Jimmy Steal states:

> A programmer must possess balance and understanding of both the science and art of show business. A station needs someone who understands that strategies and tactics are for the conference room, and fun, engagement, buzz, innovation, and exceeding listener's expectations are for over the air and online. At Emmis we look for someone who understands the job description and all of the job's duties. It is incumbent upon us to give a detailed definition of what success looks like to a prospective programmer, so an inspirational leader can positively motivate their team of talent.

FIGURE 3.15
A jingle recording session. Clustering around studio microphones enhances vocalists' performances. Courtesy of TM Studios/WestwoodOne.

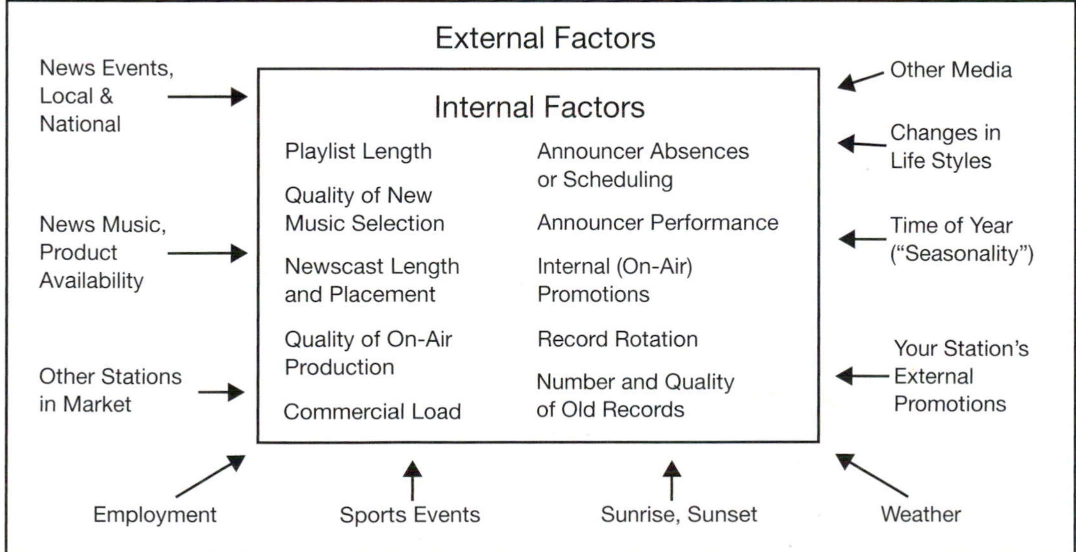

FIGURE 3.16
A model of a station's competitive environment as conceived by Arbitron. Courtesy of Arbitron.

PROGRAMMING A CLUSTER OPERATION

The widespread consolidation of the radio industry since the late 1990s has resulted in a paradigm shift in programming responsibilities. Radio clusters may consist of as many as eight stations. In this situation, one individual is usually assigned to perform the function of general supervisor of all cluster programming, and each of the stations within the cluster has a designated PD, who reports to this person—typically referred to as the director of operations. Radio corporations see it as a macrocosm/microcosm overseer design and arrangement.

As might be imagined, the challenges of programming a cluster are compounded by the very number of the stations involved. As KIMN PD Gregg Cassidy observes:

> Programming a single station is very simple versus programming a cluster. In programming a single station you have all the time necessary to evaluate all areas of your station daily. You can check your air talent each week, reevaluate your music and music rotations, be very creative with your on-air promotions, and take the necessary time to create clever and compelling production. Programming a cluster is like being a father of many children rather than one or two. Time becomes very valuable. In the simplest form, I would devote all my energy to one station per week.

Brad Carson's workday is one that exemplifies the typical routine of the cluster PD. Carson is responsible for three stations in Entercom's Memphis cluster, which includes daily stints for hosting an oldies music show and producing a sports discussion program. The key to his success, he believes, is to establish strong local ties and keep up-to-date with all aspects of his assignments. He explains, "Program directors must keep tabs on all of these things, make the music or programming sound perfect, partner with clients to effectively create ratings and revenue, hire and manage talent, perform an on-air shift in many cases, learn new ways of creating great radio and working with new technology, and having fun with your team." A glimpse at the list of typical day-in-the-life events of Brad Carson reflects these activities:

- Write voiceover scripts and schedule sessions for station voice talents.
- Conduct telephone voiceover talent review sessions, coaching them on the sound of the scripts.
- Write lines on-air talent will voice for upcoming promotions/events.
- Record commercials and personal voice elements with a production person. Discuss the situation that we can't voice a certain advertiser's script because it conflicts with another advertiser we already endorse.
- Conduct an aircheck meeting with morning-show talent.
- Manage email correspondence with network representatives of one of the stations regarding a technical issue.

- Participate in client meeting with station account executive; meet with a client we endorse.
- Schedule music log for the following day and design music log for weekend "theme."
- Execute live on-air giveaway on music station during airshift (create iPhone reminder so I don't miss it).
- Send lineup of guests and "benchmarks" for talk lineup for the following day.
- Design marketing pieces to be used online.
- Review websites and social media elements; correspond about Twitter and Facebook content with Entercom social media content manager.
- Participate in format-specific conference call with other Entercom program directors.
- Program meeting with the general manager.
- Visit with each member of the staff.
- Prepare BMI and ASCAP affidavits.
- Produce afternoon talk show in real time on sports station.
- Upload podcast from that show and prep for next day's show.
- And, last but not least, make a list for the next day's activities.

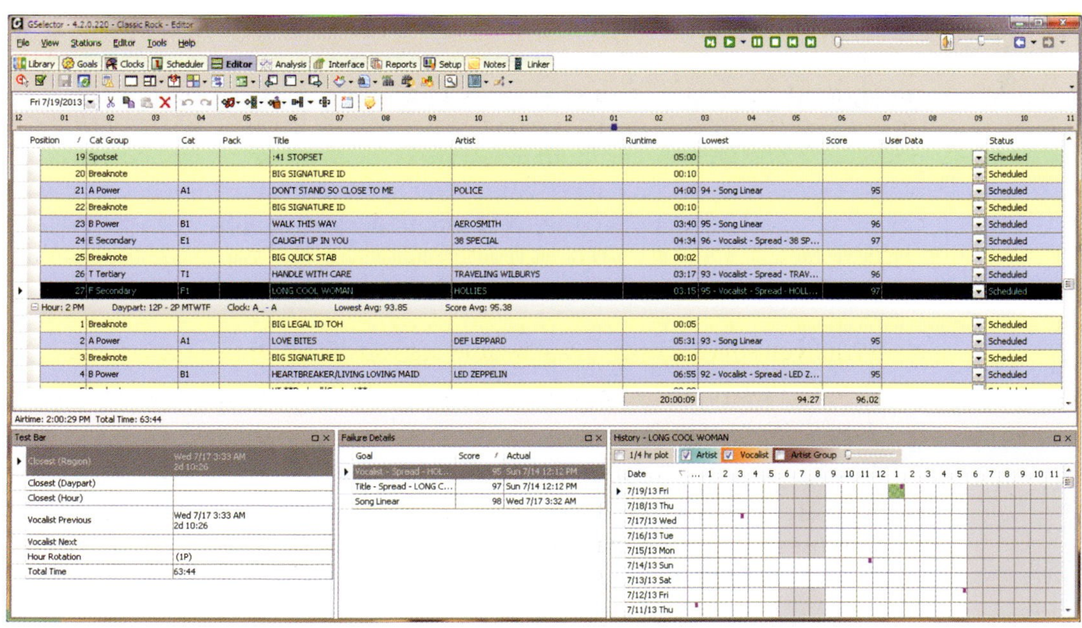

FIGURE 3.17
Music cataloguing and scheduling is managed by apps such as RCS GSelector. Courtesy of RCS.

According to WIZN/WBTZ's Matt Grasso, consolidation has created other problems for programmers:

> Ironically, if not paradoxically, many quality radio pros making top dollars were cut out in the downsizing and consolidation frenzy. This often left lesser talent in markets with clusters. Worse yet with many passionate, quality pros out of work, no one has been minding the store and developing new talent. This has become today's major challenge – finding and developing new talent. There used to be a line out the door of people wanting to be on the radio, but the perception that consolidation and downsizing have killed the job market has dramatically changed that.

SATELLITE RADIO PROGRAMMING DEPARTMENT

What follows is a brief sketch of the original concept for the organizational structure that was put into place at the time of the creation of XM Satellite radio in the early 2000s. XM's chief creative officer, the legendary programmer and consultant Lee Abrams, described how the programming area was set up prior to launch.

> I was the head overseer of programming. For original content, we had a senior vice-president of music. We had a vice-president of Talk, who handled the day-to-day operations of the non-music channels. Original Talk programming, such as Take 5 and XM Traffic, had a PD along with a staff of talent and producers. The vice-president of Talk also spearheaded the relations with third-party providers. Every cluster had a senior PD, and each channel had a PD. Channels often had music directors and deejays. A vice-president also oversaw the pure operational aspects, like computer systems and production. There was a staff of senior production directors who supervised a group of producers, aka audio animators. Supporting the animators were production assistants, who often came from the internship ranks at XM. The programming department also had a music librarian and staff that oversaw the ingestion of music into the system. Keep in mind things changed as they were tweaked to enhance the efficiency of the department. As they say, it was a work in progress.

ELEMENTS OF PROGRAMMING

In contrast with the practices of the 1950s and 1960s, few programmers today entrust the selection and scheduling of music and other sound elements to deejays and announcers. There is too much at stake and too many variables, both internal and external, that must be considered to achieve maximum results within a chosen format.

It has become a very complex undertaking, observes Andy Bloom. "For instance, all of our music is tested via callout." This important implement in the programmer's toolbox is a survey procedure for determining music preferences. So-termed because of its origins as a telephone *call-out* technique to query survey respondents, similar results today can be more efficiently obtained by using online methodologies. In any instance, the use of *song hooks* is the key to collecting useable information about listeners' interests in songs. Hooks are simply snippets edited from full-length recordings that preserve the most-recognizable or attention-grabbing portions of songs—the parts that "catch the ear" of listeners. In many instances, that portion is located in the chorus between the verses. While it's possible to create the hooks in-house, it's also common for programmers to rely on the services of a company that specializes in the creation and syndication of hooks. One such company, Hooks Unlimited, curates a library of almost 150,000 hooks readily available for use in music-testing situations, including callout, online, auditorium, and focus-group settings.

FIGURE 3.18
Hooks Unlimited is a popular source of pre-produced music hooks. Courtesy of Hooks Unlimited.

Music research takes other forms. Bloom continues, "At least one or two perceptual studies are done every year, depending on what questions we need answered. Usually a couple of sets of focus groups per year, too. Everything is researched, and nothing is left to chance." In most cases, the PD determines how much music is programmed hourly and in what rotation and when news, public affairs features, and commercials are slotted. Program wheels (also variously known as sound hours, hot clocks, and format disks)—diagrams depicting the sequence of presentation of music, commercials, and other programming elements—are carefully designed by the PD to ensure the effective presentation of on-air ingredients. In the days prior to the computerization of the on-air presentation, program wheels would be posted in the control studio to inform and guide air talent as to what is to be broadcast and at what point in the hour. Today, while the concept of the wheel is internalized within the software that manages the playout of the various program elements, the decisions about what is to be broadcast and in what order are made by the PD. Although not every station provides deejays with such specific programming schemata, today very few stations leave things up to chance since the inappropriate scheduling and sequencing of sound elements may drive listeners to a competitor. Radio programming has become that much of an exacting science. With few exceptions, stations use some kind of software-assisted formula in conveying their programming material.

According to Brad Carson, program manager for Classic Hits 94.1 KQK in Memphis, "Music stations that want to maximize rotations and use sound strategy to play the right songs the 'right' amount of times use music scheduling software programs like RCS Selector or Music Master. Each of these programs use a virtual 'clock' with songs positioned around imaging elements, commercials, and talk positions where talent/personalities either talk over song intros, between songs into cold intros or before/after commercials within a given hour."

Ed Shane observes:

> When I speak at college classes, there's always a question about why format clock hours are structured the way they are, so let me call what follows "Clock Construction 101." Arbitron diary entries show that the first quarter hour (:00–:15) gets the largest number of new entries, that is, when the radio is turned on for the first time or switched to a new station. The third quarter hour (:30–:45) gets the second largest number. The second quarter hour (:15–:30) gets the third largest number, and the fourth quarter hour (:45–:00) gets the fewest new tune-ins. That pattern is why many stations load their commercial content in the final or fourth quarter hour—trying to prevent a new listener from hearing a commercial as the first thing when tuning. Since the first quarter hour is so valuable in terms of new tune-ins, the most valuable programming elements should be placed in that segment. A music station is advised to load the first quarter hour with Power Current or Power Gold songs, songs that test the best or are the biggest hits. News stations load the latest headlines and their big talk topics into the first quarter hour.

In explaining how station personnel manage the process of song scheduling, Carson says the process begins by determining the appropriate number of songs to be scheduled within the hour.

> A certain total number of songs (this ideal number is often based off what similarly formatted stations that the station monitors from around the country use) is selected; the scheduler then codes the various aspects of those songs. Music schedulers are able to code almost every attribute of their songs including genre, era, gender, tempo, mood and even research-score ranks. Songs considered "powers" play more than various other identifiable categories. But after songs are "auto-scheduled" most program managers/music directors choose to review the entire playlist log by hand to "massage" it. For example, maybe the computer places a "power" song by the Beatles in spot #1 and the next song slotted to play is by the Rolling Stones in spot #2, due to the circumstances of that particular clock. The music scheduler then might see that and just simply "juggle" the #2-spot song by the Rolling Stones with the #3-spot song from KC and the Sunshine Band. It would then go (#1) Beatles, (#2) KC and then (#3) Rolling Stones vs. (#1) Beatles (#2) Rolling Stones then (#3) KC.

Carson notes that careful clock construction could preclude instances such as the example he cites from occurring, but also cautions that a programmer can become too prescriptive in designing the selection "rules." He explains, "With some of these music scheduling programs (like RCS Selector) it's possible to set up so many 'rules' that the program won't place songs in every slot. I think it's valuable to at the very least take a few minutes to review the log and see if there's anything out of sorts that you don't like for the brand. In today's radio, most music programmers also are doing another pass through their log to hand place imaging elements that go perfectly with the scheduled music log." In the instance of RCS software, the Selector companion program Linker integrates the station imaging content into the music schedule.

Indeed, program clocks are set up with the competition and market factors in mind. For example, programmers will devise a clock that reflects morning and afternoon drive periods in their market. Not all markets have identical commuter hours. In some cities morning drive may start as early as 5:30 am; in others it may begin at 7:00 am. The programmer sets up clocks accordingly. The clock structure parallels the activities of the community in which the station operates.

Music stations are not the only ones that use program wheels; News and Talk stations do so as well. News stations, like music outlets, use key format elements to maintain ratings through the hour. Many News stations work their clocks in 20-minute cycles. During this segment, news is arranged according to its degree of importance and geographic relevance, such as local, regional, national, and international. Most News stations lead with their top local stories. News stories of particular interest are repeated during the segment. Sports, weather, and other news-related information, such as traffic and stock market reports, constitute a part of the segment. Elements may be juggled around or different ones inserted during successive 20-minute blocks to keep things from sounding repetitious.

In the Talk format, two-way conversation and interviews fill the space generally allotted to songs in the music format. Therefore, talk wheels often resemble music wheels in their structure. For example, news is offered at the top of the hour, followed by a talk sweep that precedes a spot set. This is done in a fashion that is reminiscent of the Easy Listening format presentation.

Of course, not all stations arrange their sound hours as depicted in these pages. Many variations exist, most inspired and driven by computers, but these examples are fairly representative of some of the program schematics used in today's radio marketplace.

Program wheels keep a station on a preordained path and prevent deejays from deviating from the program-execution philosophy. As stated, each programming element—commercial, news, promo, weather, and so on—is strategically located in the sound hour to enhance flow and optimize impact. Balance is imperative: with too much deejay patter on a station promoting more music and less talk, listeners become disenchanted; with too little news and information on a station targeting the over-30 male commuter, the competition benefits. "When constructing or arranging the program clock, you have to work forward and backward to make sure that everything fits and is positioned correctly. One element out of place can become that proverbial hole in the dam. Spots, jock breaks, music—it all must be weighed before clocking. A lot of experimentation, not to mention research, goes into this," observes radio executive Lorna Ozmon.

THE BROADCAST CLOCK CREATOR

Sample Clock

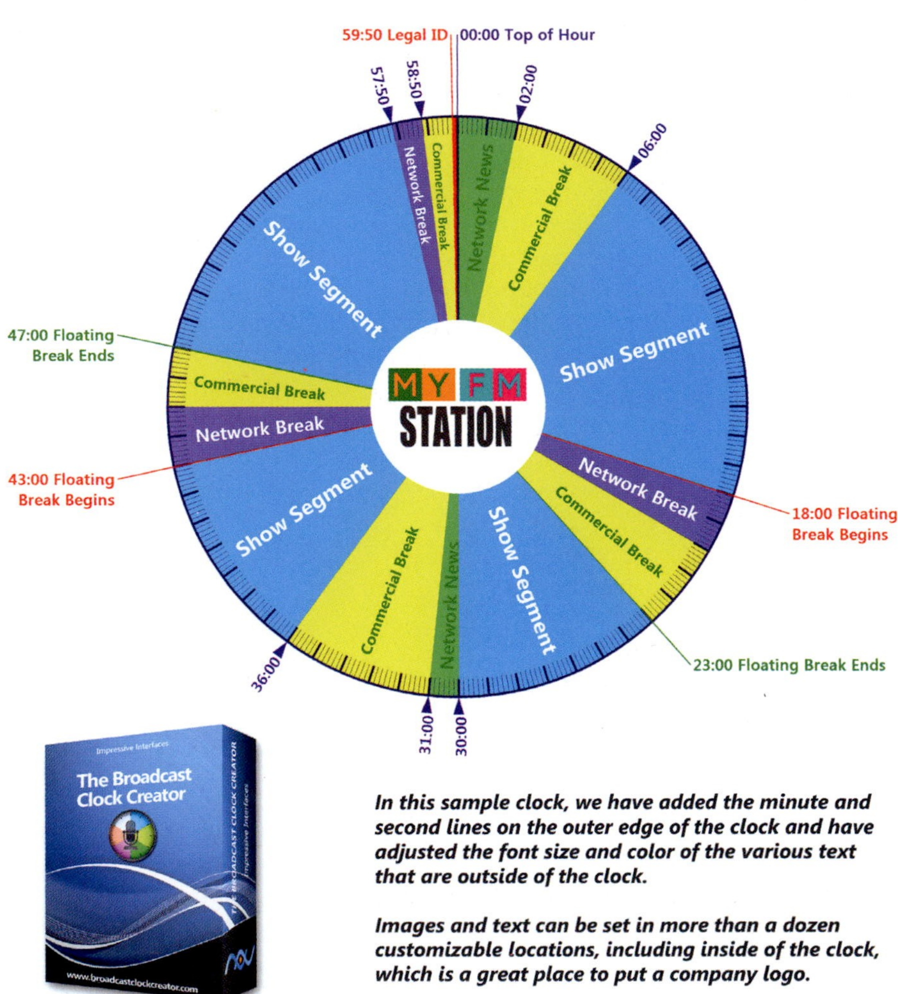

FIGURE 3.19
Software assists programmers with clock construction. Courtesy of Impressive Interfaces.

It was previously pointed out that a station with a "more music" slant limits announcer discourse to schedule additional tunes. Some formats, in particular Easy Listening/Smooth Jazz, have reduced the role of the announcer to not much more than occasional live promos and IDs. Nothing is left to chance. This also is true of stations airing the super-tight hit music format. Deejays say what appears on their monitors and move the music. At stations where deejays are given more control, wheels play a less crucial function. Outlets where a particular personality has ruled the ratings for years often let that person have more input as to what music is aired. However, even in these cases, playlists generally are provided and followed.

The radio personality has enjoyed varying degrees of popularity since the 1950s. Over the years, Top 40, more than any other format, has toyed with the extent of deejay involvement on the air. The pendulum has swung from heavy personality presence in the 1950s and early 1960s to a drastically reduced role in the mid- and later 1960s. This dramatic shift came as the result of programmer Bill Drake's attempt to streamline Top 40. In the 1970s, the air personality regained some of his or her status. WLAC programmer Dick Kent recalls how a certain percentage of listeners could be counted on to appear "at everything the station was promoting . . . and going wherever there was an opportunity to be involved with a music station's format." In the 1980s, the narrowing of hit station playlists brought about a new leanness and austerity that again diminished the jock's presence.

In the mid-1980s, some pop music stations began to give the deejay more to do. Brian Mitchell observes:

> There's sort of a pattern to it all. For a while, deejays are the gems in the crown, and then they're just the metal holding the precious stones in place for another period of time. What went on in the mid-1970s with personality began to recur in the latter part of

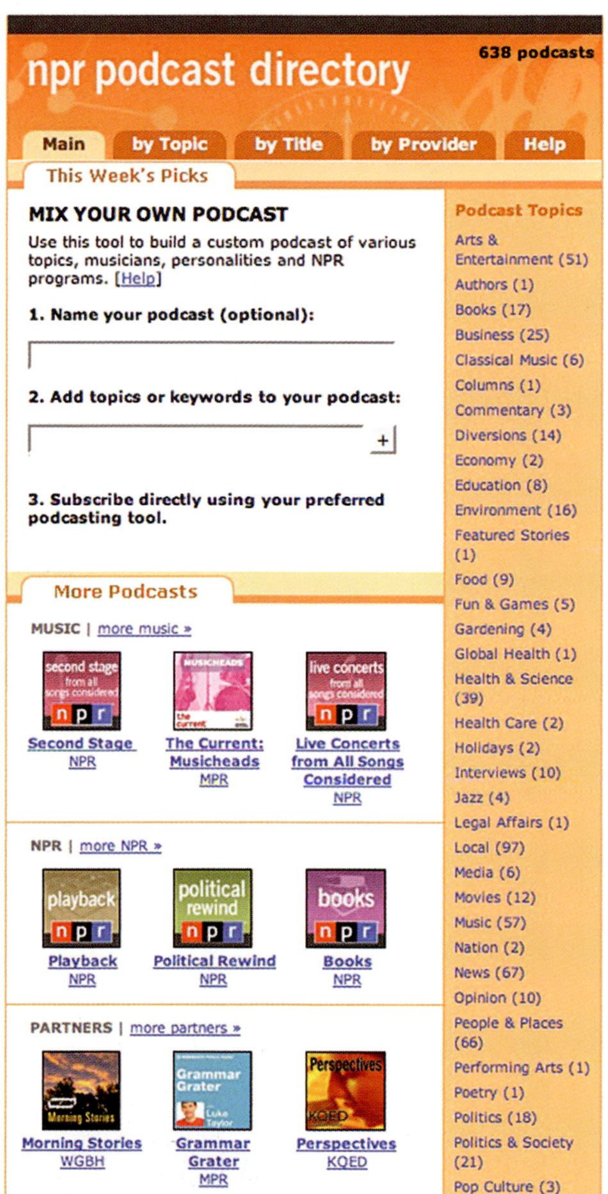

FIGURE 3.20
The use of podcasts continues to grow. Courtesy of NPR.

the 1980s. Of course, there are a few new twists in the tiara, but what it comes down to is the temporary restoration of the hit radio personality. It's a back and forth movement, kind of like a tide. It comes in, then retreats, but each time something new washes up. Deejays screamed at the teens in the 1950s, mellowed out some in the 1960s and 1970s, went hyper again in the 1980s, and conservatism regained favor in the 1990s.

INSIDERADIO.COM RADIO SHOW 2013

FORMAT TRACK TOP FORMATS IN RATED MARKETS

RECORD-SETTING GAINS FOR SPORTS AND SPANISH

The growth of spoken word formats show no signs of slowing down as sports hit a new all-time high again this year. Softer ratings and no presidential race to drive conversation and advertising led the number of news-talk stations to fall back from a peak set a year ago. Thirteen percent of commercial radio stations air a news-talk format, down 1% from 2012, with another 7% airing sports programming – meaning one-in-five commercial stations aren't playing music. After a small pullback ended a decade of continuous gains for Spanish-language formats, their growth has returned. The number of Spanish stations grew 2%, enough to set a new all-time record. The CHR format's ratings hot streak has continued during the past year, leading to a 3% jump in the number of top 40 stations. That's on top of a 7% increase a year earlier, pushing the CHR total to its highest level in two decades. After a five-year slide, interest in the country format is up, driven by surging ratings. The number of country stations is at the highest point since 2004.

Format	2004	2005	2006	2007	2008	2009	2010	2011	2012	2013
Country	2047	2022	2038	2027	2018	1995	1997	1987	2020	2042
News/Talk	1287	1326	1338	1368	1365	1416	1437	1455	1503	1453
Spanish	665	696	706	786	799	803	806	818	816	835
Sports	472	508	535	564	595	634	665	670	692	740
Classic Hits	237	271	429	477	524	582	637	657	657	678
Adult Contemporary	696	683	660	665	670	626	634	607	597	605
Top 40	502	503	484	472	472	484	495	523	559	573
Oldies	811	762	725	709	708	649	637	628	597	566
Classic Rock	451	461	456	456	474	477	481	477	477	486
Hot AC	420	374	378	373	373	409	417	435	420	428
Religion*	329	319	311	287	299	324	322	332	342	336
Rock	282	269	276	281	287	298	294	301	295	299
Adult Standards	458	404	368	369	358	327	265	251	240	227
Black Gospel	274	286	267	253	244	242	235	225	214	212
Contemp. Christian	169	172	150	153	136	162	166	166	171	172
Southern Gospel	204	206	208	204	211	209	197	188	170	172
Urban AC	140	156	167	161	161	162	159	155	152	158
Ethnic	107	115	116	115	118	121	127	131	132	142
Soft AC	319	324	302	242	223	204	173	161	156	141
R&B	157	150	136	134	135	127	128	134	132	131
Alternative Rock	100	103	108	120	121	107	99	101	102	101
Modern Rock	164	151	134	125	122	114	111	101	93	96
R&B Adult/Oldies	50	53	47	41	36	40	48	50	51	46
Variety	41	37	35	37	37	42	43	45	49	46
Pre-Teen	59	60	58	57	56	52	44	39	35	33
Jazz	88	84	78	73	60	40	38	24	36	28
Rhythmic AC				27	24	18	18	16	17	21
Gospel	35	36	32	26	26	25	26	25	23	19
Easy Listening	18	19	21	19	16	18	19	17	19	18
Classical	34	28	29	23	22	23	19	22	20	16
Modern AC	34	23	20	19	21	20	18	20	15	14
Format Not Available	1	1	11	5	7	4	16	12	12	36
TOTAL STATIONS	10651	10602	10623	10668	10718	10754	10771	10773	10814	10870

*Source: M Street Database, July 2013. Format Counts for All Commercial U.S. Stations (does not include HD stations) *Teaching, Variety*

FALL 2013 INSIDE RADIO 13

FIGURE 3.21
Tracking the trends: Top formats in Arbitron-rated markets. Courtesy *Inside Radio*.

In the first decade of the 2000s, with the pressure from so many competing audio options, high foreground personalities are beginning to look attractive once again as an antidote to the music-intensive services.

On the subject of on-air talent, Lynn Christian observes, "Requirements have changed in the past few years. Stations are not just looking for a 'pretty voice.' Today's radio management looks for talent with facile minds who are great observers—people who can listen as well as speak, plus possess the ability to demonstrate a warm and always interesting personality." On the other side of the coin, talent wants their managers to operate in a manner that makes for a positive atmosphere and experience, says Jimmy Steal. "The keys to managing talent are (1) honesty, (2) inspiration, (3) creativity, and (4) empathy."

In addition to concentrating on the role deejays play in the sound hour, the PD pays careful attention to the general nature and quality of other ingredients. Music is, of course, of paramount importance. Songs must fit the format to begin with, but beyond the obvious, the quality of the artistry and the audio mix must meet certain criteria. A substandard musical arrangement or a disc with poor fidelity detracts from the station's sound. Station imaging must integrate effectively with other programming features to establish the tone and tenor of the format. Otherwise they might have the reverse effect of their intended purpose, which is to attract and hold listeners. Commercials, too, must be compatible with the program elements that surround them.

FIGURE 3.22
Many stations have replaced local deejays with national personalities. Tom Joyner is among the most popular. Courtesy of ABC.

In all, the PD scrutinizes every component of the program wheel to keep the station true to form. The wheel helps maintain consistency, without which a station cannot hope to cultivate a following. Erratic programming in today's highly competitive marketplace is tantamount to directing listeners to other stations. At one time, Top 40 stations were the unrivaled leaders of formula programming. Today, however, even Full Service (FS) and Classic Rock outlets, which once were the least formulaic, have become more sensitive to form. The age of freeform commercial radio has long since passed, and it is doubtful, given the state of the marketplace, that it will return. Of course, stranger things have happened in radio.

A RADIO STATION ISN'T JUST A RADIO STATION ANY MORE

Peter Stewart

The business you are in is now so much more than a linear stream of in-the-moment "info-tainment," from one person to many. The live stream of today's programme (and yesterday's, and last week's) can be heard on computers and phones, but must be alongside *added value*.

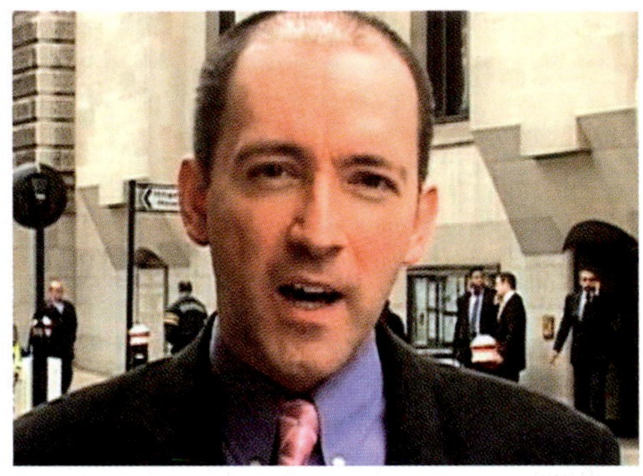

FIGURE 3.23
Peter Stewart.

That's because people aren't passive listeners any more. They are "users" of your station, who want their problems solved: "How can I buy that song, right now?" "How long will my commute home take?" "Where can I get more detail on that author you just spoke with?" "Will it rain this weekend, and if it does, what can I do with the kids that won't cost a fortune?" "How can I sound-off about the increase in the bridge toll?" . . . And they want that help right now!

The solutions you provide on your website and smartphone app will deepen their experience and engagement with your station, show and staff. So you may include a feed of local news, perhaps with the scripts, audio of the most recent bulletin, longer interviews or background information with the newsmakers, links to other sites with in-depth information and statistics; weather reports, almanacs, moving radar forecasts and webcams for whichever town is chosen; live traffic news with feeds from cameras at major junctions; local events that can be filtered according to location, date, price and theme.

You can provide background details of the songs you play, with click-throughs to download them, information on concert dates and album reviews; added background on the guests you have spoken with, how you can contact them, buy their book and possibly download a sample chapter, and links to other sites of similar interest; more information on your advertisers, their location and online discount vouchers; a forum for on-air topics to be discussed off-air with other listeners . . .

We've moved away from "radio stations": we now run businesses that can solve people's problems by providing information, thereby creating a relationship with the public . . . and, yes, making money by selling those pairs of ears and eyes to advertisers. (Absolute Radio in the UK has an online stream of music and commercials which is different from that which is broadcast. On signing up you choose preferences of music and provide details about yourself so you hear the songs you love, and the adverts are from businesses that sell what you are interested in buying. Such a personalized service means the station is truly one-to-one. Subscribers get a better experience, and the advertisers get a better response rate, and the station sales team can charge accordingly.)

The most successful radio stations are now on air, online, and on smartphone apps. And together with Facebook or Twitter, the relatively-passive *radio consumer* turns into a *participator*. If these different platforms are an integral part of your audience's lives and your station's not there, what does that say about your relevance to them? You should be doing all you can to touch your fan as often and in as many ways as possible. And have a relationship with them. Oh, and sell them advertising.

Peter Stewart has been a radio presenter, producer, reporter, news editor, and station manager, and is currently an award-winning London-based author and broadcaster for the BBC. Through face-to-face and distance coaching, and via newsletters, blogs, and books, he has advised some of the top TV and radio personalities, programmers and stations in the UK and around the world on techniques to build their audiences. He has guest lectured at various universities and colleges on broadcasting and news, and written for the BBC's *Ariel* magazine, the actors' newspaper *The Stage*, and, for ten years, a weekly column for *The Radio Magazine*.

Away from the BBC, **Peter Stewart** has authored several books on radio presentation, journalism and social media including *Essential Radio Skills* (2nd edition, Methuen Drama), *Essential Radio Journalism* (Methuen Drama), *Broadcast Journalism* (Focal Press) and (via his website) *Essential Tweeting Skills for Radio Stations*, *Find-A-Line* and *1001 Top Talking Topics*. www.PeteStewart.co.uk @TweeterStewart

STATION WEBSITES, PODCASTS AND BLOGS

In this day and age, nearly every radio station maintains a website. Most do so as an additional marketing tool, but many provide listeners with sites as a cyber-extension of their on-air signals, because so many people sit in front of their computers at work and at home for countless hours. Indeed, a station site is not only for listening, but it's a visual component of a radio station, a means of giving more sight to a once-sightless medium. As consultant Ed Shane puts it, "Social networks add an element radio has long coveted: a screen. Posting pictures via Instagram or videos via YouTube allows the audience to share the experience of an event, a live broadcast or a celebrity interview. YouTube expands from the station's network of 'followers' to the world." Says Ressen Design/Radeo Internet Radio's Darryl Pomicter: "Websites complement all terrestrial broadcast systems, supplementing and expanding content. They give stations reach they never had before—locally, nationally, and globally."

Station websites hold great value for PDs for three vastly different reasons, contends Matt Grasso, WIZN/WBTZ operations manager:

> First off, P1s [*first preference*, the dedicated listeners] spend a lot of time with your radio station, and the website is a way to keep things fresh and exciting for them. Games, exclusive Web-only promotions, staff blogs and bios all provide an exclusive, behind the scenes look at the product. Next, time spent listening (TSL) drives the ratings bus and your online broadcast

> boosts it. There are a lot of people who are procrastinating at work. Plug them into your station. Give them lifestyle news and information and watch your TSL rise. And finally, the website constitutes new inventory. You can clutter your airwaves with so much stuff. Your website is a new place to do business.

Station websites come in all shapes and sizes. That is to say, they can be simple, offering a limited number of links, and they can be highly interactive and multitiered with dozens of links. Not all sites are constructed as income streams, but more and more radio stations are viewing them as another good source of non-traditional revenue. Adding the iTunes Music Store link to their sites to allow their listeners to purchase the tunes they heard on-air was one of the first attempts to monetize the Web presence. Emmis was the first station group to do so on its stations in Chicago, Indianapolis, Austin, and St. Louis. In a more recent development, the products of Radio2Video represent the extension of traditional radio activities into non-traditional areas. In this instance, the company notes on its website that it specializes in creating "broadcast quality, high definition video advertising from radio commercials" to assist stations in taking full advantage of the enhancements that color picture and motion lend to advertising messages on stations' sites.

Larger stations and cluster operations typically hire an individual (a term frequently utilized is manager of information services [MIS] or information technology [IT] specialist) to maintain a station's Web presence. Content responsibilities are the province of other specialists (digital solutions coordinator or similar title); together these employees share responsibilities for maintaining the appearance and relevance of the website. The growing role of station sites has made it another potential career option for those interested in entering the radio field. Clearly, computer skills would rank high on the list of attributes an applicant for this position should possess, as would talent and education in technology and the graphic arts. In addition, an overall knowledge of radio programming and marketing would be of special value. Ironically, a disturbing fact emerged from a recent study conducted by Hofstra University professor Bob Papper on behalf of the Radio Television Digital News Association (RTDNA). Survey results of Web practices at News/Talk-formatted (N/T) radio stations in 2012 indicated that, across markets of all sizes, N/T stations typically delegated website-maintenance responsibilities largely to one fulltime employee and one part-timer. Whether this allocation of employee resources is sufficient for the task is questionable, considering that the successes of N/T stations depend upon the quality and quantity of information they are able to disseminate.

Although podcasts were originally designed for downloading content to iPods and MP3 players, radio stations have found them to be a value-added programming feature. Thousands of podcasts are available on the Internet, and most radio stations now offer podcasts of their on-air features on their websites. Some stations have created exclusive, podcast-only programs. Says consultant

Jason Insalaco, "Podcasting 'exclusives' can drive Web traffic and increase the time listeners spend on the website. For example, website-exclusive interviews with newsmakers, musical artists, entire unedited press conferences, or even the local high school football game can provide supplemental content for station podcasts. It's a good community service, too." Matt Grasso adds, "Podcasts are useful to station programming because it's a way to take the station with you." Grasso asserts that programmers generally were skeptical about the value of podcasting. Now, he says, "they realize that they are just another way to get even closer to the listener."

A blog is a Web page of entries from a single source/author pertaining to a particular subject or topic. The blog may have been the first social media strategy adopted by radio hosts, observes consultant Ed Shane, who notes also that blogs quickly were augmented by Facebook, Twitter, and other social networks. In early 2013, the Pew Research Center reported 67% of Americans were on Facebook, placing this site far ahead of other social platforms.

One indicator of the importance of social media as an element in the engagement of listeners, says Shane, is that NPR Digital issued social media guidelines for its member stations. "Be specific about what you want from your audience" and give the audience "a heads up on tomorrow's topics" are examples of NPR directives. The outline reminded hosts that "Your show is on the radio for one or two hours a day; it's online 24/7."

Shane says he advises his broadcast clients to "be where the listeners are" when they choose social media platforms. "If your listeners are on Facebook, that's where you engage them. If they follow news on Twitter, you want to be there, too. Post traffic information, news about celebrities—whatever they're interested in. Today, information moves at the real-time speed of Twitter, a very current content experience."

He adds that watching trends on Facebook and Twitter constitutes a form of show prep. And he cautions that all social media activity should point back to the station and its website.

Many station personalities and talk show hosts maintain blogs. Observes Insalaco:

> Blogging has become a national phenomenon. Talk show host blogs are a popular component of a station's website. Consumers are processing news at a meteoric pace via the Web, cell phones, and smartphones, so station blogs fit into this scheme. While Americans are no longer at the mercy of the network news broadcasts or the newspaper for daily information, the trend of processing news through opinion (whether a good thing or a bad thing) has developed. Radio hosts can blog about issues related to the topics discussed and the guests they have on their programs. Blogs can billboard upcoming topics and provide listeners an opportunity to interact. Also, show blogs provide additional information

and links to stories discussed on the air. Radio station blogs can feature show rundowns of the day's topics and guests so that listeners remain connected to their favorite radio personality. Blogs are easy to execute and maintain. In sum, stations that embrace blogs and podcasts will gain an upper hand in the competitive radio marketplace.

PROGRAMMING IN A NEW AGE

Ed Shane

Radio needs to think of itself in a new way. We are content creators, content developers, and content providers. Transmission and distribution are irrelevant. That's why Internet-only radio stations show so much promise. Traditional radio is a one-way medium. For much of its reign, it seemed interactive when it engaged the imagination or stimulated phone calls for talk show feedback or contesting. The new "radio" will use a variety of means to distribute content to its constituents.

FIGURE 3.24
Ed Shane.

When a radio station client of ours recently began streaming its audio via the Internet the PD was very excited, because he anticipated hearing from new listeners all over the world who could discover how good his station sounded. The president of the company that owned the station took him to the window and pointed to a house in the neighborhood nearby. "We're not streaming to be heard around the world," he told his PD. "We're streaming so the 12-year-old girl in that house will listen to our station. She doesn't listen to radio, but if she likes what you do, she'll listen on her computer."

Ed Shane, a former programmer, is CEO of Shane Media Services, which he founded in 1977, and Publisher of *Best in Texas® Music Magazine*. The company provides programming direction and custom research to radio stations and media outlets across the USA and works in virtually all formats, notably Country. Ed is the author of the college textbook *Selling Electronic Media*; of the social commentary *Disconnected America*; and of essays in *The Encyclopedia of Radio* and in *The Guide to U.S. Popular Culture*. He also contributes a regular column to *Best in Texas Music Magazine*.

THE PD AND THE AUDIENCE

Facebook, the dominant social media platform in America, continues to increase its market penetration. In the 2012 version of its celebrated *Infinite Dial* series of radio-usage studies, Arbitron estimated that 54% of Americans aged 12-plus had a personal profile on the service, up from 51% in 2011. As observed in 2011, much of that growth stemmed from increased usage by older demographics (45-plus) while the service continues to be nearly ubiquitous among online Americans aged 18–44.

The programmer, regardless of whether he or she works for a broadcast, satellite, or Internet radio station, must possess a clear perception of the type of listener the station management wants to attract. Initially, a station decides on a given format because it is convinced that it will make money with the new-found audience, meaning that the people who tune in to the station will look good to prospective advertisers. The purpose of any format is to win a desirable segment of the radio audience. Just who these people are and what makes them tick are questions that the PD must constantly address to achieve reach and retention. An informed programmer is aware that different types of music appeal to different types of people. For example, surveys have long concluded that heavy rock appeals more to men than it does to women, and that rock music, in general, is more popular among teens and young adults than it is with individuals over 40. This is no guarded secret, and certainly the programmer who is out to gain the over-40 crowd is doing themselves and their station a disservice by programming even an occasional hard rock tune. This should be obvious.

A station's demographics refer to the characteristics of those who tune in: age, gender, income, and so forth. Within its demographics, a station may exhibit particular strength in specific areas or *cells* as they have come to be termed. For example, an AC station targeting the 25–49-year-old group may have a prominent cell in women over 30. The general information provided by the major ratings surveys indicate to the station the age and sex of those listening, but little beyond that. To find out more, the PD may conduct an in-house survey or employ the services of a research firm.

Because radio accompanies listeners practically everywhere, broadcasters pay particular attention to the lifestyle activities of their target audience. A station's geographic locale often dictates its program offerings. For example, hoping to capture the attention of the 35-year-old men, a radio outlet located in a small coastal city along the Gulf of Mexico might decide to air a series of one-minute informational tips on outdoor activities, such as tennis, golf, and deep-sea fishing, which are exceptionally popular in the area. Stations have always catered to the interests of their listeners, but in the 1970s, audience research became much more oriented to lifestyle. In the 1990s, broadcasters delved further into audience behavior through psychographic research, which, by examining motivational factors, provides programmers with information beyond the purely quantitative. Perhaps one of the best examples of a station's efforts to conform to its listeners' lifestyle is *dayparting*, a topic briefly touched on in the discussion of program wheels. For the sake of illustration, let us discuss how a Classic Hits-formatted station may daypart (segmentalize) its broadcast day. To begin with, the station is targeting an over-40 audience, somewhat skewed toward men. The PD concludes that the station's biggest listening hours are mornings between 7:00 and 9:00 am and afternoons between 4:00 and 6:00 pm, and that most of those tuned in during these periods are in their cars commuting to or from work. It is evident to the programmer that the station's programming approach must be modified during drivetime to reflect the needs of the audience. Obviously, traffic reports, news and sports updates, weather forecasts, and frequent time checks are suitable fare for the station's morning audience. The interests of homebound commuters contrast slightly with those of work-bound commuters. Weather and time are less important, and most sports information from the previous night is old hat by the time the listener heads for home. Stock market reports and information about upcoming games and activities pick up the slack. Midday hours call for further modification, because the lifestyle of the station's audience is different. Aware that the majority of those listening are homemakers (in a less enlightened age this daypart was referred to as "housewife" time), the PD reduces the amount of news and information, replacing them with music and deejay conversation designed specifically to complement the activities of those tuned in. In the evening, the station redirects its programming and schedules sports and talk features, going exclusively talk after midnight. All these adjustments are made to attract and retain audience interest.

The PD relies on survey information and research data to better gauge and understand the station's audience. However, as a member of the community that the station serves, the programmer knows that not everything is contained in formal documentation. He or she gains unique insight into the mood and mentality of the area within the station's signal simply by taking part in the activities of day-to-day life. Entercom programmer Brad Carson immerses himself in work with Memphis-area non-profit organizations. Not only does he make a valuable contribution to the community, he also is able to make and sustain connections with audience members. Carson says, "I like helping local charities like St. Jude Children's Research Hospital and Special Kids and Families. I enjoy meeting listeners." A programmer with a real feel for the area in which the station is located, as well as a fundamental grasp of research methodology and its application, is in the best possible position to direct the on-air efforts of a radio station. Concerning the role of audience research, Peter Falconi says, "You can't run a station on research alone. Yes, research helps to an extent, but it can't replace your own observations and instincts." Brian Mitchell agrees with Falconi:

> I feel research is important, but how you react to research is more important. A PD also has to heed his gut feelings. Gaps exist in research, too. If I can't figure out what to do without data to point the way every time I make a move, I should get out of radio. Success comes from taking chances once in a while, too. Sometimes it's wiser to turn your back on the tried and tested. Of course, you had better know who's out there before you try anything. A PD who doesn't study his audience and community is like a racecar driver who doesn't familiarize himself with the track. Both can end up off the road and out of the race.

THE PD AND THE MUSIC

Not all radio stations have a music director. The larger the station, the more likely it is to have such a person. In any case, it is the PD who is ultimately responsible for the music that goes over the air, even when the position of music director exists. The duties of the music director vary from station to station. Although the title suggests that the individual performing this function would supervise the station's music programming from the selection and acquisition of records to the preparation of playlists, this is not always the case. At some stations, the position is primarily administrative or clerical in nature, leaving the PD to make the major decisions concerning airplay. In this instance, one of the primary duties of the music director might be to improve service from distributors representing the recorded music industry to keep the station well-supplied with the latest releases.

This can be accomplished to a great extent by maintaining close ties with the various record distributor reps.

Stations in smaller markets historically haven't been adequately serviced by record labels with new music releases and thus rely on subscription services such as HitDisc from TM Studios or Top Hits U.S.A.® from RPM, Inc. to fill in the gaps in their music libraries. TM Studio's Greg Clancy explains, "As new songs break on the charts, stations require the audio to put these songs on the air. Our HitDisc service is a delivery vehicle that assists the labels and artists by getting the music to the stations for play."

Over the years the music industry and the radio medium have formed a mutually beneficial alliance. It's been said that "politics makes strange bedfellows." That sentiment also has been often applied in describing the love/hate relationship that exists between the radio broadcasting and recorded music industries. Without the product provided by the recording companies, radio would find itself with little in the way of programming material, insofar as 90% of U.S. stations feature recorded music. At the same time, radio serves as the principal means by which the recording industry gets word of its new releases to the general public. Succinctly put, radio sells records.

Although radio stations seldom pay for their music (CDs)—recording companies send at no charge demos of their new product to most stations in return for the publicity stations provide by playing the tunes—it must pay annual licensing fees to performing rights organizations (PROs) to broadcast the copyrighted compositions of the organizations' members. Terrestrial, satellite, and online radio stations almost universally contract with as many as three PROs to manage licensing and payments for the legal public performance of copyrighted compositions: the American Society of Composers, Authors, and Publishers (ASCAP), Broadcast Music Incorporated (BMI), and SESAC (known formerly as the Society of European Stage Authors and Composers; the organization's website says this full name no longer is in use) represent the legal interests of thousands of composers and publishers whose works are performed on stations.

FIGURE 3.25
BMI is one of three prominent performing rights organizations (PROs). Courtesy of BMI.

Stations collectively negotiate through the industry's Radio Music Licensing Committee (RMLC) with the PROs to establish fair and just licensing fees. ASCAP and BMI, the two larger of the three organizations, are fee-based, with payments determined on the basis of station revenue. Both PROs offer a "blanket" license for music stations that "covers" stations' usage of all compositions within the organizations' repertories. In the case of ASCAP, the amount paid by AM and FM stations at this writing was 1.7% of annual gross income. According to ASCAP, non-commercial radio stations "pay an annual fee determined by the U.S. Copyright Office."

These fees range from a few hundred dollars at small, non-commercial, educational stations to tens of thousands of dollars at large, commercial, metro market stations. The music licensing fees paid by stations are distributed to the composers and publishers of the songs broadcast. Contrary to public perception, financial compensation for performing artists and musicians is available only to those who also compose and publish songs that receive "public performance" credit via airplay on terrestrial stations. In fact, for almost seven decades, broadcasters have regarded the publicity for performers and their record labels generated by airplay as equitable compensation.

When framing the Digital Millennium Copyright Act (DMCA), Congress moved in a new direction with respect to the matter of artist compensation. Passed in 1998, the DMCA requires owners of online music websites, including those of broadcast stations and services such as Pandora, to obtain licenses for the legal permission to disseminate copyrighted recorded content online. Permission was required not only for the right to stream copyrighted music recordings but also for commercials utilizing the talents of union members. Securing these rights required payment additional to the fees paid to the PROs for the performance rights associated with the streaming of copyrighted compositions. In sum, the obligation of stations to compensate composers, publishers, and now performers and the record labels as well, was one that many of the pioneer online webcasters were not prepared to meet. The unforeseen financial burden produced a chilling effect on the nascent online radio industry as numerous stations, unable or unwilling to pay up, shuttered their webstreams.

Since 2007 the recorded music industry has advocated passage of legislation that would levy what has been termed a "performance tax" on stations that would be collected and distributed to the community of musicians and record labels. Passage of this legislation would bring about a sea change in the industry, obligating station owners for the first time in the 80-plus-year history of the medium to pay royalties to artists for terrestrial broadcasts of copyrighted recordings. The National Association of Broadcasters (NAB) as of this writing has successfully lobbied against the measure, citing the promotional value that radio broadcasting afforded the recorded music industry as sufficient compensation and hinting to the potential for job cutbacks at the local-station level if the legislation passes.

In a move that attracted industry attention, Clear Channel Communications announced in 2012 that it agreed to share a percentage of its broadcast revenues with Nashville record label Big Machine in return for label consideration. Clear Channel anticipates the deal with the label, whose roster includes Taylor Swift, Tim McGraw, and Rascal Flatts, will propel the growth of iHeartRadio, its online content aggregator app. The company subsequently struck deals with other labels; at the time of writing, industry trade publications are reporting that Warner Music Group, Glassnote Entertainment Group, DashGo, rpm Entertainment, Naxos, Black River Entertainment, and six other labels also have signed sharing agreements with Clear Channel. In another groundbreaking deal, the 1970s-era rock band Fleetwood Mac became the first group to enter into a revenue-sharing agreement when it signed a deal in 2013 with Clear Channel. Other prominent corporate owners, notably Entercom, Greater Media, and Beasley Broadcast Group, Inc., have negotiated sharing agreements with record labels. CBS Radio created the position director/music initiatives, whose responsibilities include creating partnerships with labels for the purpose of promoting established and developing artists. These relationship-development announcements are strong indicators that the two industries are discovering the mutual benefits that can be derived through partnership agreements.

Managing the Music Library

When music arrives at the station, whether it is in physical or electronic form, the music director (sometimes more appropriately called the music librarian or music assistant) processes the recordings through the system. This may take place after the PD has screened them. Songs are categorized, indexed, and eventually added to the library if they suit the station's format. Programmer Jon Lutes suggests this approach to the classifications of songs, designating music categories in the following manner: New Music, Medium Current, Hot Current, Hot Recurrent, Medium Recurrent, Bulk Recurrent, Power Gold, Secondary Gold, Tertiary Gold, and so forth. It must be emphasized that each station approaches cataloging in its own fashion as there are no FCC rules that speak to this activity. Here is a simple example. An AC outlet receives an album by a popular female vocalist whose last name begins with an L. The PD auditions the album and decides to place three cuts into regular on-air rotation. The music director then assigns the cuts the following catalog numbers: L106/U/F, L106/D/F, and L106/M/F. L106 indicates where the album may be located in the library, either in a physical storage location or in a software database. In this case, the library is set up alphabetically and then numerically within the given letter that represents the artist's last name. In other words, this would be the 106th album found in the section reserved for female vocalists whose names begin with an L. The next symbol indicates the pace (termed "tempo") of the cut: U(p) tempo, D(own) tempo, and M(edium) tempo. Subcategorizing songs by tempo enables the programmer to adjust the pacing of the presentation. The F that follows the tempo symbol indicates the artist's gender: Female.

Playlists are then assembled and stored as a log file for playout in automated or live-assist facilities or printed for use in stations operated manually by the deejays. The music director sees that these lists are placed in the control room for use by the deejays. This last step is eliminated when the on-air studio is equipped with a computer terminal. Deejays then simply punch up the playlists designed for their particular airshifts. Ed Shane offers, "To hone the music mix for proper balance and rotation, stations use music rotation software from a variety of suppliers. The most-used software program is GSelector from Radio Computing Services (RCS), which also supplies music test analysis software, traffic software, and a digital studio-operation system" (see Figure 3.27).

Without a doubt, the use of computers in music programming has become standard, especially in larger markets where the cost of computerization is absorbed more easily. The number of computer companies selling both hardware and software designed for use by programmers has soared. Among others

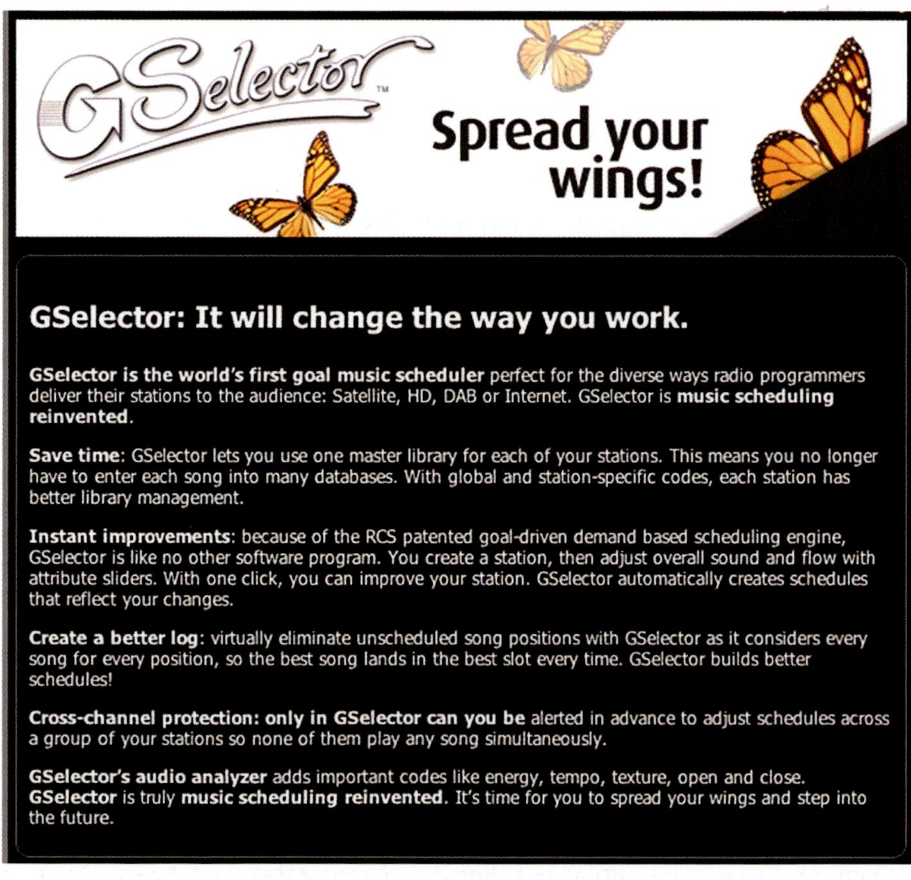

FIGURE 3.26
A host of computerized music programming services is used by the stations. Courtesy of RCS.

providing computerized music systems, Micropower Corporation's Powergold, A-Ware Software's Music Master, Music 1's Music Scheduling Software, Natural Music from Broadcast Software International's Natural Music, and the Carter Consulting product, Music Mix are some of the most successful and widely used. *Billboard,* in both its print and online versions, and *Mediabase* remain valued sources of music industry information. Format-specific chart and artist information can be found on the All Access Music Group website and in its emailed newsletters.

In light of the extensive reliance on computers, former Shane Media consultant Jon Lutes cautioned that "Music scheduling involves more than punching a few buttons on your computer keyboard. It helps to have a basic understanding of how the computer actually operates and what the particular software you are using will and will not do."

At those radio stations where the music director's job is less administrative and more directorial, this individual will actually audition and select what songs are to be designated for airplay. However, the music director makes decisions based on criteria established by the station's programmer. Obviously, a music director must work within the station's prescribed format. If the PD feels that a particular song does not fit the station's sound, he will direct the music director to remove the cut from rotation. Since the PD and music director work closely together, this seldom occurs.

Historically, a song's rotation usually is relative to its popularity, as determined by its position on national charts. For instance, songs that enjoy top ranking, say those in the Top 10, will get the most airplay on hit-oriented stations. When songs descend the charts, their rotation decreases proportionately. Former chart-toppers are then assigned another rotation configuration that initially may result in one-tenth of their former airplay, and eventually even less. In addition to the trade pubs, PDs and music directors derive information pertaining to a record's popularity from listener surveys, song download information, and numerous other sources. Stations that do not program from the current charts compose their playlists of songs that were popular in years gone by. In non-hit formats, there are no "power-rotation" categories or hit positioning schemata; a song's rotation tends to be more random, although program wheels are used. On the CHR front, Shane notes that:

> There's a major change in the way charts are constructed. The original *Billboard* Hot 100 chart was based substantially on record sales. *The Gavin Report* and other "tipsheets" used reports from radio station music directors who fed information on the positions on their own local charts, some validated by sales and requests—some not.

When *R&R* (the trade publication *Radio & Records*) was launched in 1974, its charts were also compiled from reports from radio station programmers. *R&R,* however, mixed industry news and commentary to create a niche for itself as

```
**REMEMBER: FORWARD MOMENTUM!! WHY SHOULD THE LISTENER KEEP LISTENING?**

                 ********************************
                 *           WIZN-FM            *
                 * 10 AM  Wednesday  10-23-02   *
                 ********************************
A R T I S T/A L B U M              TITLE                    RUNTIME  YR   CAT
==============================================================================

------------------------------------------------------------------------------
 00:00  LEGAL I.D.                                          5025   :08
------------------------------------------------------------------------------
STEVE MILLER BAND                TAKE THE MONEY AND RUN                 E/ 2:51
FLY LIKE AN EAGLE
------------------------------------------------------------------------------
 02:59  SHOTGUN                                             5050   :05
------------------------------------------------------------------------------
TOM PETTY                        RUNNING DOWN A DREAM                   F/ 4:23
FULL MOON FEVER                         54.00
------------------------------------------------------------------------------
 07:27  SPEED BREAK                                         5605   :08
------------------------------------------------------------------------------
J. GEILS BAND                    MUST OF GOT LOST                       D/ 6:34
LIVE BLOW YOUR FACE OUT (ON CD)         50.00
------------------------------------------------------------------------------
 14:09  POSITIONER                                          5035   :08
------------------------------------------------------------------------------
PRETENDERS                       BRASS IN POCKET(I'M SPECI              E/ 3:01
THE PRETENDERS                          50.00
------------------------------------------------------------------------------
 17:18  SHOTGUN                                             5050   :05
------------------------------------------------------------------------------
HEART                            CRAZY ON YOU                           D/ 4:54
DREAMBOAT ANNIE                         69.00
------------------------------------------------------------------------------
 22:17  BOTTOM HOUR                                         5016   :08
------------------------------------------------------------------------------
CLASH                            TRAIN IN VAIN                          E/ 3:13
LONDON CALLING                          43.00
------------------------------------------------------------------------------
 25:38  BREAK ONE/BACKSELL/LIVE PROMO                       5606  1:00
------------------------------------------------------------------------------
ERIC CLAPTON                     FOREVER MAN                            F/ 3:12
BEHIND THE SUN
------------------------------------------------------------------------------
 29:50  BOTTOM HOUR                                         5016   :08
------------------------------------------------------------------------------
MANFRED MANN'S EARTH BAND        BLINDED BY THE LIGHT                   E/ 7:07
HIGHS OF 70'S CD                        80.00
------------------------------------------------------------------------------
 37:05  BREAK TWO/PRE-SELL 10-IN-A-ROW                      5607  1:00
------------------------------------------------------------------------------
DEEP PURPLE                      HUSH                                   D/ 4:26
WHEN WE ROCK WE ROCK, WHEN WE ROLL      49.00
------------------------------------------------------------------------------
 42:31  SHOTGUN                                             5050   :05
------------------------------------------------------------------------------
```

FIGURE 3.27
Computerized logging has made station programming even more exacting a science. Courtesy of WIZN-FM.

the most important of the music trade publications in the eyes of the music (record) industry. Because the charts were based on verbal reports from local stations, the system was too easily manipulated by a station programmer who might report play but not actually play the song. This practice was known as a "paper add" because the record was added to the playlist only on paper and did not receive airplay. In 1989, *Billboard* became the first trade publication to track radio airplay as it happened and to count "spins," or plays, in compiling charts. *Billboard* and its companion publication, *Airplay Monitor*, used Broadcast Data Systems (BDS) to electronically detect airplay by matching segments of songs called "footprints" to actual play on stations monitored over the air. The practice of paper adds decreased because a song reported to *R&R* could be tracked in BDS detections. In mid-1999 both *R&R* and *The Gavin Report* (both are now defunct) began using charts based on airplay detection with information compiled by MediaBase, a monitoring service owned by Premiere Radio Networks.

Constructing a station playlist is the single most important duty of the music programmer. What to play, when to play it, and how often are some of the key questions confronting this individual. The music director relies on a number of sources, both internal and external, to provide the answers but also must cultivate an ear for the kind of sound the station is after. Some people are blessed with an almost innate capacity to detect a hit, but most must develop this skill over a period of time.

ADVICE TO PROGRAMMERS

Frank Bell

Rule 1: Follow the Listeners, Not the Format

So many people in radio get caught up in terms like CHR, Hot AC, Alternative, and AAA that they lose track of their goal: finding listeners.

Consumers of radio think in terms of "what I like" and "what I don't like." By researching your listeners' tastes and giving them what they want (as opposed to what fits the industry's definition of what they should have), you'll maximize your chances for success.

FIGURE 3.28
Frank Bell. Courtesy of Sky News.

Rule 2: Think Outside In, Not Inside Out

The fact that one company may now own several stations in a market and is capable, for example, of skewing one FM toward younger females and the other toward older females does not mean that you will automatically "dominate females."

The only reality that counts is that of the listener. If listeners feel your station serves a meaningful purpose for them, they will happily cast their Arbitron vote in your favor.

If they believe you are simply duplicating what is already available elsewhere on the dial, you will be doomed to ratings obscurity.

Rule 3: Early to Bed, Early to Rise, Advertise, Advertise, Advertise

In the Arbitron game of unaided recall, the dominant issue is "top-of-mindness," regardless of whether Arbitron is measuring unaided recall with diaries or actual behavior with Personal People Meters.

The best way to get that is through advertising your name and your station's benefits on your own air and on any other medium you can afford. Just for fun, here's a diagram I sometimes use to show first-time PDs the various factors that influence their station's ratings:

$$\frac{X - Y}{A} \times B = \text{Your Ratings}$$

X is what your station does. Y is what your direct competitors do. A represents "environmental" factors in the market, such as what's on TV during the survey, riots, floods, earthquakes, and major sporting events. B is what the rating service does. In the case of Arbitron, this would include the response rate, editing procedures, and distribution of diaries by race, age, and sex.

The most important thing to understand is that as PD, the only part of the equation you can control is X. Do the best you can to keep your station sounding compelling, entertaining, and focused on its target audience, and don't get an ulcer over those elements you can't control.

After graduating from American University in 1977, **Frank Bell** embarked on a radio adventure covering 33 years and hundreds of successful stations. Beginning as an on-air talent, he bought his first radio station with some friends at age 25 and later applied those programming, research and marketing skills as a corporate executive on behalf of privately owned companies like Keymarket Communications and publicly traded Sinclair Communications and Cumulus Media. In 2010, he joined 13 Management in Nashville to oversee radio station and record label relations for international superstar Taylor Swift.

THE PD AND THE FCC

The government is especially interested in the way a station conducts itself on the air. For instance, the PD makes certain that his or her station is properly identified once an hour, as close to the top of the hour as possible. The ID must include the station's call letters and the town in which it has been authorized to broadcast. Failure to properly identify the station is a violation of FCC rules.

Other on-air rules that the PD must address have to do with program content and certain types of features. For example, profane language, obscenity, sex- and drug-related statements, and even innuendos in announcements, conversations, or music lyrics jeopardize the station's license. The FCC prohibits indecent and profane broadcasts during certain hours of the day, and the cost for violating this rule can cost the station dearly. For example, in 2006, the Commission raised the maximum charge for offenses in this category from $32,500 to $325,000 per violation. Its issuance of notices of apparent liability for forfeiture has been on a dramatic rise for infractions surrounding on-air indecency since the early 2000s as the result of some highly publicized incidents perpetrated by radio personalities like Bubba the Love Sponge, Opie & Anthony, and Howard Stern (now beyond the reach of these rules on satellite radio). Despite the significant increase in the amount of the fine the Commission has deferred its pursuit of enforcement since 2006. On its website the FCC cites as its reason its "ongoing litigation" that is "raising questions about the Commission's indecency standard." Intervening court decisions since 2006 have promulgated additional challenges to the FCC's authority to regulate indecency.

Political messages and station editorials are carefully scrutinized by the programmer. On-air contests and promotions must not resemble lotteries in which the audience must invest to win. A station that gets something in return for awarding prizes is subject to punitive actions. Contest rules must be clearly delineated and publicized. PD eyes and ears must be attentive to station promotions that create hoaxes, which could endanger public safety. No one associated with the station may receive payment for plugging a song or album on the air. This constitutes "payola" or "plugola" and was the cause of great industry upheaval in the late 1950s. Today, PDs and station managers continue to be particularly careful to guard against any recurrence, although there have been charges that such practices still exist.

In fact, in the mid-2000s, the FCC began a formal investigation into payola allegations against four major radio groups: CBS Radio, Clear Channel, Entercom, and Citadel. It was the largest federal inquiry since the payola scandals prompted congressional hearings in 1960. Indeed, PDs must be vigilant of this illegal practice, which seems impervious to eradication.

The PD must monitor both commercial and non-commercial messages to ensure that no false, misleading, or deceptive statements are aired, and that sponsors and endorsers are properly identified, including so-called "pay for play" arrangements. Additionally, it is the PD's responsibility to ensure that the content of station promotional messages excludes any distortion of the station's ratings survey results. A station that is not number one and claims to be is lying to the public as far as the FCC is concerned, and such behavior is not condoned.

License renewal programming promises must be addressed by the PD. The proportion of non-entertainment programming, such as news and public affairs features, pledged in the station's renewal application must be adhered to, even though such requirements have been all but eliminated. A promise is a promise. If a station claims that it will do something, it must abide by its word.

The PD helps maintain the station's Emergency Alert System (EAS), making certain that proper announcements are made on the air and that the testing protocol is followed. PDs also instruct personnel in the proper procedures used when conducting on-air telephone conversations to guarantee that the rights of callers are not violated.

The station log (which ultimately is the chief engineer's responsibility) and program log (no longer required by the FCC but maintained by most stations anyway) are examined by the PD for accuracy. In addition, the station manager may assign the PD the responsibility for maintaining the station's Public Inspection File. If so, the PD must be fully aware of what documents the file is required to contain. The FCC and many state broadcast associations will provide station operators with a Public Inspection File checklist upon request. This information is available in the *Code of Federal Regulations* (47CFR73.3526) as well.

Additional programming areas of interest to the FCC include procedures governing rebroadcasts and subcarrier activities. The PD also must be aware

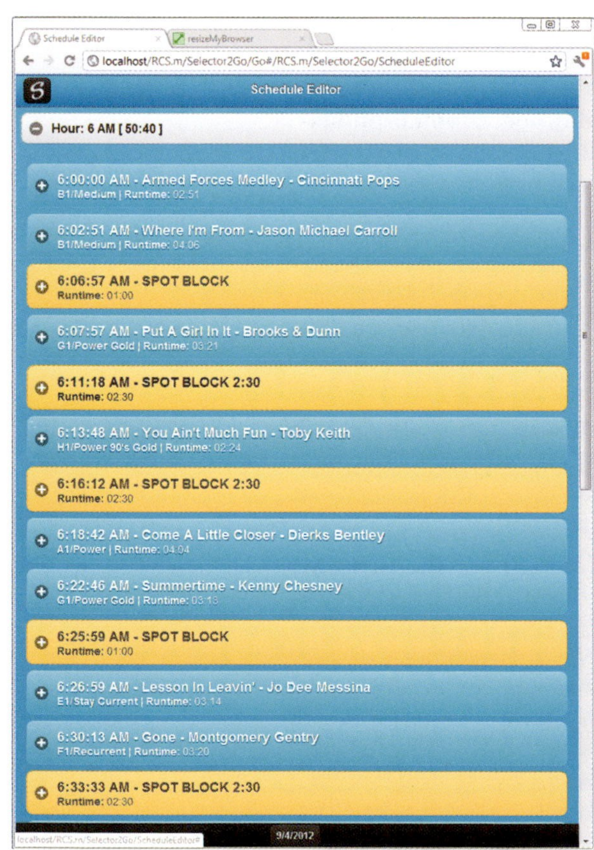

FIGURE 3.29
Music scheduling software, adapted for smartphone and tablet users. Courtesy of RCS.

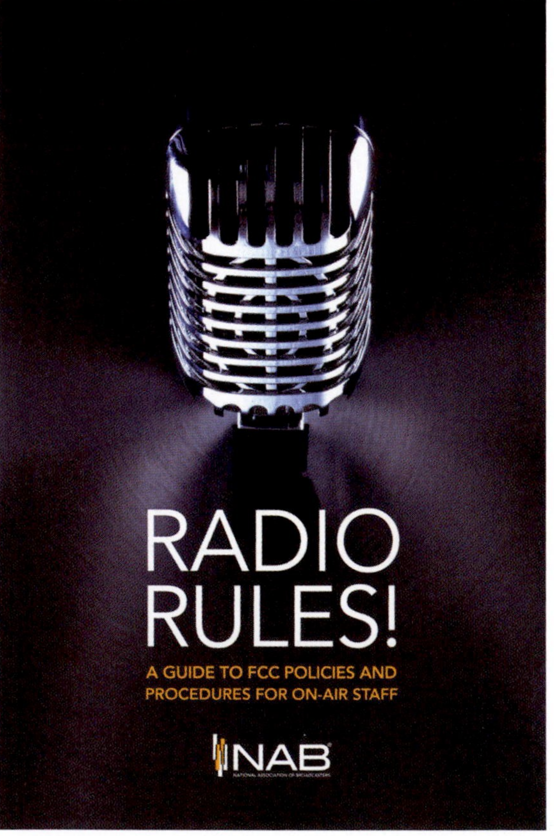

FIGURE 3.30
Cover image of *Radio Rules!* Courtesy of National Association of Broadcasters.

that the government is keenly interested in employment practices. The programmer, station manager, and other department heads are under obligation to familiarize themselves with equal employment opportunity (EEO) and affirmative action rules. An annual employment report must be sent to the FCC.

Detailed information about FCC regulations and practices of specific interests to programmers and air talent may be found in the publication, *Radio Rules! A Guide to FCC Policies and Procedures for On-Air Staff*. Published by the National Association of Broadcasters (NAB) and available from the NAB Store at nabstore.com, *Radio Rules!* is a concise reference document that examines more than two dozen topics related to programming and internal station operations.

THE PD AND UPPER MANAGEMENT

The pressures of the PD's position should be apparent by now. The station or cluster programmer knows well that his or her job entails satisfying the desires of many—the audience, government, air staff, and, of course, management. The relationship between the PD and the station or corporation's upper echelon is not always serene or without incident. Although their alliance is usually mutually fulfilling and productive, difficulties can and do occur when philosophies or practices clash. Radio legend Dick Fatherly summarized the delicate nature of the PD-GM relationship:

> Most inhibiting and detrimental to the PD is the GM who lacks a broad base of experience but imposes his opinions on you anyway. The guy who has come up through sales and has never spent a minute in the studio can be a real thorn in the side. Without a thorough knowledge of programming, management should rely on the expertise of that person hired who does. I don't mean, "Hey, GM, get out of the way!" what I'm saying is, don't impose programming ideas and policies without at least conferring with that individual who ends up taking the heat if the air product fails to bring in the listeners.

Station manager Chuck Ducoty contends that managers can enhance as well as inhibit the programmer's style:

> I've worked for some managers who give their PDs a great deal of space and others who attempt to control every aspect of programming. From the station manager's perspective, I think the key to a good experience with those who work for you is to find excellent people from the start and then have enough confidence in your judgment to let them do their job with minimal interference. Breathing down the neck of the PD is just going to create tension and resentment.

Programmer Peter Falconi believes that both the PD and the manager should make a sincere effort to get to know and understand one another. "You have

FIGURE 3.31
The Hispanic radio format attracts large and loyal audiences. Courtesy of Spanish Radio Group.

to be on the same wavelength, and there has to be an excellent line of communication. When a manager has confidence and trust in his PD, he'll generally let him run with the ball. It's a two-way street. Most problems can be resolved when there is honesty and openness."

Programmer Andy Bloom offers this observation: "Great upper management hires the best players, gives them the tools to do their job, and then leaves them alone. A winning formula."

An adversarial situation between the station's PD and upper management does not have to exist. The station that cultivates an atmosphere of cooperation and mutual respect seldom becomes embroiled in skirmishes that deplete energy—energy better spent raising revenues and ratings.

WPAT 930 AM Metro NY	
*****ALL JEWISH ALL THURSDAY NIGHT*****	
10:00–10:30 PM	**INNER MEANING WITH KIM CHEROVSKY.** Interviews on Judaism and spirituality with special guest Rabbi Jacob Jungreis
10:30–11:00 PM	**THE TOP TEN JEWISH MUSIC COUNTDOWN.** FAVORITE Jewish music of the week.
11:00–12:00 AM	**TALKLINE WITH ZEV BRENNER.** *AMERICA'S LEADING JEWISH PROGRAM. LIVE CALL IN WITH NEWSMAKER GUESTS AND CELEBRITIES MAKING HEADLINES IN THE JEWISH WORLD.*
12:00–12:30 PM	**BETWEEN THE LINES: THE TORAH CODES.** With Dr. Robert Wolf and Joel Gallis.
12:30–2:00 AM	**THE VOICE OF JERUSALEM WITH AVI. THE LATEST NEWS, SHMOOZ, AND CONTESTS LIVE FROM ISRAEL.**
2:00–3:00 AM	**THE TED SMITH SHOW.** Interview show on health and social issues.
3:00–4:30 AM	**THE TOP TEN JEWISH MUSIC COUNTDOWN.**
4:30–5:00 AM	**LIVE FROM ISRAEL.** The latest up to date news from Israel with Dov Shurin.

FIGURE 3.32
Many stations ultraniche (position) their programming. Courtesy of WPAT.

CHAPTER HIGHLIGHTS

1. The AC format, in its variations, features older pop hits (since the 1970s) and more recent songs to supplement a library of current pop standards. It appeals particularly to 25–49-year-old females, which attracts advertisers. It often utilizes music sweeps and clustered commercials. AC has spawned a variety of subgenres, including Adult Hits, Adult Standards, and iPod imitators Jack and Mike.
2. CHR features current, fast-selling hits from the Top 40. It targets teens, broadcasts minimal news, and is very promotion/contest-oriented. The introduction of Arbitron's PPM audience measurement technology suggests renewed audience interest in the format.
3. Country is the fastest growing format since the 1970s. More prevalent in the South and Midwest, it attracts a broad age group and offers a variety of subformats. Recently it has become the second-highest rated format nationally for teen listeners.
4. Easy Listening/Smooth Jazz stations evolved from the Beautiful Music stations of the 1960s and 1970s. Featuring mostly instrumentals and minimal talk, many stations have become automated and use prepackaged programming from syndicators. The primary audience is over 50. Its following has dwindled in recent years owing to myriad softer AC formats.
5. Rock or AOR stations began in the mid-1960s to counter Top 40 stations. They featured music sweeps with a large airplay library, and they played rock album cuts. News was minimal. The format attracted a predominantly male audience aged 18–34. Modern Rock and Alternative Rock are format variants.
6. All-News stations rotate time blocks of local, regional, and national news and features to avoid repetition. The format requires three to four times the staff and budget of most music operations and, due to the operating expense, the format is heard only on a few major-market stations.
7. All-Talk combines discussion and call-in shows. It is primarily a medium- and major-market format. Like All-News, All-Talk is mostly found on AM (and is the domain of conservative talkers) but is now finding a home on the FM band. All-Sports has boosted the non-music format's numbers and now is offered by several networks, including the CBS and NBC offerings that debuted in 2013.
8. The Nostalgia playlist emphasizes popular tunes from the 1940s and pre-rock 1950s, presenting its music in sweeps with a relatively low deejay profile.
9. The Oldies playlist includes hits between the 1950s and 1960s, relying on veteran air personalities. Commercials are placed randomly and songs are spaced to allow deejay patter.
10. Classic Rock concentrates on tunes once primarily featured by AOR stations. Meanwhile, Classic Hit stations fill the gap between Oldies and CHR outlets with playlists that draw from the Top 40 charts of the 1970s and 1980s.
11. UC is the "melting pot" format, attracting a heterogeneous audience. Its upbeat, danceable sound, and hip, friendly deejays attract the 18–34 age group. Contests and promotions are important.
12. Classical commercial outlets are few, but they have a loyal audience. Primarily an FM format appealing to a higher-income, college-educated (upscale, 25–49 years old) audience, Classical features a conservative, straightforward air sound.

tactics:programming
Programming Report from Shane Media Services

PROGRAM DIRECTOR - TEN TACTICS FOR SUCCESS

There are no schools to attend to become a Program Director. Many people fall into the job without a clue as to what the job really entails. Here are 10 basic points for PD success:

1. Show up. Not just for work. Show up at 2AM and visit with the overnight jock. Get to know that person in their time zone. Show up at remotes. Know how your airstaff and promotions people put on a show. Be visible both in and out of the station.
2. Listen up. You can't listen 24 hours a day, but you can tape when you must sleep. Tape the competition when you're monitoring your own shop. Don't listen as a programmer all the time. Try to slip into the attitude of your average listener to determine how well your station is delivering the format and serving your town.
3. Clean up. If you notice something wrong, why wait to make an adjustment? Eliminate small problems before they become large ones.
4. Take notes. Who's doing what in your town? Be aware of the "big picture" in your market, like an air traffic controller. If you need to make an instant adjustment, you'll be prepared.
5. Make notes. How many times have you had a brilliant idea in the middle of the night, and forgotten it by morning? Keep a note pad and pencil or mini recorder by your bed, in your car, wherever you go. A simple phrase or word jotted down quickly can bring back that concept when you've got time to develop the idea.
6. Leave notes. We are in the business of communicating, yet often do a poor job of getting a message from one end of the station to the other. Leave notes on the music log, a discrepancy sheet, a slip of paper in the phone message slot. Get in the habit of noting your thoughts to others, and watch your effectiveness as a manager improve.

FIGURE 3.33
Rules for success. Courtesy of Shane Media.

13. Religious stations are most prevalent on the AM band. Religious broadcasters usually approach programming in one of two ways. One includes music as a primary part of its presentation, whereas the other does not.
14. Ethnic stations serve the listening needs of minority groups. Black and Hispanic listeners constitute the largest ethnic audiences.
15. Full Service (FS) stations (formerly MOR) rely on the strength of air personalities and features. Mostly an AM format, FS attempts to be all things to all people, attracting an over-40 audience.
16. Niche formats, like All-Children, Business, and Tourist Radio, are popping up all over the dial as the listening audience becomes more diffused and interest grows in HD^2 stations.
17. Public and non-commercial stations typically employ a block format promoting diversity rather than a single form of programming. NPR is proactively developing its online presence and podcast library.
18. PDs are hired to fit whatever format the station management has selected. They are chosen primarily for their experience, although education level is important.
19. The PD is responsible for everything that is aired. Second in responsibility for in-house operations to the general manager (except in a cluster arrangement with a director of operations), the PD establishes programming and format policy; hires and supervises on-air, music, and production personnel; handles the programming budget; develops promotions; monitors the station and its competitors and assesses research; is accountable for news, public affairs, and sports features; and may even pull an airshift.

20. The PD's effectiveness is measured by ratings in large markets and by sales in smaller markets.

21. The PD determines the content of each sound hour, utilizing program clocks to ensure that each element—commercial, news, promo, weather, music, and so on—is strategically located to enhance flow and optimize impact. Even News/Talk stations need program clocks.

22. PDs must adjust programming to the lifestyle activities of the target audience. They must develop a feel for the area in which the station is located, as well as an understanding of survey information and research data.

23. The PD must also ensure that the station adheres to all FCC regulations pertaining to programming practices, anticipating problems before they occur. Indecent programming has resulted in huge fines, so PDs must be especially vigilant in this area.

24. Payola (plugola) has plagued the medium since the 1950s and continues to this day. The illegal pay-for-play practice requires careful monitoring by the station's PD and manager to ensure it does not occur. Large fines have been dealt to those stations violating the FCC laws governing this practice.

25. Websites, podcasts, and blogs represent a way to strengthen a station's ties to its audience.

26. Stations must pay an annual music-licensing fee to ASCAP, BMI, and/or SESAC for the privilege of broadcasting and webstreaming the copyrighted compositions of these organizations' members.

27. In the 2000s, the recording industry required that radio stations streaming music on their websites had to compensate it for such use.

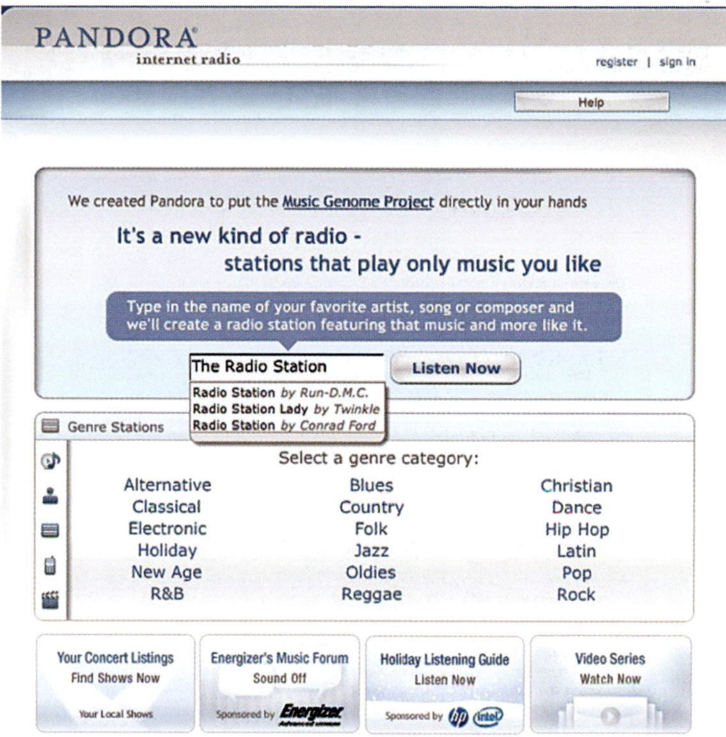

FIGURE 3.34
A source for music radio on the Internet. Courtesy of Pandora.

FIGURE 3.35
Radio illustrates its music format variety. Courtesy of Mix 98.5, WDEZ-FM, and KSSJ-FM.

FIGURE 3.36
Radio honors its legends. Courtesy Museum of Broadcast Communications.

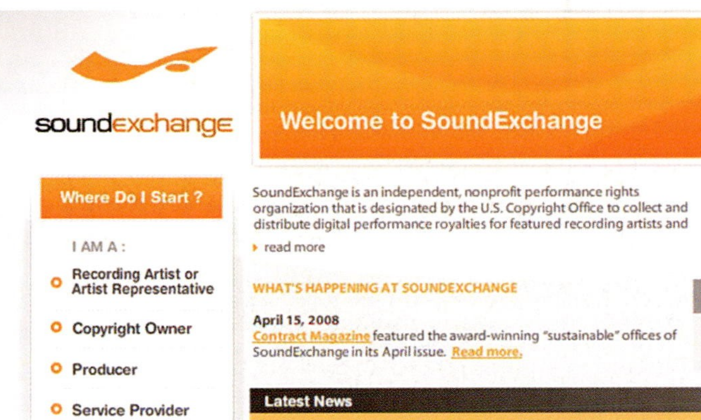

FIGURE 3.37
Protecting artists' income and rights. Courtesy of Sound Exchange.

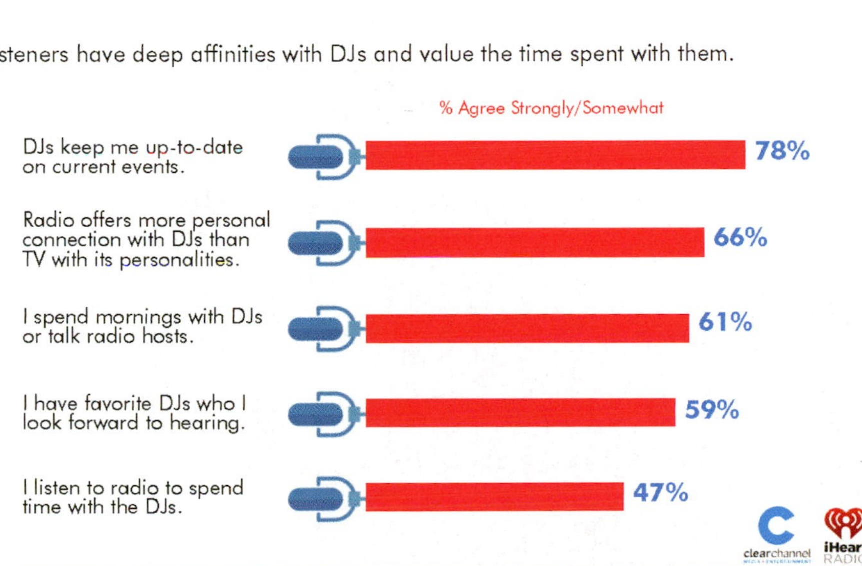

FIGURE 3.38
Reasons for explaining listener affinity with deejays is reflected in the 2013 iHeartRadio/Clear Channel study "The State of Listening Today." ©2013 Clear Channel.

SUGGESTED FURTHER READING

Adams, M.H. and Massey, K.K., *Introduction to Radio: Production and Programming,* Brown and Benchmark, Madison, WI, 1995.

Armstrong, B., *The Electronic Church,* J. Nelson, Nashville, TN, 1979.

Bender, G., *Call of the Game: What Really Goes On in the Broadcast Booth,* Bonus Books, Chicago, IL, 1994.

Broady, J., *On Air: The Guidebook to Starting a Career as a Radio Personality,* BVI, San Bernardino, CA, 2007.

Busby, L. and Parker, D., *The Art and Science of Radio,* Allyn & Bacon, Boston, MA, 1984.

Carroll, R.L. and Davis, D.M., *Electronic Media Programming: Strategies and Decision Making,* McGraw-Hill, New York, 1993.

Chapple, S. and Garofalo, R., *Rock 'n' Roll Is Here to Pay,* Nelson-Hall, Chicago, IL, 1977.

Cliff, C. and Greer, A., *Broadcasting Programming: The Current Perspective,* University Press of America, Washington, D.C., 1974 to date, revised annually.

Coddington, R.H., *Modern Radio Programming,* Tab Books, Blue Ridge Summit, PA, 1970.

DeLong, T.A., *The Mighty Music Box,* Amber Crest Books, Los Angeles, CA, 1980.

Denisoff, R.S., *Solid Gold: The Popular Record Industry,* Transaction Books, New York, 1976.

Dingle, J.L., *Essential Radio,* Peregrine Books, Marblehead, MA, 1995.

Eastman, S.T., *Broadcast/Cable Programming: Strategies and Practices,* 6th edition, Wadsworth Publishing, Belmont, CA, 2001.

Geller, V., *Beyond Powerful Radio: A Communicator's Guide to the Internet Age—News, Talk, Information & Personality for Broadcasting, Podcasting, Internet, Radio,* Focal Press, Boston, MA, 2011.

Hall, C. and Hall, B., *This Business of Radio Programming,* Billboard Publishing, New York, 1977.

Halper, D., *Full-Service Radio,* Focal Press, Boston, MA, 1991.

Halper, D., *Radio Music Directing,* Focal Press, Boston, MA, 1991.

Halper, D., *Icons of Talk Radio,* Greenwood, Westport, CT, 2008.

Hilliard, R. and Keith, M., *Dirty Discourse: Sex and Indecency in American Radio,* Iowa State Press, Ames, IA, 2003.

Hutchby, I., *Confrontation Talk: Arguments, Asymmetries, and Power on Talk Radio,* L. Erlbaum, Mahwah, NJ, 1996.

Hutchings, W., *Radio on the Road,* 8th edition, Aslan Publishing, Fairfield, CT, 2006.

James, J., *The PD Chronicles: Blatant Confessions of a Radio Guy,* Xlibris, Bloomington, IN, 2001.

Johnson, T. and Burns, A., *Morning Radio,* Johnson Publishing, Washington, DC, 1999.

Keirstead, P.A., *All-News Radio,* Tab Books, Blue Ridge Summit, PA, 1980.

Keith, M.C., *Radio Programming: Consultancy and Formatics,* Focal Press, Stoneham, MA, 1987.

Keith, M.C., *Signals in the Air: Native Broadcasting in America,* Praeger Publishing, Westport, CT, 1995.

Keith, M.C., *Sounds in the Dark: All Night Radio in American Life,* Iowa State Press, Ames, IA, 2001.

Keith, M.C., *Radio Cultures: The Sound Medium in American Life,* Peter Lang, New York, 2008.

Land, J., *Active Radio: Pacifica's Brash Experiment,* University of Minnesota Press, Minneapolis, MN, 1999.

Lochte, B., *Christian Radio: The Growth of a Mainstream Force,* McFarland, Jefferson, NC, 2006.

Lujack, L. and Jedlicka, D.A., *Superjock: The Loud, Frantic, NonStop World of Rock Radio Deejays,* Regnery, Chicago, IL, 1975.

Lynch, J. and Gillispie, G., *Process and Practice of Radio Programming,* University Press of America, Lanham, MD, 1998.

MacFarland, D.T., *The Development of the Top 40 Format*, Arno Press, New York, 1979.

MacFarland, D.T., *Contemporary Radio Programming Strategies*, Lawrence Erlbaum Associates, Hillsdale, NJ, 1990.

Maki, V. and Pederson, J., *The Radio Playbook*, Globe Mack, St. Louis, MO, 1991.

Matelski, M.J., *Broadcast Programming and Promotion Worktext*, Focal Press, Boston, MA, 1989.

McCoy, Q., *No Static: A Guide to Creative Programming*, Miller Freeman Books, Chicago, IL, 1999.

Morrow, B., *Cousin Brucie*, Morrow and Company, New York, 1987.

NAB, *The New Media Law Handbook for Radio Broadcasters*, National Association of Broadcasters, Washington, D.C., 2007.

Norberg, E., *Radio Programming: Tactics and Strategies*, Focal Press, Boston, MA, 1996.

Passman, A., *The Deejays*, Macmillan, New York, 1971.

Pierce, D., *Riding the Ether Express*, University Center for Louisiana Studies, Siana, LA, 2008.

Rhoads, B.E., et al. (eds), *Programming and Promotion*, Streamline Press, West Palm Beach, FL, 1995.

Routt, E., McGrath, J.B., and Weiss, F.A., *The Radio Format Conundrum*, Hastings House, New York, 1978.

Sauls, S.J., *The Culture of American College Radio*, Iowa State University Press, Ames, IA, 2000.

Sklar, R., *Rocking America: How the All-Hit Radio Stations Took Over*, St. Martin's Press, New York, 1984.

Utterback, A.S., *Broadcaster's Survival Guide: Staying Alive in the Business*, Chicago, IL, Bonus Books, 1997.

Utterback, A.S. and Michael, G.F., *Voice Handbook: How to Polish Your On-Air Delivery*, Bonus Books, Santa Monica, CA, 2005.

Vane, E.T. and Gross, L.S., *Programming for TV, Radio, and Cable*, Focal Press, Boston, MA, 1994.

Warren, S., *Radio: The Book*, 3rd edition, NAB Books, Washington, D.C., 1999.

Wilcox, J., *Voiceovers: Techniques and Tactics for Success*, Allworth Press, New York, 2007.

CHAPTER 4
Sales

COMMERCIALIZATION: A RETROSPECTIVE

As of the first quarter of 2013, the Radio Advertising Bureau (RAB) reported that overall radio revenue was flat at $3.5 billion. The overall health of ad-generated revenue is important because selling commercials is what keeps the majority of radio stations on the air. Selling commercials via traditional media is not the only means of generating revenue. As a result of new media technologies related to the Internet, now radio salespeople, or account executives (AE), not only sell airtime on traditional terrestrial radio but also sell advertising on digital media platforms such as Web, mobile, social, tablet, and smartphone apps associated with radio.

The salesperson sells the audience, which the station's music attracts, to the advertiser or time buyer. Radio industry experts do not predict robust growth in radio sales.

RADIO SET FOR LOW SINGLE DIGITS GROWTH PATH

Rick Ducey

In our 2013–2017 forecast for radio station revenues[1] we estimate that over-the-air revenues will grow from $14.7 billion to $16.2 billion. Digital revenues will grow from $600 million to $800 million, only about 5% of total revenues overall. We see some major groups generating as much as 20% of their revenues from digital (Web, mobile, social, tablet) platforms.

FIGURE 4.1
Rick Ducey.

In the next five years, here's the landscape I see facing radio operators:

1. **Increasing competition from digital pure plays**, e.g., Pandora, Spotify, Apple, Google, Amazon will reshape the audio market. Already, Pandora is

achieving local market ratings rivaling some radio stations. Since radio earns so much of its over-the-air revenue from local and regional accounts, it will be difficult for the pure plays to compete for ad dollars as well as listeners without local sales forces. However, the lesson we keep learning from digital is that ad spend follows the listener base and it is growing for the pure plays.

2. **Radio is not aggressive in digital platforms**: radio operators, especially the publicly held firms, see their fiduciary obligation as protecting their over-the-air revenue base. Unlike newspapers or Yellow Pages directory companies, they've faced no mortal challenges that have forced change. This encourages radio operators to pay less attention to digital platforms and use them primarily as a secondary strategy to support their over-the-air service as the primary monetization engine.

3. **Connected cars will disrupt radio**. A growing number of companies in the automotive value chain are targeting the car for new digital information and entertainment services based on one-time fees as well as recurring subscription and advertising revenues. Radio has survived satellite radio, CDs, and MP3s in the car. However, the new generation of connected car (mobile Internet) services will push the reset button and change consumer expectations for what they will have access to in-car. If radio does not adapt, innovate, or otherwise change its ways, there will be a tipping point over the next five years and radio might not be on the right side of it.

4. **Radio valuations are getting more solid**. With a rebounding and stabilizing economy, station multiples (i.e., valuation based on multiples of broadcast cash flow) are increasing. This is encouraging more station trading. With ownership changes we'll also see different operating models come into play. For the most part, radio properties are managed to relatively short-term financial goals where deployed assets are justified in cash flow on a quarterly basis.

5. **Wild card**—the broadcast radio industry may do something uncharacteristic for most industries other than high tech. There's always the possibility that either through mergers and acquisitions or spin-offs that the radio industry may disrupt itself. For example, Clear Channel, CBS and Salem have strong digital strategies. If the industry starts to see these initiatives pay off, they may quickly follow the leaders.

Rick Ducey is managing director at BIA/Kelsey. He oversees the Advisory Services, Strategy and Financial Consulting practice areas. He is an expert in digital media innovations, competitive strategies, new product development, and new business models, including digital ecosystem collaboration strategies. Prior to joining BIA in 2000, Rick Ducey was senior vice-president of NAB's Research and Information Group. Before joining NAB in 1983, he was a faculty member in the Department of Telecommunication at Michigan State University where he taught and did research in the areas of emerging telecommunication technologies and strategic market research. He also served on the graduate management faculties of George Mason University and George Washington University in telecommunications management and the University of Maryland, where he taught strategic market management and research methodologies. Rick Ducey received his PhD from Michigan State University.

[1] *Investing In Radio® Market Report*, first edition, BIA/Kelsey, Chantilly, VA, 2013.

SELLING AIRTIME

Airtime is intangible. You cannot see it or hold it in your hand. It is not like any other form of advertising. Newspaper and magazine ads can be cut out by the advertiser and pinned to a bulletin board or taped to a window as tangible evidence of money spent. Television commercials can be seen, but radio commercials are sounds flitting through the ether with no visual component to attest to their existence. They are ephemeral, or fleeting, to use words that are often associated with radio advertising. However, any informed account executive will respond to such terms by stating the simple fact that an effective radio commercial makes a strong and lasting impression on the mind of the listener in much the same way that a popular song tends to permeate the gray matter. "The so-called intangible nature of a radio commercial really only means you can't see it or touch it. There is little doubt, however, that a good spot is concrete in its own unique way. Few of us have gone unaffected or, better still, untouched by radio commercials. If a spot is good, it is felt, and that's a tangible," says former radio sales manager Charles W. Friedman.

Radio is one of the most effective means of advertising when used correctly. Of course, there is a right way and a wrong way to use the medium, and the salesperson who knows and understands the unique character of his or her product is in the best position to succeed. To the extent that a radio commercial cannot be held or taped to a cash register, it is intangible.

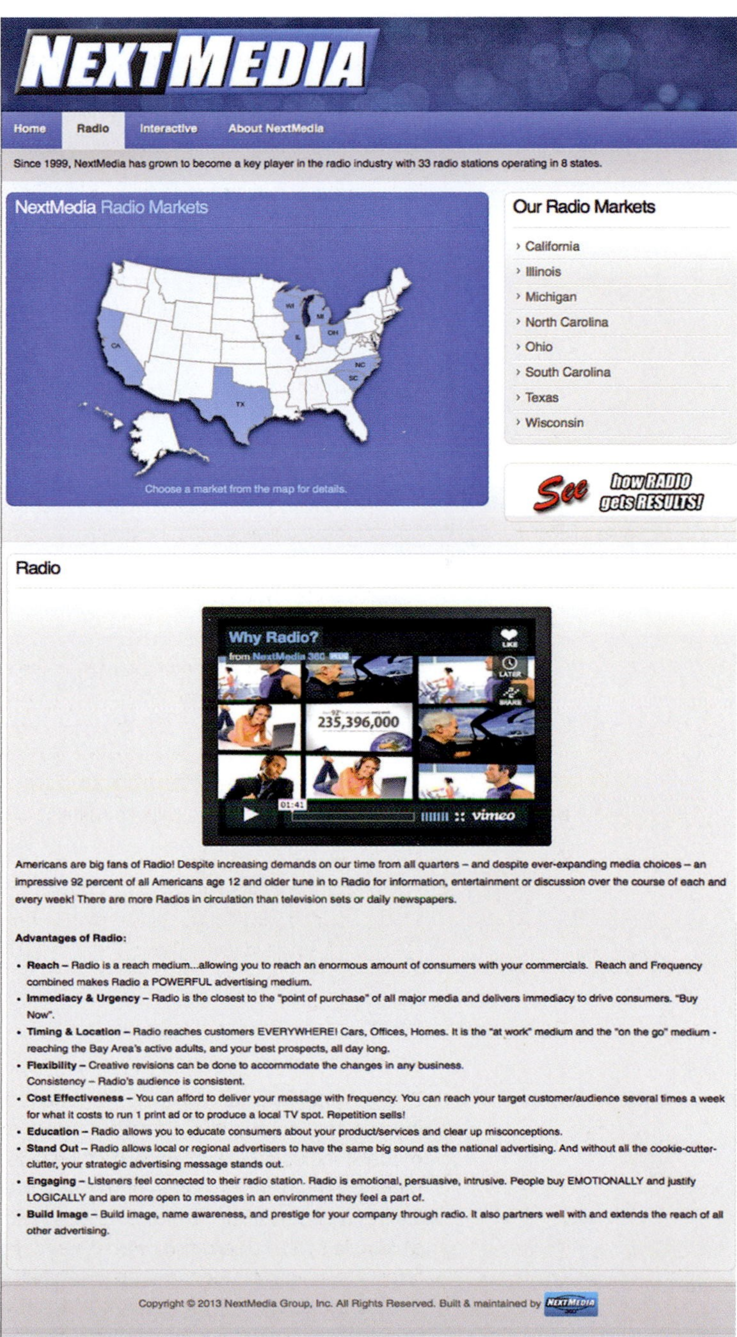

FIGURE 4.2
NextMedia explains the advantages of radio advertising to clients. Courtesy of NextMedia.

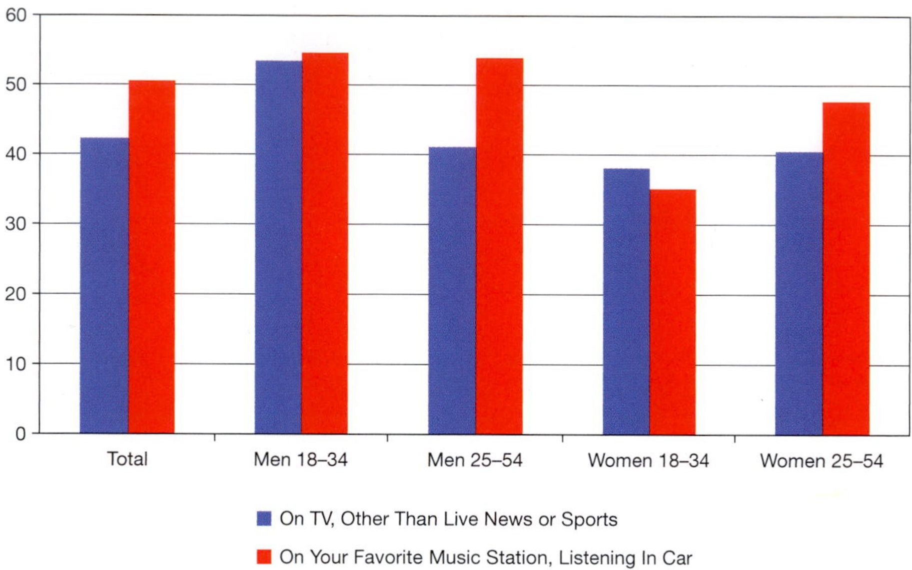

FIGURE 4.3 Radio retains through commercials (even for in-car music!) better than TV. Courtesy of NuVooDoo Media and All Access.com. www.allaccess.com/nuvoodoo/archive/15244/ad-avoidance-radio-is-the-healthiest-mass-medium.

However, the results produced by a carefully conceived campaign can be seen in the cash register. Consistent radio users, from the giant multinational corporations to the so-called mom-and-pop shops, know that a radio commercial can capture people's attention as effectively as anything crossing their field of vision. A promotional slogan from the 1950s says it best: "Radio gives you more than you can see." In 2013, one study found that radio was more effective than television at delivering consumers (or listeners) to advertisers. Radio outperformed television in every age demographic except women who were 18–34.

Consultant Ed Shane says that although over-the-air advertising remains the primary source of income for most stations, "non-traditional revenue (NTR) streams (such as a website or special events like concerts or home and garden shows) help stations realize financial goals." In that regard, GroupM Next, the division of ad giant WPP, found that online listeners of Web radio are more likely to buy products that have been advertised on Web radio and less likely to jump past ads to avoid hearing them. The same study found that the average age for Web radio listeners is 34 while the average age for traditional terrestrial radio is 47. Further, the study predicts that Web radio listening will increase as more automobiles are built with digital dashboards. In 2013, Pandora—an automated music streaming service on the Internet, launched in 2000—was reported to have gained access to the $14 billion spent on advertising annually. To compete directly with terrestrial radio, Pandora opened sales offices in 25 U.S. media markets. Pandora is likely to be a fierce competitor for radio advertising dollars considering it has nearly 66 million listeners and nearly 10% of the U.S. radio audience.

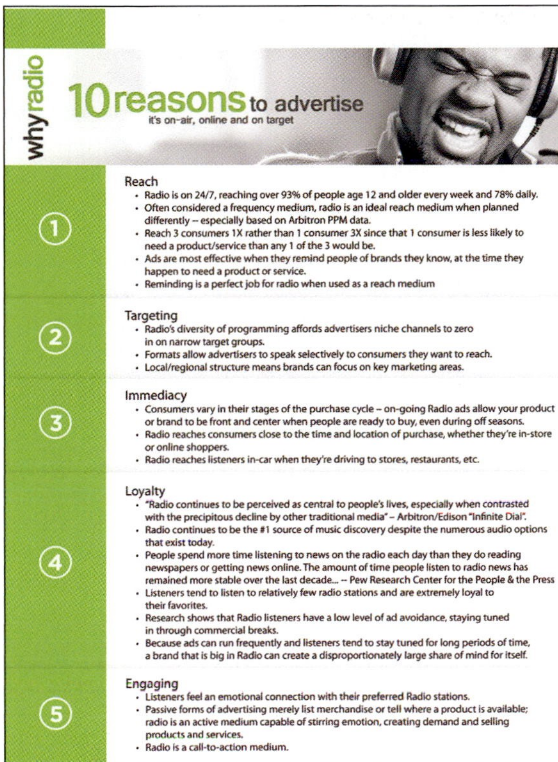

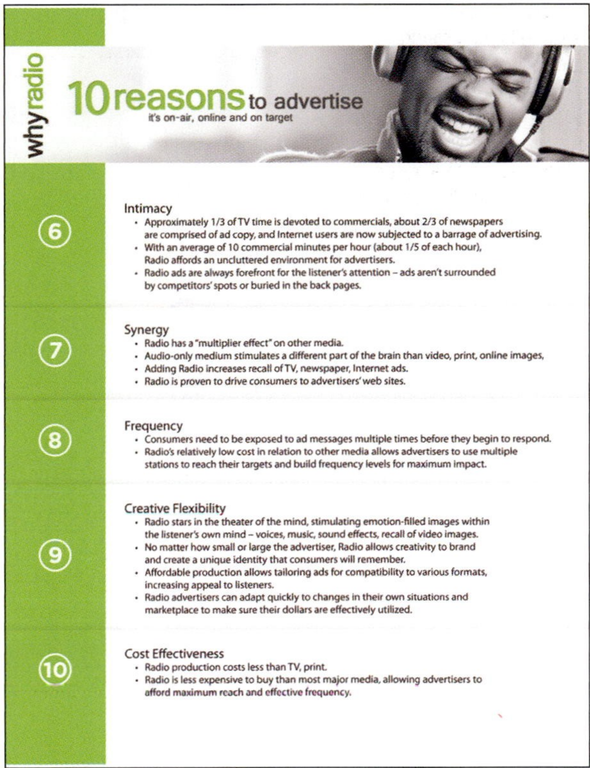

FIGURE 4.4A&B
The Radio Advertising Bureau explains ten reasons to advertise on radio.

In terms of chasing advertising dollars, the radio industry also faces challenges from the smartphone industry. An Interactive Advertising Bureau study finds that nearly 75 percent of 300 top-level brand marketing executives, currently spending money on mobile advertising, intend to increase the amount they are spending on mobile (or smartphone apps) advertising through 2015. Between the years of 2011 and 2013, the mobile budgets of these companies increased by 142 percent.

BECOMING AN ACCOUNT EXECUTIVE

A notion held by some sales managers is that salespeople are born and not made. This position holds that a salesperson either "has it" or does not, "it" being the innate gift to sell, without which all the schooling and training in the world means little. Although not all sales managers embrace this theory, many agree with the view that anyone attempting a career in sales should first and foremost possess an unflagging desire to make money, because without it, failure is almost assured.

According to RAB figures, 70% of the radio salespeople hired by stations are gone within three years; another study shows that 73% of new radio salespeople leave the business within a year. Although this sounds less than encouraging, it also must be stated that to succeed in broadcast sales invariably means substantial earnings and rapid advancement. True, the battle can be a tough one and the dropout rate is high, but the rewards of success are great.

The majority of newly hired account executives have college training. An understanding of research, marketing, and finance is important. Formal instruction in these areas is particularly advisable for persons considering a career in broadcast sales. Broadcast sales has become a familiar course offering at many colleges and universities with programs in electronic media. Research and marketing courses designed for the broadcast major also have become more prevalent. "A degree indicates a certain amount of tenacity and perseverance, which are important qualities in anyone wanting to sell radio. Not only that, but the candidate with a degree often is more articulate and self-assured. As in most other areas of radio, ten or 15 years ago fewer people had college diplomas, but the business has become so much more sophisticated and complex because of the greater competition and emphasis on research that managers actually look for salespeople with college training," says former general manager Richard Bremkamp.

Whether a candidate for a sales position has extensive formal training or not, he or she must possess knowledge of the product in order to be hired. "To begin with, an applicant must show me that they know something about radio; after all, that is what we're selling. The individual doesn't necessarily have to have a consummate understanding of the medium, although that would be nice, but they must have some product knowledge. Most stations are willing to train to an extent. I suppose you always look for someone with some sales experience, whether in radio or in some other field," said the late Bob Turley, who was a general sales manager in West Virginia.

Although not an absolute requirement, stations do prefer a candidate with sales exposure, be it selling vacuum cleaners door-to-door or shoes in a retail store. "It always makes the hiring process easier when the applicant has prior sales experience, but honestly a trained monkey can be taught to sell. What you can't teach is personality and attitude. Those are the most important traits. Everything else, I can teach them," says general manager Wolf Korgyn of KHWL-FM in Oklahoma. Weezie Kramer, Entercom's station group president, notes that experience is necessary "sometimes but not always." Kramer explains, "Particularly today as it is sometimes easier to train someone with no experience than to un-train someone's bad experience. I would also suggest that even using the term 'radio sales' does not encompass what we do. Our job is marketing solutions—and that is a relationship that is driven by understanding a client's needs and developing solutions that meet their needs (not just a sale)."

Hiring inexperienced salespeople is a gamble that a small media market radio station generally must take. The larger outlets almost always require radio sales

The Attributes, Habits and Characteristics America's Top Local Radio Salespeople Say Make Them Winners			
1.	Discipline	29.	Deliver on promises
2.	Attention to detail	30.	Very presentable personal appearance
3.	Follow-through	31.	Open minded – never stop growing
4.	Honesty	32.	Advance preparation – no winging it
5.	Listening	33.	Rarely forget to ask for the order (as opposed to rarely remembering)
6.	Timeliness, promptness		
7.	Determination	34.	Regular self-improvement. Read a lot, listen to tapes. Attend seminars.
8.	Thoroughness		
9.	Always prospecting	35.	Strong communication skills: intra-office and with clients mail/phone/in-person
10.	Creativeness		
11.	Consistently (re)discovering and fulfilling prospect/client needs		
12.	Flexibility	36.	Aggressiveness – stay with prospect/client until the job is done right
13.	Love the business	37.	Empathy/sincere caring for client's results
14.	Sincerely want their clients to succeed		
15.	Knowledge	38.	Results oriented
16.	Strong work ethic	39.	Do-it-now attitude
17.	50-plus-hour work week	40.	Keep good records
18.	Organized	41.	In office/on street early and stay late
19.	Effective time/territory management	42.	Under-promise and over-deliver
20.	Priority management/crisis avoidance techniques	43.	Get into the client's shoes, view things from client's perspective
21.	Accessible to clients/peers/management	44.	Anticipate and eliminate problems before they develop
22.	Faith in God, self, product		
23.	Unwavering enthusiasm	45.	Don't make assumptions
24.	Total personal acceptance of successes and failures	46.	Don't take anything for granted, especially your station's place in the buy
25.	Focus-focus-focus. Know what you want, what you need to do, do it		
		47.	Loyalty to company, clients, self
26.	Understanding and application of the basics of selling	48.	Keep in touch with clients, especially during their schedules
27.	Persistence	49.	Don't take rejection personally
28.	Insistence on doing the best possible job – not just "good enough"	50.	Sell ideas and solutions, not spots, flights, or packages

FIGURE 4.5
The attributes, habits, and characteristics America's top local radio salespeople say make them winners. Courtesy of Radio Ink.

credentials, a luxury that smaller stations cannot afford. Thus, they must hire untested salespeople, and there are no guarantees that a person who has sold lawn mowers can sell airtime, that is, assuming that the newly hired salesperson has ever sold anything at all. In most cases, he or she comes to radio and sales without experience and the station must provide at least a modicum of training. Unfortunately, many stations fail to provide adequate training and this also contributes to the high rate of turnover. New salespeople are commonly given two to three months to display their wares and exhibit their potential. If they prove themselves to the sales manager by generating new business, they are asked to stay. On the other hand, if the sales manager is not convinced that the apprentice salesperson has the ability to bring in the accounts, then he or she is shown the door.

During the trial period, the salesperson is given a modest draw against sales, or a "no-strings" salary on which to subsist. In the former case, the salesperson eventually must pay back, through commissions on sales, the amount that he or she has drawn. Thus, after a few months, a new salesperson may well find themselves in debt for $2,000–3,000. As a show of confidence and to encourage the new salesperson who has shown an affinity for radio sales, management may erase the debt. If a station decides to terminate its association with the new salesperson, it must absorb the loss of time, energy, and money invested in the employee. Kramer explains that "most stations remain commission-based but there is a trend towards base salary plus (either commission or commission and bonus)." But, the percentage of commission paid to salespeople varies from station size to market size. In a small media market, Korgyn says, "For us, since we're a brand new station and poor as hell, we're commission-only. We pay a flat 20% of gross sale when paid by the client. I think that is probably the norm for small market and 'owner-operator' scenarios. Two of the other local stations here in Altus, Oklahoma pay 15% commission only as well."

Characteristics that managers most often look for in prospective salespeople include ambition, confidence, energy, determination, honesty, and intelligence. "To me, the most important quality in a salesperson is the perception of being genuine and honest. If a customer trusts your salesperson, they will openly spend advertising dollars when they have them to spend. Add to that some passion, belief in the station, a touch of friendliness and a good firm handshake, and you've got the perfect salesperson," says Korgyn. Kramer asserts "the following talent themes are usually found in successful radio sellers: Command, Activator, Charisma/woo, and Strategic Communication." When hiring a salesperson, Kramer adds, "self-discipline, initiative, tenacity, goal orientation, competitive, and self-confidence" are all characteristics that are desired qualities.

Jason Insalaco, a media lawyer and former general manager, says the qualities that make a good salesperson include:

- Appreciation and genuine enthusiasm for the media brand.
- Reliability.
- Good reputation.

Insalaco asserts, "A successful salesperson works at establishing strong relationships with clients, but also maintains solid relationships with the on-air production staff, the station's on-air personalities, and the traffic department (commercial-announcement scheduling department). These fellow staff members are integral for creating an engaging sales package. If an AE works well with these other team members, then the AE will be able to deliver successfully for their clients." Korgyn says, "When I hire someone, regardless of position,

I look for a few key elements: promptness to the interview, neatness in attire (not suits and ties, just neat, attractive, and clean), a great smile that lights up the room and makes me want to smile, positive energy, and good eye-contact. If these things are there, there's a good chance everything else will fall right in line."

Friedman believes that it is important for a salesperson to have insight into human nature and behavior:

> You really must be adept at psychology. Selling really is a matter of anticipating what the prospect is thinking and knowing how best to address his concerns. It's not so much a matter of outthinking the prospective client, but rather being cognizant of the things that play a significant role in his life. Empathy requires the ability to appreciate the experiences of others. A salesperson who is insensitive to a client's moods or states of mind usually will come away empty-handed.

When hiring a salesperson, Insalaco says, "Seeking someone who has established relationships in the business and who genuinely enjoys meeting new people and forming new relationships" are important qualities.

In recent years, sales managers have recruited more heavily from within the radio station itself rather than immediately looking elsewhere for salespeople. For decades, it was believed that programming people were not suited for sales. An inexplicable barrier seemed to separate the two areas. This attitude has changed, and sales managers now give serious consideration to on-air staff who desire to make the transition into sales. Consolidation and downsizing in the 1990s also inspired multiple role playing at stations. That is to say, the morning deejay may then become the afternoon salesperson. In regard to whether deejays make successful salespeople, Korgyn says, "That depends entirely on the deejay and their personality. If they are hugely popular in the area, they might be able to ride that wave into a sale, but outside of that, if they are odd, abrasive, or weird—as many good deejays are, they will fall flat in sales. Radio deejays and salespeople just have a need for different skillsets."

The major advantage of hiring programming people to sell the station is that they have a practical understanding of the product. "A lot of former deejays make good account reps because they had to sell the listener on the product. A deejay really is a salesperson, when you get right down to it," observes broadcaster Joe Martin. Indeed the deejay has an opportunity to enter into sales because prior experience is not required. In regard to having prior sales experience, Insalaco says, "it is important to have a track record of reliability, trustworthiness, and integrity. Sales experience in any other field is helpful, but it is not required." Additionally, Insalaco says:

> Radio personalities are a helpful asset to take on sales visits to clients and potential clients. Typically, on-air personalities quickly engage the potential

> client and inject energy into a sales meeting. However, radio personalities are better behind a mic than in the role of account executive or even part-time account executive. A good salesperson understands the value of taking station talent on a sales call and should develop a positive working relationship with deejays and hosts.

Agreeing that deejays make good salespeople, Kramer keenly observes:

> While most on air talent do not want to be a sales rep they are very effective "sellers." They are selling the stationality, the brand, the music, the lifestyle, the vibe of what they do every day to their audience. They create emotional connections to their fans and that makes them terrific ambassadors for advertisers' products. They also can help build relationships and bonds with clients by making calls with our account representatives. Think about it. Our talent are our stars. Why wouldn't our clients want to mingle and connect with them like any fan?

Realizing, too, that sales is the most direct path into station management, programming people often are eager to make the shift. The trend has been greater than ever to recruit managers from the programming ranks. However, a sales background is still preferred.

The salesperson is invariably among the best-paid members of a station. How much a salesperson earns is usually left up to the individual to determine. Contrary to popular opinion, the salesperson's salary generally exceeds the deejay's, especially in the smaller markets. In the larger markets, certain air personalities' salaries are astronomical and even surpass the general manager's income, but major market sales salaries are commonly in the five- and even six-figure range. In 2013, *Inside Radio* conducted a study that found that the average annual salary for radio salespeople in media markets 200 and smaller

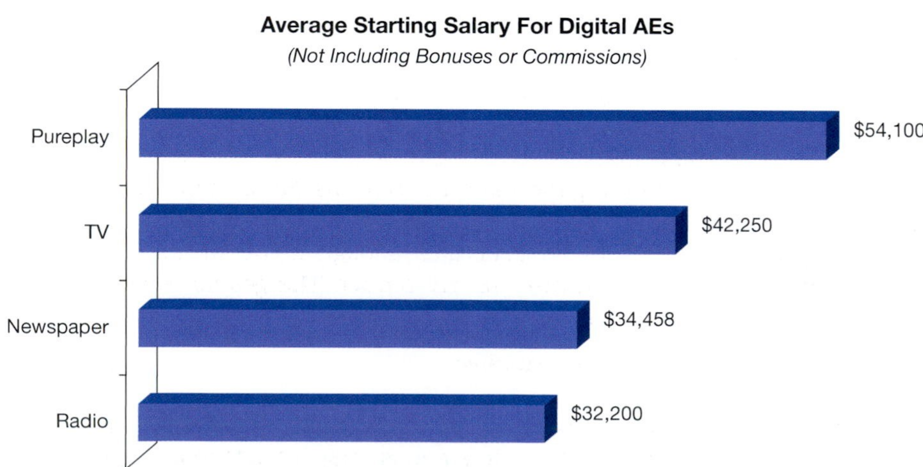

FIGURE 4.6
Starting salaries for digital account executives. Courtesy of Borrell Associates, Inc.

is $60,500 while the average annual salary in media markets one through ten is $136,700. Additionally, the rapid emergence of digital media has created opportunities for radio stations to capitalize on another revenue source which necessitates the need for digital account executives.

In 2013, Borrell Associates found that the average starting salary for a digital account executive in radio is $32,200. Borrell Associates notes that 11% of the nation's radio stations have dedicated digital sales teams and of those, 60% offer special incentive rates to increase a salesperson's salary. *Inside Radio* says, "Among those radio stations that do have digital-only reps, the team remains small with an average of fewer than three salespeople. The typical combined sales force has ten sales reps selling both on-air and online ads." A 2013 study from the Internet Advertising Bureau said that digital ad growth had set a record at $8.3 billion. Digital sales opportunities for radio to generate new revenue are plentiful.

Entry-level sales positions are fairly abundant (although station consolidation has reduced these opportunities), and stations are always on the lookout for good people. Perhaps no other position in the radio station affords an individual the opportunities that sales does, but most salespeople will never go beyond entry level in sales. Yet, for those who are successful, the payoff is worthwhile.

THE SALES MANAGER

The general sales manager (also called director of sales [DOS] in cluster operations) supervises the marketing of a station's or cluster's airtime. This person is responsible for moving inventory, which in the case of the radio outlet constitutes the selling of spot and feature schedules to advertisers. To achieve this end, the sales manager directs the daily efforts of the station's account executives, establishes sales department policies, develops sales plans and materials, conceives of sales and marketing campaigns and promotions, sets quotas, and also may sell as well.

A station's sales department customarily includes an emphasis on national, regional, and local sales. The station's or the cluster's general sales manager usually handles national responsibilities. This includes working with the station's rep company to stimulate business from national advertisers. The regional sales manager is given the responsibility of exploring sales possibilities in a broad geographical area surrounding the station or stations. For example, the regional person for an outlet in New York City may be assigned portions of Connecticut, New Jersey, and Long Island. The local sales manager at the same station would concentrate on advertisers within the city proper. The general sales manager oversees the efforts of each of these individuals.

For cluster operations, Kramer explains:

> The majority of our stations are cluster sold. However some, particularly markets where we have five or more stations, may have separate teams.

> For example, a "spoken word" team and a "music team." In a pure cluster, account executives represent all brands. We do this so that we can honestly present ourselves as marketing solutions experts who listen, discover, and solve clients' problems. If one represents the entire brand portfolio (including all of our platforms) vs. a "slice" of it, then they can solve client problems with the assets that best fit the clients' needs vs. just selling what we have.

The size of a station's sales staff varies according to its location and reach. A typical small-market radio station employs between two and four account executives, and the medium-market station averages about five. Large, top-ranked metropolitan outlets employ as many as eight to ten salespeople, although it is more typical for the major-market station to have approximately half a dozen account executives. Of course, in cluster operations where team selling often exists, these numbers will vary, as a salesperson may be selling the airtime of several stations. In cluster operations, it is not uncommon for there to be dozens of sales personnel. Kramer explains that Entercom Communications Corp., a cluster operation, has "radio stations in 23 markets that range from medium to large. Smaller markets have around ten account executives. Larger markets can have upwards of 40."

The general sales manager/DOS reports directly to the station or station cluster's general manager and works closely with the programming department in developing saleable features. Regular daily and weekly sales meetings are scheduled and headed by the sales manager, during which time goals are set and problems addressed. The sales manager also assigns account lists to members of his or her staff and helps coordinate trade and cooperative advertising (coop) deals.

As mentioned earlier, the head of the sales department is usually responsible for maintaining close contact with the station's rep company as a way of generating income from national advertisers who are handled by advertising agencies. The relationship of the sales manager and rep company is a particularly important one and will be discussed in greater detail later in this chapter. In addition, the sales manager must be adept at working ratings figures to the station's advantage for inclusion in sales promotional material that is used at both the national and local levels.

All sales come under the scrutiny of the sales manager, who determines whether an account is appropriate for the station and conditions of the sale meet established standards. In addition, the sales manager may have a policy that requires credit checks to be made on every new account and that new clients pay for a portion of their spot schedule up front as a show of good faith. Again, policies vary from station to station.

It is up to the head of sales to keep abreast of local and national sales and marketing trends that can be used to the station's advantage. This requires the sales manager to constantly survey trade magazines like *Radio Ink*, *Radio Business Report*, and *ADWEEK*, and attend industry seminars such as those conducted by the Radio Advertising Bureau (RAB). No sales department can operate in a vacuum and hope to succeed in today's dynamic radio marketplace.

FIGURE 4.7
The Radio Advertising Bureau is the sales and marketing arm of the radio industry. Courtesy of the RAB.

Statistics continue to bear out the fact that sales managers are most often recruited to fill the position of general manager. It is also becoming more commonplace for sales managers to have experience in other areas of a station's operations, such as programming and production, a factor that has become increasingly important to the person who hires the chief account executive. A 2013 *Inside Radio* study found that the average salary for the DOS in radio media markets 101+ was $91,000 while the average salary for the DOS in radio media markets one through ten was $210,000.

RADIO SALES TOOLS

Rates for airtime depend on the size of a station's listenership—the bigger the audience, the higher the rates. At the same time, the unit cost for a spot or a feature is affected by the quantity or amount purchased—the bigger the "buy," the cheaper the unit price. Clients also get discounts for consecutive week purchases over a prescribed period of time—say, 26 or 52 weeks. Although rare, a few stations publish the fees that they charge for airtime in a rate card.

Due to increased competition, stations do not always publish their rate cards since the rates might be constantly changing based on economic and market demands. John Potter, of the Radio Advertising Bureau, says:

> Few stations use published rate cards. Many are using computers with Yield Management software that automatically adjusts the rates. Some use computer spreadsheets to communicate rates internally to salespeople who write custom proposals based on the advertiser's needs. A handful that use internal rate cards are using grids so they can adjust rates by nothing more than an announcement in a sales meeting or a quick email to the sales staff. The few stations that are publishing fixed rate cards are generally small markets that have little competition other than from their local newspaper that publishes a fixed rate card.

Radio marketing expert Jay Williams, Jr., agreeing with Potter, contends that the station rate card is on its way to obsolescence, "some stations do use grid cards—but only internally—to let sellers know what grid/rates they should be quoting in their presentations. Rate cards are decreasingly shown to clients because they distract the account executive's focus from helping the client solve advertising and promotional problems and often force them into a negotiation with the client about spot rates."

RATE CARD

LET THE PACK KNOW ABOUT YOUR PRODUCT OR SERVICE

Our rates are reasonable and straightforward. Our pack of listeners is loyal and will eagerly support businesses who help to keep their favorite rock station on the air. If you want to reach the hard-working, hard-rocking, 'real' folks of Southwest Oklahoma, then you need to be advertising on KHOWL 98.7 FM.

DEMOGRAPHIC INFORMATION

License: KHWL-FM (Lone Wolf)
Frequency: FM 98.7 Mhz
Our Format: Active Rock
Target Audience: 18-34 years old
But we have listeners from under 14 to over 50.

Service Area Population: 65,000+
Median Age: 33 yrs old
Average Income: $37,394
Race: 61% White, 25% Latino, 14% Others

OUR SERVICES & RATES

30-Second Spot (Any Time, Any Quantity)	$7.50/each
60-Second Spot (Any Time, Any Quantity)	$10.00/each
Weather Sponsorship (2+ Times Per Day)	$80/month
On-Site Live Remote (Minimum 2 Hours)	$100/hour

Specific placement requests are first-come, first-served.
All of our rates are subject to change without notice.
Visit www.khowl.fm for current rates and specials.

We started this company for the love of radio and everything about it. We feel that if we provide Southwest Oklahoma with the opportunity to get excited about radio, that their excitement and enthusiasm will directly transfer to your product or service.

Everyone likes to be a part of something larger than themselves, and advertising with KHOWL 98.7 FM is your opportunity to join all of us in that sense of fulfillment and community. You won't regret your decision to make us your radio advertising partner.

Call or email us today and join the pack!

KHOWL 98.7 FM
102 W Broadway Street
Altus, Oklahoma 73521
Web: www.khowl.fm
Email: sales@khowl.fm

FIGURE 4.8
KHWL-FM, Altus, Oklahoma, rate card. Courtesy of Wolfpack Media, LLC.

Furthermore, observes WIZN's Matt Grasso:

> We never let salespeople show rate cards to clients. Rate cards force the client to try to figure out our business, radio, when radio reps should be learning about their businesses and creating customized presentations for them. Worse, clients always try to find the lowest rates on a rate card and then want to apply those rates to prime time, forcing the radio salesperson to negotiate with himself. By using computerized internal rate cards, sales management can quickly and easily adjust rates to meet demand and ensure proper inventory control.

The sales manager and station manager (DOS and market manager in cluster setups) work together to determine advertising rates, basing their decisions on ratings and what their market can support.

Planning rates for Christal

As of 5/15/13

KPRI

Dayparts	60's 5/15 - 6/2/13	6/3/13 forward :60's	:30's	May :15's	6/3 - forward :15's
M-F 6-10a	250	150	120	100	70
M-F 10a-3p	250	150	120	100	70
M-F 3-7p	250	150	120	100	70
M-Sun 6am-12mid	75	25	15	25	25
Sa / Su 10a-7p	140	40	25	35	35

Walrus

Dayparts	60's 5/15 - 6/2/13	6/3/13 forward :60's	:30's	:15's	:15's
M-F 6-10a	125	90	75	80	40
M-F 10a-3p	125	90	75	80	40
M-F 3-7p	125	90	75	80	40
M-Sun 6am-12mid	50	20	10	30	30
Sa / Su 10a-7p	100	30	25	80	40
Padres	N/A or $500		**$200**	**$150**	**$150**

Mighty 1090

Dayparts	60's 5/15 - 6/2/13	6/3/13 forward :60's	:30's	:15's	:15's
M-F 6-10a	180	140	100	100	40
M-F 10a-3p	180	140	100	100	40
M-F 3-7p	180	140	100	100	40
M-Sun 6am-12mid	50	20	20	25	25
Sa / Su 10a-7p	100	30	40	100	70

FIGURE 4.9
Radio San Diego's rate card with the account executive's sales expectations, or expected goals, listed. Courtesy of Broadcast Company of the America's Radio San Diego.

The rate card also contains its feature and spot rates.

Among the most prevalent features that stations offer are traffic, sports, weather, and business reports during different dayparts. Newscasts also are available to advertisers. Features generally include an open (introduction) and a 30- or 60-second announcement. They are particularly effective advertising vehicles because listeners tend to pay greater attention. Conditions pertaining to feature buys usually appear in the rate card: "All feature sales are subject to four weeks' notice for renewal and cancellation." A station wants to establish credibility with its features and therefore prefers to maintain continuity among its sponsors. A feature with a regular sponsor conveys stability, and that is what a station seeks.

Because the size of a radio station's audience generally varies depending on the time of day, rates for spots (commercials) or features must reflect that fact. Thus, the broadcast day is divided into time classifications: 6–10 am weekdays is typically a station's prime selling period and therefore may be designated AAA; afternoon drivetime, usually 3–7 pm, may be called AA because of its secondary drawing power. Under this system, the midday segment, 10–3 pm, would be given a single A designation, and evenings, 7–midnight, as B. Overnights, midnight–6 am, may be classified as C time. Obviously, the fees charged for spots are established on an ascending scale from C to AAA. A station may charge $300 for an announcement aired at 8 am and $45 for one aired at 2 am. The difference in the size of the station's audience at those hours warrants the contrast.

As previously mentioned, the more airtime a client purchases, the less expensive the cost for an individual commercial or unit. For instance, if an advertiser buys ten spots a week during AAA time, the cost of each spot would be slightly less than if the sponsor purchased two spots a week. A client must buy a specified number of spots to benefit from the frequency discount. A 6X rate, meaning six spots per week, for AAA 60-second announcements may be $75; the 12X rate may be $71 and the 18X rate $68, and so forth. Thirty-second spots are usually priced at two-thirds the cost of a 60-second spot. Should a client desire that a spot be aired at a fixed time—say, at 7:10 am daily—the station will tack on an additional charge, possibly 20%. Fixed position drivetime spots are among the most expensive in a station's inventory.

"I always advise my clients to buy the shortest unit of commercial time possible without compromising their message," says Bob Adams, vice-president and market manager for the Cumulus stations in York, Lancaster, and Reading, PA, whose stations sell :30 spots for 25% less than :60. "You can say the 'Pledge of Allegiance' in 20 seconds. So think of what you can say if you have the right words strung together." By buying shorter, better scripted commercials, advertisers can use the extra money to buy more frequency and get their message to more potential customers, adds Adams.

Many stations use a grid structure as Potter explained. This gives stations a considerable degree of rate flexibility. For example, if a station has five rate-level grids, it may have a range between $20 and $50 for a 60-second spot. Clients would then be given rates at the lower grid if the station had few sponsors on the air, thus creating many availabilities (places to insert commercial messages). As business increased at the station and availabilities became scarcer, the station would ask for rates reflected in the upper grids. Gridding is based on the age-old concept of supply and demand. When availabilities are tight and airtime is at a premium, that time costs more.

Grids are inventory sensitive; they allow a station to remain viable when business is at a low ebb. Certainly, when inventory prices reach a bargain level, this encourages business. For instance, during a period when advertiser activity is sluggish, a station that can offer spots at a considerable reduction stands a chance of stimulating buyer interest.

When business is brisk at a station, because of holiday buying, for example, the situation may be exploited in a manner positive to the revenue column. Again the supply-and-demand concept is at work (one idea on which capitalism is based).

Clients are offered several spot schedule plans suited for their advertising and budgetary needs. For advertisers with limited funds, run-of-station (ROS) or

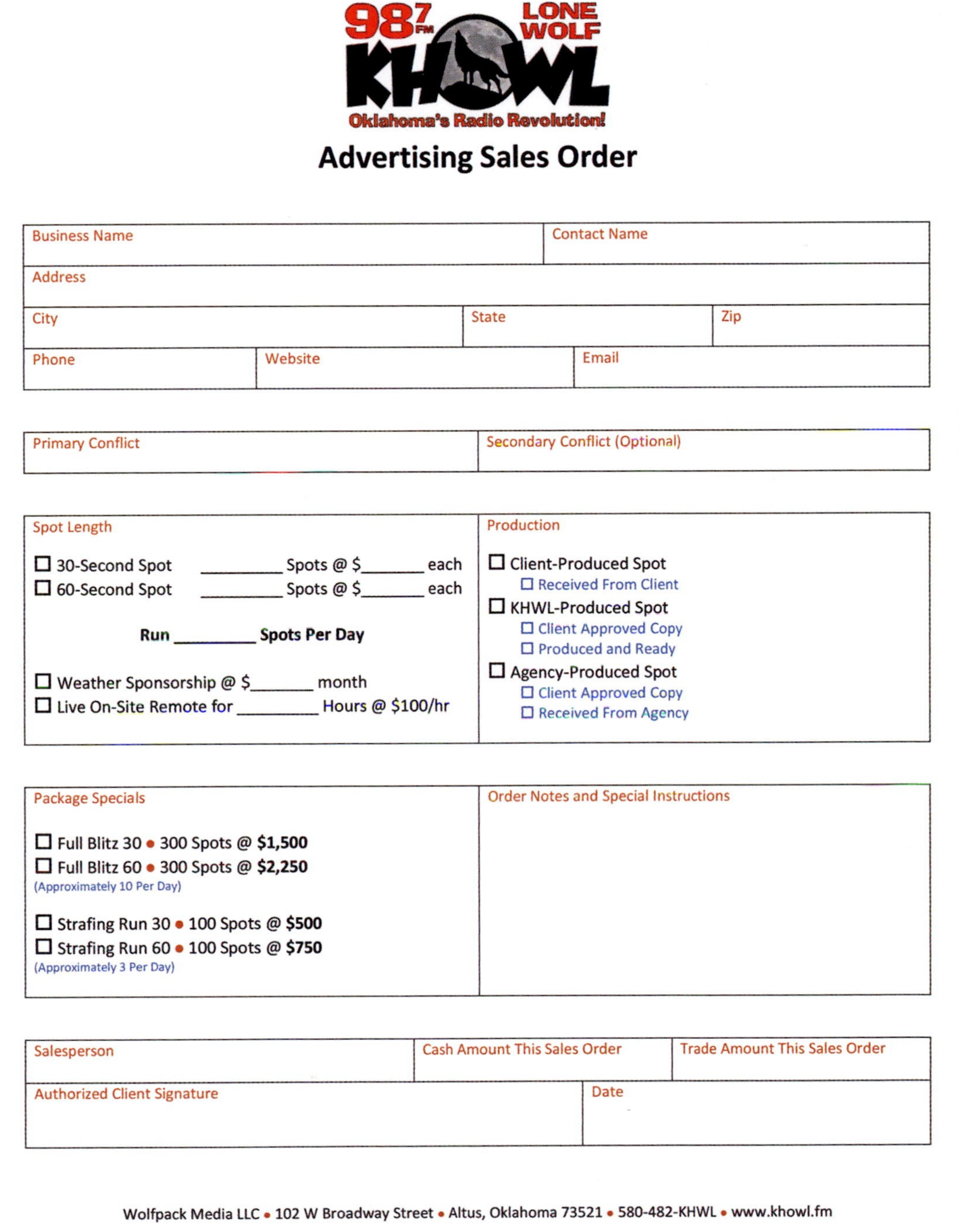

98.7 FM LONE WOLF KHOWL
Oklahoma's Radio Revolution!

Advertising Sales Order

Business Name		Contact Name
Address		
City	State	Zip
Phone	Website	Email

Primary Conflict	Secondary Conflict (Optional)

Spot Length

☐ 30-Second Spot ________ Spots @ $______ each
☐ 60-Second Spot ________ Spots @ $______ each

Run ________ Spots Per Day

☐ Weather Sponsorship @ $______ month
☐ Live On-Site Remote for ________ Hours @ $100/hr

Production

☐ Client-Produced Spot
- ☐ Received From Client

☐ KHWL-Produced Spot
- ☐ Client Approved Copy
- ☐ Produced and Ready

☐ Agency-Produced Spot
- ☐ Client Approved Copy
- ☐ Received From Agency

Package Specials

☐ Full Blitz 30 • 300 Spots @ **$1,500**
☐ Full Blitz 60 • 300 Spots @ **$2,250**
(Approximately 10 Per Day)

☐ Strafing Run 30 • 100 Spots @ **$500**
☐ Strafing Run 60 • 100 Spots @ **$750**
(Approximately 3 Per Day)

Order Notes and Special Instructions

Salesperson	Cash Amount This Sales Order	Trade Amount This Sales Order
Authorized Client Signature		Date

Wolfpack Media LLC • 102 W Broadway Street • Altus, Oklahoma 73521 • 580-482-KHWL • www.khowl.fm

FIGURE 4.10
Once ads are sold, a sales order and contract are completed and signed. Courtesy of Wolfpack Media, LLC.

best-time-available (BTA) plans are usually an option. Rates are lower under these plans because no guarantee is given as to what times the spots will be aired. However, most stations make a concerted effort to rotate ROS and BTA spots as equitably as possible, and during periods when commercial loads are light they frequently are scheduled during premium times. Of course, when a station is loaded down with spot schedules, especially around holidays or elections, ROS and BTA spots may find themselves buried. In the long run, advertisers using these plans receive a more than fair amount of choice times and at rates considerably lower than those clients who buy specific dayparts.

In *Radio Advertising's Missing Ingredient: The Optimum Effective Scheduling System* by Pierre Bouvard and Steve Marx, an innovative system is presented that improves the might of a spot schedule. According to the authors, "Optimum effective scheduling ensures that the effective reach, those hit three or more times, is at least 50% of the total reach." The idea behind optimum effective scheduling (OES) is to strengthen the impact of client buys. The OES formula is designed to heighten the efficiency of a spot buy through a system of scheduling based on ratings performance. This is accomplished by factoring a station's turnover ratio and cume.

Total audience plan (TAP) is another popular package offered clients by many stations. It is designed to distribute a client's spots among the various dayparts for maximum audience penetration, while costing less than an exclusive primetime schedule. The rate for a TAP spot is arrived at by averaging the cost for spots in several time classifications. For example, AAA $80, AA $70, A $58, B $31; thus, the TAP rate per spot is $59. The advantages are obvious. The advertiser is getting a significant discount on the spots scheduled during morning and afternoon drive periods. At the same time, the advertiser is paying more for airtime during evenings. However, TAP is very attractive because it does expose a client's message to every possible segment of a station's listening audience with a measure of cost-effectiveness.

Bulk or annual discounts are available to advertisers who buy a heavy schedule of commercials over the course of a year. Large companies in particular take advantage of volume discounts because the savings are significant.

	MON	*WED*	*FRI*
Week I	7:15	6:25	9:10
Week II	8:22	7:36	8:05
Week III	6:11	9:12	7:46
Week IV	9:20	8:34	6:52

As noted, most radio stations have gotten away or are getting away from using rate cards as internal pricing and scheduling systems have become more sophisticated and customized client presentations have become the norm. More stations now present their clients with rates for their specific schedule or with a package price for the entire schedule. Jennifer McCann, former GM of Burlington Broadcasters, shared that "While some small market stations still rely on rate cards, stations in major markets do not." Using systems similar to "yield management" systems first introduced by the airline industry, medium and larger stations often use programs such as Marketron to manage and price their spot inventory to ensure their sales goals. A radio station is usually faced with uneven and ever-changing demands on a limited amount of commercial time. Certain dayparts near the end-of-the-week, special programming, and drivetimes near holidays might be easily sold out, yet other time periods might have plenty of "avails." Using an inventory management system enables stations to continuously price their inventory by day, daypart, and even by the hour months in advance. This knowledge gives the sales department the up-to-the minute pricing and "avail" information it needs to serve the client and allows the station to maintain the maximum control of its inventory and revenue. Even in smaller markets, rate cards are not used much except as a point for negotiating. Rate cards are often confusing and focus attention on the individual spot cost rather than the total cost of an advertising campaign. To compete against other media, radio has realized the value of creating customized presentations and programs for clients that respond to their specific needs and goals. Clients and agencies sometimes do ask to see a rate card, but they are rapidly becoming extinct.

HISPANIC RADIO: BIAS IN THE BUYING PROCESS

David Gleason

In the 1970s, Spanish language radio moved into an era of rapid growth with many new stations in an increasing number of markets. As such stations began to proliferate and to register good, saleable numbers in the ratings, success was tempered by what was referred to as the "Spanish discount." This term refers to a conscious undervaluation of audience deliverability, and thus desirability, when those audiences were Hispanics.

FIGURE 4.11
David Gleason.

Such pricing pressures had long affected African American targeted stations. That market, dating back to its initial growth in the 1950s was the victim of similar "no buy" or "buy cheap" restrictions by advertisers. These buying practices came to include "No Hispanic" and "No Urban" dictates because some advertisers simply excluded ethnic media from buying consideration, while others bought ethnic radio, but exerted downward pressure on rates.

Discriminatory practices that had long existed in the buying of broadcast media targeted at African Americans and Hispanics were addressed by the FCC following a formal inquiry. In 2011, an FCC action required stations to include non-discrimination clauses in all sales contracts and the certification of compliance at the time of license renewal.

The FCC said in its Enforcement Advisory of March, 2011, "In adopting this requirement, the Commission addressed reports that some advertising contracts contain 'no urban/no Spanish' dictates that are intended to minimize the proportion of African American or Hispanic customers patronizing an advertiser's venue—or dictates that presume that African Americans or Hispanics cannot be persuaded to buy an advertiser's product or service" (FCC Advisory 2011–06).

While discriminatory buying practices are predominantly an internal decision of ad buyers, the FCC showed by this action that it was aware of such practices and that it would not tolerate them. For the ethnic-targeted broadcaster, the FCC attention was welcome. The more recent actions by the Commission reflect that agency's awareness that the practice existed and dated back many decades. In the case of Hispanic broadcasters, the "Spanish discount" is the earliest manifestation of ungrounded advertiser attitudes to the effect that listeners to Spanish language stations have lower incomes and thus "buy less," or that Hispanics are otherwise not desirable targets for advertising. This stereotype caused advertisers to apply pressure on Spanish language station rates. This is evidenced by the lower ratings to revenue conversions of Spanish language stations in nearly every market in the US. The discount mentality is not unique to Hispanic radio or to ethnic radio; "old timers" recall the "country discount" seen many, many decades ago when country stations were thought to bring low income consumers to advertisers.

David Gleason is a radio programming consultant, former EVP of Univision Radio, as well as a former owner and group manager. His website is www.americanradiohistory.com.

POINTS OF THE PITCH

Not all sales are made on the first call; nonetheless, the salesperson does go in with the hopes of closing an account. The first call generally is designed to introduce the station to the prospective sponsor and to determine the sponsor's needs. However, the salesperson should always be prepared to propose a buy that is suitable for the account. This means that some homework must be done relative to the business before an approach is made. "First determine the client's needs, as best as possible. Then address those needs with a schedule built to reach the client's customers. Don't walk into a business cold or without some sense of what the place is about," advises Charles Friedman.

Should all go smoothly during the initial call, the salesperson may opt to go for an order there and then. If the account obliges, fine. In the event that the prospective advertiser is not prepared to make an immediate decision, a follow-

FIGURE 4.12
This KHWL-FM account executive business card is used to capture the attention of the client with its creative design. In small radio media markets, the general manager is also a salesperson. Courtesy of Wolfpack Media, LLC.

up appointment must be made. The callback should be accomplished as close to the initial presentation as possible to prevent the impression made then from fading or growing cold. The primary objective of the return call is to close the deal and get the order. To strengthen the odds, the salesperson must review and assess any objections or reservations that may have arisen during the first call and devise a plan to overcome them. Meanwhile, the initial proposal may be beefed up to appear even more attractive to the client, and a "spec" tape (see the later section "Spec Spots") for the business can be prepared as further enticement.

Should the salesperson's efforts fail the second time out, third and even fourth calls are made. Perseverance does pay off, and many salespeople admit that just when they figured a situation was hopeless, an account said yes. "Of course, beating your head against the wall accomplishes nothing. You have to know when your time is being wasted. Never give up entirely on an account; just approach it more sensibly. A phone call or a drop-in every so often keeps you in their thoughts," says retired general sales manager Ronald Piro.

What follows are two checklists. The "Do" list contains some suggestions conducive to a positive sales experience, and the "Don't" list contains things that will have a negative or counterproductive effect.

DO

- Research the advertiser; be prepared; have a relevant plan in mind.
- Be enthusiastic; think positive.
- Display self-confidence; believe in yourself and the product.
- Smile; exude friendliness, warmth, and sincerity.
- Listen; be polite, sympathetic, and interested.
- Tell of the station's successes; provide testimonial material.
- Think creatively.
- Know your competition.
- Maintain integrity and poise.
- Look your best; check your appearance.
- Be objective and keep proper perspective.
- Pitch the decision-maker.
- Ask for the order that will do the job.
- Service the account after the sale.

DON'T

- Pitch without a plan.
- Criticize or demean the client's previous advertising efforts.
- Argue with the client. This just creates greater resistance.
- Bad-mouth the competition.
- Talk too much.
- Brag or be overly aggressive.
- Lie, exaggerate, or make unrealistic promises.
- Smoke or chew gum in front of the client.
- Procrastinate or put things off.
- Be intimidated or kept waiting an unreasonable amount of time.
- Make a presentation unless you have the client's undivided attention.
- Lose your temper.
- Ask for too little; never undersell a client.
- Fail to follow-up.
- Accept a "no" as final.

Checklists like the preceding ones can serve only as basic guidelines. Anyone who has spent time "on the street" as a station account executive can expand on this or any other such checklist. For the positive-thinking radio salesperson, every call gives something back, whether a sale is made or not.

TAPSCAN™

LOCAL MARKET RADIO RATINGS SOFTWARE SUITE

Radio salespeople know TAPSCAN as the software that makes it easy to tell their station's story and generate more revenue. The intuitive design is easy to use and master—if your sellers can use a mouse, they will be able to use TAPSCAN from their very first day on the job.

Powered with exclusive Maximi$er®-level data, TAPSCAN gives you access to customized demos, geographies, dayparts and multibook averages. TAPSCAN gives you an edge by making almost every part of the sale easier, from the initial presentation all the way to the hand-off to traffic.

See How We've Improved TAPSCAN!

TAPSCAN 11.2 offers a new NTR Schedule tab, enhanced research reports and more browser support.

The next planned release offers a new NTR Schedule tab, enhanced research reports and more browser support.

Contact your Nielsen Audio representative for a demo today.

With TAPSCAN, you can:

- Demonstrate the sales potential of your audience with more than 80 categories of RETAIL SPENDING POWER qualitative information
- Show advertisers the number of listeners they can reach only through your station
- See what you—and your competition—can charge to hit a requested CPP
- Find out how many spots you need to run to reach a certain frequency, based on a demo and daypart
- Determine your reach and frequency by specific demo, daypart and spot level
- Demonstrate your power against newspapers, magazines, television, cable and outdoor
- Get proposals to clients faster with e-mail-friendly PDF output
- Streamline order approval and automate the transfer to your traffic system

Data used in system:

Respondent-Level Radio Data, Summary-Level Radio Data, Black Radio Data, Hispanic Radio Data, Eastlan Radio Data

The TAPSCAN Suite may include TAPSCAN, TrafficLink®, RETAIL SPENDING POWER℠, MEDIAMASTER℠ and pdfFactory®

Want more info? Contact your account manager now!

Maximi$er®, MEDIAMASTER℠, RETAIL SPENDING POWER℠ and TrafficLink® are marks of Arbitron Inc.
TAPSCAN™ is a mark used under license.
pdfFactory® is a registered mark of FinePrint Software, LLC.

Copyright © 2013 Nielsen

FIGURE 4.13
Software designed to help ad agencies make a buy. Courtesy of Arbitron.

Overcoming common objections is a necessary step toward achieving the sale. Here are some typical "put-offs" presented to radio sales reps:

1. Nobody listens to radio commercials.
2. Newspaper ads are more effective.
3. Radio costs too much.
4. Nobody listens to your station.
5. We tried radio and it didn't work.
6. We don't need any more business.
7. We've already allocated our advertising budget.
8. We can get another station for less.
9. Business is off and we haven't got the money.
10. My partner doesn't like radio.

There are countless rebuttals for each of these statements, and a knowledgeable and skilled radio salesperson can turn such objections into positives.

LEVELS OF SALES

There are three levels from which the medium draws its sales: retail, local, and national. Retail accounts for the biggest percentage of the industry's income, more than 70%. Retail sales—also referred to as *direct sales*—involve the radio station on a one-to-one basis with advertisers within its signal area.

In this case, a station's account executive works directly with the client and earns a commission of approximately 15% on the airtime he or she sells. An advertiser who spends $1,000 would benefit the salesperson to the tune of $150. A newly hired salesperson without previous experience generally will work on a direct retail basis and will not be assigned advertising agencies until he or she has become more seasoned and has displayed some ability. Generally speaking, the smaller the radio station, the more dependent it is on retail sales, although most medium and metro market stations would be in trouble without strong business on this level. All stations, regardless of size, have some contact with advertising agencies. Here again, however, the larger a market, the more a station will derive its business from ad agencies. This level of station sales generally is classified as local. The number of advertising agencies in a market will vary depending on its size. A sales manager will divide the market's agencies among his reps as equitably as possible, sometimes using a merit system. In this way, an account executive who has worked hard and produced results will be rewarded for his efforts by being given an agency to work. The top billers—that is, those salespeople who bring in the most business—often possess the greatest number of agencies, or at least the most active. Although the percentage of commission a salesperson is accorded, typically 6–8%, is less than that derived from retail sales, the size of the agency buys usually is far more substantial.

RESOLUTIONS FOR SELLERS

(Now a perennial first-of-the-year TACTICS topic, these resolutions are designed to inspire and motivate the sales staff.)

- I will have breakfast at 7:30 AM with at least two clients a week.
- Each week, I will read a trade magazine from three client businesses.
- I will set aside one hour a day to prepare written presentations.
- One Saturday morning per month will be set aside to call on retailers.
- I will read at least one book on selling and one book on advertising each month.
- I'll carry a list of my top 10 prospects and call on at least one each day.
- I'll follow each sales presentation with a hand-written "Thank You" note.
- I will remind myself each day that 8% of sales are made after the fifth call.
- I will demonstrate to my prospects that I am willing to work for their business.
- I will always ask, "Is there something else you'd like to hear about?"
- I will remind myself each day that I am not selling time—my business is creating opportunities, processing ideas and distributing information.

FIGURE 4.14
Advice to salespeople. Courtesy of Shane Media.

The third category of station sales comes from the national level. In most cases, it is the general sales manager who works with the station's rep company to secure buys from advertising agencies that handle national accounts. Again, national business is greater for the metro station than it is for the rural. Agencies justify a buy on numbers and little else, although it is not uncommon for small market stations, which do not even appear in ratings surveys, to be bought by major accounts interested in maintaining a strong local or community image.

Producer Ty Ford observes that agency involvement has decreased in recent years because of intensified competition among the different media and the unpredictable national economy. "Increased competition from cable, television, radio, and print has forced many ad agencies out of business. Stations now frequently offer 'agency discounts' to direct-retail clients just to close the sale. Also, more retail companies are forming their own in-house agencies." Although this may be true, the ad agency is still an important factor in station revenues.

Each level of sales—retail, local, or national—must be sufficiently cultivated if a station is to enjoy maximum prosperity. Neglecting any one of these levels would result in a loss of station revenue.

PROFIT SHOULD NOT BE THE "SOLE" REASON WE ARE IN BUSINESS

Wolf Korgyn

I'd like to say that we as radio executives MUST remember that while profit is important, it should not be the sole reason we are in the business. The conglomerates have ruined radio in pursuit of the almighty dollar.

FIGURE 4.15
Wolf Korgyn.

Radio today is a mere shadow of what it once was. I have listeners every day who come into the station and marvel at how different we are and that they haven't listened to FM radio in YEARS—only to accidentally find us on the dial and never return to their iPod. This hasn't happened once or twice, but dozens of times per month over the past year. The modern listener has forgotten about music radio and has moved on to satellite, Internet, Pandora, Spotify, and, of course, their iPod devices.

Radio is in danger of going the way of the dinosaur. The only way to avoid that is to give listeners live content, live DJs, interactive shows, and most of all—passion . . . because radio is magic. No other broadcast medium touches its audience like radio. You may be broadcasting to thousands, but as a listener that DJ is talking to you. For the time that you are listening, you are not alone. That DJ is your friend, a voice you can count on being there, a reminder that you are part of something larger than yourself.

When a station voice-tracks or employs a jukebox format like Jack or Bob or John or any of the dozen or so jockless formats now popular in the industry, it strips the one thing that radio has over the alternative digital formats . . . it strips away the personality. It strips away the soul.

The best advice I can give to a radio executive in today's world—regardless of whether you are in sales, in production, or in the air-studio—is to share your *passion* with the listeners. Without passion, radio is nothing more than a jukebox with commercials, and in today's world of the Internet, satellite radio, and iPods, why would someone choose a jukebox with commercials over their own personal jukebox *without* commercials? They wouldn't. They don't.

Give listeners what Pandora, Spotify, and their iPod will never give them . . . a warm, friendly voice sharing a song, a story, a laugh, or a tear. Because *that* is what makes radio magic.

Wolf Korgyn is owner and general manager of KHWL-FM in Altus, Oklahoma.

SPEC SPOTS

One of the most effective ways to convince an advertiser to use a station is to provide a fully produced sample commercial, or "spec spot." If prepared properly and imaginatively, a client will find it difficult to deny its potential. Spec spots often are used in callbacks when a salesperson needs to break down a client's resistance. More than once, a clever spec spot has converted an adamant "no" into an "okay, let's give it a shot." Spec spots also are used to reactivate the interest of former accounts who may not have spent money on the station for a while and who need some justification to do so.

Specs also are effective tools for motivating clients to "heavy-up" or increase their current spot schedules. A good idea can move a mountain, and salespeople are encouraged by the sales manager to develop spec tape ideas. Many sales managers require that account executives make at least one spec tape presentation each week. The sales manager may even choose to critique spec spots during regularly scheduled meetings.

The information needed to prepare a spec spot is acquired in several ways. If a salesperson already has called on a prospective client, he should have a very good idea of what the business is about as well as the attitude of the retailer toward the enterprise. The station sales rep is then in a very good position to prepare a spot that directly appeals to the needs and perceptions of the would-be advertiser. If a salesperson decides that the first call on a client warrants preparing a spec tape, then he or she may collect information on the business by actually browsing through the store as a customer might. This gives the salesperson an accurate, first-hand impression of the store's environment and merchandise. An idea of how the store perceives itself, and specific information such as address and hours, can be derived by checking its website and display ad in the Yellow Pages if it has one or by examining any ads it may have run in the local newspaper. Flyers that the business may have distributed also provide useful information for the formulation of the copy used in the spec spot. Listening to commercials the advertiser may be running on another station can also give the salesperson an idea of the direction in which to move.

Again, the primary purpose of a spec spot is to motivate a possible advertiser to buy time. A spec spot that fails to capture the interest and appreciation of the individual for which it has been prepared may be lacking in the necessary ingredients. It is generally a good rule of thumb to avoid humor in a spec spot, unless the salesperson has had some first-hand experience with the advertiser. Nothing fails as abysmally as a commercial that attempts to be funny and does not come across as such to the client—thus, the saying "What is funny to one person may be silly or offensive to another."

Although spec spots are, to some extent, a gamble, they should be prepared in such a way that the odds are not too great. Of course, a salesperson who believes in an idea must have the gumption to go with it. Great sales are often inspired by unconventional concepts.

RAB Guide to Writing Great Radio Copy

Developing a great creative Radio campaign is crucial to getting results for your client but the big question is how do you do it? On the following pages you will find a 10 step plan that will help guide you through the challenges, demands and pitfalls of the copywriting process. Don't be afraid to use Radio's creative potential to the fullest and take the time needed to create great-sounding and brilliant campaigns.

STEP 1: FIND OUT WHAT THE CLIENT WANTS

I know it sounds simple and obvious but so many stations and agencies make the mistake of not listening to what their clients really want and hope to achieve with their campaign. And without understanding the real reasons behind why a potential client wants to go on the air, the commercial campaign — no matter how humorous or clever — is doomed.

STEP 2: ASK THE RIGHT QUESTIONS

So to find out what the client wants, you have to ask some questions. Some call it a Client Needs Analysis. And even though this isn't the most exciting part of the creative process, it is crucial to your success. Here are some samples:

1. Is there anything you would like to feature?
   Maybe your clients just got in a huge load of widgets and they need to sell them fast! Or maybe a certain item has a higher profit margin and it would make sense to push that product.

2. Who is your best prospect?
   This question will allow you to get into demographics and find out who they are targeting. Is it male or female or both? What percentage? Average age? Income? Profession and education level? If you represent more than one station, then these questions can help steer your client to the right "position on the dial."

3. Why do customers come to you?
   This question and others below that are similar, allow the client to tell you their story. Keep in mind that perception is reality and you should consider getting different viewpoints from co-workers, family and friends.

4. What is your single greatest competitive advantage?

5. Do you have a positioning statement?

6. What do you feel is your unique selling position?
   The USP or unique selling position (or point) is a marketing concept that allows a company to differentiate themselves from their competition.

7. What is your primary business image?

8. What's the biggest misperception you feel people have about your business?
   Sometimes this misperception can be used in the commercial to help overcome objections. For example, perhaps customers think a popular brand will automatically be too expensive. Or perhaps the potential customers feel that the location is too far away when in reality it's only a 10 or 15 minute drive.

1 of 7

FIGURE 4.16
The RAB's guidelines for salespeople to use to write effective and engaging radio spots. Please see this chapter's Appendix for more of this guide. Courtesy of the Radio Advertising Bureau.

OBJECTIVES OF THE BUY

A single spot on a radio station seldom brings instant riches to an advertiser. However, a thoughtfully devised plan based on a formula of frequency and consistency will achieve impressive results, contends former general manager John Gregory:

> It has to be made clear from the start what a client hopes to accomplish by advertising on your station. Then a schedule that realistically corresponds with the client's goals must be put together. This means selling the advertiser a sufficient number of commercials spread over a specific period of time. An occasional spot here and there doesn't do much in this medium. There's a right way to sell radio, and that isn't it.

Our "Do" and "Don't" lists of selling suggested that the salesperson "ask for the order that will do the job." They also said not to undersell an account. Implicit in the first point is the idea that the salesperson has determined what kind of schedule the advertiser should buy to get the results expected. Too often salespeople fail to ask for what they need for fear the client will balk. Thus, they settle for what they can get without much resistance. This, in fact, may be doing the advertiser a disservice, because the buy that the salesperson settles for may not fulfill declared objectives. Former sales manager Piro says:

> It takes a little courage to persist until you get what you think will do the job. There is the temptation just to take what the client hands you and run, but that technique usually backfires when the client doesn't get what he expected. As a radio sales rep, you should know how best to sell the medium. Don't be apologetic or easily compromised. Sell the medium the way it should be sold. Write enough of an order to get the job done.

To potentially increase sales, the salesperson can provide statistics to the client that show the effectiveness of radio advertising and its ability to reach large audiences at certain times of the day. A 2011 study by Arbitron found that more than 93% of the audience stays with the radio station leading into a commercial break. Studies like this counter claims that listeners change stations when commercials are aired.

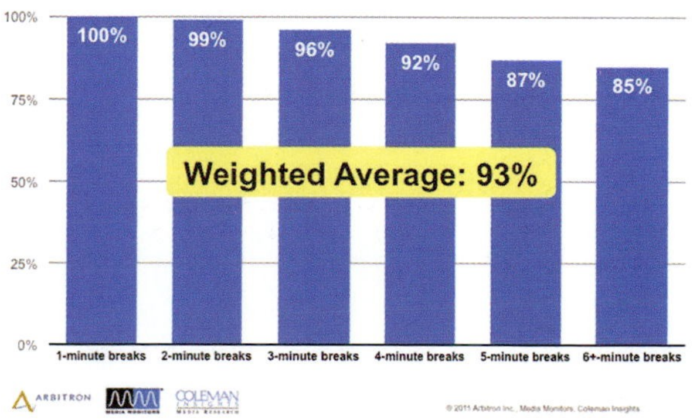

FIGURE 4.17
The majority of radio listeners continue listening through commercial breaks. Courtesy of Arbitron.

Inflated claims and unrealistic promises should never be a part of a sales presentation. Avoid "If you buy spots on my station, you'll have to hire additional salespeople to handle the huge crowds." Salespeople must be honest in their

FIGURES 4.18–4.20
Entercom uses case studies as a means to demonstrate to clients how well-planned and well-executed advertising strategies have been successful. Courtesy of Entercom Communications Corp.

ENTERCOM CaseStudies — Automotive

Local Celebrity Endorsement Drove Young Adults to Test Drive the Chevy Cruze

OBJECTIVE
Milwaukee Chevrolet Dealers wanted to create buzz around the launch of the Chevy Cruze with 18-34 year olds.

SOLUTION
Entercom Milwaukee developed an integrated marketing campaign that centered around a local radio celebrity, Kraig Karson. The endorsement campaign educated fans about the inherent benefits and compelling features of the Chevy Cruze. Kraig's endorsement brought the campaign to life with social media and digital integration including blogging and video.

TESTIMONIAL
"We have been very pleased with the results of the Kraig Karson endorsement of the Chevy Cruze and look forward to another year-long program."
— George H. Gibbs, Agency Account Director

http://bcove.me/pt33nmv4 • http://bcove.me/8k8e05dn • http://bcove.me/yg8xwimz

ENTERCOM CaseStudies — Automotive

Entercom Created Social Media Buzz and Sales Results for the Rocky Mountain Ford Dealers

OBJECTIVE
The Rocky Mountain Ford Dealers wanted to drive qualified traffic into 10 local Ford Dealers during their national "Swap Your Ride" program.

SOLUTION
Entercom Denver worked with the Rocky Mountain Ford Dealers to localize the national "Swap my Ride" campaign. Over 4 weeks local DJs "swapped" their rides and shared their driving experiences with their listeners. The campaign encouraged listener engagement by encouraging people to submit a video entry to "Win a Ride" from their local Ford dealers. Each video was viewed by the general public to create additional buzz and "votes."

RESULTS
Over the course of the campaign, the promotion created buzz in the market reaching over 1 million people and the Rocky Mountain Ford Dealers recorded a 12% sales increase over the previous year.

ENTERCOM CaseStudies — Entertainment

Online Radio Campaign Helped Jewel's "Sweet and Wild" Album Debut on Billboard's Top 10

OBJECTIVE
Jewel's record label, Big Machine Records, wanted to create heightened awareness and immediate sales for Jewel's new CD release, "Sweet and Wild".

SOLUTION
Entercom worked with Big Machine Records to develop a two-week online radio campaign to air prior to the launch of Jewel's "Sweet and Wild" CD. The online radio campaign aired across six Entercom country music radio stations.

TESTIMONIAL
"The launch was a huge success! The album debuted at #10 on Billboard Charts. We are convinced that the online radio campaign gave us the opportunity to expose this new album to the most passionate country music listeners in the U.S."
— John Zarling, Sr.
Director, New Media & National Promotion Strategy,
Big Machine Records

projections and in what a client may expect from the spot schedule they purchase. One effective strategy is to share with clients past successes.

PROSPECTING AND LIST BUILDING

When a salesperson is hired by a radio station, he or she is customarily provided with a list of accounts to which airtime may be sold. For an inexperienced salesperson, this list may consist of essentially inactive or dormant accounts, that is, businesses that either have been on the air in the past or those that have never purchased airtime on the station. The new sales rep is expected to breathe life into the list by selling spot schedules to those accounts listed, as well as by adding to the list by bringing in new business. This is called *list building*, and it is the primary challenge facing the new account executive.

A more active list, one that generates commissions, will be given to the more experienced radio salesperson. A salesperson may be persuaded to leave one station in favor of another based on the contents of a list, which may include large accounts and prominent advertising agencies. Lists held by a station's top billers invariably contain the most enthusiastic radio users. Salespeople cultivate their lists as a farmer does his fields. The more the account list yields, the more commissions in the salesperson's pocket.

New accounts are added to a sales rep's list in several ways. Once the status of the list's existing accounts is determined, which is accomplished through a series of in-person calls and presentations, a salesperson must begin prospecting for additional business. Area newspapers are a common source. When a salesperson finds an account that he wishes to add to his or her list, the account must be "declared." This involves consulting the sales manager for approval to add the account to the salesperson's existing list. In some cases, the account declared may already belong to another salesperson. If it is an open account, the individual who comes forward first usually is allowed to add it to his or her list.

Other sources for new accounts include the Internet, Yellow Pages, television stations, and competing radio outlets. Every business in the area is listed in the Yellow Pages, which contains many display ads that provide useful information. Local television stations are viewed with an eye toward their advertisers. Television can be an expensive proposition, even in smaller markets, and businesses that currently spend money on it may find radio's rates more palatable. On the other hand, if a business can afford to buy television, it often can afford to embellish its advertising campaign with radio spots. Many advertisers place money in several media—newspaper, radio, television—simultaneously. This is called a *mixed media* buy and is a proven advertising formula for the obvious reason that the client is reaching all possible audiences. Finally, accounts currently on other stations constitute good prospects because they have obviously already been sold on the medium.

In the course of an average workday, a salesperson will pass hundreds of businesses, some of which may have just opened their doors, or are about to do so. Sales reps must keep their eyes open and be prepared to make an impromptu call. The old saying "the early bird gets the worm" is particularly relevant in radio sales. The first account executive into a newly launched business often is the one who gets the buy.

A list containing dozens of accounts does not necessarily ensure a good income. If those businesses listed are small spenders or inactive, little in the way of commissions will be generated and billing will be low. The objective of list building is not merely to increase the number of accounts, but rather to raise the level of commissions it produces. In other words, a list that contains 30 accounts, of which 22 are active, is preferable to one with 50 accounts containing only 12 that are doing business with the station. A salesperson does not get points for having a lot of names on his list.

It is the sales manager's prerogative to shift an account from one salesperson's list to another's if he or she believes the account is being neglected or handled incorrectly. At the same time, certain in-house accounts, those handled by the sales manager, may be added to a sales rep's list as a reward for performing well. A salesperson's account list also may be pared down if the sales manager concludes that it is disproportional with the others at the station. The attempt to more equitably distribute the wealth may cause a brouhaha with the account person whose list is being trimmed. The sales manager attempting this feat may lose a top biller; thus, he or she must consider the ramifications of such a move and proceed accordingly. This may even mean letting things remain as they are. The top biller often is responsible for as much as 30–40% of the station's earnings.

PLANNING THE SALES DAY

A radio salesperson should make between 75 and 100 in-person calls a week, averaging 15–20 each day, if possible. This requires careful planning and organization. Ronald Piro advises preparing a day's itinerary the night before. "There's nothing worse than facing the day without an idea of where to go. A salesperson can spare himself that dreaded sensation and a lot of lost time by preparing a complete schedule of calls the night before."

Kramer adds, "A typical day/week includes prospecting, cold calling, researching client categories or info to use in presentations, going on client discovery or initial idea calls, developing creative ideas, writing presentations, making presentations, admin work related to closed business or customer service, sales training or sales meetings, a coaching one-on-one with the direct manager, and driving to appointments. A good rep will make between 12–15 face calls a week."

When preparing a daily call sheet, a salesperson, especially one whose station covers a vast area, attempts to centralize, as much as possible, the businesses to be contacted. Time, energy, and gas are needlessly expended through poor planning. A sales rep who is traveling ten miles between each presentation can get to only half as many clients as the person with a consolidated call sheet. Of course, there are days when a salesperson must spend more time traveling. Not every day can be ideally plotted. It may be necessary to make a call in one part of the city at 9 am and be in another part at 10 am. A salesperson must be where he or she feels the buys are going to be made. "Go first to those businesses likeliest to buy. The tone of the day will be sweetened by an early sale," contends Piro.

Sales managers advise their reps to list more prospects than they expect to contact. In so doing, they are not likely to run out of places to go should those prospects they had planned to see be unavailable. "You have to make the calls to make the sales. The more calls you make, the more the odds favor a sale," points out Gene Etheridge.

The telephone is one of the salesperson's best tools. Although it is true that a client cannot sign a contract over the phone, much time and energy can be saved through its effective use. Appointments can be made and a client can be qualified via the telephone. That is to say, a salesperson can ascertain when the decision-maker will be available. "Rather than travel 20 miles without knowing if the person who has the authority to make a buy will be around, take a couple of minutes and make a phone call. As they say, 'time is money.' In the time spent finding out that the store manager or owner is not on the premises when you get there, other, more productive calls can be made," says Charles Friedman.

If a client is not available when the salesperson appears, a callback should be arranged for either later the same day or soon thereafter. The prospective advertiser should never be forgotten or relegated to a call three months hence. The sales rep should try to rearrange his or her schedule to accommodate a return visit the same day, if the person to see will be available. However, it is futile to make a presentation to someone who cannot give their full attention. The sales rep who arrives at a business only to find the decision-maker overwhelmed by distractions is wise to ask for another appointment. In fact, the client will perceive this as an act of kindness and consideration. Timing is important.

A record of each call should be kept for follow-up purposes. When calling on a myriad of accounts, it is easy to lose track of what transpired during a particular call. Maintaining a record of a call requires little more than a brief notation after it is made. Notes may then be periodically reviewed to help determine what action should be taken on the account. Follow-ups are crucial. There is nothing more embarrassing and disheartening than to discover a client, who was pitched and then forgotten, advertising on another station. Sales managers usually require that salespeople turn in copies of their call sheets on a daily or weekly basis for review purposes.

SELLING PERSONALITY

Jason Insalaco

FIGURE 4.21
Jason Insalaco.

In the quickly evolving media landscape, winning radio personalities will save radio stations from advertiser erosion. Personality cannot be duplicated. A hit music single cannot sell a product or compel a listener to patronize an advertiser. A radio personality can easily accomplish this objective. A radio personality extolling the benefits of an advertiser in a live-read commercial is always more effective than the best produced spot. A live appearance or broadcast by a radio personality can bring throngs of listeners to a retail advertiser. The hottest chart-topping single can never compel and connect like radio talent. A radio personality not only entertains the listener with fresh, compelling content every day, the person behind the mic also nurtures listener loyalty and connection. Advertisers desire this "stickiness" because the more the consumer is connected to a personality, the more likely the listener will trust and heed what he or she says about a product or service.

Jason Insalaco has more than 20 years of experience in the radio industry. Throughout his tenure, he has worked as a station manager, program director, executive producer, and in other programming and production roles at radio stations in Los Angeles, San Francisco, and Boston. In addition, Jason is a media lawyer and has worked as a talent manager representing personalities from morning show radio, talk radio, and public broadcasting. He currently develops content and new media initiatives for commercial and public radio. He earned an undergraduate degree from Boston College and he obtained a law degree from Loyola Law School in Los Angeles.

SELLING WITH AND WITHOUT NUMBERS

Not all stations can claim to be number one or two in the ratings. In fact, not all stations appear in any formal ratings survey. Very small markets are not visited by Arbitron or other rating services for the simple reason that there may be only one station broadcasting in the area. An outlet in a non-survey area relies on its good reputation in the community to attract advertisers. In small markets, salespeople do not work out of a ratings book and clients are not concerned with cumes and shares. In the truest sense of the word, an account person must sell the station. Local businesses often account for more than 95% of a small market station's revenue. Thus, the stronger the ties with the community, the better. Broadcasters in rural markets must foster an image of good citizenship to make a living.

Civic-mindedness is not as marketable a commodity in the larger markets as are ratings points. In the sophisticated multi-station urban market, the ratings book is the bible. A station without numbers in the highly competitive environment finds the task of earning an income a difficult one, although there are numerous examples of low-rated stations that do very well. However, "no numbers" pretty much puts a metro area station out of the running for agency business. Agencies almost invariably "buy by the book." A station without numbers "works the street," to use the popular phrase, focusing its sales efforts on direct business.

FIGURE 4.22
Arbitron Inc. (NYSE: ARB) is an international media and marketing research firm serving the media—radio, television, cable, and out-of-home—and the mobile industry as well as advertising agencies and advertisers around the world. Arbitron businesses include measuring network and local market radio audiences across the United States. Courtesy of Arbitron.

* Please see Chapter One's discussion regarding the sale of Arbitron to Nielsen and its rebranding as Nielsen Audio.

An obvious difference in approaches exists between selling the station with ratings and the one without. In the first case, a station centers its entire presentation around its high ratings. "According to the latest Arbitron, WXXX-FM is number one with adults 24 to 39." Never out of the conversation for very long are the station's numbers, and at advertising agencies the station's standing speaks for itself. "We'll buy WXXX because the book shows that they have the largest audience in the demos we're after."

The station without rating numbers sells itself on a more personal level, perhaps focusing on its unique features and special blend of music and personalities, and so forth. In an effort to attract advertisers, non-rated outlets often develop programs with a targeted retail market in mind; for example, a home "how-to" show designed to interest hardware and interior decor stores, or a cooking feature aimed at food and appliance stores.

The salesperson working for the station with the cherished "good book" must be especially adept at talking numbers, because they are the key subject of the presentation in most situations. "Selling a top-rated metro station requires more than a pedestrian knowledge of numbers, especially when dealing with agencies. In big cities, retailers have plenty of book savvy, too," contends Piro.

Selling without numbers demands its own unique set of skills, notes WNRI's Gregory. "There are really two different types of radio selling—with numbers and without. In the former instance, you'd better know your math, whereas in the latter, you've got to be really effective at molding your station to suit the desires of the individual advertiser. Without the numbers to speak for you, you have to do all the selling yourself. Flexibility and ingenuity are the keys to the sale."

Metro Survey Area Rankings and Population

www.arbitron.com

MKT CODE	METRO 12+ RANK	TYPE	MARKET	METRO PERSONS 12+ ESTIMATED POPULATION
001	1	PPM	New York	16,033,100
003	2	PPM	Los Angeles	11,179,600
005	3	PPM	Chicago	7,910,200
009	4	PPM	San Francisco	6,377,900
024	5	PPM	Dallas-Ft. Worth	5,559,300
033	6	PPM	Houston-Galveston	5,253,500
015	7	PPM	Washington, DC	4,720,300
007	8	PPM	Philadelphia	4,547,300
047	9	PPM	Atlanta	4,487,600
013	10	PPM	Boston	4,145,900
429	11	PPM	Miami-Ft. Lauderdale-Hollywood	3,858,000
011	12	PPM	Detroit	3,790,400
039	13	PPM	Seattle-Tacoma	3,585,700
057	14	PPM	Phoenix	3,347,700
540	15	4S	Puerto Rico	3,128,300
027	16	PPM	Minneapolis-St. Paul	2,827,200
063	17	PPM	San Diego	2,729,200
087	18	PPM	Tampa-St. Petersburg-Clearwater	2,501,200
035	19	PPM	Denver-Boulder	2,486,500
321	20	PPM	Nassau-Suffolk (Long Island)[1]	(2,454,700)
021	21	PPM	Baltimore	2,373,000
017	22	PPM	St. Louis	2,318,800
051	23	PPM	Portland, OR	2,182,400
093	24	PPM	Charlotte-Gastonia-Rock Hill	2,108,900
023	25	PPM	Pittsburgh, PA	2,008,400
			TOTAL 1-25	109,460,400
379	26	PPM	Riverside-San Bernardino	1,997,700
065	27	PPM	Sacramento	1,913,000
059	28	PPM	San Antonio	1,897,800
101	29	PPM	Salt Lake City-Ogden-Provo	1,791,400
031	30	PPM	Cincinnati	1,781,400
019	31	PPM	Cleveland	1,763,800
257	32	PPM	Las Vegas	1,700,200
131	33	PPM	Orlando	1,676,600
041	34	PPM	Kansas City	1,668,100
135	35	PPM	Austin	1,586,300
215	36	PPM	San Jose[2]	(1,574,200)
045	37	PPM	Columbus, OH	1,567,700
043	38	PPM	Milwaukee-Racine	1,489,100
393	39	2S	Hudson Valley[3]	(1,487,300)
049	40	PPM	Indianapolis	1,468,300
413	41	PPM	Middlesex-Somerset-Union[4]	(1,454,800)
115	42	PPM	Raleigh-Durham	1,430,100
109	43	PPM	Norfolk-Virginia Beach-Newport News	1,390,200
077	44	PPM	Providence-Warwick-Pawtucket	1,388,700
073	45	PPM	Nashville	1,339,200
166	46	PPM	Greensboro-Winston-Salem-High Point	1,239,100
053	47	4S	New Orleans	1,222,200
299	48	PPM	West Palm Beach-Boca Raton	1,200,300
083	49	4S	Oklahoma City	1,194,300
107	50	PPM	Jacksonville	1,184,500
			TOTAL 26-50	34,201,800
			TOTAL 1-50	143,662,200
075	51	PPM	Memphis	1,122,600
061	52	PPM	Hartford-New Britain-Middletown	1,077,600
516	53	4S	Monmouth-Ocean[5]	(1,032,700)
055	54	4S	Louisville	1,009,400
105	55	4S	Richmond	1,003,700
037	56	4S	Buffalo-Niagara Falls	983,900
269	57	2S	McAllen-Brownsville-Harlingen	975,500
079	58	4S	Rochester, NY	963,800
191	59	4S	Greenville-Spartanburg	913,300
095	60	4S	Birmingham	908,100
515	61	2S	Ft. Myers-Naples-Marco Island	879,600
207	62	4S	Tucson	850,200
099	63	4S	Honolulu	843,500
067	64	4S	Dayton	836,300
069	65	4S	Albany-Schenectady-Troy	805,200
103	66	4S	Tulsa	787,800
089	67	4S	Fresno	777,200
141	68	4S	Albuquerque	749,900
127	69	4S	Grand Rapids	745,200
145	70	4S	Allentown-Bethlehem	714,800
121	71	4S	Knoxville	699,000
175	72	4S	Wilkes Barre-Scranton	696,900
071	73	4S	Des Moines	682,600
161	74	4S	El Paso	681,400
085	75	4S	Omaha-Council Bluffs	677,000
373	76	2S	Sarasota-Bradenton	652,100

TYPE: PPM – PPM, 4S – Diary Standard Continuous Measurement, 2S – Diary Standard Measurement, 2C – Diary Condensed Measurement, 2A – Diary 2-Book Average

MKT CODE (Market Code): Unique, numeric identifier for a market

[1] The Nassau-Suffolk (Long Island), NY Metro is embedded in the New York Metro.
[2] The San Jose Metro is embedded in the San Francisco Metro.
[3] Putnam, NY (population 86,300), Rockland, NY (population 262,800) and Westchester, NY (population 826,400) are included in the Hudson Valley and the New York Metro definitions.
[4] The Middlesex-Somerset-Union Metro is embedded in the New York Metro.
[5] Monmouth County (population 541,400) is included in the Monmouth-Ocean and the New York Metro definitions.

The population estimates for footnoted markets are not duplicated in the cumulative population totals.

Market Survey Schedule and Population Rankings, Fall 2013

FIGURE 4.23
Arbitron's top radio media markets ranked in the U.S. Ratings are obtained in these markets and used by radio stations and clients to effectively plan radio buys. Courtesy of Arbitron.

ADVERTISING AGENCIES

Advertising agencies came into existence more than a century ago and have played an integral role in broadcasting since its inception. Their presence continues to be felt today, but not to the extent that it was prior to the advent of television.

Agencies annually account for hundreds of millions in radio ad dollars. The long, and at times turbulent, marriage of radio and advertising agencies was, and continues to be, based on the need of national companies to convey their messages on the local level and the need of the local broadcaster for national business. It is a two-way street. From the perspective of a radio station's sales department, Kramer asserts, "The best agencies are a total advocate for the client and work with different media to create campaigns with the best possible chance for success. A great agency also listens to new ideas and presents the best of those ideas to the client. Agencies play a significant role in creating, planning, negotiating, placing, posting, and determining the ROI (return on investment) of the media placed."

Today, hundreds of advertising agencies use the radio medium. They range in size from mammoth to minute. Agencies such as McCann Erickson, Young & Rubicam (Y&R), J. Walter Thompson (JWT) Global Advertising Agency, Saatchi & Saatchi, and Leo Burnett bill in the hundreds of millions annually and employ hundreds. In December 2012, AdBrands.net estimated that 2013 would see a total of almost $160 billion spent on all advertising in the U.S., and ad agencies handle a large portion of those dollars. More typical, however, are the agencies scattered throughout the country that bill between $500,000 and $2.5 million each year and employ anywhere from half a dozen to 20 people. Agencies come in all shapes and sizes and provide various services, depending on their scope and dimensions.

The process of getting national business onto a local station is an involved one. The major agencies must compete against dozens of others to win the right to handle the advertising of large companies. This usually involves elaborate presentations and substantial investments by agencies. When and if the account is secured, the agency must then prepare the materials—audio, video, print—for the campaign and see to it that the advertiser's money is spent in the most effective way possible. Little is done without extensive marketing research and planning. The agency's media buyer oversees the placement of dollars in the various media. Media buyers at national agencies deal with station and network reps rather than directly with the stations themselves. It would be impossible for an agency placing a buy on 400 stations to personally transact with each.

There are basically three types of agencies: *full-service agencies*, which provide clients with a complete range of services, including research, marketing, and production; *modular agencies*, which provide specific services to advertisers; and *in-house agencies*, which handle the advertising needs of their own business.

The standard commission that an agency receives for its service is 15% on billing. For example, if an agency places $100,000 on radio, it earns $15,000 for its efforts. Agencies often charge clients additional fees to cover production costs and some agencies receive a retainer from clients.

The business generated by agencies constitutes an important percentage of radio's revenues, especially for medium and large market stations. However, compared to other media, such as television, radio's allocation is diminutive. The nation's top three agencies invest more than 80% of their broadcast budgets in television. Nonetheless, hundreds of millions of dollars are channeled into radio by agencies that recognize the effectiveness of the medium.

REP COMPANIES

Rep companies are the industry's middlemen. Rep companies are given the task of convincing national agency media buyers to place money on the stations they represent. Without their existence, radio stations would have to find a way to reach the myriad of agencies on their own—an impossible feat.

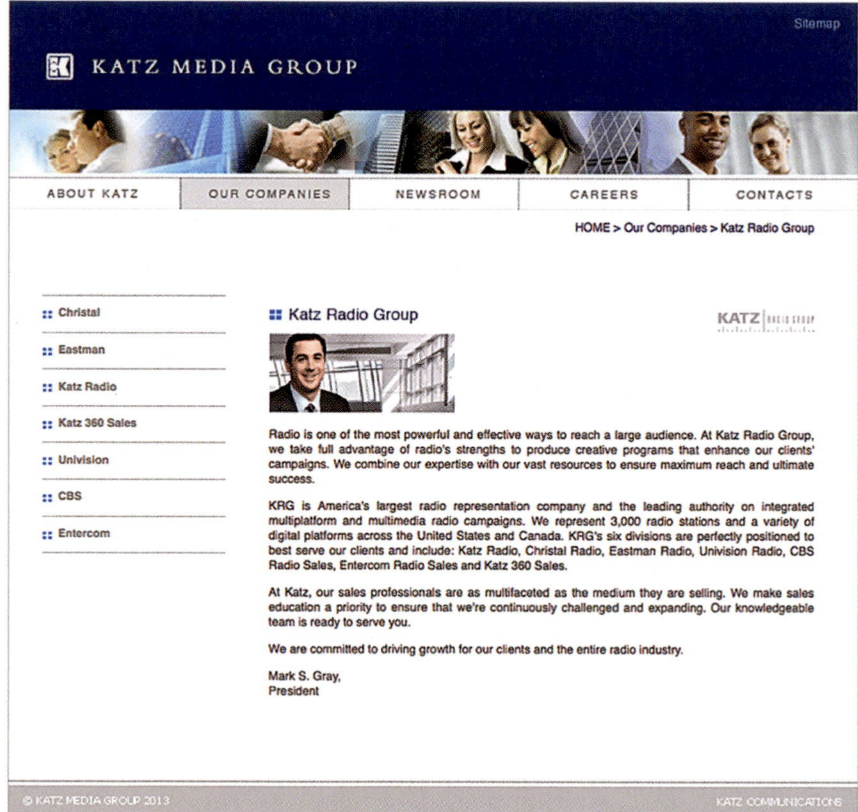

FIGURE 4.24
A rep company explains itself. Courtesy of Katz Media Group.

With few exceptions, radio outlets contract the services of a station rep company. Even the smallest station wants to be included in buys at the national level. The rep company basically is an extension of a station's sales department. The rep and the station's sales manager work together closely. Information about a station and its market are crucial to the rep. The burden of keeping the rep fully aware of what is happening back at the station rests on the sales manager's shoulders. Because a rep company based in New York or Chicago would have no way of knowing that its client station in Arkansas has decided to carry the local college's basketball games, it is the station's responsibility to make the information available. A rep cannot sell what it does not know exists. Of course, a good rep will keep in contact with a station on a regular basis simply to keep up on station changes.

There are far fewer radio station reps than ad agencies, and with the clustering of stations by radio corporations, the number of rep companies has dwindled dramatically as broadcasters assume the burden of representing themselves. Today, there are just a handful of major rep companies handling the 9,000-plus commercial stations around the country because the huge radio companies assume this function in-house. "In their heyday in the 1970s, many national and regional rep firms served individual stations and group radio owners, but because of pressures from increased costs, pressure from client stations on commission rates, and the creation of unwired network radio, an attempt to compete with the lower rates of traditional radio networks that lowered radio rates, many were forced to close or merge through the 1980s and 1990s. With consolidation, where one, two, or three groups now control most radio stations in a given market, the need for multiple reps evaporated," says Williams.

Major rep firms pitch agencies on behalf of hundreds of client stations. The large and very successful reps often refuse to act as the envoy for small market stations because of their lack of earning potential. A rep company typically receives a commission of between 5–12% on the spot buys made by agencies, and because the national advertising money usually is directed first to the medium and large markets, the bigger commissions are not to be made from handling small market outlets. Many rep companies specialize in small market stations, however, especially in the age of consolidation.

Although a small rep company may work for the agencies on behalf of numerous stations, it will seldom handle two radio outlets in the same market. Doing so could result in a rep company being placed in the untenable position of competing with itself for a buy, thus creating an obvious conflict of interest. In the past few years, many larger rep firms have taken on multiple stations in the same market due to the clustering approach of their clients.

The majority of station reps provide additional services. In recent years many have expanded into the areas of programming and management consultancy, and almost all offer clients audience research data, as well as aid in developing station promotions and designing sales materials such as rate cards.

WEBSITE, HD RADIO, AND NEW MEDIA SELLING

Websites, high-definition (HD) channels and social media have become additional sources of revenue at many stations. Stations use their websites as an additional means of generating revenue and communicating with their listeners. Indeed, a website presence is a twenty-first-century requirement and another way to add value to traditional commercial buys. Korgyn asserts:

> Websites can generate significant revenue from "banner ads" if the station has an active website. The success of a station's website and social media presence depends entirely on how tech savvy the staff is. For a website to generate any revenue, it must be updated often, offer contests and other

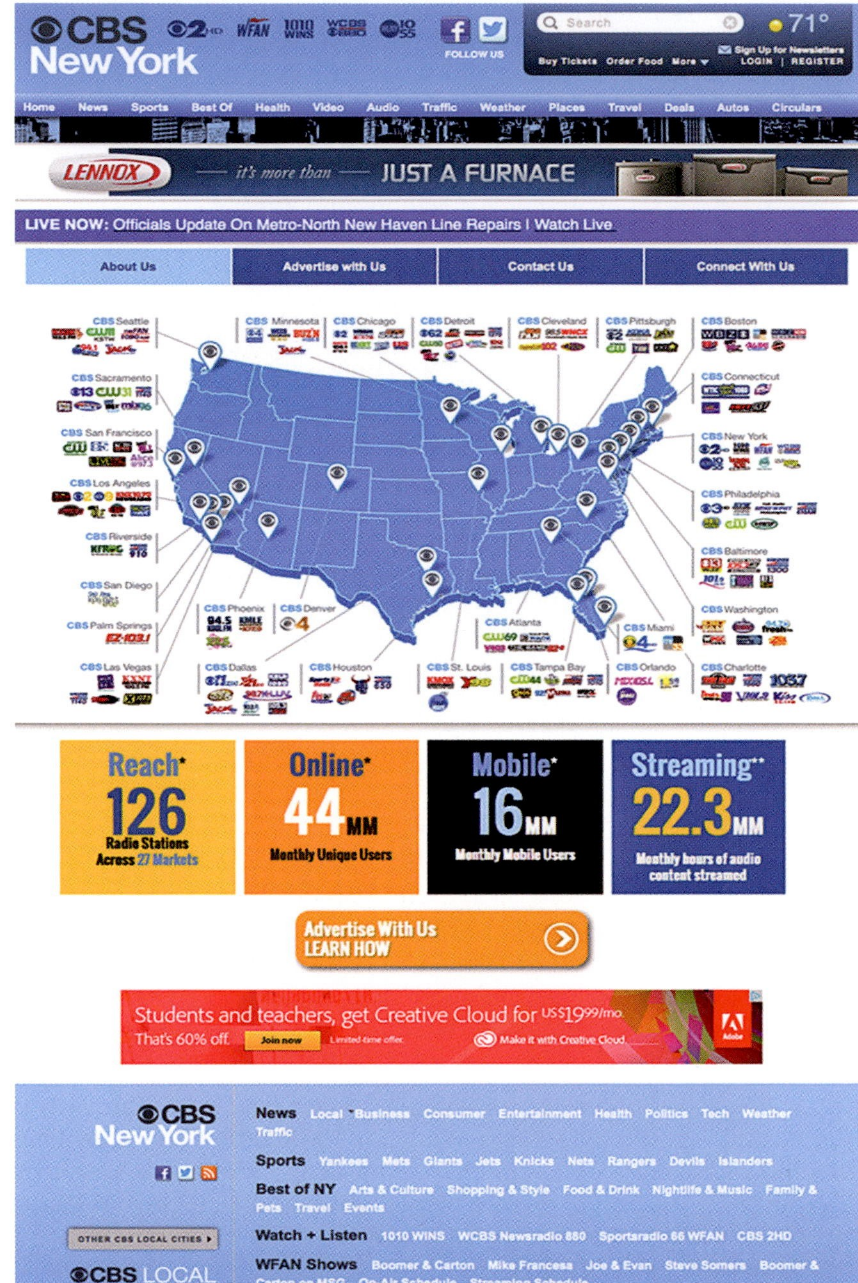

FIGURE 4.25
The CBS affiliated radio stations in New York City use their Web page to explain to businesses what the benefits would be if advertising dollars were spent on their clustered stations. Courtesy of CBS News.

> "draws" for listeners to keep coming back, and provide a fun and interactive interface. HD Radio (which we haven't implemented yet due to the robber-baron, monopolistic license pricing from iBiquity) has a great opportunity to present additional revenue streams through its "Artist Experience (AE)" screen displays. This could be used to display client ads during the commercials themselves, sponsored weather updates, sponsored contests, etc. The AE is a great tool for marketing.

Regarding online selling opportunities, Jason Insalaco says:

> Radio account executives can benefit from this source by selling additional exposure to advertisers. Another thing to keep in mind is that podcasting and streaming allow local clients of lesser means who previously could not afford a conventional broadcast schedule the chance to purchase less expensive Web commercials. Account executives can attest to the difficulty of selling the intangible (sightless) nature of radio. Web advertising helps overcome this objection. Visual banner ads allow streaming listeners to click on ads that will take them directly to a client's website. Furthermore, radio programmers now have access to immediate data to provide advertisers with the number of users streaming their station and downloading specific podcasts. The current Arbitron ratings system provides audience data four weeks later and is arguably arbitrary due to sampling inconsistencies and often erratic results. However, streaming and podcasting is a win-win for programmers who strive to retain the fickle listener and garner additional income.

One thing for broadcasters to keep in mind is that consumers do not always find online advertising welcoming or effective. A study conducted by Adobe in 2012 found that nearly a third of consumers thought online advertising was ineffective and more than half of those surveyed thought that banner ads were ineffective. The same study found that in terms of capturing a consumer's attention, radio ads were 15% more likely to capture a consumer's attention compared to online ads at 7%.

Meanwhile, it is hoped that HD side-channels (HD channels) will provide additional revenue streams for stations. While the HD adoption movement has slowed recently, expectations indicate that advertiser interest in the innovative formats emerging (and predicted to emerge) will increase. In several major markets, HD formats have already attracted sponsors seeking a more niche clientele. To maximize HD Radio's revenue potential, Kevin McNamara of RadioMagOnline.com, says:

> Let's get back to the fundamentals that worked years ago, serving the community. How about instead of putting some regurgitated music channel on the multicast channels, utilize them for providing public access to the communities within the station's service area. What I am suggesting

> here is not necessarily selling time to local businesses, rather giving time (and perhaps equipment and resources) to the communities to broadcast local events, particularly high school sports events or anything else that has relevant interest to the residents of that area . . . Would I also put this content on my streaming site? Absolutely not . . . make this content special and exclusive to the local HD Radio audience.

Newer audio media outlets such as iHeartRadio and Pandora have also experienced fluctuations in revenue. In May, 2013, Pandora reported first quarter losses of nearly $30 million accompanied by a loss of stock valuation. A quantifiable way to measure effectiveness of advertising on Pandora that goes beyond click-through rates will need to be developed. Although social media networks have not proven to be tools for generating revenue for stations yet, they may eventually. Jim Fox, operations manager and station manager for Entercom/Sacramento, stated in an interview with All Access Music Group, "I view social media as I did our old bumper sticker campaigns: I know they

Digital Sound

HD Radio broadcasts deliver crystal clear, CD-like digital audio quality to consumers.

HD2/HD3

Adjacent to traditional main stations are HD2/HD3 Channels, providing new original formats on the FM dial.

PSD

Program Service Data provides song name, artist, station ID, and other relevant data streams.

Active Alerts

Delivers critical and life saving messages during emergency situations.

Artist Experience

Visual images, such as album art of over-the -air broadcasts from HD Radio stations.

iTunes® Tagging

iTunes Tagging provides users the means to "tag" broadcast radio content for later review and purchase from the iTunes Store.

Traffic

HD Radio Digital Traffic delivers more in-depth traffic data and travel conditions – as much as 10x faster than other broadcast methods.

Instant Info

News, sports, weather and more, useful information at the touch of a button.

Bookmark

Bookmark enables users to store information about content on the radio and delivers interactive information via QR codes.

FIGURE 4.26
HD Radio transmits both audio and data to receivers providing more options for listeners and creating options for revenue streams. © 2013 iBiquity Digital Corporation; reproduced with permission from iBiquity.

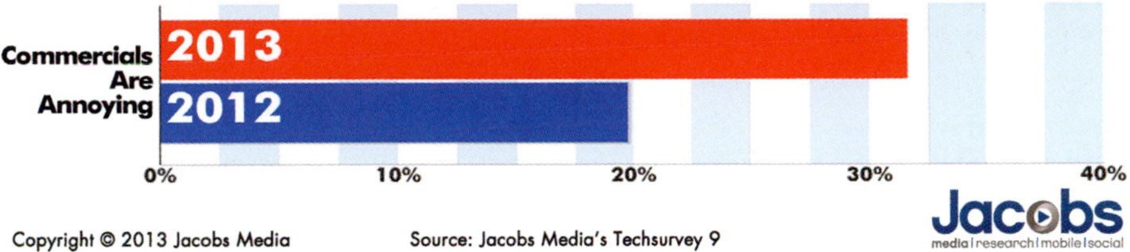

FIGURE 4.27
Research indicates that listeners are annoyed by advertising on Pandora. Courtesy of Jacobs Media.

are of value to the brand even if I can't produce any data to quantify it. KRXQ approaches social media with more than 25 years of heritage and very clearly defined personalities. KKDO tends to speak with one collective voice since it boasts 'no annoying DJs.'" The business model for online radio stations is evolving and since listeners have been accustomed to having ad-free music, the introduction of ads on Pandora has not been embraced enthusiastically by consumers.

Audio technology for podcasting has been around since the early 2000s but radio stations have failed to find a definitive way to generate revenue from podcasting.

PODCA$HING IN

Jason Insalaco

With the explosion of portable media and increased bandwidth, broadcasters have been presented with a unique opportunity to create and monetize podcasts. For the terrestrial broadcaster, podcasting typically involves the following: remove commercials, insert a pre-roll, sprinkle one or two value-added spots, and upload to the station website and iTunes. Podcasting is, in many ways, the "red-headed step-child" for traditional broadcasters. It's viewed as "important" in the industry, but often the enthusiasm is lacking for effective monetization. This results in money being left on the table for station operators.

As radio professionals strike a balance between creating original content for the podcast and merely uploading their previously aired terrestrial content on-demand, broadcasters struggle to find a way to monetize podcasting.

Whether a major radio operator or an independent podcast pioneer, a sustainable one-size-fits-all revenue model has not yet surfaced for the digital download. The podcast frontier is populated with a "Wild West" mentality—anything goes, and anything is worth a shot. Adam Carolla is one of those digital pioneers who has developed a multi-faceted approach to podcast monetization.

Adam Carolla hosts a daily podcast with a talk radio format. The podcast features topical news discussions, celebrity guests and entertaining banter at www.AdamCarolla.com. The Adam Carolla podcast officially broke the Guinness World Record for the "Most Downloaded Podcast" receiving 59,574,843 unique downloads from March 2009 to March 2011.

Carolla is a podcast trailblazer who ventured into the arena after a successful run hosting the syndicated program *Loveline* and, most recently, a syndicated morning show for CBS Radio. He launched his podcast venture only a few days after his syndicated morning show ended in February 2009, and has not looked back. Carolla explains his seamless transition: "I never actually missed a day of the show. I ended my morning show on a Friday. And on Monday, I launched my podcast and have been doing it ever since."

He monetizes his podcast using traditional live reads interspersed throughout the show along with non-traditional revenue methods—live shows, book sales, revenue shares, product sales and more.

Adam Carolla's live performances deliver steady revenue. Carolla takes his program on the road several times a month to large venues and hosts his live podcast in front of a paid audience. Typically, the Carolla live podcasts attract thousands of fans. Nearly every show is a sell-out. The live show usually features other comedians and special guests who join Carolla for the live event.

Through an innovative, revenue-sharing arrangement, Carolla sells his book and raises revenue. Carolla recently penned a *New York Times* bestseller and has published previous books and even wrote, produced, and starred in a 2007 film, *The Hammer*. In addition to using the podcast as a powerful venue to promote and sell his books and film, Carolla receives revenue share for all merchandise purchased from Amazon.com when accessed through AdamCarolla.com.

The affiliate revenue sharing model was so successful that he recently began encouraging listeners to buy not just his merchandise, but to access Amazon through his site and purchase any and all merchandise available from Amazon. As a result of the deal, he receives revenue every time someone clicks through the Amazon link on his site and purchases something. The relationship is a financial boon to his podcast operation. In fact, Carolla recently turned down a lucrative offer to take his program back to traditional radio. He credits this decision largely on the success of the Amazon revenue-share arrangement along with his other revenue generators.

"Podcast listeners are loyal," Carolla said. "Initially, I suggested that if they were going to buy something, they could click through our Amazon link to help us out. 'Wet our beaks' a bit." What began only as a slight nudge brought about a dramatic result. Listener response drastically exceeded the show's expectations. "The response has been overwhelming. The podcast listeners are driving huge numbers and the result is amazing," Carolla said.

Carolla also relies on the tried-and-true method of merchandising. He created a clever revenue generator called "Adam's Basic Cable Commentary." Fans purchase a Carolla-voiced audio track for $2.99 via AdamCarolla.com. This Carolla soundtrack accompanies campy movies such as *The Karate Kid* and *Fast & Furious*. Listeners sync up their DVDs to the Carolla Cable Commentary and enjoy entertaining riffs with Carolla and his buddies during the feature. Carolla enjoys the creativity and fun. "We don't get rich off it yet. It's more like a trickle right now, but we hope to do more of them soon," he said. He also packages the first two podcast seasons on DVD and sells box sets for $39.95 for each season. Carolla has even started his own brand of alcoholic beverage that he advertises during his program. He often hosts listener tasting events to promote his new beverage line.

Not one to leave any stone unturned, Carolla also has a subscription for the podcast—but for program archives. This type of monetization model is what the Internet world calls a "freemium." The idea behind it is that only a very small percentage of people pay, but they will more than make up for the folks who are listening for free.

Although inventive in his approach Carolla admits that, in the end, it's all about the audience. "Sponsors care about how many ears and/or eyes you are selling," Carolla said. "Whether it's a banner being dragged by a plane over a beach or someone listening to a radio or an iPod, Madison Avenue cares about the number of impressions. Whether you are selling podcast downloads or selling impressions of stadium attendees beholden to the blimp ad flying overhead with an advertisement, numbers are still the most important."

Reprinted with permission from Jason Insalaco.

Interestingly, the competition to traditional AM/FM radio has created an environment that has made the industry sensitive to the negative connotation that "terrestrial radio" has among some listeners and whether online competition should be called "radio" or "audio." Thus, *Inside Radio* reports the CEO of one major radio corporation encourages the corporation's radio sales team to not use the term "radio" when referring to online radio stations. "We tell our salespeople to call the webcasters 'Internet audio'—not 'Internet radio,'" said the CEO. Radio stations will continue experimenting with revenue models to determine what is most effective.

RADIO 2.0: TODAY'S LOCAL INTEGRATED SOLUTION PROVIDER

Weezie Kramer

Radio today integrates multiple on-air, online, and digital assets to create dynamic and solution-oriented, integrated campaigns for clients. Campaigns coordinate multiple marketing assets to engage consumers and motivate action and response from fans.

FIGURE 4.28
Weezie Kramer.

Our goal is to create great content, provide terrific entertainment and talent, and deliver it to consumers on any platform that they want to access it, whenever they want to access it.

With all of these platforms we have new ad and sponsorship opportunities that offer audio and video and display and direct to consumer revenue opportunities. We bring these elements together to create response for our clients and amplify a client's campaign to better resonate and connect with our listeners and drive results for our clients. It's interesting to note that combining multiple elements almost always increases our results for clients.

Some of radio's integrated and digital assets include:

Internet Radio

- The fastest growing segment of the radio industry, Internet radio today represents up to 15% of the total listening audience.
- Online listeners across desktop, laptop, and mobile applications tend to be among the most loyal, tech savvy, and responsive.
- Internet radio is consumed at the "point of purchase" as consumers are just a mouse click away from a client's website, a search engine, or their favorite social media site.

Internet radio is delivered on dynamic players that enhance music discovery, provide video and pictures, streaming, podcasts, and blogs, as well as contesting and e-commerce. We also have apps for iPhones and Androids and mobile websites.

Display Ads and Banner Ads

- Rich media display ads add color and ROI to a traditional campaign.
- Display ads run throughout our websites in a variety of universal sizes including 728x90, 300x100 and 300x250.

Video Pre-Rolls

- "Must see" video pre-roll and video ads provide visuals and motion that serve our most ardent fans as they opt-in to their favorite content (300x250 "video ads" are our most popular assets).
- Video pre-rolls provide an online roadblock that requires a user to view a commercial message before they can progress on the site.

Rich Media/Walk On Video

- Rich media video ads, like "walk-on" or "disruptive" video ads, launch on a radio station website page and bring additional attention and excitement to an advertisers message.
- Rich media walk-on videos are interactive, clickable and can include people, station personalities, vehicles, or more to engage the audience and encourage consumers to click to find out more.

Microsites/Landing Pages

- Creative, client branded websites and Web pages enhance an advertiser's marketing message by providing information, videos, and content specifically designed to activate the targeted demographic for the campaign.

Website Takeovers

- Daily and hourly takeovers of radio station websites can include static banner ads, visual takeovers, side bars, and more to powerfully reinforce an advertiser's message.
- Website takeovers provide an online roadblock that literally "takeover" a Web page. Visitors are inundated with an advertisers company's marketing message during a specific timeframe reinforcing an advertiser's campaign and motivating them to take action.

Social Media Activation

- Incorporating an integrated approach to promote an advertisers social media strategy drives consumer interest for an advertisers company, resulting in more followers involved in an advertisers social media extensions (i.e., Facebook, Twitter, etc.).

Mobile/Text Programs

- Combining an on-air campaign with texting can dynamically build an advertiser's brands' database.
- Text-to-win programs drive consumers into retail locations to pick up a text code and enter to win prizes and redeem special offers.
- Text alerts can be used to build a text database to share information and send daily/weekly/monthly information, tips, special offers or coupons and create an ongoing dialogue with consumers.

Loyalty Programs

- Loyalty programs give consumers an opportunity to earn points to be used towards prizes from an advertisers business, station prizes, special incentives, and more.
- Loyalty programs help create additional listener engagement by facilitating an interactive relationship which, by extension, benefits the advertiser.

Contests and Promotions

- On-air giveaways and contesting are a proven staple of radio marketing, reinforcing an advertisers objective to a highly engaged listener.
- Contests are a great way to create additional exposure and excitement for advertisers' products or offerings.

HD Radio

HD Radio offers an enhanced user experience and better fidelity. Benefits of HD Radio include:

- FM radio that sounds almost as good as a CD.
- AM radio that sounds as good as traditional FM.
- Increased listening options with multicasting.
- Tagging a song for later purchase through the iTunes Store.

And more . . .

Since 2000, **Weezie Kramer** has served as a member of Entercom's operating committee and has been responsible for operations in ten Entercom markets (Boston, Seattle, Denver, Portland, Kansas City, Milwaukee, Providence, Springfield, Madison, and Norfolk), as well as spearheading the company's reinvention efforts, where she has focused on developing enhancements to drive the company's future growth. Kramer is also a past chair of the RAB board of directors. She was the first woman to chair the RAB board, and currently serves on the RAB executive committee. She was elevated to station group president in 2013.

NON-TRADITIONAL REVENUE

One way to generate non-traditional revenue is via coop advertising. It has been estimated that more than $600 million in radio revenue comes from coop advertising—no small piece of change, indeed. Kramer explains Entercom's definition of "non-traditional" revenue as "primarily generating revenue through non ad channels or by monetizing our audience. Our connection between our fans (listeners) and our stations enables us to monetize events, experiences and assets (from concerts to bridal fairs to joining our air talent and artists we play in away destinations)." Specifically regarding coop advertising, Kramer says "We also have an e-commerce channel where we directly sell coupons and items to our audience. Likewise, due to the natural fluctuations in the nation's economy, coop opportunities remain available, but account executives have to dig deeper to find them." Kramer says, "Coop represents a nice opportunity but is often underutilized by sellers. I would estimate that the total percent of coop would be low single digits."

Coop advertising involves the cooperation of three parties: the retailer whose business is being promoted, the manufacturer whose product is being promoted, and the medium used for the promotion. In other words, a retailer and manufacturer get together to share advertising expenses. For example, Smith's Sporting Goods is informed by the Converse Running Shoes representative that the company will match, dollar for dollar, up to $5,000, the money that the retailer invests in radio advertising. The only stipulation of the deal is that Converse be promoted in the commercials on which the money is spent. This means that no competitive product can be mentioned. Converse demands exclusivity for its contribution.

Manufacturers of practically every conceivable type of product, from lawn mowers to mobile homes, establish coop advertising budgets. A radio salesperson can use coop to great advantage. First, the station account executive must determine the extent of coop subsidy a client is entitled to receive. Most of the time the retailer knows the answer to this. Frequently, however, retailers do not take full advantage of the coop funds that manufacturers make available.

In some instances, retailers are not aware that a particular manufacturer will share radio advertising expenses. Many potential advertisers have been motivated to go on the air after discovering the existence of coop dollars. Mid-sized retailers account for the biggest chunk of the industry's coop revenues. However, even the smallest retailer likely is eligible for some subsidy, and a salesperson can make this fact known for everyone's mutual advantage.

The sales manager generally directs a station's coop efforts. Large stations often employ a full-time coop specialist. The individual responsible for stimulating coop revenue will survey retail trade journals for pertinent information about available dollars. Retail associations also are a good source of information, because they generally possess manufacturer coop advertising lists. The importance of taking advantage of coop opportunities cannot be overstressed. Some stations, especially metro market outlets, earn hundreds of thousands of dollars in additional ad revenue through their coop efforts.

From the retailer's perspective, coop advertising is not always a great bargain. This usually stems from copy constraints imposed by certain manufacturers, which give the retailer a ten-second tag-out in a 30- or 60-second commercial. Obviously, this does not please the retailer who has split the cost of advertising 50/50. In recent years, this type of copy domination by the manufacturer has decreased somewhat, and a more equitable approach, whereby both parties share evenly the exposure and the expense, is more commonplace.

Coop also is appealing to radio stations because they do not have to modify their billing practices to accommodate the third party. Stations simply bill the retailer and provide an affidavit attesting to the time commercials aired. The retailer, in turn, bills the manufacturer for its share of the airtime. For its part, the manufacturer requires receipt of an affidavit before making payment. In certain cases, the station is asked to mail affidavits directly to the manufacturer. Some manufacturers stipulate that bills be sent to audit houses, which inspect the materials before authorizing payment.

Event marketing is another key form of non-traditional revenue generation. This involves the creation of a popular event, such as a food or arts festival, wherein merchants pay to be associated with it. This has become a very common and successful way for stations to make income without adding to their on-air spot loads. Says Jay Williams, Jr., "Stations are going outside the traditional spot load box and engaging in different ways to generate income." In 2012, Clear Channel collaborated with country music superstar Toby Keith to give away a Ford F-150 pickup truck. Radio listeners were required to listen to Clear Channel radio stations as well as the Clear Channel-owned iHeartRadio and were prompted to text messages using their cell phones in order to win the vehicle. Cleverly, the truck had a custom-designed Toby Keith iHeartRadio channel.

With the rapid adoption of new media technologies by consumers, non-traditional revenue potential and new opportunities have expanded. Jason

Insalaco says, "What once was considered non-traditional revenue has become expected bottom-line revenue such as advertising from streaming, podcasting, and Web impressions." Further Insalaco asserts:

> There are still opportunities for major non-traditional revenue in creating specific brand monetization opportunities with effective merchandising, licensing, and taking the program "on the road." Ironically, public radio has demonstrated the most successful examples of non-traditional revenue. For example, American Public Media's *A Prairie Home Companion* hits the road several times a month and plays to large, sold-out crowds that pay healthy ticket prices. Chicago Public Radio's *This American Life* successfully generates revenue with radio swag such as T-shirts, mugs, and posters along with creative tchotchkes including custom USB drives with 35-plus hours of content and even an original *This American Life* comic book.

Korgyn adds, "This one is a tough one really. Much of the non-traditional revenue in today's radio world is dependent on having technically savvy staff who embrace social media and the new 'digital age.' Sales opportunities exist in website banner ads, Facebook and Twitter mentions, RDS text ads and HD Radio display ads, and of course the ubiquitous 'Live Remote.'"

TRADE-OUTS

Stations commonly exchange airtime for goods, although top-rated outlets, whose time is sold at a premium, are less likely to swap spots for anything other than cash. Rather than pay for needed items, such as office supplies and furnishings, studio equipment, meals for clients and listeners, new cars, and so forth, a station may choose to strike a deal with merchants in which airtime is traded for merchandise. There are advertisers who use radio only on a trade basis. A station may start out in an exclusively trade relationship with a client in the hope of eventually converting him to cash. Split contracts also are written when a client agrees to provide both money and merchandise. For example, WXXX-FM needs two new office desks. The total cost of the desks is $800. An agreement is made whereby the client receives a $1,400 ROS spot schedule and $600 cash in exchange for the desks. Trade-outs are not always this equitable. Stations often provide trade clients with airtime worth two or three times the merchandise value to get what is needed. Thus, the saying "need inspires deals."

Many sales managers also feel that it makes good business sense to write radio trade contracts to fill available and unsold airtime, rather than let it pass unused. Once airtime is gone, it cannot be retrieved, and yesterday's unfilled availability is a lost opportunity.

CHAPTER HIGHLIGHTS

1. The anemic economy of the 2010s has contributed to the slow growth of—and at times weak status of—radio advertising. Yet, selling commercials still keeps radio stations on the air.
2. An effective radio commercial makes a strong and lasting impression on the mind of the listener.
3. A successful account executive needs: an understanding of research methods, marketing, finance; some form of sales experience; and such personal traits as ambition, confidence, honesty, energy, determination, intelligence, and good grooming.
4. Since the 1970s, programming people have made successful job transitions to sales because they have a practical understanding of the product they are selling.
5. Although an increasing number of station managers are being drawn from programming people, a sales background is still preferred.
6. The sales manager, who reports directly to the station or cluster's general manager, oversees the account executives, establishes departmental policies, develops sales plans and materials, conceives campaigns and promotions, sets quotas, works closely with the program director (PD) to develop saleable features, and sometimes sells.
7. Rates for selling airtime vary according to listenership. Rate cards are fading from the scene as new approaches to selling airtime evolve.
8. Station listenership varies according to time of day, so rate card daypart classifications range from the highest costing AAA (typically 6–10 am weekdays) to C (usually midnight–6 am). Fixed-position drivetime spots are usually among the most expensive to purchase.
9. Computerized rate cards allow rates to be quickly adjusted while using a grid structure allows for considerable rate flexibility. Grids are inventory-sensitive and they let a station remain viable when business is slow.
10. For advertisers with limited funds, ROS, BTA, or TAP are cost-effective alternatives.
11. Because few accounts are closed on the first call, it is used to introduce the station to the client and to determine its needs. Follow-up calls are made to offset reservations and, if necessary, to improve the proposal. Perseverance is essential.
12. Radio sales are drawn from three levels: retail, local, and national. Retail sales are direct sales to advertisers within the station's signal area. Local sales are obtained from advertising agencies representing businesses in the market area. National sales are obtained by the station's rep company from agencies representing national accounts.
13. A fully produced sample commercial (spec spot) is an effective selling tool. It is used to break down client resistance on callbacks, to interest former clients who have not bought time recently, and to encourage clients to increase their schedules.
14. The salesperson should commit the advertiser to sufficient commercials, placed properly, to ensure that the advertiser achieves his or her objectives. Underselling is as self-defeating as overselling.

15. New accounts are added to a salesperson's list by "prospecting" searching newspapers, Yellow Pages, television ads, competing radio station ads, and new store openings. Only open accounts may be added (those not already declared by another salesperson at the same station).

16. Because a salesperson must average 15–20 in-person calls each day, when preparing a daily call sheet it is important to logically sequence and centralize the businesses to be contacted. Also, advance telephone contacts can eliminate much wasted time.

17. Station websites, HD channels, new media technologies, and podcasts are additional opportunities for revenue at stations. The Internet is a very useful sales and prospecting tool for account executives.

18. A salesperson at a station with a high rating has a decided advantage when contacting advertisers. Stations with low or no numbers must focus on retail sales (work the street), developing programs and programming to attract targeted clients. Stations in non-survey areas must rely on their image of good citizenship and strong community ties.

19. Ad agencies annually supply hundreds of millions of dollars in advertising revenue to stations with good ratings. Media buyers at the agencies deal directly with station and network reps.

20. A station's rep company must convince national agency media buyers to select their station as their advertising outlet for the area. Therefore, the station's sales manager and the rep must work together closely.

21. Among non-traditional revenue sources are coop advertising—which involves the sharing of advertising expenses by the retailer of the business being promoted and the manufacturer of the product being promoted—and events marketing, wherein stations create events in which merchants invest their promotional dollars.

22. Rather than pay for needed items or to obtain something of value for unsold time, a station may trade (trade-out) advertising airtime with a merchant in exchange for specific merchandise.

SUGGESTED FURTHER READING

Aitchison, J., *Cutting Edge Radio: How to Create the World's Best Radio Ads*, Prentice-Hall, Englewood Cliffs, NJ, 2002.

Astor, B. and Small, J., *Direct Response Radio: The Way to Greater Profit with Measurable Advertising*, Book Surge Publishing, New York, 2008.

Baron, R. and Sissors, J., *Advertising Media Planning*, 7th edition, McGraw Hill, Columbus, OH, 2010.

Barnouw, E., *The Sponsor: Notes on a Modern Potentate*, Oxford University Press, New York, 1978.

Bergendort, F., *Broadcast Advertising*, Hastings House, New York, 1983.

Bouvard, P. and Marx, S., *Radio Advertising's Missing Ingredient: The Optimum Effective Scheduling System*, NAB, Washington, D.C., 1991.

Bovee, C. and Arena, W.F., *Contemporary Advertising*, Irwin, Homewood, IL, 1982.

Broadcast Marketing Company, *Building Store Traffic with Broadcast Advertising*, Broadcast Marketing Company, San Francisco, 1978.

Brown, D.E., *Selling Time: How to Sell Small Market Radio Advertising*, self-published by CreateSpace Independent Publishing Platform, 2009.

Burton, P.W. and Sandhusen, R., *Cases in Advertising*, Grid Publishing, Columbus, OH, 1981.

Cox, J., *Sold on Radio: Advertising in the Golden Age of Broadcasting*, McFarland, Jefferson, NC, 2008.

Culligan, M.J., *Getting Back to the Basics of Selling*, Crown, New York, 1981.

Cundiff, E.W., Still, R.R. and Govoni, N.A.P., *Fundamentals of Modern Marketing*, 3rd edition, Prentice Hall, Englewood Cliffs, NJ, 1980.

Delmar, K., *Winning Moves: The Body Language of Selling*, Warner, New York, 1984.

Diamond, B. and Frost, J., *Selling Air: How to Jump Start Your Career in Radio Sales*, iUniverse, 2008.

Dunn, W.W. and Barban, A.M., *Advertising: Its Role in Modern Marketing*, 4th edition, Dryden Press, Hinsdale, IL, 1978.

Gardner, H.S., Jr., *The Advertising Agency Business*, Crain Books, Chicago, IL, 1976.

Geskey, R., *Media Planning and Buying in the 21st Century*, 2nd edition, 20/20 Communications, LLC, Ann Arbor, MI, 2013.

Gilson, C. and Berkman, H.W., *Advertising Concepts and Strategies*, Random House, New York, 1980.

Heighton, E.J. and Cunningham, D.R., *Advertising in the Broadcast and Cable Media*, 2nd edition, Wadsworth Publishing, Belmont, CA, 1984.

Herweg, G.W. and Herweg, A.P., *Making More Money Selling Radio Advertising without Numbers*, NAB, Washington, D.C., 1995.

Hoffer, J. and McRae, J., *The Complete Broadcast Sales Guide for Stations, Reps, and Ad Agencies*, Tab Books, Blue Ridge Summit, PA, 1981.

Johnson, J.D., *Advertising Today*, SRA, Chicago, IL, 1978.

Jugenheimer, D.W. and Turk, P.B., *Advertising Media*, Grid Publishing, Columbus, OH, 1980.

Keith, M.C., *Selling Radio Direct*, Focal Press, Boston, MA, 1992.

Kelley, L.D., Jugenheimer, D.W. and Sheehan, K.B., *Advertising Media Planning: A Brand Management Approach*, 3rd edition, M.E. Sharpe, Armonk, NY, 2012.

Lane, R., King, K. and Reichert, T., *Kleppner's Advertising Procedure*, 18th edition, Prentice Hall, Upper Saddle River, NJ, 2010.

Lipsky, M., *Radio Tips*, RDR Books, Muskegon, MI, 2005.

McGee, W.L., *Broadcast Co-Op, the Untapped Goldmine*, Broadcast Marketing Company, San Francisco, CA, 1975.

Montgomery, R.L., *How to Sell in the 1980s*, Prentice Hall, Englewood Cliffs, NJ, 1980.

Murphy, J., *Handbook of Radio Advertising*, Chilton Books, Radnor, PA, 1980.

National Association of Broadcasters, *Think Big: Event Marketing for Radio*, NAB, Washington, D.C., 1994.

Prooth, V., *"Radio Advertising Doesn't Work." Says Who!* American Mass Media Corporation, New York, 2006.

Rhoads, B.E., et al. (eds), *Sales and Marketing*, Streamline Press, West Palm Beach, FL, 1995.

Sell, D., *How to Make Your Radio Advertising Work for You*, published by David Sell, 2011.

Shane, E., *Selling Electronic Media*, Focal Press, Boston, MA, 1999.

Shaver, M.A., *Make the Sale: How to Sell Media with Marketing*, Copy Workshop, New York, 1995.

Standard Rate and Data Service: Spot Radio, SRDS, Skokie, IL, published annually.

Warner, C. and Buchman, J., *Media Selling: Broadcast, Cable, Print, and Interactive*, 3rd edition, Iowa State University Press, Ames, IA, 2004.

Weyland, P., *Successful Local Broadcast Sales*, Amacom Books, New York, 2007.

RAB Guide to Writing Great Radio Copy

RAB Guide to Writing Great Radio Copy (see following pages, pp. 221–227).
Courtesy of the Radio Advertising Bureau.

FIGURE 4.29

RAB Guide to Writing Great Radio Copy

Developing a great creative Radio campaign is crucial to getting results for your client but the big question is how do you do it? On the following pages you will find a 10 step plan that will help guide you through the challenges, demands and pitfalls of the copywriting process. Don't be afraid to use Radio's creative potential to the fullest and take the time needed to create great-sounding and brilliant campaigns.

STEP 1: FIND OUT WHAT THE CLIENT WANTS

I know it sounds simple and obvious but so many stations and agencies make the mistake of not listening to what their clients really want and hope to achieve with their campaign. And without understanding the real reasons behind why a potential client wants to go on the air, the commercial campaign — no matter how humorous or clever — is doomed.

STEP 2: ASK THE RIGHT QUESTIONS

So to find out what the client wants, you have to ask some questions. Some call it a Client Needs Analysis. And even though this isn't the most exciting part of the creative process, it is crucial to your success. Here are some samples:

1. Is there anything you would like to feature?
   Maybe your clients just got in a huge load of widgets and they need to sell them fast! Or maybe a certain item has a higher profit margin and it would make sense to push that product.

2. Who is your best prospect?
   This question will allow you to get into demographics and find out who they are targeting. Is it male or female or both? What percentage? Average age? Income? Profession and education level? If you represent more than one station, then these questions can help steer your client to the right "position on the dial."

3. Why do customers come to you?
   This question and others below that are similar, allow the client to tell you their story. Keep in mind that perception is reality and you should consider getting different viewpoints from co-workers, family and friends.

4. What is your single greatest competitive advantage?

5. Do you have a positioning statement?

6. What do you feel is your unique selling position?
   The USP or unique selling position (or point) is a marketing concept that allows a company to differentiate themselves from their competition.

7. What is your primary business image?

8. What's the biggest misperception you feel people have about your business?
   Sometimes this misperception can be used in the commercial to help overcome objections. For example, perhaps customers think a popular brand will automatically be too expensive. Or perhaps the potential customers feel that the location is too far away when in reality it's only a 10 or 15 minute drive.

FIGURE 4.30

STEP 3: HELP POSITION YOUR CLIENT

Most clients on local Radio expect a measurable response from their investment on your station. Whether it's an increase in phone calls, more traffic to their store or simply more hits on their website, advertisers want something to happen. Now that you have already done your Client Needs Analysis, use that information to effectively help your client separate themselves from the competition with proper positioning.

1. Know the competition

   Who truly competes for your client's business? There may be 3 women's shoe stores in town, but if each is targeted at a different group of customers (teens, discount and upscale) then, except for some minor overlapping, they can be said to be non-competitive.

   However, if there are 3 athletic shoe stores and each carries the same brands of shoes, then all three compete directly with one another.

   Write down each competitor and a list of their perceived "strengths" or selling points such as:

   - Discount or competitive prices
   - Excellent service
   - Superior quality/variety of goods
   - Convenient locations/hours

2. Know Thyself

   Apply the same criteria when evaluating the perceived position and strengths of your client — just as you did for competitors. Remember that it may be difficult to get an accurate description of the perceived position of your client from your client. So do an informal survey with your friends, family and co-workers. Try to get a good sense of how the client is already received by customers to help you determine how you can change or enhance that image.

3. Define the Differences

   Most successful products or stores have established a very definite, easily explained and easily recognized position in the marketplace. By writing down crucial differences between competitors, you can arrive at a focal point for a commercial. After all, sometimes it's the little differences that can make a person choose one store or product over another.

STEP 4: GETTING IT ALL TOGETHER

There are several "style" categories of commercials. Don't get bogged down by always using one style for your client. Get creative by varying the elements and determining what works best for the advertiser.

1. Straightforward

   Sometimes the simplest approach works best. Imagine one effective voice delivering a well-written narrative message. This direct approach works particularly well when a positive image has previously been established and a specific event is being promoted, like a sale. In these cases, you can simply expand on or enhance the positive feelings that are already in place.

2. Music

   The use of music in commercials can be powerful since music can evoke an emotional response and create a positive feeling that transfers to the product or service. Music can also be used to tie together a mixed media campaign (TV or Internet) while aiding in recall. Music also means jingles and when done right, jingles can cut through the clutter and stick in the mind for years.

2 of 7

FIGURE 4.31

NOTE: Remember that copyrighted music that plays on your station may not be used for a recorded commercial for your client unless they pay the publisher for the rights to use that music. (That means even though that trampoline client wouldlove to use Van Halen's "Jump" as an intro to their spot, they need to acquire the rights to that song before the commercial airs. See BMI.com for more information.)

3. Slice of Life
   The "slice of life" approach allows the audience to relate personally to the commercial elements. Overhearing bits of real life conversation — between lovers, spouses, parents, neighbors — make the potential customers an active albeit silent participant instead of just a passive listener.

   If the actors in the spot strike a responsive chord, the listener is much more apt to be open to the client's offering.

   The major drawback in writing and producing slice of life spots is that they must be done extremely well to be effective. Talent must be believable and likeable or you lose credibility with the listener. Poorly written dialogue or wooden delivery will turn off the audience and have them reaching for the dial.

4. Humor
   Humor engages the listener, creates emotional responses and provides entertainment. But there are pitfalls in trying to be funny. Have you ever heard a really funny commercial that you enjoyed and when you went to tell a friend about it, you couldn't remember the product being advertised? Make humor part of the selling point.

   Also, what's funny to you, may not work for your target audience. Try to stick with universals- situations that revolve around family or intimate relationships work because these problems have the same human elements. Don't be afraid to exaggerate for comic effect. A precise true to life retelling may not be that funny but exaggeration can make people laugh and identify with the situation.

5. Testimonial
   The testimonial can be very effective in persuading a customer to try a new product or service. Affirmation by other customers can be a convincing argument and Radio is the best media for "word of mouth" advertising. Testimonials are fairly easy to produce but make sure you get your talent to relax and take their time in telling about their experience. Also, remember that a testimonial from a personality on your station is a premium spot and should always cost extra to the client.

STEP 5: OVERCOMING WRITER'S BLOCK

It's every writer's nightmare and every deadline's biggest obstacle. But there are several techniques that you can employ to overcome this looming monster. In fact, one of the first things that you can do is go back to Step 1 in this article and do your homework, ask the right questions, find out the clients wants and needs, etc. The commercial could possibly write itself once you are done. However, for those times when you can't get out of the starting gate, Jeffery Hedquist from Hedquist Productions offers these tips and tricks:

1. Sound Effects
   Randomly choose a sound effect from the production library and give yourself 2 minutes to write a commercial for your client using that effect even if it doesn't seem appropriate. Try another and do it again. Limber up your imagination and make connections between ideas that might not seem related at first. If you don't have commercial gold at this point, purposely choose a sound effect that would not normally be associated with the advertiser. For example, if the client sells office products, don't go with keyboards clicking or copy machines humming, try something different like a fire engine or a baby crying. Then, working

FIGURE 4.32

with a 2 minute deadline, force yourself to come up with some copy using that sound effect along. Once again, your mind will stretch to connect those two disparate parts of the equation and start stringing words and ideas together to bridge that gap. If you work at it, a commercial will emerge usually built around an analogy or metaphor. For example, the sound of a baby crying can represent the way we all turn into out of control babies when the office equipment doesn't work and we can't fix it. Or the fire engine could be an example of what it's like when emergencies arise in the office. Sound effects can quickly communicate and reinforce problems and solutions and create a shortcut to the minds of your audience.

2. Silence is golden
   Don't overlook the power of silence and quieter sounds. Silence can grab your attention and serve as powerful contrast to bombastic sound effects. It can also be used to highlight a solution or relieve tension.

STEP 6: GET DOWN TO BASICS – FOLLOW THESE COPYWRITING TIPS

Here is a basic list of tips to get you started:

1. Goal – Start by writing down the goal and one main point you want to get across. This step will be a huge help in deciding how you will create the commercial and what form or style it will take.

2. Elements – Next, write down the elements or information that must be in the commercial. For example, store name, address (physical and/or web), image to convey, description of merchandise, benefits to consumer.

3. Approach – Decide on how your main points and information will be communicated; how will the ideas be strung together into a coherent work of creative art?

4. Opening – Grab their attention or lose them forever. Entertain, enlighten, amuse or cause anticipation. Don't tempt the listener to tune out.

5. Simplicity – Don't use extremely complex language. Keep dialogue conversational, not stilted. Write for the ear, not for the eye. Read copy out loud.

6. Clarity – At the end of the commercial, your audience will understand exactly what you've tried to say. Don't be overly clever or you might lose your clarity. Limit the big idea to ONE per spot. No clutter.

7. Active Language – Stay away from passive verbs. If you want people to act on your commercial, choose action words.

8. Credibility – Listeners tend to follow your advice when they believe you and identify with the circumstances presented in your commercial. Write in a realistic manner, unless you are employing exaggeration or fantasy. Keep the voices credible and the talent believable.

9. Product Mention – There is no rule concerning how many times the client's name must be mentioned. Make the spot and selling process memorable.

10. Editing – You have a limited amount of time (usually 60 or 30 seconds). Write the copy and then edit it once, deleting all unnecessary words. Then, go through it again and edit even more tightly. An economy of words is essential in the commercial.

FIGURE 4.33

11. Group Efforts – Get a group together and try some brainstorming. Even useless ideas can spur successful attempts. Group thought can overcome any writer's block.

Another good checklist you can go through includes:

- Define the advertising objective — the goal of the campaign
- Define the commercial objective — the goal of the commercial
- State specific benefits — what's in it for the customer
- Make a specific offer — to get measurable results focus on one offer
- Issue a call to action — explain how/when to take advantage of the offer
- Support material — extra details needed about the product or client
- Closure — tie up loose ends and include a strong last impression

STEP 7: MAKE SURE YOUR MASTERPIECE PASSES THIS TEST

Before you do a final production of that work of art you've just produced, run through this checklist of "Copywriting Deadly Sins" provided by creative consultant, Dan O'Day.

1. SIN 1: Did you fail to attract the listener's attention?
Think of how many commercials you hear on the Radio that do not command the listener's attention. Now make sure that your commercial isn't one of them. Just think of it this way: the most important part of a print ad is the headline. In a Radio commercial, the opening line IS the headline.

2. SIN 2: Did you fail to appeal to the listener's self-interest?
The listener doesn't care about the advertiser. The listener cares about what the advertiser can do for him or her. Most copywriters make the mistake of writing about the advertiser instead of the potential customer. Make sure you have identified a need or a problem that will be filled or solved by the advertiser.

3) SIN 3: Did you fail to paint a picture?
If you think about it, Radio is actually a visual medium. Listeners convert the sound of your commercial into a mental picture that can inspire and motivate them to act upon your words. Choose those words carefully to paint a picture that will get results for your client.

4. SIN 4: Were you so clever or creative that you forgot to sell?
It happens to the best of us. A good commercial is not one that makes people laugh; it's one that motivates them to act. Make your message clear. Don't bury it in a clever idea.

5. SIN 5: Did you forget to give the listener a reason to act now?
As mentioned before, most local Radio clients are expecting tangible, measurable results from their campaigns. The copy should reach active customers who are looking for that particular product or service as well as passive customers who might be in the market soon. "Hurry to the sale soon" just doesn't cut it. Be creative and find a new way to express the offer.

FIGURE 4.34

6. SIN 6: Did you use cliché-ridden copy?
   Commercial clichés are trite and empty and don't communicate anything to the listener – don't use them. Find a way to say it fresher. It may take a little bit of time, but it's worth it to keep people from tuning out. Some common ones to avoid:

   - "Now is the time."
   - "They won't last long..."
   - "Savings throughout the store..."
   - "The sale you've been waiting for..."
   - "Conveniently located..."

7. SIN 7: Did you write too much copy?
   Avoid this common pitfall by getting in the habit of reading your copy aloud and timing yourself. The trick is to read it in a normal conversational pace. If it takes YOU seventy-five seconds to read it aloud, what makes you think your production person can do a good job with the same copy in just sixty seconds? Remember, too many words crammed into one fragile minute can be fatal.

STEP 8: LEARN HOW TO SELL YOUR IDEAS AND WIN SUPPORT

Now it's time to share your brilliant ideas with your client but there are few things to keep in mind when selling the creative and promoting the unique marketing abilities of your staff and station.

1. Don't produce a lousy spec spot.
   Sure you can hear how great it's going to sound in your head but the client is going to have a hard time hearing that "leap". In other words, don't produce a "speculative" spot unless you are certain it can sound great. Instead, present copy only and describe the commercial. If it's based on an already proven idea, play that commercial as an example of what you would like to accomplish.

2. Explain your assumptions and manage their expectations.
   Present the rationale behind your ideas. Explain why you picked that music or that announcer or that approach because you have the client's goals and expectations in mind.

3. Sell a marketing strategy, not a commercial
   This may involve the production of a campaign instead of one spot. It's important that your client understand that you are interested in increasing their sales, not just yours. By presenting a complete plan, in which creativity plays an important part, you become a member of their staff and are perceived as a hard-working player on their team.

4. Use testimonials before and after a sale.
   Provide stories of satisfied customers. These are most often in print form but you can also interview advertisers in your studio asking how the campaign or spot worked. These interviews can be edited (with permission) into great audio success stories that can be used on sales calls, presentations or possibly on air!

5. Involve production people in sales.
   Everyone benefits by seeing how the other side works. Take a production person on a sales call. Get their input and reward their productivity. In these days of consolidation, many production people can feel overworked and underappreciated. Some restaurant trade, concert tickets or even a handwritten thank you note can go a long way.

6 of 7

FIGURE 4.35

STEP 9: TIPS AND TRICKS IN TECHNICAL PRODUCTION

Technically speaking, the days of reel to reel and razor blade splicing are gone. Today's computers and audio programs are helping production directors create more spots in a shorter amount time with sound effects that would be virtually impossible a few years ago. However, faster is not necessarily better and Production Director Robert Diaz offers these tips:

1. Don't Skimp On Tools
   A great read full of emotion and enthusiasm can become lousy with a bad microphone. The good thing is that most Radio stations have decent equipment because the quality of sound is the key aspect of being "on-the-air."

2. Musical Choices
   A varied production library is a key component in creating great Radio commercials. "Sound-alike" music keeps you out of trouble when that sub sandwich client wants to use "Yellow Submarine" as their theme song. Also a library of sound effects will be handy when trying to create the right atmosphere. Keep in mind that single royalty-free tracks can now be downloaded over the Internet and all those production music files can be stored on a hard drive for easy access.

3. Stay Focused
   Finally, remember to encourage production people to stay focused and really understand what you want to convey. If they don't understand the effect you're listening for or the message you want to convey, the commercial or campaign will go nowhere-communication is essential.

STEP 10: TAKE PRIDE IN YOUR WORK AND SELL COMPETIVELY

By now, you've put in the time researching your client, learned about his or her needs, determined the message that needs to be expressed in the commercial and thought of the perfect way to do it. So now it's time to present your masterpiece.

Why not present it that way to the client?

Someone once said that a sale is a transfer of ideas. Present your idea in an exciting way and get the client excited about the sale! Position it as an answer to the client's problems or goals. Remember the creative work that you have done can literally determine the success of an account and reinforce your relationship with a client.

Nobody said it was going to be easy.

This one you know already. The challenges of developing, writing and producing great creative are many – but you can do it! There's no doubt that the key to successful creative is doing your homework and the RAB is here to help. As a member, you can check out RAB.com for more great information like Instant Backgrounds, recent articles, even "Gold Digger" reports that allow you to dig deep into demographic and lifestyle groups. Plus, there are great creative examples in our MP3 audio archive and over 2000 scripts in our commercial library just waiting to get your creative juices flowing. And the newly revised Creative Resource Directory has nearly 100 professional RAB-recommended agencies or production houses that are ready to help you get your client's commercial to the next level.

If you are not a member of RAB, visit rab.com for more information or call 1-800-232-3131!

CHAPTER 5
News

NEWS AND TODAY'S RADIO

More people claim to listen to radio for music than for any other reason, although studies are showing that this is changing due to a growing reliance on other audio media sources. The competition from other audio media sources has contributed to the loss of some listeners of radio news. The Pew Research Center's *Project for Excellence in Journalism's State of the News Media 2013* study found that news was second only to country music as the most listened-to format on radio.

The study also found that one-third of American adults said they had listened to radio news the previous day, down from 43% in 2000. The Pew study found that 1.5% of Americans age 12 and older listen to radio news on a total basis. Studies also indicate that 51% of Americans get their news from radio or logging onto a radio station's website. Local radio news stations garner primarily the 30–65 age group.

News/Talk/Info+Talk/Personality Stations Second to Country Format	
Percentage of Americans Age 12 or Older	
Country+New Country	14.1%
News/Talk/Info+Talk/Personality	12.1
Adult Contemporary+SAC	8.8
Pop Contemporary Hit Radio	7.6
Classic Hits	5.1
Classic Rock	5.0
Hot Adult Contemporary	4.4
Urban Adult Contemporary	3.9
All Sports	3.6
Rhythmic Contemporary Hit Radio	3.4
Mexican Regional	3.0

FIGURE 5.1
News/Talk/Info+Talk/Personality stations second to Country format. Courtesy of Pew Research Center.

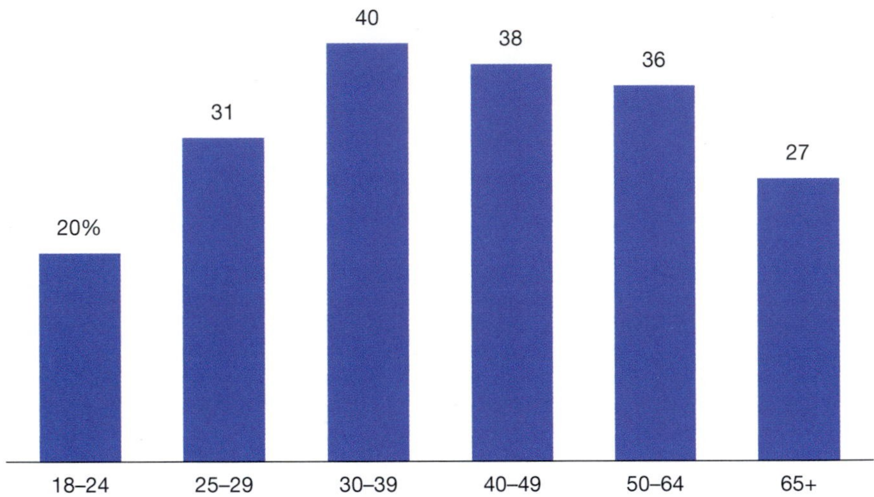

FIGURE 5.2
One-fifth of young adults listen to radio news. Courtesy of Pew Research Center.

According to Arbitron, the News/Talk/Information audience is highly educated and high-income earners. Practically all the nation's 9,000 commercial stations program news to some extent—with CBS and ABC being the primary deliverers of the news—and there are more than 2,000 stations that specialize in news programming. Radio's tremendous mobility and pervasiveness have made it an instant and reliable news source for millions of Americans.

Says former WBZ general manager (GM) Ted Jordan:

> In one sense we suffered from the same market compression as everyone else. But in other ways, it's easier today as there was more AM competition. All things considered, the news quality is as good, but now the systems in place are better, the networks we use (ABC and CBS) are better and more responsive, and the stringers are better. We used to have our own Washington, D.C., bureau because we didn't trust the networks to deliver the story. Now we can. They have really become responsive to the needs of the local stations. There is now a greater sharing of resources at our operations. We have a dotted-line relationship with WBZ TV. Their newspeople give updates on our air and our anchors appear on television. We are able to co-brand the stations and get a larger share of mind.

FIGURE 5.3
CBS Radio News logo. Courtesy of CBS News.

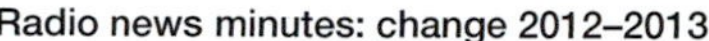

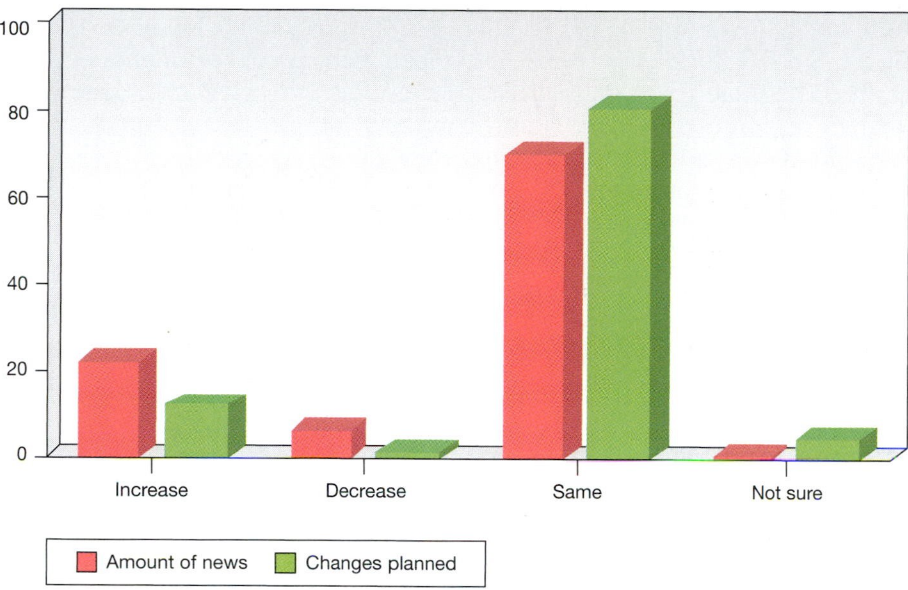

FIGURE 5.4
Changes and future plans in radio news. Reproduced by permission of the Radio Television Digital News Association.

Adds Jay Williams, "They have been able to cut costs by reallocating resources, partnering with a TV affiliate or a local newspaper, making use of portable, easy-to-use digital technology to report from the scene, and working more closely with networks and outside stringers to get follow-up reports on key stories. As to the talk that there are fewer real news sources today, I know Ted believes that isn't the case. Just the opposite, in fact."

A Radio Television Digital News Association (RTDNA) study in 2013 found that radio newsrooms reporting an increase in radio news from the previous year's study had dropped, and that more newsrooms reported an actual drop in the amount of news covered compared to the previous year's study. There was, however, an increase in the number of newsrooms who planned to keep the number of radio news minutes the same.

Ethnic news radio has also suffered in both news coverage and listenership numbers in recent years. In 2012, Disney purchased New York City's KISS and WBLS and began simulcasting the two stations. As a result of the two stations' merger, *The Tom Joyner Morning Show* and *The Michael Baisden Show*, the most listened to news and talk shows among African Americans in New York City, were cancelled.

Consultant Ed Shane argues that "Radio news is in a sad state." The deregulation of the medium since the 1980s has inspired a decline in local radio news service, according to many sources. "Listen to the news on many local stations and you're hearing announcers from out of town, feeding news from a central hub. Often the announcer has no clue about the area where he or she is being heard. On a Houston station, I heard a traffic report that originated from Dallas. The subject was traffic tie ups before the 'Oilers football game.' That was ten years after the Oilers left town and the Houston Texans dominated the hearts of Houston football fans. Outsourcing one of radio's essential services is a cost-cutting measure, and does not enhance quality." But, the same RTDNA study cited above indicated that not all is negative about radio news. A 2013 RTDNA study found that nearly 78% of radio stations cover local news with nearly 80% of AM radio stations covering local news. The good news about these findings is that the numbers are up from what the previous year's study revealed. Logically, the RTDNA study revealed that the larger the radio newsroom, the greater the amount of locally produced news.

Iconic WBZ NewsRadio 1030 continues to dominate in Boston. "There's no secret sauce, other than being completely reflective of your marketplace as WBZ has been for 90-plus years. During horrific circumstances like the Boston Massacre, WBZ is the go-to place to get news and information, and when

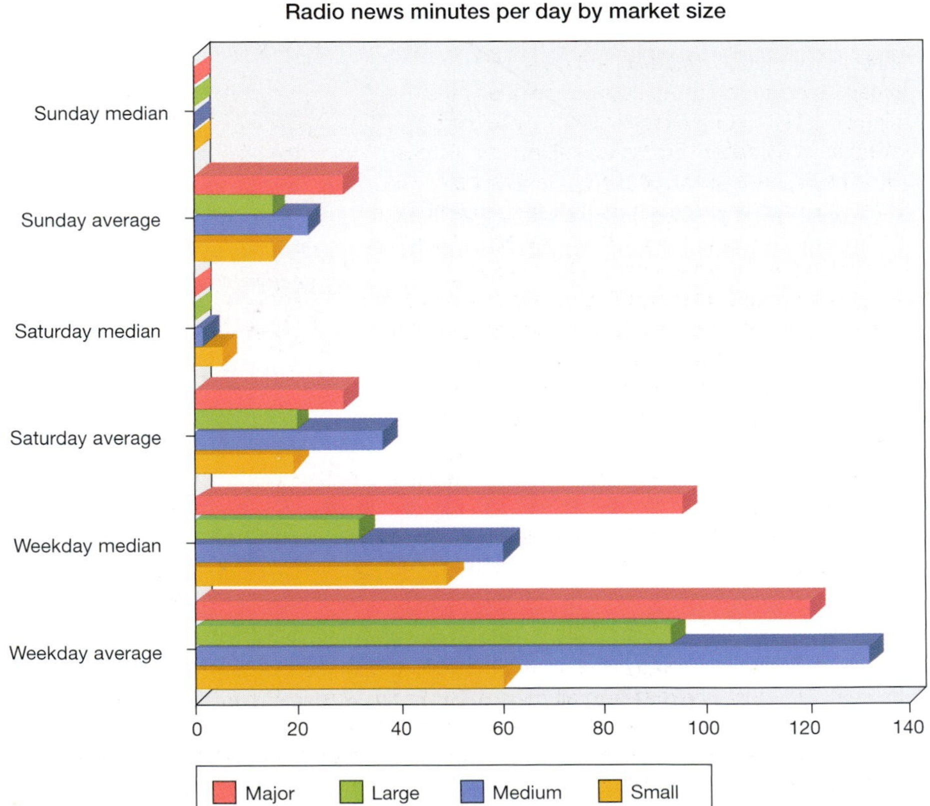

FIGURE 5.5
Hours of locally produced radio news. Reproduced by permission of the Radio Television Digital News Association.

people face difficulties and tragedies, they turn to things that they can trust, and in our case, that's WBZ Radio," said Mark W. Hannon, senior vice-president and market manager for CBS Radio, Boston. While WBZ may have been somewhat slow adjusting to the PPM world in 2009, it quickly made up ground, "creating content blocks, giving listeners an opportunity to hear more content without it being broken up, simulcasting *CBS Evening News* with Scott Pelley, who is fantastic at delivering it, and we deploy our reporters in ways we can optimize our resources" with sister station, WBZ-TV. "Our assignment desks speak with each other. This is a time of full cooperation."

Hannon suggests that "the struggle is to deliver content, adjust to technology, and respond to the new ways people are consuming news," noting that "how we get that content to consumers needs to continue to evolve . . . Twitter, social media . . . to get the content to them where they reside vs. waiting for them

LOCAL RADIO NEWS

Holland Cooke

What remains to be seen (heard) is how close the "actual" can come to the "theoretical." Theoretically, and logically, what would continue to value local radio stations to listeners and differentiate AM/FM broadcasters from iTunes, satellite radio, and the plethora of Internet-related content now becoming every-bit-as-portable via iPhone, WiMax, etc., is local content. But as a practical matter, debt now prohibits most radio station owners from delivering such content. Sadly, radio's biggest owners have treated stations like real estate. And like real estate, stations now go begging for buyers. Clearly, the theoretical fix would be uber-well-heeled buyers spotting the opportunity of a lifetime: radio's gazillion in-place receivers and the pre-existing listener habit of the demographic, which controls most wealth and, as a generation, is in the process of inheriting their parent's wealth. Baby Boomers' children are already radio's lost generation. But the real-life Homer and Marge Simpson characters, mega-consumers who fuel the U.S. economy, could be retrieved and maintained if stations offered programming more compelling than FM's race to go "All Christmas" first and AM's self-imposed typecasting as "Not from your city/you're wrong, I'm right/bad Republicans." Whether Bill Gates or other as-wealthy folk will seize this opportunity remains to be seen.

FIGURE 5.6
Holland Cooke.

Holland Cooke is a media consultant who works at the intersection of radio and the Internet. Previously, he managed all-news WTOP Radio, Washington D.C., and was vice-president of a *USA Today* new media unit. He publishes a monthly newsletter for broadcasters and digital content creators. His website is www.HollandCooke.com, and he's @HollandCooke on Twitter.

to come to us." The focus on "strengthening the brand is to embrace the technology. We're trying to get a foothold in Twitter so WBZ lives and breathes in a space where younger demographics are living." That plan is working. WBZ won the 2013 NAB Marconi Award for News Talk Station of the Year and Mark Hannon garnered the 2013 Radio Wayne award as Market Manager of the Year. The station's two networks, "ABC and CBS, have maintained great quality and continue to be great resources," Hannon says, "and the future is bright. We're back to sharing resources with WBZ-TV and the Sports Hub FM, and we're good at migrating our content to the website and online. If we stay local, reflect the market, and have great content, we'll be fine," Hannon predicts.

THE NEWSROOM

The number of individuals working in a radio station newsroom will vary depending on the size of a station, whether it is part of a cluster operation or a single outlet, and its format. While some stations have huge news operations that employ large numbers of individuals; on average, a station in a small market employs one or two full-time newspeople. Of course, some outlets find it financially unfeasible to hire newspeople. These stations do not necessarily ignore news, rather they delegate responsibilities to their deejays to deliver brief newscasts at specified times, often at the top of the hour. Stations approaching news in this manner make it necessary for the on-air person to collect news from the wire service while music is playing and broadcast it nearly verbatim—a practice known as "rip 'n' read." Little, if any, rewriting is done because the deejay simply does not have the time to do it. The only thing that persons at "rip 'n' read" outlets can and must do is examine wire copy before going on the air. This eliminates the likelihood of mistakes. Again, all this is accomplished while the music is playing.

NPR reporter Corey Flintoff warns against neglecting to examine wire copy before air-time. "We've all been caught with stuff that appears to scan at first sight but turns out to be incomprehensible when you read it."

Music-oriented stations in larger markets rarely allow their deejays to do news. Occasionally, the person jockeying the overnight shift will be expected to give a brief newscast every hour or two, but in metro markets, this is fairly uncommon. There is generally a newsperson on duty around the clock. A top-rated station in a medium market typically employs four full-time newspeople; again, this varies depending on the status of the outlet (one of a cluster of stations) and the type of programming it airs. For example, Easy Listening stations that stress music and de-emphasize talk may employ only one or two newspeople. Meanwhile, an AC station in the same market may have five people as its news staff in an attempt to promote itself as a heavy news and information outlet, even though its primary product is music. Certainly some music stations in major markets hire as many as a dozen news employees. This figure may include not only on-air newscasters but also writers, street reporters, and technical people as well. Stringers and interns also swell the figure.

During the prime listening periods when a station's audience is at its maximum, newscasts are programmed with greater frequency, sometimes twice as often as during other dayparts. The newsroom is a hub of activity as newspeople prepare for newscasts scheduled every 20–30 minutes. Half a dozen people may be involved in assembling news but only two may actually enter the broadcast booth. A primetime newscast schedule may look something like this:

Drive Coverage, am	Drive Coverage, pm
Smith 6:25 am	Lopez 3:25 pm
Bernard 7:00 am	Gardner 4:00 pm
Smith 7:25 am	Lopez 4:25 pm
Bernard 8:00 am	Gardner 5:00 pm
Smith 8:25 am	Lopez 5:25 pm
Bernard 9:00 am	Gardner 6:00 pm
Smith 9:25 am	Lopez 6:25 pm

Midday and evening are far less frenetic in the newsroom, and one person per shift may be considered sufficient.

A standard-size newsroom in a medium market will contain several pieces of audio equipment, not to mention office furniture such as desks, computers, file cabinets, and so on. The standard audio production equipment that is found in all radio station studios is used by the newsperson. The modern radio newsroom also will be equipped with various monitors to keep newspeople

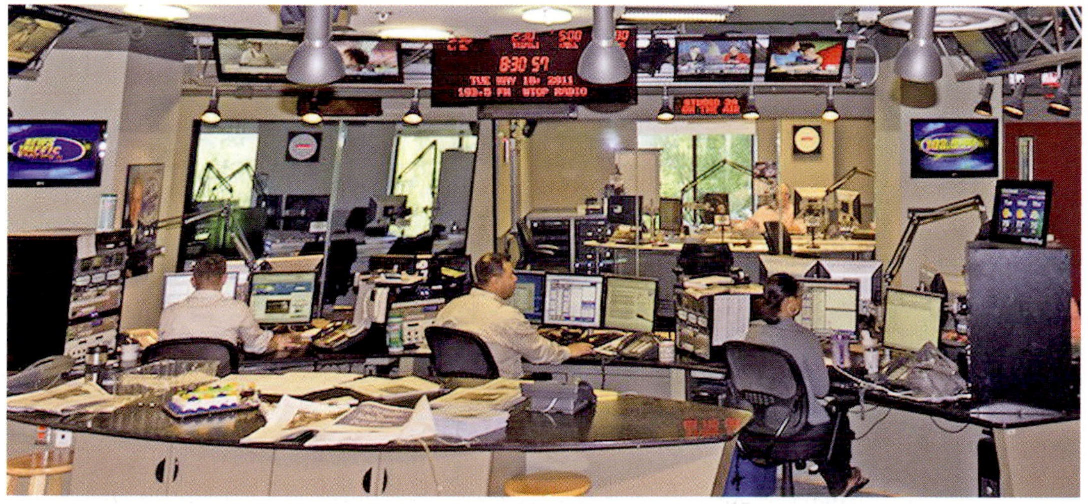

FIGURE 5.7
The WTOP newsroom and editors' desk. From left to right: film critic Jason Fraley, *Morning Drive* editor Mike Jakaitis, and editor Desiree Smith. Courtesy of WTOP-FM, Washington, D.C.

on top of what is happening at the local police and fire departments and weather bureau. Various wire service machines provide the latest news, sports, stock, and weather information, as well as a host of other data. Depending on the station's budget, two or more news services may be used. Stations with a genuine commitment to news create work areas that are designed for maximum efficiency and productivity. Jim Farley, vice-president of news and programming at WTOP, says news stations have, "Lots of computers, video monitors, and smartphones. Many of our reporters use their iPhones for reporting from the field. Oh, and a working coffee pot!"

New equipment and technology continue to streamline news coverage for radio journalists. Tim Scheld, WCBS-AM's director of news and programming stated that new technology has been an exciting addition to radio news. In a 2013 interview with *Radio Ink,* he says:

> First off, the equipment we use out on the street has changed significantly in the past ten years. Smartphones are smarter. They allow reporters to take photos, tweet, post onto Facebook, record audio, and connect via broadband to deliver high quality live audio. The technical developments in the past few years have been breathtaking, and we continue to test new avenues all the time. We are also now seeing social media play a larger role in the delivery of news to consumers. While some might consider it competition to the traditional media, I actually view it as an opportunity for us to expose our reporting and newsgathering to an audience that may not normally consider radio news as a source of information. It's an exciting time for us. Challenging, but exciting.

Indeed, a visit to WCBS-AM's website allows listeners to not only listen to the station but also "like" its Facebook page and follow its news updates on Twitter.

In situations where newsrooms have been combined and consolidated, more personnel, equipment, and space may be in evidence since the plant itself may be serving myriad signals. Cluster operation newsrooms accommodate reporters and news readers assigned to the various stations under the one roof.

News in satellite radio originates from a host of outside sources. Originally operating as two independent satellite radio entities, XM and Sirius, the two companies merged to become SiriusXM in 2007. SiriusXM provides feeds (channels) from Fox News, CNN, MSNBC, CNBC, Bloomberg Radio, BBC World Service, NPR Now, and so forth. Satellite radio is not in the business of generating news itself, so the "newsroom" (as we have been referring to it) does not exist at SiriusXM, although this may change in the future.

THE ALL-NEWS STATION

Stations devoted entirely to news programming arrived on the scene in the mid-1960s. Program innovator Gordon McLendon, who had been a key figure in the development of two music formats, Beautiful Music and Top 40, implemented All-News at WNUS-AM (NEWS) in Chicago. In 1965, Group W, Westinghouse Broadcasting, changed WINS-AM in New York to All-News and soon did the same at more of its metro outlets: KYW-AM, Philadelphia, and KFWB-AM, Los Angeles. While Group W was converting several of its outlets to non-music programming, CBS decided that All-News was the way to go at WCBS-AM, New York; KCBS-AM, San Francisco; and KNX-AM, Los Angeles. Another station that migrated to an All-News format in the 1960s was WTOP-FM in Washington, D.C., and KNX 1070 in Los Angeles.

FIGURE 5.8
WTOP logo. Courtesy of WTOP-FM, Washington, D.C.

Not long after KCBS in San Francisco began its All-News programming, another Bay City station, KGO-AM, introduced the hybrid News/Talk format in which news shares the microphone with conversation and interview features. Over the years, the hybrid approach has caught on and leads the pure All-News format in popularity. As already noted, the News/Talk format is second only to the Country music format.

FIGURE 5.9
KNX 1070 Newsradio logo. Courtesy of KNX 1070 Newsradio, Los Angeles, CA

Because of the exorbitant cost of running a news-only operation, it has remained primarily a metro market endeavor. It often costs several times as much to run an effective All-News station as it does to run one music station. This usually keeps small-market outlets out of the business. Staff numbers in All-News stations far exceed that of formats that primarily serve up music. Although a lone deejay is needed at an Adult Contemporary or Top 40 station, All-News requires the involvement of several people to keep the air sound credible. In large markets, the newsroom staff can be a large operation with many people contributing to the daily gathering and delivery of news.

Even though the cost of running a news station is high, the payback can more than justify expenditures. However, this is one format that requires a sizable initial investment, as well as the financial wherewithal and patience to last until it becomes an established and viable entity. Considerable planning takes place before a station decides to convert to All-News, since it is not simply a matter of hiring new jocks and updating the music library. Switching from a music format to All-News is dramatic and anything but cosmetic.

AM has always been the home of the All-News station. There are only a handful of FM news and information outlets. The format's prevalence on AM has grown considerably since the late 1970s when FM took the lead in listeners. The percentage of All-News and News/Talk formats on AM continued to increase in the 1980s as the band lost more and more of its music listeners to FM. However, All-News stations in a handful of metro markets keep AM at the top of the ratings charts. In the early 1990s, it was common to find one AM outlet among the leaders, and almost invariably it programmed non-music. This has

FIGURE 5.10
WTOP-FM is in a major radio market and has a very large group of individuals working to deliver the news. Courtesy of WTOP-FM, Washington, D.C.

Atlanta, GA	New York, NY
Buffalo-Niagara Falls, NY	Orlando, FL
Chicago, IL	Philadelphia, PA
Columbus, OH	Pittsburgh, PA
Detroit, MI	Roanoke-Lynchburg,VA
Erie, PA	San Francisco, CA
Ft. Myers-Naples-Marco Island, FL	San Luis Obispo, CA
Houston-Galveston, TX	Seattle-Tacoma, WA
Los Angeles, CA	Springfield, MO
Macon, GA	Tampa-St. Petersburg-Clearwater, FL
Melbourne-Titusville-Cocoa, FL	Washington, DC
Minneapolis-St. Paul, MN	Wilkes Barre-Scranton, PA

FIGURE 5.11
Arbitron radio markets with All-News formats. Courtesy Arbitron Inc. All rights reserved.

changed little in the mid-2010s. Some media observers predict that All-News will make inroads into FM as that band gives over large segments of its music audience to new media technologies. Arbitron reports there are 24 radio stations throughout the U.S. that identify themselves as having an All-News format.

All-News stations are keeping pace with technological advancements. Tim Scheld, director of news/programming at WCBS Newsradio 880 says, "The biggest, most successful radio news operations in America embraced digital long ago. They have full service, active websites and are delivering radio news via digital platforms like Tune In and Radio.com. All of the traditional news operations are expanding their brands to the digital space. The next frontier is social media."

WHAT MAKES A SUCCESSFUL NEWS RADIO STATION?

Andy Ludlum

Radio news of the present and most certainly the future has to be about one thing, it must be *local*.

FIGURE 5.12
Andy Ludlum.

Quite likely the radio we know today will become a thing of the past. If you consider the technological explosion of just the last few years, you see the methods of delivery and platforms for consuming news are constantly changing. That change will increase exponentially and we'll soon have tools and devices we can't even imagine today.

But the need for specific local information will not change. We need to know about traffic. We need to know why there's smoke in the sky. We need to know why potholes are not being fixed. We need to know why the local sales tax is so high. We need to know how elected officials are spending our tax money. We need to know where the jobs are. We need to know if a dangerous storm is bearing down on us.

I could go on, but you get the point. The communicator who remembers it is "all about local" will succeed in the future.

I have been trying over the last few years to make KNX 1070 Newsradio, with a big 50kw regional signal, even more local, not less. That's in Los Angeles, the second most populous city in the U.S. and the nation's largest media market. Every six weeks we take the entire station on location in a different community in the greater Los Angeles area. Thanks to technology, we can deliver the same services from our Wilshire Boulevard studios as we can from a city 50 miles away. These local broadcasts have been well-received by our audience, many of whom actually express surprise that a major market news station would come to where they live.

I'm fortunate. I'm at a CBS-owned All-News radio station with all the resources I need to do the job as I envision it. Elsewhere in the country, deregulation and consolidation has resulted in many small communities without any significant local news. We hear of terrible incidents where storms or tornadoes have swept through unsuspecting communities without warning. We've also heard of courageous and dedicated deejays, without any formal news training, going on the air and informing and comforting their communities.

We're also learning of the tremendous power of social media and non-traditional sources of news, especially in countries where governments have attempted to withhold or restrict free communication. We will always find ways to share the information we need. If traditional sources of news do not meet the needs of the local consumer, they will be discarded as irrelevant.

I tell young people who are just starting out now in radio news to expect that they absolutely won't be ending their careers in radio news. Instead as media technologies converge, I see the journalist of the future working in an exciting, multimedia, multiplatform environment where they are delivering their message in many ways and many formats daily. From audio podcasts to handheld video productions; from blogging to short form messaging like tweeting and texting, all will have direct and regular interaction with the audience.

The secret to great radio in the past and for information communication in the future has been that is immediate, interactive, intimate, and *local*.

Andy Ludlum is the director of News Programming at KNX 1070 Newsradio and KFWB News Talk 980 in Los Angeles, CA. He's spent more than 38 years in news and information broadcasting on radio and television. Ludlum started in radio in the 1970s as a traffic reporter in San Jose, CA. Over the years, he's been an editor, news reporter, and anchor and has worked in some great cities; San Jose, Seattle, Kansas City and, since 1995, Los Angeles. Ludlum's had the opportunity to broadcast from all over the world and cover some exceptional events, from the 1981 assassination of Anwar Sadat in Egypt, to the economic emergence of China and the rebirth of democracy in the former Soviet Union. While working in Washington state he covered the 1980 eruption of Mt. St. Helens. He's spent most of the last 25 years programming all-news or news, talk, and sports radio stations. Ludlum's stations have frequently been recognized for excellence in news broadcasting receiving three national RTDNA Edward R. Murrow Awards for Overall Excellence, local Emmys and Golden Mikes from the Radio Television News Association of Southern California. The Greater Los Angeles Chapter of the Society of Professional Journalists honored Ludlum in 2012 as a Distinguished Journalist in Radio. You can follow Andy Ludlum on Twitter at @aludlum.

THE ELECTRONIC NEWSROOM

The combined use of computers and online resources in the radio newsroom has increased to where they are now most certainly the norm. The use of computers to perform daily functions in the newsroom has quickly multiplied since they were first introduced in December 1980 at KCBS in San Francisco. Computers linked to the various wire and Internet information services are used to access primary and background data on fast-breaking stories and features. Many stations have installed touchscreen computer monitors and traditional flat-screen, high-definition television sets in on-air studios to have instant access to breaking news and weather. Instead of handheld copy, newscasters simply read from the studio monitors. The speed and agility with which news copy can be produced and edited makes a computer the perfect tool for broadcast journalists.

Radio newsrooms have fully embraced technological advances and provide a wide array of technology to its reporters to gather news and produce newscasts. Scheld describes the WCBS Newsradio 880 newsroom: "Our newsroom has telephones, televisions, Internet, and computers that can record and edit audio. We also have equipment that keeps us connected to news resources like CBS News and the *Wall Street Journal*." However, some very technologically advanced radio newsrooms still have and use very traditional broadcasting equipment. At KRLD-AM, in the fifth largest radio media market in the United States, Alice Rios, co-anchor of the KRLD-AM *Morning News* in Dallas, says the following pieces of equipment are regularly used: "An edit station where there's a computer, microphone, and a phone. Scanners, still. (Gotta love the sound of scanners in the background of old school newsrooms.) Reporters use small Marantz recorders when they go out on stories and actually many of them now have software on their phones that allow them to get interviews/audio on their smartphones. *Very* handy so that if anyone on the news staff happens to live near the scene of a breaking news story, they can go on air with audio clips, within minutes."

Furthermore, some companies provide specifically tailored software for newsrooms. "There are computer software packages these days that a newsroom

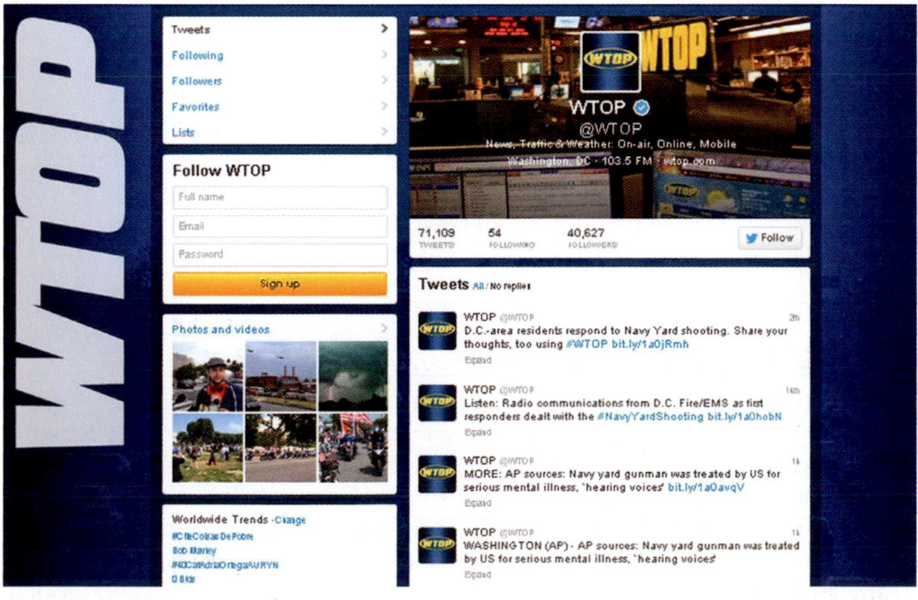

FIGURE 5.13
WTOP Twitter site. Courtesy of WTOP-FM, Washington, D.C.

can buy. In my day we used the old file and cards and Rolodex, but today newsrooms that can afford it use software to file stories, keep archives of copy, record and play actualities, and so forth," says radio consultant Donna Halper.

All newsrooms use the Internet, email, smartphone, and social media technologies. It makes sense that the information highway be accessed by a medium determined to keep its listening public informed and up-to-date. The Internet has become the best resource for information on every conceivable topic. "It is in constant use. Our brand is WTOP. Our distribution channels are radio, TV, streaming audio, wtop.com, email, text and Twitter alerts, Facebook and mobile," says Farley. As a search medium, there is none better. Data of every variety are at the fingertips of all newspeople today. The world of cyberspace has revolutionized newsgathering. Says broadcaster and academic Larry Miller, "The evolution has been from old-fashioned teletype 'wire' by landlines, to satellites, to computers and the Internet. Even audio is accessed online."

According to broadcast scholar David Reese, "Today, newsrooms use station websites to deliver news, and consumer usage patterns indicate that acquiring information this way is growing in popularity." Adds Jason Insalaco, "The listener is no longer going to remain captive to a news station to learn the day's headlines. An added plus is that many station websites offer live information on traffic flow and so forth. Station websites give outlets needed additional cache in the multimedia environment." Not all stations are effectively competing with digital news on various Web sites. Jim Farley, of WTOP-FM in Washington, D.C., says, "Some stations and groups are, others are not. Here at WTOP, we don't consider ourselves a radio station. We are a digital news organization."

The Internet has made information gathering much faster and efficient. Scheld shares, "The Internet has replaced the research department. We used to have thick books called 'reverse directories' that would provide us phone numbers in every neighborhood in our listening area so we could track down witnesses to breaking news. The internet has revolutionized our business. It puts important information at our fingertips and allows us to check facts and figures important to our stories. The internet also connects us to our listeners better than ever."

Other technology has contributed greatly to the efficiency and performance of the electronic newsroom. For instance, ISDN (Integrated Services Digital Network) significantly improved the quality of phone interviews. With ISDN, technology newsrooms can create seamless reports (in terms of audio fidelity), thus creating the impression (or illusion) that all the voices on the air come from the same studio and even from the same microphone. In 2013, when asked if radio newsrooms utilize ISDN, Andy Ludlum, director of news programming at Los Angeles's KNX 1070 Newsradio and KFWB News Talk 980, said "Yes we still use ISDN daily. We are beginning to run into problems in some parts of the country where phone companies will not install ISDN circuits, much as they have moved away from installing 8kc or higher audio circuits from point to point." Although ISDN installation is becoming problematic, Ludlum says, "There are a number of alternatives, most using high bandwidth

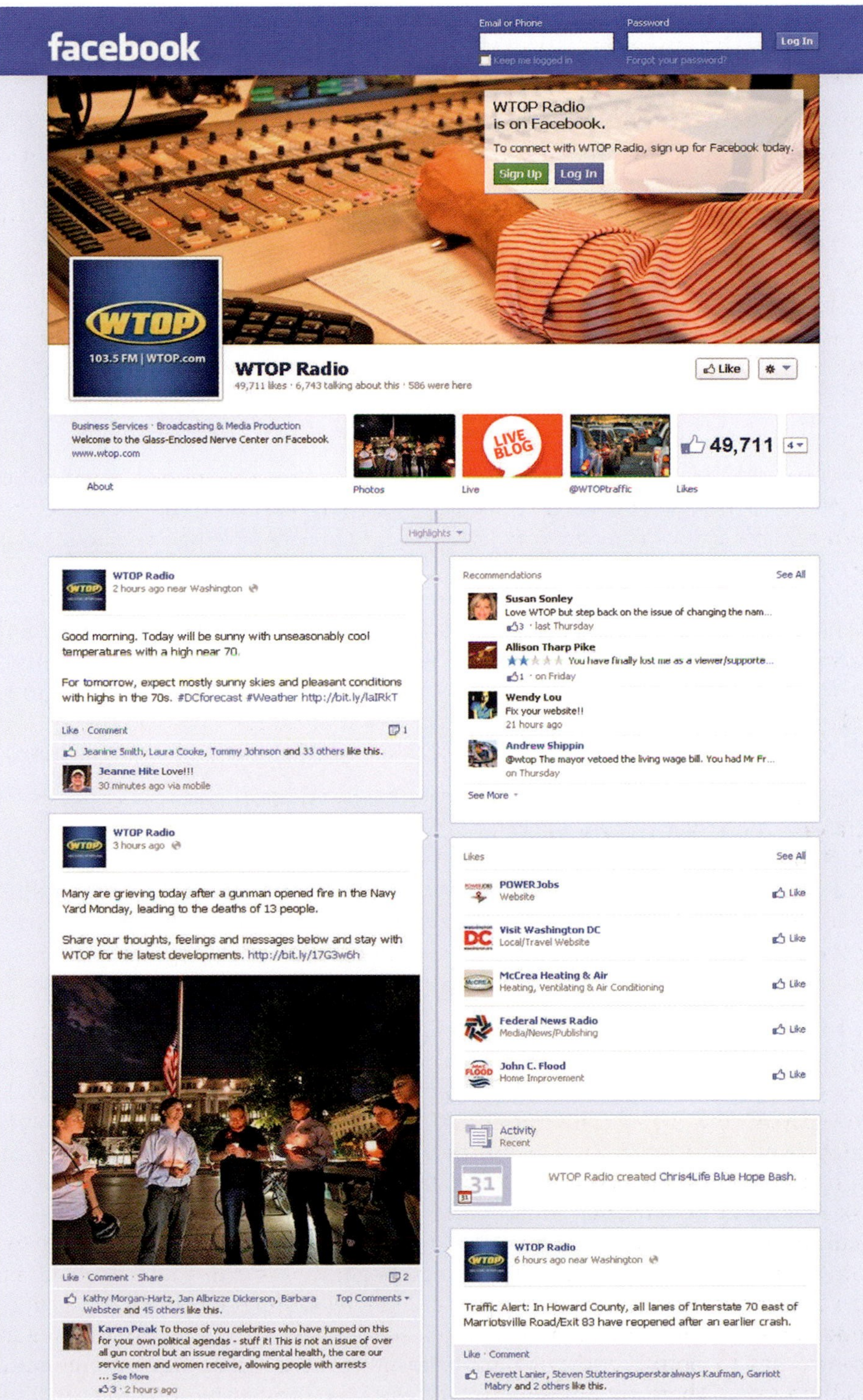

FIGURE 5.14
Facebook is used as a way to disseminate news by most stations. Courtesy of WTOP-FM, Washington, D.C.

BOSTON HERALD RADIO

Jay Williams, Jr.

Boston's second largest daily newspaper recently launched its own radio station—Boston Herald Radio. "We looked at buying stations in 2005 but the cost was too high [even for] limited signals . . . Now you can start a Web station for less than $50,000," said Jeff Magram, COO and CFO of Herald Media, Inc.

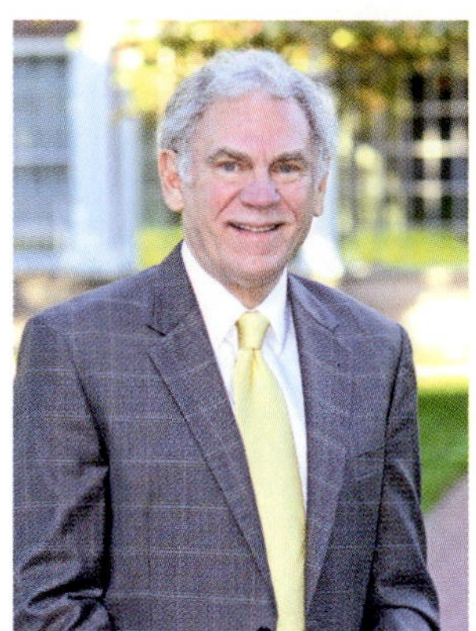

FIGURE 5.15
Jay Williams, Jr.

Faced with declining circulations, newspapers are scrambling to add platforms and extend reach, but Herald Radio firmly establishes the paper as a direct competitor for Boston's traditional radio news, talk and sports stations. Boston Herald Radio started with 12 hours a day of live, local programming featuring well-known radio hosts, but often broadcasts late for events such as the last mayoral contest, delivering political analysis and live on-scene reports as the story developed.

Magram explained the *Herald*'s rationale, "For years our columnists have been on the radio . . . then you have radio stations that rip and read *Boston Herald* stories. We talked for years about taking advantage of our own talent on our own radio station . . . and leveraging our own resources. With the explosion in smartphones, it was the right time to try a radio platform," Magram said. Boston Herald Radio can be accessed from bostonherald.com, TuneIn, *Herald* news and sports apps, iTunes Radio, and even Wi-Fi Connect in commuter trains.

FIGURE 5.16
Boston Herald Radio Studio—host's station. Courtesy of Herald Media, Inc.

"WBZ and WRKO? I think we can compete 100%; the challenge is getting people to find us and figure out how to connect to Boston Herald Radio," Magram noted. "But in terms of product and resources, we'll be just as good if not better; our depth of reporting resources is so much greater. If we were running Boston Herald Radio during the bombings, we could have had our reporters calling in, in the field on the phone, and giving information live," adding that greater listenership will happen over time as manufacturers put more Web access in cars.

FIGURE 5.17
Boston Herald Radio Studio. *Morning Meeting* show with hosts Jaclyn Cashman and Hillary Chabot and guests former Boston Mayor Ray Flynn and democratic strategist Scott Ferson. Executive producer Tom Shattuck with his back to the camera in the producer's booth. (Left to right: Hillary Chabot, Ray Flynn, Scott Ferson, and Jaclyn Cashman). Courtesy of Herald Media, Inc.

And what about the future? Magram says the relatively low-cost infrastructure—producers and hosts, the streaming vendor relationship, and a terrific software program—should allow the station to operate for a long time as it also can tap the existing news gathering, reporting and marketing resources of the *Boston Herald*. "We're no longer just a newspaper, we're a multimedia organization with 440,000 daily readers and 2.3 million unique visitors to our website. Our mission is to extend the brand beyond the existing walls, move more into digital, more into the Web, more into video both prerecorded and live streaming. There is an audience that wants our content and we need to give it to them in any fashion that they want it. We'll be driven by demand."

Jay Williams, Jr. moved from sales manager to program director to general manager of WVBF, "F-105," the station that challenged, then toppled 68WRKO to become Boston's top-rated CHR in the 1970s. "I was surrounded by incredibly talented people," he said of his early career, "it was a management tutorial that I never forgot." An entrepreneur at heart, he cofounded DMR/Interactive and developed a group of New England radio stations, managing both operations for more than 20 years. Williams is president of Broadcasting Unlimited, Inc., radio communications consultants, and serves as a trustee of Wabash College.

Internet connections such as Verizon's Fios. Using a codec, such as a Comrex Access device, you can get high quality, ISDN or studio-quality audio from remote to station. Many news operations are also using VoIP applications (Voice-over Internet Protocol)—such as Skype or broadcast applications such as LiveReportPro." Further, he notes, "while these technologies can create the 'seamless' environment you describe, I think what is most important is that they keep pace with the expectations of the audience, which is quite likely listening to us in higher fidelity than in the past. Old school remote phone or two-way audio does not sound as good on Internet streams or on digital HD broadcasts as these improved technologies. With these technologies, it is not at all uncommon anymore to have members of the team working from remote or home studios."

THE NEWS DIRECTOR

News directors, like other department heads, are responsible for developing and implementing policies pertaining to their area, supervising staff members, and handling budgetary concerns. These are basic to any managerial position.

At WTOP in Washington, D.C., the news director's responsibilities are, "Day-to-day news coverage, quality control, hiring, training, managing people," says Farley. At WCBS Newsradio 880 in New York City, "The news director is like the coach of a team. The news director is responsible for setting up his or her staff to succeed. The news director sets the tone, provides editorial direction, and coordinates news coverage for the radio station. The most important function of any news manager is to solicit ideas, and harness the potential of an entire staff," says Scheld.

The news department poses its own unique challenges to the individual who oversees its operation. These challenges must be met with a considerable degree of skill and know-how. Education and training are important. Surveys have concluded that station managers look for college degrees when hiring news directors. In addition, most news directors have, on average, five years of experience in radio news before advancement to the managerial level. In the 2013 RTDNA study, it was discovered that the average radio news director is responsible for the oversight of 2.6 stations, not just one station. Moreover, today's news directors have responsibilities beyond just overseeing the newsroom with announcing, sports, general manager and/or program director being the most likely responsibilities and titles held at the same time as overseeing the newsroom.

The news director and program director (PD) work together closely. At most stations, the PD has authority over the news department, since everything going over the air or affecting the air product is his or her direct concern and responsibility. Any changes in the format of the news or in the scheduling of newscasts or newscasters may, in fact, have to be approved by the station's programmer. For example, if the PD is opposed to the news director's plans

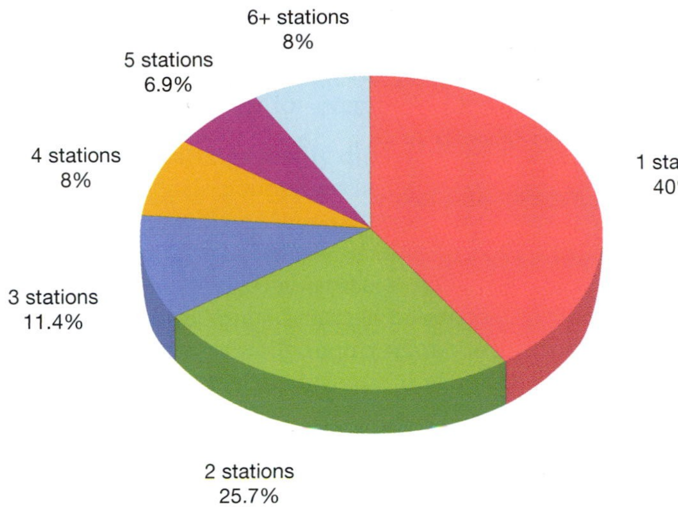

FIGURE 5.18
Number of stations per news director. Reproduced by permission of the Radio Television Digital News Association.

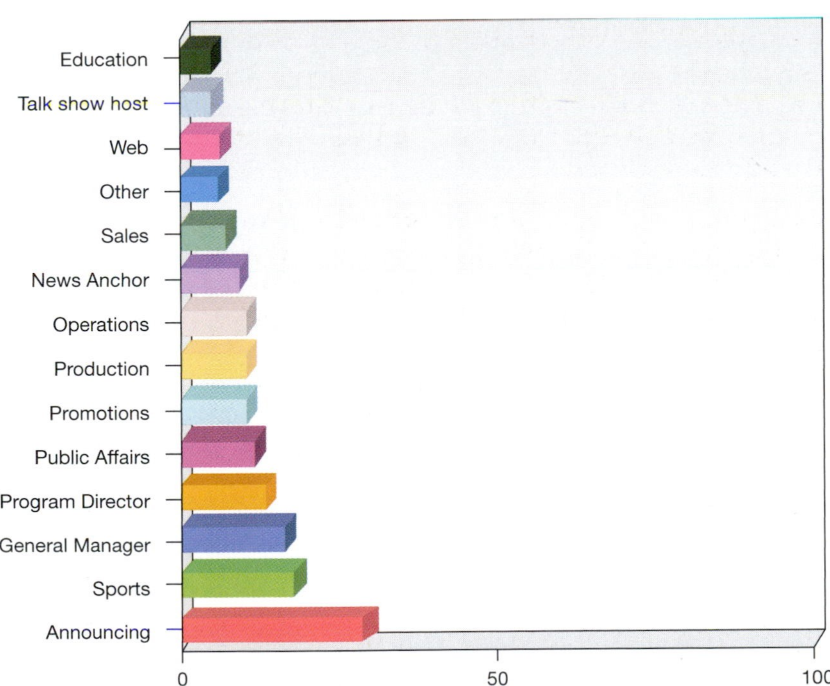

FIGURE 5.19
Other radio news director duties. Reproduced by permission of the Radio Television Digital News Association.

to include two or more recorded reports (actualities) per newscast, he may withhold approval. Although the news director may feel that the reports enhance the newscasts, the PD may argue that they create congestion and clutter. In terms of establishing the on-air news schedule, the PD works with the news director to ensure that the sound of a given newsperson is suitably matched with the time slot he or she is assigned.

Getting the news out rapidly and accurately is a top priority of the news director. "People tune to radio news to find out what is happening right now. That's what makes the medium such a key source for most people. While it is important to get news on the air as fast as possible, it is more important that the stories broadcast be factual and correct. You can't sacrifice accuracy for the sake of speed. As a radio news director, my first responsibility is to inform our audience about breaking events on the local level. That's what our listeners want to hear," says Judy Smith, who functions as a one-person newsroom at a San Antonio station. "Because I'm the only newsperson on duty, I have to spend a lot of time verifying facts on the phone and recording actualities. I don't have the luxury of assigning that work to someone else, but it has to be done."

Larry Jewett perceives his responsibilities similarly. "First and foremost, the news director's job is to keep the listener informed of what is happening in the world around him. A newsperson is a gatherer and conveyor of information. News is a serious business. A jock can be wacky and outrageous on the air and be a great success. On the other hand, a newsperson must communicate credibility or find another occupation."

Gathering local news is the most time-consuming task facing a radio news director, according to former news director Cecilia Mason:

> To do the job well you have to keep moving. All kinds of meetings—governmental, civic, business—have to be covered if you intend being a primary source of local news. A station with a news commitment must have the resources to be where the stories are, too. A news director has to be a logistical engineer at times. You have to be good at prioritizing and making the most out of what you have at hand. All too often, there are just too many events unfolding for a news department to effectively cover, so you call the shots the best way that you can. If you know your business, your best shot is usually more than adequate.

In addition to the gathering and reporting of news, public affairs programming is often the responsibility of the news director. This generally includes the planning and preparation of local information features, such as interviews, debates, and even documentaries. Ultimately, the news director's primary goal is to assure the credibility of the station's news operation. For the well-schooled and conscientious news director, this means avoiding advocacy and emphasizing objectivity. Says media scholar Indra de Silva, "So much of broadcast news today is opinion and commentary—infotainment—rather than dispassionate and unbiased reporting. That is a corruption of the long-held ideal that news should be fair and balanced. Editorializing a newscast essentially misleads the audience, which ultimately is a violation of the broadcaster's public trustee role."

WHAT MAKES A NEWSPERSON?

College training is an important criterion to the radio news director when hiring personnel. It is not impossible to land a news job without a degree, but formal education is a definite asset. In terms of a formal education, "We want people who know a lot. Smart people. A college degree helps but it alone is not a determinant of quality of work or career success," says Farley. In order to move into management, a formal education is a requirement. However, a strong desire to be in the radio industry suffices sometimes, but a formal education is always the best choice for individuals desiring a career in radio. When asked if a formal education was absolutely required to work in radio news, Rios stated:

> Not necessarily. There are several on-air personalities in our CBS Radio cluster in Dallas, who did not go to or finish college. I'd almost say half have college degrees, half do not. The thing is, those who did not get a degree in communications/RTV or journalism or political science are the people who . . . at the age of 14 and 15 started hanging out at radio stations while in high school; making copies, making coffee, etc. They just knew at an early age working in radio was their destiny. Having said that, the reason I personally believe getting a formal education is important is twofold. It's not only crucial for the experience one receives at a campus radio station (getting an internship is especially important as 90% of the time if you are a total team player and yes-(wo)man it leads to land a job at the station you intern for), but in this business—and hear me now—you *need to have a backup plan*. There is a very high turnover rate in this industry. If you are a good writer, you can always be a producer or editor in either radio or TV really. But . . . for those who think they have what it takes to be an on air reporter, or talent like the late Kidd Kraddick, I have this to say: You can have the best voice in the land. But when ratings are not good and there are changes in management . . . the person who hired you may've thought you were a rock star but the next manager might think you are mediocre at best. It would be wise to have a backup plan and consider getting a teaching certificate or . . . getting into public relations. Anything. Getting a job has a lot to do with timing and talent level. When it comes to writing though, if you are a good writer you will likely not have a hard time finding a job.

Specifically, an individual planning to enter the radio news profession should consider pursuing a broadcasting, journalism, or liberal arts degree. Courses in political science, history, economics, and literature give the aspiring newsperson the kind of well-rounded background that is most useful. As Cecilia Mason says:

> Coming into this shrinking field today, a college degree is an attractive, if not essential, credential. There's so much that a newsperson has to know. I think an education makes the kind of difference you can hear, and that's what our business is about. It's a fact that most people are more cognizant of the world and write better after attending college. Credibility is crucial in this business, and college training provides some of that. A degree is something that I would look for in prospective newspeople.

Even though education ranks high, most news directors still look for experience first. Jewett notes:

> As far as I'm concerned, experience counts the most. I'm not suggesting that education isn't important. It is. Most news directors want the person that they are hiring to have a college background, but experience impresses them more. I believe a person should have a good understanding of the basics before attempting to make a living at something. Whereas a college education is useful, a person should not lean back and point to a degree. Mine hasn't gotten me a job yet, though I wouldn't trade it for the world.

Newsman Smith agrees that "The first thing I think most news directors really look for is experience. Although I have a Bachelor of Arts degree myself, I wouldn't hold out for a person with a college diploma. I think if it came down to hiring a person with a degree versus someone with solid experience, I'd go for the latter." Scheld also acknowledges prior experience is important: Prior experience is helpful and does prepare an individual to work in the major market newsroom. Some people come into the newsroom with little news experience but they must bring in other valuable tools such as computer and audio editing skills.

Gaining news experience can be somewhat difficult in the age of downsizing and consolidation, at least more so than acquiring deejay experience, which itself is more of a challenge today than it was a decade ago. Small stations, where the beginner is most likely to break into the business, have slots for several deejays but seldom more than one for a newsperson. It becomes even more problematic when employers at small stations want the one person that they hire for news to bring some experience to the job. Larger stations place even greater emphasis on experience. Thus, the aspiring newsperson is faced with a sort of "Catch-22" situation, in which a job cannot be acquired without experience and experience cannot be acquired without a job.

One way to gain experience is through internships. WTOP-FM's Farley says, "It helps, but there's not much of a farm system out there anymore. We use a lot of interns, and their internship is in many cases an audition." Scheld agrees with Farley about the value of internships. "You do not need a college degree

FIGURE 5.20
A typical radio station news studio. Courtesy of WTOP-FM, Washington, D.C.

to work in a newsroom but it sure does help. You don't need postgraduate experience to contribute in the newsroom but any experience you bring makes you a more valuable player in the operation. The single best experience that candidates can bring to a newsroom is the internship. Internships expose you to the professional environment and are invaluable," asserts Scheld.

Agreeing with Farley about the importance of on-the-job experience and internships, Rios asserts:

> An experienced reporter or editor will nine times out of ten get a job before a recent college graduate. I'm talking about this being the case in a major market like New York, California, Chicago, or Dallas. Out of college you *must* be willing to do, and take, any job you are offered in a small(er) market. Getting that experience while you are young and single and don't have a family to consider, if only for half a year, will be the gateway into a bigger market, thus more money. Paying your dues, they call it. I just can't stress enough how important it is to be realistic, and not expect to be a news anchor in radio or TV, right out of college. Most important though, is being a good writer.

Former news director Frank Titus says that there are ways of gaining experience that will lead to a news job. "Working in news at high school and college stations is very valid experience. That's how Dan Rather and a hundred other newsmen got started. Also working as an intern at a commercial radio station fattens out the resume. If someone comes to me with this kind of background and a strong desire to do news, I'm interested."

Among the personal qualities that most appeal to news directors are enthusiasm, assertiveness, energy, and inquisitiveness. "I want someone with a strong news sense and unflagging desire to get a story and get it right. A person either wants to do news or doesn't. Someone with a pedestrian interest in radio journalism is more of a hindrance to an operation than a help," contends Mason. Titus wants someone who is totally devoted to the profession. "When you get right down to it, I want someone on my staff who eats, drinks, and sleeps news." Other needed qualities to succeed in the radio newsroom include the "ability to think on your feet, great storyteller, multimedia skills, and an incredible energy and drive," according to Farley.

On the practical side of the ledger, WCRN newsman Sherman Whitman says that typing or keyboard skills are essential. "If you can't type, you can't work in a newsroom. It's an essential ability, and the more accuracy and speed the better. It's one of those skills basic to the job. A candidate for a news job can come in here with two degrees, but if that person can't type, that person won't be hired. Broadcast students should learn to type." Meanwhile, Jewett stresses the value of possessing a firm command of the English language. "Proper punctuation, spelling, and syntax make a news story intelligible. A newsperson doesn't have to be a grammarian, but he or she had better know where to put a comma and a period and how to compose a good clean sentence. A copy of Strunk and White's *Elements of Style* is good to have around."

WCBS Newsradio's Tim Scheld agrees that writing skills are a must. "A successful radio news reporter must be a good writer. There is no substitute for good writing skills. A good reporter must also be curious. You must be skeptical, cynical, and curious. Reporters must also be great storytellers."

An individual who is knowledgeable about the area in which a station is located has a major advantage over those who are not, says Whitman. "A newsperson has to know the town or city inside out. I'd advise anybody about to be interviewed for a news position to find out as much as possible about the station's coverage area. Read back issues of newspapers, get socioeconomic stats from the library or chamber of commerce, and study street directories and maps of the town or city in which the station is located. Go into the job interview well-informed, and you'll make a strong impression."

Unlike a print journalist, a radio newsperson also must be a performer. In addition to good writing and newsgathering skills, the newsperson in radio must have announcing abilities. Again, training is usually essential. "Not only must a radio newsperson be able to write a story, but he or she has to be able to present it on the air. You have to be an announcer, too. It takes both training and experience to become a really effective newscaster. Voice performance courses can provide a foundation," says Smith. Most colleges with broadcasting programs offer announcing and newscasting instruction.

Entry-level news positions pay modestly, whereas newspeople at metro market stations earn impressive incomes. With experience come the better-paying jobs. Finding that first full-time news position often takes patience and determination. Several options are available for individuals searching for jobs in the industry such as *Broadcasting & Cable* or the RTDNA's website, which offers daily feature content along with a daily newsletter for members. Also, new media technology sites such as YouTube serve as rich places for advice on how to get a job in broadcasting. Tim Scheld's advice can be found on YouTube.

In the 2010s, radio station websites are the primary places that stations post job openings, but networking is important to secure the next job. Scheld says "All of our jobs are posted on our websites but the importance of networking cannot be overemphasized. If you are looking for work in a major market as a reporter you need to be talking to people who work in that market now and see what kind of help and advice they can provide you in terms of job possibilities. News openings are rare and most managers need to have a good idea of the top candidates for any openings at any given time."

Radio Salaries	Average	Median	Minimum	Maximum
News Director	$43,000	$35,000	$15,000	$130,000
News Reporter	37,200	33,000	17,000	110,000
News Producer	39,000	40,000	26,000	70,000
News Anchor	50,400	45,000	26,000	120,000
Sports Anchor	36,700	35,000	17,000	75,000
Sports Reporter	59,500	59,500	24,000	95,000
Web Prod/Ed	48,700	45,000	30,000	85,000

Median by Market	Major	Large	Medium	Small
News Director	$67,000	$41,500	$35,500	$30,000
News Reporter	50,000	32,000	32,500	24,000
News Producer	40,000	41,500	33,500	*
News Anchor	50,000	66,800	38,000	35,000
Sports Anchor	*	*	27,500	35,000
Sports Reporter	*	*	24,000	*
Web Prod/Ed	40,000	56,500	*	*

**insufficient data*

FIGURE 5.21
Salaries for radio news personnel. Reproduced by permission of the Radio Television Digital News Association.

WHAT IT TAKES TO WORK AT THE BOSTON HERALD CORPORATION

Jeff Magram

FIGURE 5.22
Jeff Magram.

Want to know what it takes to work at the Boston Herald Corporation? "We don't hire many 'just reporters' anymore," said Jeff Magram, COO and CFO of Herald Media, Inc. "You have to write, take pictures, create video, know social media and be able to promote yourself. It's about the quality of the video; do people care if it's not thoroughly edited, or is it about getting the content up? Maybe you could have TV that's a little bit 'rougher,' maybe you don't need to have those highly polished TV anchors," Magram muses, hinting that "Herald TV" might happen someday. And, "yes, writing is very important—what we stress is credibility and accuracy; it's paramount to us as a company. So you have to have credible sources and vet those sources."

Jeff Magram has more than 20 years of experience in the newspaper and media industry and has been the chief operating officer and CFO of Herald Media since 2001. He oversees the operations of the company and is responsible for the execution of corporate strategy. Magram is also responsible for strategic planning and has led the company through a period of organic and acquisitive growth. During Magram's tenure, Herald Media, once known exclusively as a newspaper company, has developed into a multimedia platform distributing content and providing advertising solutions in print, online, on video, and on radio. Herald Media is a multimedia company that owns and operates the *Boston Herald* newspaper, the second largest newspaper in terms of circulation in New England, bostonherald.com, a suite of online classified advertising websites (jobfind.com, homefind.com, and carfind.com) and Boston Herald Radio.

ORGANIZING THE NEWSCAST

News on music-oriented radio stations commonly is presented in five-minute blocks and aired at the top or bottom of the hour. During drivetime periods, stations often increase the length and/or frequency of newscasts. The five minutes allotted to news is generally divided into segments to accommodate the presentation of specific information. A station may establish a format that allows for two minutes of local and regional stories, one minute for key national and international stories, one minute for sports, and 15 seconds for weather information. A 30- or 60-second commercial break will be counted as part of the five-minute newscast.

The number of stories in a newscast may be preordained by program management or may vary depending on the significance and scope of the stories being reported. News policy may require that no stories, except in particular

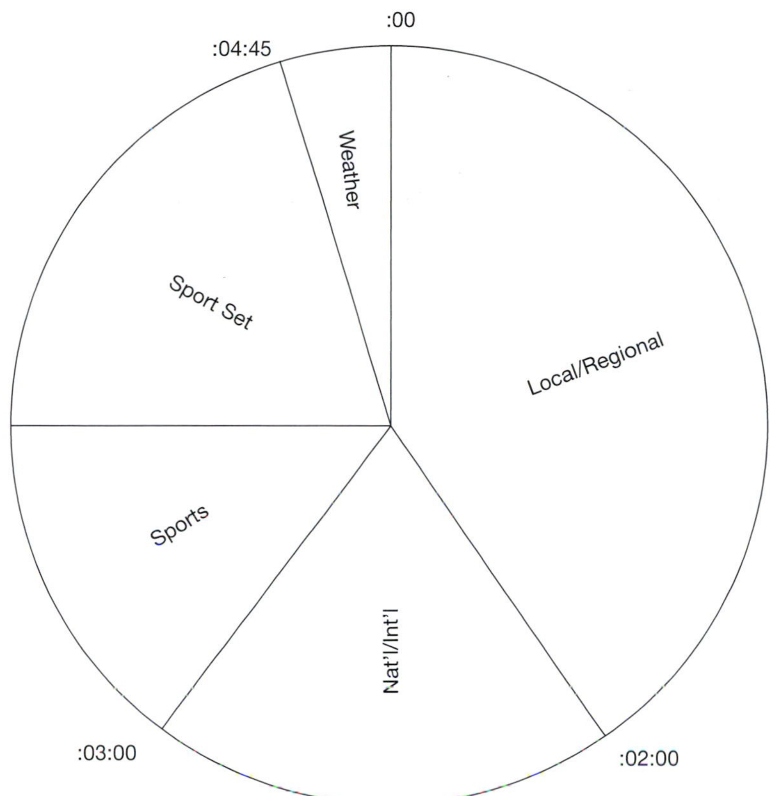

FIGURE 5.23
Five-minute newscast format clock.

cases, exceed 15 seconds. Here, the idea is to deliver as many stories as possible in the limited time available, the underlying sentiment being that more is better. In five minutes, 15–20 items may be covered. In contrast, other stations prefer that key stories be addressed in greater detail. As few as five to ten news items may be broadcast at stations taking this approach.

Stories are arranged according to their rank of importance, the most significant story of the hour topping the news. An informed newsperson will know what stories deserve the most attention. Wire services weigh each story and position them accordingly in news roundups. The local radio newsperson decides what wire stories will be aired and in what order.

Assembling a five-minute newscast takes skill, speed, and accuracy. Stories must be updated and rewritten to keep news broadcasts from sounding stale.

This often requires that telephone calls be made for late-breaking information. Meanwhile, on-the-scene voicers (actualities) originating from audio news

WBZ NEWS RADIO 1030

1170 SOLDIERS FIELD ROAD BOSTON MASSACHUSETTS 02134 TELEPHONE (617) 787-7000

WBZ NewsRadio 1030

A BRIEF DESCRIPTION

WBZ NewsRadio, the first commercially licensed station in the country, has been broadcasting to New Englanders for almost 80 years. Our award winning coverage has earned WBZ many honors including 2000's "News Station of the Year," from the Associated Press, and three recent Marconi Awards, "The Most Prestigious Radio Award Available."

WBZ has close to a million listeners weekly. The exclusive all news format creates a foreground listening environment, that delivers results for our advertisers.

Our award winning news anchors and reporters have an aggregate experience level of over 100+ years in broadcasting!

Our combined resources of both radio and television make up the largest news gathering organization in New England. Many of our radio anchors gain exposure daily on WBZ-TV 4 adding to their tremendous popularity.

WBZ highlights advertisers' messages by airing commercials as islands surrounded by news, traffic, weather or business reports. During our news, your commercial is always the first and only sixty second commercial in a commercial break.

WBZ's 50,000 watt clear channel signal reaches all of New England, and at night 38 states and six Canadian Providences. Our reach is unparalleled!

We maintain a 52 week marketing campaign promoting ourselves on TV, print, web, and at countless on-site events throughout New England.

WBZ is a leader in community involvement spearheading many events including Children's Hospital Telethon and fundraising, Call for Action, Domestic Violence and StormCenter.

WBZ is the flagship station for the Boston Bruins and the Boston Bruins Radio Network and the only place fans can catch every game every time they play.

FIGURE 5.24
A top market news station offers a profile of itself. Courtesy of Infinity.

HOW DO YOU CREATE THAT SPECIAL CONNECTION BETWEEN STATION AND LISTENER?

Tim Scheld

FIGURE 5.25
Tim Scheld.

The bond between listener and radio station is something that takes years to develop. The foundation of that bond is trust. Our job is to deliver a product that we hope will be of value to the people listening. If we do that on a consistent basis, listeners will make a conscious choice to listen to us. Over time, that develops into an implied contract that whenever there is a need, we will be there. But it's not just about having what people need; it's about how the information is conveyed. There needs to be honesty and authenticity. That comes with having news personalities who can connect with listeners. We don't put on any airs—we are real people. We laugh at a good joke, we get mad at higher tolls, we cry inside when we are faced with stories like Sandy or Newtown. We are not just providing news to our community, we are members of the community delivering news, and hopefully that comes through in what we say, how we say it, even in the questions we ask. It's all about staying connected to the community, and understanding the responsibility of being a voice for the people in that community. First and foremost, I think it's important to have a presence in the places you cover, and not just visit them in times of tragedy. That can be a challenge when you consider that in our Tri-State area we have hundreds of municipalities.

We also take seriously our responsibility to tell stories about the tremendous good going on across our listening area. These stories are the ones that provoke the most reaction and lead to new connections and new story ideas. I also feel strongly about building partnerships with community entities like the March of Dimes, WHY Hunger, the Special Olympics, and the 9/11 National Museum. These are organizations that we provide support to by helping them raise money and awareness. Another part of our commitment to the events that engage our listeners.

We run multiple events each year including several Small Business Breakfasts, "The Business of Getting into College," a Working Women's Luncheon, and a Women's Achievement Awards. These events help connect us to people in the communities we serve. They allow us to interact with listeners in a personal way and help us take the pulse of the people who listen to our station every day.

Tim Scheld is director of news and programming at New York's WCBS Newsradio 880, a job he has held since October 2003. Prior to becoming a news manager, Scheld spent 20 years working as a local radio reporter in New York City at both WOR-710AM, and then WCBS Newsradio 880. In 1994, Scheld was hired as a national correspondent for ABC News Radio where he worked until he left to take the news director position at WCBS-AM. He was part of the 2001 Peabody Award-winning coverage from ABC News of the September 11 attacks and has won numerous awards for his reporting from organizations such as the RTDNA, the New York Press Club and the New York State Associated Press Broadcasters Association.

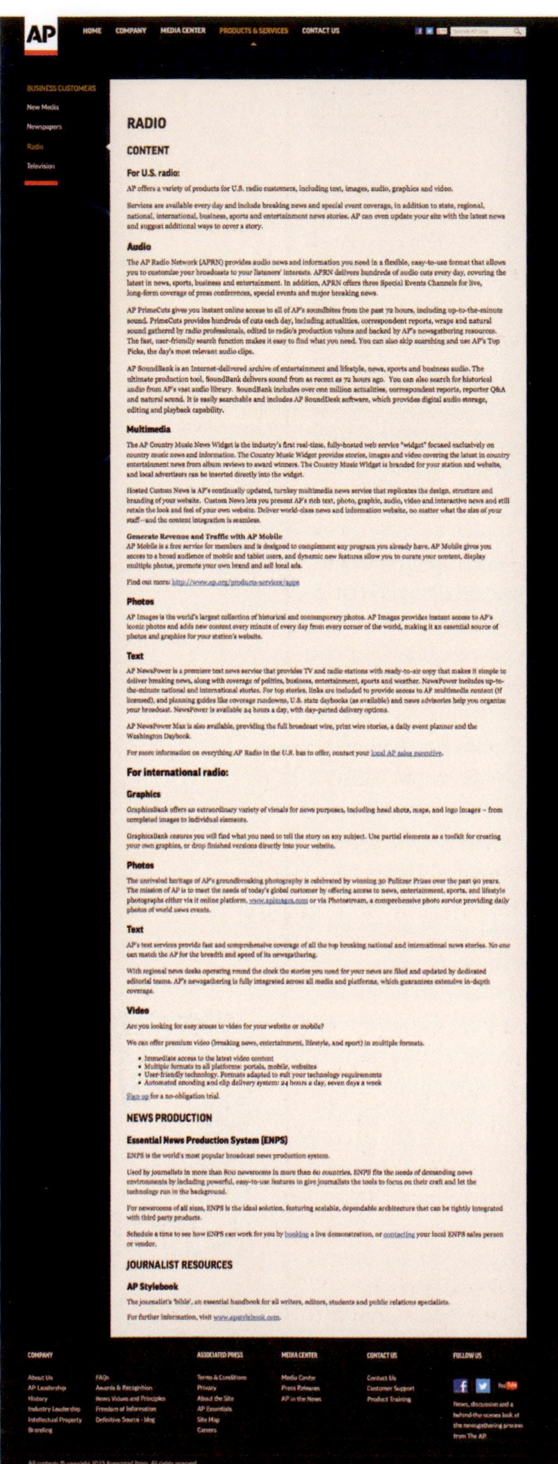

HOME COMPANY MEDIA CENTER PRODUCTS & SERVICES CONTACT US

RADIO

CONTENT

For U.S. radio:

AP offers a variety of products for U.S. radio customers, including text, images, audio, graphics and video.

Services are available every day and include breaking news and special event coverage, in addition to state, regional, national, international, business, sports and entertainment news stories. AP can even update your site with the latest news and suggest additional ways to cover a story.

Audio

The AP Radio Network (APRN) provides audio news and information you need in a flexible, easy-to-use format that allows you to customize your broadcasts to your listeners' interests. APRN delivers hundreds of audio cuts every day, covering the latest in news, sports, business and entertainment. In addition, APRN offers three Special Events Channels for live, long-form coverage of press conferences, special events and major breaking news.

AP PrimeCuts gives you instant online access to all of AP's soundbites from the past 72 hours, including up-to-the-minute sound. PrimeCuts provides hundreds of cuts each day, including actualities, correspondent reports, wraps and natural sound gathered by radio professionals, edited to radio's production values and backed by AP's newsgathering resources. The fast, user-friendly search function makes it easy to find what you need. You can also skip searching and use AP's Top Picks, the day's most relevant audio clips.

AP SoundBank is an Internet-delivered archive of entertainment and lifestyle, news, sports and business audio. The ultimate production tool, SoundBank delivers sound from as recent as 72 hours ago. You can also search for historical audio from AP's vast audio library. SoundBank includes over one million actualities, correspondent reports, reporter Q&A and natural sound. It is easily searchable and includes AP SoundDesk software, which provides digital audio storage, editing and playback capability.

Multimedia

The AP Country Music News Widget is the industry's first real-time, fully-hosted web service "widget" focused exclusively on country music news and information. The Country Music Widget provides stories, images and video covering the latest in country entertainment news from album reviews to award winners. The Country Music Widget is branded for your station and website, and local advertisers can be inserted directly into the widget.

Hosted Custom News is AP's continually updated, turnkey multimedia news service that replicates the design, structure and branding of your website. Custom News lets you present AP's rich text, photo, graphic, audio, video and interactive news and still retain the look and feel of your own website. Deliver world-class news and information website, no matter what the size of your staff—and the content integration is seamless.

Generate Revenue and Traffic with AP Mobile
AP Mobile is a free service for members and is designed to complement any program you already have. AP Mobile gives you access to a broad audience of mobile and tablet users, and dynamic new features allow you to curate your content, display multiple photos, promote your own brand and sell local ads.

Find out more: http://www.ap.org/products-services/apps

Photos

AP Images is the world's largest collection of historical and contemporary photos. AP Images provides instant access to AP's iconic photos and adds new content every minute of every day from every corner of the world, making it an essential source of photos and graphics for your station's website.

Text

AP NewsPower is a premiere text news service that provides TV and radio stations with ready-to-air copy that makes it simple to deliver breaking news, along with coverage of politics, business, entertainment, sports and weather. NewsPower includes up-to-the-minute national and international stories. For top stories, links are included to provide access to AP multimedia content (if licensed), and planning guides like coverage rundowns, U.S. state daybooks (as available) and news advisories help you organize your broadcast. NewsPower is available 24 hours a day, with day-parted delivery options.

AP NewsPower Max is also available, providing the full broadcast wire, print wire stories, a daily event planner and the Washington Daybook.

For more information on everything AP Radio in the U.S. has to offer, contact your local AP sales executive.

For international radio:

Graphics

GraphicsBank offers an extraordinary variety of visuals for news purposes, including head shots, maps, and logo images – from completed images to individual elements.

GraphicsBank ensures you will find what you need to tell the story on any subject. Use partial elements as a toolkit for creating your own graphics, or drop finished versions directly into your website.

Photos

The unrivaled heritage of AP's groundbreaking photography is celebrated by winning 30 Pulitzer Prizes over the past 90 years. The mission of AP is to meet the needs of today's global customer by offering access to news, entertainment, sports, and lifestyle photographs either via it online platform, www.apimages.com or via Photostream, a comprehensive photo service providing daily photos of world news events.

Text

AP's text services provide fast and comprehensive coverage of all the top breaking national and international news stories. No one can match the AP for the breadth and speed of its newsgathering.

With regional news desks operating round the clock the stories you need for your news are filed and updated by dedicated editorial teams. AP's newsgathering is fully integrated across all media and platforms, which guarantees extensive in-depth coverage.

Video

Are you looking for easy access to video for your website or mobile?

We can offer premium video (breaking news, entertainment, lifestyle, and sport) in multiple formats.

- Immediate access to the latest video content
- Multiple formats to all platforms: portals, mobile, websites
- User-friendly technology. Formats adapted to suit your technology requirements
- Automated encoding and clip delivery system: 24 hours a day, seven days a week

Sign up for a no-obligation trial.

NEWS PRODUCTION

Essential News Production System (ENPS)

ENPS is the world's most popular broadcast news production system.

Used by journalists in more than 800 newsrooms in more than 60 countries, ENPS fits the needs of demanding news environments by including powerful, easy-to-use features to give journalists the tools to focus on their craft and let the technology run in the background.

For newsrooms of all sizes, ENPS is the ideal solution, featuring scalable, dependable architecture that can be tightly integrated with third party products.

Schedule a time to see how ENPS can work for you by booking a live demonstration, or contacting your local ENPS sales person or vendor.

JOURNALIST RESOURCES

AP Stylebook

The journalist's 'bible', an essential handbook for all writers, editors, students and public relations specialists.

For further information, visit www.apstylebook.com.

FIGURE 5.26
Associated Press Web page listing services to its radio affiliates.
Courtesy of Associated Press

services such as Associated Press or fed by local reporters must be recorded and slotted in the newscast. "Preparing a fresh newscast each hour can put you in mind of what it must have been like to be a contestant on the old game show *Beat the Clock*. A conscientious newsperson is a vision of perpetual motion," observes Cecilia Mason.

Finally, most newspeople read their news copy before going on the air. "Reading stories cold is foolhardy and invites trouble. Even the most seasoned newscasters at metro market stations take the time to read over their copy before going on," comments Whitman. Many newspeople read copy aloud in the news studio before airtime. This gives them a chance to get a feel for their copy. Proper preparation prevents unpleasant surprises from occurring while on the air.

WIRE SERVICES—AUDIO AND INTERNET

Without the aid of the major broadcast news wire service (Associated Press), blogs, social media, and the inestimable number of news-oriented websites and television network news channels that exist (CNN, MSNBC, Fox, Drudge Report, etc.), radio stations would find it almost impossible to cover news on national and international levels. Indeed, wire service, Internet, and television are vital sources of news information to nearly all of the nation's commercial radio stations.

Both large and small stations rely on the news copy fed to them by the Associated Press (AP) considered by many in the industry as a well-respected news wire service. In AP's 2012 Annual Report, it was noted that the AP received 50 Pulitzer Prizes and had a global reach of 110 countries. It staffed news bureaus in all 50 U.S. state houses and more than 60 countries. Impressively, it provides more than 1,700 news stories a month with more than 60,000 reporters worldwide in more than 800 newsrooms. "I believe you need at least some of the resources from Associated Press to compete well. There are plenty of online and social media outlets from which to get news, but a) which ones can you trust and b) are you stealing somebody else's intellectual property?," states Farley.

The AP offers digital news packages that can be uploaded to radio station websites or shared via social media such as Twitter and Facebook. Associated Press's website states: "AP can provide breaking news and information directly to your audiences via your internal and external websites, desktops, wireless services and other interactive applications. Our extensive suite of services spans more than 30 categories of industry-targeted content to fit your digital needs."

In 2012, the Spanish Broadcasting System (SBS) announced that ten of its Spanish language stations would offer Associated Press's Spanish Online Newsfeed on their websites. "Our partnership brings the most trusted news source to our U.S. Hispanic online audience in Spanish. Multiple content verticals, like news, sports, entertainment, etc., are great additions to our network of sites," said SBS vice-president of digital sales Andrew Polsky, in an *All Access* article.

The audio cuts provided by the AP news service are an integral part of many station newscasts. Observes radio scholar Larry Miller, "When these audio clips are sent to subscribing stations, they will also send along a menu which will list the type of cut (A-actuality, V-voicer, or W-wrap), who it is, what it's about, how long it runs, and the outcue." Miller cautions that audio cuts should be used sparingly, "They should not be overused to pad out a newscast. Relevance, audio quality, and length should rule the decisions regarding how much audio to use. With the proper application of these sources, even a one-person news operation can sound like a big city newsroom."

The wire service is only one means of news gathering for radio stations. "Wire services are just part of the equation in the modern newsroom. The Internet has become an enormous and invaluable resource providing quick access to everything from maps to public records. Social media has also emerged as an important resource with many newsrooms using tools like TweetDeck to develop news tips into news stories. TweetDeck has become more important than the police scanner in our newsroom," asserts Scheld.

FIGURE 5.27
Twitter is used by most radio news stations to disseminate information. Courtesy of Twitter.com.

From 1958 to 1999, United Press International (UPI) also provided wire service and audio to radio stations via the UPI Radio Network, but it ceased its operation in 1999. Broadcast wire services came into existence in the mid-1930s, when UP (which became UPI in 1958 after merging with INS) began providing broadcasters with news copy.

FIGURE 5.28
TweetDeck is a common tool used by news stations to disseminate information. Courtesy of Twitter.com.

RADIO NETWORK NEWS

During the medium's first three decades, the terms *networks* and *news* were virtually synonymous. Most of the news broadcast over America's radio stations emanated from the networks. The public's dependence on network radio news reached its height during World War II. As television succeeded radio as the mainstay for entertainment programming in the 1950s and 1960s, the networks concentrated their efforts on supplying affiliates with news and information feeds. This approach helped the networks regain their footing in radio after a period of substantial decline. By the mid-1960s, the majority of the nation's stations used one of the four major networks for news programming.

In 1968, ABC decided to make available four distinct news formats designed for compatibility with the dominant sounds of the day. American Contemporary Radio Network, American FM Radio Network, American Entertainment Radio Network, and American Information Network each offered a unique style and method of news presentation. ABC's venture proved enormously successful. In the 1970s, more than 1,500 stations subscribed to one of ABC's four news networks.

In response to a growing racial and ethnic awareness, the Mutual Broadcasting System (MBS) launched two minority news networks in 1971. Though the network's black news service proved to be a fruitful venture, its Spanish news service ceased operation within two years of its inception. Mutual discovered that the ethnic group simply was too refracted and diverse to be effectively serviced by one network and that the Latin listeners they did attract did not constitute the numbers necessary to justify operation.

In 1973, the network also went head-to-head with ABC by offering a network news service (Mutual Progressive Network) that catered to rock-oriented stations. Mutual's various efforts paid off by making it second only to ABC in number of affiliates. After years of financial difficulties, MBS went silent in 1999, ending nearly seven decades of radio news service.

The News and Information Service (NIS) was introduced by NBC in 1975 but ended in 1977. NIS offered client stations an All-News format. Fifty minutes of news was fed to stations each hour. The venture was abandoned after only moderate acceptance. CBS, which has offered its member stations World News Roundup since 1938, and NBC have fewer than 300 affiliates apiece.

Several state and regional news networks do well, but the big three, ABC, NBC, and CBS, continue to dominate. Meanwhile, independent satellite news and information networks and the cable news services, such as CNN, have joined the field and more are planned.

The usual length of a network newscast is five minutes, during which time affiliates are afforded an opportunity to insert local sponsor messages at designated times. The networks make their money by selling national advertisers spot availabilities in their widely broadcast news. Stations also pay the networks a fee for the programming they receive.

According to Metro Network president David Saperstein, today "more and more stations are realizing the benefits that exist in outside news services, which provide the information that listeners would otherwise seek elsewhere. This allows the station to focus its marketing dollars, thus directing resources toward optimizing and maintaining what draws and keeps listeners." Of course, this latter trend has raised additional concerns about the decline in local news coverage as cited in recent RTDNA surveys. Station consolidations have resulted in the erosion of local news operations.

RADIO SPORTSCASTS

Sports is most commonly presented as an element within newscasts. Although many stations air sports as programming features unto themselves, most stations insert information, such as scores and schedules of upcoming games, at a designated point in a newscast and call it sports. Whether a station emphasizes sports largely depends on its audience. Stations gearing their format for youngsters or women often all but ignore sports. Adult-oriented stations will frequently offer a greater abundance of sports information, especially when the station is located in an area that has a major league team.

Stations that hire individuals to do sports—and invariably these are larger outlets since few small stations can afford a full-time sportsperson—look for someone who is well-versed in the subject. "To be good at radio sports, you have to have been involved as a participant somewhere along the line. That's for starters, in my opinion. This doesn't mean that you have to be a former major leaguer before doing radio sports but to have a feel for what you're talking about, it certainly helps to have been on the field or court yourself. A good sportscaster must have the ability to accurately analyze a sport through the eyes and body of the athlete," contends former radio sports director John Colletto.

Unlike news that requires an impartial and somewhat austere presentation, sportscasts are frequently delivered in a casual and even opinionated manner. "Let's face it, there's a big difference between nuclear arms talks between the United States and the Soviets and last night's Red Sox/Yankees score. I don't think sports reports should be treated in a style that's too solemn. It's entertainment, and sportscasters should exercise their license to comment and analyze," says Colletto.

Although sports is presented in a less heavy-handed way than news, credibility is an important factor, contends Colletto. "There is a need for radio sportscasters to establish credibility just as there is for newspeople to do so. If you're not believable, you're not listened to. The best way to win the respect of your audience is by demonstrating a thorough knowledge of the game and by sounding like an insider, not just a guy reading the wire copy. Remember, sports fans can be as loyal to a sportscaster as they are to their favorite team. They want to hear the stories and scores from a person they feel comfortable with."

The style of a news story and a sports story may differ considerably. Although news is written in a no-frills, straightforward way, sports stories often contain colorful colloquialisms and even popular slang. Here is an example by radio sportswriter Roger Crosley:

> The Dean College Red Demon football team rode the strong running of fullback Bill Palazollo yesterday to an 18–16 come-from-behind victory over the American International College Junior Varsity Yellow Jackets. Palazollo churned out a team high 93 yards on 25 carries and scored all three touchdowns on blasts of 7, 2, and 6 yards. The demons trailed the hard-hitting contest 16–6 entering the final quarter. Palazollo capped a 12-play 81-yard drive with his second six-pointer early in the stanza and scored the clincher with 4:34 remaining. The demons will put their 1 and 0 record on the line next Sunday at 1:30 against the always tough holy cross jayvees in Worcester.

Sportscasters are personalities, says Colletto, and as such must be able to communicate on a different level than newscasters. "You're expected to have a sense of humor. Most successful sportscasters can make an audience smile or laugh. You have to be able to ad-lib, also."

The wire services, networks, and Internet are the primary source for sports news at local stations. On the other hand, information about the outcome of local games, such as high school football and so forth, must be acquired firsthand. This usually entails a call to the team's coach or a direct report from a stringer or reporter.

RADIO NEWS AND THE FCC

The government takes a greater role in regulating broadcast journalism than it does print. Although it usually maintains a hands-off position when it comes to newspapers, the government keeps a watchful eye on radio to ensure that it meets certain operating criteria. Since the FCC perceives the airways as public domain, it expects broadcasters to operate in the public's interest.

In 2013, the FCC began an initiative called Critical Information Needs (CIN). RBR.com reports, "The FCC has a research model to study this topic with an eye toward assuring that Americans are getting the news and information they need, regardless of location, ethnicity or any other factor." The CIN study will focus its radio study on stations with News/Talk formats.

The FCC requires that radio reporters present news factually and in good faith. Stories that defame citizens through reckless or false statements may not only bring a libel suit from the injured party but action from the FCC, which views such behavior on the part of broadcasters as contrary to the public's interest. Broadcasters are protected under the First Amendment and therefore have certain rights, but as public trustees, they are charged with the additional responsibility of acting in a manner that benefits rather than harms members of society.

Although the FCC tends to take a hands-off approach, broadcasters still believe there are things the FCC can do to create an environment that is conducive to radio stations covering the news. "I believe the FCC should allow more cross-ownership of radio, TV and newspaper as a means of sharing news resources and costs. Exemptions should be made to keep newspaper and broadcast news organizations viable," says Farley.

Broadcasters are free to express opinions and sentiments on issues through editorials. However, to avoid controversy, many radio stations choose not to editorialize even though the FCC encourages them to do so.

NEWS ETHICS

The highly competitive nature of radio places unusual pressure on newspeople. In a business where being first with the story is often equated with being the best, certain dangers exist. Being first at all costs can be costly indeed if information and facts are not adequately verified. As previously mentioned, it is the radio journalist's obligation to get the story straight and accurate before putting it on the air. Anything short of this is unprofessional. Rios says:

> I'd have to say the state of radio these days is very good. As always the beauty of news radio is whether you are listening at home or in your car when there's breaking news, we can get the information on air instantly, once confirmed. That is the advantage we will always have over television news. What is happening though because of the Internet is . . . stories are out there that you see and want to run with, but as always you *have* to verify any story before running it. Have we been burned before? Yes, especially with sensational, pop culture stories. We are much more careful and thorough with stories that are important to our local audience.

The pressures of the clock, if allowed, can result in haphazard reporting. If a story cannot be sufficiently prepared in time for the upcoming news broadcast, it should be withheld. Getting it on-air is not as important as getting it on-air correctly. Accuracy is the newsperson's first criterion. News accounts should never be fudged. It is tantamount to deceiving and misleading the public. "It's the responsibility of everyone who we hire from producers to reporters, to understand the mission of getting the facts straight before putting something on the air. It is part of the culture of the radio station to verify the facts of a story before putting it on the air to the best of our ability," says Scheld.

News reporters must exhibit discretion not only in the newsroom but also when on the scene of a story. It is commendable to assiduously pursue the facts and details of a story, but it is inconsiderate and insensitive to ignore the suffering and pain of those involved. For example, to press for comments from a grief-stricken parent whose child has just been seriously injured in an accident is callous and cruel and a disservice to all concerned, including the station the newsperson represents. Of course, a newsperson wants as much information as possible about an incident, but the public's right to privacy must be respected. As Rios says:

> You can learn to become a good reporter, but instinct has a lot to do with it. Instinct in knowing what questions to ask in an interview. Sensitivity as well. You will inevitably cover a funeral. Tough assignment, trying to get an interview with a friend or loved one about the death of a toddler or teen, for example. It's all in the approach and genuine sincerity. And knowing when and when *not* to push for an interview. Schmoozing with police on the scene of a story or police communications liaison is never a bad thing. Make friends with police. Most importantly though is being able to *paint a picture*, through words and sound. Radio is theatre of the mind. The listeners have to imagine the story while they're driving or washing dishes at home.

CODE OF ETHICS

PREAMBLE

Professional electronic journalists should operate as trustees of the public, seek the truth, report it fairly and with integrity and independence, and stand accountable for their actions.

PUBLIC TRUST

Professional electronic journalists should recognize that their first obligation is to the public.

Professional electronic journalists should:

- Understand that any commitment other than service to the public undermines trust and credibility.
- Recognize that service in the public interest creates an obligation to reflect the diversity of the community and guard against oversimplification of issues or events.
- Provide a full range of information to enable the public to make enlightened decisions.
- Fight to ensure that the public's business is conducted in public.

FAIRNESS

Professional electronic journalists should present the news fairly and impartially, placing primary value on significance and relevance.

Professional electronic journalists should:

- Treat all subjects of news coverage with respect and dignity, showing particular compassion to victims of crime or tragedy.
- Exercise special care when children are involved in a story and give children greater privacy protection than adults.
- Seek to understand the diversity of their community and inform the public without bias or stereotype.
- Present a diversity of expressions, opinions, and ideas in context.
- Present analytical reporting based on professional perspective, not personal bias.
- Respect the right to a fair trial.

INDEPENDENCE

Professional electronic journalists should defend the independence of all journalists from those seeking influence or control over news content.

Professional electronic journalists should:

- Gather and report news without fear or favor, and vigorously resist undue influence from any outside forces, including advertisers, sources, story subjects, powerful individuals, and special interest groups.
- Resist those who would seek to buy or politically influence news content or who would seek to intimidate those who gather and disseminate the news.
- Determine news content solely through editorial judgment and not as the result of outside influence.
- Resist any self-interest or peer pressure that might erode journalistic duty and service to the public.
- Recognize that sponsorship of the news will not be used in any way to determine, restrict, or manipulate content.
- Refuse to allow the interests of ownership or management to influence news judgment and content inappropriately.
- Defend the rights of the free press for all journalists, recognizing that any professional or government licensing of journalists is a violation of that freedom.

TRUTH

Professional electronic journalists should pursue truth aggressively and present the news accurately, in context, and as completely as possible.

Professional electronic journalists should:

- Continuously seek the truth.
- Resist distortions that obscure the importance of events.
- Clearly disclose the origin of information and label all material provided by outsiders.

Professional electronic journalists should not:

- Report anything known to be false.
- Manipulate images or sounds in any way that is misleading.
- Plagiarize.
- Present images or sounds that are reenacted without informing the public.

INTEGRITY

Professional electronic journalists should present the news with integrity and decency, avoiding real or perceived conflicts of interest, and respect the dignity and intelligence of the audience as well as the subjects of news.

Professional electronic journalists should:

- Identify sources whenever possible. Confidential sources should be used only when it is clearly in the public interest to gather or convey important information or when a person providing information might be harmed. Journalists should keep all commitments to protect a confidential source.
- Clearly label opinion and commentary.
- Guard against extended coverage of events or individuals that fails to significantly advance a story, place the event in context, or add to the public knowledge.
- Refrain from contacting participants in violent situations while the situation is in progress.
- Use technological tools with skill and thoughtfulness, avoiding techniques that skew facts, distort reality, or sensationalize events.
- Use surreptitious newsgathering techniques, including hidden cameras or microphones, only if there is no other way to obtain stories of significant public importance and only if the technique is explained to the audience.
- Disseminate the private transmissions of other news organizations only with permission.

Professional electronic journalists should not:

- Pay news sources who have a vested interest in a story.
- Accept gifts, favors, or compensation from those who might seek to influence coverage.
- Engage in activities that may compromise their integrity or independence.

ACCOUNTABILITY

Professional electronic journalists should recognize that they are accountable for their actions to the public, the profession, and themselves.

Professional electronic journalists should:

- Actively encourage adherence to these standards by all journalists and their employers.
- Respond to public concerns. Investigate complaints and correct errors promptly and with as much prominence as the original report.
- Explain journalistic processes to the public, especially when practices spark questions or controversy.
- Recognize that professional electronic journalists are duty-bound to conduct themselves ethically.
- Refrain from ordering or encouraging courses of action that would force employees to commit an unethical act.
- Carefully listen to employees who raise ethical objections and create environments in which such objections and discussions are encouraged.
- Seek support for and provide opportunities to train employees in ethical decision-making.

In meeting its responsibility to the profession of electronic journalism, RTDNA has created this code to identify important issues, to serve as a guide for its members, to facilitate self-scrutiny, and to shape future debate.

FIGURE 5.29
RTDNA Code of Ethics. Reproduced by permission of the Radio Television Digital News Association.

Objectivity is the cornerstone of good reporting. A newsperson who has lost his or her capacity to see the whole picture is handicapped. At the same time, the newsperson's job is to report the news and not create it. Although maintaining objectivity is the goal, it is not always possible. Scheld asserts, "Reporters do have to maintain objectivity in delivering the facts of a story but there is no way we can completely divorce ourselves from the emotions that come from some stories. If our baseball team wins the championship, and our city celebrates, we get caught up in the excitement. If we witness tragedy such as the terrible shootings in Newtown, we cannot help but deliver this news with a sense of personal trauma. There is no way around it. Our listeners want us to be authentic." Agreeing with Scheld, Rios states, "Objectivity, is critical. You have to present both sides of controversial stories and *never* let your personal stance on any topic be obvious. And never run a controversial story without getting both sides. We actually had a news anchor who would literally skip a story that had anything to do with the political party opposite to the one he sided with. He would always use the excuse that he simply ran out of time to do the opposing view story. He ultimately got fired."

The mere presence of a member of the media can inspire a disturbance or agitate a volatile situation. Staging an event for the sake of increasing the "newsiness" of a story is not only unprofessional but illegal. Groups have been known to await the arrival of reporters before initiating a disturbance for the sake of gaining publicity. It is the duty of reporters to remain as innocuous and uninvolved as possible when on an assignment. Recall Indra de Silva's comment earlier about the need for news to be presented in a thoughtful and conscientious way.

Several industry associations, such as RTDNA and the Society of Professional Journalists, have established codes pertaining to the ethics and conduct of broadcast reporters. "The codes of professional conduct are important for an organization. The idea is for our work to benefit the public good. We need to do our jobs in a fair minded way motivated by a pursuit of the truth. Any reminder of those pillars is a good thing," says Scheld.

TRAFFIC REPORTS

Traffic reports are an integral part of drivetime news programming at many metropolitan radio stations. Although providing listeners with traffic condition updates can be costly, especially air-to-ground reports that require the use of a helicopter or small plane, they can help strengthen a station's community service image and also generate substantial revenue. To avoid the cost involved in airborne observation, stations sometimes employ the services of local auto clubs or put their own mobile units out on the roads. A station in Providence, Rhode Island, broadcasts traffic conditions from atop a 20-story hotel that overlooks the city's key arteries. Fixed cameras at key traffic locations are also used.

Says David Saperstein, "Companies like Metro Network provide stations with outside traffic reporting services in a manner that is more cost- and quality-effective than a station handling it themselves."

Traffic reports are scheduled several times an hour throughout the prime commuter periods on stations primarily catering to adults, and they range in length from 30–90 seconds. The actual reports may be done by a station employee who works in other areas of programming when not surveying the roads, or a member of the local police department or auto club may be hired for the job. Obviously, the prime criterion for such a position is a thorough knowledge of the streets and highways of the area being reported.

NEWS IN MUSIC RADIO

In the 1980s, the FCC saw fit to eliminate the requirement that all radio stations devote a percentage of their broadcast day to news and public affairs programming. Opponents of the decision argued that such a move would mark the decline of news on radio. In contrast, proponents of the deregulation commended the FCC's actions that allow for the marketplace to determine the extent to which non-entertainment features are broadcast. In the late 1980s, RTDNA expressed the concern that local news coverage had declined. This, they said, had resulted in a decrease in the number of news positions around the country. Supporting their contention they pointed out that several major stations, such as KDKA, WOWO, and WIND, had cut back their news budgets.

But, WCRN news director Sherman Whitman believes that the radio audience wants news even when a station's primary product is music. "The public has come to depend on the medium to keep it informed. It's a volatile world and certain events affect us all. Stations that aim to be full-service cannot do so without a solid news schedule."

"Responsible broadcasters know that it is the inherent duty of the medium to keep the public apprised of what is going on," claims Larry Jewett. "While radio is primarily an entertainment medium, it is still one of the country's foremost sources of information. Responsible broadcasters—and most of us are—realize that we have a special obligation to fulfill. The tremendous reach and immediacy that is unique to radio forces the medium to be something more than just a jukebox."

News director Frank Titus believes that stations will continue to broadcast news in the future. "There might be a tendency to invest less in news operations, especially at more music-oriented outlets, as the result of the regulation change and rampant consolidations, but news is as much a part of what radio is as are the deejays and songs. What it comes right down to is people want news broadcasts, so they're going to get them. That's the whole idea behind the commission's actions. There's no doubt in my mind that the marketplace will continue to dictate the programming of radio news."

News director Roger Nadel concurs. "As the age of the average listener increases, even people tuning in to 'music' stations find themselves in need of at least minimal doses of news. So long as those stations are doing well financially, owners can be content to maintain some kind of a news operation. News is not likely to disappear; not even at music stations."

Competition from the wave of new audio services has also influenced the role of news in terrestrial radio.

CHAPTER HIGHLIGHTS

1. A study by the Radio Television Digital News Association indicates that news radio is second only to country music radio when listeners are searching for a station to listen to for entertainment and information.
2. The size of a station's news staff depends on the degree to which the station's format emphasizes news, the station's market size, the emphasis of its competition, and station consolidations. Small stations often have no newspeople and require deejays to use "rip 'n' read" wire service copy.
3. Large news staffs may consist of newscasters, writers, street reporters, and tech people, as well as stringers and interns.
4. Computers in radio newsrooms are used as links to the various wire, news, audio, and Internet outlets for reading news copy on the air, and as computers for writing and storing news. Software is available to newsrooms for archiving and other purposes.
5. The news director, who works with and for the PD, supervises news staff, develops and implements policy, handles the budget, ensures the gathering of local news, is responsible for getting out breaking news stories rapidly and accurately and plans public affairs programming. News directors also hold multiple jobs at some stations depending on the size of the market in which the station is located.
6. News directors seek personnel with both college education and experience. However, finding a news slot at a small station is difficult since its news staffs are small, so internships and experience at high school and college stations are important. In addition, such personal qualities as enthusiasm, aggressiveness, energy, inquisitiveness, typing skills, a knowledge of the area where the station is located, announcing abilities, and a command of the English language are assets.
7. News stories must be legible, intelligible, and designed for effortless reading. They should sound conversational, informal, simple, direct, concise, and organized.
8. Actualities (on-the-scene voicers) are obtained from news service feeds, online sources, and by station personnel at the scene.
9. The FCC expects broadcasters to report the news in a balanced and impartial manner. Although protected under the First Amendment, broadcasters making reckless or false statements are subject to both civil and FCC charges.
10. Ethically, newspersons must maintain objectivity, discretion, and sensitivity.

11. The FCC's deregulation of news and public affairs programming in the 1980s, widespread station clustering in the 1990s and 2000s due to consolidation, and emerging new media technologies have prompted concerns by industry officials and others that radio news service is on the decline if not on the cusp of extinction.

SUGGESTED FURTHER READING

Anderson, B., *News Flash: Journalism, Infotainment, and the Bottom-Line Business of Broadcast News*, Jossey-Bass, San Francisco, CA, 2004.

Barnas, F. and White, T., *Broadcast News Writing, Reporting, and Producing*, 6th edition, Focal Press, Burlington, MA, 2013.

Bartlett, J. (ed.), *The First Amendment in a Free Society*, H.W. Wilson, New York, 1979.

Bittner, J.R. and Bittner, D.A., *Radio Journalism*, Prentice Hall, Englewood Cliffs, NJ, 1977.

Bliss, E.J., *Now the News*, Oxford Press, New York, 1991.

Bliss, E.J. and Hoyt, J.L., *Writing News for Broadcast*, 3rd edition, Columbia University Press, New York, 1994.

Block, M., *Broadcast News Writing for Professionals*, Marion Street Press, Oak Park, IL, 2005.

Block, M. and Durso, J., *Writing News for TV and Radio: The New Way to Learn Broadcast Newswriting*, CQ Press, Washington, D.C., 2010.

Boyd, A., *Broadcast Journalism*, 5th edition, Focal Press, Boston, MA, 2008.

Boyer, P.J., *Who Killed CBS?* Random House, New York, 1988.

Charnley, M., *News by Radio*, Macmillan, New York, 1948.

Chantler, P. and Stewart, P., *Essential Radio Journalism: How to Produce and Present Radio News (Professional Media Practice)*, Bloomsbury Methuen Drama, New York, 2009.

Cox, J., *Radio Journalism in America: Telling the News in the Golden Age and Beyond*, McFarland & Company, Jefferson, NC, 2013.

Culbert, D.H., *News for Everyman: Radio and Foreign Affairs in Thirties America*, Greenwood Press, Westport, CT, 1976.

Day, L.A., *Ethics in Media Communications*, Wadsworth Publishing, Belmont, CA, 1991.

Fang, I., *Those Radio Commentators*, Iowa State University Press, Ames, IA, 1977.

Fang, I., *Radio News/Television News*, 2nd edition, Rada Press, St. Paul, MN, 1985.

Friendly, F.W., *The Good Guys, The Bad Guys, and the First Amendment: Free Speech vs. Fairness in Broadcasting*, Random House, New York, 1976.

Frost, C., *Reporting for Journalists*, Routledge, New York, 2002.

Garvey, D.E., *News Writing for the Electronic Media*, Wadsworth Publishing, Belmont, CA, 1982.

Geller, V., *Beyond Powerful Radio: A Communicator's Guide to the Internet Age—News, Talk, Information & Personality for Broadcasting, Podcasting, Internet, Radio*, Focal Press, Burlington, MA, 2011.

Gibson, R., *Radio and Television Reporting*, Allyn & Bacon, Boston, MA, 1991.

Gilbert, B., *Perry's Broadcast News Handbook*, Perry Publishing, Knoxville, TN, 1982.

Hall, M.W., *Broadcast Journalism: An Introduction to News Writing*, Hastings House, New York, 1978.

Hilliard, R.L., *Writing for Television, Radio, and New Media (Broadcast and Production)*, Wadsworth, Boston, MA, 2011.

Hitchcock, J.R., *Sportscasting*, Focal Press, Boston, MA, 1991.

Hood, J.R. and Kalbfeld, B. (eds), *The Associated Press Handbook*, Associated Press, New York, 1982.

Hunter, J.K., *Broadcast News*, C.V. Mosby Company, St. Louis, MO, 1980.

Johnston, C., *Election Coverage: Blueprint for Broadcasters*, Focal Press, Boston, MA, 1991.

Kalbfeld, B., *Associated Press Broadcast News Handbook*, McGraw Hill, New York, 2001.

Keirstead, P.A., *All-News Radio*, Tab Books, Blue Ridge Summit, PA, 1980.

Keirstead, P.A., *Computers in Broadcast and Cable Newsrooms*, Erlbaum, Mahwah, NJ, 2005.

Mayeux, P., *Broadcast News Writing and Reporting*, Waveland Press, Chicago, IL, 2000.

Nelson, H.L., *Laws of Mass Communication*, Foundation Press, Mineola, NY, 1982.

Raiteri, C., *Writing for Broadcast News*, Roman & Littlefield, Lanham, MD, 2005.

Shrivastava, K.M., *Broadcast Journalism in the 21st Century*, New Dawn Press, Elgin, IL, 2004.

Simmons, S.J., *The Fairness Doctrine and the Media*, University of California Press, Berkeley, CA, 1978.

Stephens, M., *Broadcast News: Radio Journalism and an Introduction to Television*, Holt, Rinehart and Winston, New York, 1980.

Wenger, D. and Potter, D., *Advancing the Story: Broadcast Journalism in a Multimedia World*, CQ Press, Washington, D.C., 2007.

Wulfemeyer, K.T., *Broadcast Newswriting*, 2nd edition, Iowa State University Press, Ames, IA, 2003.

CHAPTER 6
Research

WHO IS LISTENING?

As early as 1929, the question of listenership was of interest to broadcasters and advertisers alike. That year Cooperative Analysis of Broadcasting (CAB), headed by Archibald M. Crossley, undertook a study to determine how many people were tuned to certain network radio programs. Information was gathered by phoning a preselected sample of homes. One of the things the survey found was that the majority of listening occurred in the evening between 7:00 and 11:00 pm. This became known as radio's "primetime" until the 1950s.

On the local station level, various methods were employed to collect audience data, including telephone interviews and mail-out questionnaires. However, only a nominal amount of actual audience research was attempted during the late 1920s and early 1930s. For the most part, just who was listening remained something of a mystery until the late 1930s.

In 1938, C.E. Hooper, Inc. began the most formidable attempt up to that time to provide radio broadcasters with audience information. Like Crossley's service, Hooper also used the telephone to accumulate listener data. CAB relied on listener recall; Hooper, however, required that interviewers make calls until they reached someone who was actually listening to the radio. This approach became known as the "coincidental" telephone method. Both survey services found their efforts limited by the fact that 40% of the radio-listening homes in the 1930s were without a telephone.

As World War II approached, another major ratings service, known as the Pulse, began to measure radio audience size. Unlike its competitors, the Pulse collected information by conducting face-to-face interviews. Interest in audience research grew steadily throughout the 1930s and culminated in the establishment of the Office of Radio Research (ORR) in 1937. Funded by a Rockefeller Foundation grant, the ORR was headed by Paul F. Lazarsfeld, assisted by Hadley Cantril and Frank Stanton. The latter would go on to assume the presidency of CBS in 1946 and would serve in that capacity into the 1970s. Over a ten-year period, the ORR published several texts dealing with audience research findings and methodology. Among them were Lazarsfeld and Stanton's multivolume *Radio Research*, which covered the periods of 1941–1943 and 1948–1949. During the same decade, Lazarsfeld also published book-length reports on the public's attitude toward radio: *The People Look at Radio* (1946) and *Radio Listening in America* (1948). Both works cast radio in a favorable light by concluding that most listeners felt the medium did an exemplary job. The Pulse and Hooper were the prevailing radio station rating services in the 1950s as the medium worked at regaining its footing following the meteoric rise of television. In 1965, the American Research Bureau (later to be known as Arbitron) began measuring radio audience size through the use of a diary, which required respondents to document their listening habits over a seven-day period. By the 1970s, Arbitron reigned as the leading radio measurement company, whereas Hooper and Pulse faded from the scene.

To provide the radio networks and their affiliates and advertisers with much-needed ratings information, Statistical Research, Inc., of New Jersey, introduced Radio's All Dimension Audience Research (RADAR) in 1968. The company gathered its information through telephone interviews with more than 6,000 households. In the 1990s, Arbitron retained its hold on first place among services measuring radio audiences, especially since the demise of Birch/Scarborough, which gained considerable acceptance following its debut in the late 1970s. In 1991, this audience measurement company became yet another victim of the economic malaise. Arbitron's supremacy in the business carried forward into the new millennium, due in large part to advancements the company made in measuring listenership across multiple platforms. In September, 2013 Nielsen Holdings N.V. finalized its acquisition of Arbitron in a deal reported by *The Wall Street Journal* to be valued at $1.3 billion. Nielsen is widely known for its television-audience measurement service and, according to information made public at the time of the announcement, regards Arbitron as a viable business partner that can assist the company in extending its services to the measurement of electronic media consumption out-of-home. Arbitron has since been rebranded as Nielsen Audio. However, because the company-provided promotional materials used to illustrate this text had yet to transition to the new name and corporate imaging at the time of this writing, the name "Arbitron" is retained throughout.

Ratings companies must be reliable, and credibility is crucial to success. Therefore, measurement techniques must be tried and true. Information must be accurate, since millions of dollars are at stake. In 1963, the Broadcast Rating Council was established to monitor, audit, and accredit the various ratings companies. The Council created performance standards to which rating services are expected to adhere. Those that fail to meet the Council's operating criteria are not accredited. A non-accredited ratings service will seldom succeed. In 1982, the Broadcast Rating Council was renamed the Electronic Media Planning Council to reflect a connection with the ratings services dealing with the cable television industry.

Renamed the Media Rating Council (MRC) in 1997 to include Internet constituencies, the MRC's declared purposes are:

1. To secure for the media industry and related users audience measurement services that are valid, reliable, and effective.
2. To evolve and determine minimum disclosure and ethical criteria for media audience measurement services.
3. To provide and administer an audit system designed to inform users as to whether such audience measurements are conducted in conformance with the criteria and procedures developed.

ON AUDIENCE RESEARCH

Ed Cohen

Radio research always responds to the needs of the business. The primary research in the industry is the Nielsen radio ratings, a survey-based description of the amount of audience and time spent with stations and the overall medium that can be used as the "currency" for the advertising buy/sell process. Estimates are provided for demographic groups (age/gender combinations), time periods, and local and national geographies. Subscribers also use the data for programming purposes, in addition to the buy/sell.

FIGURE 6.1
Dr. Ed Cohen. Courtesy of Nielsen.

A couple of trends are emerging. Radio has taken on a broader definition beyond AM and FM stations. In addition to transmitting over the air, radio stations are streaming their broadcasts over the Internet, pure play music services and aggregators are emerging, podcasts, and other audio sources are affecting the research paradigm. The result is a rise in "census-based" measurement for online audio consumption, taking data from either the source (servers sending out streams) and/or the receiver (information from the device).

Another trend is cross-platform information. Most content providers reach their audiences over multiple platforms and in a number of formats such as audio, video, and text. If the content provider is available wherever their consumer wants them, they want to capture their entire audience. The measurement aspects of cross-platform are not simple, but will be part of the landscape in radio's new world.

Ed Cohen, PhD, is vice-president of measurement innovation at Nielsen.

FIGURE 6.2
The Portable People Meter™ is the newest method for tracking listening. Courtesy of Arbitron.

THE RATINGS AND SURVEY SERVICES

The extreme fragmentation of today's listening audience, created by the almost inestimable number of stations and formats, makes the job of research a complex but necessary one. All stations, regardless of size, must put forth an effort to acquaint themselves with the characteristics of the audience, says Edward J. Noonan, codirector, Survey Research Associates. "A station cannot operate in a vacuum. It has to know who is listening and why before making any serious programming changes." Today, this information is made available through several ratings services and research companies. More stations depend on Arbitron audience surveys than any other.

Since the collapse of Birch/Scarborough, broadcasters have had little choice but to subscribe to Arbitron—that or go without the listening estimates on which so many agencies and advertisers rely. However, the radio audience survey industry has begun to expand, if only slowly. For example, in recent years, additional listener/ratings services have begun to emerge. AccuRatings is one example. It began to measure audiences in major metropolitan areas in the mid-1990s. Eastlan Ratings, which began in 1999, specializes in serving the smaller-market broadcaster. The company provides audience estimates to client stations located in 90 cities nationwide, ranging from Alaska to Florida. Whereas Arbitron utilizes electronic measuring devices and diaries to gather data from listeners, Eastlan relies on the telephone recall methodology. Similar companies were beginning to surface to the relief of many broadcasters concerned with Arbitron's hold. Arbitron's dominance has indeed caused anxiety in the radio community. Many managers and programmers were more than disturbed by the withdrawal of the alternative Birch measurement service from the marketplace. Arbitron covers more than 270 markets ranging in size from major to small. Arbitron claims more than 2,700 radio clients and a staff of 3,000 interviewers who collect listening information from two million households across the country. All markets are measured at least once a year during the spring; however, larger markets are measured on an ongoing basis year round. Until the early 1980s, metro markets traditionally were rated in the spring and fall. However, six months between surveys was considered too long in light of the volatile nature of the radio marketplace.

To determine a station's ranking, Arbitron follows an elaborate procedure. First, the parameters of the area to be surveyed are established. Arbitron sees fit to measure listening both in the city or urban center, which it refers to as the Metro Survey Area (MSA), and in the surrounding communities or suburbs, which it classifies as the Total Survey Area (TSA). MSAs are organized mostly along the boundaries established by the federal government's Metropolitan Statistical Areas; TSAs define geographic areas that subsume the Metro Survey Area and include additional counties or parishes. These areas are further delineated into Designated Market Areas (DMAs®), a geographic subdivision scheme developed by Nielsen Media Research for the purpose of identifying county and parish placements within markets. Once the areas to be measured have been ascertained, the next thing Arbitron does is select a sample base composed of individuals to be queried regarding their listening habits. The following paragraphs describe procedures Arbitron has used for many years to gather listening information using a paper, pamphlet-styled diary it supplies to panelists; more information about its emerging passive electronic measurement system is provided later in this chapter. Arbitron conducts its surveys over a three- to four-week period, during which time new samples are selected weekly.

When the sample has been established, a letter is sent to each targeted household. The replacement letter informs members of the sample that they have been selected to participate in a radio-listening survey and asks for their cooperation. Within a couple of days after the letter has been received, an Arbitron interviewer calls to describe the purpose of the survey as well as to determine how many individuals aged 12 or older reside in the household. Arbitron places more than four million telephone calls annually in its effort to recruit survey panelists. Upon receiving the go-ahead, Arbitron mails its seven-day survey diary, which requires respondents to log their listening activities. A monetary premium, consisting of an incentive stipend of a dollar or two accompanies the document. The diary is simple to deal with, and the information it requests is quite basic: time (day/part) tuned to a station, station call letters, program name or dial setting; whether AM or FM, and where listening occurred—car, home, work, or elsewhere. Although the diary asks for information pertaining to age, sex, and residence, the actual identity or name of those participating is not requested.

Prior to the start of the survey, a representative of Arbitron makes a pre-survey follow-up telephone call to those who have agreed to participate. This is done to make certain that the diary has been received and that everyone involved understands how to maintain it. Another follow-up call is made during the middle of the survey week to ascertain if the diary is being kept and to remind each participant to return it promptly upon completion of the survey. Panelists are provided with toll-free telephone and online assistance to help them should questions about the process arise. Outside the metro area, follow-ups take the form of a letter. The diaries are mailed to Columbia, Maryland, where optical character readers (OCRs) scan the diaries and prepare the data for processing and computation.

Arbitron claims that 65 of every 100 diaries it receives are usable, a remarkable compliance percentage considering that the company mails almost two million diaries each year. Diaries that are inadequately or inaccurately filled out are not used. Upon arriving at Arbitron headquarters, diaries are examined by editors and rejected if they fail to meet criteria. Any diary received before the conclusion of the survey period is immediately voided, as are those that arrive more than 12 days after the end of the survey period. Diaries with blank or ambiguous entries also are rejected. Those diaries that survive the editors'

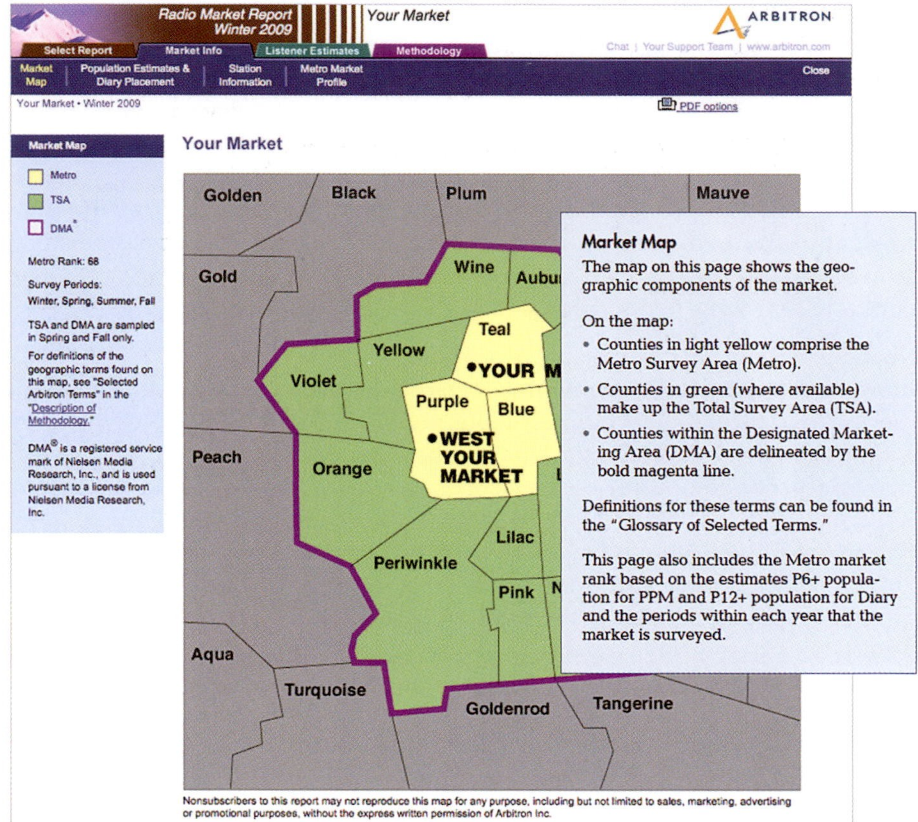

FIGURE 6.3
Page from an Arbitron Radio Market Report containing an explanation of what constitutes the survey area. Courtesy of Arbitron.

scrutiny are then processed through the computer, and their information is tabulated. Computer printouts showing audience estimates are sent to subscribers. Prior to 2006, subscribing stations received a printed report (the "book") within a few weeks after the last day of the survey. Today, Arbitron disseminates the information electronically, preserving the "look" of the "book" while shortening the time between processing and delivery.

Arbitrends, a computerized service designed to feed data to stations, has been made available to subscribers since the 1990s. Information regarding a station's past and current performances and those of competitors is available at the touch of a finger. Breakouts and tailor-made reports are provided on an ongoing basis by Arbitrends to assist stations in the planning of sales and marketing strategies. The survey company has more than 13 billion characters reserved on computer disk packs. Arbitron also makes available its Arbitrends Rolling Average Printed Reports to those stations without computers. To date, Arbitron has prepared more than 380,000 radio market reports.

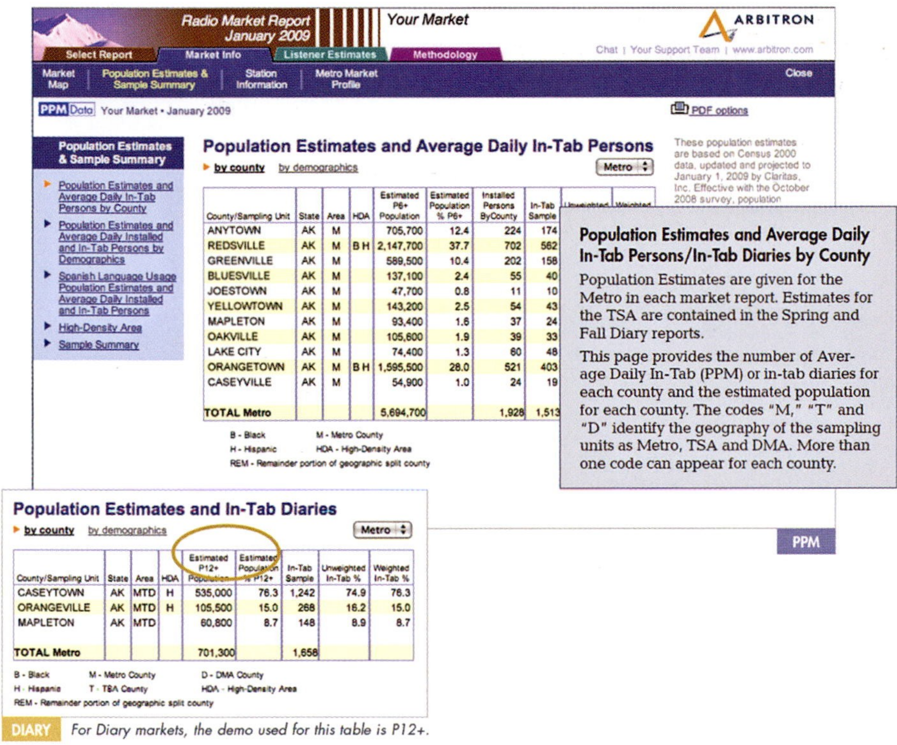

County/Sampling Unit	State	Area	HDA	Estimated P6+ Population	Estimated Population % P6+	Installed Persons ByCounty	In-Tab Sample
ANYTOWN	AK	M		705,700	12.4	224	174
REDSVILLE	AK	M	B H	2,147,700	37.7	702	562
GREENVILLE	AK	M		589,500	10.4	202	158
BLUESVILLE	AK	M		137,100	2.4	55	40
JOESTOWN	AK	M		47,700	0.8	11	10
YELLOWTOWN	AK	M		143,200	2.5	54	43
MAPLETON	AK	M		93,400	1.6	37	24
OAKVILLE	AK	M		105,600	1.9	39	33
LAKE CITY	AK	M		74,400	1.3	60	48
ORANGETOWN	AK	M	B H	1,595,500	28.0	521	403
CASEYVILLE	AK	M		54,900	1.0	24	19
TOTAL Metro				5,694,700		1,928	1,513

B - Black
H - Hispanic
M - Metro County
HDA - High-Density Area
REM - Remainder portion of geographic split county

County/Sampling Unit	State	Area	HDA	Estimated P12+ Population	Estimated Population % P12+	In-Tab Sample	Unweighted In-Tab %	Weighted In-Tab %
CASEYTOWN	AK	MTD	H	535,000	76.3	1,242	74.9	76.3
ORANGEVILLE	AK	MTD	H	105,500	15.0	268	16.2	15.0
MAPLETON	AK	MTD		60,800	8.7	148	8.9	8.7
TOTAL Metro				701,300		1,658		

B - Black
H - Hispanic
M - Metro County
T - TSA County
D - DMA County
HDA - High-Density Area
REM - Remainder portion of geographic split county

FIGURE 6.4
Arbitron sample explanation of diary correlations with populations. Courtesy of Arbitron.

Ever evolving its services, Arbitron rolled out another online product for its radio clients in 2006. In an announcement on its website, it stated:

> Arbitron Inc., in conjunction with comScore Media Metrix, a division of comScore Networks, Inc., has established a new audience measurement system designed to provide traditional broadcast ratings for the online radio industry. The service provides customers with Average Quarter-Hour and Cume audience estimates for standard dayparts and demographics. The comScore Arbitron Online Ratings service is based on approximately a quarter of a million U.S. participants within the comScore global consumer panel. Using proprietary and patent-pending technology, comScore passively and continuously captures the online behavior of these panelists, including online radio listening behavior.

Arbitron's most formidable rival in recent years was Birch/Scarborough, headquartered in New Jersey. As a radio audience measurement service, Birch provided clients with both quantitative and qualitative data on local listening patterns, audience size, and demographics. Birch interviewers telephoned a

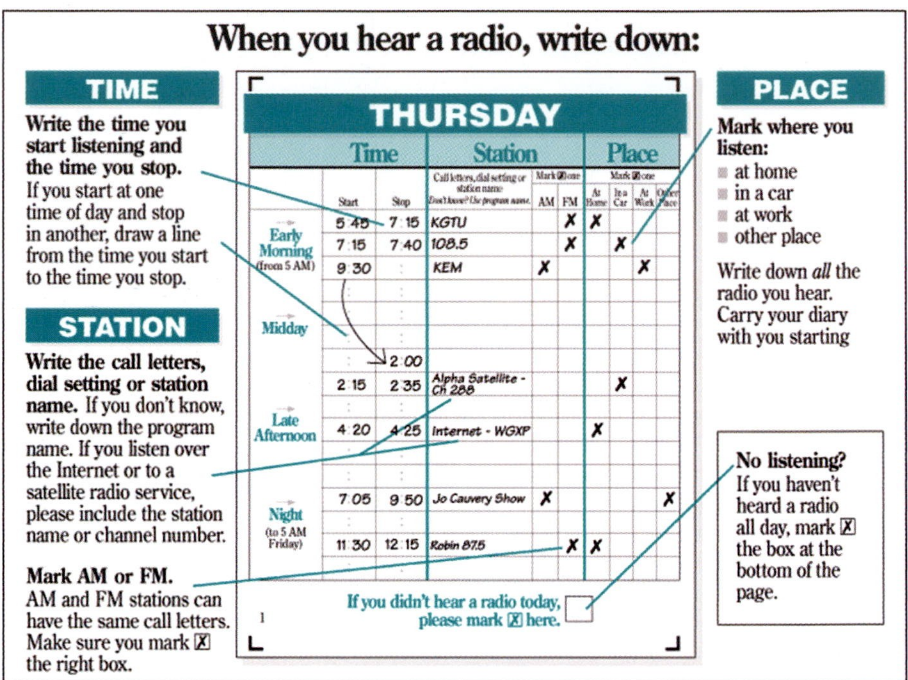

FIGURE 6.5
Instructions for filling out a diary to document AM, FM, and satellite radio listening. Accuracy is important. Courtesy of Arbitron.

pre-balanced sample of households during the evening hours, seven days a week, to acquire the information they needed. "Respondents aged 12 or older were randomly selected from both listed and nonlisted telephone households. These calls were made from highly supervised company toll-free long-distance facilities," noted Phil Beswick, vice-president of the defunct Birch/Scarborough broadcast services. The sample sizes varied depending on the size of the market being surveyed. For example, Birch/Scarborough contacted approximately 1,100 households in a medium market and between 2,000 and 8,000 in major metro markets. A wide range of reports were available to clients, including the *Quarterly Summary Report*, estimates of listening by location, county by county, and other detailed audience information that were similar in size and scope to the products issued by Arbitron. Fees for Birch/Scarborough services were based on market size. Birch provided subscribers with general product consumption and media usage data. In late 1994, Arbitron purchased 50% of the Scarborough Research Corporation, with plans to offer stations expanded data about their listeners.

Dozens of other research companies throughout the country (among them Coleman Insights Media Research, Bolton Research Corporation, Mark Kassof & Company, Spectrum Research, Inc., Frank N. Magid Associates, Inc., Decision Information Resources, Inc., Paragon Media Strategies, Shane Media Services,

FIGURE 6.6
Audio listening occurs across a variety of delivery platforms. Courtesy of Arbitron.

International Demographics, Inc./The Media Audit, Media Psychology Research Center, Gallup, Inc., Ipsos MediaCT, Mediabase®, TAPSCAN™ and others cited herein) provide broadcasters with a broad range of useful audience information. While some of them use approaches similar to Arbitron (and the former Birch) to collect data others use different methods to provide the broadcast, satellite, and online radio industries with an array of both qualitative and quantitative research information. "Southeast Media Research offers four research methods: focus groups, telephone studies, mail intercepts, and music tests," explains Don Hagen, the company's president. Christopher Porter, senior research analyst at Surrey Research, says that his company uses similar techniques.

Meanwhile, audience researcher Dick Warner claims that the telephone recall method is the most commonly used and effective approach to radio audience surveying. "The 24-hour telephone recall interview, in my estimation, yields the most reliable information. Not only that, it is quick and current—important factors in a rapidly moving and hyperdynamic radio marketplace."

On the subject of music testing, Coleman Research's Rebecca Reising notes that her company's approach is unique. "We developed FACT, short for Fit Acceptance and Compatibility Test. FACT's proprietary research methods and sophisticated databases make it much more powerful, reliable, and useful than old-fashioned music testing methods. As quick and efficient as old tests, FACT provides a sophistication of interpretation of music tests not offered by any other research company."

In the hyperactive radio industry arena, both traditional and novel audience survey techniques must ultimately prove themselves by assisting stations in their unrelenting quest for stronger ratings numbers.

QUALITATIVE AND QUANTITATIVE DATA

Since their inception in the 1930s, ratings services primarily have provided broadcasters with information pertaining to the number of listeners of a certain age and gender tuned to a station at a given time. It was on the basis of these quantitative data that stations chose a format and advertisers made a buy.

Due to the explosive growth of the electronic media in recent years, the audience is presented with many more options, and the radio broadcaster, especially in larger markets, must know more about his intended listeners to attract and retain them. Subsequently, the need for more detailed information has arisen. TroyResearch is an example of a research firm that focuses on qualitative rather than quantitative audience information. Since the late 1990s this has assisted stations by gathering data about audiences and music preferences, conducting its inquiries online. Ten years ago, a station that was shooting for a top spot in the ratings surveys had to be concerned with more than simply the age and sex of its target audience. Competitive programming strategies were being built around an understanding and appreciation of the lifestyles, values, and behavior of those listeners sought by a station. CEO Mike Henry of Paragon Media Strategies says the industry has undergone "seismic change" in the ways that research is performed and utilized. The rules by which stations operated at the turn of the millennium, he believes, are today either different, or non-existent. He summarizes the changes in a series of seven observations:

1. There has been a major reduction in the amount of primary research used by radio for programming purposes. Most stations get no primary research for programming in the average year.
2. A major increase in the amount of secondary research used by radio has occurred. For instance, polling monitors have replaced music testing procedures for most stations.
3. There is new reliance on using Arbitron (and Media Monitors's Mscore) for research and not just for ratings.
4. There is an increasing reliance on the utilization of "in-house" and "self-selected sample" research tools (e.g., online studies among the station database, new music testing panels . . . resulting in as much marketing as research).
5. Reliance on new media feedback mechanisms, led by Facebook and Twitter.
6. Increased reliance on consultants who tell radio stations what to do rather than having the stations invest more money on researching the thoughts of listeners.

7. Research today in radio is focused squarely on sales research and its use for driving sales rather than on programming research and its use in driving ratings.

How have the changes Henry enumerated affected day-to-day life inside the radio station? He expressed the opinion that in most instances the program director (PD) is now the station's "programming research director" and all the responsibility for gathering research depends upon the PD's best judgment. This situation, he asserts, is a budgetary issue. "As you can imagine," he says, "the quality and reliability of station programming research has fallen off the cliff."

FROM PAPER TO ELECTRONIC MEASUREMENT: THE PORTABLE PEOPLE METER™

Another approach to measuring station listenership has emerged in the form of Arbitron's Portable People Meter™ (PPM®). While Arbitron's website states that the conventional paper diary method of tabulating audience size "will likely continue to be used successfully for years to come," the company has made significant strides in migrating to passive, electronic audience measurement. The technology, says Emmis Communications leader Jeff Smulyan, "is long overdue." He adds, "We are finally getting credit for the huge audience we felt we had all along in Arbitron's previous methodology. In Los Angeles, for example, one of our Emmis station's cume was up 70% and our other Emmis station cume has almost quadrupled. That's a lot of people listening to us that we were not getting credit for." No longer will survey participants take an active role in recording their listening activities. The PPM does it by detecting electronically coded tones embedded into the signal transmissions by radio stations. Arbitron supplies stations with encoding devices that incorporate the tones into their broadcasts. Special circuitry "masks" the tones in such a way as to make them imperceptible to listeners yet recognizable by the PPM unit. Differentiation among stations within markets occurs without confusion because each station transmits its own unique, Arbitron-assigned coded tone. Think of it as a station's individualized "fingerprint"—no two stations within a given market utilize the same tonal coding protocol.

This cell phone-sized device is worn or carried by survey participants (Arbitron terms them "panelists") for an agreed-upon period of time. PPM technology approximates human hearing in the sense that reproduced sound from stations must be of sufficient volume in order to be "heard" by humans and "sampled" by the unit. Every 30 seconds the PPM makes a record of stations' identifier codes, storing the information. Arbitron retrieves the data electronically, using home-office telephone circuits that connect to the devices and poll the data. The company then creates timely reports for distribution to radio station subscribers.

Arbitron introduced the PPM in 2006. Considering the fact that the company began using the traditional seven-day, paper diary in 1965, its conversion to electronic data-gathering represented an historic landmark. Within a year's time, however, members of the radio broadcasting community were being joined by industry observers in directing criticisms toward Arbitron, citing problems with methodology and sample sizes. Arbitron proceeded in 2008 with PPM rollout experiments in other major markets. Following its New York City test, Arbitron elicited criticism over its method for recruiting panelists. Insufficient representation of certain racial and ethnic minorities, claimed New York attorney general Andrew Cuomo, led to inaccurate ratings and a subsequent reduction in advertising revenue for stations that programmed to Hispanics and African Americans. Dissatisfaction with PPM in other markets led to the formation of the PPM Coalition, an industry group whose membership consisted of the National Association of Black Owned Broadcasters (NABOB), the Spanish Radio Association, Univision, and others. The Coalition appealed to the FCC for assistance in resolving its dissatisfactions with PPM. Arbitron and the Coalition, with the assistance of the U.S. House of Representatives Oversight and Government Reform Committee, mended their relationship, pledging to work collaboratively in the future.

Following its 2013 acquisition of Arbitron, Nielsen Audio announced its intention to enlarge its sample sizes in PPM markets, increasing the number of panelists by 6%. Additionally, the firm will escalate its efforts to empanel sufficiently representative pools of African American and Hispanic listeners. Historically, these panelists have proved difficult to recruit.

A multiple-year investment in PPM research and development culminated in a successful rollout when CBS contracted the use of the device in 35 of its markets. Beasley Broadcast Group and Spanish Broadcasting System did likewise. On the heels of these deals, four other major radio groups—Bonneville International Corporation, Emmis Communications Corporation, Greater Media, Inc., and Lincoln Financial Media—signed multiyear contracts for PPM radio ratings. When PPM received approval from the Media Ratings Council, the announcement signaled to the industry that the device was likely here to stay.

Ed Shane predicts the PPM may never be employed in small markets. "I daresay small markets will never see PPM because of the cost of implementation. It's a much more important element in the sales process in large markets because of the transactional nature of buying. The smaller the market, the more selling is based on relationships and—most importantly—on results at the cash register."

Tripp Eldredge, president and CEO of DMR/Interactive, offers his views as to why the PPM is superior to the old paper method of gathering audience data:

> The PPM is both passive and longitudinal. Both qualities lead to a superior methodology. Because it's passive, it doesn't rely on the memory or consciousness of the respondent to gather data and more importantly

> report it correctly. The diary relies on proper station identification as well as proper reporting of behavior on a quarter-hour by quarter-hour basis. Because it's longitudinal, it provides much more stable results for the time periods most relevant to advertisers and broadcasters. Much of the differences in the diary methodology can be a result of sampling error, depending on the time period in question. The meter eliminates much of the instability due to randomness because it's kept for an average of six months. Also, the long-term nature of the meter may serve to eliminate the survey bias inherent in the diary process.

There are some important new insights the PPM will provide that result from its longitudinal nature. One very important new benefit is the ability to track loyalty and brand-switching over time. The diary process would infer the preferred station through the week-long measurement. The First Preference (P1) is the station that gets the majority of a consumer's listening. P1 drives the majority of a station's AQH (average quarter hour) listening. However, the diary could not track the changes in P1 from week to week or month to month.

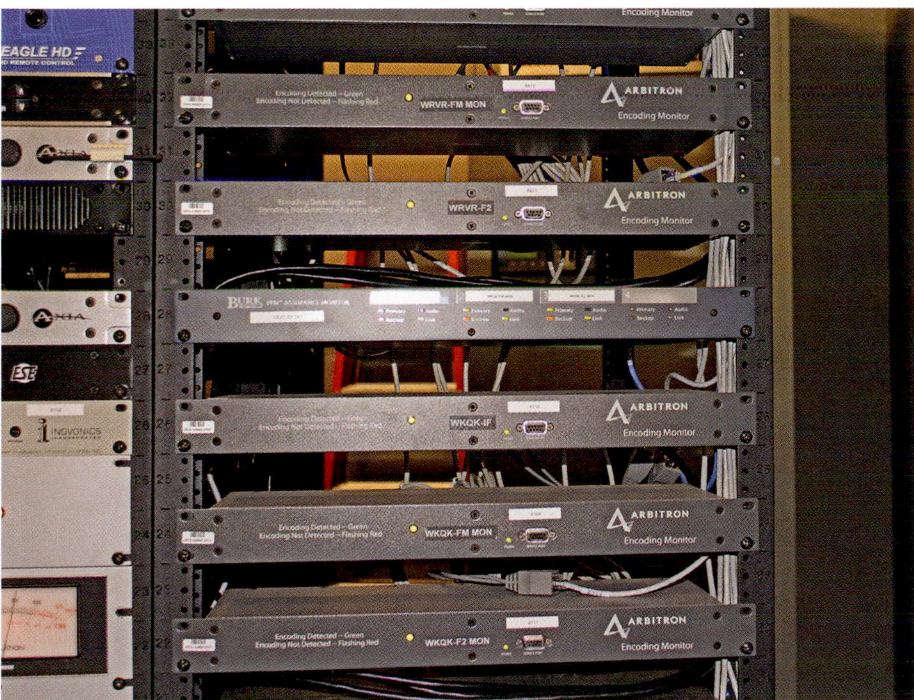

FIGURE 6.7
A station cluster's arrangement of Portable People Meter™ encoder monitoring equipment. These devices detect the presence or absence of the PPM encoding tones transmitted by stations and received by listeners' PPM devices. Alarm circuitry in the monitor signals a station engineer in the event of PPM-encoder malfunction. Courtesy of Entercom Radio Memphis.

The meter can because it tracks the same consumers from day to day, etc. This new metric will provide new and better feedback to programmers and potentially advertisers as they begin to understand how loyalty impacts listening and how it is impacted by programming and marketing components.

Eldredge observes that the PPM is not without its shortcomings:

> Currently, the PPM shows an approximately 20% decrease in AQH listening to many stations. In a related note, the overall time spent listening to radio is lower, although there are about double the total audiences of stations. The meter shows that there are far more people tuning into a station than the diary has shown. Because there are more people identified, the average time spent listening is lower. That's not necessarily a shortcoming of the PPM as much as it is an indication that the diary was not able to pick up about half of the actual stations tuned, resulting in consumers inadvertently overstating their listening volumes to the stations they remembered.

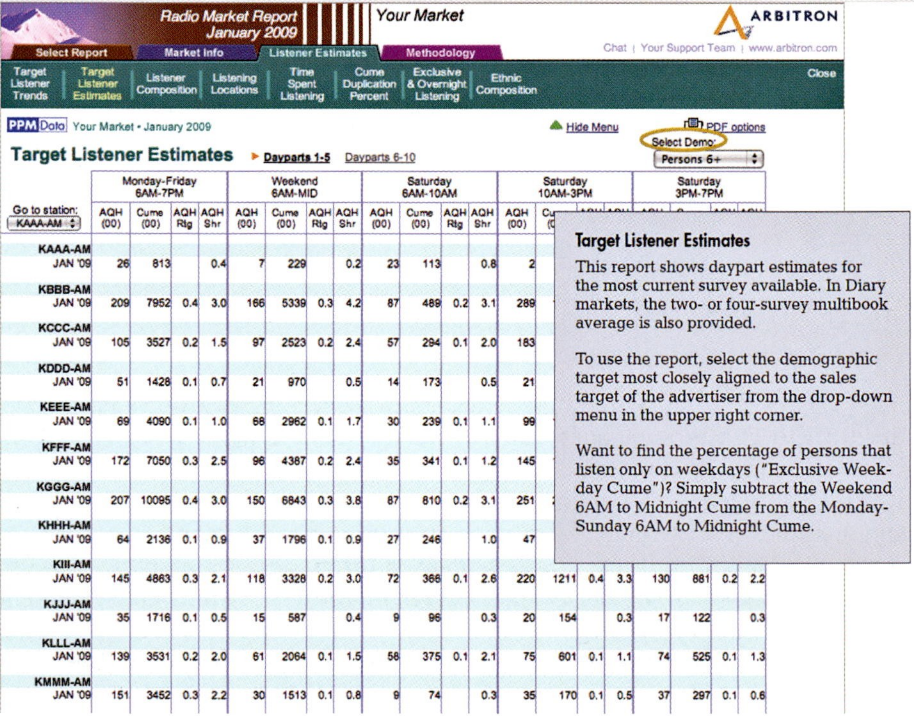

	Monday-Friday 6AM-7PM				Weekend 6AM-MID				Saturday 6AM-10AM				Saturday 10AM-3PM				Saturday 3PM-7PM			
	AQH (00)	Cume (00)	AQH Rtg	AQH Shr	AQH (00)	Cume (00)	AQH Rtg	AQH Shr	AQH (00)	Cume (00)	AQH Rtg	AQH Shr	AQH (00)	Cume (00)	AQH Rtg	AQH Shr	AQH (00)	Cume (00)	AQH Rtg	AQH Shr
KAAA-AM JAN '09	26	813		0.4	7	229		0.2	23	113		0.8	2							
KBBB-AM JAN '09	209	7952	0.4	3.0	166	5339	0.3	4.2	87	489	0.2	3.1	289							
KCCC-AM JAN '09	105	3527	0.2	1.5	97	2523	0.2	2.4	57	294	0.1	2.0	183							
KDDD-AM JAN '09	51	1428	0.1	0.7	21	970		0.5	14	173		0.5	21							
KEEE-AM JAN '09	69	4090	0.1	1.0	68	2962	0.1	1.7	30	239	0.1	1.1	99							
KFFF-AM JAN '09	172	7050	0.3	2.5	96	4387	0.2	2.4	35	341	0.1	1.2	145							
KGGG-AM JAN '09	207	10095	0.4	3.0	150	6843	0.3	3.8	87	810	0.2	3.1	251							
KHHH-AM JAN '09	64	2136	0.1	0.9	37	1796	0.1	0.9	27	246		1.0	47							
KIII-AM JAN '09	145	4863	0.3	2.1	118	3328	0.2	3.0	72	366	0.1	2.6	220	1211	0.4	3.3	130	881	0.2	2.2
KJJJ-AM JAN '09	35	1716	0.1	0.5	15	587		0.4	9	96		0.3	20	154		0.3	17	122		0.3
KLLL-AM JAN '09	139	3531	0.2	2.0	61	2064	0.1	1.5	58	375	0.1	2.1	75	601	0.1	1.1	74	525	0.1	1.3
KMMM-AM JAN '09	151	3452	0.3	2.2	30	1513	0.1	0.8	9	74		0.3	35	170	0.1	0.5	37	297	0.1	0.6

FIGURE 6.8
Arbitron estimates show where a station stands in its market. Courtesy of Arbitron.

Radio Market Report January 2009 | Your Market

Select Report | Market Info | Listener Estimates | Methodology

Target Listener Trends | Target Listener Estimates | Listener Composition | Listening Locations | Time Spent Listening | Cume Duplication Percent | Exclusive & Overnight Listening | Ethnic Composition

PPM Data Your Market • January 2009

Target Listener Trends

Go to station: KAAA-AM	Monday-Sunday 6AM-MID				Monday-Friday 6AM-10AM				Monday-Friday 10AM-3PM				Mo
	AQH (00)	Cume (00)	AQH Rtg	AQH Shr	AQH (00)	Cume (00)	AQH Rtg	AQH Shr	AQH (00)	Cume (00)	AQH Rtg	AQH Shr	AQH (00)
KAAA-AM													
~JAN '09	17	900		0.3	26	305		0.4	28	477		0.4	23
~HL '08	13	747		0.3	23	238		0.4	20	474		0.3	18
~DEC '08	14	913		0.3	27	406		0.4	23	568		0.3	15
~NOV '08	17	1281		0.3	29	359	0.1	0.4	32	742	0.1	0.4	21
~OCT '08	16	1261		0.3	28	448		0.4	26	814		0.4	23
KBBB-AM													
~JAN '09	178	10276	0.3	3.4	175	3346	0.3	2.6	158	3626	0.3	2.4	306
~HL '08	188	10596	0.3	3.7	157	3230	0.3	2.8	192	4672	0.3	2.8	278
~DEC '08	176	10080	0.3	3.4	168	2978	0.3	2.6	173	3977	0.3	2.5	226
~NOV '08	180	11450	0.3	3.2	163	3373	0.3	2.2	161	4077	0.3	2.2	264
~OCT '08	167	10657	0.3	3.0	162	2682	0.3	2.2	165	3779	0.3	2.3	219
KCCC-AM													
~JAN '09	88	4941	0.2	1.7	89	1798	0.2	1.3	116	1861	0.2	1.7	106
~HL '08	94	5008	0.2	1.9	71	1450	0.1	1.3	174	2452	0.3	2.6	125
~DEC '08	95	5287	0.2	1.8	67	1486	0.1	1.0	140	2300	0.2	2.1	129
~NOV '08	97	5299	0.2	1.7	61	1725	0.1	0.8	143	2157	0.3	2.0	126
~OCT '08	116	5118	0.2	2.1	77	1549	0.1	1.1	168	2256	0.3	2.4	138

FIGURE 6.9
Sample page from an Arbitron *Radio Market Report* tracks listenership trends. Courtesy of Arbitron.

Other devices have challenged the PPM. Smartphones, which were making the transition to mainstream adoption in the mid-2000s, were being touted as potential media measurement devices given their ubiquity and expanding service capabilities. In 2006, The Media Audit, an operational division of International Demographics, Inc., teamed with Ipsos, a multinational research company to explore the feasibility of using a smartphone for audience measurement purposes. Houston, Texas, was the location chosen for the test. Stations in the nation's sixth-largest radio market began prepping for the test. Later that year, Arbitron took legal steps to keep The Media Audit/Ipsos from entering the ratings business, citing their smartphone technology as an infringement on the patented PPM technology. In separate agreements, The Media Audit and Ipsos both agreed to withdraw from efforts to engage in smartphone audience measurement for the next three years and, as of this writing, have not announced intentions to return.

In terms of what the PPM means to on-air personnel, Jason Insalaco posits the view that

> early results indicate music is winning over deejay patter. Consequently, programmers of struggling morning shows are pulling back their personalities from the usual bits, interviews, and banter and offering more music-intensive morning programming. However, PPM data also indicates that strong morning show personalities are continuing to exhibit success equal to, if not greater than, AQH compared to the old diary methodology. The early lessons of PPM are that the new measurement device highlights the strengths and weaknesses of the station. If a morning show was underperforming according to the diaries, it will likely become even more flaring under PPM. Programmers have a large amount of weekly data at their fingertips with PPM. It also is showing that midday and afternoon drive listening is reaching audience levels sometimes equal to morning drive. As programmers become more comfortable with PPM, they will take more risks on the air. If the early data shows that something new is not working, programmers can quickly change course without having to wait months to discern a trend as they did under the previous diary system.

IN-HOUSE RESEARCH TECHNIQUES

Research data provided by the major survey companies can be costly. For this reason and others, stations frequently conduct their own audience studies. Although stations seldom have the professional wherewithal and expertise of the research companies, they can derive useful information through do-it-yourself surveys, creating questionnaires for landline telephone, online, face-to-face, and mail surveys.

Telephone surveying has traditionally been a commonly used method of deriving audience data on the station level. It is generally less costly than the other forms of in-house research, and sample selection is less complicated and not as prone to bias. It also is the most expedient method. There are, however, a few things that must be kept in mind when conducting call-out surveys. One, not everyone has a phone and many numbers are unlisted. This shortcoming, however, can be easily overcome through the use of software capable of generating lists of randomized telephone numbers. Another limitation of this method is the public's wariness of phone solicitations for interviews, the result of fear that the ultimate objective of the caller is to sell something. The public is inundated by phone solicitors (of both the human and robo-call, computerized varieties). Finally, extensive interviews are difficult to conduct over the phone. Five to ten minutes usually is the extent to which an interviewee will submit to questioning. Callout interview seminars and instructional materials are available from a variety of sources, including the telephone company itself.

Internet and email services provide another valuable means for those radio stations that survey their audiences. Many stations employ computers for callout research purposes. There are many obvious benefits, interactivity and archiving foremost among them. The face-to-face or personal interview also is a popular research approach at stations, although the cost can be higher than call-out, especially if a vast number of individuals are being surveyed in an auditorium setting. The primary advantages of the in-person interview are that questions can be more substantive and greater time can be spent with the respondents. Of course, more detailed interviews are time-consuming and usually require refined interviewing skills, both of which can be cost factors.

Mail surveys, in both paper and electronic forms, can be useful for a host of reasons. To begin with, they eliminate the need to hire and train interviewers. This alone can mean a great deal in terms of money and time. Because no interviewers are involved, one source of potential bias also is eliminated. Perhaps most important is that individuals questioned through the mail are somewhat more inclined toward candor since they enjoy greater anonymity. The major problem with the mail survey approach stems from the usually low rate of response. One in every five questionnaires distributed may actually find its way back to the station. The length of the questionnaire must be kept relatively short and the questions succinct and direct. Complex questions create resistance and may result in the survey being ignored or discarded.

Large and major market outlets usually employ someone to direct research and survey efforts. This person works closely with upper management and department heads, especially the program director (PD) and sales manager (SM). These two areas require data on which to base programming and marketing decisions. At smaller outlets, area directors generally are responsible for conducting surveys relevant to their department's needs. A case in point would be the PD who plans a phone survey during a special broadcast to help ascertain whether it should become a permanent program offering. To accomplish this task, the programmer enlists the aid of a secretary and two interns from a local college. Calls are made, and data are collected and analyzed.

The objective of a survey must be clear from the start, and the methodology used to acquire data should be as uncomplicated as possible. Do-it-yourself surveys are limited in nature, and overly ambitious goals and expectations are seldom realized. However, in-house research can produce valuable information that can give a station a competitive edge. Today, no radio station can operate in a detached way and expect to prosper.

Every station has numerous sources of information available to it. Directories containing all manner of data, such as population statistics and demographics, manufacturing and retailing trends, and so on, are available online, at the public library, city hall, chamber of commerce, and various business associations. The American Marketing Association and American Research Foundation also possess information designed to guide stations with their in-house survey efforts.

RESEARCH DEFICITS

Although broadcasters refer deferentially to the ratings surveys as the "book" or "bible," the stats they contain are audience-listening estimates—no more, and, it is hoped, no less. Since their inception, research companies have been criticized for the methods they employ in collecting audience listening statistics. The most prevalent complaint has had to do with the selection of samples. Critics have charged that they invariably are limited and exclusionary. Questions have persisted as to whether those surveyed are truly representative of an area's total listenership. Can 1% of the radio universe accurately reflect general listening habits? The research companies defend their tactics and have established a strong case for their methodology.

In the 1970s, one criticism directed to ratings companies at a time when the wired, landline telephone was the primary means of contact, was their neglect in recruiting minorities to participate in surveys. In efforts to rectify this deficiency, both Arbitron and Birch established special sampling procedures. The survey companies also had to deal with the problem of measuring Spanish-speaking people. Arbitron found that using the personal-retrieval technique significantly increased the response rate in the Spanish community, especially when bilingual interviewers were used. The personal-retrieval technique did not work as well with blacks, since it was difficult to recruit interviewers to work in many of the sample areas. Thus, Arbitron used a telephone retrieval procedure that involved callbacks to selected households over a seven-day period to document listening habits. In essence, the interviewer filled out the diaries for those being surveyed. In the 1980s, Arbitron implemented Differential Survey Treatment (DST), a technique designed to increase the response rate among blacks and later, among Hispanic listeners who, historically, were under-represented ethnicities in Arbitron's surveys. The company became more intensive and proactive in its telephone-recruitment efforts to induce minorities into participating on panels. Another incentive tactic was to increase the amount of the premium (financial compensation) Arbitron offers its panelists. The survey company provides incentives over the customary $1–2 compensation. Up to $5 is paid to some respondents of certain black households. DST employs follow-up calls to retrieve diaries.

During its years of operation, Birch/Scarborough Research employed special sampling procedures and bilingual interviewers to collect data from the Hispanic population. According to the company, its samples yielded a high response rate among blacks. Thus, Birch did not use other special sampling controls. Ethnic listening reports containing average quarter-hour and cume estimates for Hispanics, blacks, and others were available from the company in a format similar to that of its Capsule Market Report.

Both survey companies employed additional procedures to survey other non-telephone households, especially in markets that have a large student or transient population. In the late 1970s, a Boston station targeting young people

FULL STUDY • EXCLUSIVELY FOR ARBITRON CLIENTS

Radio Today 2013
How America Listens to Radio

FIGURE 6.10
Title page of Arbitron's comprehensive annual report on radio listenership across formats. Courtesy Arbitron.

complained that Arbitron failed to acknowledge the existence of more than 200,000 college students who did not have personal phone listings. The station, which was rated among the top five in the market at the time, contended that a comprehensive survey of the city's listening audience would bear out the fact that they were, in fact, number one.

Similar complaints of skewed or inconclusive surveys persist today, but the procedures and methods used by the major radio audience research companies, although far from perfect, are more effective than ever. Christopher Porter says the greatest misconception about research data is that they are absolutes etched in granite:

> The greatest fallacy is that research findings are gospel. This goes not only for the quantitative studies but for focus groups as well. Regardless of the methodology, any findings should be used as a "gut adjuster," rather than a "gut replacer." Sampling error is often ignored in a quantitative study, even in an Arbitron report. When we report that 25% of a sample feels some way about something, or when a station with a 4.1 beats one with a 3.8 in a book, most station managers and PDs take all these statistics at face value.

FIGURE 6.11
The Radio Advertising Bureau provides radio station data for use in attracting advertisers.
Courtesy of RAB.

Rip Ridgeway, former vice-president of Arbitron Ratings, believes that stations place too much emphasis on survey results. "I think that station hierarchy puts too much credence on the ratings estimates. They're an indicator, a sort of report card on a station's performance. They're not the absolute end-all. To jump at the next numbers and make sweeping changes based on them generally is a big mistake."

Former station manager Lorna Ozmon, founder of Ozmon Media, Inc., concurs with both Porter and Ridgeway and warns that research should help direct rather than dictate what a station does. "I use research, rather than letting it use me. The thing to remember is that no methodology is without a significant margin of error. To treat the results of a survey as gospel is dangerous. I rely on research to provide me with the black-and-white answers and depend on myself to make determinations on the gray areas. Research never provided a radio station with the glitter to make it sparkle."

Station general manager (GM) Richard Bremkamp also expresses concern over what he perceives as an almost obsessive emphasis on survey statistics. "The concern for numbers gets out of hand. There are some really good-sounding stations out there that don't do good book, but the money is in the numbers. Kurt Vonnegut talks about the 'Universal Will to Become' in his books. In radio that can be expanded to the Universal Will to Become Number One. This is good if it means the best, but that's not always what it means today."

The proliferation of data services has drawn criticism from broadcasters who feel that they are being oversurveyed and overresearched. When Arbitron introduced its computerized monthly ratings service (Arbitrends), the chairman of its own radio advisory council opposed the venture on the grounds that it would cause more confusion and create more work for broadcasters. He further contended that the monthly service would encourage short-term buying by advertisers. Similar criticism was lodged against Birch/Scarborough's own computerized service, BirchPlus. However, both services experienced steady growth.

Compounding the task of audience surveying, says Ed Shane, is the fact that "lower response rates are affecting all research." Continues Shane:

> Telephone research operations have the same problem because people are burned out on solicitation by phone. For a recent research project, we made 20,100 phone calls to yield 405 respondents. As already indicated, some researchers suggest turning to the Internet for surveys. It's sure convenient, because the respondents come to the researcher. However, until Internet usage levels are as ubiquitous as the telephone used to be, the sample generated from Internet surveys is not projectable across the population as a whole.

David Pearlman concurs. "Audience research is increasingly hard to acquire. Response rates are the foremost issue facing Arbitron, or anyone else measuring listening or consumer habits." The temporal nature of research results also helps to illustrate the story of the difficulties of acquiring meaningful, correct information. It is a situation, as Dave Van Dyke, president and CEO of Bridge Ratings LLC says, that dictates the strategy adopted by his company. Bridge Ratings LLC, he explains, "was founded on and continues to pursue the most accurate consumer media consumption data possible. We have invented some new matrixes while combining them with tried and true research methodologies. Our research is revolutionary in the sense that it truly captures media consumption at a moment in time. That is why we do constant, on-going field work for many of the world's largest and most influential media companies and investment firms." The accelerated pace of technological change makes it difficult to pinpoint listener response at any given moment. Van Dyke elaborates, "One of the benefits of our methodologies is its ability to recognize how fast-changing technology is impacting entertainment media. That ability to capture behaviors as a snapshot is why our clients are consistently asking for more studies because they know how quickly behaviors change." Adds consultant Gary Begin, "Until PPM or some other methodology is fully realized, getting diary-keepers to make accurate entries will largely depend on their remembering a station's name or frequency, and that, as we well know, is a dubious business."

Adding to all this, notes Shane, is the fact that "radio research has been all but eliminated from station budgets as simply too costly. That leaves little understanding of the audience and its needs and desires."

FIGURE 6.12
Consultants use strategic-marketing techniques in developing campaigns for improving station performance. Courtesy of DMR/Interactive.

HOW AGENCIES BUY RADIO

The primacy of numbers perhaps is best illustrated through a discussion of how advertising agencies place money on radio stations. It is the media buyer's job to effectively and efficiently invest the advertiser's money—in other words, to reach the most listeners with the budget allotted for radio use. According to media buyer Lynne Price, the most commonly employed method determines the cost per point (CPP) of a given station. Lynne explains the procedure:

> A media buyer is given a budget and a gross rating point (GRP) goal. Our job is to buy to our GRP goal, without going over budget, against a predetermined target audience, i.e., adults 25 to 54, teens, men 18 to 34, etc. Our CPP is derived by taking the total budget and dividing by the GRP goal, or total number of rating points we would like to amass against our target audience. Now, using the CPP as a guideline, we take the cost per spot on a given station, and divide by the rating it has to see how close to the total CPP the station is. This is where the negotiation comes in. If the station is way off, you can threaten not to place advertising until they come closer to what you want to spend.
>
> The other method used to justify station buys is cost per thousand (CPM). Using this technique, the buyer determines the cost of reaching 1,000 people at a given station. The CPM of one station is then compared with that of another's to ascertain efficiency. To determine a station's CPM, the buyer must know the station's average quarter-hour audience (AQH persons) estimate in the daypart targeted and the cost of a commercial during that time frame. The following computation will provide the station's CPM: by dividing the number of people reached into the cost of the

commercial, the CPM is deduced. Thus, the lower the CPM, the more efficient the buy. Of course, this assumes that the station selected delivers the target audience sought. Again, this is the responsibility of the individual buying media for an agency. It should be apparent by now that many things are taken into consideration before airtime is purchased.

WHAT A RESEARCH COMPANY DOES

Ted Bolton

Bolton Research is a quantitative research company—our main objective is to get the opinions of radio listeners on virtually anything having to do with the programming and marketing of a given station (or future station). There are several methods we use to get the info:

FIGURE 6.13
Ted Bolton.

- **Perceptual studies.** These are in-depth surveys that gather opinions on issues such as music preferences, station personalities, and competitors. All respondents are included based on their age, listening habits (e.g., favorite station), favorite music types, ethnicity, county of residence, and anything else of importance to the station (client). These surveys run 15–20 minutes. Respondents are selected at random. We also do tracking studies, which include respondents from the original survey and which measure changes in opinion (usually six months out from the original survey). Perceptual studies are the foundation of research because they provide overall market information: perceptions of the client's station and its competitors, which the station uses to make programming, marketing, and sales decisions. The information gathered also aids us in designing a research program for the station.

- **Music and program testing.** There are several commonly used methods for testing music and program elements.

  1. *Auditorium testing*. This is the industry standard for testing music that may be aired on the station. Respondents are screened according to station listenership, and paid an incentive between $35 and $50, depending on the market size. The typical test involves 100–150 respondents; they are usually split into two groups. Each group gathers at a hotel, where they listen on speakers to 350–400 hooks (five to ten seconds of a song, the most memorable part). In total, 700–800 hooks will be tested. The respondents score each hook, using a 1–5 (or similar) scale. They also note if they are familiar with the song, and give it a "burn score" if they're tired of hearing the song.

     Bolton Research does "Personalized Music Tests" (PMT) instead of auditorium tests. Respondents in a PMT come to a facility at a time of their choice, and they test the hooks on portable music players with headphones. We've found that we have a better turnout than the auditorium tests and that the results are better because each respondent hears the hooks the same way (in an auditorium, respondents are at different distances from the speakers) without distractions from other listeners. Auditorium tests are still the industry standard, however.

2. *Perceptual analyzer tests*. In both of the previous methods, responders typically score hooks with paper and pencil. The data then must be coded and tabulated before the client sees the results. A recent development, perceptual analyzer tests, gives a client instant information. As the scores are given, the computer produces an instant, continuous EKG-like graph that shows averages for different groups—a station's "core" listeners and its competitors' listeners, for instance. We've found this method (we call the test "BoltScan") to be most useful in testing music in the original order that it actually aired, thereby showing us both popular songs that keep listeners tuned in, and the stuff that causes tune-out. It works the same way for testing morning shows, comedy bits, and so on.

3. *Call-out music research*. This is a staple of radio programming. Respondents of a specific age and listening group—typically core listeners in a tight age range—are called at home and asked to score 25–30 hooks. The test is obviously short and can be conducted biweekly or even weekly. This information is most useful for trending the familiarity, popularity, and burnout of songs (usually new songs) over time. Callout is a task often assigned to station interns, but a number of research companies offer the service as well.

4. *Focus groups and listener panels*. Focus groups are, of course, used for all kinds of consumer product testing, and radio is no exception. Again, respondents are screened for age and listenership. Chosen participants are paid a small incentive and come to a focus group facility or hotel room in groups of 8–12. Station staff observe while the moderator asks respondents about their likes and dislikes of station attributes, including music preferences, personalities, competing stations, etc. Listener panels are more informal and are usually done in-house by the station. Respondents are recruited on the air or from the station's database. Again, respondents are asked for their opinions about the station.

4a. *Web-based research*. Listeners can be recruited via the Web to participate in perceptual and music testing research. In some cases respondents are offered incentives. This vastly improves upon the quality of the sample base. However, many stations make use of optional opt-in type study where listeners are asked to become part of a "Listener VIP Club." The quality of any sample is highly dependent upon the incentives that, in turn, have an impact on response rates.

5. *Statistics*. Although some complicated statistical methods are sometimes used, the vast majority of data analysis involves "descriptive" statistics: frequency and average scores. Frequency is a computation of how many people fit into a category or choose a given response to a question. Averages (mean, median, and mode) are measures of average or typical performance. For most research reports, these basic statistics are enough. Some more sophisticated statistics are used to look for relationships and differences between groups: correlation ANOVA (analysis of variance), t-tests, chi-square, and cluster and factor analysis. For instance, we often use cluster analysis to separate respondents into distinct groups, such as modern rock and classic rock lovers. This helps a station to determine which artists are unique elements in a specific audience's tastes.

Why do research? Not every radio programmer is a convert to the gospel of research. It is expensive, and stations are always on a tight budget. Many programmers have done just fine using experience and their gut to get them through. In addition, as people become more guarded with their privacy, both in terms of personal information and home invasion with the telephone, research becomes a more difficult and expensive proposition.

Yet, the market intelligence research provides is vital to the stations. Research provides information that can make the gut feeling more of a sure thing or tell you that your gut is all wrong. Even the best research is useless if it's not studied and properly applied. Also, shoddy research *can* do a lot more harm than good. As is the case with most things in life, you frequently get what you pay for.

Ted Bolton has more than 25 years of experience in helping companies create marketing strategies that accelerate the acceptance and diffusion of entertainment content and new media technologies for a wide range of applications. He founded Bolton Research Corporation and it has grown to become one of the leading media/technology research firms in the U.S., serving AT&T, Time Warner, CBS, NBC, ABC, Comcast, Banc One, Clear Channel Communications, and others.

Dr. Bolton's dissertation invented a predictive modeling algorithm for new technology adoption and diffusion that is still in use today. At Bolton Research he led the industry in new media product testing, predictive modeling, consumer ethnography, and a wide assortment of seminal music and artist testing techniques. His passion for media, advertising, music, and information technologies is based on the premise that technologies only work if people integrate them into their existing way of life.

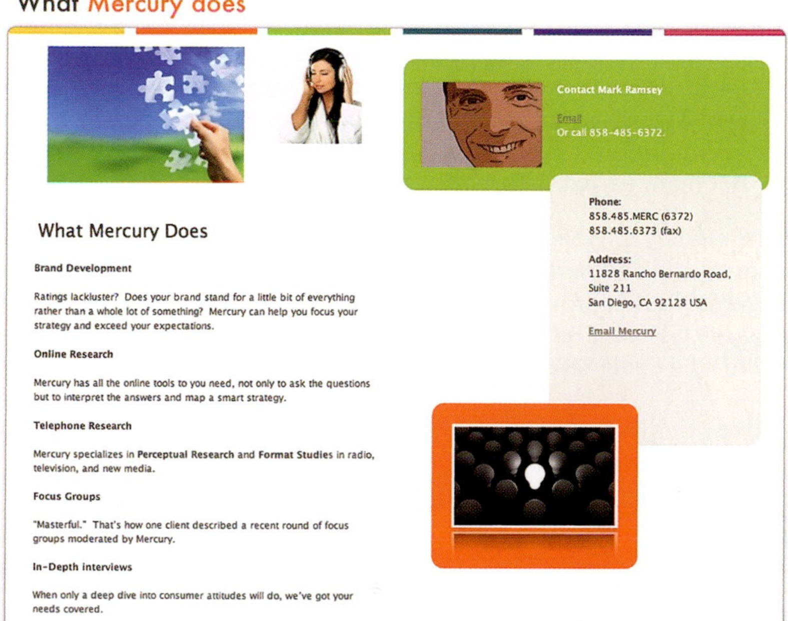

FIGURE 6.14
Research companies aid station efforts to locate advertisers. Courtesy of Mercury Research.

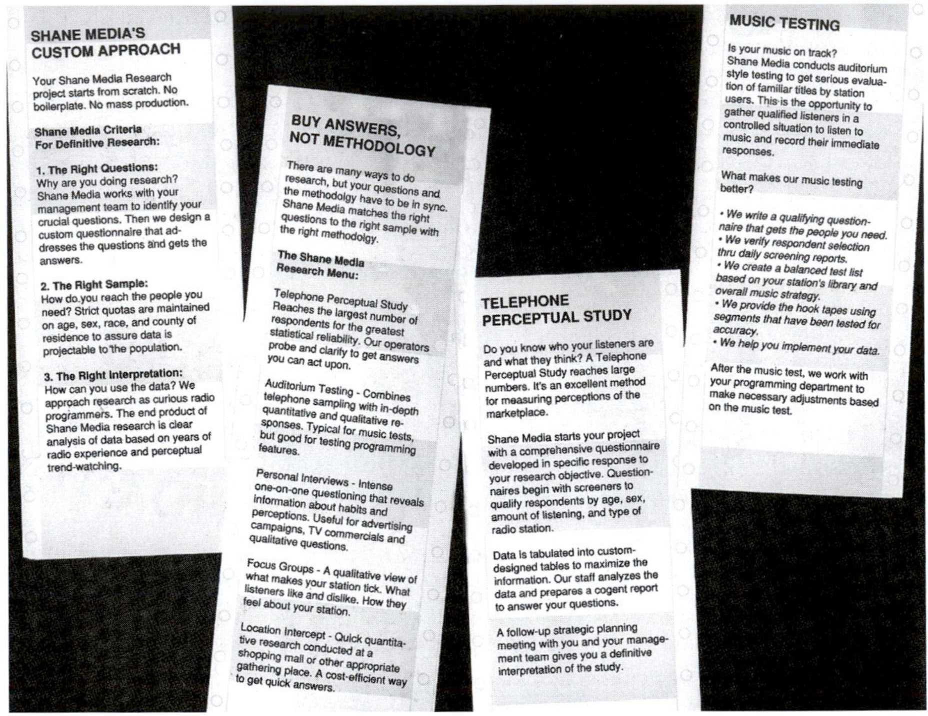

SHANE MEDIA'S CUSTOM APPROACH
Your Shane Media Research project starts from scratch. No boilerplate. No mass production.
Shane Media Criteria For Definitive Research:
1. The Right Questions:
Why are you doing research? Shane Media works with your management team to identify your crucial questions. Then we design a custom questionnaire that addresses the questions and gets the answers.
2. The Right Sample:
How do you reach the people you need? Strict quotas are maintained on age, sex, race, and county of residence to assure data is projectable to the population.
3. The Right Interpretation:
How can you use the data? We approach research as curious radio programmers. The end product of Shane Media research is clear analysis of data based on years of radio experience and perceptual trend-watching.
BUY ANSWERS, NOT METHODOLOGY
There are many ways to do research, but your questions and the methodology have to be in sync. Shane Media matches the right questions to the right sample with the right methodolgy.
The Shane Media Research Menu:
Telephone Perceptual Study Reaches the largest number of respondents for the greatest statistical reliability. Our operators probe and clarify to get answers you can act upon.
Auditorium Testing - Combines telephone sampling with in-depth quantitative and qualitative responses. Typical for music tests, but good for testing programming features.
Personal Interviews - Intense one-on-one questioning that reveals information about habits and perceptions. Useful for advertising campaigns, TV commercials and qualitative questions.
Focus Groups - A qualitative view of what makes your station tick. What listeners like and dislike. How they feel about your station.
Location Intercept - Quick quantitative research conducted at a shopping mall or other appropriate gathering place. A cost-efficient way to get quick answers.
TELEPHONE PERCEPTUAL STUDY
Do you know who your listeners are and what they think? A Telephone Perceptual Study reaches large numbers. It's an excellent method for measuring perceptions of the marketplace.
Shane Media starts your project with a comprehensive questionnaire developed in specific response to your research objective. Questionnaires begin with screeners to qualify respondents by age, sex, amount of listening, and type of radio station.
Data is tabulated into custom-designed tables to maximize the information. Our staff analyzes the data and prepares a cogent report to answer your questions.
A follow-up strategic planning meeting with you and your management team gives you a definitive interpretation of the study.
MUSIC TESTING
Is your music on track? Shane Media conducts auditorium style testing to get serious evaluation of familiar titles by station users. This is the opportunity to gather qualified listeners in a controlled situation to listen to music and record their immediate responses.
What makes our music testing better?
• We write a qualifying questionnaire that gets the people you need.
• We verify respondent selection thru daily screening reports.
• We create a balanced test list based on your station's library and overall music strategy.
• We provide the hook tapes using segments that have been tested for accuracy.
• We help you implement your data.
After the music test, we work with your programming department to make necessary adjustments based on the music test.

FIGURE 6.15
Many consultants provide a host of research services to their clients. Courtesy of Shane Media.

THE FUTURE OF RESEARCH IN RADIO

Most experts agree that the role of research in radio will continue to grow despite the trend toward downsizing and clustering. They base their predictions on the ever-increasing fragmentation and niching of the listening audience, which makes the jobs of targeting and positioning more complex. "The field of broadcast research has grown considerably in the past two decades, and there is every reason to suspect that the growth will continue. As demographic targets and formats splinter, there will be an increasingly greater need to know. Much of the gut feel that has propelled radio programming will give way to objective research that is based on a plan," contends Dwight Douglas.

Christopher Porter sees the fragmentation and niching as creating a greater demand for research. "With the inevitability of more competition in already overcrowded markets, the need to stay abreast of market developments is critical. Yes, the role of research will continue to grow."

Although the role of research in the programming of large-market stations is significant to in-house methods, claims Ed Noonan. "Professional research services can be very costly. This will keep research to a minimum in lesser markets, although there will be more movement there than in the past. Callout research will continue to be a mainstay for the small station."

"Cost-effective ways to perform and utilize sophisticated psychographic data have made the computer standard equipment at most stations, small and large alike. Research is becoming a way of life everywhere, and computers and station websites are an integral part of the information age. Computers encourage more do-it-yourself research at stations, as well, and websites allow for the collection of data and the interaction with audience," contends WGAO station manager Vic Michaels.

Gary Begin contends that advances in research technology also will continue to improve the nature and quality of research. "As with the portable ratings devices now being touted, we'll see more improvement in methodology and a greater diversity of applicable data as the result of high-tech innovations. I think the field of research will take a quantum leap in the years to come. It has in the past, but the size of the leap will be greater into the 2000s."

Today it is common for stations to budget 5–10% of their annual income to the research, and Christopher Porter believes it will probably increase. "As it evolves," he says, "it is likely that the marketplace will demand that more funds be allocated for research purposes. Research may not guarantee success, but it's not getting any easier to be successful without it."

Research has been a part of radio broadcasting since its modest beginnings in the 1920s, and it appears that it will play an even greater role in the operations of stations as the new century deepens.

THE ROLE OF RESEARCH

Warren Kurtzman

Research plays a more vital role in the success of radio stations than at perhaps any other time since our firm's founding nearly 35 years ago. Globalization and the increased diversification of nearly every country we work in have created greater fragmentation in listener tastes. These developments, coupled with the technology-fueled explosion in media choices available to consumers, have increased the complexity of the marketplaces most radio stations compete in exponentially.

FIGURE 6.16
Warren Kurtzman.

When markets are more complex it makes successfully programming, positioning, and marketing of radio stations harder. Our experience is that stations are most successful at attracting large audiences when they are well-known, possess brand attributes with which listeners want to affiliate and are strongly associated with types of content for which large appetites exist. That is where research comes in—it helps radio managers objectively understand the tastes of audiences and the degree to which their stations and their competitors are associated with the brand attributes and content listeners desire the most.

In recent years, this complex environment has become even more challenging to navigate due to the introduction of electronic audience measurement in many markets, such as the Portable People Meter (PPM) system utilized in the largest markets in the United States and Canada. Prior efforts to measure audience sizes through written diaries and telephone interviews generally meant that stations that were well-known and positively branded could count on regularly finishing atop the ratings. Electronic audience measurement has taught us that building a strong brand is not enough; to be a ratings leader, a radio station must be strongly branded *and* must deliver content on a moment-by-moment basis that is compelling as possible.

It is not enough, however, to do more research in response to these factors. Research must adapt to the changing habits of consumers and must focus on delivering insights that are customized to the needs and objectives of each radio station. That has resulted in the development of many more tools than radio stations had at their disposal as recently as a decade ago. For example, the PPM measurement system has led to the development of more sophisticated research services for evaluating content on the minute-by-minute—and, in some cases the second-by-second—level.

Thus, research's role in radio remains vital. It is a key "science" that complements the "art" of creative programmers and managers and produces successful radio stations around the world.

Warren Kurtzman was named president and chief operating officer of Coleman Insights in August 2008 after serving as a vice-president since joining the firm in May 1995. He works directly with dozens of clients and oversees the day-to-day operations of the company, which helps media companies in North America, South America, Europe, and Asia build strong brands and develop great content through consumer research. His background includes 11 years in radio station management and media research with Strategic Radio Research, Arbitron, Inc., WUUU/Utica, New York, and WVBR/Ithaca, New York. Kurtzman holds a Bachelor of Science degree in policy analysis from Cornell University in Ithaca, New York, and a Master's in business administration from New York University. He resides in Raleigh, North Carolina with his wife, two children and two dogs.

CHAPTER HIGHLIGHTS

1. Beginning in the late 1920s, surveys were conducted to determine the most popular stations and programs with various audience groupings. Early surveys (and their methods) included C.E. Hooper, Inc. (telephone), CAB (telephone), and the Pulse (in-person). In 1968, RADAR (telephone to 6,000 households) began to provide information for networks. The current leader among local market audience surveys is Arbitron (PPM and week-long diary) which was purchased by Nielsen and rebranded as Nielsen Audio in 2013.
2. In 1963, the Broadcast Rating Council was established to monitor, audit, and accredit ratings companies. In 1982, it was renamed the Electronic Media Planning Council to reflect its involvement with cable television ratings. Renamed the Media Rating Council in 1997, it now represents Internet constituencies, as well as radio, TV, cable, and print.
3. Arbitron measures listenership in the MSA, that is, the city or urban center, and the TSA, which covers the surrounding communities.
4. A station's primary listening locations are designated as the DMA®.
5. The Arbitron seven-day diary logs time tuned to a station; station call letters or program name; whether AM, FM, or satellite; where listening occurred; and the listener's age, gender, and area of residence.
6. From the late 1970s to the early 1990s, Birch/Scarborough gathered data by calling equal numbers of male and female listeners aged 12 and over. Clients were offered seven different report formats, including a computerized data retrieval system. The company went out of business on December 31, 1991.
7. With today's highly fragmented audiences, advertisers and agencies are less comfortable buying just ratings numbers and look for audience qualities. Programmers must consider not only the age and gender of the target audience but also their lifestyles, values, and behavior.
8. The PPM is a cell phone-sized device that records radio audience listening patterns. Its creator, Arbitron, hopes it will eventually replace its long-used seven-day paper diary. The cell phone may well serve to record radio-listening habits as well.
9. Criticisms about underrepresented minority panelists in the early history of PPM measurement led to the formation of the PPM Coalition by industry representatives to improve media relationships with Arbitron.
10. Arbitron successor Nielsen Audio has announced intentions to increase PPM sample sizes and focus on improving efforts to recruit African American and Hispanic panelists.
11. Station in-house surveyors use telephone, computer, website, face-to-face, and mail methods.
12. Media buyers for agencies use station ratings to determine the most cost-effective buy for their clients. Two methods they use are the cost per rating point (CPP) and the cost per thousand (CPM).
13. Ratings estimates are a quantitative indicator of audience response to programming. Qualitative research outcomes about listener preferences (notably, recorded music) serve to inform the thinking of and the decisions made by programmers.

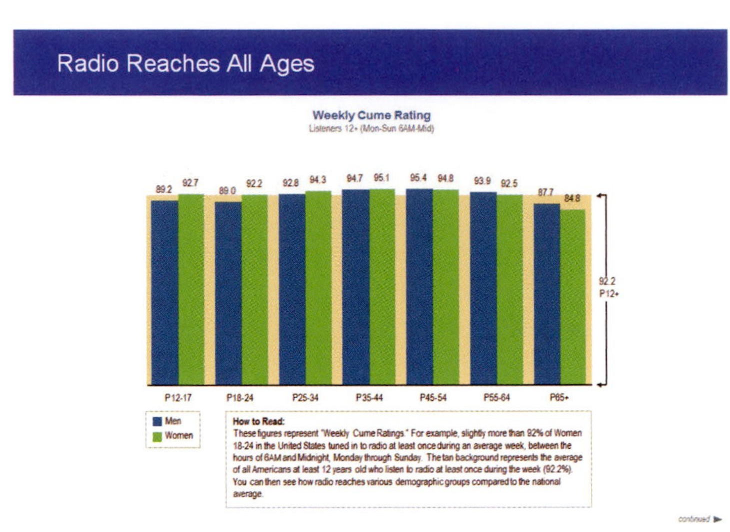

FIGURE 6.17
Arbitron data gives radio stations information to attract advertisers. Courtesy of Arbitron.

FIGURE 6.18
Websites offer stations enormous research opportunities. Courtesy of Mark Kassof & Company.

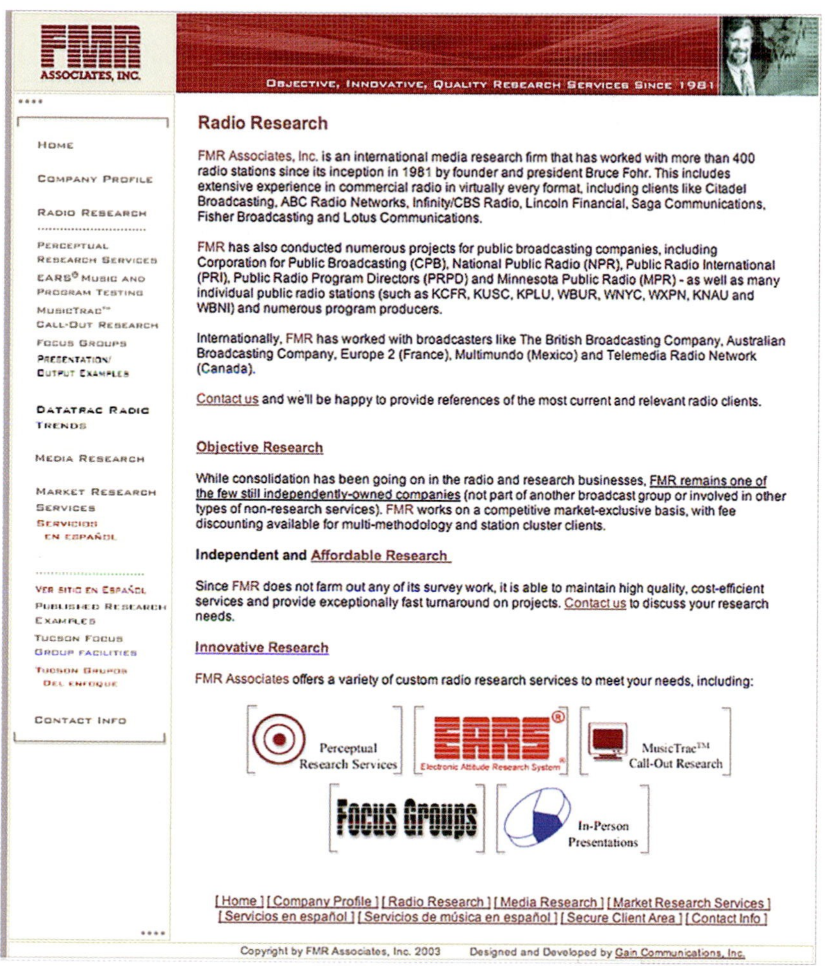

FIGURE 6.19
Companies such as FMR Associates provide radio stations with important research data. Courtesy of FMR Associates.

WAAA-FM	Custom Local Callout Sample Report	Kelly Music Research, Inc.

	Custom Local Callout	*Sample Report*	Grade				Mean				Burn				Unfamiliar				Total	Total	Total	Total
	Song	Artist	Male	Female	25–34	35–44	Male	Female	25–34	35–44	Male	Female	25–34	35–44	Male	Female	25–34	35–44	Grade	Mean	Burn	Unfam
1	Boys Round Here	Blake Shelton	86	90	87	89	4.00	4.10	4.04	4.07	21%	17%	21%	17%	3%	0%	4%	0%	88	4.05	19%	2%
2	Runnin' Outta Moonlight	Randy Houser	83	91	85	89	3.83	4.10	3.86	4.07	7%	14%	11%	10%	0%	0%	0%	0%	87	3.97	10%	0%
3	Crash My Party	Luke Bryan	82	89	89	82	3.79	4.07	4.11	3.77	24%	28%	25%	27%	0%	0%	0%	0%	86	3.93	26%	0%
4	Aw Naw	Chris Young	78	92	85	85	3.71	4.21	4.00	3.93	17%	10%	7%	20%	3%	0%	4%	0%	85	3.96	14%	2%
5	Done	The Band Perry	77	93	88	82	3.59	4.28	4.04	3.83	28%	24%	32%	20%	0%	0%	0%	0%	85	3.93	26%	0%
6	Parking Lot Party	Lee Brice	84	86	88	83	3.83	3.97	4.00	3.80	28%	21%	18%	30%	0%	0%	0%	0%	85	3.90	24%	0%
7	Don't Ya	Brett Eldredge	81	89	83	87	3.85	4.03	3.92	3.97	17%	31%	29%	20%	7%	0%	7%	0%	85	3.95	24%	3%
8	Get Your Shine On	Florida Georgia Line	81	87	80	87	3.72	3.97	3.71	3.97	34%	28%	36%	27%	0%	0%	0%	0%	84	3.84	31%	0%
9	Night Train	Jason Aldean	80	86	81	85	3.85	3.97	3.81	4.00	14%	14%	21%	7%	7%	0%	4%	3%	83	3.91	14%	3%
10	Mine Would Be You	Blake Shelton	78	87	81	83	3.68	4.04	3.81	3.90	7%	14%	14%	7%	3%	3%	4%	3%	82	3.86	10%	3%
11	See You Again	Carrie Underwood	77	87	83	81	3.59	4.00	3.82	3.77	34%	24%	39%	20%	0%	0%	0%	0%	82	3.79	29%	0%
12	Redneck Crazy	Tyler Farr	78	83	79	81	3.74	3.83	3.81	3.77	21%	28%	29%	20%	7%	0%	7%	0%	80	3.79	24%	3%
13	Round Here	Florida Georgia Line	77	83	75	85	3.55	3.89	3.56	3.87	14%	14%	21%	7%	0%	3%	4%	0%	80	3.72	14%	2%
14	Sunny and 75	Joe Nichols	79	80	77	82	3.75	3.79	3.73	3.80	10%	17%	18%	10%	3%	3%	7%	0%	80	3.77	14%	3%
15	Point At You	Justin Moore	80	79	79	79	3.69	3.66	3.68	3.67	21%	28%	25%	23%	0%	0%	0%	0%	79	3.67	24%	0%
16	Southern Girl	Tim McGraw	77	81	73	85	3.64	3.76	3.48	3.90	14%	17%	25%	7%	3%	0%	4%	0%	79	3.70	16%	2%
17	It Goes Like This	Thomas Rhett	75	80	76	80	3.52	3.72	3.54	3.70	17%	14%	18%	13%	0%	0%	0%	0%	78	3.62	16%	0%
18	Carolina	Parmalee	78	77	76	78	3.66	3.70	3.61	3.75	10%	21%	29%	3%	0%	7%	0%	7%	77	3.68	16%	3%
19	All Kinds Of Kinds	Miranda Lambert	73	81	74	79	3.46	3.82	3.50	3.79	21%	10%	21%	10%	3%	3%	0%	7%	77	3.64	16%	3%
20	That's My Kind of Night	Luke Bryan	71	81	74	78	3.44	3.76	3.62	3.60	28%	24%	21%	30%	7%	0%	7%	0%	76	3.61	26%	3%
21	Don't Let Me Be Lonely	The Band Perry	74	76	77	73	3.45	3.87	3.72	3.56	17%	10%	14%	13%	0%	21%	11%	10%	75	3.63	14%	10%
22	Stay	Florida Georgia Line	68	81	80	70	3.71	3.89	3.88	3.75	0%	0%	0%	0%	30%	10%	11%	27%	75	3.81	0%	20%
23	Sweet Annie	Zac Brown Band	73	76	73	76	3.46	3.67	3.48	3.64	24%	10%	32%	3%	3%	7%	4%	7%	74	3.56	17%	5%
24	Red	Taylor Swift	73	73	72	75	3.46	3.45	3.41	3.50	28%	31%	32%	27%	3%	0%	4%	0%	73	3.46	29%	2%
25	Radio	Darius Rucker	75	71	71	75	3.54	3.73	3.61	3.63	17%	10%	25%	3%	3%	24%	18%	10%	73	3.62	14%	14%
26	Drunk Last Night	Eli Young Band	71	71	71	71	3.50	3.73	3.61	3.60	17%	0%	11%	7%	10%	24%	18%	17%	71	3.60	9%	17%
27	We Were Us	Keith Urban	72	69	69	72	3.38	3.61	3.52	3.45	28%	3%	21%	10%	0%	21%	18%	3%	71	3.48	16%	10%
28	Wasting All These Tears	Cassadee Pope	71	68	73	67	3.39	3.44	3.56	3.29	24%	17%	25%	17%	3%	14%	11%	7%	70	3.42	21%	9%
29	Chillin It	Cole Swindell	69	66	65	71	3.42	3.57	3.43	3.54	17%	3%	18%	3%	10%	28%	25%	13%	68	3.49	10%	19%
30	Everything I Shouldn't Be …	Thompson Square	68	67	69	67	3.35	3.65	3.55	3.42	21%	3%	14%	10%	10%	31%	21%	20%	68	3.48	12%	21%
31	I Can't Change The World	Brad Paisley	60	75	65	70	2.93	3.76	3.24	3.39	24%	17%	21%	20%	3%	14%	11%	7%	67	3.32	21%	9%
32	Everybody's Got Somebody …	Hunter Hayes	64	69	68	66	3.15	3.50	3.38	3.26	28%	7%	21%	13%	7%	17%	14%	10%	67	3.31	17%	12%
33	Friday Night	Eric Paslay	63	68	64	67	3.25	3.89	3.71	3.40	10%	10%	11%	10%	17%	38%	39%	17%	66	3.52	10%	28%
34	Days of Gold	Jake Owen	63	66	65	64	3.07	3.68	3.48	3.19	31%	3%	11%	23%	3%	34%	25%	13%	64	3.32	17%	19%
35	Whatever She's Got	David Nail	56	69	66	60	3.00	3.71	3.43	3.29	10%	0%	0%	9%	30%	30%	22%	36%	63	3.36	5%	30%

FIGURE 6.20

Results of a music test using the callout research method. The test and its report are customized to a client station's specifications. Courtesy of Kelly Music Research.

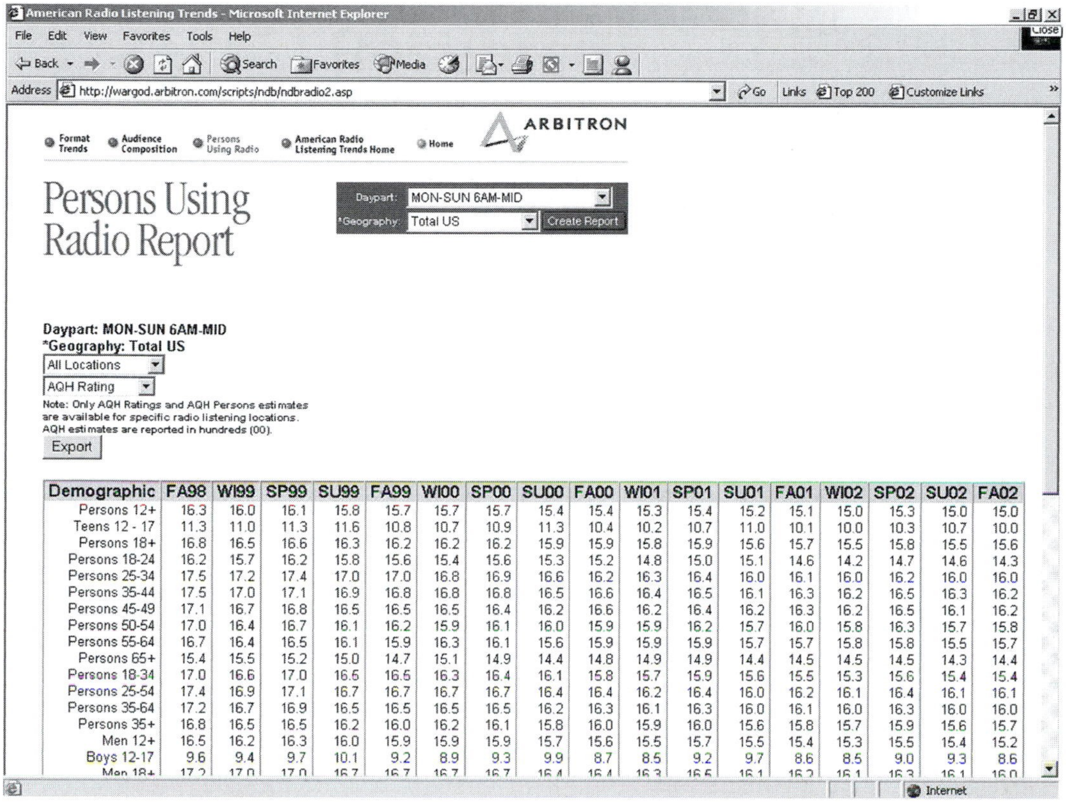

American Radio Listening Trends - Microsoft Internet Explorer

http://wargod.arbitron.com/scripts/ndb/ndbradio2.asp

Format Trends · Audience Composition · Persons Using Radio · American Radio Listening Trends Home · Home

ARBITRON

Persons Using Radio Report

Daypart: MON-SUN 6AM-MID
*Geography: Total US

Create Report

Daypart: MON-SUN 6AM-MID
***Geography: Total US**

All Locations
AQH Rating

Note: Only AQH Ratings and AQH Persons estimates are available for specific radio listening locations. AQH estimates are reported in hundreds (00).

Export

Demographic	FA98	WI99	SP99	SU99	FA99	WI00	SP00	SU00	FA00	WI01	SP01	SU01	FA01	WI02	SP02	SU02	FA02
Persons 12+	16.3	16.0	16.1	15.8	15.7	15.7	15.7	15.4	15.4	15.3	15.4	15.2	15.1	15.0	15.3	15.0	15.0
Teens 12 - 17	11.3	11.0	11.3	11.6	10.8	10.7	10.9	11.3	10.4	10.2	10.7	11.0	10.1	10.0	10.3	10.7	10.0
Persons 18+	16.8	16.5	16.6	16.3	16.2	16.2	16.2	15.9	15.9	15.8	15.9	15.6	15.7	15.5	15.8	15.5	15.6
Persons 18-24	16.2	15.7	16.2	15.8	15.6	15.4	15.6	15.3	15.2	14.8	15.0	15.1	14.6	14.2	14.7	14.6	14.3
Persons 25-34	17.5	17.2	17.4	17.0	17.0	16.8	16.9	16.6	16.2	16.3	16.4	16.0	16.1	16.0	16.2	16.0	16.0
Persons 35-44	17.5	17.0	17.1	16.9	16.8	16.8	16.8	16.5	16.6	16.4	16.5	16.1	16.3	16.2	16.5	16.3	16.2
Persons 45-49	17.1	16.7	16.8	16.5	16.5	16.5	16.4	16.2	16.6	16.2	16.4	16.2	16.3	16.2	16.5	16.1	16.2
Persons 50-54	17.0	16.4	16.7	16.1	16.2	15.9	16.1	16.0	15.9	15.9	16.2	15.7	16.0	15.8	16.3	15.7	15.8
Persons 55-64	16.7	16.4	16.5	16.1	15.9	16.3	16.1	15.6	15.9	15.9	15.9	15.7	15.7	15.8	15.8	15.5	15.7
Persons 65+	15.4	15.5	15.2	15.0	14.7	15.1	14.9	14.4	14.8	14.9	14.9	14.4	14.5	14.5	14.5	14.3	14.4
Persons 18-34	17.0	16.6	17.0	16.6	16.5	16.3	16.4	16.1	15.8	15.7	15.9	15.6	15.5	15.3	15.6	15.4	15.4
Persons 25-54	17.4	16.9	17.1	16.7	16.7	16.7	16.7	16.4	16.4	16.2	16.4	16.0	16.2	16.1	16.4	16.1	16.1
Persons 35-64	17.2	16.7	16.9	16.5	16.5	16.5	16.5	16.2	16.3	16.1	16.3	16.0	16.1	16.0	16.3	16.0	16.0
Persons 35+	16.8	16.5	16.5	16.2	16.0	16.2	16.1	15.8	16.0	15.9	16.0	15.6	15.8	15.7	15.9	15.6	15.7
Men 12+	16.5	16.2	16.3	16.0	15.9	15.9	15.9	15.7	15.6	15.5	15.7	15.5	15.4	15.3	15.5	15.4	15.2
Boys 12-17	9.6	9.4	9.7	10.1	9.2	8.9	9.3	9.9	8.7	8.5	9.2	9.7	8.6	8.5	9.0	9.3	8.6
Men 18+	17.2	17.0	17.0	16.7	16.7	16.7	16.7	16.4	16.4	16.3	16.5	16.1	16.2	16.1	16.3	16.1	16.0

FIGURE 6.21 *(Above)*
Demographic information is still the coin of the realm in audience research despite a much more qualitative orientation by advertisers. Courtesy of Arbitron.

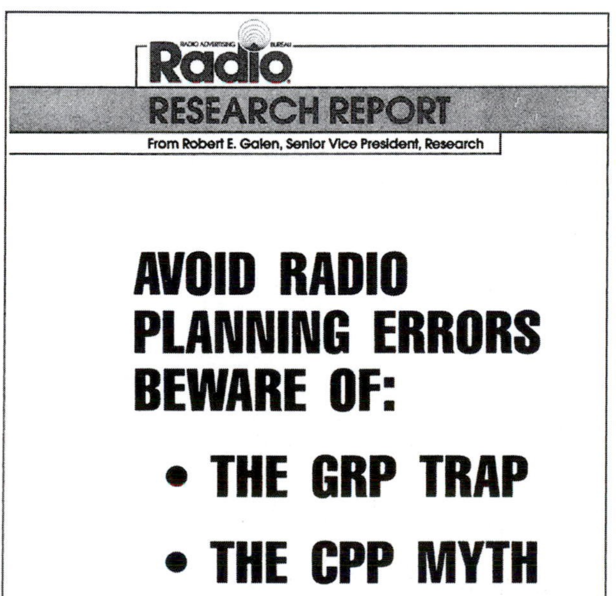

FIGURE 6.22
Some broadcasters contend that there are inherent failures in across-the-board GRP/CPP buying by agencies. RAB publishes this report to caution against the pitfalls of buying formulas. Courtesy of RAB.

SUGGESTED FURTHER READING

Arbitron Company, Portable People Meter 101 (online tutorial), http://www.arbitrontraining.com/training/ppm101/ppm101_Start.htm.

Balon, R.E., *Radio In the 90s*, NAB Publishing, Washington, D.C., 1990.

Bartos, R., *The Moving Target, What Every Marketer Should Know about Women*, The Free Press, New York, 1982.

Berger, A.A., *Media and Communication Research Methods*, Sage, Beverly Hills, CA, 2008.

Broadcast Advertising Reports, Broadcast Advertising Research, New York, periodically.

Broadcasting Yearbook, Broadcasting Publishing, Washington, D.C., 1935 to 2010 (ceased publication).

Bryant, J., *Media Effects: Advances in Theory and Research*, 3rd edition, Routledge, New York, 2008.

Buzzard, K., *Chains of Gold: Marketing the Ratings and Rating the Markets*, Scarecrow Press, Lanham, MD, 1990.

Buzzard, K., *Electronic Media Ratings*, Focal Press, Boston, MA, 1992.

Chappell, M.N. and Hooper, C.E., *Radio Audience Measurement*, Stephen Day Press, New York, 1944.

Compaine, B., et al., *Who Owns the Media? Confrontation of Ownership in the Mass Communication Industry*, 2nd edition, Knowledge Industry Publications, White Plains, NY, 1982.

Duncan, J., *American Radio*, Author, Kalamazoo, MI, twice yearly.

Duncan, J., *Radio in the United States: 1976–82: A Statistical History*, Author, Kalamazoo, MI, 1983.

Eastman, S.T., *Research in Media Promotion*, LEA, Mahwah, NJ, 2000.

Electronic Industries Association, *Electronic Market Data Book*, EIA, Washington, D.C., annually.

Fletcher, J.E. (ed.), *Handbook of Radio and Television Broadcasting: Research Procedures in Audience, Programming, and Revenues*, Van Nostrand Reinhold, New York, 1981.

Gunter, B., *Media Research Methods*, Sage Publishing, Beverly Hills, CA, 2000.

Jamieson, K.H. and Campbell, K.K., *The Interplay of Influence: Mass Media and Their Publics in News, Advertising, and Politics*, Wadsworth Publishing, Belmont, CA, 1983.

Jensen, K.B., *Handbook of Media and Communications Research*, Routledge, New York, 2002.

Katz, H., *The Media Handbook: A Complete Guide to Advertising Media Selection, Planning, Research, and Buying*, 4th edition, Routledge, New York, 2010.

Lazarsfeld, P.F. and Kendall, P., *Radio Listening in America*, Prentice Hall, Englewood Cliffs, NJ, 1948.

McDowell, W., *Troubleshooting Audience Research*, NAB, Washington, D.C., 2000.

National Association of Broadcasters, *Radio Financial Report*, NAB, Washington, D.C., 1955 to date, annually.

National Association of Broadcasters, *Audience Research Sourcebook*, NAB Publishing, Washington, D.C., 1991.

Park, D.W. and Pooley, J. (eds), *The History of Media and Communication Research*, Peter Lang, New York, 2008.

Radio Facts, Radio Advertising Bureau, New York, published annually.

Shane, E., *Selling Electronic Media*, Focal Press, Boston, MA, 1999.

Webster, J.G., Phelan, P. and Lichty, L.W., *The Theory and Practice of Audience Research*, 3rd edition, Lawrence Erlbaum Associates, Mahwah, NJ, 2006.

Wimmer, R.D. and Dominick, J., *Mass Media Research: An Introduction*, 10th edition, Wadsworth Publishing, Belmont, CA, 2014.

CHAPTER 7
Promotion

PROMOTIONS—PRACTICAL AND BIZARRE

The idea behind any promotion is to win listeners. Over the years, stations have used a variety of methods, ranging from the conventional to the outlandish, to accomplish this goal. "If a promotion achieves top-of-the-mind awareness in the listener, it's a winner. Granted, some strange things have been done to accomplish this," admits Mississippi broadcaster Bob Lima. Today, radio stations also use the Internet to market themselves. Stations have elaborate websites with colorful graphics to catch the reader's attention, giveaways, and announcements of upcoming contests, concerts, and photos of winners of the most recent contests to encourage more listenership. Stations have even adopted new media/social media technologies by inviting listeners to friend the station on its Facebook page and follow the station on Twitter or Instagram. Stations will use whatever technology and platform needed to communicate with and potentially gain more listeners.

Promotions designed to captivate the interest of the radio audience have inspired some pretty bizarre schemes. In the 1950s, Dallas station KLIF placed overturned cars on freeways with a sign on their undersides announcing the arrival of a new deejay, Johnny Rabbitt. It would be hard to calculate the number of deejays who have lived atop flagpoles or in elevators for the sake of a rating point.

FIGURE 7.1
Stations promote their image. Courtesy of Wolfpack Media, LLC.

In the 1980s, the shenanigans continued. To gain the listening public's attention, a California deejay set a world record by sitting in every seat of a major league ballpark that held 65,000 spectators. In the process of the stunt, the publicity-hungry deejay injured his leg. However, he went on to accomplish his goal by garnering national attention for himself and his station. Another station offered to give away a mobile home to contestants who camped out the longest on a platform at the base of a billboard. The challenge turned into a battle of wills as three contestants spent months trying to outlast each other. In the end, one of the three was disqualified, and the station, in an effort to cease what had become more of an embarrassment than anything else, awarded the two holdouts recreational vehicles.

Today, promotions have gotten edgier, especially on those stations featuring "shock jock" shows. Things can and do get out of hand when personalities go to the extreme to draw listeners' attention with on-air pranks and giveaways. Prior to migrating to satellite, Howard Stern held all manner of scatological promotions and contests, many centered around women removing their clothes, and Opie and Anthony asked listeners to have sex in public places. This ultimately got them removed from the air, thus proving there are limits to what a station can do to get attention from an audience. Of course, after a successful stint (or exile) on satellite radio, the duo was hired back by terrestrial radio—proving again that ratings matter most. The tone and tenor of station promotions have certainly changed over the decades, notes Larry Miller. "Although occurring in what now seems a gentler and kinder world, my personal favorite is the one about a station in LA in the early 1950s that sent out a 'free Valhalla Oil credit card' to listeners. Well, there was no such oil company, but loyal listeners nevertheless spent a good deal of time searching for a Valhalla gas station. Everybody had a laugh."

Reporter Peg Harney offers testimony that the bizarre still occurs in radio promotions:

> As a publicity stunt and also to get people to use the local public library, a station in Ft. Worth, Texas, a couple years back announced it had hidden cash in small denominations in the fiction section. Approximately 800 people descended on the library and proceeded to pull books off the shelves looking for the money. The library had not been notified that the station was going to make the announcement, and it was totally taken by surprise. The librarian said that approximately 4,000 books were pulled from the shelves—some of them had pages torn out—and that people were climbing on the bookcases and making a tremendous mess. The station was forced to make a public apology, and it promised full financial restitution.

One of the most infamous examples of a promotion gone bad occurred when a station decided to air-drop dozens of turkeys to a waiting crowd of listeners in a neighborhood shopping center parking lot. Unfortunately, the station discovered too late that turkeys are not adept at flying at heights above 30 feet. Consequently, several cars were damaged and witnesses were traumatized as turkeys plunged to the ground. This promotion-turned-nightmare was fictionalized in an episode of the television sitcom *WKRP in Cincinnati*.

Even worse is when a death occurs as a result of a station's promotional stunt. In Sacramento, California, in 2007, at KDND, the station held a "Hold your Wee for a Wii" contest. It required contestants to drink as much water as possible without relieving themselves. A young mother of three children, for whom she was trying to win the Wii video game system, died after drinking two gallons of water. As a result of the death, ten employees lost their jobs. *The Washington Post* reports, "The standard argument made by radio executives is that listeners who participate in stunts are adults and ought to take responsibility for their own actions."

In an effort to increase listenership, in 2011, a Canadian radio station had a contest offering its listeners an opportunity to win a baby. LifeSiteNews.com reported the station's program director as saying, "one in six people have trouble conceiving, and we know that our audience—we target females between the age of 25 and 54—is dealing with the issue of conceiving right now, and so we wanted to give them the opportunity to have a baby of their own." The contest was designed to pay for in vitro fertilization (IVF).

FIGURE 7.2A&B
Radio stations will do whatever is necessary to attract listeners and appeal to their targeted demographic. This was a promotional event designed for female listeners. Courtesy of Hot 89.9, Ottawa, Ontario.

In 2009, WRXL in Virginia held a contest called "Marriage Bailout 09" in which it gave listeners free divorces via an arrangement with a local attorney.

The list of glitches and botched promotions is seemingly endless. In the late 1960s, a station in central Massachusetts asked listeners to predict how long its air personality could ride a carousel at a local fair. The hardy airman's effort was cut short on day three when motion sickness got the best of him and he vomited on a crowd of spectators and newspaper photographers. A station in California came close to disaster when a promotion that challenged listeners to find a buried treasure resulted in half the community being dug up by overzealous contestants. In Massachusetts, a station invited listeners to retrieve money-filled balloons dropped by helicopters into the surf, and contestants came close to drowning as the balloons floated out to sea.

These promotions did indeed capture the attention of the public, but in each case, the station's image was somewhat tarnished. The axiom that any publicity, good or bad, is better than none at all can get a station into not only hot water, but legal problems contends station promotion director Chuck Davis. "It's great to get lots of exposure for the station, but if it makes the station look foolish, it can work against you."

The vast majority of radio contests and promotions are of a more practical nature and run without too many complications.

Promotions that involve prizes, both large and small, spark audience interest, says Rick Peters, CEO of Bluewater Broadcasting. "People love to win something or, at least, feel that they have a shot at winning a prize. That's basic to human nature, I believe. You really don't have to give away two city blocks, either. A listener usually is thrilled and delighted to win a pair of concert tickets."

Although numerous examples can be cited to support the view that big prizes get big audiences, there is also ample evidence that low-budget giveaways, involving T-shirts, albums, tickets, posters, dinners, and so forth, are very useful in building and maintaining audience interest. In fact, some surveys have revealed that smaller, more personalized prizes may work better for a station than the high-priced items. Concert tickets, iPods, and dinners-for-two rank among the most popular contest prizes, according to surveys. Cheaper items usually also mean more numerous or frequent giveaways. In 2013, *Inside Radio* reports, "At the top of the list is a tangible value proposition to the listener, such as giving away concert tickets, gift cards, or other items of value. O'Reilly Auto Parts provides $25 and $50 gift cards and offers sale specials. Also frequently mentioned is the opportunity for listeners to meet their favorite personality, live entertainment or a sound system, activities and street visibility to draw passersby in."

The Internet and social media technologies have forced stations to place more of an emphasis on promotions and marketing for stations. Brian Foster, vice-president of NextMedia, which operates radio stations in eight states, says, "The number of options have grown at break-neck speed. While you used to compete against the station across the street, you now must battle against thousands of options with varying degree of personalization." Facebook and Twitter are commonplace on radio station websites. "Social media has become the new age billboard. Street presence is also critical, this would include fairs, concerts, etc.," says Foster.

"RADIO + SOCIAL MEDIA = ?"

Lori Lewis

FIGURE 7.3
Lori Lewis. Courtesy of Lori Lewis.

All too often, we see brands approaching social with basic questions such as "How do I get more followers?" or "How can I generate revenue from it?" And while there's certainly nothing wrong with wanting a large social fan base or creating a secondary revenue stream, the fact of the matter is that social media is personal for people. Coming at social with "What can it do for me?" contradicts the interactive nature of these platforms.

There's a human element to social that is overlooked. Therefore brands should have a human approach—not a common thinking bottom-line undertaking. When brands only look at social (and its fans) based on what it can do for them, they come up short of being an effective social brand. So in order to avoid some of the more popular social misconceptions, let's start with the following principles to consider:

Social Media is Not a Silver Bullet

Social in isolation will not grow your brand. None of your plans should be simply social—rather the combination of owned, earned, shared, and paid media. Social is there to make more of a personal impact between the station and the fan—strengthening the brand's perceived value.

Vanity Metrics—A Brand's Favorite Sin

The amount of "Likes" or "followers" you accrue does not equate to brand impact nor does it measure the quality and depth of your fan relationships. Affinity trumps "likes" and tweets. But to build affinity, you must speak the language of your fans and emulate *their* dialogue—not that of radio promos and pitches. Be present and connected socially and disciplined enough to not stray from what fans value about your station with random posts and tweets. It's the station's behavior that will make you memorable or forgettable. And at the end of the day it's about how many fans you converted from the social sites and apps that you essentially "rent" over to the assets you "own" (AM/FM stick, database, website, app, etc . . .)—not the vanity metric.

"Social Natives" Do Not Correlate to Business Sense

Many times, the people speaking for our great radio brands socially are not required to have brand voice sophistication or even perspective on what went into building the brand in the first place. They are speaking for brands socially because they either fall into that "native social/digital" generation or worse, they "know" social because they've been "doing it" for a while. But having social media "knowledge" does not mean they have the maturity and common sense necessary to speak in a brand's singular voice. *Doing* social and *being* social are two very different things. Find people who love acknowledging fans and being social.

Building a Believable Social Brand

When it comes to building great radio brands, we work on the fundamentals: research, putting the right people in place, and having a plan. It's intuitive to us to build dynamic radio stations with that discipline. But when it comes to building a social brand, we're not as buttoned up. And radio's approach to social may actually be stunting its growth in the space. Social is personal. Real people don't go on these platforms with the idea of helping you get ratings or generate revenue. They are there to interact with their friends—not brands. But they will participate with you—once you've built anticipation and trust.

We Are Not Entitled to a Social Fan Base

We may have remarkable traditional brands that fans come to every day and even participate with—but when it comes to having believability in the social space, you can't force trust. This next line you read may sound like common sense, but it's not common practice.

Never Underestimate the Power of the Personal Touch

Too often we see celebrities or companies (sometimes even radio stations and personalities) brushing off fans—as if we're entitled to pick and choose who we respond to—if we even bother to respond at all. But understanding what it takes to build and sustain a social fan base is critical as this space grows and becomes an even bigger part of people's lives. The memorable brands in this space have identified what it takes to go beyond the ordinary and create meaningful fan experiences. They know it's about looking further than their own needs and serving the fans first.

You'll also notice three common themes that run through an effective social brand's presence and behavior:

1. **Validation:** Making people feel that they have been seen and heard.
2. **Inspiration:** When there's more care in your content selection than cat videos, and you create or curate content that correlates with what *fans* experience as the essence of your brand, you confirm their reality by sharing what it is they value.
3. **Information:** Telling your fans something they don't already know—especially with breaking news or commonly shared stories—elevates your brand authority.

We are operating radio stations in a world that has been coined as "permanent beta"—it's the mindset that everything (even our own self) is a work in progress, never finished. Because of this "permanent beta" digital and social world there may be no way we will ever master social sites or apps. Things will always be changing. But if you get the fundamentals and the appropriate behavior down, future changes will have minimal effect on your overall strategy. That's because you will have crafted the art of serving. And you don't have to take it from me. Take it from the fans that have been followed on Twitter by their favorite deejay or radio station or those that actually get a response on Facebook.

The social space isn't about persuading fans to listen to you as much as it is fitting your brand into their conversations and making a commitment to use these platforms to make

Gavin Buck @Gbuck12
@JaxonWMMR just followed me! My life now has value!!!
Expand

D&G @DanielleGudino
Not only has one of my favorite stations @91X been following me. I now have the @91XTicketThief following me too... #youwillbecaught

Sarah @lilbunEfoofoo
Yep. I'm gonna dork out on you again. @robin_roth is now following me. Been listening to her on @91X since the 80s!
#dreamsdocometrue

Oliver_Stoned @3rdCoastStoner
Now followed by the one & only @wcsx!!! The number 1 classic rock station in this galaxy or any other! #RockCity

FIGURE 7.4
Being followed by a deejay on Twitter can have a real impact on listeners.

Jeri Simpson
Is the bonus code for the week not working for other people too?

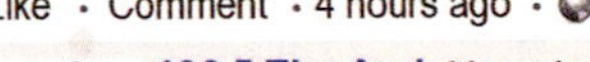

106.5 The Arch Yours is the first report of a problem - we're checking.
4 hours ago · Like

Jeri Simpson I love that you guys stay on top of your fb. It's great customer service!
4 hours ago · Unlike · 1

FIGURE 7.5
Listeners also value a response to their Facebook comments.

their lives better. Making them feel seen and heard. That's the real currency today—allowing people to feel like they have a voice. When we take the time to commit to acknowledging them, wonderful things happen. The greatest "best practice" for social media can be summed up in three words: every person counts.

Lori Lewis's radio career spans more than 20 years starting out as an on-air talent at high profile stations such as Active Rock WXTB (98ROCK) Tampa, FL to a decorated program director for stations such as Rock B104/Baltimore, Maryland. In 2008, Lewis moved back to her home town Green Bay, Wisconsin, and created a new position in radio, serving as multimedia content manager executing a comprehensive digital and social program for Midwest Communications. In March 2011, Lewis was tapped by Jacobs Media to serve as director of digital and social strategies. As a strategist, Lewis collaborates and assists brands with fan development on digital and social platforms. She teaches behaviors behind every platform, and analyzes what channels will meet the goals of each client to strengthen the long-term health of their assets, and increase the bottom line.

THE PROMOTION DIRECTOR'S/MANAGER'S JOB

Promotions Coordinator Opening in Seattle!!!!

Dby salem » Wed Sep 25, 2013 3:33 pm

Would you like to start your day knowing that you work in an environment that reflects your personal values and advances your career goals? If this is you, Salem Communications Seattle believes you can achieve great things at Christian Teaching and Talk stations KGNW 820AM (English), KNTS 1680AM (Spanish), KKOL 1300AM Business News Talk station and KLFE 1590AM Conservative Talk

CAREER OPPORTUNITY:
Salem Communications is a leading broadcaster of religious programming and informative talk. The company owns and operates commercial radio stations in major markets throughout the United States. Salem Communications in Seattle, Washington is seeking a qualified Promotions & Marketing Coordinator to work with the Salem Seattle Management team for strategic planning for our radio stations.

DUTIES:
-Plan promotional events, including set up and breakdown of equipment, provide support and interact with listeners
-Coordinate contests/giveaways.
-Assist with budget and order promotional supplies/giveaways.
-Organize and execute station remotes and events as well as coordinate talent.
-Lead and attend weekly promotions meeting
-Develop and maintain annual Promotions calendar. Create, update and distribute event calendars every week.
-Organize staff meetings and luncheons as well as client parties and meetings.
-Interface with corporate PR department – provide info on station activities/events.
-Arrange trade advertising.
-Design &/or create new forms, flyers, tickets, info sheets, awards, etc...
-Build and maintain active database of churches.
-Assist with maintaining and updating web sites.
-Design email blasts and maintain email database using third party software.
-Assist the GSM and sales team with entry of orders in Traffic Software
-Help maintain company vehicle: Fuel van for events and remotes, keep clean inside and out.
-Provide Reception back-up when needed and other duties as assigned

[b]JOB REQUIREMENTS:
-A passion for our station formats
-Proficient in Word, Excel, Outlook, Photo Shop, Publisher, and Illustrator.
-Professional Public appearance.
-Must be 21 years of age and able to operate a company vehicle, have a valid driver's license.
-Ability to lift 50lbs and able to stand for long periods of time at events and work weekends and evenings.
-Excellent communication and presentation skills.
-Ability to multi-task, have exceptional organization skills.
-Excellent verbal and written skills.
-A team player, high energy and a positive attitude.
-Must be able to work nights and week-ends if needed.
-Knowledge of media and sales experience a plus but for the right candidate, we are willing to provide training in radio ad sales.
-BILINGUAL (ENGLISH/SPANISH) A PLUS!!!!!

Compensation: depends on experience, along with a full benefits package and a positive work environment.

CONTACT INFORMATION: Jobs@salemradioseattle.com or fax 206-777-3236
(Emails or faxes only. Please provide position title of interest, resume and cover letter)

Salem Communications is an Equal Opportunity employer

FIGURE 7.6
A job ad for a promotions coordinator gives an idea of the qualifications needed to do the job. Courtesy of All Access Music Group, Inc.

Not all stations employ a full-time promotion director. But most stations designate someone to handle promotional responsibilities. At small outlets, the program director (PD) or even the general manager (GM) assumes promotional chores. Larger stations and station clusters with bigger operating budgets typically hire an individual or individuals to work exclusively in the area of promotion. "At major-market stations, you'll find a promotion department that includes a director and possibly assistants. In middle-sized markets, such as ours, the promotion responsibility is often designated to someone already involved in programming," says Bob Lima. Overall, the economy dictates the amount of promotion positions available. When asked if today's job market is robust, Foster says, "No, budget realities have limited the growth of this particular segment inside of the radio stations."

Observes Ed Shane: "Some promotion managers consider themselves 'marketing directors.' There are two levels of job responsibility for promotion people. Some are glorified 'banner hangers,' who make sure the grunt work is done at a station promotion or a live broadcast. Others are true department heads who exhibit leadership and vision within their operations."

Indeed the promotion director's responsibilities are manifold. Essential to the position are a knowledge and understanding of the station's audience. A background in research is important, contends Grube. "Before you can initiate any kind of promotion you must know something about who you're trying to reach. This requires an ability to interpret various research data that you gather through in-house survey efforts or from outside audience research companies. You don't give away beach balls to 50-year-old men.

Ideas must be confined to the cell group you're trying to attract." Agreeing with Grube, Foster asserts knowing the radio station's audience is an essential part of the job. "They are the verb to the program director's noun. They are in charge of activating the vision and communicating with the station's P1 listeners (brand warriors)," says Foster about the relationship between the listeners and the promotion director.

Writing and conceptual skills are vital to the job of promotion dirvector, says veteran radio executive Charlie Morriss:

> You prepare an awful lot of copy of all types. One moment you're composing press releases about programming changes, and the next you're writing a 30-second promo about the station's expanded news coverage or upcoming remote broadcast from a local mall. Knowledge of English grammar is a must. Bad writing reflects negatively on the station. The job also demands imagination and creativity. You have to be able to come up with an idea and bring it to fruition.

tactics: promotions

A Promotions Report from Shane Media

PROMOTIONAL PITFALLS

If you don't consider every detail when putting a promotion together, expect headaches. Here are common promotion mistakes encountered by the Promotion Marketing Association:

Contradiction between the selling copy and the official rules.

If your promo copy says "win a trip anywhere in America," and the rules say "continental U.S.," you're in trouble when the winner opts for Hawaii.

The photo or illustration of the prize doesn't match the prize exactly.

In a printed ad or Web promotion page, show the prize you intend to give away. Even a change of color (especially on a car) can cause a problem when the winner comes to claim the prize.

Expenses are not explained.

If you say "all expenses paid," the winner may expect a new wardrobe or to have the pets boarded while they take the prize trip. Name specific expenses you'll cover or set a dollar limit to avoid ambiguity.

Over-estimating the value of a prize.

Whatever you pay for the prize, there's always the possibility that the winner could get it cheaper. Airfare's a good example. A cross country trip at $3,000 could be had for $2,000 and the consumer might demand full value. Report a $3,000 prize to the I.R.S. and the winner claims $2,000, there's more trouble. Use a phrase like "full retail value."

Using descriptive words without knowing the established meanings.

"Luxury" and "deluxe" are travel industry words that set a standard for expectations. Don't give a stay at a "luxury" hotel and book a Day's Inn.

Copy rules from someone else's contest or using last year's rules.

There's always a minor detail that is unique to the situation. Check the law and whether it has changed since the last play of the contest.

Allowing retailers to handle entries without guidance.

A promotional partner needs to be as vigilant about security and abuse as you do. Provide detailed instructions on how to handle entry boxes and forms.

Launching the promotion before you have the prizes.

Secure the prize first and you never worry about a product that's behind on production, a retailer who fails to deliver, or a winner who shows up sooner than you expected.

FIGURE 7.7
Cautionary words from a consultant. Courtesy of Shane Media.

Chuck Davis agrees with Morriss and adds that although the promotion person should be able to originate concepts, a certain number of ideas come from the trades and other stations. "When this is the case, and it often is, you have to know how to adapt an idea to suit your own station. Of course, the promotion must reflect your location. Lifestyles vary almost by region. A promotion that's successful at a station in Louisiana may bear no relevance to a station with a similar format in Michigan. On the other hand, with some adjustments, it may work as effectively there. The creativity in this example exists in the adaptation."

Foster says the job of the promotion director has changed. "It has morphed. The 'old school' promotion directors used to seek out opportunities and partnerships that allowed stations to promote their brand. However, with the complexity of today's marketplace this position has become more of a facilitator. We need to get back to being proactive and not reactive with this position."

Promotion directors must be versatile. A familiarity with graphic art is generally necessary, insofar as the promotion director will be involved in developing station logos and image IDs for advertising in the print media, on billboards, on social media, and websites. The promotion department also participates in the design and preparation of visuals for the sales area.

The promotion director's job should include an extreme comfort level with social media and how it is used to enhance engagement with the audience. Social media is the province of the promotion director because it extends the engagement of the station brand across new media platforms. Facebook creates conversation and connection between the station and its listeners, building excitement for a contest. Twitter allows instant updates on breaking news, contests, and promotional events.

The acquisition of prize materials through direct purchase and trades is another duty of the promotion person, who also may be called on to help coordinate sales coop arrangements. "You work closely with the sales manager to arrange tie-ins with sponsors and station promotions," contends Morriss.

Like other radio station department heads, it is the promotion director's responsibility to ensure that the rules and regulations established by the FCC, relevant to the promotions area, are observed. This will be discussed later in the chapter, in the section "Promotions and the FCC."

Of course, it is important that a promotion director maintains a high level of communication with other station personnel, particularly the program director and sales manager, who are almost always an integral part of a promotion's execution and implementation. Everyone should be in the know about contests and promotions. Possessing the ability to work collaboratively with colleagues is another required skill in this position. "You must work well with a team but still be able to lead the station towards events and opportunities that will benefit the brand," asserts Foster.

TYPES OF PROMOTIONS

There are two primary categories of station promotions: on-air and off-air. The on-air category will be examined first since it is the most prevalent form of radio promotion. Broadcasters already possess the best possible vehicle to reach listeners, and so it should come as no surprise that on-air promotion is the most common means of getting the word out on a station. The challenge confronting the promotion director is how to most effectively market the station so as to expand and retain listenership. To this end, a number of promotional

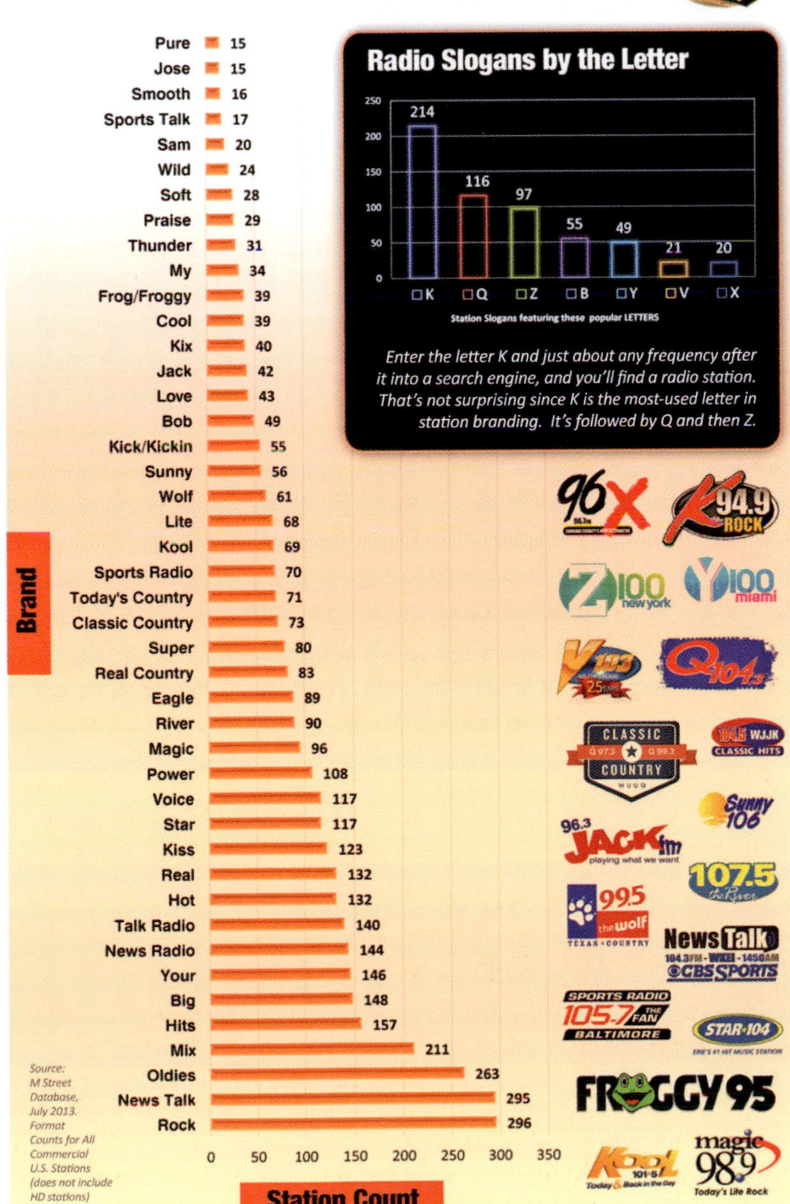
RADIO'S BIGGEST BRANDS
Radio Slogans by the Letter
214 K
116 Q
97 Z
55 B
49 Y
21 V
20 X
Station Slogans featuring these popular LETTERS
Enter the letter K and just about any frequency after it into a search engine, and you'll find a radio station. That's not surprising since K is the most-used letter in station branding. It's followed by Q and then Z.
Brand
Pure 15
Jose 15
Smooth 16
Sports Talk 17
Sam 20
Wild 24
Soft 28
Praise 29
Thunder 31
My 34
Frog/Froggy 39
Cool 39
Kix 40
Jack 42
Love 43
Bob 49
Kick/Kickin 55
Sunny 56
Wolf 61
Lite 68
Kool 69
Sports Radio 70
Today's Country 71
Classic Country 73
Super 80
Real Country 83
Eagle 89
River 90
Magic 96
Power 108
Voice 117
Star 117
Kiss 123
Real 132
Hot 132
Talk Radio 140
News Radio 144
Your 146
Big 148
Hits 157
Mix 211
Oldies 263
News Talk 295
Rock 296
0 50 100 150 200 250 300 350
Station Count
Source: M Street Database, July 2013. Format Counts for All Commercial U.S. Stations (does not include HD stations)

FIGURE 7.8
Slogans are used to brand and market the radio station. Courtesy of *Inside Radio*.

devices are employed, beginning with the most obvious—station call letters. "The value of a good set of call letters is inestimable," says former station manager Richard Bremkamp, Jr. "A good example is the call letters of a station I once managed which have long been associated with the term 'rich' and all that it implies: 'Hartford's Rich Music Station—WRCH.'"

Call letters convey the personality of a station. For instance, try connecting these call letters with a format: WHOG, WNWS, WEZI, WODS, WJZZ, WIND, and WHTS. If you guessed Country, News, Easy Listening, Oldies, Jazz, Talk, and Hits, you were correct. The preceding call letters not only identify their radio stations but they convey the nature or content of the programming offered.

Larry Miller adds:

> Anything that can be made to spell "KISS" is always a favorite with listeners, starting with a KISS station in the Northwest back in the 1950s. Other similar calls include "Magic" for a soft AC, "Zoo" for a wild and crazy CHR or Hot AC, or "Rock" as in K-Rock. In Hawaii, calls that spell Hawaiian words have always been popular, such as K-POI. In the early 1970s, the ABC group of O&O FMs changed call letters to reflect "hip" or local culture with calls like KLOS in LA or KSFX in San Francisco or WRIF in Detroit or WPLJ (white port and lemon juice) in New York.

When stations do not possess call letters that create instant recognition, they often couple their frequency with a call letter or two, such as JB-105 (WPJB-FM 105) or KISS-108 (WXKS-FM 108). This also improves the retention factor. Slogans are frequently a part of the on-air ID. "Music country—WSOC-FM, Charlotte," "A touch of class—WTEB-FM, New Bern," and "Texas best rock—KTXQ-FM, Fort Worth" are some examples. Slogans exemplify a station's image. When effective, they capture the mood and flavor of the station and leave a

FIGURE 7.9
The slogan, "the Buzz," is used on this station's vehicle. Courtesy of WBTZ.

FIGURE 7.10
The KISS-FM van. Courtesy of SCS Unlimited and KISS-FM.

strong impression in the listener's mind. It is standard programming policy at many stations to announce the station's call letters and even its slogan each time a deejay opens the microphone. This is especially true during ratings sweeps when survey companies ask listeners to identify the stations they tune into. "If your calls stick in the mind of your audience, you've hit a home run. If they don't, you'll go scoreless in the book. You've got to carve them into the listener's gray matter and you start by making IDs and signatures that are as memorable as possible," observes Rick Peters.

Jay Williams, Jr., observes that call letters are being used less and less in the digital age. "Stations identify themselves using their frequencies (92.5) today more than their call letters. This has become the case since the radio dial became digitized. The emphasis is now more numerical than alphabetical. Even the alphanumeric approach (Magic 92) has faded in favor of simply stating the station's frequency."

It is a common practice for stations to "bookend"—place call letters and/or frequencies before and after all breaks between music. For example, "WHJJ: Stay tuned for a complete look at local and national news at the top of the hour on WHJJ." Deejays also are told to graft the station call letters onto all bits of information: "92.9 Time," "102.5 Temperature," "102.5 Weather," and so on. There is a rule in radio that call letters can never be overannounced. The logic behind this is clear. The more a station tells its audience what it is tuned to, the more apt it is to remember, especially during diary-based rating periods. In markets measured by the Portable People Meter (PPM), constant repetition of call letters is not necessary because PPM is based on proximity of the meter carrier to a signal, not on call letter recall. Stations in the top 50 markets reduced call letter mentions and other talk elements in response to the technology.

On-air contests are another way to capture and hold the listener's attention. Contests must be easy to understand (are the rules and requirements of the contest easily understood by the listener?) and possess entertainment value (will non-participants be amused even though they are not actually involved?). A contest should engage the interest of all listeners, players and non-players alike.

A contest must be designed to enhance a station's overall sound or format. It must fit in, be compatible. Obviously, a mystery sound contest requiring the broadcast of loud or shrill noises would disrupt the tranquility and continuity of an Easy Listening station and result in tune-out.

Successful contests are timely and relevant to the lifestyle of the station's target audience, says Lima. "A contest should offer prizes that truly connect with the listener. An awareness of the needs, desires, and fantasies of the listener will help guide a station. For example, giving away a refrigerator on a hot hit station would not really captivate the 16-year-old listener. This is obvious, of course. But the point I'm making is that the prizes that are up for grabs should be something the listener really wants to win, or you will have apathy."

FIGURE 7.11
The WTOP news van wrapped with WTOP call letters, frequency, website, and logo. Courtesy of WTOP-FM.

The importance of creativity already has been stated. Contests that attract the most attention often are the ones that challenge the listener's imagination, contends Morriss. "A contest should have style, should attempt to be different. You can give away what is perfectly suitable for your audience, but you can do it in a way that creates excitement and adds zest to the programming. The goal of any promotion is to set you apart from the other guy. Be daring within reason, but be daring."

On-air promotion is used to inform the audience of what a station has to offer: station personalities, programs, and special features and events. Rarely does a quarter-hour pass on any station that does not include a promo that highlights some aspect of programming:

- "Tune in to WXXX's *News at Noon* each weekday for a full hour of . . ."
- "Irv McKenna keeps *Nightalk* in the air midnight to six on the voice of the valley—WXXX. Yes, there's never a dull moment . . ."
- "Every Saturday night WXXX turns the clock back to the 1980s to bring you the best of the golden oldies . . ."
- "Hear the complete weather forecast on the hour and half-hour throughout the day and night on your total service station—WXXX . . ."

On-air promotion is a cost-efficient and effective means of building an audience when done correctly, says John Grube. "There are good on-air promotions and weak or ineffective on-air promotions. The latter can inflict a deep wound, but the former can put a station on the map. As broadcasters, the airtime is there at our disposal, but we sometimes forget just how potent an advertising tool we have."

Marketing expert Andrew Curran points to another area of promotion:

> A stealth promotion might include members of the station database and is something that only the people eligible to win know is going on. For example, a station might announce a name three times a day for a chance to win $1,000. "We'd like to thank John Smith for listening to Classic Rock WXYZ." Then this person would have 20 minutes to call in and win and since only he can win, he's not competing with the whole city to get through on the phone. Plus, he feels important that he's eligible to win a special contest from the station. In the end, of course, a great promotion makes people want to tune in to the station.

VFIGURE 7.12
Billboards catch the attention of commuters. Courtesy of Rock 102.

Radio stations employ off-air promotional techniques to reach people not tuned in. One traditional form is using billboards. Billboards are a popular form of outside promotion. To be effective, they must be both eye-catching and simple. Only so much can be stated on a billboard, since people generally are in a moving vehicle and have only a limited amount of time to absorb a message.

Placement of the billboard also is a key factor. To be effective, billboards must be located where they will reach a station's intended audience. Although an All-News station would avoid the use of a billboard facing a high school, a rock music outlet may prefer the location.

Bus cards are a good way to reach the public. Cities often have hundreds of buses on the streets each day. Billboard companies also use benches and transit shelters to get their client's message across to the population. Outside advertising is an effective and fairly cost-efficient way to promote a radio station, although certain billboards at heavy traffic locations can be extremely expensive to lease.

Newspapers are used by stations to reach and target a newspaper's reading demographic. In large metro areas, alternative newspapers, such as the *Boston Phoenix*, are very effective in delivering certain listening cells. The *Phoenix* enjoys one of the largest readerships of any independent press in the country. Its huge college-age and young professional audience makes it an ideal promotional medium for stations after those particular demographics. Although the readership of the more conventional newspapers traditionally is low among young people, it is high in older adults, making the mainstream publications useful to stations targeting the over-40 crowd.

Newspapers with large circulations provide a great way to reach the population at large. They also can be very costly, although some stations are able to trade airtime for print space. Newspaper ads must be large enough to stand out and overcome the sea of advertisements that often share the same page.

FIGURE 17.13A
A WTOP bus-back advertisement with DC Metro. Courtesy of WTOP-FM.

FIGURE 17.13B
Close-up of the advertisement.

Television is a costly but effective promotional tool for radio. A primary advantage that television offers is the chance to target the audience that the station is after. An enormous amount of information is available pertaining to television viewership. Thus, a station that wants to reach the 18–24-year-olds is able to ascertain the programs and features that best draw that particular cell.

The costs of producing or acquiring ready-made promos for television can run high, but most radio broadcasters value the opportunity to actually show the public what they can hear when they tune to their station. WBZ-AM in Boston used local television extensively to promote its former morning personality

FIGURE 7.14
A station showcases its on-air talent. Courtesy of WIZN.

FIGURE 7.15
Boston Herald Radio newspaper ad. Courtesy of Herald Media, Inc.

Dave Maynard and its current sunrise news team. Ratings for the station have been consistently high, and management points to their television promotion as a contributing factor.

The Pew Research Center found that by 2013, 85% of Americans had access to the Internet. Accordingly, it is no surprise that the Internet is one of the most frequent means of off-air promotion for stations in the 2010s. Listeners expect radio stations to have websites that contain all types of information such as bios and photos of the on-air staff, contest rules, links to social media such as Facebook and Twitter so that listeners can follow their favorite radio stations via new media technologies and their smartphones. *Inside Radio* reported in 2013:

> In addition to a significant on-air push, clients increasingly expect stations to promote appearances on Facebook, Twitter, and via their email database. But for stations doing dozens of appearances a week, that's not always feasible so some clients negotiate social media up front. Appearance recaps, including photos, are also seen as essential. So is effective communication between the account executive, the promotion department and the talent. Some agencies set up pre-appearance conference calls. Others dispatch an event coordinator to the store to work with the station team.

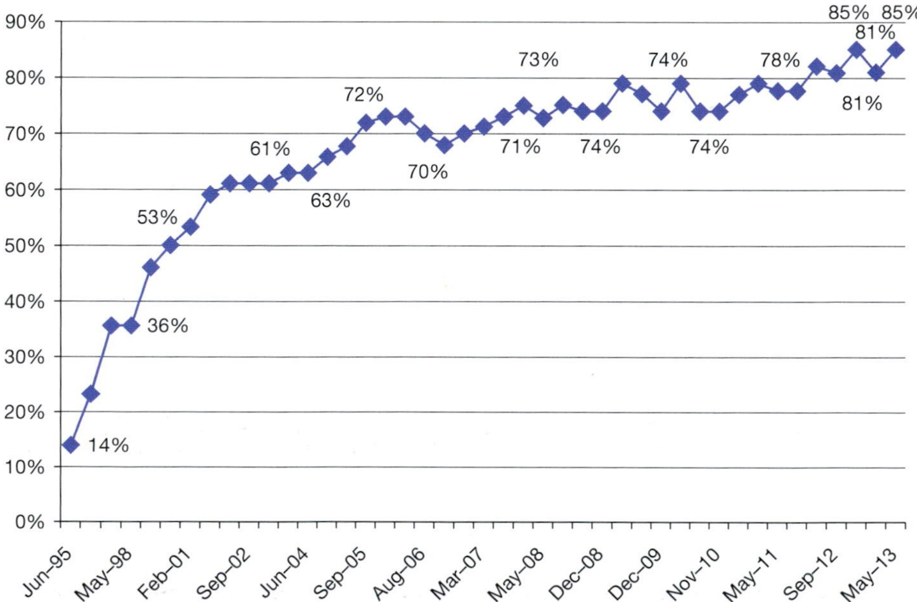

FIGURE 7.16
Internet adoption is high. Radio stations must utilize the Internet to communicate with listeners. Courtesy of the Pew Internet & American Life Project Surveys.

Mix 94.1 Canton's Best Mix! Think pink!

MIX 94.1 | FAN CLUB | ON-AIR | CONTESTS | EVENTS | DEALS | MIX 411 | WEATHER | LISTEN LIVE

Like 0

SAVE THE DATES ...
Mix 94.1's special dates, special activities, special programming!
Mark your calendars!

Join DeLuca for the Grand Opening Celebration of the newest Romeo's Pizza Location at 4887 Portage Street NW, Canton 44708!

Chow down with DeLuca from 2pm-4pm and don't miss your chance to win tickets to The Factory of Terror, The Pro Football Hall of Fame, and the Cavaliers Vs. Bobcats at the Canton Civic Center. Plus, a chance to win free pizza for a year! And, Romeo's will be having a grand opening special exclusively on Saturday. Get a large, one topping, carry out pizzas for only $10! So join us for the grand opening celebration at Romeo's Pizza this Saturday, October 4th at 4887 Portage St. NW in Canton!

News-Talk 1480 WHBC Supports Mercy Service League's Harvest Ball 2013! Saturday, October 12th. Benefit: Mercy Dental Services and General Practice Residency Endowment. Click through for details.

News-Talk 1480 WHBC & Mix 94.1 Supports Making Strides Against Breast Cancer Walk. 10am Sunday, October 27th, Canton McKinley High School. Join Mix 94.1's Kayleigh Kriss and celebrate people who have battled breast cancer, increase awareness about the disease and raise money for the American Cancer Society to save more lives! Click through for details and registration.

News-Talk 1480 WHBC & Mix 94.1 @ Light Up Downtown! Thursday, December 5th, 5:30pm-8:30pm, Central Plaza South and Downtown Canton. Take a magical journey with Christopher Pop-In-Kins, Santa's Official Children's Elf, as he pops in again this year. All of your favorite holiday characters will visit from wonderful winter wonderlands and through smiles, laughs and song, encourage everyone to enjoy the heart of the holiday. The entire News-Talk 1480 WHBC and Mix 94.1 family will be on hand with treats and a meet and greet!

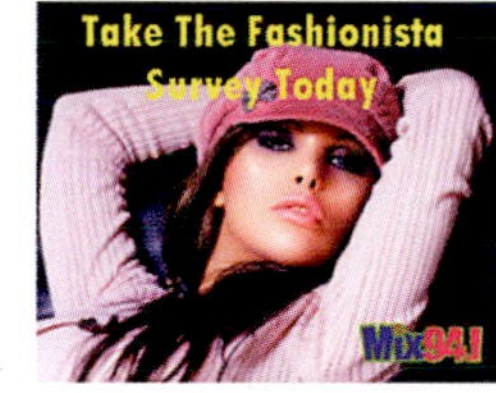

Mix 94.1 ON DEMAND

TWITTER

FACEBOOK

TEXT

CONTACT US

STUDIO LINE

AUDIO VAULT

LISTEN LIVE

FIGURE 7.17
Mix 94.1 uses its Web page to promote the station using Facebook, Twitter, texting via smartphones, and other new media technologies. Courtesy of NextMedia Group, Inc.

BUILD A RADIO WEBSITE THAT GETS RESULTS

Glenn Halbrooks

A radio website should include more than a station's telephone number and stock photos of recording artists. Strengthen your radio station's brand by connecting with your audience in ways that aren't possible over the airwaves and track your results using the latest web analytics tools.

1. Give Your Radio Website a Local Look

As more radio stations switch from local in-studio programming to syndicated shows, it's easy for a station to appear generic—on-air and online. Design your radio website to reflect your community by including backgrounds, banners and photos showing familiar landmarks. Even if your station hasn't produced any memorable on-air radio personalities, it will appear that your station is a bedrock of your city and not just a station from anywhere, U.S.

2. Use Local News to Keep Your Radio Website Fresh

Even the most loyal on-air listeners need a reason to keep coming back to your website. Use local news to keep your site looking fresh every time someone clicks on it. If your station doesn't produce news on its own, form a partnership with a local television station or newspaper to post their stories on your site. Beyond traditional news, listing area gas prices or movie times also creates local content that will keep people interested.

3. Strengthen Your Identity with Music Industry News

The on-air radio station format needs to be reflected on your website. Beyond your logo and slogan, strengthen your brand through music industry news. These tidbits can be promoted by your announcers on the air to drive people to the site—"Wait till you see Cher's latest revealing outfit—we have photos on our website that you have to see!"

4. Post Your Playlist

Since the day the first song was played on radio, a listener has asked, "I wonder what's the name of that song and who sings it?" You can answer those questions by having a constantly updated playlist on your site. The software you choose can let users hear the song again online, add it to their personal playlist or even buy it.

5. Create a Listeners' Club

Everyone likes to feel like a VIP. By creating a listeners' club on your website, you build loyalty among your audience members while making them feel special. Your on-air announcers should direct people to your site, where they fill out a club form to get discounts, tickets and other offers through their email. The questions you ask on the form can give you instant research—like the hometown, age and gender of your listeners, and their favorite music artists, all for free.

6. Turn Listeners into Winners through Contests

Radio contests have been a staple at most stations for decades. Whether you give away prizes on the air or online, you should require people to use your site to sign up. That keeps your staff from having to sort through letters and postcards or taking information over the phone. As with listeners' clubs, you can design an online sign-up form to get research information—like what time of day a person listens to your station, who's their favorite announcer and which songs they wish you'd play.

7. Allow Your Audience to Listen Online

In years past, office workers would have had to put a radio on their desk to hear you while on the job. By allowing your audience to listen through your site, you keep them connected anywhere they have Internet service. While they have your site pulled up to hear the music, hopefully they'll also click around to check out your other content.

8. Interact through Social Media and Polls

Social media platforms like Facebook and Twitter give your audience a way to talk about your station. Make sure to display the latest posts on your website so that you can capitalize on the buzz happening on your Facebook and Twitter pages. This provides another opportunity for on-air promotion of your site—"What did you think of the *American Idol* finale—post your comments and read what others are saying. Go to our site to get the links!" A website poll can achieve the same goal of interaction —"The latest Lady Gaga song? Smash or trash? Go to our site to tell us!"

9. Add Apps for Listeners on the Go

Smartphone apps are quickly becoming a must for most media websites. Make sure you don't turn away your listeners by failing to offer them. When your audience downloads an app for their iPhone, Android, BlackBerry, or other mobile device by going to your website, you don't lose them when they're away from their radio. Even if you can't offer specific apps, designing a mobile site that works on all phones is another option. It gives users a stripped down, easy to read site for their small screen size.

10. Connect with Your Community

You already know that the most successful radio stations do more than play music from a studio, they put their people out into the community to become a vibrant part of listeners' lives. Your radio website can highlight your efforts around town. Publish a photo gallery from a concert, post a sign-up form for a charity walk, or just embed YouTube videos of your crew doing something crazy with your listeners during an outstanding radio remote. Reinforce your community commitment by making sure it's showcased on your site.

11. Offer Advertisers New Ways to Reach Their Customers

Building a more loyal audience is great, but creating new opportunities for your advertisers is just as important. By using your site, they can move beyond 15- or 30-second audio-only commercials. Your sales department can create half-price deals, photo galleries of cars for sale, or video tours of clothing boutiques. Now your advertising clients aren't limited to sound only—if you take time to brainstorm how to use your website to bring them better results.

For decades, radio stations have strived to avoid static on the air. Today, you also want to avoid a static radio website so even if your listeners have infinite music choices, they pick your station as their favorite.

Stations give away thousands of items displaying station call letters and logos annually. Among the most common promotional items handed out by stations are posters, T-shirts, calendars, key chains, coffee mugs, music hit lists, book covers, pens, and car litter bags. The list is vast.

Plastic card promotions have done well for many stations. Holders are entitled to a variety of benefits, including discounts at various stores and valuable prizes. The bearer is told to listen to the station for information as to where to use the card. In addition, holders are eligible for special on-air drawings.

Another particularly effective way to increase a station's visibility is to sponsor special activities, such as fairs, sporting events, and theme dances, and to participate in parades and concerts. Hartford's Big Band station, WRCQ-AM, has received significant attention by presenting an annual music festival that has attracted more than 25,000 spectators each year, plus the notice of other media, including television and newspapers.

Personal appearances by station personalities and interaction with listeners by the radio personalities are always effective means to reach listeners while utilizing forms of off-air promotion. Remote broadcasts from malls, beaches, and the like also aid in getting the word of the station out to the public.

FIGURE 7.18
WTOP advertises at Nats Park during a Washington Nationals baseball game. Courtesy of WTOP-FM.

FIGURE 7.19
WTOP scoreboard advertising at the Verizon Center during a Washington Capitals hockey game. Courtesy of WTOP-FM.

FIGURE 7.20
WTOP served as a media sponsor for the 2013 National Memorial Day Parade. Courtesy of WTOP-FM.

FIGURE 7.21
San Diego's The Mighty 1090 doing a live remote. Courtesy of Broadcast Companies of America.

FIGURE 7.22
Walrus 105.7 FM doing a live remote that gives listeners a chance to win. Courtesy of Broadcast Companies of America.

One last means of marketing a station is offered by Jay Williams, Jr., co-founder of DMR/Interactive and president of Broadcasting Unlimited:

> Promotion and marketing have never been more critical. In the current economy, stations have to do everything they can to draw and hold an audience. Direct marketing through mail and/or by telephone is a very cost-effective way to target an audience and to keep a station in front of radio listeners, especially during rating periods. Telepromoting is becoming more prevalent. Directed or targeted marketing makes sense because stations must be more effective with what they have. The business of radio is changing. Audiences are fragmenting, brand loyalties are eroding. Mass marketing is losing its impact. Person-to-person or individualized marketing delivers tangible results.

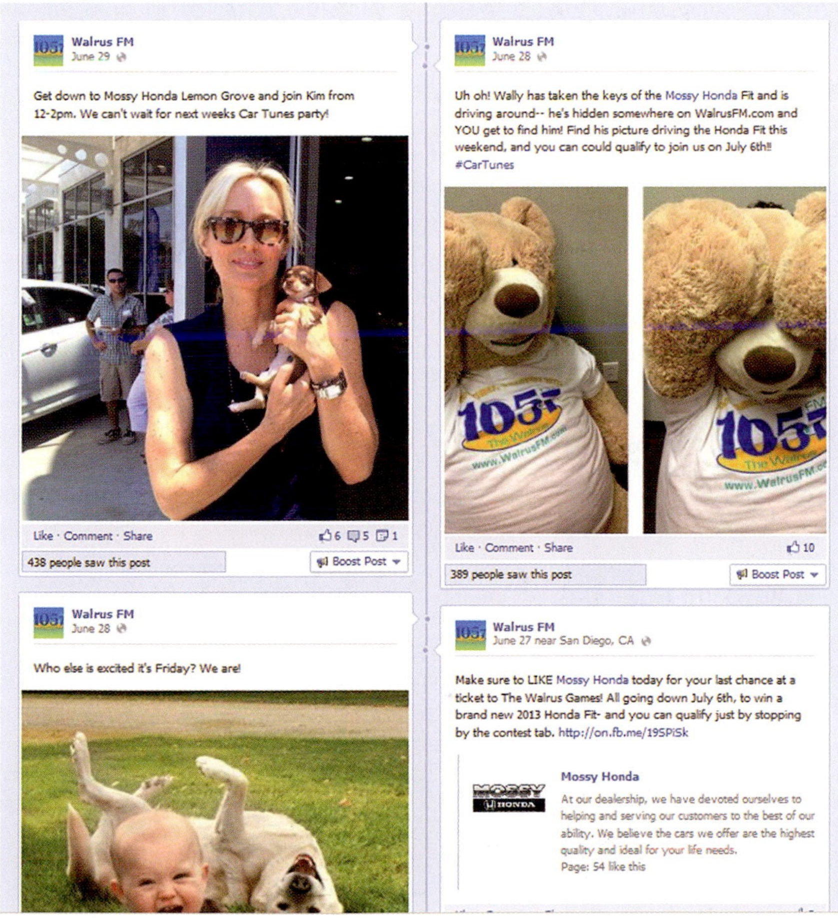

FIGURE 7.23
Social media such as Facebook is used to give listeners an opportunity to win prizes on the radio. Courtesy of Broadcast Companies of America.

Ed Shane concurs with Williams, adding, "Direct marketing is the wave of the one-to-one future. Connections through Facebook, Twitter, and other social media allow stations easy access to listener ideas and feedback. Engagement through social media, when used effectively, will achieve the same result as direct mail, telemarketing, and database management."

FIND A PARADE AND JOIN

Ed Shane

Promotion is an extension of your station's brand experience aimed at your target listener. It gets listeners directly involved with an activity or event that builds audience or enhances the image of your outlet and your advertiser's business.

As a programmer, I first ask the following question about any promotion: What are we trying to achieve? Reduced to the simplest terms, there are three goals:

1. Cume—building audience.
2. Time spent listening—holding onto audience.
3. Image—making the station memorable to the audience.

FIGURE 7.24
Ed Shane.

If the station is not trying to achieve at least one of the three, the promotion has no value.

The next question: Who's the target? The bottom line of any promotion is that it should be in sync with the needs and expectations of the audience. If the promotion doesn't resonate with your station's target listener, there'll be no benefit.

The final question: What's the desired consumer response? Do we want them to listen? (I hope so. Too many promotions fail in this aspect.)

Note that none of this involves how many Twitter followers a station has collected or how many Facebook friends.

The same questions apply to promotions conducted via new media or social media as apply to old fashioned call-in-to-win promotions or live broadcasts from a retail location.

Twitter is a "news channel" that is perfect for calling attention to a new contest or promotion in an engaging, conversational way. Twitter allows for instant updates on contesting and promotional events. Facebook is a "conversation channel" that connects with listeners on what appears to be a personal level. It's also an easy way to get listener feedback on ideas. No social medium should be used on its own to drive a promotion unless it brings the strategy back to the three basic questions—especially the questions about driving new or extended listenership.

The hazard in concentrating too much on social media is that the station doesn't own its Facebook friends or its Twitter followers. Facebook and Twitter do. If they decide to change strategy, they can do what they want with your customers' information.

Too many stations have used social media as a backstop against declining promotion budgets. Consolidation caused radio companies to reduce expenditures to make clusters more profitable. Often the promotion budget was among the first to disappear. This was exacerbated by the recession of 2008–2012, as stations further reduced the amounts spent on outreach advertising and on promotional activities alike. Even bumper stickers, once a mainstay of local promotional efforts, were no longer prolific.

In spite of the reductions in budgets, promotion is vital to radio as it connects with its communities.

If there's no money, find a parade and get in front of it.

Make sure it's a parade your audience wants to join.

Ed Shane, as CEO of Houston-based Shane Media, is a programming and research advisor to radio in markets of all sizes.

PROMOTIONS IN THE DIGITAL ERA

With an 85% adoption rate among Americans, the Internet has had a profound impact on the way radio stations promote themselves in the 2010s. The technological advances that have accompanied the Internet have made some promotional strategies antiquated while other, newer strategies have been found to be very effective. DMR/Interactive's senior vice-president/co-founder Catherine Jung says, "For the most successful radio stations, the Internet has become a visual and interactive element of the brand. Many station sites now offer unique entertaining elements like videos, best-of podcasts, blogs and more." DMR/Interactive's chief executive officer, Tripp Eldredge adds, "It has also provided a powerful way to target current and new listeners. As a result, promotions that simply relied on 'be the nth caller' are giving way to digital registrations with instant-win components and frictionless sharing. That said, there continues to be a surprising amount of stations that have not evolved to the listener-centric, interactive approach. They tend to view the Internet as simply an extension to their transmitters."

Relying on the Internet and social media technologies has required stations to modify organizational structures at both single stations and clustered stations to technologically support the new promotional approaches. DMR's chief operating officer, Andrew Curran notes:

> Having unsuccessfully experimented with adding "webmaster" to the station engineer's duties, most have now evolved into a two-level model. The infrastructure and technology is developed and deployed via a corporate group. They set standards, evaluate technology, and implement the tools and best practices. At the local station level, there are usually a few people designated as the "digital team" whose primary responsibilities span from sales to programming to marketing. In a few large-operator

> cases, it's a completely separate group operating relatively separately from the local station.

Many social media promotions are used by stations to communicate with listeners effectively. Jung asserts, "Many have experimented with rewards programs, song research panels, text messaging, and mobile apps to extend their brands into these areas." Determining successful and effective Internet promotion strategies can be challenging due to the uniqueness of the technology. "In fact," Eldredge says, "the challenge is defining and measuring success. Traditionally, the definition is related to ratings increases and revenue growth. Because there are now so many more variables, operators have a much more difficult time distilling out what components or tools are effective." Curran says, "We guide clients with an overall philosophy of identifying and engaging across many touch points with who matters most to your format and station brand. With that in mind, technologies such as social media platforms and apps that provide fans with the opportunity to create and share content along with the ability to connect with each other fuel the most engagement and sharing activity." Jung adds:

> Several clients of ours used the shared-participation gaming to create a bridge between traditional promotion and the social sphere. For example, the game of concentration was used to create a groundswell of participation and connection across social media, digital, and on-air. The shared participation of helping each other with the game created a deep and real connection between the participating listeners. The powerful outcome was that these listeners all credited the station with helping them create these amazing new relationships.

Smartphones such as iPhones, Androids, and BlackBerries are in the hands of nearly every consumer. It's important for radio stations to determine how to effectively target these consumers because not all demographics use all features of smartphones. For example, Jung observes, "Part of the answer here depends on the format. For youthful formats like CHR and Hip Hop, texting and mobile is a large part of their focus with promotions. It's a smaller percentage, but growing for most other formats. Like everything, it's important to know your key listeners and how they engage with smartphones. What they would like to see. Now more than ever, it's important to be listener-centric." For users of smartphones and social media technologies, the simple act of sharing content is important to consumers. "On another level, many listeners who were not participating enjoyed watching the content and sharing created by those that were. This organic content generation provided a unique asset for the station and its listener community resulting in record-level sharing across the social networks, great content that could be repurposed on the air, and record ratings for the station," Curran noted.

As communication has become so much more interactive, with the listener/consumer (the old broadcasting, top-down model) increasingly becoming a participant/content provider, radio will best adapt to this change by empowering the listeners. Eldredge suggests:

> The more that station brands can empower the listeners to create, express, and share with other listeners, the more powerful the station brands can become. When listeners start to connect with other listeners through helping, creating, sharing, etc., they credit the station for that relationship-building. Stations that help listeners build relationships and enhance the relationships they already have will set themselves apart from the old-guard of "we broadcast, you listen." Similarly, programmers and air-talent that deeply understand their core listeners will naturally be able to respond and evolve their products and offerings more effectively. Knowing the life of the core consumer has never been more critical as you decide where to invest your limited time and money.

Employees working in the twenty-first-century radio station promotions department must not only be technologically savvy, but also have a keen understanding of people and their use of technology. Eldredge asserts, "A key skill is being able to know how to deeply understand the listeners, particularly the most important listeners of a station-brand. The ability to know tools and strategies to discover and synthesize listeners' tastes, activities, preferences, sharing patterns, etc. will set you apart because most stations and groups are simply employing tactics without setting a listener-centric strategy." Curran adds, "In addition, promotions teams often work across the cluster, so you have to be able to understand and generate success across multiple formats."

SALES PROMOTION

Promoting a station can be very costly, as much as half a million dollars annually in some metro markets. To help defray the cost of station promotion, advertisers are often recruited. This way both the station and the sponsor stand to benefit. The station gains the financial wherewithal to execute certain promotions that it could not do on its own, and the participating advertiser gains valuable exposure by tying in with special station events. Stations actually can make money and promote themselves simultaneously if a client purchases a substantial spot schedule as part of a promotional package. Says Larry Miller, "An effective promotional campaign should try to include a sales component, in part to help allay the costs of advertising. If it's done right, it will bring in new business for the station."

There are abundant ways to involve advertisers in station promotion efforts. They run the gamut from placing advertisements and coupons on the station's Web page to joining the circus for the day; for example, "WXXX brings the 'Greatest Show on Earth' to town this Friday night, and you go for half price just by mentioning the name of your favorite radio station—WXXX." The ultimate objective of a station/sponsor collaborative is to generate attention in a cost-efficient manner. If a few dollars are made for the station along the way, all the better.

As stated previously, the promotion director also works closely with the station's sales department in the preparation and design of sales promotion materials, which include items such as posters, coverage maps, ratings breakouts, flyers, station profiles, rate cards, and much more.

A challenging economy and increased pressure from media other than radio made advertiser participation in promotion vital. Consultant Ed Shane says he regularly cautions his client stations to make sure advertiser involvement doesn't override the needs of the station. "We often lose 'ownership' of our promotions because our enthusiasm for getting a sponsorship clouds our view of the goals we set out in the first place. Promotions should be a win-win partnership."

BUDGETING PROMOTIONS

Marketing expert Andrew Curran opens this section with his views on the challenges of finding resources to promote a station:

> In my experience, since revenue growth in radio has been relatively flat in recent years, marketing budgets are often the first thing to cut, especially in the third and fourth quarters of the year when a company needs to hit its financial numbers. In addition, it seems that stations seem to get the most marketing money when the ratings are down and instant results need to be delivered to get revenue up. Certainly this makes for some tense campaigns and often—if the promotion is successful and ratings go up—marketing dollars are moved to another station that is in need of help rather than allowing the original station to strengthen its position with additional marketing.

Obviously, cost projections are included in the planning of a promotion. The promotion director's budget may be substantial or all but non-existent. Stations in small markets often have minuscule budgets compared with their giant metro market counterparts. But then again, the need to promote in a one- or two-station market is generally not as great as it is in multistation markets. To a degree, the promotion a station does is commensurate with the level of competition.

A typical promotion at an average-size station may involve the use of newspapers plus additional handout materials, such as stickers, posters, buttons, and an assortment of other items depending on the nature of the promotion. Television and billboards may also be utilized. Each of these items will require an expenditure unless some other provision has been made, such as a trade agreement in which airtime is swapped for goods or ad space.

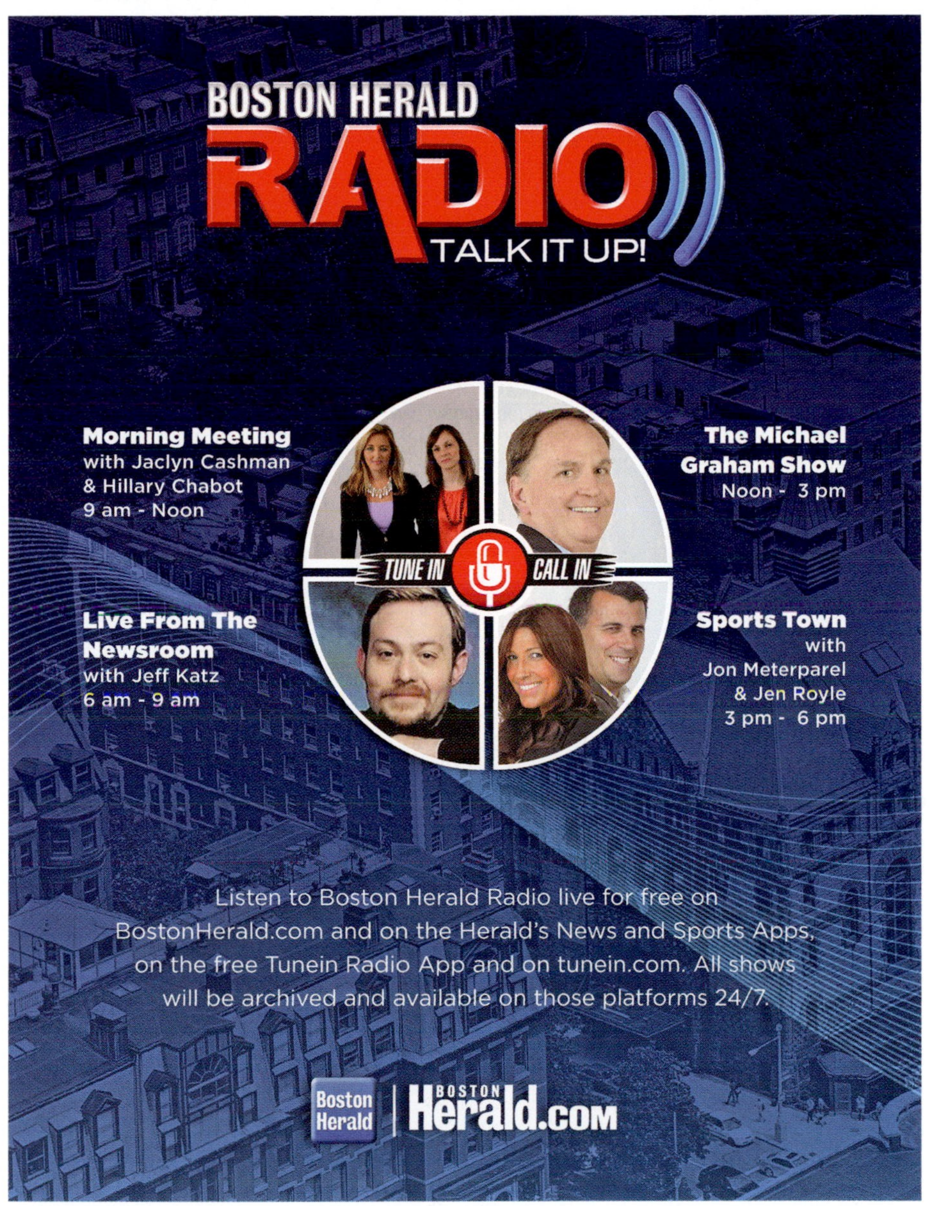

FIGURE 7.25
Stations showcase their on-air talent. Courtesy of Herald Media, Inc.

The cost involved in promoting a contest often constitutes the primary expense. When WASH-FM in Washington, D.C., gave away $1 million, it spent $200,000 to purchase an annuity designed to pay the prize recipient $20,000 a year for 50 years. The station spent nearly an equal amount to promote the big giveaway. Most of the promotional cost resulted from a heavy use of local television. In the early 1980s, KHTZ-FM in Los Angeles spent more than $300,000 on billboards and television to advertise its dream-house giveaway. The total cost of the promotion approached half a million dollars. The price tag of the house was $122,000. Both of these high-priced contests accomplished their goals—increased ratings. In a metro market, one rating point can mean $1 million in ad revenue. "A promotion that contributes to a two- or three-point jump in the ratings is well worth the money spent on it," observes Rick Peters.

The promotion director works with the station manager in establishing the promotion budget. From there, it is the promotion director's job to allocate funds for the various contests and promotions that are run throughout the station's fiscal period. "The idea is to control the budget and not let it control you. Obviously computers have been a big help in this respect," states Marlin R. Taylor, who also contends that large sums of money need not be poured into promotions if a station is on target with its programming.

> In 1983, the Malrite organization came to New York and launched Z-100, a contemporary hit-formatted outlet, moving it from "worst to first" in a matter of months. They did a little advertising and gave away some money. I estimate that their giveaways totaled less dollars than some of their competitors spent on straight advertising. But the station's success was built on three key factors: product, service, and employee incentives. Indeed, they do have a quality product. Second, they are providing a service to their customers or listeners, and, third, the care and feeding of the air staff and support team are obvious at all times. You don't necessarily have to spend a fortune on promotion.

Larry Miller agrees, "A really good promotion director can do effective promotions without spending a lot of money. First, utilize 'on air' promotions; second, trade out for stuff like contest prizes and newspaper advertising. You can do a lot for very little through a combined effort with programming."

Since promotion directors are frequently expected to arrange trade agreements with merchants as a way to defray costs, a familiarity with and understanding of the station's rate structure is necessary. Trading airtime for use in promotions is less popular at highly rated stations that can demand top dollars for spots. Most stations, however, prefer to exchange available airtime for goods and services needed in a promotion, rather than pay cash.

PROMOTIONS AND THE FCC

Although the FCC has dropped most of its rules pertaining to contests and promotions, it does expect that they be conducted with propriety and good judgment. The basic obligation of broadcasters to operate in the public interest remains the primary consideration. Section 73.1216 of the FCC's rules and regulations (as published in the *Code of Federal Regulations*) outlines the dos and don'ts of contest presentations.

Stations are prohibited from running a contest in which contestants are required to pay in order to play. The FCC regards as lottery any contest in which the elements of prize, chance, and consideration exist. In other words, contestants must not have to risk something to win.

Contests must not place participants in any danger or jeopardize property. Awarding prizes to the first five people who successfully scale a treacherous mountain or swim a channel filled with alligators certainly would be construed by the FCC as endangering the lives of those involved. Contestants have been injured and stations held liable more than once. In the case of the station in California that ran a treasure hunt resulting in considerable property damage, it incurred the wrath of the public, town officials, and the FCC. In a more tragic example of poor planning, a listener was killed during a "find the disk jockey" contest. The station was charged with negligence and sustained a substantial fine.

Stations are expected to disclose the material terms of all contests and promotions conducted. These include the following:

- entering procedures;
- eligibility requirements;
- deadlines;
- when or if prizes can be won;
- value of prizes;
- procedure for awarding prizes;
- tie-breaking procedures.

The public must not be misled concerning the nature of prizes. Specifics must be stated. Implying that a large boat is to be awarded when, in fact, a canoe is the actual prize would constitute misrepresentation, as would suggesting that an evening in the Kon Tiki Room of the local Holiday Inn is a great escape weekend to the exotic South Seas.

The FCC also stipulates that any changes in contest rules must be promptly conveyed to the public. It makes clear, too, that any rigging of contests, such as determining winners in advance, is a direct violation of the law and can result in a substantial penalty, or even license revocation.

WHAT TO INCLUDE IN "OFFICIAL RULES"

The official rules are a contract between the station as sponsor of the contest and the participant. There's no one way to draft official rules, but there are certain elements that most legal advisors recommend:

1. Methods of entry, including alternate methods, if necessary to avoid lottery "consideration."
2. Limitations on the number of entries, if applicable.
3. Prohibition of facsimile entries.
4. Method of determining winners.
5. Odds of winning.
6. Eligibility: age, residence, exclusion of employees and/or families of the station, sponsors, and other parties
7. Duration: the beginning and end dates for entry, when game pieces are available and when winner's lists will be available.
8. Limitation on liability.
9. Disclaimer of liability on lost, late, or misdirected mail or electronic entry.
10. "Void where prohibited" clause.
11. Responsibility for taxes on prizes.
12. Legal documents, as needed: Affidavit of eligibility and liability, permission to use name and images in publicity releases.
13. Unclaimed prizes. Not awarded, subject to "second chance" drawing, given to an alternate or runner-up, or other disposition.
14. Reservation of publicity rights.
15. Entries become the property of the station or sponsor.
16. Judges' decisions are final.
17. Disclaimer for printing or typographical errors that assures that no more than the advertised number of prizes will be awarded.
18. Minors clause, if needed, to restrict the game to those over 18.
19. Fraud/malfunction clause to allow station to disqualify anyone for tampering.
20. Availablility of the winner's list.

FIGURE 7.26
Stations are expected to make contest rules clear to the public. Courtesy of Shane Media.

Although the FCC does not require that a station keep a contest file, most do. Maintaining all pertinent contest information, including signed prize receipts and releases by winners, can prevent problems should questions or a conflict arise later.

Stations that award prizes valued at $600 or more are expected by law to file a 1099-MISC form with the IRS. This is done strictly for reporting purposes, and stations incur no tax liability. However, failure to do so puts a station in conflict with the law.

CHAPTER HIGHLIGHTS

1. To keep listeners interested and tuned in, stations actively promote their image and call letters. Small-market stations promote themselves to compete for audience with other forms of media. Major-market stations use promotion to differentiate themselves from competing stations.
2. Radio recognized the value of promotion early and used print media, remote broadcasts, and billboards to inform the public. Later, ratings surveys proved the importance of effective promotions. Today, radio stations use Web pages and social media such as Facebook and Twitter to promote station activities, programming, and contests.
3. Greater competition because of the increasing number of stations and monthly audience surveys means today's stations must promote themselves continually.
4. The most successful (attracting listenership loyalty) promotions involve large cash or merchandise prizes.
5. A successful promotion director possesses knowledge and understanding of the station's audience; a background in research and marketing, writing, and conceptual skills; the ability to adapt existing concepts to a particular station; and a familiarity with graphic art. The promotion director is responsible for acquiring prizes through trade or purchase and for compliance with FCC regulations covering promotions.
6. On-air promotions are the most common method used to retain and expand listenership. Such devices as slogans linked to the call letters and contests are common.
7. To "bookend" call letters means to place them at the beginning and conclusion of each break. To "graft" call letters means to include them with all informational announcements.
8. Contests must have clear rules and must provide entertainment for players and non-players alike. Successful contests are compatible with the station's sound, offer prizes attractive to the target audience, and challenge the listener's imagination in order to win.
9. Off-air promotions are intended to attract new listeners. Popular approaches include billboards, bus cards, newspapers, television, discount cards, giveaway items embossed with call letters or logo, deejay personal appearances, special activity sponsorship, remote broadcasts, direct mail, and telemarketing. Station websites are promotional tools.
10. To offset the sometimes-substantial cost of an off-air promotion, stations often collaborate with sponsors to share both the expenses and the attention gained.

11. FCC regulations governing promotions are contained in Section 73.1216. Basically, stations may not operate lotteries, endanger contestants, rig contests, or mislead listeners as to the nature of the prize.

SUGGESTED FURTHER READING

Bergendorff, F.L., *Broadcast Advertising and Promotion: A Handbook for Students and Professionals*, Hastings House, New York, 1983.

Dickey, L., *The Franchise: Building Radio Brands*, NAB Publications, Washington, D.C., 1994.

Donnelly, W.J., *Planning Media: Strategy and Imagination*, Pearson Education, New York, 1995.

Eastman, S.T., Klein, R.A. and Ferguson, D., *Media Promotion and Marketing for Broadcasting, Cable, and the Internet*, Focal Press, Burlington, MA, 2006.

Gompertz, R., *Promotion and Publicity Handbook for Broadcasters*, Tab Books, Blue Ridge Summit, PA, 1977.

Johnson, A., *The Radio Sponsorship and Promotions Handbook: Creative Ideas for Radio Campaigns*, Saland Publishing, New York, 2007.

Macdonald, J., *The Handbook of Radio Publicity and Promotion*, Tab Books, Blue Ridge Summit, PA, 1970.

Matelsi, M., *Broadcast Programming and Promotion Work Text*, Focal Press, Boston, MA, 1989.

National Association of Broadcasters, *Best of the Best Promotions, III*, NAB Publications, Washington, D.C., 1994.

National Association of Broadcasters, *Casinos, Lotteries, and Contests*, NAB Publications, Washington, D.C., 2007.

Nickels, W., *Marketing Communications and Promotion*, 3rd edition, John Wiley & Sons, New York, 1984.

Peck, W.A., *Radio Promotion Handbook*, Tab Books, Blue Ridge Summit, PA, 1968.

Ramsey, M., *Fresh Air: Marketing Gurus on Radio*, iUniverse, Lincoln, NE, 2005.

Rhoads, B.E., et al. (eds), *Programming and Promotions*, Streamline Press, West Palm Beach, FL, 1995.

Roberts, T.E.F., *Practical Radio Promotions*, Focal Press, Boston, MA, 1992.

Savage, B., *Perry's Broadcast Promotion Sourcebook*, Perry Publications, Oak Ridge, TN, 1982.

Shane, E., *Selling Electronic Media*, Focal Press, Boston, MA, 1999.

Stanley, R.E., *Promotions*, 2nd edition, Prentice Hall, Englewood Cliffs, NJ, 1982.

CHAPTER 8

Traffic and Billing

THE AIR SUPPLY AND PROGRAM LOGS

What was printed here 25 years ago remains a fact today: a station sells airtime—that is its inventory, its product. The volume or size of a given station's inventory depends chiefly on the amount of time it allocates for commercial matter. For example, some stations with Adult Contemporary and Easy Listening formats deliberately restrict or limit commercial loads as a method of enhancing overall sound and fostering a "more music, less talk" image.

A full-time station has more than 10,000 minutes to fill each week. This computes to approximately 3,000 minutes for commercials, based on an 18-minute commercial load ceiling per hour. In the eyes of the sales manager, this means anywhere from 3,000 to 6,000 availabilities or slots—assuming that a station sells 60- and 30-second spot units—in which commercial announcements are inserted.

From the discussion in all the previous chapters, it should be apparent that inventory control and accountability at a radio station are no small jobs. They are, in fact, the primary duties of the person called the traffic manager. And, the position of traffic manager is pivotal enough in a radio station that it has its own professional association, the Traffic Directors Guild of America (TDGA). The guild's mission is "To foster pride in our unique profession, and to promote the contributions we provide to the Radio and Television Broadcasting Industry. The Traffic Directors Guild seeks to enhance our member careers through information, cooperative services and education." It is a non-union organization whose goal is to serve revenue management scheduling professionals, accounts receivable, continuity, operations and business management personnel. The TDGA website also lists employment opportunities for traffic directors.

THE TRAFFIC MANAGER

Vicki Nichols, traffic manager for Emmis Indianapolis, says the traffic manager's responsibility is, in its simplest form, "to manage inventory in a way that maximizes revenue." A daily log is prepared by the traffic manager (also referred to as the traffic director). This document is at once a schedule of programming elements (commercials, features, and public service announcements [PSAs]) to be aired and a record of what was actually aired. It serves to inform the on-air operator of what to broadcast and at what time, and it provides a record for, among other things, billing purposes.

Let us examine the process involved in logging a commercial for broadcast beginning at the point at which the salesperson writes an order for a spot schedule.

1. The salesperson writes an order and returns it to the station.
2. The sales manager then checks and approves the order.
3. The sales secretary enters the order into the computer software.
4. Copies of the formalized order are distributed to the traffic manager, sales manager, billing, salesperson, and client and/or accessed by these individuals via the station's software database.
5. The order is placed in the traffic scheduling book or entered into the computer for posting to the log by the traffic manager using highly specialized programming software.
6. The order is logged, commencing on the start date according to the stipulations of the buy.

FIGURE 8.1
Here's how station program logs look when printed to paper. These days the commercial info generally goes electronically to the air studio automation. Courtesy of RadioTraffic.com

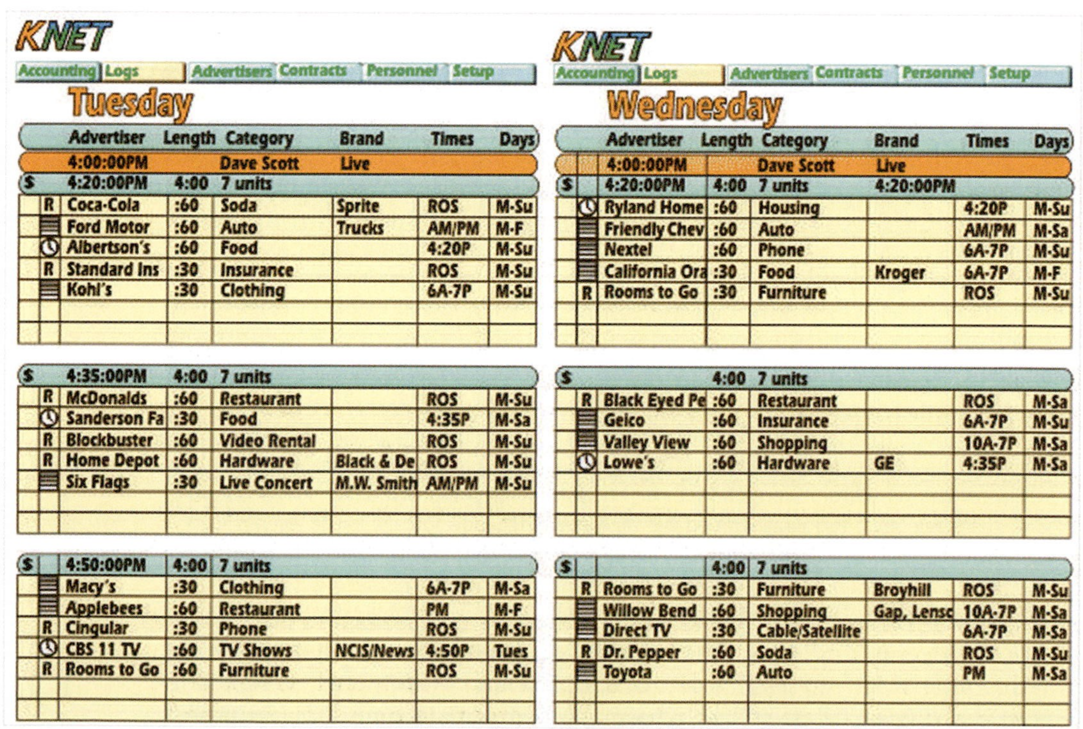

KNET

Accounting | Logs | Advertisers | Contracts | Personnel | Setup

Tuesday

	Advertiser	Length	Category	Brand	Times	Days
	4:00:00PM		Dave Scott	Live		
$	4:20:00PM	4:00	7 units			
R	Coca-Cola	:60	Soda	Sprite	ROS	M-Su
	Ford Motor	:60	Auto	Trucks	AM/PM	M-F
	Albertson's	:60	Food		4:20P	M-Su
R	Standard Ins	:30	Insurance		ROS	M-Su
	Kohl's	:30	Clothing		6A-7P	M-Su
$	4:35:00PM	4:00	7 units			
R	McDonalds	:60	Restaurant		ROS	M-Su
	Sanderson Fa	:30	Food		4:35P	M-Sa
R	Blockbuster	:60	Video Rental		ROS	M-Su
R	Home Depot	:60	Hardware	Black & De	ROS	M-Su
	Six Flags	:30	Live Concert	M.W. Smith	AM/PM	M-Su
$	4:50:00PM	4:00	7 units			
	Macy's	:30	Clothing		6A-7P	M-Sa
	Applebees	:60	Restaurant		PM	M-F
R	Cingular	:30	Phone		ROS	M-Su
	CBS 11 TV	:60	TV Shows	NCIS/News	4:50P	Tues
R	Rooms to Go	:60	Furniture		ROS	M-Su

KNET

Accounting | Logs | Advertisers | Contracts | Personnel | Setup

Wednesday

	Advertiser	Length	Category	Brand	Times	Days
	4:00:00PM		Dave Scott	Live		
$	4:20:00PM	4:00	7 units	4:20:00PM		
	Ryland Home	:60	Housing		4:20P	M-Su
	Friendly Chev	:60	Auto		AM/PM	M-Sa
	Nextel	:60	Phone		6A-7P	M-Su
	California Ora	:30	Food	Kroger	6A-7P	M-F
R	Rooms to Go	:30	Furniture		ROS	M-Su
$		4:00	7 units			
R	Black Eyed Pe	:60	Restaurant		ROS	M-Sa
	Geico	:60	Insurance		6A-7P	M-Su
	Valley View	:60	Shopping		10A-7P	M-Sa
	Lowe's	:60	Hardware	GE	4:35P	M-Sa
$		4:00	7 units			
R	Rooms to Go	:30	Furniture	Broyhill	ROS	M-Su
	Willow Bend	:60	Shopping	Gap, Lensc	10A-7P	M-Sa
	Direct TV	:30	Cable/Satellite		6A-7P	M-Sa
R	Dr. Pepper	:60	Soda		ROS	M-Su
	Toyota	:60	Auto		PM	M-Sa

FIGURE 8.2
Marketron logo. Courtesy of Marketron.

Although the preceding is both a simplification and generalization of the actual process, it does convey the basic idea. Keep in mind that not all stations operate in exactly the same manner. The actual method for preparing a log will differ also from station to station depending on whether it is done manually or by computer and whether the station is in a large or a small market. Only an extremely small number of stations still use the manual system to generate logs and, of those who still create them manually, they often simplify the process by preparing a master or semi-permanent log containing fixed program elements and even long-term advertisers. Short-term sponsors and other changes will be entered on an ongoing basis. This method significantly reduces the time involved. Once the log is prepared, it is then copied and distributed. Again, to emphasize, due to technological advancements with computers and software, manually creating traffic logs is an antiquated system and is very rarely used in the early 2010s. Rather, station program logs are computer-generated and more streamlined for the broadcast day. There are a number of companies available to broadcasters who offer traffic and billing software such as Marketron.

Dave Scott, president and CEO of RadioTraffic.com, a leading provider of traffic and billing software, says "RadioTraffic.com has salespeople who call virtually every radio station on a regular schedule. Our research shows that computers and traffic and billing software are ubiquitous, probably over 99% penetration. A very, very small number generate a log in Excel or Word but we have not heard of any stations trying to log with QuickBooks or similar accounting software. Those stations would be the very small listener-supported outlets such as public radio, Christian, or foreign language stations." Emily Stephens, director of marketing at Marketron, one of the nation's leading traffic and billing software companies, agrees with Scott saying, "We would estimate that 1–2 % of stations may manually manage scheduling ads and billing. The availability of low-cost, specialized software has influenced this practice."

The vast majority of stations use highly sophisticated computer software. There are many benefits to using computer software to schedule commercial traffic and generate billing invoices. Particularly, Scott says the following are the benefits:

1. Sending invoices to advertisers is a business necessity. Many advertisers require bills from broadcasters to show specific dates and times each ad aired (like long distance phone bills used to show).
2. Equally important is the need to accurately schedule the commercials that each advertiser has purchased within the days and dayparts specified within the orders. Scheduling involves many placement factors such as separating competing products and merchants an appropriate time span away from

each other, not airing commercials for one advertiser at the same time on following days nor multiple ads too close together

3. In network shows, the commercial breaks are a specific length (that varies in different programs) and the ads aired must match the network time available very closely. If a station has not sold the required commercial time, it must fill with promos or public service.
4. Traffic and billing software accomplishes that easily and automatically.

It is the traffic manager's responsibility to see that an order is logged as specified and that each client is treated fairly and equitably. A sponsor who purchases two spots, five days a week, during morning drivetime, can expect to receive good rotation for maximum reach. It is up to the traffic manager to schedule the client's commercials in as many quarter-hour segments of the daypart as possible. The effectiveness of a spot schedule is reduced if the spots are logged in the same quarter-hour each day. If a spot is logged at 6:45 am daily, it is only reaching those people tuned at that hour each day. However, if on one day it is logged at 7:15 am and then at 8:45 am on another, and so on, it is reaching a different audience each day. It also would be unfair to the advertiser who purchased drivetime to have spots logged only prior to 7:00 am, the beginning of the prime audience period. Most stations have a rotation chart that indicates when commercial breaks will be taken so that the traffic software can schedule the commercials.

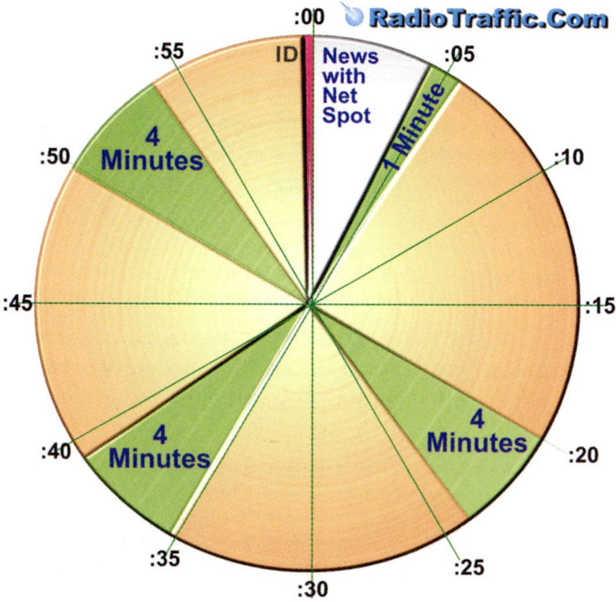

FIGURE 8.3
Designated placement of commercials in four-minute availabilities.
Courtesy of RadioTraffic.com.

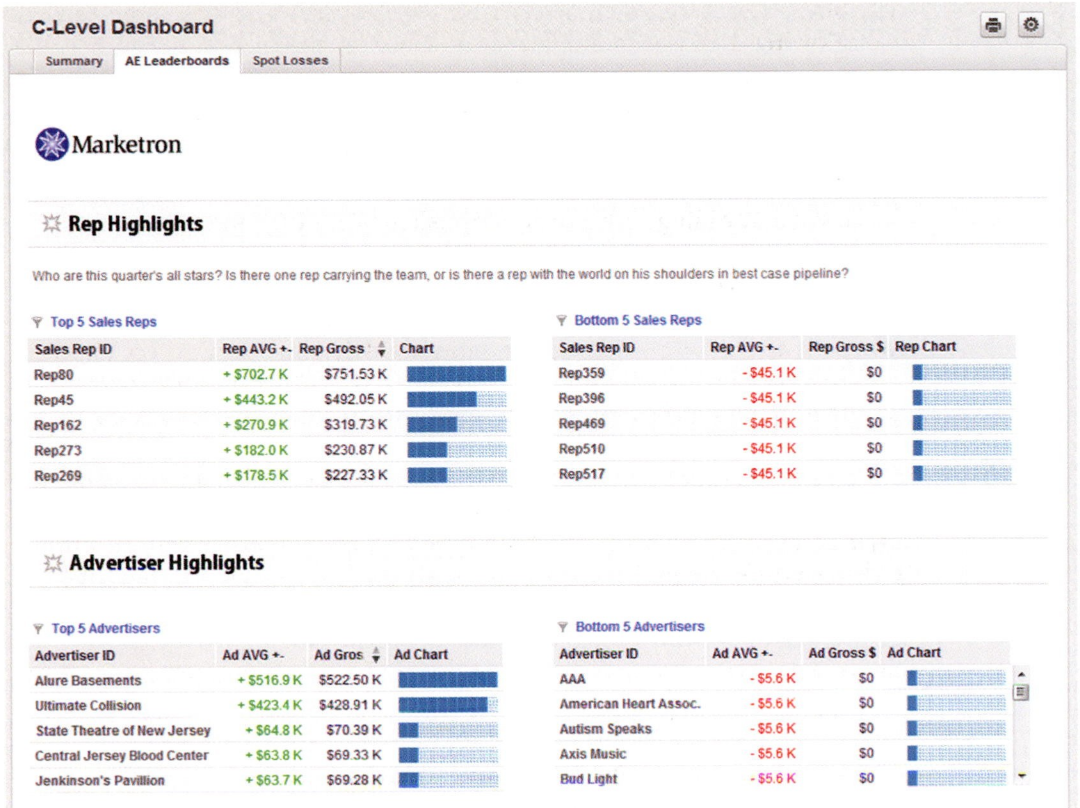

FIGURE 8.4
Insight is Marketron's reporting service and allows for customizable ad-hoc reporting. This screenshot is of a C-level dashboard that was customized to the executive's specific needs. Dashboards can include performance reports, pacing to financial goals, and trends at the station and market level. Courtesy of Marketron.

Using the traffic and billing software, the traffic manager maintains a record of when a client's spots are aired to help ensure effective rotation. Another concern of the traffic manager is to keep adequate space between accounts of a competitive nature. Running two restaurants back-to-back or within the same spot set would likely result in having to reschedule both at different times at no cost to the client. In addition to using the traffic software, the traffic manager designates certain times within the hour in which commercial breaks will occur.

It also falls within the traffic manager's purview to make sure that copy and the production of the commercial(s) are in on time. Most stations have a policy requiring that commercial material be on hand at least 48 hours before it is scheduled for broadcast. Traffic manager Carol Bates of Providence, Rhode Island, says that getting copy before the air date can be a problem. "It is not unusual to get a commercial or copy a half-hour before it is due to air. We ask that copy be in well in advance, but sometimes it's a matter of minutes.

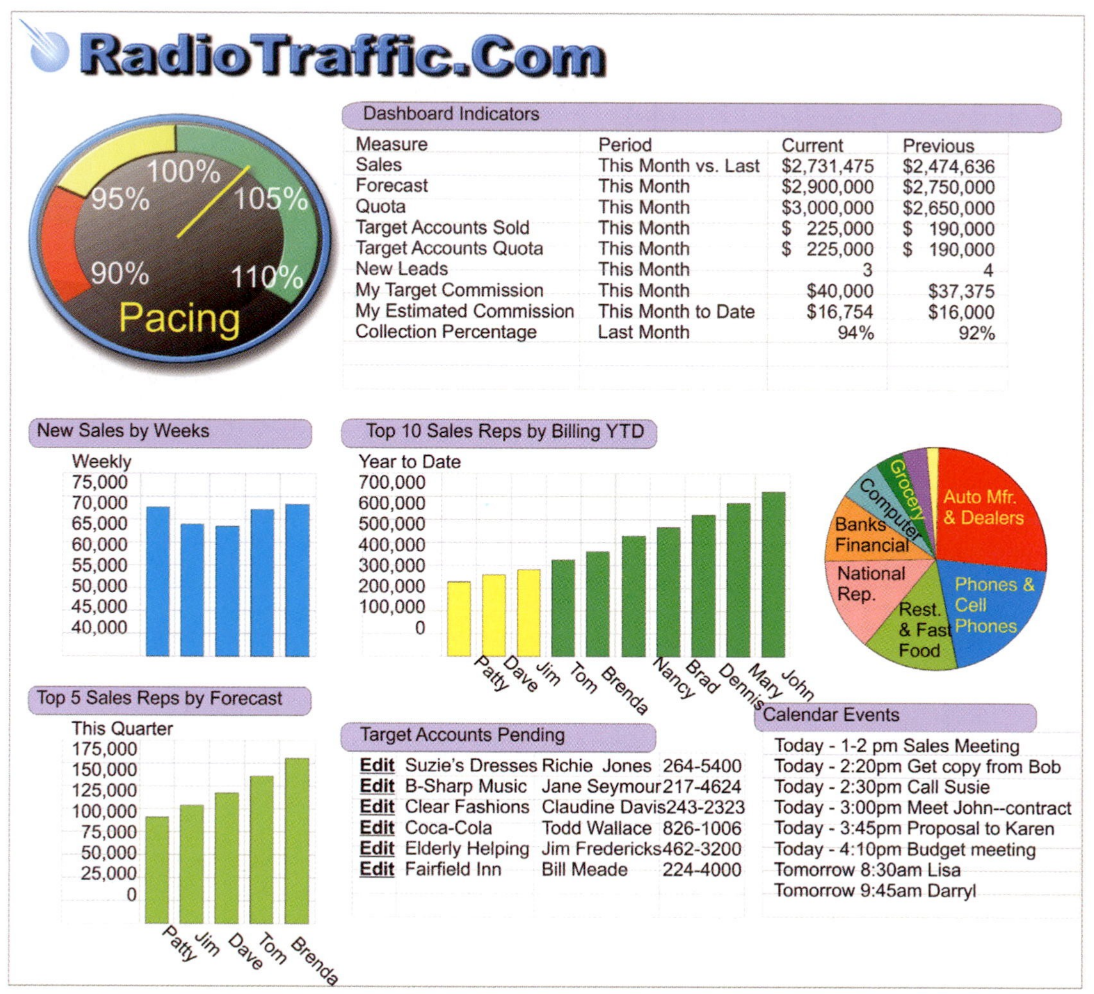

FIGURE 8.5
Computer software lets station sales managers monitor their team's sales success. Each salesperson's dashboard shows their individual pacing, keeping their teammates' financials private. Courtesy of RadioTraffic.com

No station is unfamiliar with having to make up spots due to late copy. It's irritating but a reality that you have to deal with."

Station traffic manager Jan Hildreth says that holiday and political campaign periods can place added pressure on not only the traffic person, but also the salesperson. "The fourth quarter is the big money time in radio. The logs usually are jammed, and availabilities are in short supply. The workload in the traffic department doubles. Things also get pretty chaotic around elections. It can become a real test for the nerves. Of course, there's always the late order that arrives at 5 pm on Friday that gets the adrenaline going." Traffic and billing

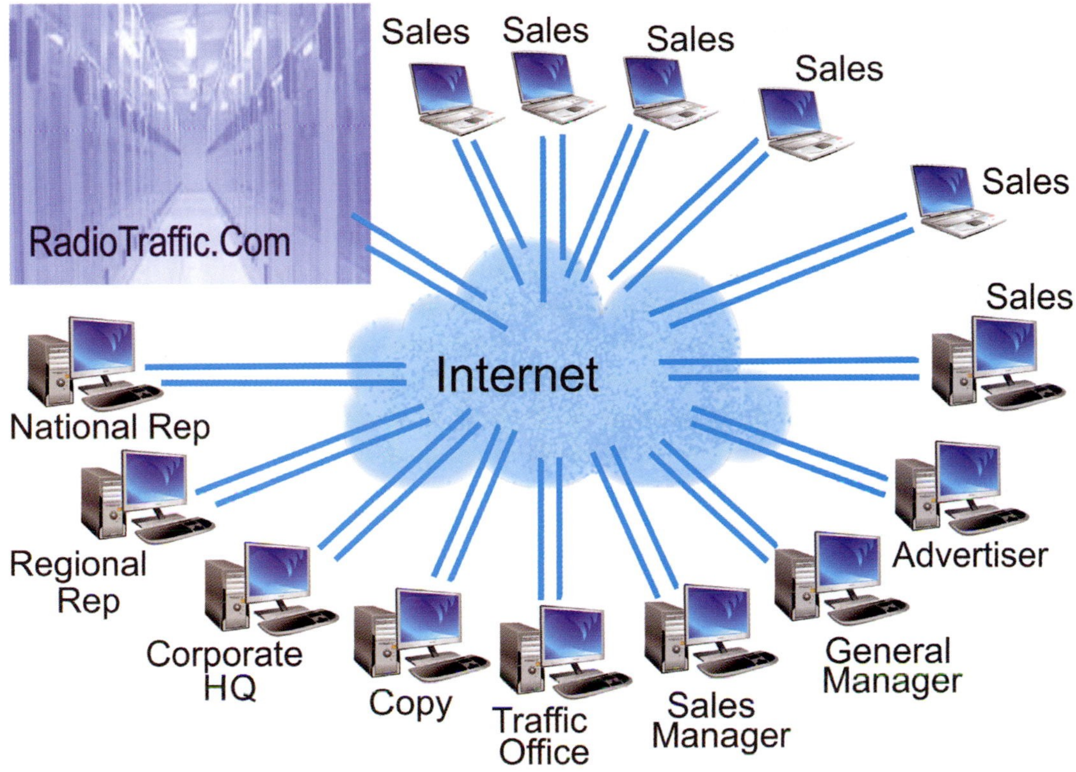

FIGURE 8.6
With multiuser cloud-based traffic and billing software, everyone from sales staff to advertiser or agency to outside rep firms and corporate headquarters see overall pacing dashboards and can drill down to individual salespeople, orders, and any advertiser. Courtesy of RadioTraffic.com.

software enables a salesperson along with station management to constantly monitor the amount of sales being made and whether financial targets are being met for both the station and the individual salesperson.

There are few station relationships closer than that of the traffic department with programming and sales. Programming relies on the traffic manager for the logs that function as scheduling guides for on-air personnel and need to be uploaded into the automation systems that are used by many stations to broadcast both commercials and music. Sales depends on the traffic department to inform it of existing availabilities and to process orders onto the air. "It is crucial to the operation that traffic has a good relationship with sales and programming. When it doesn't, things begin to happen. The program director (PD) has to let traffic know when something changes; if not, the system breaks down. This is equally true of sales. Traffic is kind of the heart of things. Everything passes through the traffic department. Cooperation is very important," observes radio station traffic manager Barbara Kalulas.

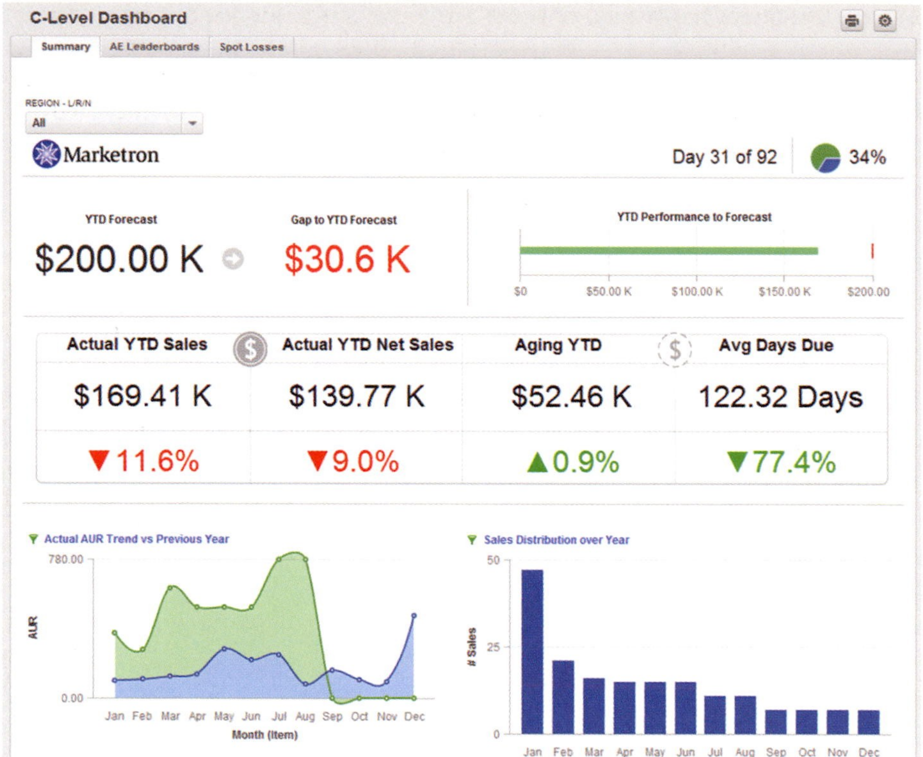

FIGURE 8.7
Insight reporting can also be managed at the AE level at a station and helps sales teams track their progress against goals and look at dashboards for pacing, sales, and more. Courtesy of Marketron.

THE TRAFFIC MANAGER'S CREDENTIALS

A college degree usually is not a criterion for the job of traffic manager. This is not to imply that skill and training are not necessary, and more commonly everybody at a radio station has at least some college education. Nichols agrees:

> I don't believe any school teaches traffic/continuity, even the schools that have "communications" courses. It's a job you learn by doing, if someone will give you a chance to learn. I don't think any young person goes to college thinking "I'll take a communications course, so I can be a traffic manager!" It's usually by accident or happenstance that we fall into these jobs. It also takes someone who enjoys the puzzles of making too many spots fit into too few avails. Someone who is a self-starter, who can work under pressure, and do more than one thing at a time. Organized people do well in this field.

Obviously, the demands placed on the traffic manager are formidable, and not everyone is qualified to fill the position. "It takes a special kind of person to effectively handle the job of traffic. Patience, an eye for detail, plus the ability to work under pressure and with other people are just some of the qualities the position requires," notes radio executive Bill Campbell.

Traffic managers must be well-organized so they can keep up with the hectic pace at radio stations. Nichols asserts certain times of the year are much busier than others for various reasons. "In Indianapolis, May is a huge month for us, since my stations carry the Indy 500 race. Weeks that contain holidays are usually very busy as well as the beginning of the school year, and of course, the car dealers! Oh, my, the car dealers!" Not only must traffic managers be well organized to do their own responsibilities, but sometimes colleagues in the station need some gentle reminding that paperwork is needed in the traffic manager's office to process sales orders. Nichols says, "Our team sends out lists of missing copy to all the sellers several times a week. They follow that up with emails and/or calls to specific sellers regarding particular pieces of copy that are missing."

Computer skills are vital to the job. A familiarity with computers and traffic and billing software has become an absolute requirement because, as noted, most stations have given up the manual system of preparing logs in favor of the more efficient, computerized method.

Many traffic people are trained in-house and come from the administrative or clerical ranks. Even though traffic salaries generally exceed that of purely secretarial positions, this is not an area noted for its high pay, as Nichols comments:

> Salaries will vary greatly between companies and between markets. Small-market stations, which have less revenue generated than do stations in larger markets, will pay less. The bigger the market and the bigger the gross revenue of the station, and the number of stations the traffic professional handles will all impact salary. Tenure, experience, and number of people in the department all have an impact. I'd say beginners would start at $25,000–30,000 in a market the size of Indianapolis. I've been doing it for about 35 years, in Birmingham, Atlanta, and now in Indianapolis. My current salary is about $62,000.

Traffic managers frequently make the transition into sales or programming. The considerable exposure to those particular areas provides a solid foundation and good springboard for those desiring to make the change. Moreover, the transition from programming is natural and a good collaborative relationship between the two departments is helpful. Nichols asserts, "It's very important, because we all have a part to play in making clients, listeners and internal customers happy with the end result."

PIONEER IN TRAFFIC/BILLING SOFTWARE DEVELOPMENT

Dave Scott

Dave Scott started as an amateur radio "ham operator" as a teen, building his own transmitters. At the University of Michigan engineering studies took a back seat to being on-the-air part-time at the student station and each of the five commercial stations in the area at one time or another.

Three years later, he was engineer and rock deejay for a year in Greenville-Spartanburg, South Carolina, and for another year in Albany, New York. Then eight years in St. Louis radio on-the-air and behind-the-scenes management, where he eventually got into part-ownership.

FIGURE 8.8
Dave Scott.

He became a programmer for stations nationwide for a radio station jingle company in Dallas, consulting up to 400 stations. He became president and grew the company to produce other products for radio stations including music and commercial scheduling software, music libraries on CD, computerized CD jukeboxes for automated shifts, a comedy service for morning shows and special 60- and 30-second instrumental beds for commercial production. The company bought out two competitors and went public as TM Century, which still exists under new owners as TM Studios in Dallas.

Scott left to start Scott Studios, which built computerized commercial players and deejay automation for radio stations. This company grew larger than the competitors over his 12 years, selling 16,000 studio workstations to 4,600 stations. After he sold, it was bought by Google, who sold it to WideOrbit.

In 2005 Scott started RadioTraffic.com, which now sells commercial traffic and billing software to about 800 stations.

Traffic managers, according to Nichols, must have an eye for details:

> Attention to detail, and the ability to work within deadlines. We are interrupted many times in a day, so refocusing on the task at hand is important. We have salespeople from multiple stations, their sales managers, and programming folks, and also, though not as much, folk from the accounting office, coming or calling and emailing with requests and questions. It's an on-demand kind of office. But the main goal, the main purpose, is to schedule commercials in the middle of this busy atmosphere.

Although the traffic manager is expected to handle many responsibilities, the position generally is perceived as more clerical in nature than managerial.

DIRECTING TRAFFIC

Computers vastly enhance the speed and efficiency of the traffic process. Computers store enormous amounts of data, retrieve information faster than humanly possible, and schedule and rotate commercials with precision and equanimity, to mention only a few of the features that make the new technology especially adaptive for use in the traffic area. Stephens says the primary benefit for radio stations to use traffic and billing software is, "the traffic and billing system is the inventory and revenue management system for any broadcaster. As such, the better tools it gives its users, the better they may manage their operation and the more profitable they will be."

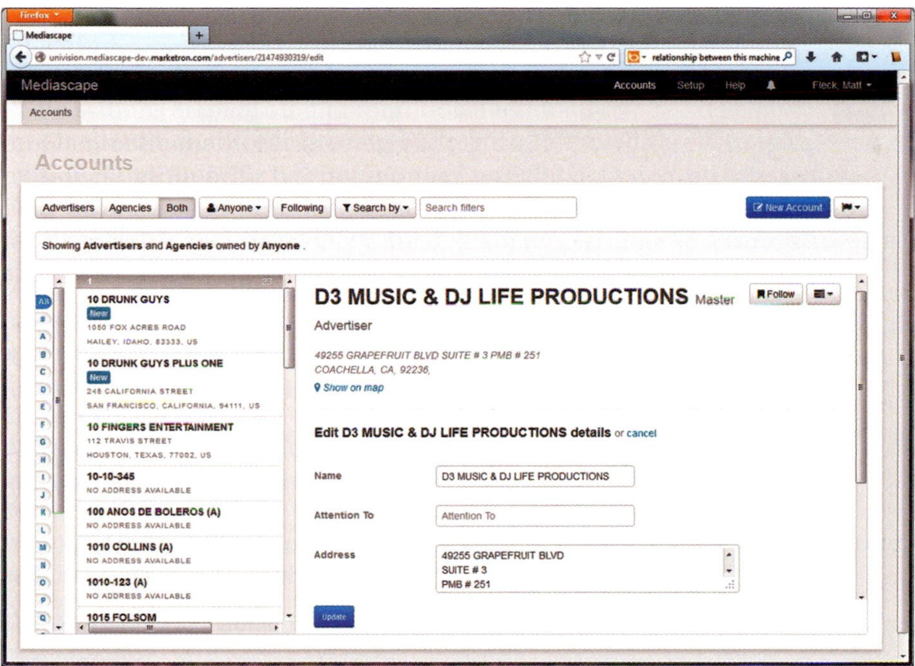

FIGURE 8.9
Mediascape Accounts: Manage the contact details for all of the accounts, corporate wide or follow those accounts that are of interest. Courtesy of Marketron.

Although the initial financial expenditure in computers is substantive and the hardware is expensive to maintain, computers nonetheless are a wise investment for radio stations, according to Nichols. "Fewer employees are needed to produce the same volume of work. What used to be the responsibility of many is now pared down to smaller staffs. Although some companies have pared it down *too* small, expecting unrealistic volume of work from too few employees. I won't name the companies (but Emmis is not one of them)."

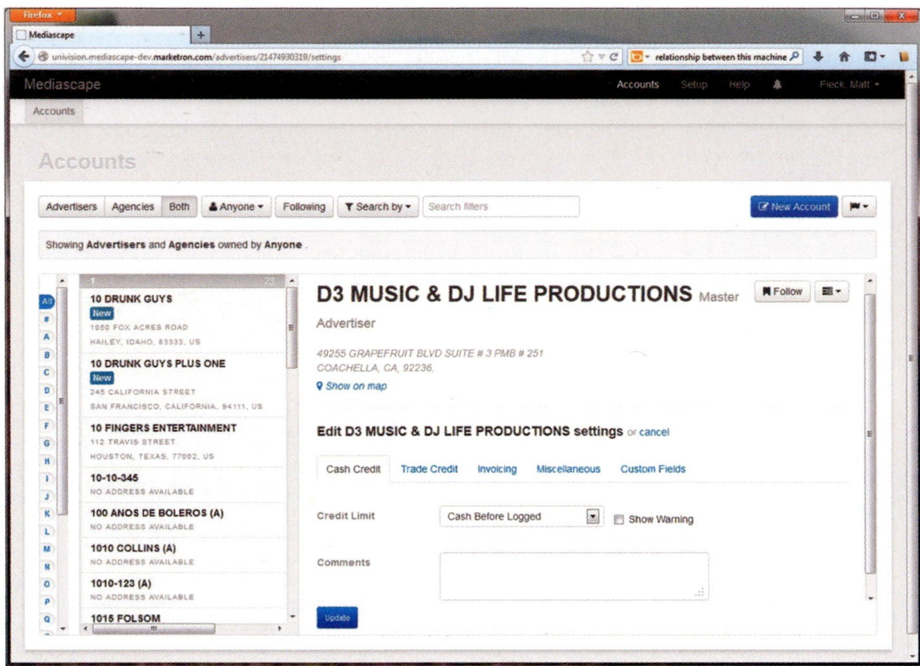

FIGURE 8.10
Mediascape Accounts: Centrally controlled, for maximum salability, the traffic system settings for every market from one, central location. Courtesy of Marketron.

Computers are an excellent tool for inventory control and managing files, contends former broadcast computer consultant Vicki Cliff:

> Radio is a commodity not unlike a train carload of perishables, such as tomatoes. Radio sells time, which is progressively spoiling. The economic laws of supply and demand are classically applied to radio. Computers can assist in plotting that supply-and-demand curve in determining rates to be charged for various dayparts at any given moment.

Inventory control is vital to any business. Radio is limited in its availabilities and seasonal in its desirability to the client. In a sold-out state, client value priorities must be weighted to optimize the station's billing. All things being equal, the credit rating of the client should be the deciding factor. Computers can eliminate the human subjectivity in formulating the daily log.

Despite the costs, many stations across the nation have transitioned to software to manage their traffic and billing procedures. In a 2013 interview with *Talkers*, Jeff Haley, the CEO of Marketron, a leading provider of traffic and billing software for radio stations, explained how his company helps stations, "While technology like ours can enable radio stations to streamline their operations, when it comes to sales, it still needs a human touch to make the deal. With

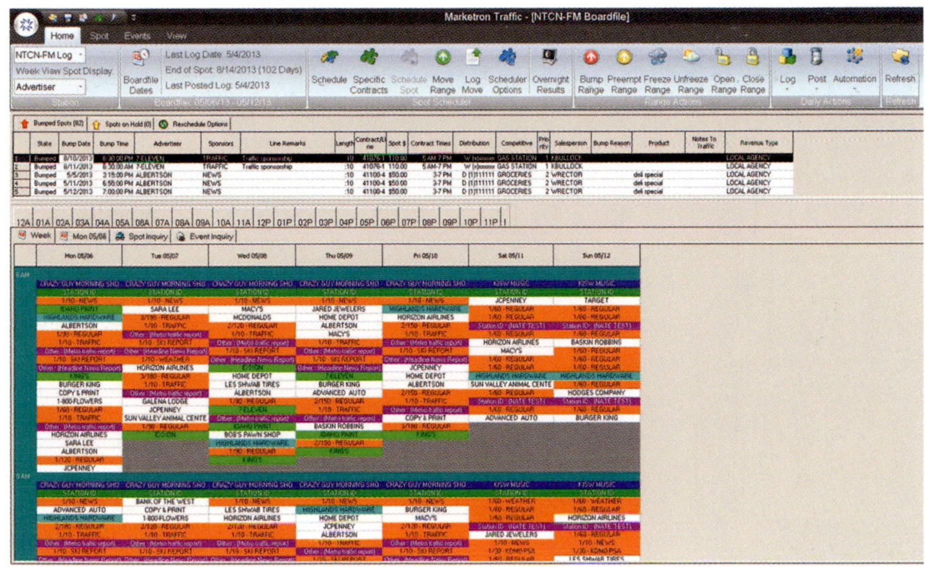

FIGURE 8.11
The Boardfile is the area in which Marketron traffic managers manage their logs. This screenshot is in weekly view allowing spots to be moved across hours, days, or weeks along with other features geared to maximize the revenue for every log.

Marketron on board, a station's sales reps are able to save time on data keeping and management, and pull together more sophisticated packages to suit each advertiser, leveraging all available platforms, and markets."

The computer and traffic software can increase a station's efficiency. Haley says:

> For example, Mediascape customers who take advantage of our Network Connect service routinely save between two and eight hours of work time per station per week through the benefit of integrations with network providers such as Dial Global, Premiere, Cumulus, and others which replace what was once a very labor-intensive and manual process with an automated workflow. We can demonstrate the same efficiencies in a variety of areas of our customers' operations such as digital sales, billing activities, and reporting where once highly manual and complex processes are becoming automated and simplified, freeing time to focus on truly critical functions and unlocking tremendous value for our customers.

In an interview in *Radio Ink,* WPOC-FM's Jim Dolan observed that "The move right now is toward putting your sales force in the field armed with laptops and instantaneous online access to inventory, availability, and contract information." The traffic software will continue to improve the efficiency of the station's traffic and billing department. Scott anticipates a number of technological developments to continue improving efficiency.

FIGURE 8.12
A handheld chart of unsold air time on an iPhone (or any smartphone) as seen by advertising salespeople. Courtesy of RadioTraffic.com.

Specifically, Scott expects software will be:

1. Better, faster and cheaper! We're in the information age and radio stations and the advertisers who support them demand accurate, timely information. Broadcasting is proven to respond in cases of disasters, both natural and man-made, and those involve virtually instantaneous rescheduling of programming and commercials.
2. Since the advent of smartphones and tablets we're in a new BYOD era (BYOD = bring your own device). Examples include iPads and tablets and smartphones of all flavors. This means an advertising salesperson in the field can get any info they need on their own device without having to phone someone back at the station to look it up on the station's computer.
3. With RadioTraffic.com, sales managers can approve pending orders, salespeople can reprint invoices or ad copy, print or inform advertisers about their past and future commercials on most any smartphone, tablet computer, laptop, or desktop computer with Internet connectivity.

Agreeing with Scott, Stephens says, "The companies who own radio stations are almost all multimedia outlets these days and they certainly will be even more so in the future. Every station will have their traditional, terrestrial signal, their streaming channel, their website, and likely even mobile or other as yet undeveloped media types. To be successful in this world they will need to be able to sell, manage, and report on all of their media properties through a single portal."

Various types of traffic and billing software are available. Several companies, most notably Radio Traffic, Marketron, Harris Osi-Traffic, Wide Orbit, Natural Broadcast Systems, and ACI Media, specialize in providing broadcasters with software packages. Prices for computer software vary depending on the nature and complexity of the software program.

Compatible hardware is specified by the software manufacturer. Most all traffic and billing software is PC compatible. The traffic and billing software companies have not yet developed Apple-compatible software. When asked about that, Scott said: "I've researched this question repeatedly and at this time [mid-2013], no traffic software is available for any Apple computers that generates commercial logs or invoices."

In terms of the PC-versus-Apple platform discussions about traffic and billing software, Stephens says:

> Generally, solutions available are "client server" applications dependent on the client operating system to function, with the Microsoft Windows operating system being the most prevalent. These apps have been enabled to run in other environments using Citrix and other software emulation tools. New applications are being designed to be browser-based and capable of running on any operating system including the major desktop OSs (Windows, Linux, Mac OS, etc.) and modern mobile devices (iOS, Android, Windows Mobile, and BlackBerry), allowing users to access information at any time, from anywhere on any device.

Notes Jay Williams, Jr.:

> Traffic and accounting for stations are increasingly cloud-based—this gives management, sales, traffic, and bookkeeping access to identical, real-time information from any device, anywhere. And some stations are including their CRM [customer relationship management] programs so everyone can view the most recent client contact, when and how much was sold, how the order is scheduled, and if management has approved the order. Cloud-based data virtually eliminates problems of multiple or misplaced orders, gives management immediate and complete detail of inventory and revenue, and provides better operational security, too.

TRAFFIC IN CLUSTERS

In the age of widespread station clustering, it is common for a centralized traffic (and billing) department to handle the work of several outlets that are owned by the same company or group. In this case, the staff of the "hub" department (the one handling all of the work) may be enlarged to accommodate the increased demands. Obviously, this also means that the traffic departments at the various stations in the cluster are no longer necessary and therefore are typically eliminated. Nichols says, "In our cluster all traffic and invoicing is handled on site by the accounting department. Some processes are handled by the corporate office, which happens to be in our building. Corporate does payroll and all HR functions and AP." To meet the needs of the various stations in the cluster a salesperson must sell airtime, a number of software programs are available to help the salesperson meet his/her goals.

Using scheduling and billing software within station clusters creates a need for a large staff to oversee the complex operations. Nichols shares:

> We have four terrestrial stations, one FM translator, and a statewide radio network. I supervise four people: one who is traffic manager for two stations (I do logs for the other two stations, and the FM translator); two

> are continuity directors who handle all the copy/audio/scripts that run both on air and on streaming, and one of them also is the network coordinator; and one part-time person who helps with everything. The sellers have access to their own information in Marketron (projections, bumps, times reports, copies of invoices). I generate and distribute inventory reports (to show managers and sellers what inventory is sold/available) every day.

Williams adds, "Consolidation and technology have provided opportunities for savings in traffic, bookkeeping, engineering, production, and other internal operations. Technology soon will allow stations to automatically accept and schedule orders directly from approved clients and agencies; the acceptance of this 'offer-buy-schedule' software will streamline the traffic-billing process even more."

Dave Scott, CEO of RadioTraffic.com, further discusses the impact of consolidation of radio station traffic operations:

> In the era when an owner could only have two stations in a market (prior to the 1996 Telecom Act), one traffic person often did all the "back room" commercial scheduling and billing for two stations. So six or seven stations would have had three or four people. After consolidation, it's not unusual for seven stations to have one or two people handling all commercial scheduling and billing. This has been possible partly through combination sales (where one or two sales people handle sales of ads for six, seven, or eight stations) and partly through more efficient traffic and billing software (made so one order entry process could get all the details into all six, seven, or eight stations).

Some of this has been due to the multitasking aspect of Windows software and some due to faster and more powerful multicore desktop computers, along with the advent of networking of several computers together so all sales people could do some order entry.

What we do at our company is take multiple station operation two steps further. First, RadioTraffic.com software is Internet-enabled, so sales people don't have to phone in to find out about unsold availabilities. This is important because ad time is perishable. You can't sell the time a few minutes ago if you didn't sell it in advance.

Internet connectivity also means sales people don't have to drive back to the station to get new orders or change orders entered by traffic people. They can do so with any computer or the Internet anywhere. That includes laptop computers with wireless Internet access, any computer at an Internet café, and any PDA with wireless Internet. Station people and clients have secure access to full account information from any Internet computer, just the way as one has account info from their bank or credit card company. Here at Radio-Traffic.com we also offer client invoices, affidavits, and statements that talk.

FIGURE 8.13
When traffic and billing software users first turn on their computer, many see graphics showing financial performance like this for a general manager or sales manager. Staff sales people would see only their own results for privacy. Courtesy of RadioTraffic.com.

Merely click on the day and time of any commercial and you can hear an air-check playback of it along with what came before and after, all over the Internet. All this makes traffic run smoothly in cluster situations.

WHAT IS TRAFFIC? (NO, WE MEAN THE "OTHER" *TRAFFIC*)

Larry Keene

No, this broadcast traffic person doesn't go up in the chopper to report on drivetime gridlock on the freeway, interstate, or high volume arteries. Broadcasting actually has two areas involving the word "traffic." We are the "other one," although and in a way, we do control what goes where, when, and under what conditions.

Our traffic is the revenue management specialist. And the truly successful managers will confirm you should never underestimate the value of the traffic professional when the campaigns are handed off from sales and creative for insertion into the financial funnel controlled by the revenue management specialists of traffic.

We're guessing about how we got so lucky to be stuck with the name "traffic" in our titles, but possibly because we are the incoming receiver of placement duties from sales, programming, technicians, promotion, marketing, production, and management. The incoming is like a major freeway intersection in Los Angeles all transitioning to directed streams of . . . well, traffic seems the most appropriate word to describe it—we are, the traffic cop, traffic controller, traffic director or manager that directs it to its proper destination.

Please realize that air traffic controllers, highway traffic officers and broadcast traffic personnel all function in a similar manner . . . hundreds of planes heading for the airport terminal, hundreds of vehicles on the highways headed for different destinations, and hundreds of programs and commercials trying to find their "avails" on the program log.

Our key employees in "traffic" involve the scheduling of programs, commercial content, program teasers, promotional announcements, and all the other components that comprise what is heard on the audio of your favorite stations, website, or wireless-delivered content.

It seems fairly simple to us, but it's confusing to others, especially when someone in an elevator asks you what you do. Be prepared for a blank stare when you say, "I'm the traffic director or traffic manager. At WXXX."

It's easy to say that you schedule the programs and commercials on your favorite radio stations—but that inevitable moment or two of silence from the person that had asked you what you do always feels slightly awkward. The truth is you're in charge of a multitasking highly complex revenue center that links all of the program segments for the station audience.

You may have heard of the buzzword "STEM," which is an acronym for science, technology, engineering, and mathematics. Traffic is a little of each, rather than a reliance on just one of the four. However, those of us involved in the profession tend to think it's a little more of science and math, and then blended with computer technology and engineering.

From the outside, many will say, you have limited amounts of inventory made up of "spaces" or avails for commercials, promos and items pre-committed to networks or required legal items such as required station identifications, etc. Your job, outsiders believe, is to put the inventory into the available spaces and your job is done. If only it was that easy.

You and your tools must calculate which items have the priorities over others. You must try to avoid having competitors running back-to-back; most days there are more items than there are spaces.

The program director has given instructions that the commercial sets cannot be longer than *x* number of minutes, so you must decide how to combine the varying lengths of 10-, 15-, 20-, 30- and 60-second announcements can be combined before a "clutter" factor causes audience tune-out.

Another consideration is avoiding having the same announcer's voice of several announcements in a row. Scientifically speaking, you lose listener credibility if it's the same voice telling you what to buy three or four times in a row. All of the foregoing items blend together. Fortunately, computer software helps immeasurably—but the "human factor" is alive and well and comes into play more often than non-traffic personnel realize.

When it's all over, you also need to confirm that all commercials or revenue-producing items ran within the time frames that were dictated by the original orders received from agencies and a wide host of sales personnel. (That's continuity, but it's crucial to your tasks, too.) Stations need to promote themselves and their programs—you're the person that verifies the "promos" are ready to roll at the right time.

Next day, the traffic staff does it all over again. Actually, you're the key multitasker that maximizes the revenue for the sales department, confirms that all the commercial, promotional, legal, and programming segments are not only properly scheduled but that they are all in-house and in-place for on-demand playback. While every duty is important, maximizing the revenue takes the number-one priority position.

And, in today's world, that entire procedure is usually needed for not just one, but multiple stations including subchannels (like HD2, HD3, etc.), website audio streaming, display ads, banners and boxes on your stations' websites, mobile feeds, and—as the disk jockeys like to say—the list goes on and on.

And, if you think that's confusing, consider the many titled positions within the traffic department (although traffic director and traffic manager seem to be the more commonly used): TDGA tends to prefer the all-inclusive title of traffic professional. There are, at least 30 different titles in traffic; all could be summarized as "traffic." That's like saying Baskin-Robbins and Ben & Jerry's have so many flavors from which to choose. To most of us, simply put—they're all "ice cream." And to our colleagues in management, sales, creative, talent, and technical, they think all of our titles are all just "traffic."

Larry Keene is a 56-year veteran of the radio business, ranging from on-air personality, program manager, producer of the *Joe Pyne Show*, the Miss America Radio Network for 25 years, sales manager, traffic manager, general manager, owner of two radio groups, executive board member of NAFMB, NRBA, president of NJBA for three terms, national sales manager of a major traffic software vendor, founder of TDGA. He is the author of the *TDGA Radio-TV Glossary of Broadcast Terms*, a 100-plus page volume of approximately 1,250 terms and definitions, etc. (considered by many to be the "back office bible" of broadcasting terms).

BILLING

At most stations, advertisers are billed for the airtime they have purchased after a portion or all of it has run. Few stations require that sponsors pay in advance. It is the job of the billing department to notify the advertiser when payment is due. Al Rozanski, former business manager of WMJX-FM, Boston, explains the process involved once a contract has been logged by the traffic department. "We send invoices out twice monthly. Many stations bill weekly, but we find doing it every two weeks cuts down on the paperwork considerably. The first thing my billing person does is check the logs to verify that the client's spots ran. We don't bill them for something that wasn't aired. Occasionally a spot will be missed for one reason or another, say a technical problem. This will be reflected on the log because the on-air person will indicate this fact." Nichols explains the process in Indianapolis:

> I generate logs for the next day. On the next day, I reconcile and post the previous day's logs. On Mondays, the accounting department invoices all orders that have expired during the previous week (after all logs are posted). On the Monday following the end of broadcast calendar month,

[the individual responsible for billing] invoices everything that ran in the month. Then [the individual in the billing department] and the business manager run tons of revenue reports, balancing the receivables (payments from advertisers) against the invoices. I think at some point during the month they send statements to clients who have not remitted checks in a timely manner.

Although some stations still send invoices via traditional mail, the radio industry has also utilized email as a means to deliver invoices. "Local merchants are now more accustomed to receiving invoices by email, rather than waiting for a bill to come in the mail," says Scott.

Not all radio stations have a full-time business manager on the payroll. Thus, the person who handles billing is commonly responsible for maintaining the station's financial records or books as well. In this case, the services of a professional accountant may be contracted on a regular periodic basis to perform the more complex bookkeeping tasks and provide consultation on other financial matters.

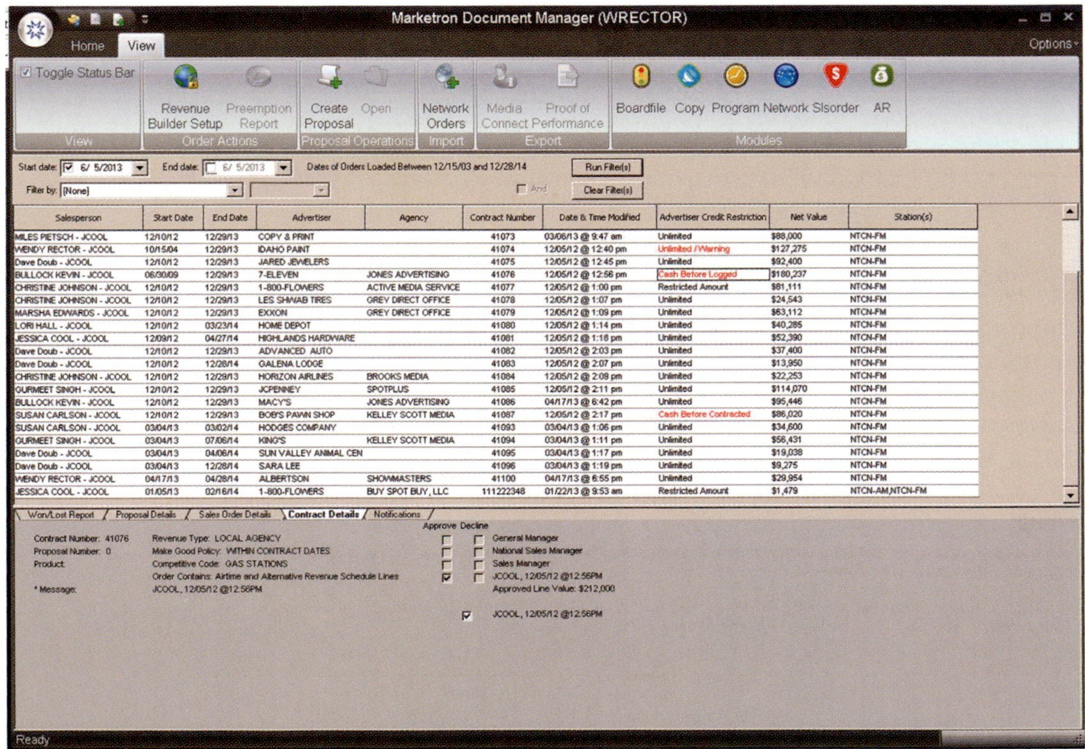

FIGURE 8.14
Marketron's Document Manager serves as an electronic desktop and approval queue for all contracts in the system from a status of pending through historical. Courtesy of Marketron.

STANDARD TERMS AND CONDITIONS

1 Approvals. Station reserves the right to approve all advertising, which approval shall not be unreasonably withheld. Advertiser agrees that advertisements and promotions which it runs in accordance with this Agreement shall be in accordance with applicable rules and policies established from time to time by Station.

2. Commercial Content. Station assumes no responsibility, obligation or liability with respect to the content or style of the advertising provided by the Advertiser and Advertiser agrees to indemnify Station for any liability which may result from broadcasting said commercial. In an effort to provide the community with wholesome entertainment, Station reviews all programming and commercials which it places for broadcast, and reserves the right to reject any particular advertisement provided by Advertiser. See station's production guidelines for a thorough detail of stations commercial policies.

3. Additional Requested Broadcasts. Except as otherwise agreed to in writing, if Advertiser continues to request that Station broadcast advertising beyond that specified herein, additional broadcasts shall be considered a part of this contract, at the rate established by the Station from time to time, and otherwise subject to these terms and conditions, until otherwise agreed to in writing.

4. Confirmations and Cancellations. All contracts and revisions are scrutinized for accuracy prior to mailing. Upon receipt of station contracts by Advertiser, it is Advertiser's responsibility to notify Station of any possible discrepancy. If Station receives no notice within seven (7) days of issue, the contract or revision will be considered correct and Advertiser will be responsible for payment. Station requires two (2) weeks notice of cancellation.

5. Trademarks and Non-Exclusivity. This Agreement does not grant Advertiser the rights to use tradenames, trademarks or service marks of Station. No merchandising, promotional or other special consideration, nor any product category exclusivity or other protection regarding any broadcast, will be provided by Station in connection with the scheduled advertising unless specifically set forth in this Agreement.

6. Failure to Broadcast Commercials. Advertiser acknowledges that commercials occasionally may not be broadcast when scheduled due to events beyond the reasonable control of Station. in the event scheduled advertising is not broadcast when scheduled. Station shall be entitled to place advertising on a subsequent, comparable broadcast, on a "make good" basis. In no event shall Station be liable for any consequential or incidental damages relating to its failure to air scheduled advertising.

7. Execution by Agency. If this Agreement is entered into by an Advertising Agency on behalf of an Advertiser, said Agency jointly and severally undertakes the obligations of Advertiser hereunder.

8. Massachusetts Law. This Agreement is made and entered into in Massachusetts and shall be interpreted, construed and enforced in accordance with the laws of the Commonwealth of Massachusetts.

CREDIT POLICY

1. Extension of Credit. Standard Station credit policy is cash in advance for Advertiser's first order, pending approval of credit, and said credit will not be extended without a completed and signed credit application from Advertiser on file.

2. Credit limits. Individual credit limits are established at the sole discretion of Station and are subject to review from time to time.

COMMISSIONS AND DISCOUNTS

1. Agency Commissions. Commissions will be paid by Station only to established Advertising Agencies in good standing.

PAYMENTS

1. Payments. Standard Station payment policy is that all invoices are due and payable net thirty (30) days from receipt of invoice.

2. Late Charges. Any amounts due Station from Advertiser not paid within (30) days of receipt of invoice are subject to a five percent (5%) late payment charge.

3. Collections. In the event of any collection action or litigation to collect amounts due from Advertiser, Station shall be entitled to reasonable cost of collection and attorneys fees as determined by the Court.

FIGURE 8.15
Terms and conditions of an advertising buy. Courtesy of WXLO-FM.

Accounts that fail to pay when due are turned over to the appropriate salesperson for collections. If this does not result in payment, a station may use the services of a collection agency. Should its attempt also fail, the station likely would write the business off as a loss at tax time. The standard payment policy for radio stations is "payable net thirty (30) days from receipt of invoice." Late charges, collection action, and ultimately litigation could ensue if payment is not made for the messages advertised. Nichols states, "It's the salesperson's responsibility to collect past due amounts from their accounts, I believe, until it gets so past due it needs the attention of a collections agent."

Dave Scott adds the cluster angle to the preceding:

> In the era of group ownership a seamless automatic consolidation of financial reporting from clusters of stations in different cities, states, and regions, as well as national totals, is needed. Previously, clusters would combine their stations and fax weekly reports to headquarters. Now, group owners know their own pacing on an hour-by-hour basis, just the way a chain retailer would have their cash registers tied together for consolidated sales pacing and restocking.

THE FCC AND TRAFFIC

Although the FCC eliminated program log requirements in the early 1980s as part of the era's formidable deregulation movement, it ushered in new, more lenient ownership rules that have had an impact on radio station commercials and billing. Because of deregulation, Stephens says "FCC decisions that relate to media ownership rules have had an enormous impact on traffic and billing at stations. The increased consolidation of media companies affect the way that radio inventory is sold and managed by creating larger station clusters and a desire for many of the larger media groups to centralize operations. Often the result is traffic managers handling more stations and increased workloads."

Although stations are no longer required to retain a program log under existing rules, some sort of document is still necessary to inform programming personnel of what is scheduled for broadcast and to provide information for both the traffic and billing departments pertaining to their particular functions. A program log creates accountability. It is both a programming guide and a document of verification. Before the FCC deregulatory efforts of the 1980s, radio stations were expected to maintain a formal program log, which—in addition to program titles, sponsor names, and length of elements—reflected information pertaining to the nature of announcements (commercial material, PSA), source of origination (live, recorded, network), and the type of program (entertainment, news, political, religious, other). Failing to include this information on the log could have resulted in punitive actions against the station by the FCC.

Today, there are no stipulations regarding the length of time that logs must be retained. Before the elimination of the FCC program log regulations, stations were required to retain logs for a minimum of two years. Today most stations still hold onto logs for that amount of time for the sake of accountability, and with computers as archive sources, logs may be kept indefinitely without creating physical space issues. Scott adds, "The FCC requires honesty and accuracy in financial matters, but good business practices usually are fully as motivating."

CHAPTER HIGHLIGHTS

1. Each commercial slot on a station is called an *availability*. Availabilities constitute a station's saleable inventory.
2. The traffic manager (or traffic director) controls and is accountable for the broadcast time inventory.
3. The traffic manager prepares a log to inform the deejays and board operators of what to broadcast and at what time.
4. The traffic manager is also responsible for ensuring that an ad order is logged as specified, that a record of when each client's spots are aired is maintained, and that copy and production commercials are in on time.
5. Programming relies on the traffic manager for the logs that function as scheduling guides for on-air personnel; the sales department depends on the traffic manager to inform them of existing availabilities and to process orders onto the air.
6. Although most traffic people are trained in-house and are drawn from the administrative or clerical ranks, they must possess patience, an eye for detail, the ability to work under pressure, and keyboarding skills.
7. Traffic departments use sophisticated computers and scheduling and billing software to enhance speed and efficiency. Therefore, traffic managers must be computer knowledgeable.
8. In many instances, station ownership consolidation (clustering) has eliminated individual station traffic and billing departments and a single traffic hub within the cluster prepares logs and sponsor invoices for all the stations. In some cases, outside companies have assumed the task.
9. Based on the spots aired and depending upon each station's preference, as recorded and verified by the traffic department, the billing department sends invoices weekly or via email to each client. Invoices are sometimes notarized for clients with coop contracts.
10. Since the FCC eliminated program log requirements in the early 1980s, stations have been able to design logs that inform programming personnel of what is scheduled for broadcast and that provide necessary information for the traffic and billing departments.

SUGGESTED FURTHER READING

Diamond, S.Z., *Records Management: A Practical Guide*, AMACOM, New York, 1983.

Doyle, D.M., *Efficient Accounting and Record Keeping*, Wiley Small Business Series, New York, 1978.

Heighton, E.J. and Cunningham, D.R., *Advertising in the Broadcast and Cable Media*, 2nd edition, Wadsworth Publishing, Belmont, CA, 1984.

Hunter, J. and Thiebaud, M., *Telecommunications Billing Systems*, McGraw-Hill, New York, 2002.

Keith, M.C., *Selling Radio Direct*, Focal Press, Boston, MA, 1992.

Muller, M., *Essentials of Inventory Management*, American Management Association, New York, 2011.

Murphy, J,. *Handbook of Radio Advertising*, Chilton, Radnor, PA, 1980.

Schreibfeder, J., *Achieving Effective Inventory Management*, Effective Inventory Management, Dallas, TX, 2005.

Shane, E., *Selling Electronic Media*, Focal Press, Boston, MA, 1999.

Slater, J., *Simplifying Accounting Language*, Kendall-Hall Publishing, Dubuque, IA, 1975.

Warner, C. and Buchman, J., *Broadcast, Cable, Print, and Interactive*, Iowa State University Press, Ames, IA, 2003.

Wild, T., *Best Practice in Inventory Management*, John Wiley & Sons, New York, 1998.

Zeigler, S.K. and Howard, H.H., *Broadcast Advertising: A Comprehensive Working Textbook*, 2nd edition, Grid Publishing, Columbus, OH, 1990.

CHAPTER 9
Production

A SPOT RETROSPECTIVE

The transition from analog to digital audio technology ushered radio into a new era in mixing and sound imaging. A typical radio station—whether it be broadcast, satellite, or Internet—produces thousands of commercials, public service announcements (PSAs), and station-promotion messages (promos) annually. Additionally, stations will mix a vast array of positioning messages designed to create and reinforce stations' images with their audiences.

Collectively, radio insiders refer to commercial audio messages as "spots." The term "spot" denotes a brief message, typically 60 seconds or fewer in duration, that contrasts its brevity with the approach utilized in the early days of the medium. In the 1920s, most paid announcements consisted of lengthy speeches on the virtues of a particular product or service. In the absence of suitable recording technologies, the general practice was to read the commercial script, or "copy," live. Perhaps the most representative of the commercials of the period was one of the first ever to be broadcast, which lasted more than ten minutes and was announced by a representative of a real estate firm from Queens, New York. Aired live over WEAF in 1922, by today's standards the message would sound more like a classroom lecture than a broadcast advertisement. Certainly, no snappy jingle or ear-catching sound effects accompanied the episodic announcement.

Most commercial messages resembled that lengthy real-estate pitch until 1926. On Christmas Eve of that year, four singers introduced the radio jingle by gathering around the microphone to deliver a musical tribute to Wheaties cereal. It took several years, however, before singing commercials became commonplace. For the most part, commercial production during the medium's first decade was relatively mundane. The reason was twofold: the government had resisted the idea of blatant or direct commercialism from the start, which fostered a low-key approach to advertising, and the medium was just in the process of evolving and therefore lacked the technical and creative wherewithal to present a more sophisticated message.

Things changed by 1930, however. The austere, no-frills pitch, occasionally accompanied by a piano but more often done a cappella, was gradually replaced by the dialogue spot that used drama or comedy to sell its product. A great deal of imagination and creativity went into the writing and production of commercials, which were presented live throughout the 1930s. The production demands of some commercials equaled and even exceeded those of the programs they interrupted. Orchestras, actors, and lavishly constructed sound effects commonly were required to sell a chocolate-flavored syrup or a muscle liniment. By the late 1930s, certain commercials had become as famous as the favorite programs of the day. Commercials had achieved the status of pop art.

Still, the early studios where talent labored to intone the sponsors' messages were primitive by today's standards. So-termed "production rooms" were technologically unsophisticated performance studios. Sound effects were mostly improvised show by show, commercial by commercial, in some cases using the actual objects with which sounds were identified. Glass was shattered, guns fired, and furniture overturned as the studio's on-air light flashed. Before World War II, few sound effects were available on records. It was just as rare for a station to broadcast prerecorded commercials, although the 78-rpm acetate disc—known as an "electrical transcription" and usually abbreviated as an "e.t."—and magnetic wire recordings were used by certain major advertisers. The creation of vinyl discs in the 1940s inspired more widespread use of the e.t. for radio advertising purposes. Today, sound effects are imported from CDs and downloaded from the Internet where they are stored on computer hard drives.

The live spot was the mainstay at most stations into the 1950s, when two innovations brought about a greater reliance on the prerecorded message. Magnetic recording tape and 33-1/3 rpm long-playing (LP) records revolutionized radio production methods. Recording tape brought about the greatest transformation and, ironically, was the product of Nazi scientists, who developed acetate recorders and tape for espionage purposes. The adoption of magnetic tape by radio stations was costlier and thus occurred at a slower pace than 33-1/3 rpm disc use, which essentially required a turntable modification to accommodate playing the slower speed.

Throughout the 1950s, advertising agencies grew to rely on LPs. By 1960, magnetic tape recorders were a familiar piece of studio equipment. Initially, prerecorded spot announcements were played on air directly from reel-to-reel tape decks, similar or identical to the machines on which the messages had been recorded. While this technique was versatile it was also cumbersome—it required the deejay to manually thread the ribbon of magnetic tape through the guides of the playback deck and then shuttle the tape to locate the beginning of the recorded message and prepare it for playback. This practice, termed "cueing," was similar to the technique deejays utilized to prepare vinyl records on turntables for airplay. Stations relied more and more on prerecorded commercials following the introduction of the cartridge tape deck. "Cart machines" modernized control room procedures thanks to their ease of use. By enclosing the magnetic tape within small, plastic cartridges, developers of the "cart machine" freed deejays from the burdens of loading, cueing, and unloading tape on bulky, cumbersome reel-to-reel decks. Self-cueing carts enabled deejays to play out short-form, recorded program elements with ease. Commercial spots, PSAs, jingle IDs, sound effects, and other program features could be easily selected at random from the cart library and played (or "fired") on-air at the push of a button. Such rapid sequencing helped to quicken the pace, and revolutionized the sound of 1960s-era Top 40 stations. Magnetic tape also fueled the development of automated radio by replacing the deejay with prerecorded programming served up to listeners via automatically sequenced reel-to-reel and cartridge tape machines. While "automated radio" endured much criticism for its lack of personality and spontaneity, it nonetheless did away with live announcements entirely and minimized the possibility for on-air mistakes to occur.

Commercials themselves became more sophisticated sounding since practically any scenario one could imagine could be accomplished on tape. Perhaps, no individual in the 1960s more effectively demonstrated the unique nature of radio as an advertising medium than did Stan Freberg. When, through skillful writing and the clever use of sound effects, Freberg transformed Lake Michigan into a basin of hot chocolate, dolloped with a 700-foot-high mountain of whipped cream, and crowned with a 10-ton maraschino cherry dropped from the sky by Royal Canadian Air Force planes, no one doubted the feat.

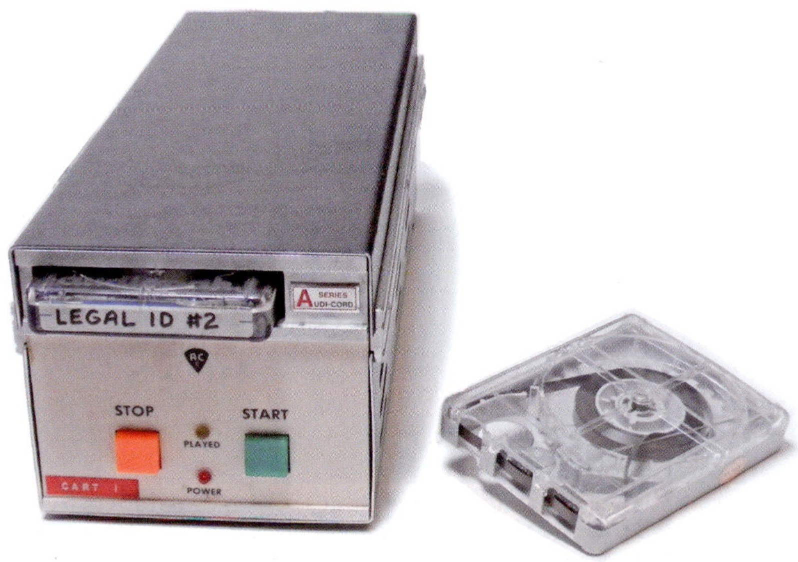

FIGURE 9.1
A broadcast cartridge tape deck and its companion endless-loop, magnetic recording tape "cart." Courtesy of Thomas A. White.

Today, the sounds of millions of skillfully prepared commercials trek through the ether and into the minds of practically every man, woman, and child in America. Good writing and inventive production are what make the medium so successful.

FORMATTED SPOTS

In the 1950s the medium took to program *formatting* to survive and prosper. Today listeners are offered myriad sounds from which to choose; there is something for practically every taste. Stations concentrate their efforts on delivering a specific format, which may be defined as Adult Contemporary,

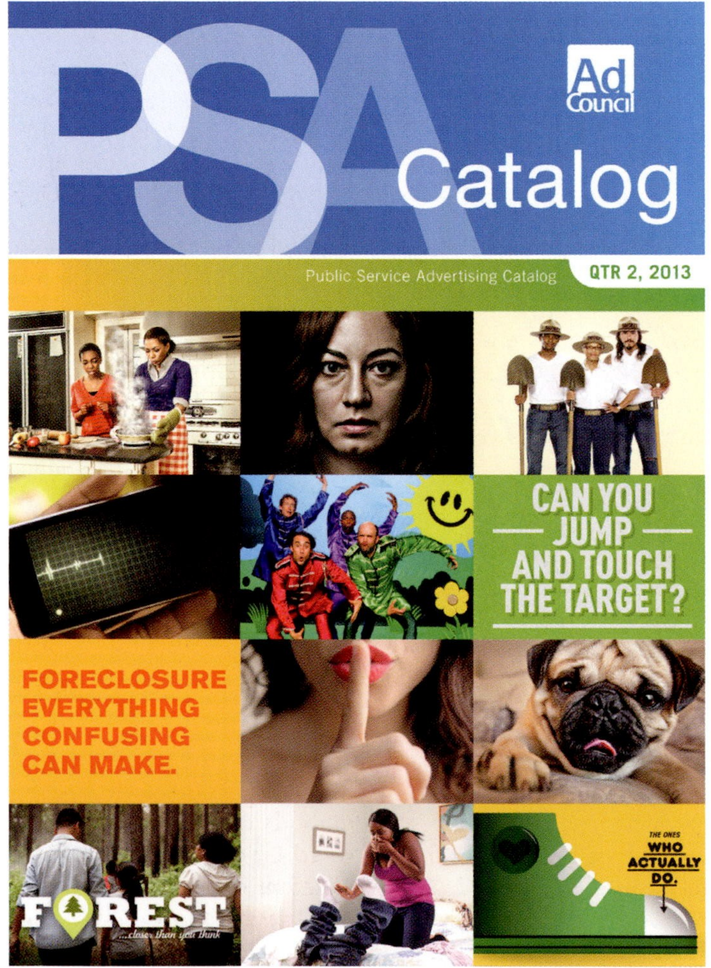

FIGURE 9.2
This catalog, issued quarterly, informs stations about public service campaigns and announcements available from the Ad Council. Courtesy of the Ad Council.

Country, Modern Rock, or any one of a dozen others. As you will recall from the discussion in Chapter 3, each format has its own distinctive sound, which is accomplished through a careful selection and arrangement of compatible program elements. To this end, commercials attempt to reflect a station's format. In the age of consolidation, says Larry Miller, "There is a tendency to do one-size-fits-all at the advertising agency level. In-house local retail may be more customized to fit the format." The need to match the presentation styles of message and the music extends to prerecorded PSAs produced and distributed by the Ad Council. This not-for-profit agency frequently develops public service campaigns utilizing format-specific production styles, content and talent.

THE PRODUCTION ROOM

In general, metro market stations and clusters employ a fulltime production person (known variously as production director, production manager, production chief, and more recently as chief imager or creative services director). This individual's primary duties are to record voice-tracks and mix commercials and PSAs. Other duties involve the maintenance of the station's production libraries of background music "beds" and sound effects and the mixdown of promotional material and special programs, such as public affairs features, interviews, and documentaries.

Stations that do not have a slot for a fulltime production person divide this work among the on-air staff. In this case, the program director (PD) often oversees production responsibilities, or a deejay may be assigned several hours of production duties each day and be called the production director.

At most medium and small outlets, on-air personnel take part in the production process. Production may include the simple transfer of an advertising agency spot into the station's computerized program-automation system, a mixdown that requires a single, instrumental music bed underneath a 30-second voicer, or a multielement mixdown of a 60-second two-voicer with sound effects and several bed transitions. Station production can run from the mundane to the exciting and challenging (mixing a commercial in such a way as to convey the message through a confluence of sounds).

Most production directors in this digital age often are called imaging directors, and are recruited from the on-air ranks, having acquired the necessary studio dexterity and know-how to meet the demands of the position. In addition to the broad range of mixdown skills required by the job, a solid knowledge of editing techniques is essential. The production director is routinely called on to make gatekeeping decisions about content ranging from rudimentary replacements to performing more complex editing chores, such as the rearrangement of elements in a 60-second concert promo.

The production/imaging director works closely with many people but perhaps most closely with the program director. The person responsible for production

FIGURE 9.3
Audio mixing in a joint studio/control room.
Courtesy of Wheatstone.

is expected to have a complete understanding of the station's programming philosophy and objective. This is necessary because commercials constitute an element of programming and therefore must complement the format execution, achieving compatibility with the music, the personalities, and the overall sound of the station. A production person must be able to determine when an incoming commercial clashes with the station's image. When a question exists as to the spot's content appropriateness or suitability, the program director will be called on to make the final judgment, because it is he or she who is ultimately responsible for what gets on the air. In the final analysis, station production is a product of programming. In most broadcast organizations, the production director answers to the program director. It is a logical arrangement given the relationship of the two areas.

The production/imaging director also works closely with the station copywriter. Their combined efforts can make or break a commercial. The copywriter conceives of the concept and the producer brings it to fruition. The traffic department also is in close and constant contact with production, because one of its primary responsibilities is to see that copy gets processed and is made available in the on-air studio at the time when it is scheduled for broadcast.

Once again the extensive clustering of station facilities in the age of consolidation finds many production responsibilities centralized. By now many radio groups have established one production hub to mix the spots of their other outlets, especially when in the same market. Typically, this has resulted in the downsizing of individual station production staff and the elimination of comprehensive mixdown studios at these sites.

THE STUDIOS

A radio station has two kinds of studios: on-air and production. Both share basic design features and have comparable equipment. Additionally, production studios often are arranged and configured to serve as back-ups in the event that technical difficulties render the on-air studio inoperable. In cluster operations where stations are colocated, there is often a single primary production facility. For ease of movement and accessibility, audio equipment is commonly situated in a configuration consistent with the intended position of the person

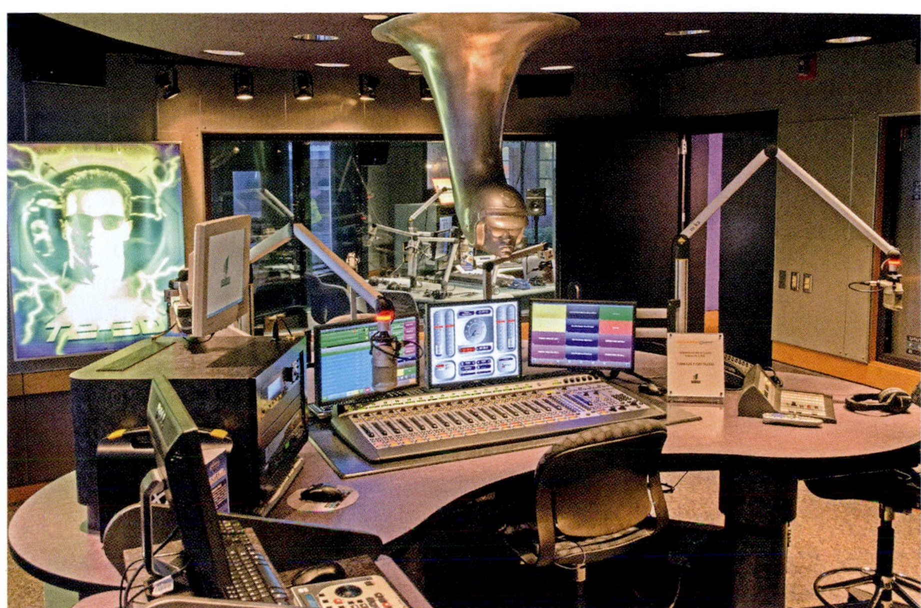

FIGURE 9.4
Terminator 2-themed broadcast studio at Universal Orlando accommodates multiple guests. Courtesy of the Telos Alliance.

who operates the equipment. "Standing" arrangements help to promote and sustain deejay momentum and are commonly utilized at stations with high-energy formats. Alternately, studios designed for "seated" operation tend to put announcers into a more relaxed mood and elicit a subdued pace. The important role that well-designed studio furniture plays in contributing to a successful, creatively productive environment must be underscored.

Says David Holland, a designer with Omnirax Furniture Company:

> Studio furniture is an integral part of any radio station with an impact that is financial, strategic, and personal. A clear idea of a studio's function will set the tone for decisions involving size of the space, shape of the furniture and equipment requirements. As the trend in equipment is clearly towards smaller and more powerful, the largest determinant of the size of the furniture is the number of people the studio needs to support. Careful consideration must be paid to relationships between "board ops" and talent, hosts and guests, screener and producer, etc. Both sound and sight lines must be maintained so that the studio functions as a cohesive whole. Proper attention to the design of the furniture affects everything from the sound over the airwaves and ergonomics of the working environment to the ease of installing and maintaining equipment.

While the casual observer attaches significance to the aesthetic appeal of the studio layout, Holland explains the importance of understanding how station engineers interact with studio furniture. "Well-designed furniture," Holland states, "pays careful attention to engineering requirements. At today's pace, equipment gets replaced sooner, talent may come and go—even ownership changes, but it is universally true that wire will still need to go everywhere to sustain the studio's operation. Engineers are at the heart of the station and furniture that supports their function will last for many years."

In-person visitors and webcam viewers alike must be favorably impressed with the layout and appearance of studios. Holland continues:

> Studio furniture can and should reflect a station's personality and brand. It is a given that studio furniture must be rugged to accommodate a rotating corps of staff and guests in a 24/7 environment. But it is equally important that the furniture have an aesthetic and functional appeal to attract and impress talent, advertisers, and sponsors. Shape, materials, color, and hardware are some of the many elements that combine and interplay in successful furniture design. Functionally designed furniture supports the strategic goals of superior sound, ergonomics and engineering. And great looking furniture promotes personal pride of ownership and radio station morale.

The standard equipment found in radio studios includes microphones, an audio console (commonly referred to as the "board"), and computer workstations (on-air studios are usually networked to the production studio). This computer would also contain automation software (such as BE AudioVAULT® FleX™, RCS Zetta®, or similar), video display monitors, CD playback decks, digital effects

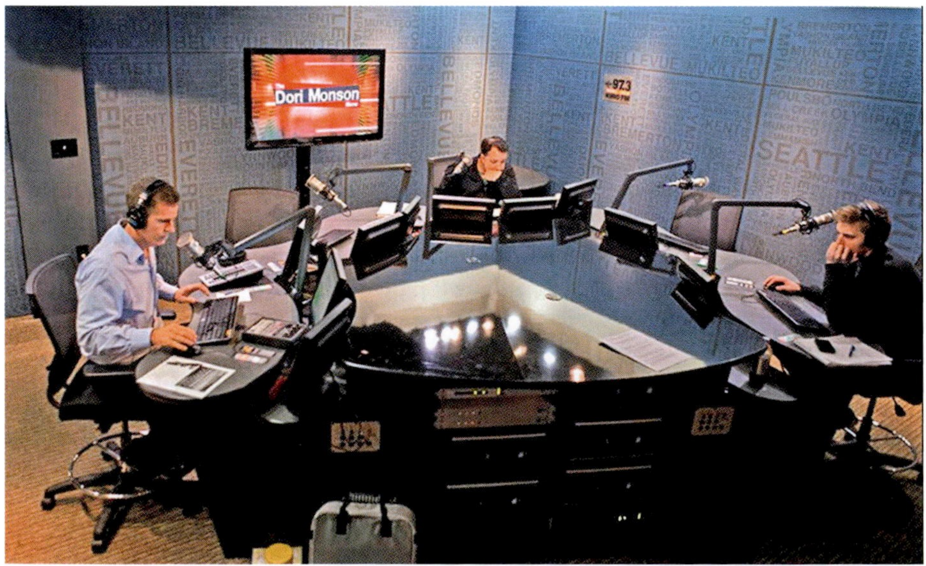

FIGURE 9.5
Careful attention to furniture design, construction, and layout results in successful ergonomic interaction between talent and equipment. Courtesy of KIRO Radio and Omnirax Furniture Company.

processors, so-called hybrid systems to enable telephone-conversation broadcasts, and external patch panels (digital consoles typically have these built in).

FIGURE 9.6
This deejay is working "combo," serving simultaneously as talent and board operator. Courtesy of Wheatstone.

AUDIO CONSOLE

The audio console is the centerpiece, the very heart of the radio station. In its 2013 *Source Book & Directory*, the trade publication *Radio World* lists more than three dozen audio console manufacturers. Although design characteristics and configurations vary, the basic components and functions remain relatively constant. Consoles in all different sizes and shapes support the operations of stations ranging in size from the largest major-market group clusters to the smallest mom-and-pop AM daytimers. Characteristics and features common to all consoles include inputs that permit audio energy to enter the console and outputs through which audio energy is fed to other locations, VU or loudness meters that measure the amount or level of sound energy, pots (faders) that control gain (the quantity of sound energy), switches for designating the destinations of the audio signals, controls to adjust the volume of the in-studio monitor loudspeakers, and, occasionally, master gain pots for the purpose of controlling general output levels (see Figures 9.7–9.9).

In recent years audio console technology has veered significantly from the old-school analog method of audio-signal manipulation. Today's modern approach is fueled by computerization and networking. Consoles and audio sources communicate using IP-Audio technology. Clark Novak, of manufacturer Telos Systems/Axia Audio, notes that the designation AoIP (Audio over Internet Protocol) is occasionally used in this context, although the usage is incorrect. He explains:

> This is a bit of a misnomer. Although AoIP tends to get used as shorthand for any device that sends audio over a network, the studio network typically has nothing to do with the Internet. A more accurate name for studio networking is IP-Audio, which denotes that you are using IP addressing to route audio to specific destinations within a studio network that's closed to the outside world. AoIP is appropriate, however, when applied to remote codecs (like our Z/IP ONE, the Comrex Access, or the Tieline remote codecs) that use the Internet to send audio to and from distant locations.

Every audio source, from studio microphones to automation program-playout systems to incoming remote-broadcast pickup signals, is instantly routable and made available not only to any input fader on the studio console, but equally important, to *any* studio's console that is connected to the local network. Equally important, the data that accompany the digital audio signal, such as the logic commands used to control device functions (e.g., audio playback start/stop control), also routes automatically from source to destination. Deejays, for instance, can be assured that their personalized vocal settings on microphone processors are automatically applied to the appropriate microphone regardless of the studio from which they operate. AoIP offers superior flexibility to show producers and on-air talent for managing audio control among grouped stations and provides significant layers of redundancy to assist station engineers in maintaining the integrity of operations whenever equipment failures occur

FIGURE 9.7
This control board features analog-scale VU meters. Courtesy of Arrakis Systems.

FIGURE 9.8
A low-profile console featuring IP networking. Courtesy of Wheatstone.

FIGURE 9.9 (*Above*) Multiple console configurations address specific station requirements and budgets. Courtesy of the Telos Alliance.

FIGURE 9.10 Studio equipped with turntables. Note the vinyl LP library, at left. Courtesy of the Telos Alliance.

FIGURE 9.11A&B
Talent stations: The turret-style (left) and surface-mount (right) panels provide air talent with immediate access to a microphone cough switch, headphone volume control, and other studio monitoring functions. Courtesy of Wheatstone.

or routine maintenance is performed. Some thoughts about console functionality, as viewed from the board operator ("board-op") perspective: the use of linear, or *slide,* faders is nearly universal in the modern console. Sliding faders began displacing the *rotary* pot design widely used until the 1970s. The popularity of the slide fader is due in part to its slim design. A clustered row of faders minimizes the arm-stretching gymnastics required of deejays to operate some of the older-style, rotary-pot control boards.

The *cue* function of the console enables the deejay or board-op to privately monitor audio signals. Telos/Axia's Novak observes that use of the term "cue" to denote this mode of operation is slowly falling out of favor: "The TV term 'preview,'" he says, "is beginning to make its way into radio alongside the old 'cue' term. Axia uses 'Preview' on all of our consoles in place of 'cue,' and some other manufacturers do as well." Regardless of the term applied to this function, its monitoring provisions are supported by a low-power amplifier and loudspeaker/headphone arrangement that enables the board operator to be able to hear sounds originating from in-studio audio playback equipment that ranges from records to digital automation systems as well as to the incoming sounds of network-program feeds. Onboard intercom/talkback systems similarly permit the monitoring of audio signals originating externally from the studio without distributing them to other destinations. The setup and preparation of the sound sources facilitates their introduction into the mixdown sequence.

The modular nature of newer consoles permits a high level of customization and technical sophistication. Depending upon format, budget, and other considerations, consoles may be equipped with modules for controlling and monitoring telephone call-in shows and with circuitry for managing the equipment associated with profanity deletion.

COMPUTERS AND SOFTWARE

Computers are the soul of the audio studio—both on-air and production. Observes Vic Michaels:

> Studio computers would contain editing software, like Pro Tools or Adobe Audition. The on-air computer would also contain automation software, such as Audio Vault. It would also possess Selector, which is needed to tell the Audio Vault system what to play. At my station, we have three computers in production: one is for Audio Vault automation, the second is for Selector music software, and the third is for editing on Pro Tools. All three are networked to the on-air computer. Everything now is "audio files." When one makes a commercial or records a song off a CD, it becomes an audio file that can be moved from computer to computer.

Computerization has all but eliminated the need for standalone audio-playback devices in the control room. Although some stations continue to utilize analog and digital "cart"-style playback decks for the reproduction of short-duration program elements the more common practice today is to rely on a computerized automation system to manage the playout. Songs, commercials, PSAs, promotional/imaging productions and other show elements can be easily imported into the on-air automation system and then conveniently and randomly accessed at the time when they are needed. Contrast this environment with the on-air studio of yesteryear, where the deejay frantically cued vinyl records on turntables and retrieved plastic tape "carts" from storage racks for insertion into playback decks. Computerization frees the deejay of these cumbersome, repetitive tasks—time that can be better utilized in show development and presentation.

The aforementioned AudioVAULT is one of several software systems that have proven worthy of standing up to the day-to-day rigors encountered in the control room. Similar products—including Zetta, WideOrbit Automation for Radio, Dalet Radio Suite, Enco DAD, and others—merge the production and playout functions, bringing to the table a host of on-screen features for simplifying operations while adding production value to the presentation. Systems typically include easily editable program log displays that allow for immediate addition, deletion and rearrangement of songs, commercials, and other program elements. Virtual "cart decks" assist deejays by making short-duration audio files accessible for playback. Audio recorders make simple work of recording, editing and playing back telephone call-ins. Web-surfing during the course of a show is facilitated by a system's built-in browser.

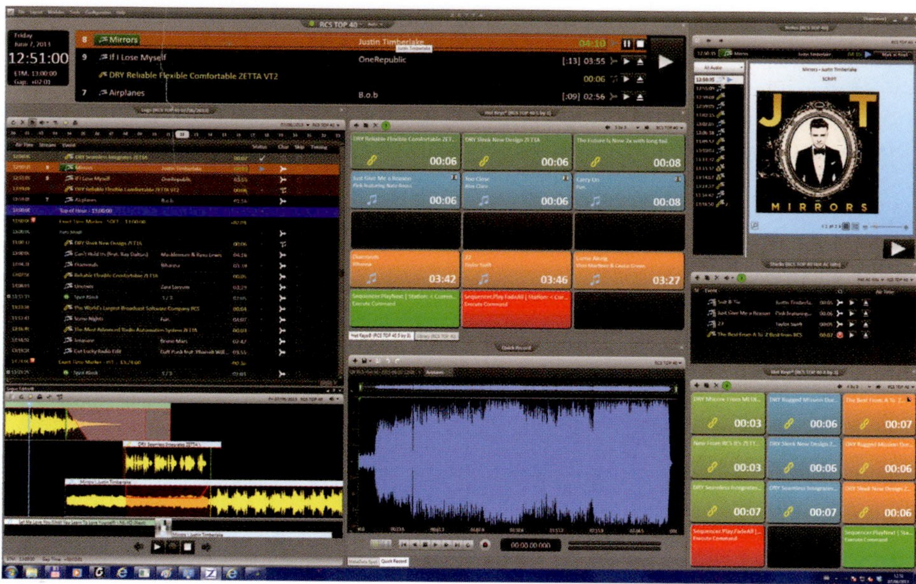

FIGURE 9.12
RCS automated playout system Zetta. Colored "HotKeys" provide instant playback access to select audio files. Courtesy of RCS.

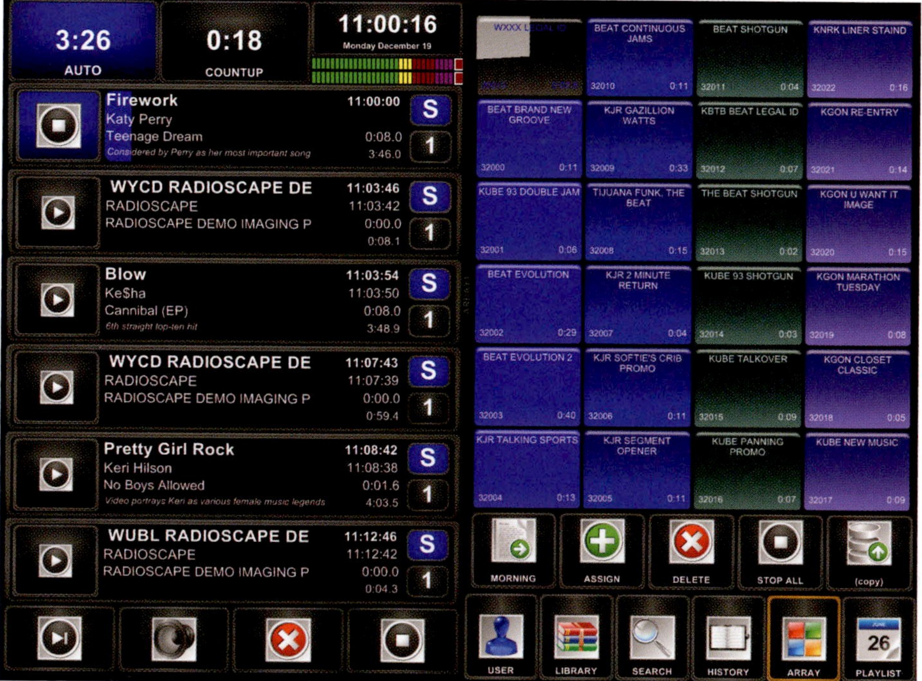

FIGURE 9.13
Enco's "DAD"—Digital Audio Delivery—automation software displays songs in sequential playback order. Courtesy of Enco.

FIGURE 9.14
The recorder feature of the Arrakis Digilink-HD automation system enables deejays to quickly capture phone calls for immediate playback. Courtesy of Arrakis Systems.

More recently, another category of software has found its way into station operations. Programs such as the Telos ProFiler and the OMT Technologies iMedialogger are replacing the cassette tape deck for "skimming" and program-archival purposes. Cassette "skimmers" are recording devices that are dedicated to the sole function of documenting the on-air content by making recordings of broadcasts whenever microphones are open. The recording commences whenever a microphone is switched on; it ceases when the mic is turned off. "Skim" tapes thus provide program directors and other managers with accurate recordings of deejay performances that exclude music and commercials. PDs are thus able to quickly and efficiently review the performances of on-air talent without having to navigate around the extraneous content. Today, this activity is easily performed on dedicated computers running program-archival software. In addition to managing the "skim" function the software can operate in "log" mode, making simultaneous "skim" and continuous recordings that document the entire broadcast, second-by-second. Because these functions are managed under software control, the recorded audio files may be accessed over the Internet readily and securely by out-of-market personnel, including group PDs and programming consultants.

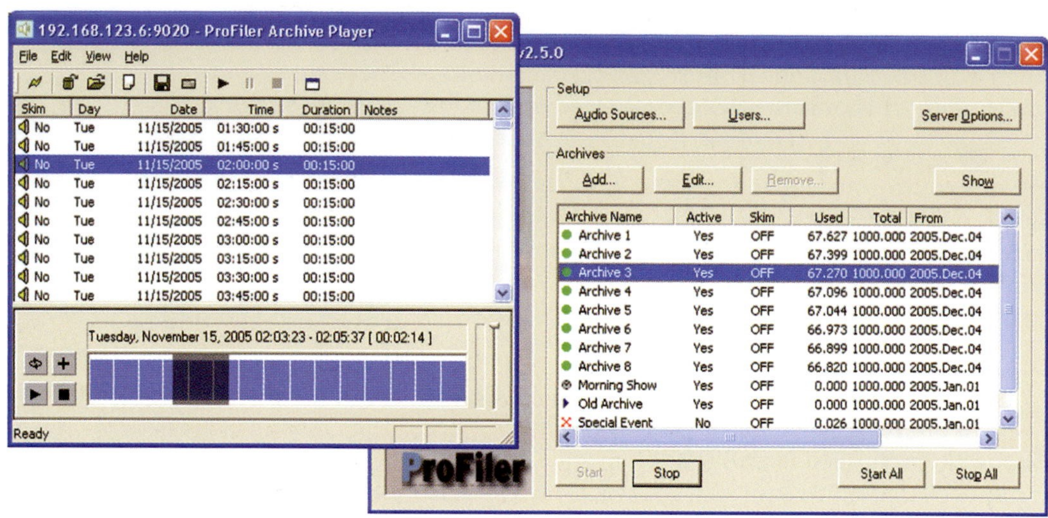

FIGURE 9.15
Air monitoring: Skimming and logging functions performed by ProFiler. Courtesy of the Telos Alliance.

VOICE-TRACKING

In the age of station ownership consolidation and studio clusters, radio corporations are finding it cost-efficient to feed their stations prerecorded voices. These days as much station announcing takes place away from the station as it does within the local studio. Radio companies hire off-premise announcers to meet stations' voicing needs, so there is less and less origination of on-site deejay patter. Utilizing the voice-tracking technique, the deejay creates the illusion of being physically present in the control room, announcing the songs and playing the commercials in real time. In reality, all voicing is prerecorded; the system correlates the voice recordings with the song playlist and delivers the mix to listeners. One announcer may be the voice of multiple stations, each supplied with deejay patter custom-created to the specific needs of the local market. Satellite feeds and the Internet-delivered audio populate local station airwaves with out-of-town voices.

Voice-tracking, of course, can just as readily be performed by in-house announcers. When voice-tracking is done at the station level, it ramps up efficiency, providing more multitasking opportunities for station personnel. Says Ed Shane, "Voice-tracking is an ideal productivity tool, allowing air talent to prerecord their air shifts in order to use their work time producing commercials, appearing live at sponsor locations, or doing a variety of jobs other than waiting for songs to end in order to deliver a ten-second talkover."

Voice-tracking has generated concern because the ranks of announcers are being thinned out. Jackie O'Brien, director of operations at Metro Networks, observes:

> The field of radio broadcasting has changed tremendously over the past few years. Many positions have been lost due to the innovation of voice-tracking. While this may be a cost-efficient way to run a radio group, it has taken away the personality of the service. When I started in broadcasting, I felt the position was more than the sound of my own voice. There was a commitment made to service the public with news, information, and a little entertainment. This meant staying on through a snowstorm or covering local elections. It also meant talking the occasional lonely heart out of suicide. I've been at Metro Networks for four years. In that time, I've watched old positions I held in radio disappear to voice-tracking.

Critics cite the loss of spontaneity associated with a truly "live" presentation as detrimental to the quality of service. Further, the practice of recording comments in advance of their broadcast makes it difficult to deliver accurate time checks, weather forecasts and up-to-the-minute information. On the other hand, proponents of voice-tracking—notably station owners and management—cite the improved operator efficiencies that automation enables. Experienced talent can record (or *track*) a typical three-hour airshift in less than 30 minutes, making them available for assignment to perform other station duties such as

FIGURE 9.16
Voice-tracking and other production activities are supported by this studio. Courtesy of Entercom Radio Memphis.

production and promotion. Tracking can assist owners in economizing on personnel salaries because fewer employees are required to staff the station. It bears noting that automating the radio broadcast was first accomplished more than 50 years ago, and the arguments, both pro and con, presented in this discussion are just as viable today as when they were first asserted in the 1960s. Despite concern for the impact voice-tracking has on the announcing profession and radio localism, more and more stations are using it, and the future would suggest that this practice—for better or worse—will grow.

STANDALONE RECORD/PLAY DECKS

As the ongoing evolution of audio technology progresses, it is not uncommon even today to find control and production rooms sporting an intermixture of analog and digital record/playback decks. Few would argue that analog magnetic tape's best days have passed. Nonetheless, certain stations find it convenient to maintain and support a working reel-to-reel or cartridge tape system, even if it's only to facilitate the digitization of legacy station archival recordings. Manufacturers experimented with several digital technologies in the 1990s seeking to find a viable replacement for the venerable analog cart machine. Equipment manufacturers introduced machines designed to write digital data files to removable storage media, including floppy disks, mini-discs, random-access memory and, eventually, directly to hard disks. These next-generation "cart machines" appealed to producers. Says station manager Vic Michaels, "They replaced the old-line carts, because they were faster, programmable, visual, digital, and competitively priced." Companies like Sony, Tascam, Denon, and Otari manufactured the mini-disc machine, which replaced the traditional analog cart machine at most stations—and subsequently became yet another victim of the computer age. Updated versions of two legacy digital devices from 360 Systems—the Instant Replay 2 and the Short/cut 2000—remain popular with deejays and show producers. Unlike most PC-based audio-playout arrangements, the 360 Systems are dedicated-function units. These easy-to-operate decks feature real-button operation, providing reaffirming, tactile responses to operators when hectic conditions in the studio demand split-second decision executions.

FIGURE 9.17
A professional, two-track, reel-to-reel analog tape deck. Courtesy Thomas A. White.

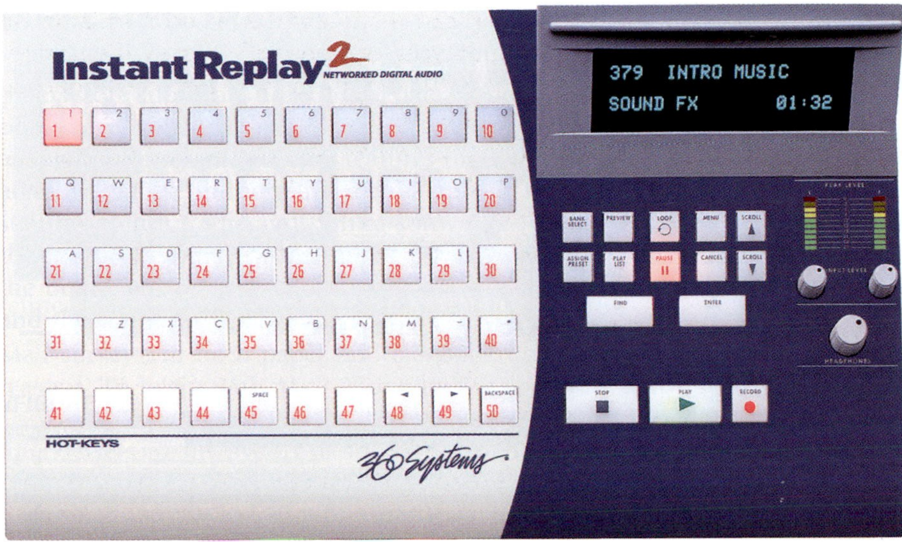

FIGURE 9.18
This successor to the analog cartridge tape recorder/reproducer offers instant playback access to 1,000 digital audio cuts. Courtesy 360 Systems®.

COMPACT DISCS

Compact disc players entered the radio production studio in the 1980s. Although CD players have been largely displaced by PC-based playout systems, their value as a piece of production equipment has not entirely vanished. Observes Skip Pizzi:

> Digital audio had its greatest initial acceptance as CD hardware, to the point where it was estimated that more than half of the radio stations in the U.S. used CDs to some extent. In major markets, this figure rose steeply. Many of these stations programmed music exclusively from CD, or nearly so. The practice of providing promotional copies of new releases on CD by record companies (following an earlier period of general reluctance to do so) became common practice. Second- and third-generation professional CD players aided in the process of acceptance [see Figure 9.20].

CD players employ a laser beam to read encoded data at a rate of 4.3218 million bits per second. A compact disc is 4.7 inches wide and 1.2 mm thick, and players are quite light and compact as well. This feature alone makes them attractive to broadcasters. But what makes a CD player most appealing to broadcasters is its superior sound. Compact disc players offer, among other features, far greater dynamic range than recorded vinyl or analog magnetic tape. CD audio reproduction has a characteristically lower signal-to-noise ratio than does analog-style reproduction, resulting in a more pristine and less-distorted sound quality. They also eliminate the need for physical contact during cueing, and erratic speed irregularities are virtually non-existent.

Because digital discs are specially coated, they are more resistant to damage than are analog discs. This is not to suggest that CDs are impervious; they are not. In fact, the majority of CD-related problems stem from the discs themselves and not the players. Despite initial claims of the invincibility of the digital disc, experience has shown that mishandling of discs is courting disaster. CDs cannot be mistreated—that is, used as Frisbees or placemats for peanut butter sandwiches—and still be expected to work like new. The simple fact is that, although compact discs are more resistant to damage, they can be harmed.

A CD reads a disc from its core outward, moving from 500-rpm on the inside to 200-rpm on the outer edge of the disc. Most CD players feature a variety of effect options, which can be of particular use to a production mix. Accessing cuts on a CD player is quick and simple, although excerpting segments from a track for inclusion in a mixdown can be somewhat less expedient. Nonetheless, CD players are still useful in the production studio. Compact discs are a wonderful source for bed music (music that serves as background under voiced copy) and sound effects.

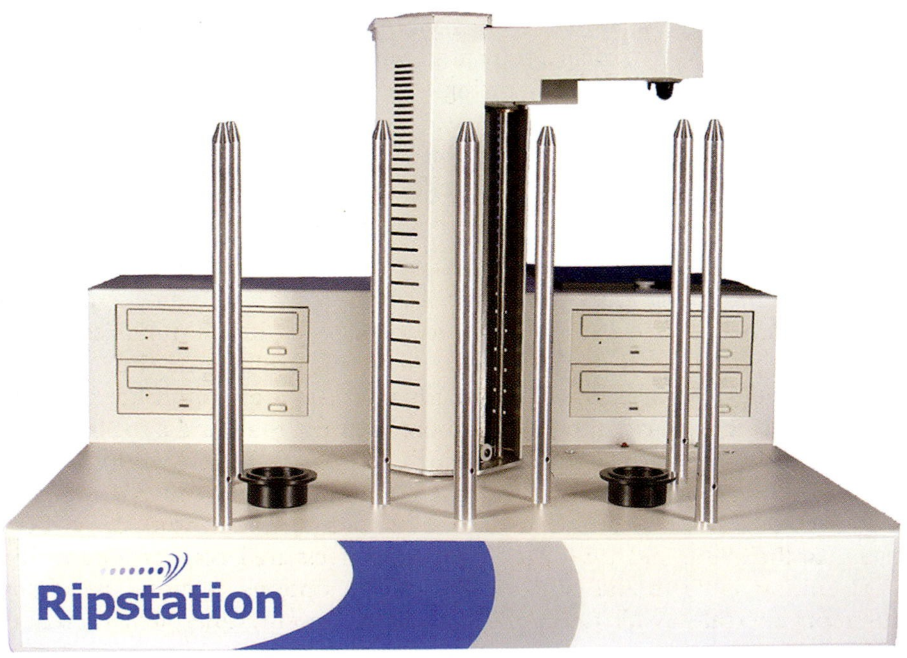

FIGURE 9.19
Automated CD track-ripper facilitates digital audio file extraction. Courtesy of MF Digital.

Working with a CD unit is anything but complicated. Press a button and a tray ejects (on top-loaded models a door pops open). A disc is placed into the tray, and the press of the same button returns the tray and disc into the player. The operator then selects the track to be played and presses the appropriately numbered button. The audio rolls.

Burnable CD units (CD-R and CD-RW) are prominent in the production room. CD-Rs allow one-time burning, whereas CD-RWs are rewritable and thus can be burned and erased repeatedly.

FIGURE 9.20
CD players cart players continue to be used in some studios. Courtesy of Denon.

COMPRESSORS, EQUALIZERS, AND AUDIO PROCESSING

"There are three domains of audio," says producer Ty Ford. "They are amplitude, frequency, and time." Some stations alter amplitude to create the illusion of being louder without actually changing level. This is called compressing the signal. Production people use compressors to enhance loudness as well as to eliminate or cut out ambient noise, thus focusing on specifics of mix. Compression often is used as a method of getting listeners to take greater notice of a piece of production and as a remedy to certain problems (see Figure 9.22).

Equalizers (EQs) work the frequency domain of audio by boosting and/or reducing the pitch frequencies across the sound spectrum. EQs allow producers to correct problems such as boomy bass tones or high-pitched tinniness as well as to create parity between different elements of production. They are also useful in creating special effects. Equalization now can be accomplished onboard (within audio console circuitry) and outboard (either by a standalone hardware unit or within a software application such as Pro Tools or Audition). Most audio processors are time-domain devices. Outboard units, often referred to as "effects processors" or simply as "boxes," became popular production room fixtures in the 1980s and 1990s. Today, special effects are largely created within audio editing software and enhanced by plug-in options. Stations use digital processors to create a wide range of effects such as reverb, time/pitch alteration, and flange.

In the last few years, radio stations have become increasingly interested in what audio processors have to offer their mixes. Today these boxes are a familiar,

FIGURE 9.21
Screens, screens everywhere: Multiple video monitors display important studio-operations parameters. Courtesy of the Telos Alliance.

often integral, item in production rooms at the majority of stations. Their value in the creation of commercials, PSAs, promos, and features is inestimable. The use of samplers and synthesizers is common in radio production rooms too. Samplers let a production person load a studio audio source (recorder, live mike) into its built-in microprocessor and then manipulate the digitized data with the aid of a synthesizer keyboard to create a multitude of effects. Samplers are wired to an audio console so that the sounds they produce may be integrated into mixdown. Samplers are also found in certain audio effects processors with musical instrument digital interface (MIDI). A sample is a digital recording of a small bit of sound.

FIGURE 9.22
Digital effects processor. Courtesy of Lexicon.

"A lot of musical instrument (MI) gear has been introduced into the radio production studio. Synths, samplers, and sequencers are pretty commonplace today," notes Ty Ford.

PATCH PANELS AND ROUTING SWITCHERS

A patch panel consists of rows of jacks (receptacles) that have been wired to inputs and outputs connected to various external sources—studios, equipment, remote locations, network lines, and so forth. Patch panels essentially are routing devices that allow for items not directly wired into an audio console to become a part of a broadcast or production mixdown. Routing switchers represent another method for distributing audio signals within and across studios. These standalone devices are usually centrally located and rack-mounted for easy access. Equipment input and output connections are accomplished easily by means of push-button selection. Today, says Vic Michaels, "Patch panels are still utilized but not as frequently as before. Use is based on a station's needs. Digital consoles now have internal patch capabilities built right into the console so one can patch in certain effects or sources to any channel" (see Figure 9.23). "And, of course, with an IP-Audio network," Clark Novak explains, "routing any output to any input systemwide can be easily accomplished in several different ways:

1. You can use a software application that has a graphic cross-point representation onscreen that allows you to pick an input and output and route

FIGURE 9.23
Interconnections among consoles, processors, telephone systems, and monitors converge with Livewire™ networking technology. Courtesy of the Telos Alliance.

one to the other; this is common to both AoIP and older TDM routing switchers alike.

2. There are also hardware appliances that mount in studio or TOC racks that allow users to select from a list of inputs and outputs and switch them. Again, these are common to both TDM and AoIP routing systems.
3. Some systems allow the station engineer to build graphical interfaces, or 'user panels,' which can be displayed on a studio computer monitor. These panels typically have a preselected set of routing choices that allow the air talent to pick from a preapproved menu of routing operations."

MICROPHONES

Microphones are designed with different pickup patterns (see Figure 9.25). Omnidirectional microphones are sensitive to sound from all directions (360°), whereas bidirectional microphones pick up sound from two directions (180°). The unidirectional microphone draws sound from only one path (90°), and because of its highly directed field of receptivity, extraneous sounds that enter the microphone from the sides and the rear tend to be rejected. This feature has made the unidirectional microphone popular in both the control and production studios, where generally one person is at work at a time. Most studio consoles possess two or more microphone inputs so that additional voices can be accommodated when the need arises

Omnidirectional and bidirectional microphones often are used when more than one voice is involved. For instance, an omnidirectional may be used for the broadcast or recording of a roundtable discussion, and the bidirectional during a one-on-one interview.

Announcers must be aware of a microphone's directional features. Proper positioning in relation to a microphone is important. Being outside the path of a microphone's pickup (off-mic) affects sound quality. At the same time, operating too close to a microphone without using proper breath control can

FIGURE 9.24
The look of microphones in the 1920s. Courtesy of Jim Steele.

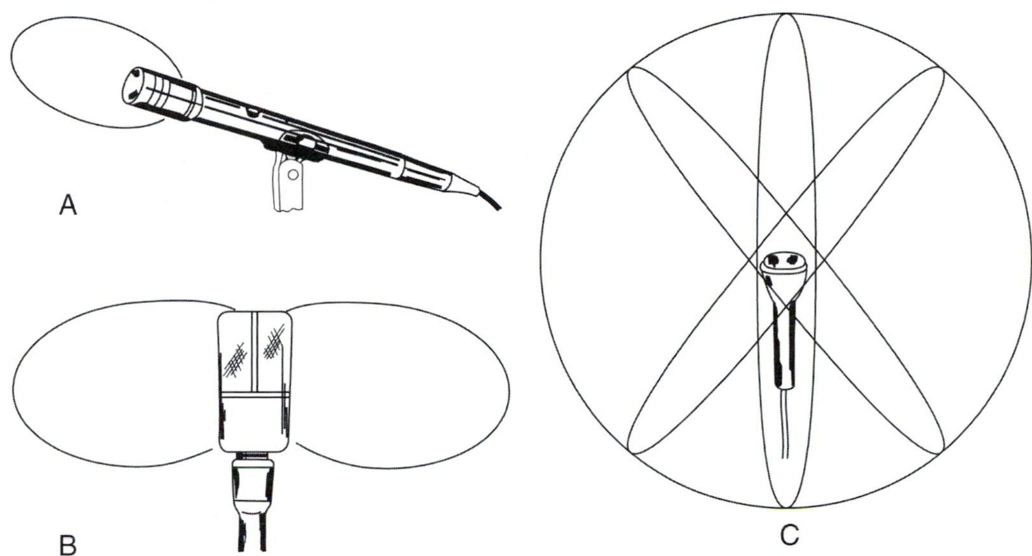

FIGURE 9.25
Microphone pickup patters: (A) unidirectional, (B) bidirectional, and (C) omnidirectional.

FIGURE 9.26
The RCA model 77DX ribbon microphone was a favorite of many deejays in the mid-twentieth century. Its design enhances low-frequency response, accentuating the resonance of the male voice. Courtesy of Randal Crow and Chuck Bethea.

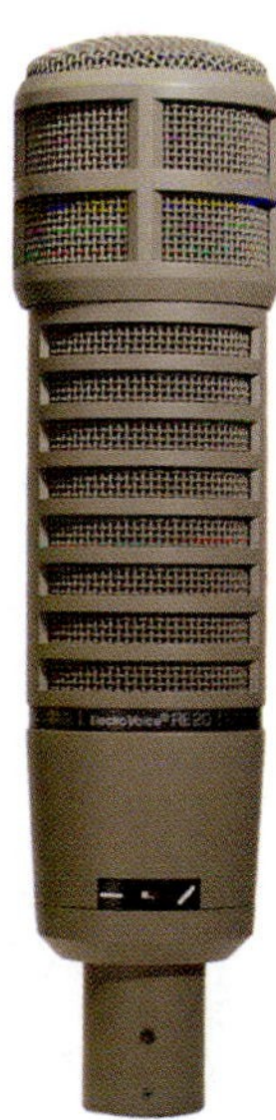

FIGURE 9.27
The rugged Electro-Voice RE20 dynamic cardioid microphone is frequently seen in contemporary studios. Courtesy of Electro-Voice.

result in distortion, known as popping and blasting. Keeping a hand's length away from a microphone and "working" the mic slightly off the center axis of pickup will usually prevent this from occurring. Windscreens and blast filters may be attached to a microphone to help reduce distortion.

TELEPHONES

The telephone instrument and the service that supports it have been essential tools to radio broadcasting since the medium's beginning and are routinely utilized in both studio and remote applications. Due in part to a rise in the popularity of the Talk format and also in part to advancements in technology, studio telephone systems have become increasingly more sophisticated and complex. Decades ago the broadcast of a caller's voice was a technically unsophisticated arrangement. A simple, direct electrical connection between a telephone desk set and an input fader on the control board was all that was needed. It was a cumbersome arrangement that often left the deejay juggling the phone handset while trying to sustain other control room operations.

Today the phone-conversation broadcast is a streamlined operation, supported by digital circuitry and operating under computer-system control. Air talent no longer fumbles with the telephone receiver; incoming caller audio is directed into headphones while outgoing studio conversation is picked up through studio microphones and relayed to callers. Technical fidelity is much-improved and minimizes the effect of the psychoacoustic phenomenon termed "listener fatigue" which can result in listener tune-out.

FIGURE 9.28
Producers of talk shows utilize telephone hybrid equipment such as this six-line system. Courtesy of the Telos Alliance.

REMOTE PICK-UP (RPU)

Remote broadcasts are a mainstay of radio stations regardless of market size. From coverage of professional sports contests to program origination from the county fair to the grand opening of the newest used-car dealership, broadcasters have been there, mics in hand, to bring all the details to listeners.

In the previous millennium it was common for stations to have mobile control room studios, either custom-constructed at the remote broadcast location or built into vehicles, to put the magic of creating a radio broadcast on full display in front of audiences. The opportunities for listeners to be able to put a face to a voice, grab an autographed deejay photo, and participate in on-the-scene contests were attractive lures, and in many instances retail businesses were all-too-willing to pay for the privilege of hosting stations and their personalities. As popular music formats transitioned from AM to FM in the 1970s and 1980s, competing stations realized the difficulties of replicating the high-fidelity sonic quality of their studio broadcasts at remote-broadcast sites. Stations began dispatching talent to the remote locations with just their microphones, opting to originate the music playback in-house. In more recent times, audience interest in seeing how radio broadcasts are engineered has been lessened by the ubiquitous personal computer: playing digital music files with computer software, after all, is not too much different in the home as it is in the station control room.

That being said, the remote broadcast remains a staple of many stations' schedules. Studio-to-remote site interconnection initially was accomplished using dedicated telephone circuits. During the 1960s, stations began using wireless VHF transceiving equipment to deliver audio. Transceivers manufactured by George Marti became ubiquitous staples for remote broadcasting, and products bearing his name continue to be widely used to achieve short-hop (typically up to 30 miles) connection. Manufacturers of remote pick-up equipment continue to embrace advances in technology, exploiting the capabilities of the Internet and cellular telephone networks. The result is a variety of products that are becoming increasingly more lightweight, portable, and feature-laden. A current generation of portable RPUs combines the audio amplification and control features of a remote mixer with dedicated computer circuitry and modems, packaged in desktop and handheld configurations. High-fidelity audio and interruptible feedback (IFB) capabilities make possible the origination of remote broadcasting with sophistication and listenability.

ISDNs are digital phone lines that bring voices and other audio to studios with near-perfect sound quality. Because voice-tracking has become the means by which so many stations fill their airwaves, ISDN connections have become invaluable.

As production director Matt Grasso observes, "The day of the scratchy cell phone or muddy dedicated line is over. Your talent sounds like they are right in the studio. If they are at a club, not only can they talk, but they can broadcast the

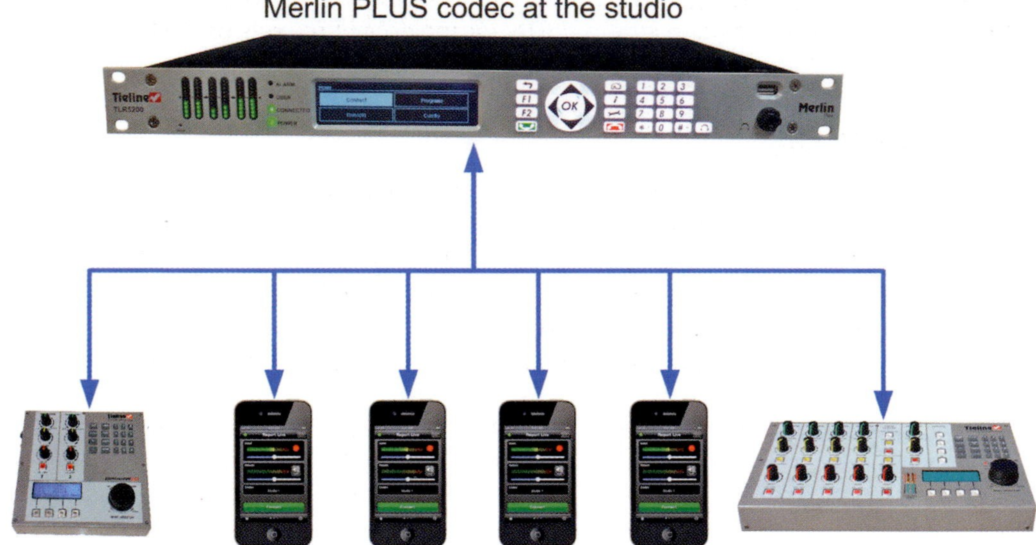

FIGURE 9.29
Mixer-style and Android-based encoders relay remote audio to studio receiver. Courtesy of Tieline.

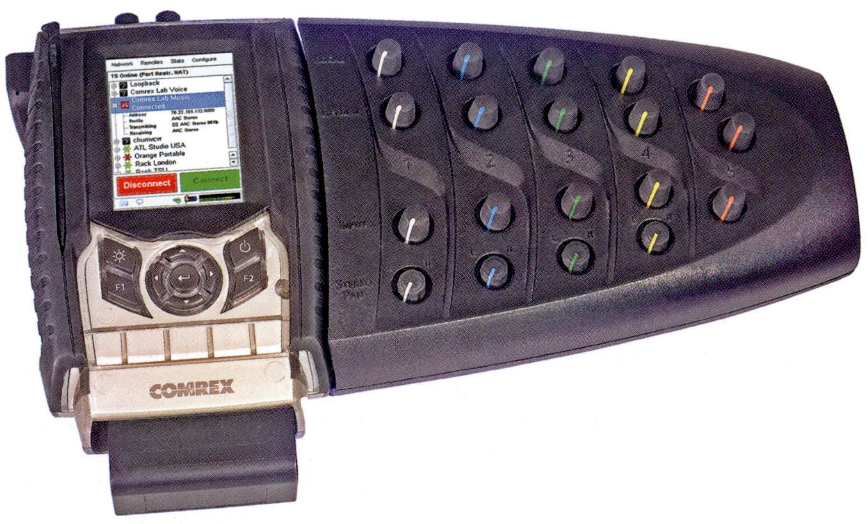

FIGURE 9.30
A dockable mixer extends the capabilities of this remote codec to five microphone- or line-level inputs. Courtesy of Comrex.

music they are playing there right over the air with the same quality you would get from a CD player in the main studio. ISDN means no reel-to-reels or DATs coming to a station via snail mail either."

DIGITAL EDITING

Old-school, physical tape editing is a lost art that ranged from effecting a simple repair to constructing a complicated rearrangement of sound elements. Today the old razor-blade approach to cutting and splicing tape is all but ancient history, having lost ground to "non-destructive," tapeless digital methods.

Computers handle the bulk of editing in the production room. This tapeless approach involves loading audio into a RAM or hard disc and making edits via a monitor (with the aid of a mouse, a keyboard, or a console). Although this technology has been costly in the past, today prices are quite affordable, motivating more and more stations to convert to the tapeless studio. Computerized audio workstations were once perceived as the studio of the future, but they are the studio of today.

FIGURE 9.31
Ultimately portable podcasting: Simply add a laptop to this mic/headset/software package. Courtesy of Focusrite.

COPYWRITING

Poet Stephen Vincent Benet, who wrote for radio during its heyday, called the medium "the theater of the mind." Indeed, the person who tunes in to radio gets no visual aids but must manufacture images on his or her own to accompany the words and sounds being broadcast. The station employee who prepares written material is called a copywriter. A copywriter's job consists primarily of writing commercials, promos, and PSAs, with the emphasis on the first of the three.

Not all stations employ a fulltime copywriter. This is especially true in small markets where economics dictate that salespeople write on behalf of their own advertisers' accounts. Deejays also are called on to pen commercials. At stations with bigger operating budgets, a fulltime copywriter often will handle the bulk of the writing chores.

Copywriters must possess a complete understanding of the unique nature of the medium, a familiarity with the audience for which the commercial message is intended, and knowledge of the product being promoted. A station's format will influence the style of writing in a commercial; thus, the copywriter also must be thoroughly acquainted with the station's particular programming approach. Commercials must be compatible with the station's sound. For instance, copy written for Lite AC usually is more conservative in tone than that written for Modern Rock stations, and so on.

Here's an example from WXXX "Home of the Hits":

> (SFX: Bed in) TJ's Rockhouse, Mart Street, Downtown Boise, presents Cleo and the gang rocking out every Friday and Saturday night. At TJ's there's never a cover or minimum, just a good time. Sunday Idaho's monarchs of rockabilly, Jobee Lane, raise the roof at TJ's. You better be ready to shake it, because nobody stands still when Jobee Lane rocks. Thursday is half-price night, and ladies always get their first drink free at Boise's number one club for fun and music. Take Main to Mark Street and look for the house that rocks, TJ's Rockhouse. (SFX: Stinger out)

And another example, this one's from WYYY "Soothing Sounds":

> Elegant dining is just a scenic ride away. (SFX: Bed in and under) The critically acclaimed Viscount (vy-count) Inn in Cedar Glenn offers patrons an exquisite menu in a setting without equal. The Viscount's 18th-century charm will make your evening out one to remember. Jamison Longley of the *Wisconsin Register* gives the Viscount a four-star rating for service,

FIGURE 9.32
This console features 12 mixing channels in a compact desktop layout. Courtesy of Wheatstone.

cuisine, and atmosphere. The Viscount (SFX: Royal fanfare) will satisfy your royal tastes. Call 675–2180 for reservations. Take Route 17 north to the Viscount Inn, 31 Stony Lane, Cedar Glenn.

Some basic rules pertain to the mechanics of copy preparation. First, copy is word-processed and double-spaced for ease of reading. Next, left and right margins are set at one inch. Sound effects are noted in parentheses at that point in the copy where they are to occur. Proper punctuation and grammar are vital, too. A comma in the wrong place can throw off the meaning of an entire sentence. Be mindful, also, that commercials are designed to be heard and not read. Keep sentence structure as straightforward and uncomplicated as possible. Maintaining a conversational style will improve comprehension of the client's message.

Timing a piece of copy is relatively simple. There are a couple of methods: one involves counting words, and the other counting lines. In the first approach, 25 words would constitute ten seconds; 75 words, 30 seconds; and 150 words, one minute. Counting lines is an easier and quicker way of timing copy. This method is based on the assumption that it takes, on average, three seconds to read one line of copy from margin to margin. Therefore, nine to ten lines of copy would time out to around 30 seconds, and 18–20 lines to one minute. Of course, production elements such as sound effects and beds must be included as part of the count and deducted accordingly. For example, six seconds worth of sound effects in a 30-second commercial would shorten the amount of actual copy by two lines.

Because everything written in radio is intended to be read aloud, it is important that words with unusual or uncommon pronunciations be given special attention. Phonetic spelling is used to convey the way a word is pronounced. For instance: "Dinner at the Fo'c'sle (Foke'-sil) Restaurant in Laitone (Lay'-ton) Shores is a sea adventure." Incorrect pronunciation has resulted in more than one canceled account. The copywriter must make certain that the announcer assigned to voice-track a commercial is fully aware of any particularities in the copy. In other words, when in doubt spell it out.

Excessive numbers and complex directions are to be avoided in radio copy. Numbers, such as an address or telephone number, should be repeated and directions should be as simple as possible. The use of landmarks ("across from city hall . . .") can reduce confusion. Listeners are seldom in a position to write down something at the exact moment they hear it. Copy should communicate, not confuse or frustrate.

Of course, the purpose of any piece of copy is to sell the client's product. Creativity plays an important role. The radio writer has the world of the imagination to work with and is limited only by the boundaries of his own.

FIGURE 9.33 *(Above)* From the remote broadcast location an operator can control the studio console with this software app. Courtesy of Wheatstone.

Before

Track 1	VOICE
Track 2	BED #1
Track 3	SFX
Track 4	BED #2

After

Track 1	VOICE
Track 2	BED #1
Track 3	SFX #1
Track 4	SFX #2

FIGURE 9.34 Editing a multitrack involves adding or deleting tracks. Here BED 2 is replaced by SFX 2 on track 4.

ANNOUNCING TIPS

Although the radio announcer ranks have dwindled as radio companies consolidate and downsize their staffs and employ voice-tracking to serve multiple stations, thousands of men and women in this country still make their living before the microphone. In few other professions is the salary range so broad. A beginning announcer may make little more than minimum wage, whereas a seasoned professional in a major market may earn a salary in the six-figure range.

Although announcer salaries can be very modest in smaller markets, the financial rewards tend to be substantial at metro market stations, which can afford to pay more. Of course, competition for the metro market station positions is keener, and expectations are higher. "You have to pay your dues in this profession. It's usually a long and winding road. It takes time to develop the on-air skills that the big stations want. It's hard work to become really good, but you can make an enormous amount of money, or at least a very comfortable income, when you do," says radio personality Mike Morin.

The duties of an announcer vary depending on the size or ranking of a station. In the small station, announcers generally fill news and/or production shifts as well. For example, a midday announcer at WXXX, who is on the air from 10 am until 3 pm, may be held responsible for the 4 and 5 pm. newscasts, plus any production that arises during that same period. Meanwhile, the larger station may require nothing more of its announcers than to record voiceovers. Of course, the preparation for an airshift at a major-market station can be very time-consuming.

An announcer must, above all else, possess the ability to effectively read copy aloud. Among other things, this involves proper enunciation and inflection, which are improved through practice. Programmer Bill Towery contends that the more a person reads for personal enjoyment or enrichment, the easier it is to communicate orally. "I'd advise anyone who aspires to the microphone to read, read, read. The more the better. Announcing is oral interpretation of the printed page. You must first understand what is on the page before you can communicate it aloud. Bottom line here is that if you want to become an announcer, first become a reader."

Having a naturally resonant and pleasant-sounding voice certainly is an advantage. Voice quality still is very important in radio. There is an inclination toward the voice with a deeper register. This is true for female announcers as well as male. However, most voices possess considerable range and with training, practice, and experience even a person with a high-pitched voice can develop an appealing on-air sound. Forcing the voice into a lower register to achieve a deeper sound can result in injury to the vocal chords. "Making the most of what you already have is a lot better than trying to be something you're not. Perfect yourself and be natural," advises Morin.

Relaxation is important. The voice simply is at its best when it is not strained. Moreover, announcing is enhanced by proper breathing, which is only possible when one is free of stress. Initially, being "on-mic" can be an intimidating experience, resulting in nervousness that can be debilitating. Here are some things announcers do to achieve a state of relaxation:

1. Read copy aloud before going on the air. Get the feel of it. This will automatically increase confidence, thus aiding in relaxation.
2. Take several deep breaths and slowly exhale while keeping your eyes closed.
3. Sit still for a couple of moments with your arms limp at your sides. Tune out. Let the dust settle. Conjure pleasant images. Allow yourself to drift a bit, and then slowly return to the job at hand.
4. Stand and slowly move your upper torso in a circular motion for a minute or so. Flex your shoulders and arms. Stretch luxuriously.
5. If possible, remain standing during your delivery. When seated, check your posture. Do not slump over as you announce. A curved diaphragm impedes breathing. Sit erect, but not stiffly.
6. Hum a few bars of your favorite song. The vibration helps relax the throat muscles and vocal chords.
7. Give yourself ample time to settle in before going on. Dashing into the studio at the last second will jar your focus and shake your composure.

In most situations, an accent—regional or otherwise—is a handicap and should be eliminated. Contrary to the misperceptions, most radio announcers in the South do not have a drawl, and the majority of announcers in Boston put the

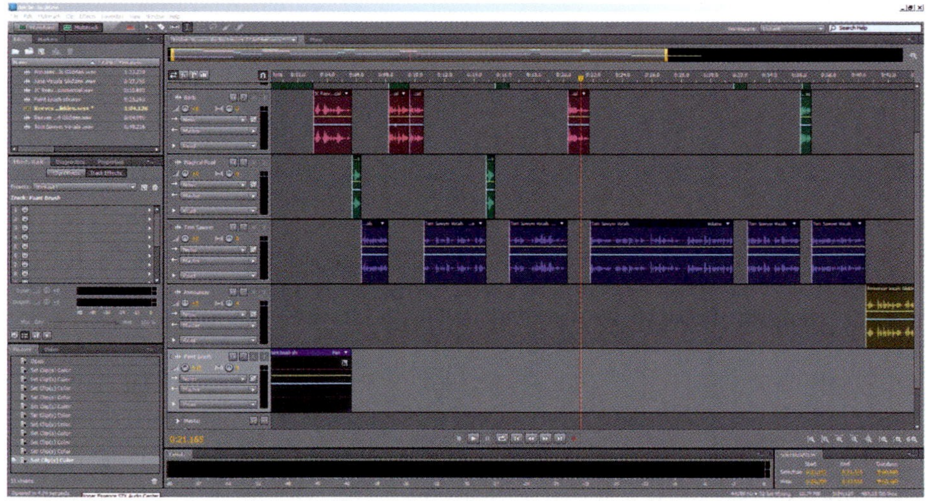

FIGURE 9.35
A multitrack audio layout in Adobe Audition. Producers isolate individual audio elements into separate tracks to achieve greater control over the sound of the final mix. Courtesy of Audra Wiant and Richard Withers.

"r" in the word "car." A noticeable or pronounced accent will almost always put the candidate for an announcer's job out of the running. Accents are not easy to eliminate, but with practice they can be overcome.

THE SOUND LIBRARY

Music is used to enhance an advertiser's message—to make it more appealing, more listenable. The music used in a radio commercial is called a *bed* simply because it supports the voice. It is the platform on which the voice is set. A station may bed thousands of commercials over the course of a year. Music is an integral component of the production mixdown.

Today, sound libraries are almost always delivered via downloads. However, many stations still derive bed music from other sources. Demonstration CDs (demos) sent by recording companies to radio stations are a familiar source when used with appropriate copyright permissions, since few actually make it onto playlists and into on-air rotations. These CDs are particularly useful because the music is unfamiliar to the listening audience. Known tunes generally are avoided in the mixdown of spots because they tend to distract the listener from the copy. However, there are times when familiar tunes are used to back spots. Nightclubs often request that popular music be used in their commercials to convey a certain mood and ambiance.

Movie soundtrack CDs are another good place to find beds because they often contain a variety of music, ranging from the bizarre to the conventional. They also are an excellent source for special audio effects, which can be used to great advantage in the right commercial.

On-air CDs are screened for potential production use as well. Although several tracks may be placed in on-air rotation and thereby eliminated for use in the mixdown of commercials, some cuts will not be programmed and therefore will not be available for production purposes.

Syndicated bed music libraries are available at a price and are widely used at larger stations. The All Access Music Group online directory contains a complete listing of production companies offering bed music libraries. TM Studios in Dallas is an established and highly regarded source of production music and station-imaging materials. According to TM's Greg Clancy, "Stations need a variety of musical elements to support the position and image they wish to create. Clients may need production music to put behind a commercial for a local client. They may need pieces of music or sound effects to support a voiced 'liner' that says the station name. Whatever their needs, we can help."

Creating a stylistic musical identity for a station poses a unique set of challenges to a jingle producer. At TM, Clancy says, the inspiration for a theme can come from "anywhere." He explains the jingle idea may originate in "the deep recesses of a composer's brain" or may be influenced by "styles that represent the current playlist of a particular station. Some programmers want the sound of

106.7 WIZN **PRODUCTION ORDER** 99.9 The Buzz

Client SMITH HDWARE AE KEITH

STATION: WIZN (WBTZ) (:30) :60

START DATE 9-14 END DATE 11-21

ROTATION INSTRUCTIONS Equal
(How many versions? 2)

✓ PRODUCE USING ATTACHED COPY
___ ADD TAG TO EXISTING SPOT
___ SPEC SPOT
___ NEED A CASSETTE

DUB FROM:
MP3 ✓
DGS___
Spot Taxi___
Other___

SEND DUB TO: KALO
(via MP3) via reel
Address: ___

APPROVALS:
___ NO APPROVAL NEEDED
✓ NEEDS APPROVAL
CONTACT:___
PHONE NUMBER:___
___ OK TO LEAVE ON VOICE MAIL AND PUT ON THE AIR

OTHER INSTRUCTIONS Use Bill on VT

FOR PRODUCTION USE ONLY
Music/SFX___
Date/Time Produced___
Date/Time Approved___

CART NUMBERS
WIZN___
Buzz___

FIGURE 9.36
Production order. Courtesy of WBTZ.

FIGURE 9.37
Instrumentalists perform their parts during a production-music recording session. Courtesy of TM Studios and WestwoodOne.

the jingles to sound like the music played on the station, and some want the jingles to stand out from the format playlist by being completely different." The process begins with ideation:

> We typically start with a brief from the client, outlining structural and stylistic needs. He might have specific needs, such as requiring several themes to support his morning show. He might need traffic and news opens and beds . . . just depends on what the client wants. We also listen intently to how he wants the jingles to sound, and how he will use them. We typically create demos to make sure we are going down the correct path, then go into full instrumental production. The vocals are usually the last layers to be recorded, then mixing and mastering begin.

Additionally, a search of the Internet will yield lists of audio production sources. The majority of stations continue to lift beds from in-house CDs.

Music used for production purposes is catalogued so that it can be located and reused. Syndicated libraries come fully catalogued. When catalogs and sound files are stored side-by-side in a station computer database, producers can easily and readily identify, locate and integrate into a mix the appropriate track that can make the spot both memorable and effective. If a file exists for a bed that is not in current use and the bed is appropriate for a new account, then either a fresh file will be prepared or the new information will be added into the existing file.

No production studio is complete without a commercial sound effects library, but in the digital age, many effects are made in-house. Sound effects libraries can be purchased for as little as $100, or they can cost thousands. The quality and selection of effects vary accordingly. Specially tailored audio effects also are available for imaging purposes, enabling stations to create unique sound signatures for promos and sweepers. Libraries can run into the thousands but can add a unique touch to a station's sound.

WRITE GREAT COPY

Good copy is essential for successful advertising. To make certain the ad will attract customers for your client, remember these points:

1) Make your first sentence count. Does it provoke interest? Does it demand attention? Does it create a mood? If your first sentence doesn't have it, you've lost your best chance at getting the listeners' attention.

2) Keep your copy simple. The most eloquent thoughts are expressed in few words. If good writers can express complex emotions such as "love" simply, why are convoluted sentences needed to sell a leather coat? Cogent copy takes time and effort. The results are worth it.

3) Write for one person. Don't use words like "many of you" that refer to a lot of people listening. Radio isn't TV; people listen and respond to radio as individuals. Make your copy personal.

4) Eliminate the details. Store hours, telephone numbers, the credit cards they accept are useful in newspaper ads, not on radio. People don't listen to radio with a scratch pad handy. These details take up space and won't motivate anyone to buy anything.

5) Use a "locator." Store addresses are hard to remember, harder to visualize where they might be. Listeners relate better to "locators"—places they know or can easily find. "Across from the fairgrounds" will be remembered, "1365 N. King Street" likely won't be.

6) Focus on one thought or idea. What is the single most important thing you want the listener to know? Make it personal, make it entertaining, make it exciting—but concentrate on one theme idea. Never resort to a laundry list of services or use cliches.

7) Create and consistently use a phrase that "positions" the business or product. This will help the listener recall the business and why he/she should go there. Examples: Chevy Trucks: "Like a Rock"; Fox News Channel, "Fair and Balanced"; "Dude, you're gettin' a Dell."

8) After you've written the copy, read it aloud to someone else. Find out what they remembered. You may need to revise it.

BROADCAST MARKETING CONSULTANTS • 35 Main Street, Wayland, Massachusetts 01778 • 508/653-7200 • Fax 508/653-4088

FIGURE 9.38
Tips on writing effective copy. Courtesy of Broadcasting Unlimited.

CHAPTER HIGHLIGHTS

1. The first radio commercials aired in 1922.
2. Early commercials were live readings: no music, sound effects, or singing.
3. Dialogue spots, using drama and comedy to sell the product, became prominent in the 1930s. Elaborate sound effects, actors, and orchestras were employed.
4. With the introduction of magnetic recording tape and 33_ LPs in the 1950s, live commercial announcements were replaced by prerecorded messages.
5. The copy, delivery, and mixdown of commercials must be adapted to match the station's format to avoid audience tune-out.
6. The production director (imaging director) records voice tracks, mixes commercials, PSAs, and station-imaging content. The director maintains the bed music and special effects libraries, mixes promotional material and special programs, and performs basic editing chores.
7. At smaller stations the production responsibilities are assigned part-time to on-air personnel or the program director.
8. The production director usually answers to the program director and works closely with the copywriter and the traffic manager.
9. For ease of movement and accessibility, both on-air and production studio equipment are arranged in a U-shape. The equipment and cabinetry can be configured to accommodate announcers who either are standing or seated.
10. The audio console (board) is the central piece of equipment. It consists of inputs, which permit audio energy to enter the console; outputs through which audio energy is fed to other locations; VU meters, which measure the level of sound; pots (faders), which control the quantity (gain) of sound; monitor gains, which control in-studio volume; and master gains, which control general output levels.
11. When operating the console in cue or preview mode, the operator can listen privately to various audio sources without channeling them through an output.
12. Digital audio hardware such as the 360 Systems Instant Replay 2 and Short/cut 2000 devices and automation software programs have replaced the standard analog cartridge tape deck. They let producers digitally mix and archive extensive amounts of audio.
13. Compact disc players use a laser beam to decode the disc's surface, which eliminates stylus and turntable noises, distortion, and record damage.
14. Audio processors, samplers, digital carts, and MIDI enhance a radio production studio's product. Virtual processing effects are available in software such as Adobe Audition and Pro Tools, which have these features built in.
15. A patch panel is a routing device, consisting of inputs and outputs, connecting the audio console with various external sources. Analog and digital technologies are utilized to manage signal routing, which occurs within the console as well as externally.
16. Microphones are designed with different pickup patterns to accommodate different functions: omnidirectional (all directions), bidirectional (two directions), and unidirectional (one direction).

17. Telephone technology has been central to the operation of radio stations since the beginning. Telephone equipment is especially important to the operation of talk-intensive formats.

18. Remote broadcasting is common and remains a widespread practice for news and sports coverage, and entertainment program origination. Wired and wireless telephone services are routinely utilized with remote pickup units (RPUs) to deliver audio signals to the main studio.

19. Audio editing ranges from simple repairs to complicated rearrangements of sound elements. The formerly popular razor-cut splicing approach to tape editing has been replaced by non-destructive computer and multitrack methods.

20. Digital audio workstations, which rely on computer technology and software (Pro Tools and Adobe Audition are very popular), are currently used in a vast number of radio production studios.

21. The station copywriter, who writes the commercials, promos, and PSAs, must be familiar with the intended audience and the product being sold. The station's format and programming approach influence the style of writing. Copy should be word-processed, double-spaced, and have 1-inch margins. Sound effects are noted in parentheses, and phonetic spellings are provided for difficult words.

22. Aspiring announcers must be able to read copy aloud with proper inflection and enunciation. A naturally resonant and pleasant-sounding voice without a regional accent is an advantage.

FIGURE 9.39
The production person remains the station's true artist whether the studio is cutting-edge digital or old-world analog. Courtesy of WIZN.

FIGURE 9.40
Founding *Keith's Radio Station* author Dr. Michael C. Keith sits in what was regarded as a state-of-the-art studio in 1980. Courtesy Boston College.

23. The practice of voice-tracking is reducing the number of announcing jobs. More and more, local station announcing originates elsewhere, especially in cluster operations and when stations are a part of major station groups.

24. Every station maintains a sound library for use in spot mixdowns. Commercially produced sound effects, bed music collections, and unfamiliar cuts from CDs and the Internet (and even LPs) are common source materials. Digital equipment and computer workstations allow producers to create their own in-house effects.

SUGGESTED FURTHER READING

Adams, M.H. and Massey, K., *Introduction to Radio: Production and Programming*, Brown and Benchmark, Madison, WI, 1995.

Alburger, J.R. and Hall, M., *The Art of Voice Acting*, Focal Press, Boston, MA, 2002.

Alten, S.R., *Audio in Media*, 8th edition, Wadsworth Publishing, Belmont, CA, 2007.

Alvear, J., *Web Developer.com Guide to Streaming Multimedia*, Wiley, New York, 1998.

Baker, J., *Secrets of Voice-Over Success: Top Voice-Over Actors Reveal How They Did It*, 2nd edition, Sentient Publications, Boulder, CO, 2009.

Ballou, G., *Handbook for Sound Engineers*, 3rd edition, Focal Press, Boston, MA, 2008.

Bartlett, B., *Stereo Microphone Techniques*, Focal Press, Boston, MA, 1991.

Campbell, T., *Wireless Writing in the Age of Marconi*, University of Minnesota, Minneapolis, MN, 2006.

Derry, R., *Audio Editing with Adobe Audition 2.0: Broadcast, Desktop and CD Audio Production*, Focal Press, Boston, MA, 2006.

Ford, T., *Advanced Audio Production Techniques*, Focal Press, Boston, MA, 1993.

Garrigus, S. R., *Sound Forge 8 Power!: The Official Guide*, Cengage Learning, Independence, KY, 2005.

Hausman, C., et al., *Announcing: Broadcast Communicating Today*, 5th edition, Wadsworth Publishing, Belmont, CA, 2003.

Hausman, C., et al., *Modern Radio Production: Production Programming & Performance*, 9th edition, Wadsworth Publishing, Boston, MA, 2013.

Hilliard, R.L., *Writing for Television, Radio, and New Media (Broadcast and Production)*, 10th edition, Wadsworth Publishing, Boston, MA, 2011.

Hoffer, J., *Radio Production Techniques*, Tab Books, Blue Ridge Summit, PA, 1974.

Hyde, S.W., *Television and Radio Announcing*, 11th edition, Pearson, Boston, MA, 2008.

Kaempfer, R. and Swanson, J., *The Radio Producer's Handbook*, Allworth Press, New York, 2004.

Keith, M.C., *Broadcast Voice Performance*, Focal Press, Boston, MA, 1989.

Keith, M.C., *Radio Production: Art and Science*, Focal Press, Boston, MA, 1990.

Labelle, B., *Background Noise: Perspectives on Sound Art*, Continuum International Publishing, London, 2006.

Mack, S., *Hands-On Guide to Webcasting: Internet Event and AV Production*, Focal Press, Boston, MA, 2006.

McLeish, R., *Radio Production*, 5th edition, Focal Press, Boston, MA, 2005.

Mott, R.L., *Radio Sounds Effects*, McFarland Publishing, Jefferson, NC, 2005.

National Association of Broadcasters, *Guidelines for Radio Continuity*, NAB Publishing, Washington, D.C., 1982.

National Association of Broadcasters, *Guidelines for Radio Copywriting*, NAB Publications, Washington, D.C., 1993.

Nisbet, A., *The Technique of the Sound Studio*, 4th edition, Focal Press, Boston, MA, 1979.

Nisbet, A., *The Use of Microphones*, 3rd edition, Focal Press, Boston, MA, 1989.

Oringel, R.S., *Audio Control Handbook*, 6th edition, Focal Press, Boston, MA, 1989.

Orlik, P.B., *Broadcast/Cable Copywriting*, 7th edition, Allyn & Bacon, Boston, MA, 2003.

Pohlmann, K.C., *Advanced Digital Audio*, SAMS, Indianapolis, IN, 1991.

Priestman, C., *Web Radio: Radio Production for Internet Streaming*, Focal Press, Boston, MA, 2002.

Reese, D.E., et al., *Broadcast Announcing Worktext*, Focal Press, Boston, MA, 2005.

Rumsey, F., *Tapeless Sound Recording*, Focal Press, Boston, MA, 1990.

Rumsey, F., *Digital Audio Operation*, Focal Press, Boston, MA, 1991.

Sauls, S.J. and Stark, C.A., *Audio Production Worktext: Concepts, Techniques, and Equipment*, 7th edition, Focal Press, Burlington, MA, 2013.

Watkinson, J., *Digital Audio and Compact Disc Technology*, 3rd edition, Focal Press, Boston, MA, 1995.

CHAPTER 10

Engineering

CHARACTERISTICS OF AM AND FM STATIONS

AM and FM stations are located at different points in the electromagnetic spectrum: AM stations are assigned frequencies between 540 and 1700 kHz on the Standard Broadcast band, and FM stations are located between 88.1 and 107.9 MHz on the FM band.

Ten kilohertz (kHz) separate the carrier frequencies of AM stations and there are 200 kHz separations between FM station frequencies. FM broadcasters utilize 30 kHz for over-the-air transmissions and are permitted to provide a secondary content-delivery channel, termed a "subsidiary communications authority (SCA)" transmission to subscribers on the remaining frequency. The larger channel width provides FM listeners a better opportunity to fine-tune

FIGURE 10.1
Digital audio processors are the centerpiece of this cluster's master control operation. Courtesy of Entercom Radio Memphis.

their favorite stations as well as to receive broadcasts in stereo. To achieve parity, AM broadcasters developed a way to transmit in stereo, and by 1990 hundreds were doing so. The fine-tuning edge still belongs to FM, because its sidebands (15 kHz) are three times wider than AM's (5 kHz).

FM transmission occurs at a much higher frequency (millions of cycles per second) compared to AM (thousands of cycles per second). At such a high frequency, FM is immune to the low-frequency emissions that plague AM. Although a car motor or an electric storm will generally interfere with AM reception, FM is static free. Broadcast engineers have attempted to improve the quality of the AM band, but the basic nature of the lower frequency makes AM simply more prone to interference than FM. FM broadcasters see this as a key competitive advantage and referred to AM's ill-fated move in the 1980s to stereo as "stereo with static."

Signal Propagation

The paths of AM and FM signals differ from one another. Ground waves create AM's primary service area as they travel across the earth's surface. High-power AM stations are able to reach listeners hundreds of miles away during the day. At night AM's signal is reflected by the atmosphere (ionosphere), thus creating a skywave that carries considerably farther, sometimes thousands of miles. Skywaves constitute AM's secondary service area.

In contrast to AM signal radiation, FM propagates its radio waves in a direct (line-of-sight) pattern. FM stations are not affected by evening changes in the atmosphere and generally do not carry as far as AM stations. A high-power FM station may reach listeners within an 80- to 100-mile radius because its signal weakens as it approaches the horizon. Because FM outlets radiate direct waves, antenna height becomes nearly as important as power. In general, the higher an FM antenna, the farther the signal travels

Skywave Interference

The fact that AM station signals travel greater distances at night is a mixed blessing. Although some stations benefit from the expanded coverage area created by the skywave phenomenon, many do not. In fact, more than 2,000 radio stations around the country must cease operation near sunset, and thousands more must make substantial transmission adjustments to prevent interference. For example, many stations must decrease power after sunset to ensure non-interference with others on the same frequency: WXXX-AM is 5 kW during the day, but at night it must drop to 1 kW. Another measure designed to prevent interference requires that certain stations direct their signals away from stations on the same frequency. Directional stations require two or more antennas to shape the pattern of their radiation, whereas a non-directional station that distributes its signal evenly in all directions needs only a single antenna. Because of its limited direct wave signal, FM is not subject to the post-sunset operating constraints that affect most AM outlets.

Station Classifications

To guarantee the efficient use of the broadcast spectrum, the FCC established a classification system for both AM and FM stations. Under this system, the nation's 15,000-plus radio outlets operate free of the debilitating interference that plagued broadcasters prior to the Radio Act of 1927.

FM Station Class	Reference (Maximum) Facilities for Station Class (see 47 CFR Section 73.211) ERP (in kW) / HAAT (in meters)	FM Protected or Primary Service Contour		Distance to Protected or Primary Service Contour (km)	Distance to 70 dBu (or 3.16 mV/m) City Grade or Principal Community Coverage Contour (see 47 CFR Section 73.315) (km)
		dBu	mV/m		
Class A	6.0 kW / 100 meters	60 dBu	1.0 mV/m	28.3 km	16.2 km
Class B1	25.0 kW / 100 meters	57 dBu	0.71 mV/m	44.7 km	23.2 km
Class B	50.0 kW / 150 meters	54 dBu	0.50 mV/m	65.1 km	32.6 km
Class C3	25.0 kW / 100 meters	60 dBu	1.0 mV/m	39.1 km	23.2 km
Class C2	50.0 kW / 150 meters	60 dBu	1.0 mV/m	52.2 km	32.6 km
Class C1	100.0 kW / 299 meters	60 dBu	1.0 mV/m	72.3 km	50.0 km
Class C0 (C-zero)	100.0 kW / 450 meters	60 dBu	1.0 mV/m	83.4 km	59.0 km
Class C	100.0 kW / 600 meters	60 dBu	1.0 mV/m	91.8 km	67.7 km

FIGURE 10.2

FM station classes. Courtesy of the Federal Communications Commission.

AM classifications are as follows:

- **Clear Channel:** A clear channel is one on which stations are assigned to serve wide areas. These stations are protected from objectionable interference by other radio stations within their primary service areas and, depending on the class of station, their secondary service areas.
- **Class A station:** A Class A station is an unlimited time station that operates on a clear channel and is designed to render primary and secondary service over an extended area and at relatively long distances from its transmitter. Its primary service area is protected from objectionable interference from other stations on the same and adjacent channels, and its secondary service area is protected from interference from other stations on the same channel (see § 73.182). The operating power shall not be less than 10 kW nor more than 50 kW (see also § 73.25(a)). Class A stations have no time restrictions on hours of operation. Among the pioneer, or oldest, clear channel stations in the country are KDKA, WBZ, WSM, and WJR.
- **Class B station:** A Class B station is an unlimited time station that is designed to render service only over a primary service area. Class B stations are authorized to operate with a minimum power of 0.25 kW (or, if less than 0.25 kW, an equivalent RMS antenna field of at least 141 mV/m at 1 km) and a maximum power of 50 kW, or 10 kW for stations that are authorized to operate in the 1605–1705 kHz band.
- **Class D station:** A Class D station operates either daytime, limited time, or unlimited time with nighttime power less than 0.25 kW and an equivalent RMS antenna field of less than 141 mV/m at 1 km. Class D stations shall operate with daytime powers not less than 0.25 kW nor more than 50 kW. Nighttime operations of Class D stations are not afforded protection and must protect all Class A and Class B operations during nighttime hours. New Class D stations that had not been previously licensed as Class B will not be authorized.

- **Regional channel:** A regional channel is one on which Class B and Class D stations may operate and serve primarily a principal center of population and the rural area contiguous thereto.
- **Local channel:** A local channel is one on which stations operate unlimited time and serve primarily a community and the suburban and rural areas immediately contiguous thereto.
- **Class C station:** A Class C station is a station operating on a local channel and is designed to render service only over a primary service area that may be reduced as a consequence of interference in accordance with § 73.182. The power shall not be less than 0.25 kW nor more than 1 kW. Class C stations that are licensed to operate with 0.1 kW may continue to do so.

Part 73, Section 73.21 of the *Code of Federal Regulations* provides more details on AM station classifications.

FCC efforts to mitigate situations for certain stations that either were creating or affected by excessive interference resulted in the frequency allocation of new AM band space. Termed the *expanded band,* the frequencies between 1610 and 1700 kHz were reallocated by the FCC for the purpose of allowing certain stations

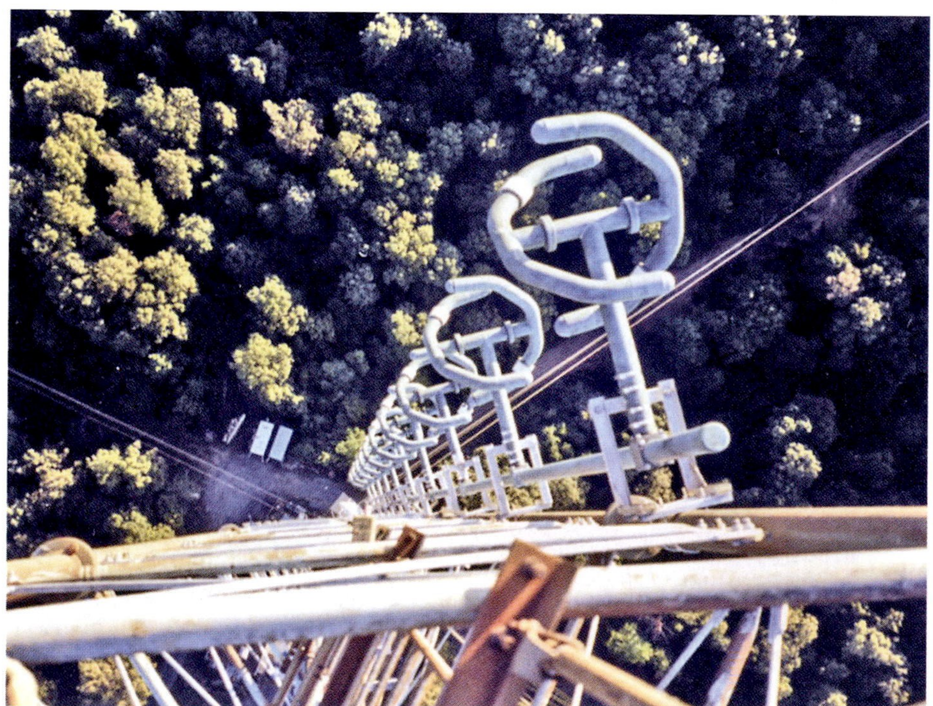

FIGURE 10.3
An FM transmitting antenna, as viewed from its tower position 700 feet above ground. The antenna structure consists of 12 elements (bays) that enable the station to achieve an effective radiated power (ERP) of 100 kW. Courtesy of Thomas A. White.

to migrate from the existing *standard band* to less-congested dial positions. During the period 1997–1998 the FCC issued permits for *expanded band* operation to 65 stations.

FM classifications include the following:

FIGURE 10.4
FM transmitters of power capacities ranging from 3.5 to 40 kW. Courtesy of Nautel.

- **Class C:** The most powerful FM outlets with the greatest service parameters, these stations may be assigned a maximum effective radiated power (ERP) of 100 kW and a tower height of up to 1,968 feet. Class C radio waves carry, on average, 70 miles from their point of transmission.
- **Class B:** These stations operate with less power—up to 50 kW—than Class Cs and are intended to serve smaller areas. The maximum antenna height for stations in this class is 492 feet, and signals generally do not reach beyond 40–50 miles.
- **Class A:** The least powerful of commercial FM stations; they seldom exceed 3 kW ERP (except in select cases where a ceiling of 6 kW is imposed) and 328 feet in antenna height. The average service contour for stations in this category is 10–20 miles.
- **Class D:** Originally set aside for noncommercial stations with 10 W ERP, this type of station was most apt to be licensed to a school or college.

FIGURE 10.5
Engineer refers to visual display prior to adjusting transmitter operating parameters. Courtesy of Nautel.

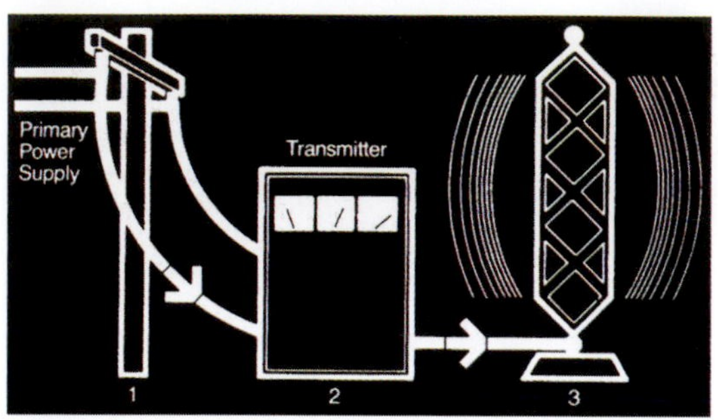

FIGURE 10.6
Stations receive their power from conventional utility companies. From *FCC Broadcast Operator's Handbook.*

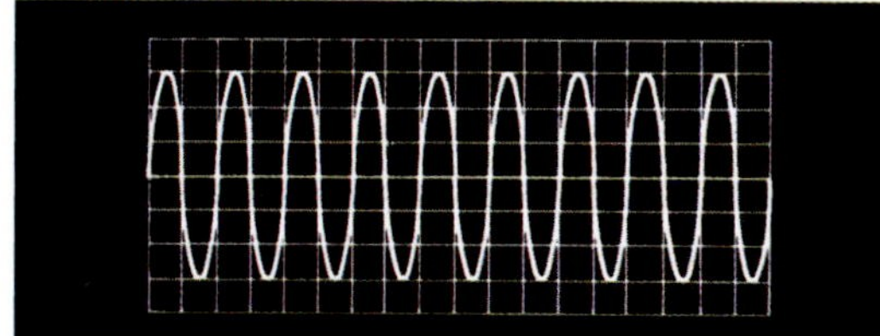

FIGURE 10.7
Unmodulated (undisturbed) carrier. *From FCC Broadcast Operator's Handbook*, Figure 5–1.

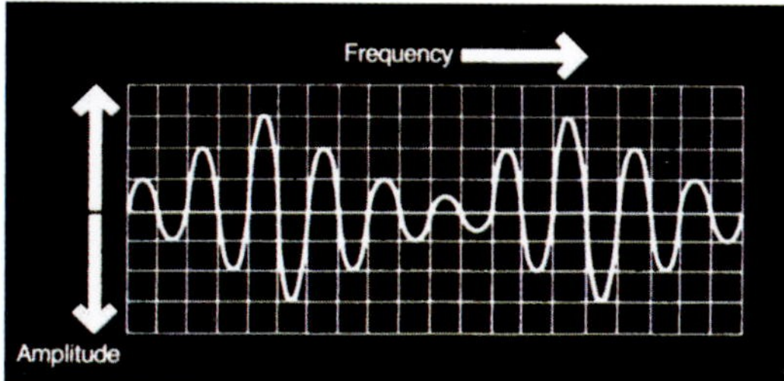

FIGURE 10.8
Amplitude modulated (AM) carrier. From *FCC Broadcast Operator's Handbook*, Figure 5–2.

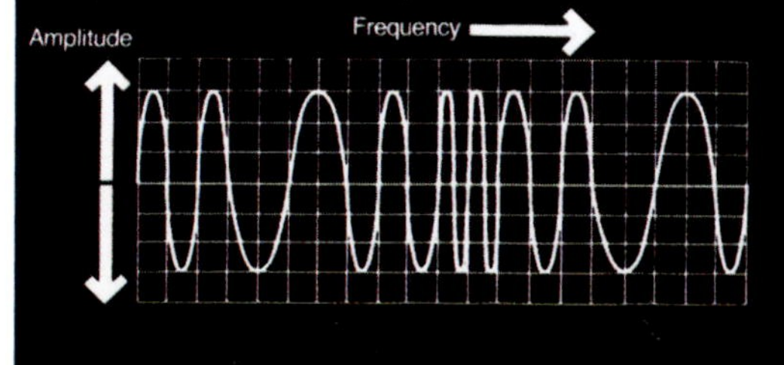

FIGURE 10.9
Frequency modulated (FM) carrier. From *FCC Broadcast Operator's Handbook*, Figure 5–4.

In the 1980s, the FCC introduced new classes of FM stations under Docket 80–90 in an attempt to provide several hundred additional frequencies, and more subclasses were added later. They are as follows:

- **Class C0:** These stations transmit with up to 100 kW of effective radiated power (ERP) from an antenna of no more than 1,476 feet in height.
- **Class C1:** Stations granted licenses to operate within this classification may be authorized to transmit up to 100 kW ERP with antennas not exceeding 981 feet. The maximum reach of stations in this class is about 50 miles.
- **Class C2:** The operating parameters of stations in Class C2 are close to Class Bs. The maximum power granted Class C2 outlets is 50 kW, and antennas may not exceed 492 feet. Class C2 stations reach approximately 35 miles.
- **Class C3:** These stations operate with shorter antennas and with power that does not exceed 25 kW ERP.
- **Class B1:** The maximum antenna height permitted for Class B1 stations (328 feet) is identical to Class As; however, Class B1s are higher-powered, and are permitted a maximum 25 kW ERP. Class B1 signals carry 25–30 miles.

Low-Power FM (LPFM) station classifications include the following:

- **Class L1:** 50–100 W ERP.
- **Class L2:** 1–10 W ERP.

In view of the ongoing revisions made to FM classifications, we suggest you consult Section 73.211 of the current *Code of Federal Regulations*. At the time of this writing the FCC had been petitioned to create a new Class C4. The petition proposed allowing stations to operate with a maximum effective radiated power of 12,000 watts with a maximum antenna height of 328 feet.

FIGURE 10.10
Compact, rack-mounted webcasting equipment processes, encodes, and streams digital audio. Courtesy of the Telos Alliance.

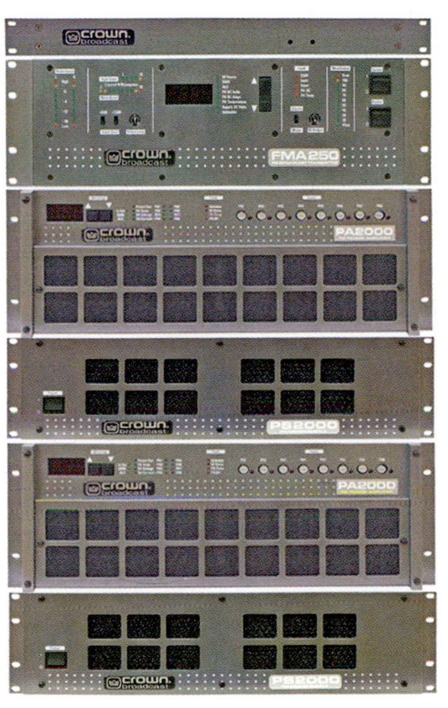

FIGURE 10.11
Multiple components combine electrically to produce up to 4 kW of transmitting power. Courtesy of Crown Broadcast IREC.

SATELLITE AND INTERNET RADIO

Satellite Radio

Satellite radio signals come from more than 22,000 miles out in space. Two companies, Sirius Satellite Radio and XM Satellite Radio, began operating in the early 2000s and merged in 2008. Although former XM Satellite Radio's initial transponders (two Boeing HS 702 satellites) were set aloft in a geostationary orbit, Sirius Satellite Radio's first birds (three SS/L-1300 satellites) rotate in an elliptical pattern ensuring that each satellite spends around 16 hours over the United States. As of this writing, SiriusXM reported that a total of nine active and reserve satellites were orbiting, although the earliest ones launched were nearing the end of their useful service periods.

VLF (Very Low Frequency) 30 kHz and below	— *Maritime use*
LF (Low Frequency) 30 kHz to 300 kHz	— *Aeronautical/maritime*
MF (Medium Frequency) 300 kHz to 3000 kHz	— *AM, amateur, distress, etc.*
HF (High Frequency) 3 MHz to 30 MHz	— *CB, fax, international, etc.*
VHF (Very High Frequency) 30 MHz to 300 MHz	— *FM, TV, satellite, etc.*
UHF (Ultra High Frequency) 300 MHz to 3000 MHz	— *TV, satellite, CB, DAB (proposed), etc.*
SHF (Super High Frequency) 3 GHz to 30 GHz	— *Satellite, radar, space, etc.*
EHF (Extreme High Frequency) 30 GHz to 300 GHz	— *Space, amateur, experimental, etc.*

FIGURE 10.12
Radio spectrum table.

Offering CD-quality digital radio, these satellite radio signals are beamed to homes, cars, and portable receivers serving more than nearly 24 million subscribers. Satellite radio uses the S-band (2.3 GHz) for its digital audio radio service (DARS). Both services keep a satellite ready for launch in the event one of their satellites malfunctions. Program origination from ground stations are uplinked to the satellites and then relayed to terrestrial end users (subscribers). Receivers unscramble the incoming signals, which offer more than 100 channels each. In addition, the signals contain encoded data for display on receivers allowing listeners to see what is being broadcast (artist, song, etc.). Ground repeaters are employed when needed to strengthen incoming satellite signals. An international satellite radio service called WorldSpace utilizes the L-band to provide digital audio to Africa and Asia. According to former XM Satellite's chief programmer, Lee Abrams, the operation's technical department consists of four key areas: studios, hardware development, satellites and repeaters, and IT.

Internet Radio

Since the 1990s, radio has been available over the Internet. There are two types of Internet radio stations: those generated by broadcast stations and those that exist solely online. In the case of the first category, stations typically simulcast their broadcast signals over the Internet. The second category of Internet station is typically more eclectic in its programming offerings, because the formatting constraints prevalent in broadcast radio do not exist in the independent, cyber-only outlets.

Thanks to the Internet, college radio is experiencing a surge of interest. Institutions can avoid the hurdle of obtaining FCC licensing and can establish Internet-only (I-O) stations at minimal expense. Backbone Networks Corporation specializes in assisting college broadcasters in navigating the technological waters of online radio, enabling students and staff to devote their time and energies to program development. Paul Kamp, vice-president for business development and counsel for Backbone, cites economics as the allure of online radio. He observes, "Internet economics is helping to drive the shift toward Internet radio. A new station does not need to apply for an FCC license or purchase or lease time on a broadcast tower for broadcasting in a particular region. They only need to have the ability to generate and manage 168 hours of programming a week and all that it entails."

Unlike traditional terrestrial stations, whose reach and operating parameters are limited, technology imposes no geographical limitations in Internet radio.

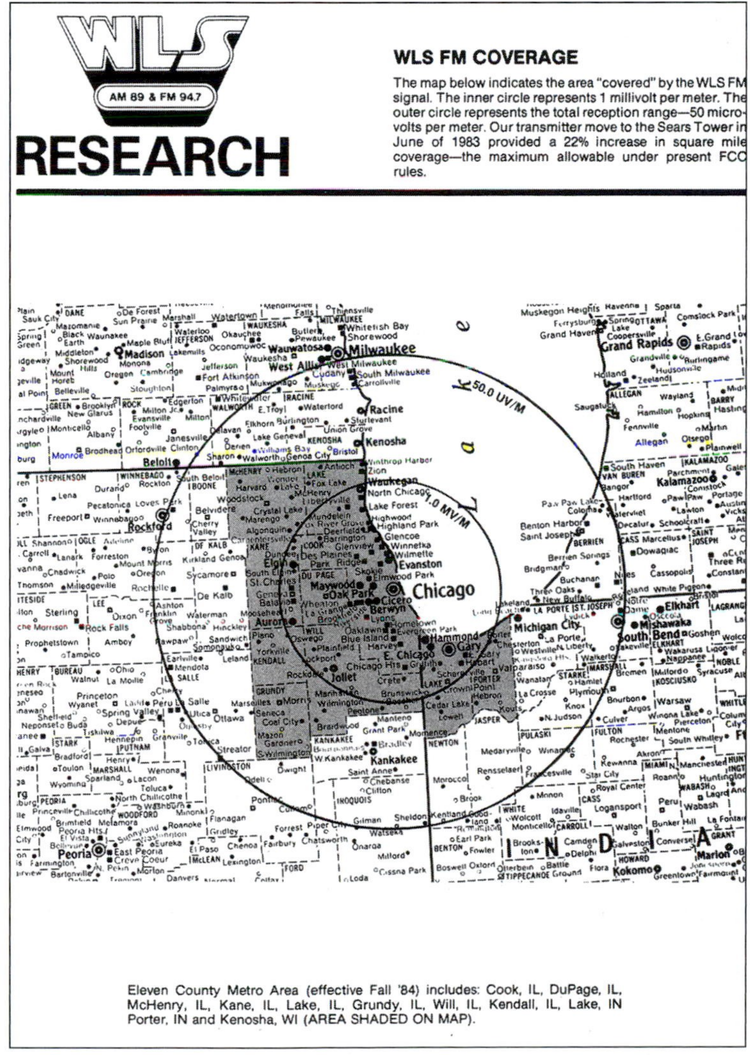

FIGURE 10.13
Coverage maps show where a station's signal reaches. Courtesy of WLS.

FM vs. AM: Technical Considerations

If electrical signals could be seen, they would look like the figures shown here. (Actually, they *can* be seen, on an instrument called an oscilloscope, which resembles a small television set.) If one were to whistle into a microphone with a pure low-frequency audio tone, the microphone would convert the voice into an electrical signal like Fig. 1.

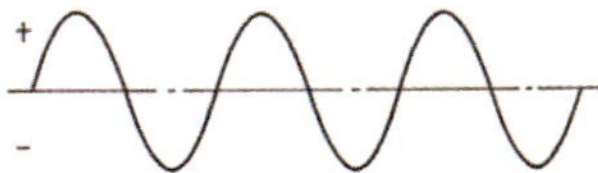

Figure. 1. A pure audio tone converted into an electrical signal.

Figure. 2. A carrier wave produced by a radio transmitter.

An essential portion of a radio transmitter produces a much higher frequency electrical signal called the carrier wave like Fig. 2. To transmit intelligence, the radio transmitter must somehow superimpose the voice signal on the carrier wave, a process called modulation. (The radio receiver *demodulates,* or separates the desired audio signal from the carrier wave.)

Amplitude modulation or AM was the first type of modulation developed, early in the 20th century. When the amplitude or height of the carrier is changed in time with the audio signal, the result would look like Fig. 3

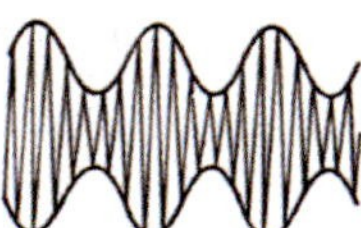

Figure 3. An amplitude modulated radio signal.

Figure 4. A frequency modulated radio signal, modulated by the same audio signal as in Fig. 3.

Instead of modulating the amplitude of the carrier, one can use the audio signal to change the *frequency* of the carrier, and that is frequency modulation. If the carrier were frequency modulated by the same audio signal as in Fig. 3, the result would look like Fig. 4. The frequency increases and decreases, but the amplitude of the modulated signal stays constant. The same intelligence has been transmitted. Of course a symphony concert with its multitude of sounds would produce a much more complicated looking waveform.

Questions About AM vs. FM:

Why is FM more static-free than AM?

Static is caused by things like lightning discharges or electrical discharges from nearby motors or other electrical devices, and those discharges produce small bursts of radiated energy. The

FIGURE 10.14A&B

The difference between the two bands. Courtesy of Brian Belanger, Radio and Television Museum.

AM receiver picks up the bursts of static along with the desired signal and adds them together. Static shows up as sharp vertical peaks (spikes) on the modulated waveform, and AM radios respond to them. However, in an FM receiver, the amplitude of the signal does not matter—only changes in frequency matter—so there is no static with FM.

If it is better, why didn't people use FM in the early days of radio?

AM was discovered first, and tends to be simpler. In the early days of radio, mathematicians thought they had "proved" that FM would not work as well as AM, but their analyses were oversimplified. E. H. Armstrong showed that if one used a sufficiently wide bandwidth, FM works just fine. For FM to work well, a much wider channel (bandwidth) is required than with an AM station. At the frequencies used in the AM broadcast band (roughly 550 to 1700 kilohertz) there is insufficient spectrum "space" to permit the wide channels needed for FM, but there is sufficient channel space available at the higher frequencies now used for FM (88 to 108 Megahertz). Another problem was that in the early days of radio, the vacuum tubes then available did not work well at the high frequencies where FM needed to operate. Another benefit of FM: the wider channels occupied by FM stations can accommodate modulation with wider frequency excursions than those from AM stations, so FM stations broadcast with much higher fidelity.

Why can you sometimes hear far away stations on AM but not on FM?

That has to do not with the difference between AM and FM, but rather *the different radio propagation conditions* in the AM band vs. the FM band. At the frequencies used in the AM broadcast band, signals can bounce off the ionosphere, especially at night, and be reflected back to earth at considerable distances from the transmitter, as shown in the figure below. But signals at the much higher frequencies used for FM generally do *not* bounce off the ionosphere, and so FM reception is limited to more or less a line-of-sight path.

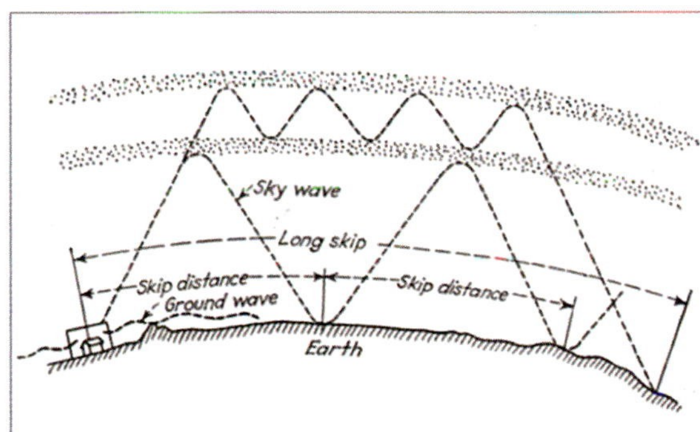

Figure 5. Charged particles in the ionosphere can reflect radio signals, which can then come back to earth quite some distance away from the transmitter.. These reflected signals often shows up at the frequencies used in the AM broadcast band, especially at night, but NOT at the much higher frequencies used for FM.

FIGURE 10.14A&B
continued

However, in certain, rare instances, broadcasters have restricted access to their online streams to listeners located within the station's terrestrial coverage area in efforts to minimize distribution and copyright-fee expenses.

With Internet access, anyone anywhere can enjoy the medium. An Internet station emanating from Dayton, Ohio, may be heard in Bangkok, Thailand, and tens of thousands of broadcasts are available. Kamp explains the magnitude of scale thusly: "The worldwide broadcast capability of Internet radio enables the broadcaster to broadcast to a targeted niche and still have a large audience. For example, you may only be able to reach one million listeners in the greater Dayton, Ohio, area with a Polka broadcast. Yet you can reach more than one billion people with an Internet radio station."

Unlike terrestrial and satellite radio, Internet radio has the capability of providing a full range of visual data, such as photos, text, video, and links. Interactivity also adds further cache to the medium's appeal, which has been battling issues regarding the use of copyrighted music through the decade. "As internet radio grows outside of music radio and into other types of content," Kamp notes, formats such as "Talk, Public Radio, Sports and other specialized content that is created or owned by the station's Internet radio should find some substantial growth and provide some interesting programming."

The process of distributing an Internet radio signal is not complex. Internet radio operations possess an encoding computer, which converts the audio into data packets that are routed to an end-user's Internet-connected device. In the span of just more than a decade, Internet radio has escaped its desktop-computer tether. "In the early 1990s," Kamp explains, "you needed a computer with high speed Internet access to decode the streams in order to listen. Today the Internet is available on a myriad of devices like smartphones, tablets, and specialized Internet radio receivers made by traditional home audio manufacturers."

Broadcasters are turning to the Internet as a reliable and economical way to insert their stations into on-the-scene coverage of local community events. Remote broadcasting, according to Kamp, is easily accomplished because the Internet has lowered the barriers to entry. "Internet or cloud-based solutions enable a very small remote system to be sent to the field instead of provisioning an ISDN line in the past. This frees the broadcasters from their studio, enabling them to go out into the community to broadcast events. This allows the broadcaster to get back to serving their community."

DIGITAL AUDIO BROADCASTING (HD RADIO™ TECHNOLOGY)

Radio has been undergoing a technological metamorphosis. Analog signal processing and transmission is being supplemented by digital processing and transmission, a manipulation that codifies the analogous audio signal into the digits zero and one for broadcast. The reason for the transformation is simple: better and more evolved sound. Broadcast stations employ digital technology in order to compete with audio alternatives, such as MP3 players, satellite radio, and mobile music services.

The Federal Communication Commission decided in 2002 on a technology referred to as "in-band, on-channel" (IBOC) for digital AM and FM broadcasting. IBOC enables a "hybrid" mode of operation, allowing stations to simultaneously transmit over their existing frequency assignments both analog and digital signals. The advantage is that no additional frequency spectrum is required for implementing the digital signal. A unique feature of IBOC is its ability to support multiple transmission channels. Thus, while the main digital channel replicates the programming heard on the station's original primary channel, two additional FM channels are available for originating discrete, alternate programming.

In its decision the FCC approved iBiquity Digital Corporation as the sole provider of IBOC technology. iBiquity developed and branded its system as HD Radio™ and licenses its technology to broadcasters in the United States, Mexico and other countries. The term "HD Radio" itself is *not* an abbreviation of the term "high definition radio." More explicitly, as iBiquity indicates on its website, "'HD Radio™' and the HD Radio logo are proprietary trademarks of iBiquity Digital Corporation. The 'HD' in HD Radio™ is part of iBiquity Digital's brand name for its advanced digital AM/FM system." Furthermore, as the site informs readers, "It does not mean hybrid digital or high-definition digital; both of these are incorrect."

Although the present system of analog broadcasting essentially replicates sound waves (with inherent shortcomings), digital converts sound waves into a low-bandwidth bit-stream of zeroes and ones. In digital, sound waves are assigned numeric values and become coded pulses.

Simply put, in digital, sounds are mathematically quantified. Digital technology is capable of greater frequency response and dynamic range than is possible with analog transmission, notably AM. Thus, more audio information is conveyed to the listener, who hears more. Another positive feature from the broadcast operator's perspective is the fact that digital signals do not require as much power as analog signals do.

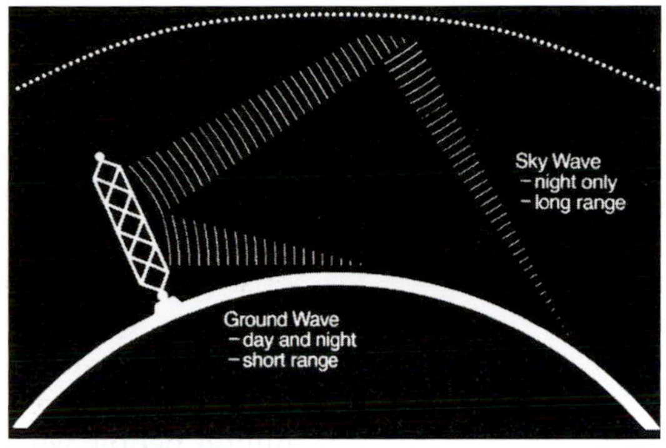

FIGURE 10.15
AM signal radiation. From *FCC Broadcast Operator's Handbook*, Figure 3–2.

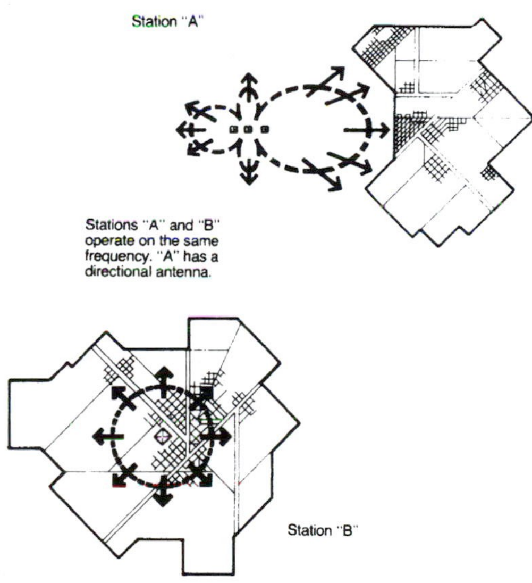

FIGURE 10.16
Non-directional and directional antenna radiation. From *FCC Broadcast Operator's Handbook*, Figure 7–2.

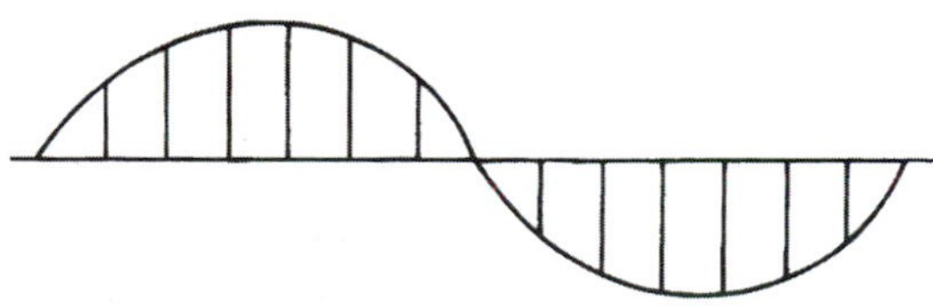

FIGURE 10.17
In digital processing of sound, an analog waveform is quantified, that is, given a numeric binary value.

Because the technology is incompatible with existing AM-FM radios, listeners must acquire technology-compatible HD Radio receivers in order to receive the digital signal. During the first decade of HD Radio broadcasting some observers expected the existing analog system of AM and FM broadcasting to become passé. Others predict that analog broadcasting will be around for a few more years and that, if digital becomes the pre-eminent broadcasting system, analog AM and FM stations will still be out there—that is, until the FCC no longer perceives them as providing a viable service. In any event, the conversion to digital appears to be inevitable. Analog broadcasting will go the way of the turntable.

Radio engineer Aaron Reed expresses his views on the issues that will confront the full implementation of digital radio:

> Dealing with the political boondoggle and the necessary paradigm shift in how "radio" will be done after its implementation (from the technical changes necessary to augment the programming delivery to the altering of the way people think of radio as a mostly one-way medium) will prove a major challenge to any engineer. Couple that with station managers demanding they be digital because "the other guy is" but then balking at the hefty price and you can see the problems. It won't be easy, and inevitably many stations will try to do it on the cheap and fail because DAB is not something that can be done incrementally. Just saying your station is digital is not going to get the listeners. Something far more radical in

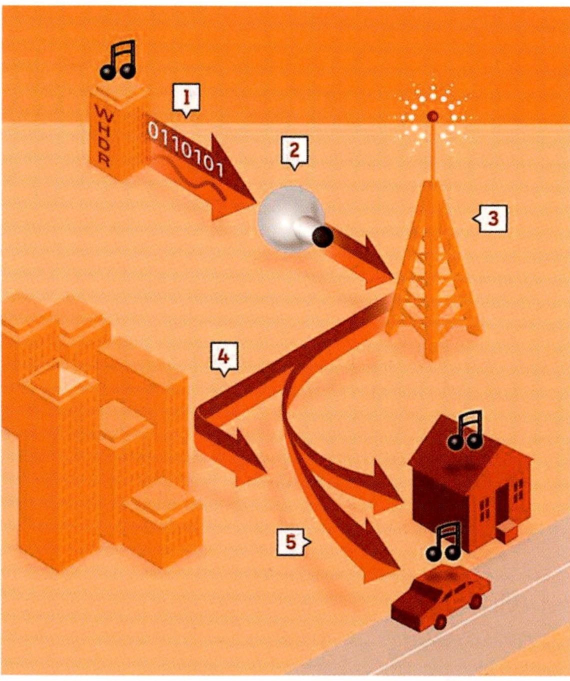

1. Analog and Digital signals sent separately
2. Signals combined prior to transmission
3. Composite signal transmitted by station
4. Multipath distortion only affects analog
5. Signal compatible with both analog and digital radios – only digital radios receive multicast channels

FIGURE 10.18
How HD Radio works. Courtesy of iBiquity. © 2013 iBiquity Digital Corporation; reproduced with permission from iBiquity.

> the programming services that stations offer will be required. The potential is there. Whether engineers and their moneymen are willing to do it is the big question.

BECOMING AN ENGINEER

Most station managers or chief engineers look for experience when hiring technical people. Formal training such as college ranks high but not as high as actual hands-on technical experience. Kevin McNamara, director of engineering at Beasley Broadcasting Group states:

> A good electronics background is preferred, of course. This doesn't necessarily mean ten years of experience or an advanced degree in electronic engineering, but rather a person with a solid foundation in the fundamentals of radio electronics, perhaps derived from an interest in amateur radio, computers, or another hobby of a technical nature. This is a good starting point. Actually, it has been my experience that people with this kind of a background are more attuned to the nature of this business. You don't need a person with a physics degree from MIT, but what you do want is someone with a natural inclination for the technical side. Ideally speaking, you want to hire a person with a tech history as well as some formal in-class training.

Chief engineer Jim Puriez concurs:

> A formal education in electronics is good, but not essential. In this business if you have the desire and natural interest, you can learn from the inside out. You don't find that many broadcast engineers with actual electronics degrees. Of course, most have taken basic electronics courses. Most are long on experience and have acquired their skills on the job. While a college degree is a nice credential, I think most managers hire tech people on the basis of experience more than anything else.

Entercom/Memphis chief engineer Skip Reynolds says the evolving nature of the business underscores the need for intelligent, skilled technologists. "Broadcasting as we know it is changing rapidly," he observes, "but the fact remains: radio is a one-to-many medium. That means there will still be transmitters, towers, studios for local origination, and remote facilities for local sporting events. That also means there are a lot of opportunities for engineers!"

Reynolds adds, "As you start out you may find the opportunity to specialize a bit, whether it be studio or transmitter maintenance, IT/computers or maybe producing sporting events. You probably will get to participate in larger projects like a studio rebuild or maybe installing a transmitter."

Equally important, in his opinion, is the need for engineers to achieve the delicate balance between work and home. Cultivating positive professional associations with co-workers is important, but it must be achieved without compromising the integrity of relationships with family or succumbing to personal sacrifice. "Above all," he says, "keep a cheerful and cooperative attitude. Prioritize your work. Be creative by finding better ways to accomplish a goal. Finally, pace yourself by allowing time for yourself and family."

Station engineer Sid Schweiger also cites experience as the key criterion for gaining a broadcast engineer's position. "When I'm in the market for a tech person, I'll check smaller market stations for someone interested in making the move to a larger station. This way, I've got someone with experience right from the start. The little station is a good place for the newcomer to gain experience."

In his column in *Radio World* (June 9, 1999), editor Paul J. McLane lamented the dearth of young people entering the field and the need for specialists with various technical and computer skills. Wrote McLane, "Fluency never stops. People I respect say radio engineers should learn to think large, and that goes for digital audio and data training."

Numerous schools and colleges offer formal training in electronics and information technology (IT). The number shrinks somewhat when it comes to those institutions actually providing curricula in broadcast engineering. However, a number of technical schools do offer basic electronics courses applicable to broadcast operations. The Society of Broadcast Engineers (SBE) also provides

FIGURE 10.19
Station engineer at the workbench. Courtesy of Jack Zibluk.

valuable education and knowledge certification for engineering talent. Members of SBE chapters in markets across the US convene regularly, providing information and education for the novice technician and the advanced engineer alike. A good way to learn more about how to become a station engineer is by contacting a nearby chapter and arranging to attend a meeting. That's how Luke Lukefahr, IT engineer for Clear Channel/St. Louis found entry into the industry. Lukefahr recalls:

> The Society of Broadcast Engineers has helped me immensely. When I attended my first meeting as a student in college I was able to meet a group of engineering professionals that worked in a market that I had only dreamed of working. Meeting so many different engineers allowed me to get my name out and show that even though I was young, I had a passion to learn as much as I could about broadcast engineering. By attending SBE meetings you not only get your name out, you have access to years of knowledge from a group of professional engineers. SBE also offers different educational programs and certifications which help engineers gain more knowledge about current and future broadcasting equipment.

For Lukefahr, SBE membership offers more than education:

> What really impressed me about the SBE is that it's like a family; the engineers that are members are not out for each other's jobs, they are just a group of people that are there to help. The engineer that hired me is a member of the chapter where I attended my first meeting. During my first interview with Clear Channel he said that he recognized my name. SBE gave me the chance to get my foot in the door. I still attend SBE meetings and I plan on becoming a certified broadcast networking technologist (CBNT).

While affirming his belief in the value of SBE membership, Lukefahr reflects on this early stage of his career, observing, "If I had to go back and change one thing I would have joined SBE during my freshman year of college because I would have become better-rounded in my knowledge of broadcast and IT equipment."

Before August 1981, the FCC required that broadcast engineers hold a First-Class Radiotelephone license. To receive the license, applicants were expected to pass an examination. An understanding of basic broadcast electronics and knowledge of the FCC rules and regulations pertaining to station technical operations were necessary to pass the lengthy examination. Today a station's chief engineer (also called chief operator) need possess only a Restricted Operator Permit. Those who held First-Class licenses prior to their elimination now receive either a Restricted Operator Permit or a General Radiotelephone license at renewal time.

ENGINEERING: CHALLENGING, REWARDING, IN DEMAND

Paul McLane

Are you interested in a career in radio broadcasting technology?

Radio has been going through something of an existential crisis brought on by significant new competition and changes in how people consume audio. Broadcast engineering, too, has been challenged to ask itself fundamental questions. You might help reinvent this job category. Here are a few things you should know:

FIGURE 10.20
Paul McLane. *Radio World* photo by Jim Peck.

Radio broadcasting is a field chronically short of new tech talent. Organizations need people skilled in electronics and RF transmission technology, particularly as older generations of engineers retire. Ralph Hogan, recently the president of the Society of Broadcast Engineers, cited "the loss of retiring engineers from the industry at an alarming rate." That's troubling for industry; it's an opportunity for you.

The skillset required has evolved to incorporate aspects of information technology, new media platform integration, radio data services, and other sectors. But while radio companies can find IT candidates with relative ease, they need people who combine an IT mindset with a willingness to work in RF, mechanical structures, and traditional electronics. I believe that if you embrace a broad scope of technology, you will offer a potential employer a powerful combination.

Paul Brenner, senior vice-president and chief technology officer of Emmis Communications, compares today's engineer to "a Renaissance IT guy."

"I always tell young talent to respect the RF guys, learn from them, they can keep you from getting hurt and teach the requirements of an FCC-regulated business," Brenner told me. But whether you choose to come at the career from an RF or information technology perspective, "IT is part of the fabric of delivering radio; so be entrepreneurial in your approach to solving problems with technology."

Why be a broadcast engineer? You'll play with technology and get paid for it. You can gratify your "problem-solver" itch. You'll work with large-scale systems and media platforms. You'll learn about, and be challenged regularly by, new systems and approaches. You'll play a key role that companies find hard to fill, providing an additional measure of job security. Should you prove capable, you'll quickly earn enhanced responsibility. You may work independently or with little supervision. You may manage a capital expenditure budget and have the opportunity to build a studio, transmission facility or network. You will have ample opportunity to "be the hero" should systems fail. If you learn to think strategically, you'll have more access to organizational decision-makers than many employees enjoy.

Gary Kline, senior vice-president of engineering and IT for Cumulus Media, notes the constant, "on-call" nature of the job, which he considers thrilling. "It's broadcasting and media and news and entertainment, and it is exciting. Along with that excitement and 24/7 atmosphere comes additional responsibility." He notes that there could be thousands, even millions of listeners to the systems you build. "Take New York City, for example. Build a studio in NYC and the audience is huge."

Also, you'll have the chance to help redefine what it means to be a broadcast engineer. Promising technologists have a particular opportunity to achieve right now, as radio is working to reinvent its role in the dashboard and smartphone. As we see with Clear Channel's iHeartRadio platform or Cumulus's alignment with digital music company Rdio, broadcasters are exploring non-traditional media where your skills can be put further to the test.

What are downsides of radio engineering? Typical complaints include long hours, a broad range of skills to master, conditions that may be dangerous to the untrained, a lack of respect in some organizations, and (ironically, given demand) a pay scale that is low relative to other technical fields.

Sometimes the job is not sexy. Veteran engineer Tom Ray wrote on the Talkers.com website that many young people "have no desire to be on call, to crawl around in swampy fields after hours, to service transmitters that can kill them, not to mention the fact that one can encounter a snake or other creepy crawly thing walking into the door of the transmitter building." Yes, those experiences can be part of the job; they can also be part of the pleasure of it, depending on your personality. And they can be weighed against the thrills of turning on a new transmitter, installing a network using audio over IP or helping a radio station expand its content distribution beyond FM or AM.

Not many educational institutions teach broadcast-specific implementations of RF, traditional electronics, IT infrastructure, and network-based tools. It's OK to come into the field with a basis in one area and then seek to build your skills through field experience and industry training.

Support for career development is improving. For example the SBE offers an online "university" with courses in IP networking, streaming, FCC enforcement, audio processing, FM and AM systems, voice telco networks, RF safety, and disaster recovery. A few state broadcast associations offer programs to encourage engineers; the Alabama Broadcasters Association is particularly active. The SBE has a well-respected certification program to help engineers demonstrate expertise.

The largest U.S. commercial radio company, Clear Channel Media and Entertainment, employs some 400 engineers. It recently created an electrical engineering coop program that offers college students an opportunity to expand their abilities with hands-on training with technologies and operations at Clear Channel stations. Students alternate semesters working in the coop system and then returning to school to pursue their degrees; a few qualify for scholarships. The company separately created a Market Engineering Development Program that offers employees one-on-one coaching, education and testing, along with special project experience —the goal is to advance participants quickly into market engineering manager roles.

Clear Channel Executive vice-president of engineering and systems integration Jeff Littlejohn stated in the announcement that the company wants to make a strategic investment in the future of broadcast engineering: "We hope to attract and expose new talent to the ever-changing world of radio while also fostering the growth and development of our existing employees." Cumulus Media similarly has engineering mentoring programs. To me, such programs are evidence that our field offers ample opportunity to ambitious, technically minded students.

In considering opportunities, also remember the newer entities that challenge the traditional definition of radio, such as SiriusXM, Pandora, or the long list of companies that offer streaming or online content services. These firms may not rely on traditional over-the-air infrastructure; but they too hire technical candidates and are part of the expanding world of radio.

Some see today as a scary time in radio; others see exciting opportunity. Without question, however, the field offers professional opportunities to the student of electronics, the tinkerer, the technically savvy digital native. Resources are available to help a student develop industry-specific skills not found on the college curriculum.

Paul McLane is editor in chief of *Radio World*, the news source for radio managers and engineers, and editorial director of the Broadcast & Video Group of NewBay Media, overseeing publications including *Radio* magazine, *TV Technology*, *Government Video* and the NAB Show *Daily News*. He was a journalist for Delmarva Broadcasting Co. and held sales and marketing management positions with Radio Systems Inc. and Bradley Broadcast & Pro Audio. Contact him at pmclane@nbmedia.com.

It is left to the discretion of the individual radio station to establish criteria regarding engineer credentials. Many do require a General Radiotelephone license or certification from associations, such as the Society of Broadcast Engineers (SBE) or the National Association of Radio and Telecommunications Engineers (NARTE), as a preliminary means of establishing a prospective engineer's qualifications.

Communication skills rank highest on the list of personal qualities for station engineers, according to McNamara:

> The old -stereotype of the station "tech-head" in white socks, chinos, and shirt-pocket pen holder weighed down by its inky contents is losing its validity. Today, more than ever, I think, the radio engineer must be able to communicate with members of the staff from the manager to the deejay. Good interpersonal skills are necessary. Things have become very sophisticated, and engineers play an integral role in the operation of a facility, perhaps more now than in the past. The field of broadcast engineering has become more competitive, too, with the elimination of many operating requirements.

Because of a number of regulation changes in the 1980s, most notably the elimination of upper-grade license requirements, the prospective engineer now comes under even closer scrutiny by station management. The day when a "1st phone" was enough to get an engineering job is gone. There is no direct "ticket" anymore. As in most other areas of radio, skill, experience, and training open the doors the widest.

Because the very landscape of radio has changed as the result of the Telecommunications Act of 1996, station clusters abound. This means a chief engineer or director of a cluster's technical operation has formidable responsibilities. Instead of keeping one station on the air, this person may have as many as eight signals to watch over. In cluster operations, there may be several experienced engineers on site or one senior engineer who directs the duties of several techs and producers.

AUTOMATION PATENT UPDATE — Page 6

NewBay Media

RADIOWORLD

JUNE 5, 2013 | The News Source for Radio Managers and Engineers | $2.50 | RADIOWORLD.COM

INSIDE

LOVE THY GENERATOR

• In the wake of monster weather, Curt Yengst details how you can make sure you've done proper upkeep before storms hit. — **Page 22**

HIKING THE APPALACHIAN TRAIL

• A Buyer's Guide entirely about apps! — **Page 26**

MUCH ADO ABOUT MILLENNIALS

• A younger generation is poised to take over radio broadcast … they can handle it, argues WSUM(FM)'s general manager — **Page 38**

Globally, Digital Radio Progresses

Various technologies fit various needs, but digital has forward momentum

BY T. CARTER ROSS

No longer an oddity, digital radio in many corners of the world is becoming an important part of the mediascape and a next step in the evolution of content delivery.

From maturing markets in Europe to a massive developing network in India, for digital radio broadcasting the focus is moving from tests and trials to implementation, promotion and growth.

In February the European Broadcasting Union issued Recommendation R 138, laying forth the goal of moving forward with digital radio, primarily the DAB+ version of Eureka-147, across the continent. The EBU membership includes all the large, well-established public-service broadcasting companies in Europe, so while this is not a mandate, it does have institutional weight behind it. Most European public-service broadcasting companies have active DAB services or, at the least, trial services on the air.

EBU RECOMMENDATION

While recognizing that different countries are at various stages of digital deployment, EBU R 138 calls for "immediate deployment" using DAB+ in VHF band III and, in areas where DAB coverage is not practical, the DRM30 and/or DRM+ system.

Both the Eureka-147 and DRM families are open standards published by the European Telecommunications Standards Institute. The WorldDMB Forum is the main promoter of DAB/DAB+ technology, while the Digital Radio Mondiale Consortium is the primary promoter of DRM30/DRM+.

"This is a relatively new document and too early to measure the effect. We must also remember that it is a recommendation and not a directive," said WorldDMB President Jørn Jensen. "However we believe it will be useful for countries who are in doubt about the future of broadcasting in Europe."

The DRM Consortium welcomed the inclusion of a recommendation for the DRM systems.

(continued on page 10)

Courtesy DRM Consortium

At BES Expo 2013 in New Delhi, India, NXP Semiconductors demonstrated a multistandard chipset that can support DRM30, DRM+, DAB, DAB+, T-DMB and HD Radio on AM and FM. In the picture are Karthik Ramesh of NXP and DRM Marketing Director Radu Obreja (holding the chip).

FIGURE 10.21
Radio World is the go-to source of news for radio managers and engineers. Courtesy of *Radio World.*

THE SOCIETY OF BROADCAST ENGINEERS

Wayne Pecena

FIGURE 10.22
Wayne Pecena.

The Society of Broadcast Engineers (SBE) was organized in 1964 and is the only member organization solely devoted to furthering and representing the interests of broadcast engineering and related technology fields. The society offers a wide range of services and programs to the radio and TV broadcast engineering community, whether you are a beginner or an experienced professional.

The SBE Certification Program is one of the most visible programs offered by the Society. Prior to the early 1980s, a Federal Communications Commission (FCC) First-Class Operators License was the benchmark for substantiating the knowledge and skill level of the Broadcast Engineer. Upon the FCC eliminating the requirement for a Broadcast Engineer to hold a First-Class License, the evaluation of an engineer's skill and competence fell on the shoulders of the station licensee. The SBE Certification Program was developed and has become the premier technology certification program in the broadcast industry. Annual salary surveys conducted by *Radio* magazine have shown that those holding SBE Certifications receive higher annual median pay than those non-certified by 36–48%, depending upon the market size.

Fifteen SBE Certifications cover the beginner Operator Level to the Professional Engineering level, with focus in both radio and TV fields. The certified radio operator (CRO), the certified broadcast technologist (CBT), the certified audio engineer (CAE), the certified senior radio engineer (CSRE), and the certified professional broadcast engineer (CPBE) are such certification levels offered by the SBE. In addition, specialty endorsements are available in fields such as AM directional specialist (AMD) and digital radio broadcast specialist (DRB). The certified broadcast network engineer (CBNE) certification is the latest certification offering and recognizes the importance and growth of IT in the industry. Demonstration of technical knowledge through a structured testing program is the foundation of all levels of certification. The more advanced certification levels also have experience requirements.

Professional development programs are a cornerstone of services offered by the SBE. Programs available include online webinars, online SBE University classes, and in-person presentation held at Ennes Workshops throughout the country. The Ennes Workshop held each year at the National Association of Broadcasters (NAB) annual convention is one of the premier professional development offerings of the SBE in cooperation with NAB. SBE programs range from the beginner in the field to programs focused upon furthering the knowledge of the seasoned broadcast engineer. The SBE Leadership Program is a unique professional development program focused upon preparing the broadcast engineer for leadership and management roles in the industry.

Additional programs offered to the membership include legislative representation, group insurance, frequency coordination services, and an online job opportunities listing service. The SBE Store offers a wide range of discounted technology books, Certification preparation guides (CertPreview), operator handbooks, and numerous SBE logo items.

The SBE certification lapel pins are a popular item to recognize one's SBE certification accomplishments.

Today, the SBE serves members in a wide range of technology fields ranging from the studio audio production operator to the chief engineer in the radio, TV, cable, and postproduction related fields. As the SBE approaches 50 years of service to the broadcast technology field, it is well positioned with services and programs focused upon serving the broadcast technology community for the next 50 years.

FIGURE 10.23
Society of Broadcast Engineers logo. Courtesy of SBE.

The SBE website www.sbe.org provides a wealth of information regarding SBE programs and services. Consider joining the SBE. Student memberships are available and become active in more than 115 local SBE chapters across the US. Stay in touch with the SBE through social media outlets Facebook, LinkedIn, and Twitter.

Wayne M. Pecena is the assistant director of educational broadcast services in the Office of Information Technology at Texas A&M University. He has 40 years of broadcast and telecommunications engineering experience and holds B.S. and M.S. degrees from Texas A&M University. Pecena is certified by SBE as certified professional broadcast engineer and a certified broadcast network engineer. He serves on the SBE board of directors as the education committee chair and was named the 2012 SBE Educator of the Year. He is a frequent SBE speaker on IP networking topics for the broadcast engineer.

THE EMERGENCY ALERT SYSTEM

Much has changed in the way broadcasters provide information to the public in times of imminent or immediate threats to life and property. The Conelrad (for Control of Electromagnetic Radiation) system came into existence following World War II as the nation and the world entered the nuclear age. Its 1963 successor, the Emergency Broadcast System (EBS), empowered the U.S. president to take control of electronic communications in the event of war or national emergency. A 1976 revision to the system endorsed its use during state and local emergencies, and in many parts of the U. S. activation of the EBS became commonplace during times of threatening weather occurrences. The role of EBS was thus enlarged so as to provide not just the president but also heads of state and local government with a way to communicate with the public in the event of a major emergency. By the 1990s, EBS too was viewed as outmoded. Rapid advancement and deployment of digital technologies underscored the need for a next-generation, automated warning system.

In 1994, the FCC announced the Emergency Alert System (EAS) as the successor to the EBS. Initially intended to layer the fundamental mission of the EBS over a modernized distribution system, today the FCC describes EAS on its website as

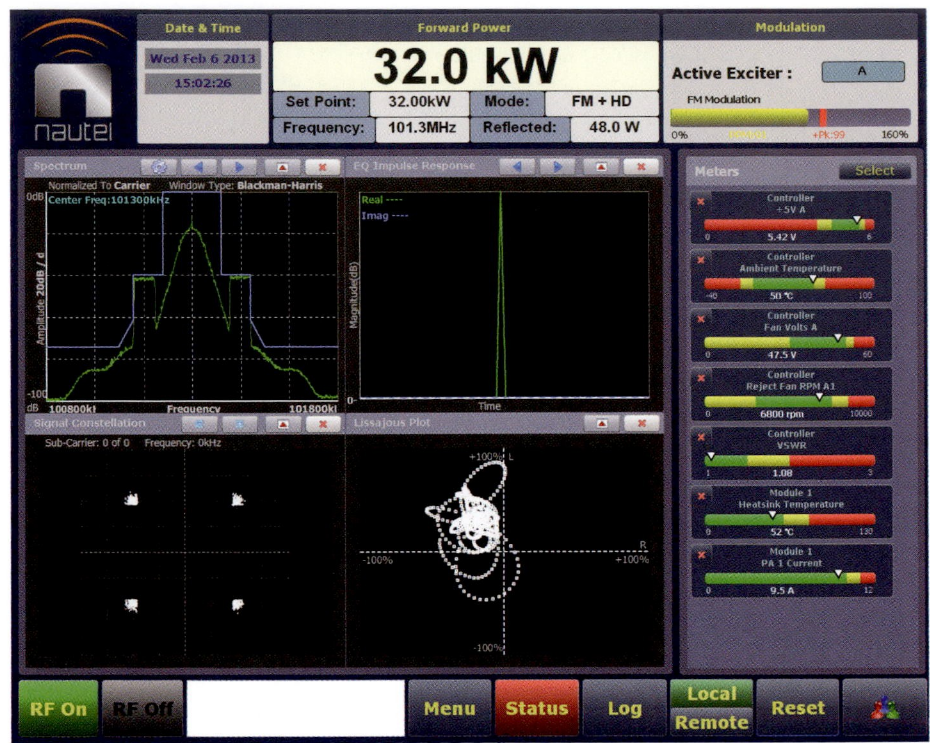

FIGURE 10.24
This transmitter user-interface screen offers both local and remote-site control capabilities, including the instrumentation and monitoring functions. Courtesy of Nautel.

Name	NORAD ID	Int'l Code	Launch date	Period [minutes]	Action
SIRIUS FM-6	39360	2013-058A	October 25, 2013	1436.1	Track it
XM-5	37185	2010-053A	October 14, 2010	1436.1	Track it
SIRIUS FM-5	35493	2009-034A	June 30, 2009	1436.1	Track it
XM-3	28626	2005-008A	March 1, 2005	1436.1	Track it
XM-1	26761	2001-018A	May 8, 2001	1436.1	Track it
XM-2	26724	2001-012A	March 18, 2001	1436.1	Track it
SIRIUS 3	26626	2000-077A	November 30, 2000	1436	Track it
SIRIUS 2	26483	2000-051A	September 5, 2000	1436	Track it
SIRIUS 1	26390	2000-035A	June 30, 2000	1436.1	Track it

FIGURE 10.25
Satellites have limited life expectancies. This table lists both original and replacement SiriusXM satellites. Courtesy of www.n2yo.com.

> a national public warning system that requires broadcasters, cable television systems, wireless cable systems, satellite digital audio radio service (SDARS) providers, and direct broadcast satellite (DBS) providers to provide the communications capability to the President to address the American public during a national emergency. The system also may be used by state and local authorities to deliver important emergency information, such as AMBER [America's Missing: Broadcast Emergency Response] alerts and weather information targeted to specific areas.

The Federal Emergency Management Agency (FEMA) makes funds available to private and commercial stations designated to remain on the air before, during, and after an authentic emergency through the Broadcast Station Protection Plan. Broadcast facilities that cooperatively participate with FEMA in this arrangement are termed Primary Entry Point (PEP) stations. According to the FEMA website:

> PEP stations also serve as the primary source of initial broadcast for a Presidential Emergency Alert Notification (EAN). PEP stations are equipped with additional and back up communications equipment and power generators designed to enable them to continue broadcasting information to the public during and after an event. The Integrated Public Alert and

FIGURE 10.26
Engineer "rides gain" on deejay mic during a remote broadcast originating from the Bonnaroo Music and Arts Festival. Courtesy of the Telos Alliance.

Warning System (IPAWS) Program Management Office (PMO) is expanding the number of participating broadcast stations across the nation to directly cover over 90 percent of the U.S. population. IPAWS PMO is modernizing existing PEP stations with next generation alert and warning equipment to include Common Alert Protocol (CAP) compliance equipment, and Internet Protocol enabled equipment. The IPAWS PMO continues to complete the integration of satellite data transmission paths as a diverse path for EAS message delivery from FEMA to PEP stations. An XM Radio transmission path was completed in the first quarter of 2010, and direct satellite connectivity became available to the national PEP stations in the third quarter of 2010. PEP station expansion will help ensure that under all conditions the President of the United States can alert and warn the public.

FEMA anticipates that 90% of the nation's population will be within range of one of 77 PEP stations when the plan is fully implemented in 2015.

Today EAS embraces many of these revisions, as well as additional innovations and procedures. A nationwide system test conducted in 2011 revealed

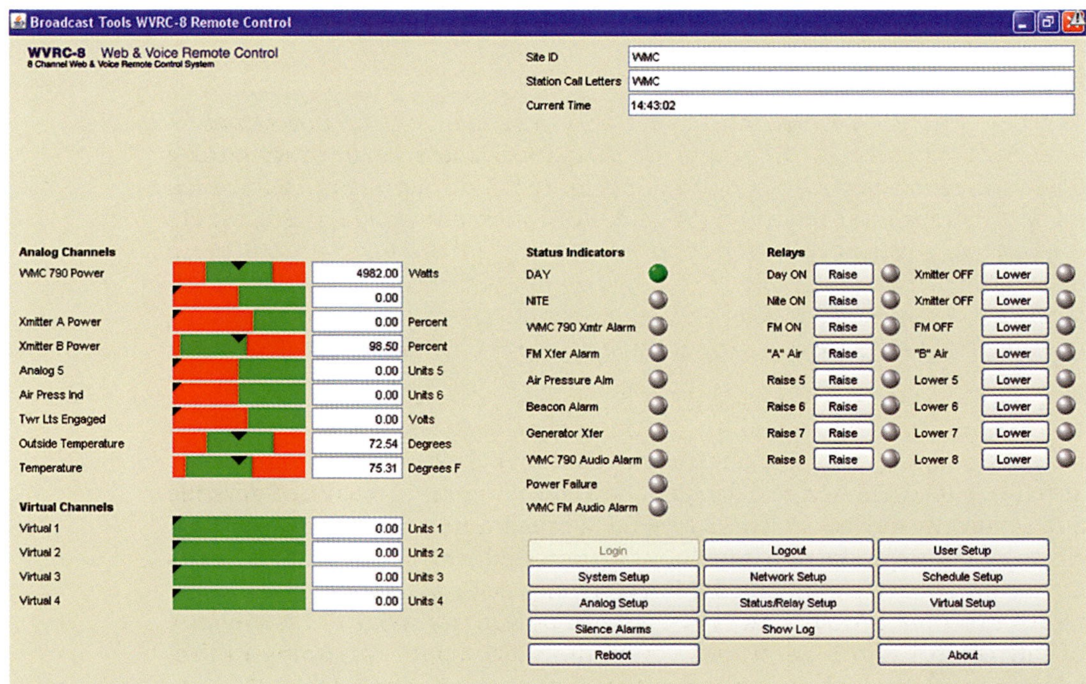

FIGURE 10.27
AM and FM transmitter operating parameters are indicated by this software-based monitoring system. Sensors measure power levels, AM antenna radiating patterns, the integrity of FM transmission-line pressure and the function of the tower light beacons. This product automatically notifies a station engineer by telephone if any parameter exceeds prescribed tolerances. Courtesy of Entercom Radio Memphis.

weaknesses in the system, notably the fact that some stations were not within the reception range of a PEP station. As of this writing, another test is anticipated but a date has yet to be announced. Another instance of innovation was FEMA's 2013 addition of Premiere Radio Networks as a PEP facility. Programming supplied by this Clear Channel-owned subsidiary is estimated to reach more than 190 million listeners each week. In sum, EAS remains a system under scrutiny and evaluation as world events, such as 9/11, the hurricanes Katrina and Sandy, and devastating tornadoes in Alabama, Missouri and Oklahoma increase the need for an effective emergency alert system.

EAS Operating Handbook

The *EAS Operating Handbook* states in summary form the actions to be taken by personnel at EAS Participant facilities upon receipt of an EAN (Emergency Action Notification), an EAT (Emergency Action Termination), tests, or state and local area alerts. It is issued by the FCC and contains instructions for the above situations. A copy of the *Handbook* must be located at normal duty positions or EAS equipment locations when an operator is required to be on duty and be immediately available to staff responsible for authenticating messages and initiating actions (see 70 FR 71033, November 25, 2005).

AUTOMATION

The FCC's decision in the mid-1960s requiring that AM/FM operations in markets with populations of more than 100,000 originate separate programming 50% of the time provided significant impetus to radio automation. Before then combo stations, as they were called, simulcast their AM programming on FM primarily as a way of curtailing expenses. FM was still the poor second cousin of AM. (In the late 1980s, the FCC dropped most of its simulcast prohibitions. Since then many stations have resorted to simulcasting as a means of dealing with the realities of fierce competition and a declining AM market.)

Responding to the rule changes, many stations resorted to automation systems as a way to keep expenses down. Interestingly enough, however, automation for programming, with its emphasis on music and de-emphasis on chatter, actually helped FM secure a larger following, resulting in increased revenue and stature. By the late 1970s, however, FM broadcasting, with its high-fidelity, stereophonic reproduction capabilities, surpassed AM in listenership. Criss Onan, an active veteran of automation equipment sales and former broadcaster, recalls this time period as an era of reversal of fortunes. With the ascendancy of interest in FM, station owners veered from automation, returning to live-talent operation and its promise for increased revenues. Onan recalls:

> The declining listening to AM stations caused owners to investigate more cost-effective ways to produce programming. Programming services were created to utilize lowering satellite time rates to deliver 24/7 long-form music programming in several different formats. Although personal

computers (PCs) were relatively expensive, station owners deployed them to insert local advertising spots in satellite program commercial breaks. The FCC's relaxation of ownership limits spurred increased sales of hard-drive automation systems. Being able to record an advertising spot once and have it instantly available in any studio for any station was much more efficient than having numerous tape decks with multiple tape copies of the same spot.

Prior to the arrival of PC-based automation, the purchase of a tape-based, electro-mechanically operated system represented a substantial economic investment. Automation's appeal to owners, despite its hefty up-front expense, was to save them money by cutting the costs for staffing their stations.

Onan cites the declining cost of PC-based systems as an instigator for the increase in automation utilization. "Today," he estimates, "almost all stations use hard drive-based automation systems." Another economic incentive that spurred interest in using automation as a means for containing expenses, Onan explains, was "the US economic recession in the late 2000s, which caused a significant advertising revenue reduction for most stations. Combined with high debt service from escalating station sale values, owners have aggressively consolidated station operations. This has caused a loss of jobs in the industry." Owners embraced technology as a way to improve voice-talent productivity. "Voice-tracks in some dayparts on commonly owned stations in a market are now frequently recorded by the same talent," Onan observes. This mode of operation is not isolated solely to stations within a cluster. He continues, "Talent may also record voice tracks for the owner's other markets. Even independently contracted talent, producing content from home studios, is being used. This is possible using moderately fast Internet connections."

Automated stations are not full walk-away operations. They employ operators as well as announcers and production people to oversee activities. The extent to which a station uses automation often directly influences its staffing needs. Obviously, a fully automated station will employ fewer programming people than a partially automated outlet. For additional insight on this topic refer to Chapter 11, Appendix A by Phil Barry, senior vice-president/general manager for WestwoodOne 24/7 Formats.

It bears noting that the production of entertainment programming might have been the first aspect of studio operations to benefit from online connectivity, but other activities have since tapped into the Web's capabilities for the convenience and versatility it offers. Criss Onan chronicles the history of this paradigm shift and its effects on other day-to-day station operations:

The production of advertising spots is being consolidated to regional centers by some owners as is the gathering, generation, and delivery of news. Scheduling of advertising spots and music is also being consolidated to regional centers or even national centers by owners.

FIGURE 10.28A&B
Equipment rack in a cluster operation includes audio processing and monitoring devices. Courtesy of Entercom Radio Memphis.

Stations in all size markets may be minimally staffed or entirely unstaffed during some dayparts such as overnights and weekends. Transmitter remote control systems automatically contact an on-call, designated operator if a parameter exceeds a specified tolerance.

What form will the next-generation automation system take? "In the future," Onan speculates, "scheduling and automation play-out functions may reside in the Internet 'Cloud' hosted by service providers rather than provided by technical infrastructure at the radio station's site."

FIGURE 10.29
New product designs undergo extensive testing in the Wheatstone Sound Lab. Courtesy of Wheatstone.

CHAPTER HIGHLIGHTS

1. AM stations are assigned frequencies between 535 and 1705 kHz, with 10 kHz separations between frequencies. AM is disrupted by low-frequency emissions, can be blocked by irregular topography, and can travel hundreds of mile along surface level ground waves, or thousands of miles along nighttime sky waves.
2. Because AM station signals travel greater distances at night, to avoid skywave interference, more than 2,000 stations around the country must cease operation near sunset. Thousands more must make substantial nighttime transmission adjustments (decrease power), and others (directional stations) must use two or more antennas to shape the pattern of their radiation.
3. FM stations are assigned frequencies between 88.1 and 107.9 MHz, with 200 kHz separations between frequencies. FM is static free, with direct waves (line-of-sight)

FIGURE 10.30
Stations that generated 50 kW promoted their greater coverage areas. Courtesy of WHAS.

carrying up to 80–100 miles. Both AM and FM stations are licensed for eight years as of this writing.

4. To guarantee efficient use of the broadcast spectrum and to minimize station-to-station interferences, the FCC established three classifications for AM stations and eight classifications for FM. Lower classification stations are obligated to avoid interference with higher classification stations. Recent FCC actions have created more subclassifications.

5. Satellite radio employs both geosynchronous (XM) and elliptical (Sirius) orbits from more than 22,000 miles in space. When necessary, ground repeaters are used to strengthen signals.

6. The digital-audio technology trademarked as HD Radio enhances the listening experience, offering superior frequency response and greater dynamic range. New spectrum space may be allocated to accommodate the digital service. Industry observers are divided in their opinions as to when HD Radio will supplant analog transmission.

FIGURE 10.31
An electro-mechanical controller sequenced the playback of analog reel-to-reel and cartridge tapes in this 1970s-era automation system. Courtesy Chuck Conrad, Chalk Hill Educational Media, Inc.

7. Educational opportunities for prospective broadcast engineers include programs of instruction offered by colleges and universities, trade and technical schools and the Society of Broadcast Engineers (SBE).
8. A station's chief engineer (chief operator) needs experience with basic broadcast electronics and information technology, as well as a knowledge of the FCC regulations affecting the station's technical operation. The chief must install, maintain, and adjust equipment, and perform weekly inspections and calibrations. Other duties may include training techs, planning maintenance schedules, and handling a budget.
9. A Proof of Performance involves checking the station's technical performance: frequency response, harmonic distortion levels, FM noise level, AM noise level, stereo separation, crosstalk, and subcarrier suppression.
10. The Emergency Alert System (EAS) (formerly the Emergency Broadcast System [EBS]), implemented after World War II, provides the president of the United States with a means of communicating with the public in an emergency. Over time, the role of the service has been expanded to include information about severe weather and, more recently, AMBER alerts. Stations must follow rigid instructions both during periodic tests of the system and during an actual emergency.

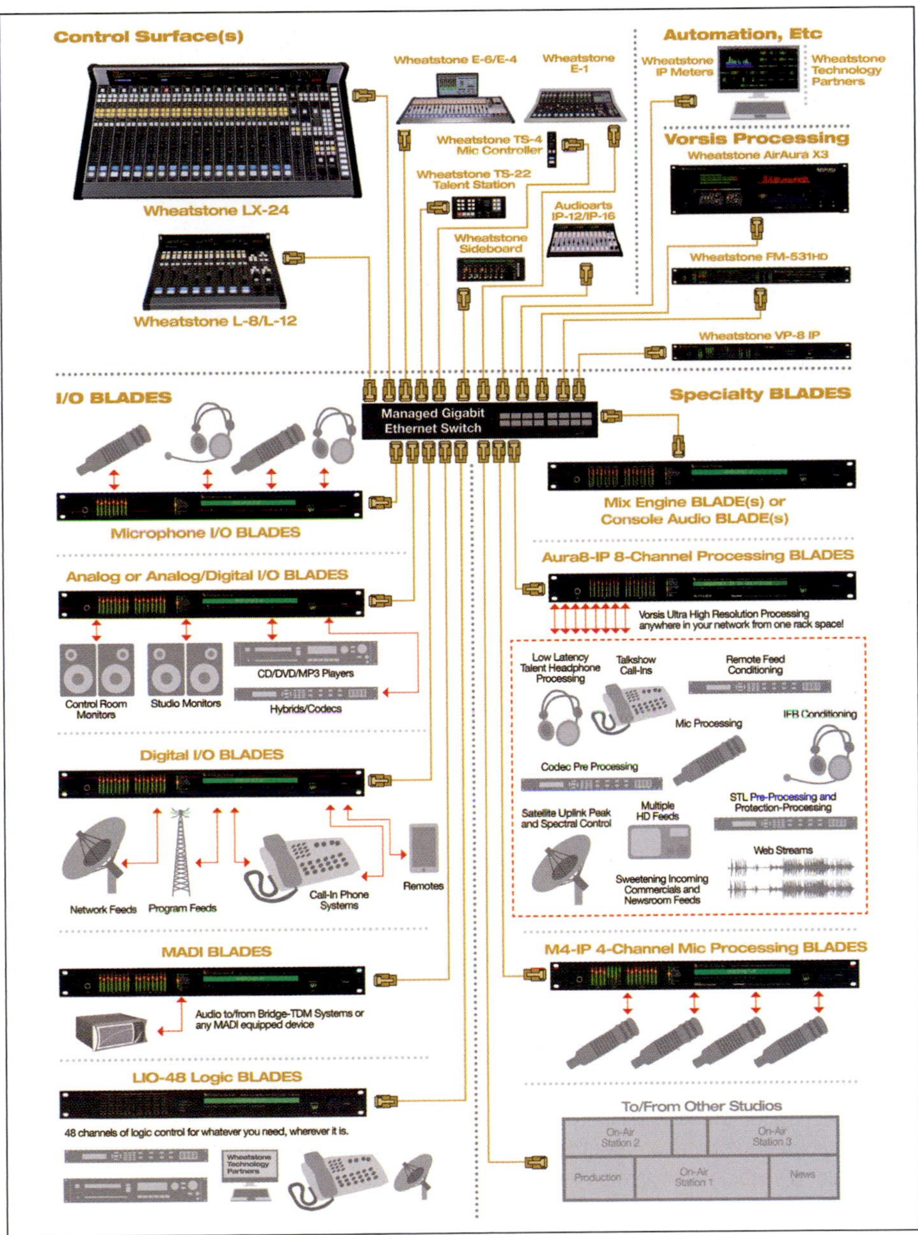

FIGURE 10.32
This protocol for networking studios provides flexibility for managing operations in station clusters. Courtesy of Wheatstone.

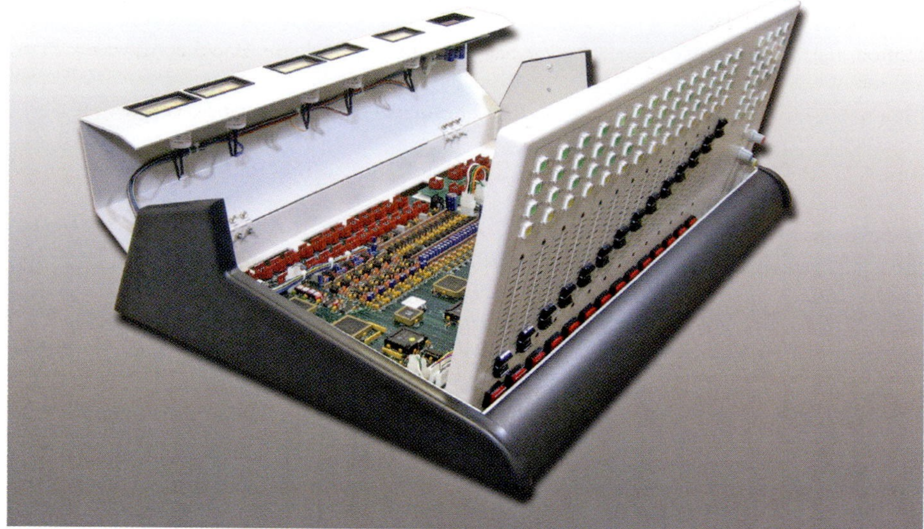

FIGURE 10.33
The engineer's view: a peek "under the hood" of a broadcast console. Courtesy of Arrakis Systems.

11. Many of today's commercial stations are fully or partially automated. Computer-assisted automation reduces staffing costs but requires investment in equipment. Automated programming elements are aired when metadata embedded with audio files issue commands to execute file playout. At many stations, satellite programming services use computers (at both uplink and downlink sites) to control station automation systems.
12. Direct satellite-fed stations need little equipment because programming originates at the syndicator's studios.
13. The FCC requires that a station's license and the permits of its operators be accessible in the station area.

SUGGESTED FURTHER READING

Abel, J.D. and Ducey, R.V., *Gazing into the Crystal Ball: A Radio Station Manager's Technological Guide to the Future*, NAB, Washington, D.C., 1987.

Antebi, E., *The Electronic Epoch*, Van Nostrand Reinhold, New York, 1982.

Butler, A., *Practical Tips for Choosing and Using Consulting and Contract Engineers*, NAB Publications, Washington, D.C., 1994.

Cheney, M., *Tesla: Man out of Time*, Prentice Hall, Englewood Cliffs, NJ, 1983.

Considine, D.M. (ed.), *Van Nostrand's Scientific Encyclopedia*, Van Nostrand Reinhold, New York, 1983.

Davidson, F.P., *Macro: A Clear Vision of How Science and Technology Will Shape Our Future*, William Morrow, New York, 1983.

Ebersole, S., *Broadcast Technology Worktext*, Focal Press, Boston, MA, 1992.

Grant, A.E., *Communication Technology Update*, Focal Press, Boston, MA, 1995.

Hilliard, R.L., *FCC Primer*, Focal Press, Boston, MA, 1991.

Hoeg, W. and Lauterbach, T. (eds), *Digital Broadcast Audio: Principles and Application of Digital Radio*, 2nd edition, Wiley, Hoboken, NJ, 2003.

Hong, S., *From Marconi's Black-Box to the Audion*, MIT Press, Cambridge, MA, 2001.

Mirabito, M. and Morgenstern, B., *The New Communication Technologies*, 2nd edition, Focal Press, Boston, MA, 1994.

Morton, D.L., Jr., *Sound Recording: The Life Story of a Technology*, Johns Hopkins University Press, Baltimore, MD, 2006.

National Association of Broadcasters, *Broadcast Engineering*, NAB Publications, Washington, D.C., 2008.

Noll, E.M., *Broadcast Radio and Television Handbook*, 6th edition, Howard Sams, Indianapolis, IN, 1983.

Priestman, C., *Web Radio: Radio Production for Internet Streaming*, Focal Press, Boston, MA, 2005.

Reed, J.H., *Software Radio: A Modern Approach to Radio Engineering*, Prentice-Hall, Englewood Cliffs, NJ, 2002.

Regal, B., *Radio: The Life Story of a Technology*, Greenwood, Westport, CT, 2005.

Reitz, J.R., *Foundations of Electromagnetic Theory*, Addison-Wesley, Reading, MA, 1960.

Roberts, R.S., *Dictionary of Audio, Radio, and Video*, Butterworths, Boston, MA, 1981.

Sarkar, T.K., et al. (eds), *History of the Wireless*, Wiley-Interscience, New York, 2006.

Starr, W., *Electrical Wiring and Design: A Practical Approach*, John Wiley & Sons, New York, 1983.

Watkinson, J., *The Art of Digital Audio*, Focal Press, Boston, MA, 1992.

Wilson, D., *A Broadcast Engineering Tutorial for Non-Engineers*, NAB, Washington, D.C., 1999.

Wurtzler, S.J., *Electronic Sounds: Technological Change and the Rise of Corporate Mass Media*, Columbia University Press, New York, 2007.

CHAPTER 11

Consultants and Syndicators

RADIO AID

Radio consultants have been around almost from the start, but it was not until the medium set a new course following the advent of television that the field grew to real prominence. By the 1960s, consultants were directing the programming efforts of hundreds of stations. In the 1970s, more than one-third of the nation's stations enlisted the services of consultants. The number of stations increased from 2,000 in the 1950s to more than 12,000 in the 1990s. As formats emerged and splintered, the number of consultants rose, too; their duties enlarged to include providing counsel about music selection, audience research, and marketing. Independent consultancies experienced a reversal of fortunes in the aftermath of the 1996 ownership-rules changes as several large group owners relocated the responsibilities to in-house advisors. Today, the field of radio consultancy has shrunk substantially due to the corporatization of the radio industry.

Former radio consultant Kent Burkhart observed:

> Since consolidation many of the small consulting companies have shut their doors. Most of the large consulting companies with lots of assets (meaning an exclusive format, research partners, marketing connections, etc.) have done well financially . . . but not as well as before. Prior to consolidation our company [Burkhart/Abrams] was charging a certain fee for each station in a group. However, since consolidation many groups have hired one chief programming executive for a lot less money than the aforementioned fee per station.

Longtime pro Mark St. John, co-founder with Guy Zapoleon of Zapoleon Media Strategies, affirms Burkhart's observation about the changes consolidation have visited upon the consultancies:

> Consolidation has definitely had a major impact on our business. The two major chains, Clear Channel and Cumulus, do not hire outside consultants for the most part. They have highly evolved internal structures to oversee programming efforts. For example, we have worked for Clear Channel and its previous incarnations in the past but that dwindled down to basically one market, New York, for which Guy still consulted until he joined the company directly. The good news is that there are many smaller companies that are doing great things in medium and small markets—by being live and local and really engaging in their communities. Working with these broadcasters is eminently rewarding. I believe as the economy improves and more financing becomes available these broadcasters will have an opportunity to expand as the major companies spin off markets below 50. This represents a tremendous upside for independent consultants.

Consultant Donna Halper shares a similar view of the impact of consolidation on her profession:

> It's certainly affected radio consulting. With fewer independent stations that means radio conglomerates are relying more on voice-tracking and syndication. It used to be that consultants trained and developed talent in small and medium markets, but these days a company might simulcast the same programs on two or more of their stations or use voice-tracking from another city to give the impression that a live and local personality is on the air. They may also have an in-house person who oversees the stations. Yet, this saves the companies money on hiring talent (and also saves them from hiring a consultant), but it also presents a problem. Many of these companies are not planning for the future.

Joel Raab, of Joel Raab Associates, is another consultant who sees opportunities for growth. Regarding the impact of corporatization on his consultancy, which specializes in servicing Country-formatted stations, Raab observes, "From my perspective, I could argue that it has helped. My business is as strong as ever."

With respect to the need for identifying and cultivating the talents of air personalities, Halper observes:

> Veteran talkers like Rush Limbaugh and Dave Ramsey will not live forever, and without developing new talent, who will take their place? As we witnessed during the 9/11 and Hurricane Katrina crises, people *do* want live and local radio, yet in many markets, there are no local personalities at all. Sooner or later somebody will have to start developing talent again and creating radio stations that are unique. We are already raising a generation of young adults who don't rely on radio the way their parents did.

Millennials, according to this successful consultant and educator, typically "find radio boring, with too many commercials and the same songs over and over. To get these people back (and I do believe it can be done) radio needs to return to its roots and get involved with the community again. As a consultant and someone who loves radio, I hope we will see more local personalities and more local programming. Radio needs to get back to being a friend again."

Echoing Halper's sentiments, consultant Doug Erickson says:

> The biggest challenge for radio consultants today is the corporate resistance to new ideas. As radio has become a consolidated industry, it has become more conservative in many ways. General managers and program directors feel more pressure to make the "right" choice and this often leads to making the "safest" choice—which is not always in the best interest of the station. As a consultant I try to make station management aware of the risks of doing nothing innovative. If terrestrial radio is to continue to be a part of the daily lives of most people, it must find a new way to remain personal and relevant, and it must do as much to touch the hearts of listeners as it does their ears.

"Professionals running radio stations want to win," Mark St. John observes, "and that is why we are hired in the first place. They are always willing to listen and act in order to achieve that goal. That doesn't mean throwing caution to the wind on highly speculative formats, although it does happen to varying degrees of success. But there is always willingness to accept change in order to grow ratings and revenue." Reluctance by managers to pursue new approaches and ideas *can* be overcome, says Raab. "My experience with GMs is that they *will* take risks, as long as you can show them that those risks have a good chance of paying off. It helps if you can give a real-life example in which a certain idea has worked. It's all about dollars and cents."

Calling upon her considerable experience enables consultant Valerie Geller to reconcile the risk-aversion mentality philosophically: "Risk is always a challenge. Radio is a creative process. While the fear of failure can loom even larger in a tight economy, if you want to win, you have to try new things. Risk is part of the game." She concedes the uncertainty by analogizing the radio business with a social institution: "Yes, radio is a risky business, but so is getting married (which statistically has a 50% failure rate) but that doesn't stop people from getting married." She notes that in her seminal text, *Beyond Powerful Radio—A Communicator's Guide to the Internet Age*, "the emphasis is on taking those risks in a very calculated way. The book specifically shows you how to maximize your creative risk to achieve potential success. Often my job as a consultant is to help clients get to the place where they can appreciate the benefits of risking and succeeding. But it's harder for some than for others."

Meanwhile, consultant Gary Berkowitz says that consolidation has not impacted his business greatly but admits it has taken its toll on the field. "I still fly more than 100,000 miles a year, so I'd say things are pretty good. Plus, many consultants left the business and took local programming jobs, so there are fewer of us out there. In all seriousness, there is no doubt that it has changed." Mark St. John, on the other hand, reports that travel time at his consultancy has diminished in recent years:

> Clients kept us engaged but whereas we used to travel to the market anywhere from 2–4 times yearly, now it is typically 0–1 time. The slack is taken up by a dramatic increase in online meetings which are a very efficient way to conduct business. We also conduct coaching sessions via Skype. These technologies allow for fewer face-to-face meetings and still get the job done. Of course, face time is always valuable because even though many clients have been with us for years it is always beneficial to spend time in the market with the staff. This is more important with newer clients in the early stages of development.

Also, from the perspective of Juan Carlos Hidalgo, who consults Spanish radio, the market for his services is strong:

> It's been a fascinating experience working for stations in major markets, such as Los Angeles, Chicago, and San Francisco, where you have all the tools, like research and marketing budgets to complement programming efforts. At the same time in the smaller markets that I consult, I have to rely more on creativity due to the limited budgets and tools. The dynamic of these two different situations keeps me on the cutting edge of doing new and exciting things to improve the performance of my client radio stations. Consolidation hasn't impacted my business. Maybe in the future.

Whether the radio consultancy function will be completely absorbed by corporations remains to be seen. However, consultants continue to play an important role in the shaping and management of the medium today. Observes prominent radio consultant George Burns:

> The principal role of radio consultants has evolved considerably since Mike Joseph started the whole thing in the 1950s. We began by being very specifically task-oriented. A consultant was assumed to have greater expertise at the job than anyone that the station could afford fulltime. Currently consultants serve primarily as outside (and, it is hoped, impartial) monitors of station progress. The job is to assure management that everything possible is being done to maximize the station's potential. If something is not functioning properly or needs to be changed, consultants are expected to give voice to these concerns. Over the years, the job has become infinitely more complex. Musical and non-musical aspects of programming have spread widely apart. Research has become a separate discipline. And lately, the marketing side of radio has achieved

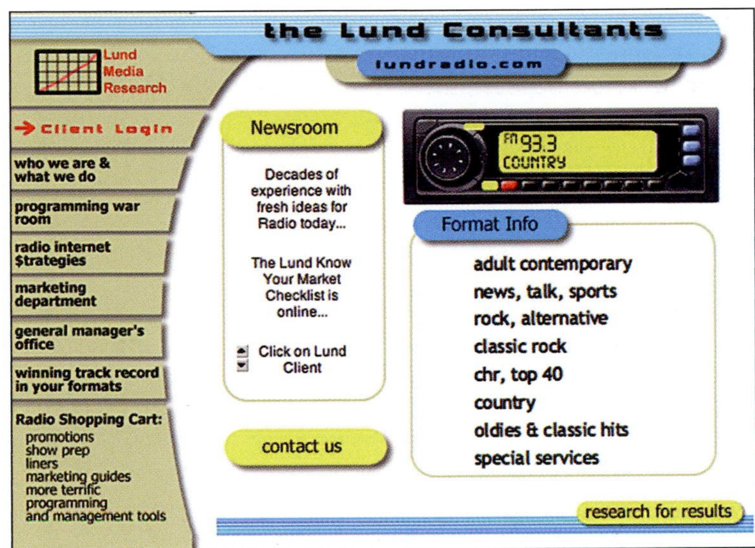

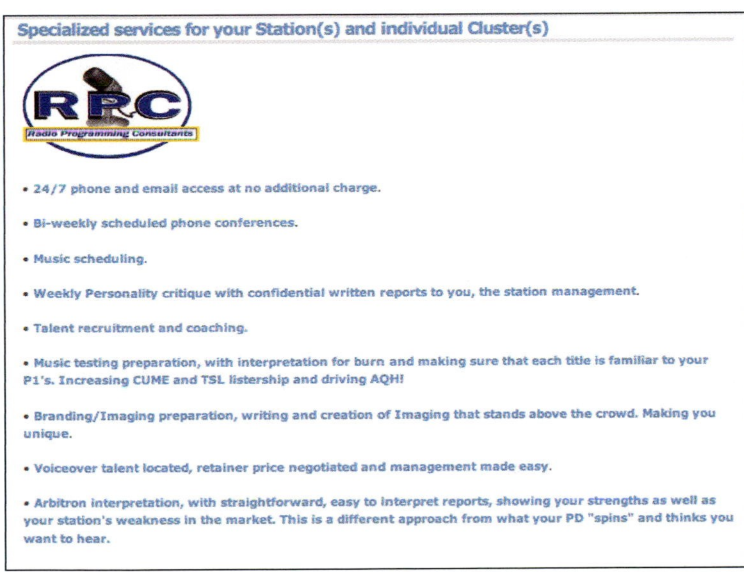

FIGURE 11.1A&B
There are an abundance of radio consulting services from which stations can choose. Courtesy of Lund Consultants.

a "life of its own." Different consultants approach each station's progress from varying points of view. Specialization was inevitable.

Stations use consultants for various reasons, says Fred Jacobs, president of Jacobs Media: "Stations realize that they need an experienced, objective ear to make intelligent evaluations. Consultants are also exposed to ideas and innovations from around the country that they can bring to their client stations. As radio has become more competitive, stations understand that their need for up-to-date information about current trends in programming and marketing has increased."

Dave Scott, former president of Century 21 Programming (now TM Studios), Dallas, Texas, adds that a lack of research expertise on the local station level prompts many stations to use consultants. "It takes a lot of resources to assess a market and prescribe a course of action. Most stations do not have the wherewithal." Mark St. John elaborates on the scarcity of resources at stations, observing that

> budgets for research have gone way down over the last five years. It is a matter of priority. Stations that routinely did annual perceptual studies now do them only if there is a market change that warrants it or not at all. Stations that did annual music testing have either diminished it or cut it out as well. Traditional callout formerly was ubiquitous and has been converted to online music testing utilizing station listener databases at a much lower cost. Even so, we have access to lots of different kinds of research and are able to channel that knowledge to the benefit of the client. That increases our value so that they can take advantage of trends without having a large research budget. Research is generally not done in house anymore—it is difficult to set up and monitor and the results could be questionable. Better to leave research to the people who are set up to do it properly.

Donna Halper agrees with Scott and St. John, adding, "Consultants give their client stations an objective viewpoint and another experienced person's input. Consultants are support people, resource people, who bring to a situation a broader vision rather than the purely local perspective. Consultants (and not just out-of-work PDs who call themselves consultants but in reality aren't) have a lot of research, information, and expertise they can make available to a client with an ailing station."

Fewer than 100 broadcast consultants are listed in the various media directories around the country. More than half of this number specializes in radio. Says Ed Shane, "I remember a time when there were 250 programming consultants listed in the *R&R* directory, which was, until 2009, a twice-yearly publication of the defunct trade magazine *Radio & Records*. The number has tumbled since consolidation. One-man shops that couldn't make it as clients were swallowed by competing companies. Some consulting firms merged. Others folded to go in-house as brand managers at major broadcast companies." Joel Raab views the shift from independency to corporate employment as beneficial to both parties, serving to make programming at the owner level stronger. St. John views the moves to corporate employment by these former independents as good for his business. As he sees it, "some of the top programming minds in

America from Mike McVay to Steve Smith to Guy Zapoleon are now working inside companies. That trend is likely to continue and has to be viewed as a positive for those of us remaining as independent consultants!"

In general, consultancy companies average around 20–30 employees but may be composed of as few as two or three and in some cases are a one-person operation. Many successful program directors also provide consultancy to stations in other markets in addition to their regular programming duties. A growing number of station rep companies provide their client stations consultancy services for an additional fee. Again, in the age of station consolidation and massive radio groups, consultancy often originates in-house. One of the distinct benefits that major corporations accrue, according to Valerie Geller, is exclusivity. She explains, "One advantage from the corporate perspective: When you hire somebody to work for you, he or she won't be available to be hired by your competitors to work against you." She regards the impact of corporate hiring on the profession as minimal, reasoning that "hiring a company in-house 'group' consultant has solved some problems for certain station groups, it has not fundamentally changed the nature of the work we do."

CONSULTANT SERVICES

Stations hire program consultants to improve or strengthen their standings in the ratings surveys. Consultant Valerie Geller works with a wide-ranging clientele of station and individual clients. Geller views the ownership-consolidation issue from a different perspective. Her services are constantly in demand; it's the nature of the way business is transacted, she reports, that has changed:

> Consolidation or not, it's busy. I work with a lot of independently owned stations and projects, but due to the corporate consolidation and station cutbacks, I'm finding that I'm on the road constantly. If a program director, producer, or news director recognizes that he or she does not have the time to train or develop his or her staff, that's when I get the call to help, either with a workshop or seminar session or individual coaching work. I also began offering a series of one-on-one coaching sessions "by the hour," which makes it easy and more affordable for managers to hire outside help to aircheck their talent. Another big change is that individual talent, or on-air personalities, who are invested in improving their own performances, often hire me independently, and pay for their coaching sessions on their own dime. Many are willing to invest in their career growth and development because they recognize the importance of building themselves as a "brand name" across multiple platforms, regardless of the station for which they are working. Usually that happens if their PDs or managers are stretched so thin that they are overloaded with other work and unable to offer the guidance that talent needs in order to grow. So again, it's been very busy.

An outside consultant may share general program decisions with the station's PD or may be endowed with full control over all decisions affecting the station's sound, contends Halper. "I have as little or as much involvement as the client desires. Depending on the case, I can hire and train staff (or fire staff), design or fine-tune a format." Consultant responsibilities alternate between the external and internal aspects of station operations. Halper reports that in some instances she may be charged with reviewing a station's visual appearance, offering "suggestions about improving the station's visibility." She adds, "It's amazing how many stations have a boring website, or a logo that looks outdated." In other situations her role is to

> simply motivate and direct deejays, which is actually anything but simple. I can also prevent an owner from implementing a really bad idea: having had years of experience, I know what works and what does not. Whatever a station wants, as a professional consultant I can provide. Usually, I make recommendations and then the owner or GM decides whether or not I will carry them out. At some of my stations, I've functioned as the acting PD, for all intents and purposes. At other client stations, I've been sort of the unofficial mother figure, providing support, encouragement, and sometimes a much-needed kick in the behind.

The stations Joel Raab consults that operate outside the larger markets tend to need basic programming and audience-relationship guidance. "In smaller markets, we are doing more music scheduling than ever for stations, as staff cutbacks and quality control issues have necessitated more involvement on our part. More time is spent advising clients regarding social media usage and concerns."

Among other services, Fred Jacobs says his company offers:

> in-market visits for monitoring and strategizing; ongoing monitors of client competition from airchecks or station 'listen lines'; critiques of on-air talent, assistance/design of music scheduling and selection; computer programs that assist with promo scheduling, database marketing, and

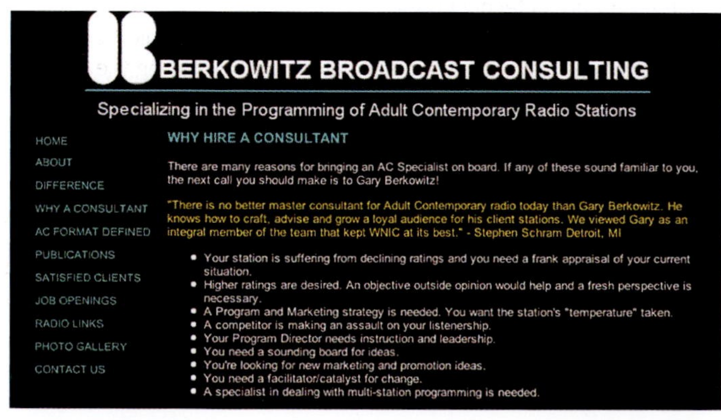

FIGURE 11.2
Consultants make a dramatic difference at many stations. Courtesy of Berkowitz Broadcast Consultants.

morning show preparation; design of off-air advertising and coordination with production; and design/implementation of market research for programming, image, and music.

Most consultant firms are equipped to provide either comprehensive or limited support to stations. "In some cases, consultants offer a packaged 'system for success' in the same way a McDonald's hamburger franchise delivers a 'system for success' to an investor. The consultant gets control. In other instances, consultants deliver objective advice or research input to a station more on a one-to-one basis. This parallels the role of most accountants or attorneys in that the decisions are still made by the station management, not the consultant," notes Dave Scott.

Following an extensive assessment of a station's programming, a consultant may suggest a major change. "After an in-depth evaluation and analysis, we may conclude that a station is improperly positioned in its particular market and recommend a format switch. Sometimes station management disagrees.

STATION CONSULTING

Gary Berkowitz

The principal reason stations hire consultants is the experience, knowledge, and wisdom that is not always available to them on a local basis. Today's program directors have more responsibility than ever including multiple station programming, airshifts, managing digital, etc. When I get involved, I focus in on one station, develop a strategy, and make sure that strategy is being followed. Consolidation has been around long enough that we've figured out what it means to the field of radio consultants. I've always believed that if you can help people get better ratings, which in turn convert into revenue, they will want to use you. There are still many broadcasters who need the savvy of solid consultants. As far as the effects of all the new audio technologies on the consultancy profession, it has not been as significant as one might think. Radio stations are still judged by the ratings and ratings are still determined by having the best sounding and best-marketed product. Terrestrial radio still fights for every ad dollar available, so the ratings are now more important than ever.

FIGURE 11.3
Gary Berkowitz.

Gary Berkowitz has been involved in every aspect of the operation and management of high quality, financially successful radio stations. During his 35-year career the Emerson College graduate's responsibilities have taken him from on-air personality to music and program director. He established Berkowitz Broadcast Consulting in 1990 to help Adult Contemporary (AC) radio stations achieve higher ratings. Today, Gary Berkowitz represents North America's highest rated ACs, owned by major groups including CBS Radio and Greater Media. Berkowitz Broadcast Consulting is based in Detroit, Michigan.

They're the consultants for companies that "don't use consultants."

They're our station's secret weapon.

- Today's # 1 stations choose Shane Media for programming.
- Now, a full menu of research services, too.
- Our 20th Year of thinking ahead!

SHANE MEDIA
(713) 952-9221
Radio Programming and Research
www.shanemedia.com

FIGURE 11.4
Consultants offer various services to stations. Courtesy of Shane Media.

Changing formats can be pretty traumatic, so there is often resistance to the idea. A critique more often recommends that adjustments be made in an existing format than a changeover to a different one. There are times when a consultant is simply called upon to assist in the hiring of a new jock or newsperson. Major surgery is not always necessary or desired," says Halper.

Today, the majority of stations in major and medium markets switching formats do so with the aid of a consultant (or an in-house programming executive in cluster situations). According to the National Association of Broadcasters (NAB), 3–5% of the nation's stations change formats each year. Consultant fees range from hundreds to thousands of dollars per day, depending on the complexity of the services rendered and the size of the station and its market.

CONSULTANT QUALIFICATIONS

Most consultants begin as broadcasters. Some successfully programmed stations before embarking on their own or joining consultancy firms. According to the late Rick Sklar, a fabled major-market programmer and founder of the advisory firm Sklar Communications, consultants who have a background in the medium have a considerable edge over those who do not. "The best way to fully understand and appreciate radio is to work in it. As you might imagine, radio experience is very helpful in this business." Jacobs agrees with Sklar. "Ideally a consultant should have a successful background in programming, with expertise in a number of areas, including research, sales, marketing, and promotion. Technology conversancy is important, too, opines Mark St. John. In order to make the successful leap from radio broadcaster to consultant, a person should "have impressive technical skills, especially with music programming software, e.g. Selector or Music Master, and be able to collect and present myriads of data and provide context to that data."

"The key word is *success*," Jacobs insists. "A solid track record in a number of different market situations is invaluable." He adds, "Consultants also need to have strong communication and tracking skills to best work with a variety of clients in markets around the country." Not all consultants have extensive backgrounds in the medium. Most do possess a thorough knowledge of how radio operates on all its different levels, from having worked closely with stations and having acquired formal training in colleges offering research methodology, audience measurement, and broadcast management courses. "A solid education is particularly important for those planning to become broadcast consultants. It is a very complex and demanding field today, and it is becoming more so with each passing day. My advice is to load up. Get the training and experience up front. It is very competitive out there. You make your own opportunities in this profession," says Dave Scott.

Consultants almost universally agree that possessing outstanding "people skills" is a must for success in the profession. "Consulting requires an ability to deal with all kinds of people and to address a wide range of emotions. Decisions—

for example, about changing formats—sometimes result in drastic personnel changes. A consultant must be adept at diplomacy but must act with conviction when the diagnosis has been made. Major surgery is invariably traumatic, but the idea is to make the patient, the station, healthy again. You can't let your own personal biases or tastes get in the way of what will work in a given market," observes Halper. Dave Scott shares Halper's sentiments. "A consultant, like a doctor, must be compassionate and at the same time maintain his objectivity. It is our intention and goal as a program consultant service to make our client stations thrive. As consultants, we're successful because we do what we have to do. It's not a question of being mercenary. It's a question of doing what you have to do to make a station prosper and realize its potential."

Consultant company executives also consider wit, patience, curiosity, sincerity, eagerness, competitiveness, and drive—not necessarily in that order—among the other virtues that the aspiring consultant should possess. Geller emphasizes the absolute need for forthrightness and transparency in observing the characteristics that successful consultants must exhibit. Principal among the qualifications is "A willingness to tell the truth, even when it's not easy, or comfortable" and the ability to empathize with the client while sustaining respect for them. Gary Berkowitz adds, "All of those things are important. Indeed experience, integrity, and honesty top the list, as does the ability to tell clients what you really think versus what they might want to hear." As Joel Raab puts it, the successful consultant possesses "the ability to cut through to the heart of issues and the courage to tell the truth as you know it. Clients want and expect you to disagree with them."

QUALIFICATIONS OF SUCCESSFUL CONSULTANTS

Valerie Geller

Veteran Valerie Geller has consulted stations in all 50 states and 33 foreign countries. What qualifications does she believe a successful consultant should possess? Here are her observations.

FIGURE 11.5
Valerie Geller.

- **Have knowledge, experience, and a successful track record:** The people who hire you like to know that you've had past successes—and a lot of them! I began consulting after working for years in the business. My background includes small market radio news in Wyoming, to major market on air and management positions—including that of executive producer, news director and program director at stations in Los Angeles (KFI), San Francisco (K101), and New York (WABC).
- **Focus on one thing at a time:** Consulting allows you the luxury to hone in on what you like to do. For me, it's working with talent and programming to help strengthen on

air performance and help people better focus their content to more effectively engage audiences. That for me is one of the most satisfying parts of this job. The other part I love is finding and developing talent.

- **Flexibility:** When you work as a consultant, try as you might, you can't "make" people change. They have to want to. Your job as a consultant is to suggest, advise, and counsel. So if you are only happy when you have complete control of the product, consulting might not be the job for you.
- **Learn from others:** Back when I was employed at radio stations, I had an opportunity to work with a lot of different consultants. From some I learned what to do, and from others, what not to do. Radio is an art form. Good consultants listen. They have knowledge of the station and what else is available to audiences in the market. They take into account the strengths and qualities of each individual on staff. They also need to understand the market's idiosyncrasies to be effective. You can't just come to town with a bag of tricks. Each station and staff has unique problems and challenges.

Finally, as a colleague once said to me: "it costs nothing to be nice." Performers are famous for having fragile egos, so, I try when I can, to be gentle—although it's not always possible. And, since I've worked in just about every aspect of this business, on and off the air, I have genuine empathy for what my clients experience on a daily basis.

To sum up the qualifications, it's important to have:

1. Knowledge and the ability to listen and to understand what's right, what's wrong, and importantly, how to work with "what is."
2. Empathy and a desire to do right by the client.
3. A willingness to tell the truth, even when it's not easy, or comfortable.
4. The experience to assess a complex situation quickly, and recognize dynamics.
5. The ability to be open to new ideas and willing to re-engage others with their own ideas, or interest them in new ones.

Valerie Geller is president of Geller Media International, a broadcast consulting firm working with news, talk, information, and personality programming for radio and television throughout the world. Geller coaches talent, leads "Creating Powerful Communicators" workshops and seminars, and has helped more than 500 stations in 33 countries develop and grow their audiences by training communicators to work more effectively. She is a much-in-demand conference and keynote speaker and seminar leader and is the author of four books about broadcasting. Her latest, *Beyond Powerful Radio—A Communicator's Guide to the Internet Age*, is available from Focal Press.

CONSULTANTS: PROS AND CONS

There are as many opponents of program consultants within the radio industry as there are advocates. Broadcasters who do not use consultants argue that local flavor is lost when an outsider comes into a market to direct a station's programming. Joel Raab sees things differently. He views the consultant/

management relationship as a collaborative process. "A good consultant," in his opinion, "presents input and ideas that must flow through the filter of the local management's experience. I would argue that a well-consulted, well-executed station will sound more local, as outside input mixed with inside insight is a very powerful combination."

Donna Halper contends that, in employing a consultant, local flavor may be sacrificed to some degree but believes that most professional consultants are sensitive to a station's local identity:

> Some consultants do clone their stations. Others of us do not. In fact, I'd say most do not. For those of us who recognize local differences, there need not be any loss whatsoever as a consequence of consultant-recommended changes. But the hits are pretty much the hits, and good radio is something that Tulsa deserves as well as Rochester. So I do try to localize my music research and acquire a good feel for the market I'm working in. But as far as basic rules of good radio are concerned, those don't vary much no matter what the market is. It's important for a station to reflect the market it serves, and I support my clients in that. Because I work out of Boston doesn't mean that my AOR client in Duluth should sound like a Boston album rocker. It should sound like a solid AOR station that could be respected in any city but fits the needs of Duluth.

Consultant Dwight Douglas says that localization is essential for any radio station and that consultants are amply aware of this fact:

> It is an industry axiom that a station must be a part of its environment. An excellent station will be uniquely local in relating to its audience. That tends to take the form of news, weather, sports, public service, general information, and jock talk. A good consultant will free a station from music worries and allow it to concentrate on developing local identity. We work hard at customizing formats to suit the geodemographics or lifestyles of the audiences of our client stations.

"When stations hire consultants," Valerie Geller says, "they do so, because they need or want to change. If things are *not* working to plan or if there is a problem, a consultant can offer help to move the station up a notch with a valuable and objective set of outside eyes and ears. It's easy to lose perspective if you get too close to the product. That's where the consultant can help. But a consultant should not direct programming." Drawing upon years of national and international experience, she concludes that:

> Audiences leave if programming does not inform, entertain, or inspire them. If the content is not relevant, or if they are bored, listeners will tune out. There are three principles that work, no matter the country or the culture: 1. Tell the truth; 2. Make it matter; and 3. Never be boring!

> A lot of the work I do, and certainly the content of all four of my books, is based on these principles. That being said, a good consultant is someone who listens, has insight and clarity of vision, enough background and experience to recognize dynamics, and can offer a map of practical ideas based on having worked with many stations. While a consultant can help you craft the map, you and your station still have to take the journey.

The late, well-respected programmer and air personality Mikel Hunter observed, "No station should simply turn itself over body and soul to a consultant. Local flavor does not have to be sacrificed if a station has a strong PD and a general manager who doesn't insist that the PD merely follow the consultant's suggestions. A station should not let itself become a local franchise. Consultants are a valuable resource, but both the station and the consultant must pool their wisdom to make the plan work." Zapoleon's Mark St. John continues the discussion, explaining how he projects himself into the activities of his client stations:

> I have always considered myself as another member of the staff. We work together to build a strategy that is customized for every situation. Everybody needs to buy in to the strategy and then we closely monitor its execution to make sure we achieve our goals. It is harder to do it this way, but it means that the local flavor remains intact and every station sounds like it is truly connected to its market.

Jacobs strikes a similar note of caution regarding the importance of local connection:

> With a consultant, a station can conceivably lose some of its localness if there isn't adequate effort to give it a hometown flavor. But the loss of local presence is far more likely with satellite-delivered formats. Consultants need to work closely with station management (and vice versa) to find local ties and signposts, because listeners care most about what's happening in their town. It's always important to understand that there are regional differences in taste, personalities, and music. Many high-powered on-air personalities would be hard-pressed to duplicate their success in another market.

The cost factor is another reason why some stations do not use consultants. "Consultants can be expensive, although most consultants scale their fees to suit the occasion, that is, the size of the market. A few hundred dollars a day can be exorbitant for many smaller stations. But the cost of the research, analysis, and strategy usually is worth the money. I believe that a station, in most cases, gets everything it pays for when it uses a consultant. It's worth investing a few thousand to make back a million," contends Dwight Douglas.

Dave Scott believes that certain stations can become too dependent on consultants. "A consultant is there to provide support and direction when

Donna Halper & Associates
Radio Programming Consultants
304 Newbury St., #508
Boston, MA 02115
(617) 766–0666

QUESTIONS I AM OFTEN ASKED ABOUT HIRING A CONSULTANT

1. What kind of station would hire a consultant?

All kinds! From major market #1 stations that want to stay that way to new stations that need help choosing a format or hiring staff.

2. Aren't most consultants just out-of-work Program Directors?

Not today. Competition is too intense. Most of us who have stayed in the consulting field have years of experience in one thing: CONSULTING.

3. Should I hire a 'big name' consultant?

Since the majority of consultants today are experienced, you should choose one based on what his/her areas of expertise are. Interview a few consultants and you will see that each has some speciality – whether its a certain format (some consultants prefer to do only one format) or a certain market size. Choosing the right consultant for your station is an important decision, and you shouldn't do it on name alone.

4. What can a consultant offer my station that my own people can't provide?

First, consultants aren't there to replace your people, nor do they want them to look bad. While staff changes may result from the recommendations of a consultant, our first purpose is to offer you an UNBIASED, outside overview of how your station sounds, both its strengths and its weaknesses.
We work WITH your people, providing research, guidance, training, market studies, etc. Often, because we are not caught up in the day-to-day cirumstances, we can offer a fresh, objective point of view.

5. What are the benefits of HALPER & ASSOCIATES?

I'm glad you asked. We've been in business since 1980. (Before that, Donna Halper spent 13 years in major markets as an announcer, Music Director, PD, news reporter, and writer/producer of special programming.) Our specialties include critiques/positioning studies, staff training and motivation, and talent development. We work in markets of all sizes, but we are best-known for our ability to turn around failing small and medium market stations. We also do motivational seminars, and are expert at handling morale problems. Unlike some consultants who only do one format, Halper & Associates can show success stories in AC, Gold, CHR, Urban, Classic Rock, Full-Service/M-O-R, and Country.
SINCE 1980, OVER 90% OF OUR CLIENTS HAVE SHOWN RATINGS GROWTH.
And, our critiques and market studies have been used by some of the biggest and best companies.
Also, Halper & Associates has experience with Canadian radio, and we have consulted in Puerto Rico.

6. Can you promise results for every client?

No consultant wins 'em all, although we'd like to. But, our slogan has always been "NO PROMISES ... JUST RESULTS." We are proud of our many satisfied clients and our renewal rate is quite high. Many of our clients say they would never use another consultant. So, when its time to think about a consultant, choose DONNA HALPER & ASSOCIATES. We can get results for you. To find out more, call us at 617–786–0666. We'll give you the attention you might not get from the "big names," affordable rates, and, most important, you can count on us to make a positive impact on your station and its staff!
DONNA HALPER GETS RESULTS!!!

FIGURE 11.6
Consultant's response to commonly asked questions. Courtesy of Donna Halper and Associates.

needed. If a station is infirm, it needs attention, perhaps extensive care. However, when a station regains its health, an annual or semi-annual checkup is usually sufficient. A checkup generally can prevent problems from recurring."

Statistically, those stations that use programming consultants more often than not experience improved ratings. In case after case, consultants have taken their client stations from bottom to top in many of the country's largest markets. Of course, not all succeed quite so dramatically. However, a move from eleventh place to sixth in a metro market is considered a noteworthy achievement and has a very invigorating effect on station revenue. "The vast majority of consultants benefit their clients by increasing their position in the ratings book. This means better profits," notes Halper, who has improved the ratings of 90% of her client stations during three decades of consulting. Improving a station's ratings, of course, is not always an objective for the smaller-market stations, and consultants such as Halper are sensitive to the needs of these stations' operators. "Even in non-rated markets," Halper indicates, "a better sounding station is likely to attract more listeners, and more advertisers too."

A Good Consultant Can Make A Difference...

With so many good consultants out there, it can be a difficult task to choose the one who is right for your station. To help you make such an important decision, **HALPER & ASSOCIATES** offers a few facts about what we can do for you:

1. **HALPER & ASSOCIATES** has gotten results for our clients since 1980. Our staff and our reputation are solid.

2. **HALPER & ASSOCIATES** has success stories in nearly every format, from CHR to Urban, Gold to Classic Rock, Country to AC, News and MOR. We've helped turn around many stations — both AM's and FM's. Recently, for example, we took a declining Urban/CHR from a 5.3 to an 8.4 in one year. An AC client of ours has grown from a 13.0 to a 17.1 in two years. Since 1980, over 90% of our clients have shown ratings increases. Many are now #1 or #2.

3. **HALPER & ASSOCIATES** gets results in markets of all sizes, from the East Coast to the West Coast, Canada and Puerto Rico. We have clients in major and large markets, but we have become known for our work in small and medium markets. We understand the special challenges of these markets and can make an impact even if you don't have a huge promotion budget or a legendary air staff.

4. **HALPER & ASSOCIATES** offers more than just better ratings. Our specialty is motivation and talent development. We can help to bring out the best in your staff, handle morale problems, or give your department heads the training and input they need to do their jobs more effectively. We are also known for our thorough market analyses, critiques and positioning studies. We can help you find the right format, or fine tune the one you now have.

5. **HALPER & ASSOCIATES** never clones stations or deals in fad formats. Each of our clients is unique. We are there whenever you need us.

No promises. Just results.

Donna Halper and Associates
Radio Programming Consultants
304 Newbury Street #506
Boston, Mass. 02115
(617) 786-0666

FIGURE 11.7
Consultant promotional piece. Courtesy of Donna Halper and Associates.

About the future of radio consultancy, George Burns says:

> I see the role of consultants undergoing considerable change in the next few years. The rules of ownership and the very principles under which our industry is organized are altering radically. Consultants will probably take even more of an advisory role and have less involvement in the day-to-day operations of a station. The new and larger broadcasting companies, in all size markets, will keep expertise in-house and rely less on outside input in these areas. I see consultants operating at "higher levels" in the future. They will be working on organization, continuing education, motivation, compensation, human resources, and other "top management" concerns. Consultants, I believe, will become more policy oriented and less concerned with ground level activities.

PROGRAM SUPPLIERS

One part art, one part technology: what the glib, personality-driven, DJ approach did to revolutionize program presentation in the 1950s, so did the emergence of "automated" radio during the 1960s. In a triumph of technology, automation systems enabled station operators to minimize the need for human intervention by storing music, commercials, weather announcements, and other program elements on magnetic recording tape and scheduling them for future on-air playback. Because the nature of the process for automating the broadcast was technically sophisticated, the circumstances motivated station management to seek out syndicator services that could, for a fee, provide the station with libraries of prerecorded music and instructions for format execution. Today, digital storage devices have displaced the analog tape-playback systems of yesteryear. When properly executed, the automated format of today can sound so lifelike as to be virtually indistinguishable from live programming. In addition to numerous independent syndicators many of the large radio corporations create programming for distribution to their own stations, relaying real-time program content by satellite and Internet. As a result, fewer independent 24-hour format suppliers exist today. As Jay Williams observes:

> Consolidation changed the syndication business; two of the largest syndicators are now owned by the biggest station groups. Perhaps because their own stations are now clients, or perhaps because individual stations are reluctant to rehire staff after the recession, or maybe it's because national advertisers are increasing their support, but syndicated programming and products have improved and become more popular. Once relegated to late nights and weekends, syndicated shows have found their way to every daypart including morning drive. And as syndicators have become more adept at creating flexible, customized original programming, that trend will continue.

Williams adds that syndicated programming can benefit stations even in the major markets by tapping into the successes of nationally recognized TV personalities. "For major market radio managers, the opportunity to have a nationally known TV personality such as Ryan Seacrest or Billy Bush host middays or evenings on their station, especially as these radio shows feature timely interviews with entertainers and recording artists that may be unavailable to own their local talent, these additional advantages make syndication even more attractive."

It has been estimated that over half of the country's radio outlets have purchased syndicated programming of some type, which may consist of as little as a series of one- or two-minute features or as much as a 24-hour, year-round station format. Longtime program specialist Dick Ellis cites economics as the primary reason why stations resort to syndicators. "When I programmed for Peters Productions they supplied high-quality programming and engineering at a relatively low cost." The expertise provided by Peters, Ellis notes, focused on programming and engineering, with the objective of enabling station management to focus on managing external operations. "All of this, he summarizes, frees the local operator to concentrate his efforts on promotion and, of course, sales."

Both economics and service motivate radio stations to contract syndicators, contends former Satellite Music Network (now operated by Cumulus Media Networks and branded as "Music Radio") programmer Lee Abrams. Stations were "attracted to our affordable, high-quality programming. It's just that simple. Syndies provided an excellent product within a cost-effective context. Their expertise in delivering niche concepts was very appealing to radio operators."

Equally as prominent are the providers of the 24-hour automated formats, companies that specialize in dayparted and occasional special-event programming to meet specific broadcaster needs. Every part of the broadcast day is served by syndicators, and morning drive in particular, observes Ed Shane. "Syndicated morning shows are widespread and proliferating. There are almost too many to keep track of. At a quick glance, you've got Bob and Sheri, John Boy and Billy, Bob and Tom, The Tom Joyner Show, Steve Harvey, Yolanda Adams, Free Beer and Hot Wings, Big D and Bubba, and on and on." For smaller-market stations, syndicated programs offer several distinct advantages, as Jay Williams explains. According to him:

> The advantages of airing outside programming are compelling especially for small and medium-market radio stations. It might cost $30,000 or more for a local operator to create a home-grown morning show with two people, but that includes risks. The local morning show may not be successful, the talent may not get along, or perhaps worse, the local show is so successful the talent is lured away to a larger market. Yet for that same amount of money, a station can choose a successful syndicated

> morning show like Bob and Tom or Elvis Duran and eliminate their management worries. That alone makes syndication an appealing option especially for non-programming oriented station owners and managers.

SYNDICATOR SERVICES

The name "Drake-Chenault" was synonymous with the 24/7, tape-based program syndication business in the late 1960s. Founded by legendary programmer Bill Drake and business partner Gene Chenault, D-C distinguished itself from the various instrumental music-format syndicators of the day, notably Schulke Radio Productions and Bonneville, by incorporating recorded song-and-artist deejay intro and outro announcements into the music presentation. Embellishing an automated music format with deejay announcements is commonplace today, but it was quite a technological achievement for D-C, whose signature automated format, "HitParade," predated today's digitized voice-tracking technique by several decades.

The major program syndicators of the tape-based era prospered in the 1970s through the 1990s, usually marketing several distinctive, fully packaged radio formats. "In its heyday, Peters Productions made available a complete format service with each of their format blends. They were not merely a music service. Their programming goal was the emotional gratification of the type of person attracted to a particular format," says Dick Ellis, whose former company offered a dozen different formats, including Beautiful Music, Easy Listening, Standard Country, Modern Country, Adult Contemporary, Standard MOR, Super Hits, Easy Contemporary, and a country and contemporary hybrid called Natural Sound.

Century 21 Programming also was a leader in format diversity, explains Dave Scott. "Our inventory included everything from the most contemporary super hits sound to several Christian formats. We even offered a full-time Jazz format. We had programming to fit any need in any market."

The demand for syndicator product has paralleled, if not exceeded, the increase in the number of radio outlets since the l960s. Again, the new millennium has brought a change in the field of program syndication with the large radio corporations often assuming the responsibilities for program production inhouse. Syndication of the personality-driven programs in the contemporary marketplace is dominated by only a handful of companies, led by Premiere Radio Networks. Premiere is a subsidiary of Clear Channel Communications, the largest owner/operator of radio stations in the U.S. According to its website, Premiere Networks:

> syndicates 90 radio programs and services to more than 5,000 radio affiliations and reaches over 190 million listeners weekly. Premiere is the number one audio content provider in the country and features the following personalities: Rush Limbaugh, Jim Rome, Ryan Seacrest,

Glenn Beck, Bob & Tom, Delilah, Steve Harvey, Blair Garner, George Noory, John Boy and Billy, Big Tigger, Sean Hannity, Elvis Duran, Jason Lewis, Randi Rhodes, Nikki Sixx, Kane, and others.

Observes Ed Shane, "The key to using syndicator or network programming is to make it sound like it belongs to the station. Even big personality shows like Rush and Sean Hannity can make use of local avails and bumpers for personalized call letters and promos." Today United Stations Radio Network, Salem Music Network, Radio Disney, and Learfield Communications serve the industry with specialized programming features ranging from rock concerts to play-by-play sports coverage.

Also playing a prominent role in the program-syndication marketplace are the producers of fulltime music formats. Using satellites and the Internet to distribute programming to client stations, syndicators of these 24/7 formats typically provide a near-turnkey entertainment package that includes real-time delivery of DJ-hosted music and custom-tailored station imaging elements such as IDs, liners, breaks and sweepers. Top-caliber DJ talent ensures that the overall presentation has a major-market "sound." WestwoodOne, a leading provider, makes available a variety of program formats, including Country, Adult

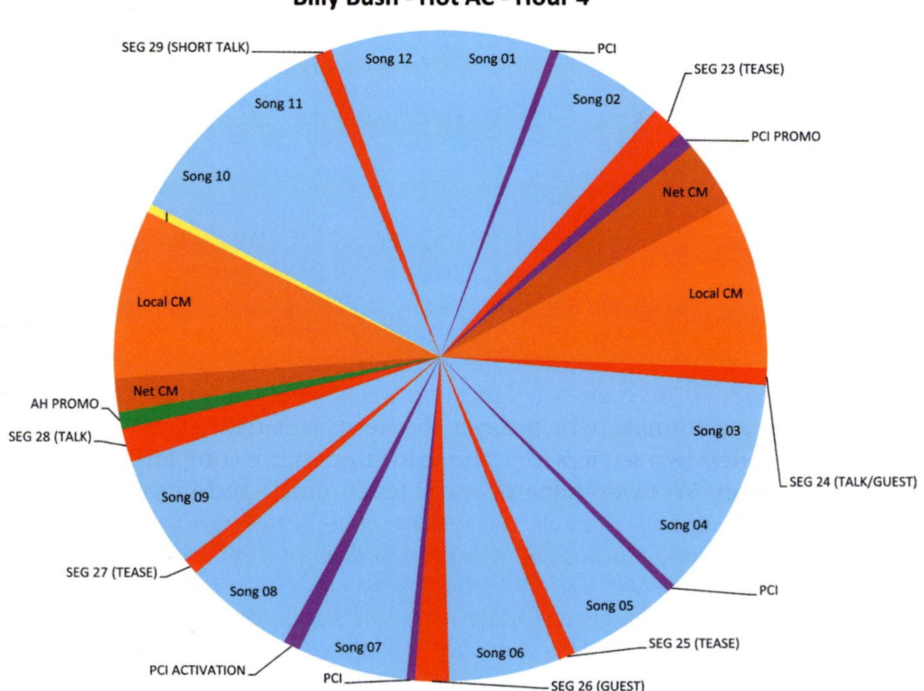

FIGURE 11.8
Program clock for an hour of Billy Bush's syndicated music program. Courtesy of NBCU and Jay Williams.

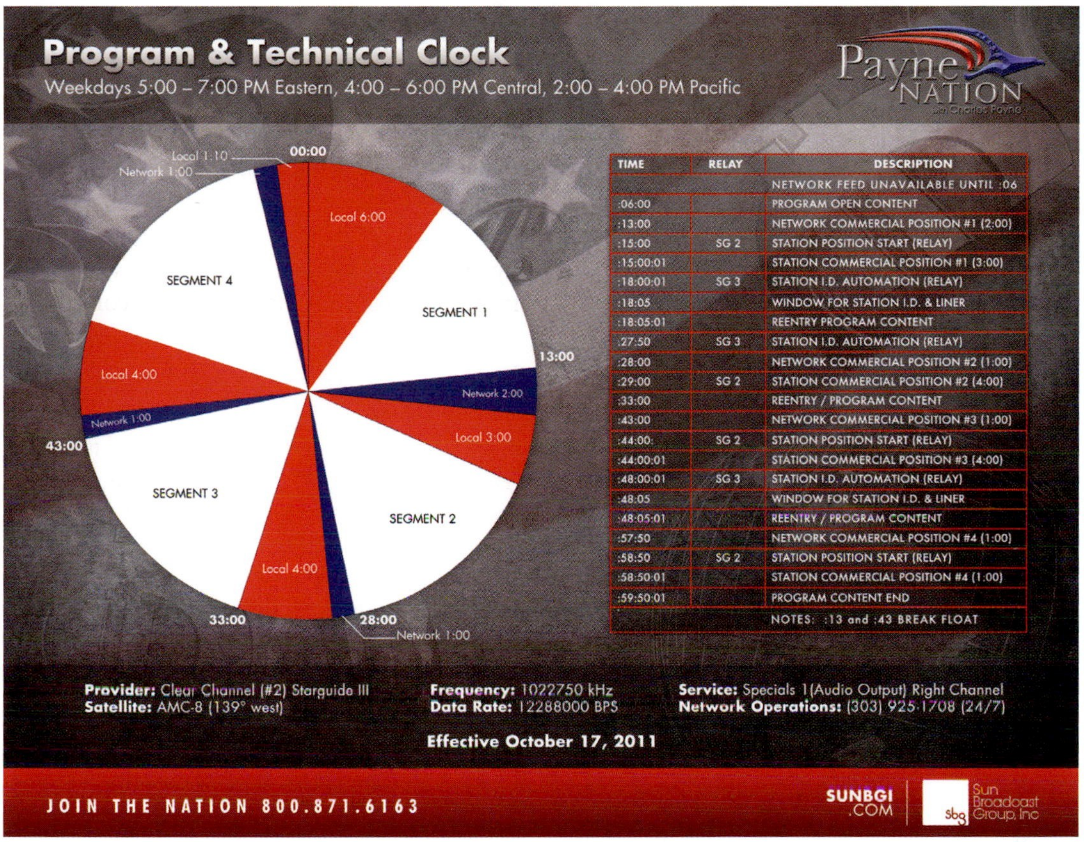

TIME	RELAY	DESCRIPTION
		NETWORK FEED UNAVAILABLE UNTIL :06
:06:00		PROGRAM OPEN CONTENT
:13:00		NETWORK COMMERCIAL POSITION #1 (2:00)
:15:00	SG 2	STATION POSITION START (RELAY)
:15:00:01		STATION COMMERCIAL POSITION #1 (3:00)
:18:00:01	SG 3	STATION I.D. AUTOMATION (RELAY)
:18:05		WINDOW FOR STATION I.D. & LINER
:18:05:01		REENTRY PROGRAM CONTENT
:27:50	SG 3	STATION I.D. AUTOMATION (RELAY)
:28:00		NETWORK COMMERCIAL POSITION #2 (1:00)
:29:00	SG 2	STATION COMMERCIAL POSITION #2 (4:00)
:33:00		REENTRY / PROGRAM CONTENT
:43:00		NETWORK COMMERCIAL POSITION #3 (1:00)
:44:00:	SG 2	STATION POSITION START (RELAY)
:44:00:01		STATION COMMERCIAL POSITION #3 (4:00)
:48:00:01	SG 3	STATION I.D. AUTOMATION (RELAY)
:48:05		WINDOW FOR STATION I.D. & LINER
:48:05:01		REENTRY / PROGRAM CONTENT
:57:50		NETWORK COMMERCIAL POSITION #4 (1:00)
:58:50	SG 2	STATION POSITION START (RELAY)
:58:50:01		STATION COMMERCIAL POSITION #4 (1:00)
:59:50:01		PROGRAM CONTENT END
		NOTES: :13 and :43 BREAK FLOAT

FIGURE 11.9
Syndicated talk shows, such as the business-based *Payne Nation*, also follow a structured program clock. Courtesy of Sun Broadcast Group and Jay Williams.

Contemporary, Rock, Classic Hits, Adult Standards and Hispanic. The network structures the presentation in such a way as to make it equally suitable for "round-the-clock" or dayparted (nights and weekends) use. In addition to the satellite-delivered formats, which target the needs of smaller-market stations, the company offers two services for stations in larger, more-competitive markets. In both instances, WestwoodOne provides tested music and imaging services, customized to the specific market. As far as the on-air personalities are concerned, it's up to each station to decide whether to employ local announcers or utilize out-of-market talent operating from the company's centralized studio. In the latter instance, WestwoodOne personalities utilize station-supplied, localized information about events, promotions, and weather in recording station-specific voice tracks. Relayed individually to each client station over the Internet and automatically integrated into the station's customized digital automation system, the voice tracks impart a major-market feel to broadcasts in locations where the talent-employment expense would otherwise be cost-prohibitive.

Two innovative variations on syndicated Top 40 have attracted recent media attention. Jelli embraces an alternative take on the traditional programming model. Music playlists are determined not in the typical fashion by professional station personnel but rather by Jelli listeners across the United States. In an interview with *USA Today*, co-founder Michael Dougherty says he conceived Jelli as a response to the question, "What if Google ran a radio station?" The result is a crowdsourced approach to music selection and scheduling. Listeners connect with the service's website to scan a list of songs and vote either their approval ("Rocks") or rejection ("Sucks"). The Jelli website listed more than two dozen affiliated stations in mid-2013, located in markets ranging in size from Minneapolis and San Francisco to Metropolis, Illinois, and Clovis, New Mexico. In some markets Jelli is heard fulltime; in others, stations utilize it in selected dayparts, most commonly in evenings. The viability of an audience-curated radio station music library remains to be seen as it competes for listeners in a digital music landscape where Spotify and Pandora stream from libraries of millions of songs instantly, and on-demand.

Another syndicated format to put a new spin on the CHR presentation is gaining traction. According to co-developer Mike Henry, CEO of Paragon Media Strategies, the service is "a patent-protected CHR format called QuickHitz." He describes QuickHitz as an innovative approach to traditional CHR. Its notable feature is song brevity. In a departure from stations that typically present a dozen or so songs within a 60-minute period, Henry says QuickHitz "plays 24 songs an hour using edited versions of the songs." With an average song-length of two minutes and stopsets of three minute-maximum lengths, QuickHitz promises to deliver twice the number of tunes played by typical CHR stations. While this approach may infuse the presentation with variety and vitality, it has been observed that in doubling the number of songs listeners are presented with an increased number of opportunities for rejecting songs and tuning out. "New Music U-Turn" is a format feature where the audience provides input into the selection and testing of potential hits. Unlike Jelli, where listeners feed information directly to the syndicator's website, "U-Turn" picks are determined by listener-submitted data to the third-party website SoundOut.

FIGURE 11.10
Jelli logo. Courtesy of Jelli.

FIGURE 11.11
QuickHitz logo. Courtesy Mike Henry and QuickHitz.

ABOUT JELLI

Mike Dougherty

FIGURE 11.12
Mike Dougherty.

It is well publicized that the media business is undergoing rapid evolution. Over the last ten years we've seen major segments of media, communication and consumption reinvented via the Web. The telephone, the VCR, and the book are examples of everyday things that have been fundamentally changed by rethinking them and connecting them to a Web platform. In fact, the places we go to purchase media are no longer "places" but rather "user experiences."

As we move into the second decade of this transformation, the social Web is bringing a new wave of reinvention. But there hasn't been much innovation in the radio industry in decades. Radio is massive, reaching hundreds of millions of people weekly, and generating hundreds of billions of listening hours while serving trillions of audio ads each year. However it remains a one-way broadcast medium, with no feedback loop and antiquated measurement. Internet streaming radio services show a path to the future but still represent less than 10% of all listening to radio, and transforming our radio experience in cars with wireless data networks will take time to reach scale.

At Jelli, we believe radio is social in its DNA. Radio's shared listening experience builds local community around a favorite station. We had an idea: what would happen if we could reinvent the radio, using the social Web? Could we make you think of your radio in a new way? How would you participate? Beyond music, what type of content from the Web would be available? Could we make it fun? Could we extend some of the proven concepts of radio, such as the request show, such as contests, and certainly community, but rethink all of it from the ground up?

Our team did not come from a radio background. My co-founder Jateen Parekh was the first employee on the Amazon Kindle project, reinventing the book, and had been on the engineering team that developed the first digital video recorder before that, reinventing the VCR. I had been working at a company called Tellme, a speech applications company (before Apple's Siri) that sought to reinvent what is possible with the phone. We were acquired by Microsoft for this reason.

We both shared a passion for music, audio and radio. We were excited enough to leave great jobs at large, stable companies in the middle of the deepest recession since the Great Depression, to join an unfunded startup to reinvent what is possible in radio!

"Don't Change the Station, Change the Song."

We designed a platform to help local stations amplify the strength of their local community, by allowing their listeners to engage with the station and each other in fundamental ways. We developed a "crowdsourced" radio platform, giving control of the song choices to the people. Since we had no radio experience, we didn't know what we couldn't do. So we just created something we wished we could do with the radio. We designed Jelli with elements taken from Internet radio, with a few twists.

Jelli enables everyone to be a DJ, and the entire terrestrial broadcast is shaped by the audience in real time. Users can choose a song seconds before it plays. To control what plays, you vote using the station's website or an iPhone or Android app. The results are transparent. Each vote adds a "plus 1" or "minus 1" to the score. The highest score wins, and when you vote you help your song bubble up to the top of the list. We added some fun game mechanics as well. One example is our rock meter. It is sort of like thumbs up/thumbs down on Internet radio services, but more social. More like a tug of war. In fact, if enough listeners hate a song, the song is yanked in mid-stream like the Gong Show. We hooked all of this action up to Facebook and Twitter, so users could share their actions with their friends, amplify community, and drive listeners to the broadcast, increasing ratings and tune-in.

We also filed several patents for our concepts and technology, some which were granted by the USPTO in early 2013.

Moving from "Did it Run?" to "Did it Resonate?"

In late 2011, the second phase of our evolution commenced, when we were approached by large radio advertising agencies to apply our platform capabilities to terrestrial radio advertising.

Radio is a very efficient medium to provide reach for clients, and it is a "must buy" for certain brands to achieve their goals. However, it has been hampered by lack of real-time data to measure the effectiveness of those dollars. This is becoming a bigger issue as more clients buy online and mobile campaigns, which highlight further the lack of real-time data in offline media like radio or TV.

Just as our cloud-based platform serves music on the air in real time, it can also deliver radio spots on the air on stations across the U.S., logging these offline impressions and immediately providing access to clients about their campaign progress. In addition we have real-time audience data that can show how the listeners are reacting to the campaigns, and we can integrate a radio spot seamlessly with online and mobile triggers to measure conversion and ROI.

We help radio stations create a great community, driving up engagement and ratings. We can invite brands into that experience. Radio spots become interactive, and the community can engage with brands via radio in ways that were impossible before. The social engagement is measured and available in real time, driving significant insight, also a first for the medium.

As of June 2013, we are deployed at more than 175 affiliates reaching over 27 million people weekly. Our social programming platform has received hundreds of millions of votes, more than 11 votes per minute per station. In addition, we have even developed research that correlates social engagement with ratings.

We're just starting in creating something new with something old. We look forward to what the next ten years of reinvention will bring.

Mike Dougherty is the chief executive officer and co-founder of Jelli, a social radio platform that combines the reach of radio with the engagement of the Web. He has 20 years of experience with online and mobile services and corporate development. Recently, Jelli launched a next-generation advertising platform that automates the delivery of audio advertising on traditional broadcasts while providing real-time measurement, accountability, and analytics to broadcasters and advertisers. Dougherty was named a radio industry Power Player by All Access and has appeared on CNBC's *Squawk Box* and G4TV.

Syndicators assist stations during the installation and implementation stage of a format and provide training for operators and other station personnel. Comprehensive operations manuals are left with subscribers as a source of further assistance.

Syndicators offer programs on a barter basis, for a fee without presold spots (commercial announcements) or for a fee containing spots. Leasing agreements generally stipulate a minimum two-year term and assure the subscriber that the syndicator will not lease a similar format to another station in the same market. Should a station choose not to renew its agreement with the syndicator, all material must be returned unless otherwise stipulated.

The majority of format syndicators also market production libraries, jingles, and special features for general market consumption.

News coverage is another form of program content to which the syndication model of distribution has been applied with success. GRNlive was initially established as Global Radio News in the late 1990s. The organization embraced the Internet as a marketplace for news audio collection and distribution. CEO Henry Peirse described its early days in terms of its approach, which differed from similar organizations. GRN, he explained, was "more than rip and read with clips on subscription." Rather, it was "a pay as you use international news service with content supplied by a vast network of freelance reporters all over the world. The idea was to give radio stations freedom to create news bulletins to suit their audience and use the Internet as the marketing, delivery and sales tool."

Peirse continues:

> When the first Internet bubble burst in the early 2000s, GRN reconstituted itself to act as a management network for freelance reporters globally. Over the years they used the technology they pioneered as a distributor for a wide variety of radio and audio clients. But the business now is the network of reporters who can provide live interviews, audio, research, video, stills, fixing and anything else a news publisher or broadcaster (radio and TV) might need in an age of depleted newsroom resources.

FIGURE 11.13
GRNlive: A non-subscription, alternative approach to the network-distribution model for gathering and distributing news internationally. Courtesy of Henry Peirse and GRNlive.

He describes GRNlive as an organization that achieves the efficiencies of networked newsgathering operations yet requires no agency subscription in order to participate. "Arguably," he says, this approach is "still ahead of its time but the model fits into the existing schematic of newsrooms and is growing into the new world of information publishers, be they brand name broadcasters or influential websites."

What is the difference between a network and a syndicator? Phil Barry explains, "There's no practical difference between the two, at least not as far as the public is concerned. The 'network' designation stems from the old, what we used to call 'wired' networks like ABC, CBS, (full-service offerings, etc.) of the day, as opposed to standalone shows, or services. Nowadays, within the industry, the differentiation is more likely a reference to whether the commercial inventory is sold inside, or outside of RADAR," the Arbitron-provided network-radio measurement service. Barry explains, "From an advertising sales perspective, 'network' often refers to inventory sold as part of a RADAR grouping, and inventory not part of RADAR is referred to as sold in 'syndication.' Nonetheless, there isn't a hard and fast definition that applies in every case. WestwoodOne, for example, refers to itself as a 'network,' but some of the shows are sold in 'syndication.'"

HARDWARE REQUIREMENTS AND QUALITY

Now that digital audio is a mature technology, it is rare indeed for a station to receive network or syndicated programming by any means other than satellite and Internet. An NAB survey concluded that more than three-quarters of the nation's stations receive some form of satellite programming. Advancements to Internet Protocol (IP) technology also have led to changes in the methods of content delivery.

Satellite-fed syndicator programs are often archived for later replay. Drew Carey of Premiere Radio Networks discusses the procedure for doing so for one of his company's programs, *The Bob & Tom Show*. Carey says that the program is designed to air in its entirety for the full four hours as sent. *The Bob & Tom Show* airs live 6:00 am to 10:00 am in the Eastern time zone. Stations in the Central time zone have the option to air the show live 5:00 am to 9:00 am or delayed by one hour, 6:00 am to 10:00 am. Stations in the Mountain and Pacific time zones air the show on a delayed basis, carrying it either from 5:00 am to 9:00 am or 6:00 am to 10:00 am, depending upon their competitive situation. Since May 20, 2009, *The Bob & Tom Show*, and all Premiere Radio Network programming, has been aired using the X-Digital PRO4-P digital audio receiver. This receiver is equipped to deliver multiple audio services in high-quality digital audio. It has been designed to make use of all the digital communication features available today, and to be upgraded to take advantage of the technologies of tomorrow. By programming the receiver, stations can receive *The Bob & Tom Show* live, or record it and then air the show, from the receiver, at the desired local time. All XDS PRO4-P digital audio receivers are connected to the Internet. This feature provides Premiere Radio Networks with addressability, enabling it to upload market-specific network commercials to the receiver and then play these network commercials within network programming, broadcasting localized messages dependent upon the affiliates' locations. The end result provides market-targeted delivery of commercials for the show's advertisers. In the predigital days of syndication technology, show delivery and format execution were all too often hit-or-miss affairs. For instance, subaudible audio tones embedded into the program for the purposes of switching off the network and cueing the insertion of the affiliated station's

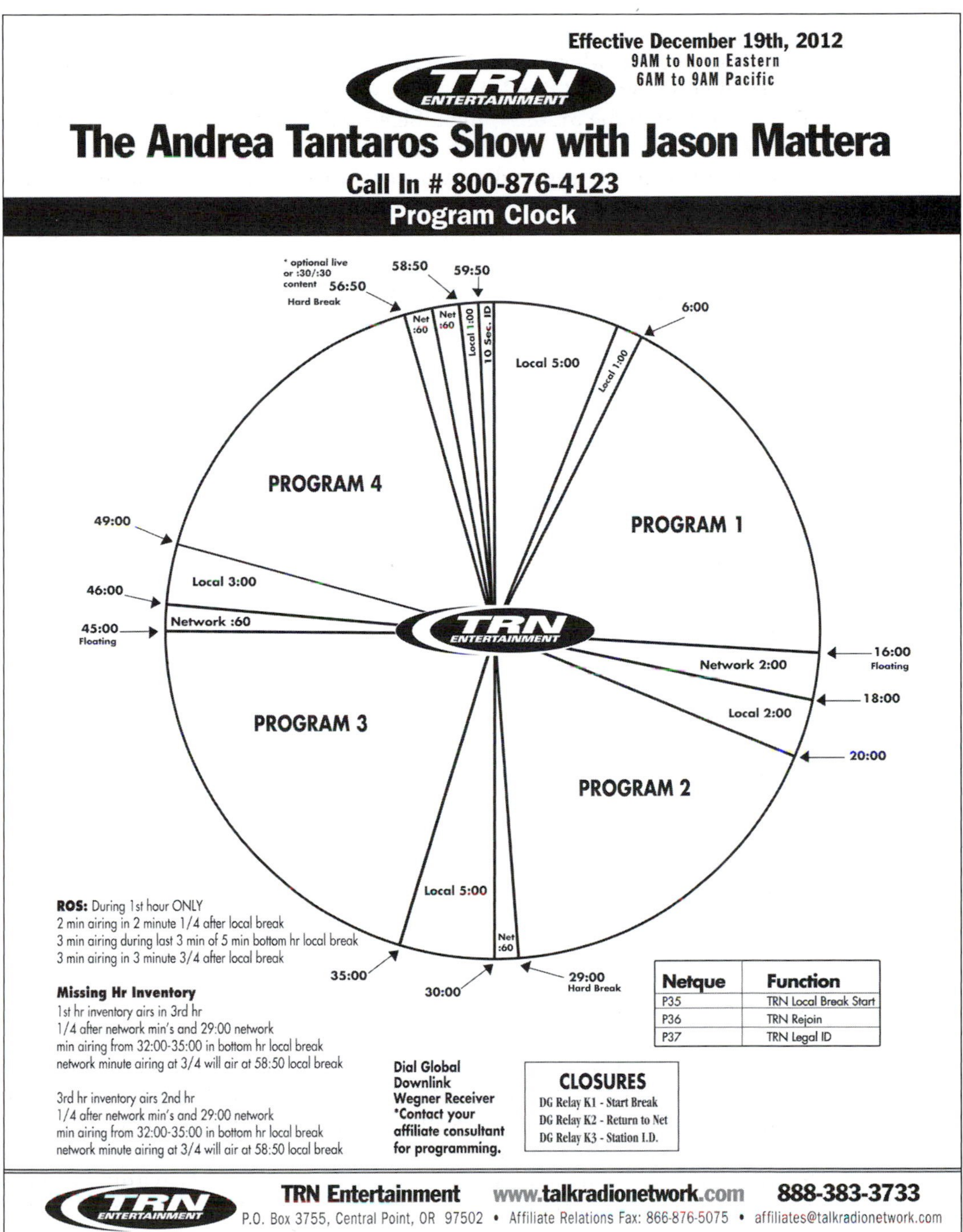

FIGURE 11.14

The nationally syndicated *Andrea Tantaros Show* includes availabilities for affiliate cutaways twice per hour. Courtesy of Sun Broadcasting Group and Jay Williams.

local programming didn't always function as planned. "We've come a long way from 'hard clocks,' space junk and satellite dishes on the roof, and crossing our fingers hoping that the 'tones' will fire correctly," quipped Matt Grasso, operations manager at Hall Communications in Burlington, VT. He added, "Increasing download speeds, codecs, ISDN lines and FTP servers have made syndication more flexible and station-friendly." Grasso adds:

> A local station operator can log into the syndicator's server and quickly click and drag the voice tracks onto the station's computer. That means you can easily play your own music format with Ryan Seacrest hosting the show. Best of all, there's no "hard clock," so even if the syndicated show is set up for 12 commercials an hour, you can easily drop a song and add more spots. Many syndicated shows like Ryan Seacrest also offer a local news feel, too. And you've got other options with an FTP server and evergreen-style breaks.

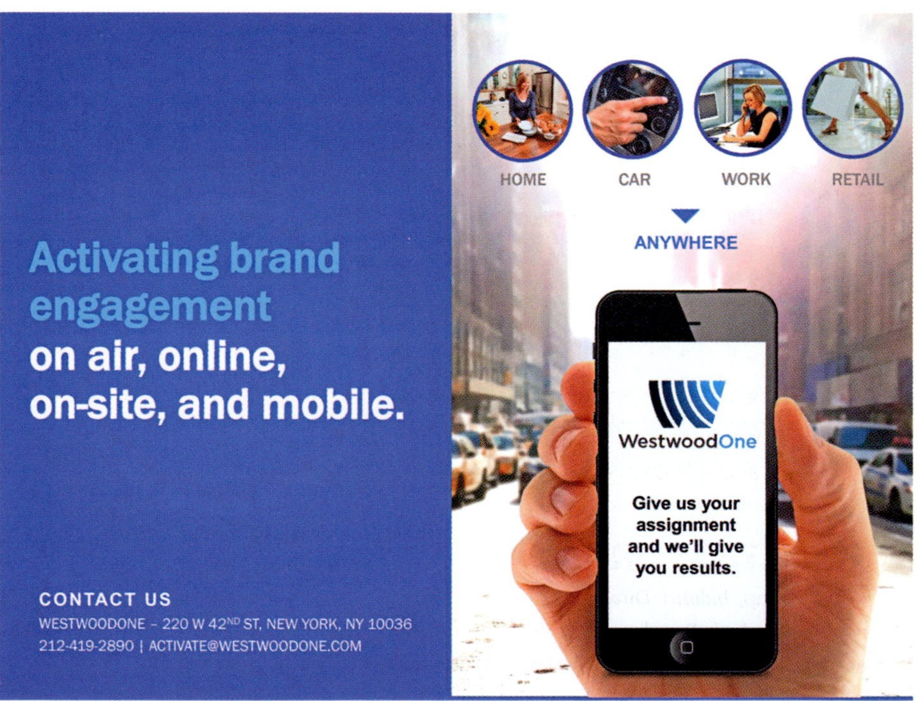

FIGURE 11.15
The importance of reaching listeners across all platforms is emphasized by this network. Courtesy of WestwoodOne.

CHAPTER HIGHLIGHTS

1. The significant increase in stations and formats created a market for consultants. Today, the ranks of radio consultants have been reduced due to consolidation and major radio companies typically have their own in-house consultant in the form of an experienced programming executive.
2. Consultants provide various services, including market research, programming and format design, hiring and training of staff, staff motivation, advertising and public relations campaigns, news and public affairs restructuring, social media strategies, and technical evaluation (periodic airchecks of sound quality).
3. Aspiring consultants should acquire background experience in the medium, solid educational preparation, and strong interpersonal skills.
4. Station executives opposed to using consultants fear losing the station's local flavor, becoming a clone of other stations, and having to justify the substantial expense.
5. Investments by stations in research have fallen off markedly.
6. Statistically, stations using programming consultants more often than not experience improved ratings.
7. Increased use of programming syndication is related to the increased use of computers and satellites. Most of the nation's stations purchase some form of syndicated programming.
8. Syndicated programs are generally cost-effective, of high quality, and reliable, thus allowing smaller stations to achieve a metro station sound.
9. Program syndicators provide a variety of test-marketed, satellite- and Internet-delivered radio formats—from Country to Top 40 to Religious. Services may include music, breaks, promos, customized IDs, and even promotions.
10. While some program syndicators charge fees for their programs, others barter (swap) programming in return for access to a station's commercial airtime inventory.
11. Networks and syndicators are essentially one and the same.

SUGGESTED FURTHER READING

All Access Group, *Industry Directory*, www.allaccess.com.

Broadcasting Yearbook, Broadcast Publishing, Washington, D.C., 1935 to 2010 (ceased publication).

Crouch, S., *No Static: A Guide to Creative Radio Programming*, Backbeat Books, San Francisco, CA, 2002.

Deweese, S.B., *Radio Syndication: How to Create, Produce, and Distribute Your Own Show*, Elfin Cove Press, Bellevue, WA, 2001.

Fornatale, P. and Mills, J., *Radio in the Television Age*, Overlook Press, Woodstock, NY, 1980.

Geller, V., *Creating Powerful Radio*, Focal Press, Boston, MA, 2007.

Hall, C. and Hall, B., *This Business of Radio Programming*, Billboard Publishing, New York, 1977.

Howard, H.H. and Kievman, M.S., *Radio and Television Programming*, Grid Publishing, Columbus, OH, 1983.

Inglis, A.F., *Satellite Technology*, Focal Press, Boston, MA, 1991.

Keith, M.C., *Radio Programming: Consultancy and Formatics*, Focal Press, Boston, MA, 1987.

Kempner, M.A., *Can't Wait Til Monday Morning: Syndication in Broadcasting*, Rivercross Publishing, Orlando, FL, 1998.

Mirabito, M.M. and Morgenstern, B.L., *New Communication Technologies: Applications, Policy, and Impact*, 4th edition, Focal Press, Boston, MA, 2000.

The Radio Programs Sourcebook, 2nd edition, Broadcast Information Bureau, Syosset, NY, 1983.

Series, Serials, and Packages, Broadcast Information Bureau, Syosset, NY, annually.

Shane, E., *Selling Electronic Media*, Focal Press, Boston, MA, 1999.

Vane, E.T. and Gross, L.S., *Programming for TV, Radio, and Cable*, Focal Press, Boston, MA, 1994.

Wasserman, P., *Consultants and Consulting Organization Directory*, 3rd edition, Gale Research, Detroit, MI, 1976.

APPENDIX A

Music Format Syndication

A History and Primer

PHIL BARRY, SVP/GM WESTWOOD ONE 24/7 FORMATS

FIGURE 11.16
Phil Barry. Courtesy of Phil Barry.

Radio music format syndication started in the mid-1960s, with the Beautiful Music format being the first one to make its way on newly licensed FM stations. Syndicators like TM Programming, Bonneville, Drake-Chenault, Century 21, etc., embraced the concept of providing radio stations with 10-inch reel-to-reel tapes that contained the music, with the stations producing and running recorded promos and liners. There were a dozen or more of these "syndication" houses by the mid-1970s.

There was new demand for content, resulting from the FCC's licensing of new FM stations. These were, in most cases, co-owned by AM stations (which dominated the ratings of the day). Those operators who were granted these FM licenses wanted to program them economically, since listenership to FM was minimal. Even so, it provided the basis for format syndication and distribution that continues to this day.

The technology required to broadcast those formats utilized primitive automation systems operating sequential-play tape machines. Gradually, computer technology over the years supplanted the analog tape systems. We went from reel-to-reel tape, to CDs, and now, to hard-drive-based Windows or Linux-based automation systems.

FIGURE 11.17
WestwoodOne: Music, news, talk, sports, and programming-services provider. Courtesy of WestwoodOne.

Along a parallel path, as satellite delivery of network programming was replacing telephone landlines, satellite-delivered formats made their debut around 1981. Two companies, Satellite Music Network (SMN, later sold to ABC/Disney and now owned by Cumulus Media) and Transtar (later acquired by WestwoodOne) launched around the same time, their mission being to create "live" radio stations, with disc jockeys, promotions, and much of the other essential content, created and delivered in a turnkey, ready-for-broadcast fashion. Transtar and SMN were later joined by Jones Radio Networks and Waitt Radio (offering a more localized version; stations simply inserted liners, commercials, news, and other locally originated content into the pre-configured "clock"). It operated much the same way network television did (and still does): nationally originated programming with time slots where the local affiliate inserted content. There was one big difference: most of these formats were disguised as local radio stations. To the listener, there was no reason to believe it all wasn't originating from the station down the street. There was no national branding attached. It was up to the radio station to paste their local brand onto the incoming satellite delivered content, and present it as their own.

As consolidation impacted radio station ownership, the same happened with syndication. Eventually, through acquisitions and fallout, most of those companies were rolled up into the company now known as WestwoodOne.

WestwoodOne continues to develop and distribute these three distribution platforms: DG TOTAL, DG LOCAL, and DG CUSTOM.

DG TOTAL is the satellite delivered, turnkey 24/7 format, distributed much like it has been since 1981 when SMN and Transtar began. It is provided via a barter business model (typically, the program service is exchanged for two minutes per hour of commercial inventory). The only significant difference now, in terms of delivery, is that digital technology allows the network/syndicator to customize the commercial content to the market. An example would be a big network advertiser like Home Depot. With locations across the country, in January, an affiliate in the Northeast would run a spot for a snow blower sale, while in Florida, patio furniture commercials air. The old model had the same copy airing everyplace. DG Total consists of ten different music formats.

DG CUSTOM is the successor to the syndicated reel-to-reel formats distributed by Drake-Chenault, TM, Bonneville, etc. This is more of a do-it-yourself model now. The syndication company provides the nationally created content (usually an hour-by-hour music log, a music library, and imaging); the station provides their own local personalities and integrates other local content. The music logs integrate seamlessly into the station's automation system, executing music playback in the process. These elements are generally updated weekly, and created for 25 different music formats. Approaches can be either generic or uniquely customized to a particular market.

DG LOCAL is the successor to Waitt Radio. This is a patented approach that includes a dedicated automation system (STORQ), the music library and imaging. There are two big differences between DG LOCAL and the TOTAL approach.

One is that the deejays in the DG LOCAL studio complex customize up to three of the breaks per hour for each station (including local weather). Through unique, online access we call EZ Localize, the station communicates to the network—as often as it wants—the specific information they want the DG LOCAL jocks to talk about on the air. Within seconds, it's available for the jock to execute. The breaks they record are then transmitted, via satellite, to the individual stations, and air within a few minutes of their creation. This allows a station to remain continuously connected to their local community, through the personalities, while taking advantage of the cost-efficiency inherent with syndication.

The second advantage is the totally flexible clock, which results from the entire format streaming from the locally placed STORQ system. There is built-in program-schedule flexibility because there are no network "windows" or timed elements to hit. The top of hour ID falls at a natural break in programming, etc.

The service may or may not include the customized breaks, depending on the size of the station and whether they're willing to pay the additional cost, but the flexible clock is part of the service for all clients of DG LOCAL.

With the industry's push toward "live and local" content (to separate terrestrial radio from Pandora, iTunes Radio, etc.) this approach allows the syndicator to completely customize the dynamic content, while staying efficient by producing some static content which all stations utilize.

Phil Barry, a native of Detroit and 32-year veteran of the radio network/syndication business, is currently senior vice-president/GM for WestwoodOne's 24/7 format business, based in Denver. Previously, Phil served as group vice-president/GM for Jones Radio Networks 24/7 formats, as Jones Radio's vice-president for programming, as vice-president for programming for Drake-Chenault, and as a programmer/consultant at TM Programming. Barry's radio experience includes PD and on-air stints in Phoenix and Detroit. He attended Delta College near Saginaw, MI.

APPENDIX B

Syndication

Interview with Tom Griswold, of *The Bob & Tom Show*, Indianapolis; conducted by Jay Williams, Jr.; "quotations" are from Tom Griswold.

- Show is delivered to 123 stations nationwide via satellite.
- It's distributed by Premiere Networks (owned by Clear Channel).
- Interesting note . . . Premiere used to have separate salespeople for certain shows and they are now moving to a model where all the sales people will sell all the shows.
- Shows are fed live from 6:00 am to 10:00 am Eastern time, with three six-minute breaks per hour for local programming (commercials, news updates, etc.). Some stations, mostly in the Mountain States or on the West Coast, will delay the broadcast to fit their morning time slots.
- Bob and Tom try to entertain and don't focus on their local area at all. "If you listen to the show, you wouldn't know where we were here" (Indianapolis). Tom doesn't think syndicated shows like *Bob & Tom* will replace local shows but believes "there will be a mix of local and syndicated shows. There is still a big demand for a lot of local content."
- "We tip-toed into it (syndication) starting out with three affiliates. But the show took off quickly. One magazine had voted us as one of the 'most stolen-from radio shows in America,' and it was great to be able to get our show out there."
- Preparing for a show: "There's at least one aspect that's easier. If you make a comment about a local institution, it could cost your station billings from some advertiser who gets upset. But when you're getting material from all over the nation, rarely do you get negative feedback. And there's a lot more ammo to choose from nationally—you don't have to rely on what happened at the local school board."
- Live is very important. "I could listen to tapes or CDs, but I listen to radio just to keep in touch."

APPENDIX C

Here She Comes

Reproduced in this Appendix are portions of the results of the 2012 edition of Alan Burns and Associates' annual research into the attitudes and usage patterns of female radio listeners. Internationally recognized media consultant Alan Burns analyzed more than one million discrete pieces of data collected in 2012 collected online from more than 2,000 women nationwide aged 15 to 54. While the results of the study are too comprehensive to be reproduced in their entirety, Figure 11.19 reveals two sets of findings to illustrate the type of information that consultancies such as this one provide to clients. Alan Burns and Associates makes available the entire dataset at the website www.burnsradio.com.

FIGURE 11.18
Alan Burns. Courtesy of Alan Burns.

Alan Burns is founder and CEO of Alan Burns and Associates, a worldwide media consulting firm that has advised more than 200 radio stations and large groups, including ABC, CBS/Infinity, Emmis, and Clear Channel Communications, and radio clients in the U.S., Europe, Scandinavia, the Middle East, Australia, and New Zealand. In addition to its work in commercial radio, Alan Burns and Associates has used its marketing, research, and creative skills to advise clients such as DMX Cable, the Corporation for Public Broadcasting, and major record labels such as Atlantic, Elektra, and RCA. Burns has been a pioneer in the use of audience research in radio, having conducted, among other firsts, the first cluster analysis project in the industry. He co-authored the radio industry bestseller *Morning Radio: A Guide to Developing On-Air Superstars* (1999).

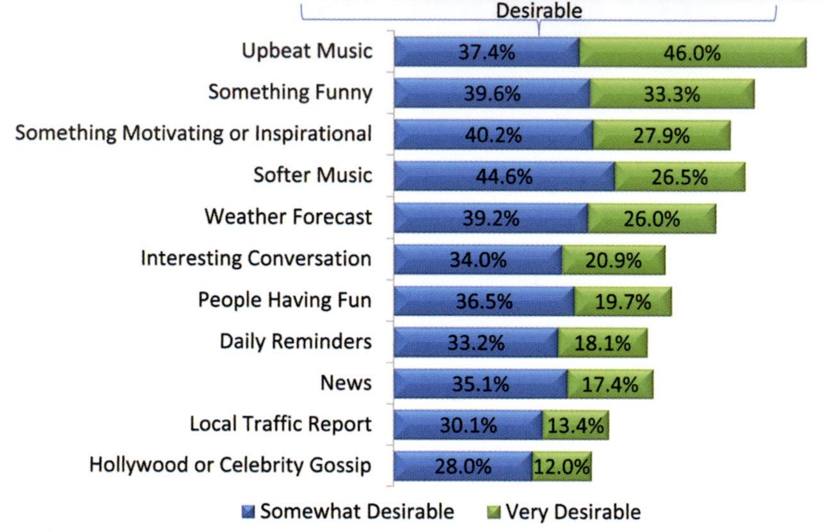

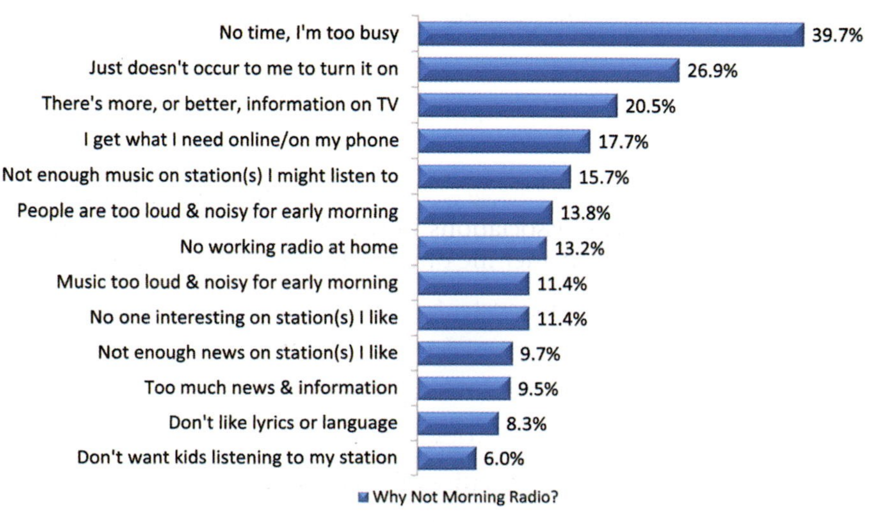

FIGURE 11.19A&B
Tables appearing in *Here She Comes* reflect morning media usage by study respondents. Courtesy of Alan Burns and Associates.

Glossary

AAA Adult Album Alternative format; also known as "Triple-A."

AAC Advanced Audio Coding used for digital audio.

ABC American Broadcasting Company; network.

AC Adult Contemporary format.

Account executive Station or agency salesperson.

Actives (Active Audience) Listeners who call radio stations to make requests and comments or in response to contests and promotions.

Actuality Actual recording of news event or person(s) involved.

Ad Council National clearinghouse for public service announcements.

Adjacencies Commercials strategically placed next to a feature.

Ad-lib Improvisation; unrehearsed and spontaneous comments.

Affidavit Statement attesting to the airing of a spot schedule.

Aircheck Recording of live broadcast.

All Access An online trade publication produced by the All Access Music Group.

Alternate Broadcast Inspection Program (ABIP) A collaboration between the FCC and state broadcast associations in which the station goes through a mock inspection modeled after the one conducted by FCC field inspectors.

AM Amplitude modulation; method of signal transmission using Standard Broadcast band with frequencies between 535 and 1605 (1705) kHz.

AMAX Enhanced AM receiver developed by the NAB.

AMBER alert America's Missing: Broadcast Emergency Response.

Analog Continuous variation in quantity of sound waves and current.

Announcement Commercial (spot) or public service message of varying length.

AoIP Audio over Internet Protocol.

AOR Album-Oriented Rock radio format.

AP Associated Press; wire and audio news service.

Apps Abbreviation for a software application used on mobile devices.

Arbitron Audience measurement service to determine the number of listeners tuned to area stations. It was sold to Nielsen and rebranded as Nielsen Audio.

ASCAP American Society of Composers, Authors, and Publishers; music licensing service.

Attenuate Reduce signal; decrease levels or output.

Audio Sound; modulation.

Audio Ad Center A CBS Radio digital platform designed for advertisers to purchase online audio advertising.

Audio animator Term used by satellite radio for production person.

Audition tape Telescoped recording showcasing talents of air person.

Auditorium test Research method involving large-room survey of panelists about song preferences.

Automation Equipment system designed to play prepackaged programming.

AWRT American Women in Radio and Television.

Back announce Recap of preceding music selections.

Barter Exchange of airtime for programming or goods.

BEA Broadcast Education Association.

Bed Music behind voice in commercial.

Blasting Excessive volume resulting in distortion.

Blend Merging of complementary sound elements.

Blog Internet journal or diary page of personality or talk host.

BM Beautiful Music radio format.

BMI Broadcast Music Incorporated; music licensing service.

Board op Control board operator.

Book Term used to describe rating survey document; "bible."

Branding Establishing station identity and value.

Bridge Sound used between program elements.

BTA Best-time-available, also run-of-station (ROS); commercials logged at available times.

Bulk eraser Tool for removing magnetic impressions from recording tape.

Bumper Music played to intro segments on talk programs and features.

Call letters Assigned station identification beginning with "W" east of the Mississippi and "K" west.

Call-out Music research conducted by calling panelists to play song snippets and document responses. See **hook.**

Capstan Rotating shaft in analog recorders that drives tape motion.

Cart Plastic cartridge containing a continuous loop of recording tape.

CCC Clear Channel Communications.

CFR *Code of Federal Regulations.*

Chain broadcasting Forerunner of network broadcasting.

CHR Contemporary Hit Radio format.

Classic Hits Radio format; preferable to the descriptor "Oldies" in some usages.

Clear Channel FCC-designated AM service classification for stations authorized to serve wide areas at high power.

Clock Wheel indicating sequence or order of programming ingredients aired during one hour.

Clustering Combining the operations of several stations.

Codec Audio encoding and decoding equipment.

Cold Background fade on last line of copy; descriptive term for denoting the manner in which a song (or other recording) ends.

Combo Announcer with engineering duties; AM/FM operation.

Commercial Paid advertising announcement; spot.

Compact disc (CD) Digital recording using laser beam to decode surface.

Compression Manipulation of audio dynamic range for the purpose of managing amplitude; manipulation of digital audio files utilizing a bit-reduction technique for the purpose of decreasing file size.

Console Audio mixer consisting of inputs, outputs, toggles, meters, and pots; board.

Consolidation. See **clustering**.

Consultant Station advisor or counselor; "radio doctor."

Control room Center of broadcast operations from which programming originates; air studio.

Cool out Gradual fade of bed music at conclusion of spot.

Coop Arrangement between retailer and manufacturer for the purpose of sharing radio advertising expenses, so-called because of its "Cooperative" feature.

Copy Advertising message; continuity; commercial script.

CPB Corporation for Public Broadcasting.

C-QUAM Compatible—Quadrature Amplitude Modulation bridged the gap between AM stereo and HD Radio.

CRB Copyright Review Board.

CRM Customer Relationship Management.

CRMC Certified Radio Marketing Consultant.

Crossfade Fade-out of one element while introducing another.

Cue Signal for the start of action; to prepare a device to play a recorded audio element using a console's on-board loudspeaker to monitor the signal.

Cue burn Distortion at the beginning of a record cut resulting from heavy cueing.

Cume The average number of persons listening to a particular station for at least five minutes during a 15-minute period.

DAB Digital audio broadcasting.

DARS Digital Audio Radio Service.

DAT Digital audio tape.

Dayparts Periods or segments of broadcast day: for example, 6:00 am to 10:00 am, 10:00 am to 3:00 pm, 3:00 pm to 7:00 pm.

Daytimer AM station required to sign on the air at or after local sunrise and leave the air at or near sunset.

Dead air Silence where sound usually should be; absence of programming.

Deejay Host of radio music program; announcer; disk jockey.

Demagnetize. See **erase**.

Demographics Audience statistical data pertaining to age, sex, race, income, and so forth.

Digital Convergence of analog waveform to numerical code.

Direct Broadcast Satellite (DBS) Powerful communications satellite that beams programming to receiving dishes at earth stations.

Directional Station transmitting signal in a preordained pattern so as to protect other stations on similar frequency.

Distortion Audio garble.

DMA Designated market area.

DMX Digital music satellite service.

Dolby Noise reduction system.

Donut spot Commercial in which copy is inserted between segments of music.

DOS Director of sales.

Double billing Illegal station billing practice in which client is charged twice.

Downloading Gathering audio or video from the Internet for local storage.

Downsizing Reducing staff by combining functions and departments.

Drivetime Radio's primetime: 6:00 am to 10:00 am and 3:00 pm to 7:00 pm.

DST Differential Survey Treatment.

Dub Copy of recording; duplicate (dupe).

EAN/EAT Emergency Alert Notification/Emergency Alert Termination (via EAS).

Eastlan Audience measurement service specializing in smaller markets using telephone-recall methodology.

EBS/EAS Emergency Broadcast System/Emergency Alert System.

Edit To alter composition of recorded material; splice.

ENG Electronic newsgathering.

Equalization Manipulation of frequency spectrum; also known as "EQ."

Erase Wipe-clean magnetic impressions; degauss, bulk, deflux, demagnetize.

ERP (1) Effective radiated power; (2) tape head configuration: erase, record, playback.

ET Electrical transcription.

Ethnic Programming for minority group audiences.

Facebook An online social networking site created in 2004 by Harvard student Mark Zuckerberg.

Fact sheet List of pertinent information on a sponsor.

Fade To slowly lower or raise volume level; descriptive term for denoting the manner in which a song (or other recording) ends.

FCC Federal Communications Commission; government regulatory body with authority over radio operations.

Feedback Recycling of audio signal; reamplification.

Fidelity Relative comparison between original sound and its mediated reproduction.

Fixed position Spot routinely logged at a specified time.

Flight Advertising air schedule.

FM Frequency modulation; method of signal transmission using 88 to 108 MHz band.

Format Type of programming a station offers; arrangement of material, formula.

Frequency Number of cycle-per-second excursions of an electrical sine wave.

Full Service Format featuring a balance of music, personality and information elements. See **MOR.**

Fulltrack Recording utilizing entire width of tape.

Gain Volume; amplification.

Generation Dub; dupe.

Grease pencil Soft-tip marker used to inscribe recording tape for editing purposes.

Grid Rate card structure based on supply and demand.

Ground wave AM signal traveling the earth's surface; primary signal.

HD™ iBiquity Digital Corporation-trademarked term denoting advanced digital AM-FM broadcasting.

HD2, HD3 HD Radio frequency side-channels.

Headphones Speakers mounted on ears; headsets, cans.

Hertz (Hz) Cycles per second; unit of electromagnetic frequency.

HLT Highly leveraged transaction.

Hook The catchiest or most memorable portion of a song; a snippet used in conducting music research of listener preferences.

Hot Overmodulated.

Hot clock Wheel indicating when particular music selections are to be aired.

Hype Exaggerated presentation; high intensity, punched.

IBEW International Brotherhood of Electrical Workers; union.

IBOC In-Band, On-Channel.

ID Station identification required by law to be broadcast as close to the top of the hour as possible; station break. Announcement wording consists of FCC-assigned call letters followed by city of license.

iHeartRadio A computer and smartphone application that allows for online audio listening owned by Clear Channel Communications.

Imager Audio production person; an imaging director.

Input Terminal receiving incoming current.

Inside Radio An online trade publication examining all aspects of the radio industry.

Institutional Message promoting general image.

I-O Internet-Only radio station.

iPad Portable tablet computer.

IPAWS Integrated Public Alert and Warning System.

iPod Portable media player.

IPS Inches per second; tape speed: 3.75, 7.5, 15, 30 IPS.

IRT Internet radio tuner.

ISDN Integrated Services Digital Network.

IT Information technology.

ITU International Telecommunications Union; world broadcasting regulatory agency.

iTunes A computer and smartphone application that allows for online audio listening by Apple.

Jack Plug for patching sound sources; patch-cord, socket, input.

Jack format Programming emulating iPod sound mix.

Jelli Service mark denoting a proprietary programming strategy involving crowd-sourcing for music selection and scheduling.

Jingle Musical commercial or promo; signature, logo.

Jock See **deejay**.

JRAM *Journal of Radio and Audio Media.*

KDKA Radio station first to offer regularly scheduled broadcasts (1920).

Kilohertz (kHz) One thousand cycles per second; AM frequency measurement, kilocycles.

K-Love Contemporary Christian music service operated by the not-for-profit Educational Media Foundation.

Leader tape Plastic, metallic, or paper tape used in conjunction with magnetic tape for marking and spacing purposes.

Level Amount of volume units; audio measurement.

Licensee Individual or company holding license issued by the FCC for broadcast purposes.

Line Connection used for transmission of audio; phone circuit.

Line-of-sight Path of FM signal; FM propagation.

Liner Recorded vocal promo used to ensure adherence to a station image. See **sweeper.**

Liner card Written on-air promo used to ensure adherence to station image; prepared ad-libs.

Live copy Material read over air; not prerecorded.

Live tag Postscript to taped message.

LMA Local Marketing (or Management) Agreement.

Local channels Class D AM stations found at high end of band: 1200 to 1600 kHz.

LP Long-play phonograph record.

LPFM Low power FM.

Make-good Replacement spot for one missed.

Market Area served by a broadcast facility; DMA.

Master Original recording.

Master control. See **control room**.

MBS Mutual Broadcasting System; defunct radio network.

Megahertz (mHz) Million cycles per second; FM frequency measurement, megacycles.

Mergers Consolidation or combining of assets and resources.

Mini-disc machines Digital cart decks employing floppy disc technology for audio reproduction and archiving.

MIS Manager of information systems.

MIW Mentoring and Inspiring Women in Radio.

Mixdown Integration of sound elements to create desired effect; production.

MMD Mobile multimedia device.

MMS Mobile music services.

Mobile device A small handheld device with a computer screen that has most of the capabilities of a standard computer.

Monitor Studio speaker; aircheck.

Mono Single or full-track sound; monaural, monophonic.

MOR Middle-of-the-Road radio format.

Morning Drive radio's primetime daypart: 6:00 am to 10:00 am.

MP3 Digital audio file format.

MRC Media Ratings Council.

MSA Metro survey area; geographic division in radio survey.

Multitasking Performing several duties.

Multitracking Recording sound-on-sound; overdubbing, stacking tracks.

Music sweep Several selections played back-to-back without interruption; music segue.

NAB National Association of Broadcasters.

NABET-CWA National Association of Broadcast Employees and Technicians-Communications Workers of America.

NABOB National Association of Black Owned Broadcasters.

NAEB National Association of Educational Broadcasters.

Narrowcasting Directed programming; targeting specific audience demographic.

NBC National Broadcasting Company; network.

Network Broadcast entity providing programming to affiliates: NBC, CBS, ABC.

Network feed Programs sent via telephone lines or satellites to affiliate stations.

New media Digital technology that allows consumers to access information anytime and anywhere.

News block Extended news broadcast.

Nielsen Parent company of Nielsen Audio.

Nielsen Audio Formerly Arbitron.

NPR Formerly National Public Radio.

NRSC National Radio Systems Committee.

NTR Non-traditional revenue.

O&Os Network or group owned and operated stations.

OES Optimum Effective Scheduling.

Off-mike Speech or other sound occurring outside a microphone's pickup pattern.

Out-cue Last words in a line of recorded copy.

Output Transmission of audio or power from one location to another; transfer terminal.

Overdubbing. See **multitracking**.

Overmodulate Exceed standard or prescribed audio levels: pinning VU needle.

P1, P2, P3 Nielsen Audio scale of a station's time spent listening (TSL).

Packaged Canned programming; syndicated, prerecorded, taped.

Pandora A computer and smartphone application that allows for online audio listening.

Passives (passive audience) Listeners who do not call stations in response to contests or promotions or to make requests or comments.

Patch Circuit connector; cord, cable.

Patch panel Jack board for connecting audio sources: remotes, studios, equipment; patch bay.

PBS Public Broadcasting System.

PDA Personal Digital Assistant.

PEP (Emergency Alert System) Primary Entry Point (station).

Pinch roller Rubber wheel that presses recording tape against capstan.

Playback Reproduction of recorded sound.

Playlist Roster of music for airing.

Playout Sequenced reproduction of program elements by software-based automation equipment.

Plug (1) To promote; (2) audio connector.

Podcast Online archived/posted audio available for downloading.

Popping Break-up of audio due to gusting or blowing into mic; blasting.

Portable People Meter (PPM)™ Arbitron's proprietary electronic audience measurement device.

Positioner Brief statement used on-air to define a station's position in a market.

Pot Potentiometer; volume control knob, gain control, fader, attenuator.

Preview To privately audition or monitor an audio source. See **cue.**

Production. See **mixdown**.

Production room Studio dedicated to the purpose of creating recorded program material and commercials, usually for subsequent broadcast.

Promax Broadcast promotion and marketing executives association.

Promo Live or recorded announcement featuring details about an upcoming program to elicit listenership.

PSA Public service announcement; non-commercial message.

Psychographics Research term dealing with listener personality, such as attitude, behavior, values, opinions, and beliefs.

Public Inspection File Stations are required by the FCC to maintain certain documentation related to the station's license.

Punch Emphasize; stress.

R&R (now-defunct) *Radio & Records* magazine.

RAB Radio Advertising Bureau.

Rack Prepare or set up for play or record: "rack it up;" equipment container.

RADAR® Radio's All Dimension Audience Research; nationwide measurement service by Nielsen Audio.

RAIN *Radio and Internet Newsletter.*

Rate card Radio station statement of advertising fees and terms; rarely used today.

Rating Estimated audience tuned to a station; size of listenership, ranking.

RCA Radio Corporation of America; NBC parent company.

Rdio A computer and smartphone application that allows for online audio listening.

RDS/RBDS Technology that enables AM and FM stations to send data to "smart" receivers, allowing them to perform several automatic functions.

Recut Retake; rerecord, remix.

Reel-to-reel Analog recording machine with supply and take-up reels.

Remote Broadcast originating away from station control room.

Reverb Echo; redundancy of sound.

Rewind Speeded return of recording tape from take-up reel.

Ride gain Monitor level; observe VU meter display.

Rip 'n' read Airing copy unaltered from wire.

rpm Revolutions per minute: 33-1/3 45_, and 78 rpm.

RPU Remote Pick-Up.

RTDNA Radio Television Digital News Association.

Run-of-station (ROS) See **BTA**.

SAG-AFTRA Screen Actors Guild-American Federation of Television and Radio Artists.

Satellite Orbiting device for relaying audio from one earth station to another; DBS, Comsat, Satcom.

SBE Society of Broadcast Engineers.

SCA Subsidiary Communication Authorization; subcarrier FM.

Secondary service area AM skywave listening area.

Segue Uninterrupted flow of recorded material; continuous.

SESAC Society of European Stage Authors and Composers; music licensing service.

SFX Abbreviation sound effect.

Share Percentage of station's listenership compared to competition; piece of audience pie.

Side-channel An additional HD channel or frequency.

Signal Sound transmission; RF. Signature theme; logo, jingle, ID.

Simulcast Simultaneous broadcast over two or more frequencies.

SiriusXM Satellite radio service; subscriber-based audio program source.

Skim To record a deejay performance or a recording of same.

Smartphone A mobile phone with advanced computing capabilities.

Smooth Jazz Radio format emphasizing elements of jazz and pop music.

Sound Imager Audio producer, animator.

Spec spot Specially tailored commercial used as a sales tool to help sell an account.

Splice To join ends of recording tape with adhesive; edit.

Splicing bar Grooved platform for cutting and joining recording tape; edit bar.

Sponsor Advertiser; client, account, underwriter.

Spot set Group or cluster of announcements; stop set.

Spotify A computer and smartphone application that allows for online audio listening.

Spots Commercials; paid announcements.

Station Broadcast facility given specific frequency by FCC.

Station identification See **ID**.

Station log Document containing specific operating information as outlined in Section 73.1820 of the FCC *Rules and Regulations*.

Station rep Company acting on behalf of local stations to national advertising agencies.

Stereo Multichannel sound; two program channels.

Stinger Music or sound effect finale preceded by last line of copy; button, punctuation.

STL Studio-Transmitter Link.

Straight copy Announcement employing unaffected, non-gimmicky approach; institutional.

Streaming Delivering media content via the Internet.

Stringer Field or on-scene reporter.

Subliminal Advertising or programming not consciously perceived; below-normal range of awareness, background.

Sustain Descriptive term for denoting the manner in which a song (or other recording) ends.

Sweeper Transitional recorded jingle between program elements used to ensure adherence to a station image. See **liner**.

Syndicator Producer of purchasable program material.

Tablet A mobile, hand-held computer.

Tag See **live tag**.

Tagging device Allows listener to buy songs they hear on radio.

Talent Radio performer; announcer, deejay, newscaster.

Talk Conversation and interview radio format.

TAP Total audience plan; spot package divided between specific dayparts: AAA, AA, A.

Tape speed Movement measured in inches per second: 3.75, 7.5, 15 IPS.

TDGA Traffic Directors Guild of America.

Telescoping Time-reducing compression technique applied to audio to achieve a desired length; technique used in audition tapes and concert promos, editing.

TFN Till further notice; without specific kill date.

Trade-out Exchange of station airtime for goods or services.

Traffic Station department responsible for scheduling sponsor announcements. Transmit to broadcast; propagate signal; air.

TSA Total survey area; geographic area in radio survey.

Twitter An online social networking site, created in 2006, that allows individuals to microblog using 140 characters or less.

UC Urban Contemporary format.

UHF Ultra-high frequency.

Underwriter. See **sponsor**.

UNESCO United Nations Educational, Scientific and Cultural Organization.

Unidirectional mic Microphone designed to favor sound pick-up from a single direction; cardioid, studio mic.

UPI United Press International; news service.

VOA Voice of America.

VT Voice track.

Voiceover Talk over sound.

Voicer Voice of news reporter.

Voice-tracking Prerecorded deejay comments inserted into broadcasts at prescribed times under software-automation control.

Volume Quantity of sound; audio level.

Volume control See **pot**.

VU Meter gauge measuring units of sound.

WARC World Administrative Radio Conference; international meeting charged with assigning spectrum space.

Web radio Online radio station.

Website Internet site.

WestwoodOne Radio programming network and syndicator.

Wheel See **clock**.

Wi-Fi Wireless Internet access.

Windscreen Microphone filter used to prevent popping and distortion arising from air movement across diaphragm.

Wireless telegraphy Early radio used to transmit Morse code.

Wow Distortion of sound created by inappropriate speed; miscue.

Wrap Open and close voicers in actuality.

Index

X

Y

Z

Page intentionally left blank

Page intentionally left blank

Page intentionally left blank

Page intentionally left blank

Page intentionally left blank

Page intentionally left blank

Page intentionally left blank

Page intentionally left blank

Page intentionally left blank

Page intentionally left blank

Page intentionally left blank

Page intentionally left blank

Page intentionally left blank